CWAP®
Certified Wireless Analysis Professional
Official Study Guide

David A. Westcott

David D. Coleman

Peter Mackenzie

Ben Miller

WILEY

Wiley Publishing, Inc.

Acquisitions Editor: Jeff Kellum
Development Editor: Thomas Cirtin
Technical Editor: Jerome Henry
Production Editor: Eric Charbonneau
Copy Editor: Kim Wimpsett
Editorial Manager: Pete Gaughan
Production Manager: Tim Tate
Vice President and Executive Group Publisher: Richard Swadley
Vice President and Publisher: Neil Edde
Media Project Manager 1: Laura Moss-Hollister
Media Associate Producer: Josh Frank
Media Quality Assurance: Doug Kuhn
Book Designer: Judy Fung
Compositor: Craig Johnson, Happenstance Type-O-Rama
Proofreaders: Marcus Burton; Jen Larsen, Word One
Indexer: Ted Laux
Project Coordinator, Cover: Katie Crocker
Cover Designer: Ryan Sneed

For general information on our other products and services or to obtain technical support, please contact our Customer Care Department within the U.S. at (877) 762-2974, outside the U.S. at (317) 572-3993 or fax (317) 572-4002.

Wiley also publishes its books in a variety of electronic formats. Some content that appears in print may not be available in electronic books.

Library of Congress Cataloging-in-Publication Data

CWAP : certified wireless analysis professional official study guide : exam PW0-270 / David Westcott ... [et al.]. — 1st ed.
      p. cm.
   ISBN-13: 978-0-470-76903-4 (pbk.)
   ISBN-10: 0-470-76903-3 (pbk.)
   ISBN: 978-1-118-07521-0 (ebk)
   ISBN: 978-1-118-07523-4 (ebk)
   ISBN: 978-1-118-07522-7 (ebk)

1. Wireless LANs—Examinations—Study guides. I. Westcott, David, 1962- II. Title: Certified wireless analysis professional official study guide.
 TK5105.78.C929 2011
 621.384076—dc22
                        2010053542

Dear Reader,

Thank you for choosing *CWAP: Certified Wireless Analysis Professional Official Study Guide (PW0-270)*. This book is part of a family of premium-quality Sybex books, all of which are written by outstanding authors who combine practical experience with a gift for teaching.

Sybex was founded in 1976. More than 30 years later, we're still committed to producing consistently exceptional books. With each of our titles, we're working hard to set a new standard for the industry. From the paper we print on, to the authors we work with, our goal is to bring you the best books available.

I hope you see all that reflected in these pages. I'd be very interested to hear your comments and get your feedback on how we're doing. Feel free to let me know what you think about this or any other Sybex book by sending me an email at nedde@wiley.com. If you think you've found a technical error in this book, please visit http://sybex .custhelp.com. Customer feedback is critical to our efforts at Sybex.

Best regards,

Neil Edde
Vice President and Publisher
Sybex, an Imprint of Wiley

To Janie, Jennifer, and Samantha. Thank you for being part of my journey through life.
—David A. Westcott

To my kids, Brantley and Carolina, you have made your father proud.
—David D. Coleman

To my granddad, the late Jim Mackenzie, for the influence he had in my life.
—Peter Mackenzie

To my patient, witty, and wise mother, Ellen, who instilled in me a love for storytelling and all things creative. To my father, Doug, who has been a role model and calming influence when I have needed it most. And to Chioma, my sweet Lovie and the sine qua non of my life.
—Ben Miller

Acknowledgments

I would like to thank my in-laws Ann and John Barrett for providing us with a wonderful home this past year while ours was being built. Thank you, Janie, Jennifer, and Samantha, for your patience and understanding of my life on the road. To my parents, Kathy and George, thank you for almost always being willing to hop in the car and drive four hours to give a helping hand or to attend one of our many parties. I also want to say thank you to Devin Akin for introducing me to wireless in one of the first CWNA classes ten years ago, to Chris Leach for hiring me as a wireless networking trainer seven years ago, and to Carolyn Cutler for keeping me busy for the past three years.

—David A. Westcott

I would once again like to thank my children, Brantley and Carolina, for their patience and understanding of their father throughout the writing of yet another book. I love you kids very much. I would also like to thank my mother, Marjorie Barnes, and my stepfather, William Barnes, for many years of support and encouragement. I would also like to thank my brother, Rob Coleman, for all his help and support over the years.

—David D. Coleman

First and foremost, I would like to thank the God who created and sustains me and whose love and grace brings meaning and purpose to my life. I would like to thank my wife, Sarah, for the unconditional love and support she has shown me throughout the writing of this book. I would like to thank my children, Luke and Joshua, for bringing a smile to my face when I needed it the most, and I would like to thank my parents, Richard and Heather, for always believing in me.

I would like to thank my colleagues Alistair Meakin and Peter Quinn for their support during my professional career at MarQuest. I would also like to thank Riaz Khan at WildPackets and Janice Spampinato at Case Technologies for their support and contribution to this book.

—Peter Mackenzie

To begin, it is best to start at the beginning. Thank you, Ignacio De La Torre, for starting me on the path toward a career in wireless networking. You sure pick wireless professionals better than you pick fantasy football quarterbacks. Thank you, Devin Akin, whose great gift is to inspire the ordinary into the extraordinary. I was there when you taught the world's first CWAP course, and I'm still trying to recover. Mike Walsh, thank you for taking a chance on a 28-year-old to write a seven-figure-a-year wireless training curriculum. Also, thank you for leveling with me when I was full of it. I must thank Tori Easterly for fighting for me in spite of my orneriness and against me when that orneriness needed reins. And thank you for reminding me that hockey is great. Great thanks must be given to Jeff Kellum and Tom Cirtin for guiding me through this project. They helped me turn scattered thoughts into something legible. And finally, a hearty shout-out to a man full of good ideas and good humor, GT Hill. If I had to pick one man as my partner in a wireless venture or to ride shotgun as I plunder the local Chick-Fil-A, GT would be that man.

—Ben Miller

Writing *CWAP: Certified Wireless Analysis Professional Official Study Guide* has been an adventure from the start. We would like to thank all of the following individuals for their support and contributions during the entire process.

We must first thank our acquisitions editor at Sybex, Jeff Kellum, for initially finding us and bringing us onto this project five years ago. Jeff is an extremely patient and understanding editor who occasionally sends a nasty email message. We would also like to thank our development editor, Thomas Cirtin.

Although he was not available to be one of the official authors of this book, we must thank Keith Parsons for the work he did on the spectrum analysis chapter. His knowledge and insight was instrumental in helping to understand and bring together a complicated topic.

We would also like to thank everyone from the CWNP program (www.cwnp.com). You should be proud of the internationally renowned wireless certification program that you have developed. It has been a pleasure working with all of you the past decade. A special thanks goes to Marcus Burton for his feedback and content review.

We would also like to thank the following individuals and companies for their support and contributions to the book:

Aerohive Networks (www.aerohive.com)—Devin Akin and Paul Levasseur

AirMagnet (www.airmagnet.com)—Dilip Advani, Chia Chee Kuan, and Joey Kuo

Aruba Networks (www.arubanetworks.com)—Chris Leach, Kevin Hamilton, Carolyn Cutler, and Susan Wells

CACE Technologies (www.cacetech.com)—Janice Spampinato

Fluke Networks (www.flukenetworks.com)—Carolyn Carter, Dan Klimke, and Lori Whitmer

Meru Networks (www.merunetworks.com)—Kamal Anand

Motorola (www.motorola.com)—Ralf Deltrap, Bryan Harkins, and David Thomas

NetStumbler (www.netstumbler.com)—Marius Milner

Wi-Fi Alliance (www.wifi.org)—Kelly Davis-Felner and Krista Ford

WildPackets (www.wildpackets.com)—Stephanie Temples

—The Authors

About the Authors

David A. Westcott is an independent consultant and technical trainer with more than 25 years of experience in information technology, specializing in wireless networking and security. In addition to providing advice and direction to corporate clients, David has been a certified trainer for more than 17 years, providing training to government agencies, corporations, and universities around the world. David was an adjunct faculty member for Boston University's Corporate Education Center for more than 10 years and has developed and delivered courses on wireless networking, wireless mesh networking, wired networking, and security.

Since installing his first wireless network in 1999, David has become a Certified Wireless Network Trainer, Administrator, Security Professional, and Analysis Professional. David is also a member of the CWNE Roundtable, a selected group of individuals who work with the CWNP Program to provide direction for the CWNE exam and certification. David has earned certifications from Cisco, Aruba Networks, Microsoft, EC-Council, CompTIA, and Novell. David lives in Concord, Massachusetts. A licensed pilot, he enjoys flying his Piper Cherokee 180 around New England when he is not flying around the world commercially. David is CWNE #7 and can be reached via email at david@westcott-consulting.com.

David D. Coleman is the global training manager for Aerohive Networks, www.aerohive.com, creators of the award-winning cooperative control wireless LAN (WLAN) architecture. David is in charge of Aerohive training programs for all partners and customers throughout the globe. David has instructed IT professionals from around the globe in wireless networking administration, wireless security, and wireless frame analysis. The company he founded 10 years ago, AirSpy Training (www.airspy.com), specialized in corporate Wi-Fi training, and he has worked with Aruba Networks, Avaya, Cisco Networks, Motorola AirDefense, and Polycom. He has trained numerous computer security employees from various law enforcement agencies, the U.S. Marines, the U.S. Army, the U.S. Navy, the U.S. Air Force, and other federal and state government agencies. David has written multiple books and white papers about wireless networking, and he is considered an authority on 802.11 technology. When he is not traveling, David resides in Atlanta, Georgia. David is CWNE #4, and he can be reached via email at mistermultipath@gmail.com. You can also follow David online via Twitter at www.twitter.com/mistermultipath.

Peter Mackenzie is currently the head of technical operations for U.K. company MarQuest, where he is the principle instructor for both the CWNP and WildPackets Academy courses. Peter is also a certified Motorola instructor. Peter has taught courses in various countries around the globe. When not instructing courses, Peter provides consultancy services specializing in wireless networking and network analysis to many industries including local government, education, and retail. Peter also heads up the wireless installation team at MarQuest working with many different wireless vendors and holding many of their certifications, along with the vendor-neutral CWNE and CWNT certifications. Peter is CWNE #33 and is a member of the CWNE Roundtable. Peter can be reached at pmackenzie@marquest.com.

Ben Miller is a wireless services professional based in Los Angeles, California. Ben is an active trainer and writer covering a variety of topics pertinent to wireless LANs. He authors Sniff WiFi (www.sniffwifi.com), a blog about practical wireless protocol analysis and security. Ben is the course director for the Global Knowledge Wireless Curriculum, overseeing course development, instructor readiness, and equipment testing for Wireless LAN Foundations and Wireless LAN Security and Analysis. He was a guest speaker for the Information Systems Security Association (ISSA) – New England chapter event on wireless local area network security. In addition, he has been an advisor to the CWNP Program and a contributor to the CWNP Forum for vendor-neutral wireless certifications. In his spare time, Ben is a feature writer covering mixed martial arts and professional wrestling for the *Wrestling Observer* and a story editor for No Trace Camping, a production company based in Los Angeles. He graduated from the University of Southern California in 1999 with a bachelor's of science degree in chemical engineering with an emphasis in polymer science. He is also CWNE #12.

Contents at a Glance

Contents

Table of Exercises

Foreword

The finalization of the 802.11n standards in September 2009 appears to have been the starting point for tremendous technology evolution in the Wi-Fi industry all through 2010. Today we see coverage and capacity capabilities at lowered price points that were unheard of just a few years ago. Wireless equipment manufacturers are no longer concerned with simply providing automatic control of channel and power settings. Today's centralized wireless network controllers provide quality of service (QoS) management, load balancing between adjacent access points, band steering (where an 802.11n client device is moved from a 2.4 GHz channel to a more optimal 5 GHz channel), and more. Real-time location services, sophisticated rogue device detection and blocking, geo-fencing, packet analysis, and other overlay technologies are riding on top of the Wi-Fi network infrastructure.

The Wi-Fi engineer in today's marketplace is challenged to be better educated than may have been necessary a few years ago. I've often said that manufacturers' data sheets can look like the result of collaboration between three marketing people and one engineer. Separating hype from reality can only be accomplished when you can hold a manufacturer's claim or performance implication up to the measuring rod of core operational characteristics and the laws of physics. It's that level of engineering detail that you'll find in the pages of this *Study Guide*.

There are two categories of things to learn. First, you have to understand what the IEEE came up with when it specified 802.11 operational behavior in the various standards. You're learning the logic and rules that were developed by a bunch of smart engineers. Second, you have to understand some aspects of electromagnetic wave propagation and the associated laws of physics. You're learning the logic and rules that are part of nature. It's this combination of rules and laws that provides the basis for fully understanding the way Wi-Fi works, how it interoperates, why it fails, and how to isolate, describe, mitigate, and repair problems. You'll also be equipped to separate the hype from the reality when you're assessing any of the numerous vendor claims in the marketplace.

Connect802 has had the opportunity to work with customers across the United States during on-site RF surveys, equipment installation, and postinstallation support and troubleshooting. We've seen the proverbial "good, bad, and ugly." As a Certified Wireless Network Professional Premier Certified Solutions Provider and with multiple CWNP-certified engineers on staff, our company has seen the differentiation that CWNP certification makes in the field and in competitive sales situations. When we work with someone who has demonstrated their knowledge and experience through the CWNP certification program, we know we're going to be working with someone who has technical competence. That person should be you.

The scope and depth of content in the CWAP exam are considered the basis for your continued engineering growth in the Wi-Fi space. The goal is not to simply "pass the test" but, rather, to learn and internalize what's being presented. We all agree that what you have in your hands is a fundamental starting point and a core "springboard" for everything else you'll be learning about RF engineering and wireless data communication in the future. Enjoy, learn, and have fun!

Joe Bardwell
President/Chief Scientist
Connect802 Corporation

Introduction

If you have purchased this book or if you are thinking about purchasing this book, you probably have some interest in taking the Certified Wireless Analysis Professional (CWAP) certification exam or in learning more about what the CWAP certification exam is about. We would like to congratulate you on this next step in the wireless certification process, and we hope that this book can help you on your journey. Wireless networking is one of the hottest technologies on the market. As with many fast-growing technologies, the demand for knowledgeable people is often greater than the supply. The CWAP certification is one way to prove that you have the knowledge and skills to support this growing industry. This *Study Guide* was written with that goal in mind.

This book was written to help teach you about analyzing wireless networking so that you have the knowledge needed not only to pass the CWAP certification test but also to support and troubleshoot wireless networks. We have included review questions at the end of each chapter to help you test your knowledge and prepare for the test. We have also included labs, white papers, videos, and presentations on the CD to further facilitate your learning.

Before we tell you about the certification process and requirements, we must mention that this information may have changed by the time you are taking your test. We recommend you visit www.cwnp.com as you prepare to study for your test to determine what the current objectives and requirements are.

WARNING Do not just study the questions and answers! The practice questions in this book are designed to test your knowledge of a concept or objective that is likely to be on the CWAP exam. The practice questions will be different from the actual certification questions. If you learn and understand the topics and objectives, you will be better prepared for the test.

About CWAP and CWNP

If you have ever prepared to take a certification test for a technology that you are unfamiliar with, you know that you are not only studying to learn a different technology but probably also learning about an industry that you are unfamiliar with. Read on, and we will tell you about CWNP.

CWNP is an abbreviation for *Certified Wireless Network Professional*. There is no CWNP test. The CWNP program develops courseware and certification exams for wireless LAN technologies in the computer networking industry. The CWNP certification program is a vendor-neutral program.

The objective of CWNP is to certify people on wireless networking, not on a specific vendor's product. Yes, at times the authors of this book and the creators of the certification will talk about, demonstrate, or even teach how to use a specific product; however, the goal is the overall understanding of wireless, not the product itself. If you learned to drive a car, you had to physically sit and practice in one. When you think back and reminisce, you probably do not tell someone you learned to drive a Ford; you probably say you learned to drive using a Ford.

There are seven wireless certifications offered by the CWNP program:

CWTS: Certified Wireless Technology Specialist   The CWTS certification is an entry-level enterprise WLAN certification and a recommended prerequisite for the CWNA certification. This certification is geared specifically toward WLAN sales professionals, project managers, networkers, and support staff who are new to enterprise Wi-Fi.

CWNA: Certified Wireless Network Administrator   The CWNA certification is a foundation-level Wi-Fi certification; however, it is not considered an entry-level technology certification. Individuals taking this exam (exam PW0-104) typically have a solid grasp on network basics such as the OSI model, IP addressing, PC hardware, and network operating systems. Many candidates already hold other industry-recognized certifications, such as the CompTIA Network+ or Cisco CCNA, and are looking for the CWNA certification to enhance or complement existing skills.

CWSP: Certified Wireless Security Professional   The CWSP certification exam (PW0-200) is focused on standards-based wireless security protocols, security policy, and secure wireless network design. This certification introduces candidates to many of the technologies and techniques that intruders use to compromise wireless networks and that administrators use to protect wireless networks. With recent advances in wireless security, WLANs can be secured beyond their wired counterparts.

CWDP: Certified Wireless Design Professional   The CWDP certification exam (PW0-250) is a professional-level career certification for networkers who are already CWNA certified and have a thorough understanding of RF technologies and applications of 802.11 networks. This certification prepares WLAN professionals to properly design wireless LANs for different applications to perform optimally in different environments.

CWAP: Certified Wireless Analysis Professional   The CWAP certification exam (PW0-270) is a professional-level career certification for networkers who are already CWNA certified and have a thorough understanding of RF technologies and applications of 802.11 networks. This certification prepares WLAN professionals to be able to perform, interpret, and understand wireless packet and spectrum analysis.

CWNE: Certified Wireless Network Expert   The CWNE certification is the highest-level certification in the CWNP program. By successfully completing the CWNE requirements, you will have demonstrated that you have the most advanced skills available in today's wireless LAN market. The CWNE exam (PW0-300) focuses on advanced WLAN analysis, design, troubleshooting, QoS mechanisms, spectrum management, and extensive knowledge of the IEEE 802.11 standard as amended.

CWNT: Certified Wireless Network Trainer   Certified Wireless Network Trainers are qualified instructors certified by the CWNP program to deliver CWNP training courses to

IT professionals. CWNTs are technical and instructional experts in wireless technologies, products, and solutions. To ensure a superior learning experience for customers, CWNP Education Partners are required to use CWNTs when delivering training using official CWNP courseware.

How to Become a CWAP

To become a CWAP, you must do the following three things: agree that you have read and will abide by the terms and conditions of the CWNP confidentiality agreement, pass the CWNA certification test, and pass the CWAP certification test.

 You can find a copy of the CWNP confidentiality agreement online at the CWNP website.

When you sit to take the test, you will be required to accept this confidentiality agreement before you can continue with the test. After you have agreed, you will be able to continue with the test, and if you pass the test, you are then a CWAP.

The information for the exam is as follows:

- Exam name: Wireless Analysis Professional
- Exam number: PW0-270
- Cost: $225 (in U.S. dollars)
- Duration: 120 minutes
- Questions: 60
- Question types: Multiple choice/multiple answer
- Passing score: 70 percent (80 percent for instructors)
- Available languages: English
- Availability: Register at Pearson VUE (www.vue.com/cwnp)

When you schedule the exam, you will receive instructions regarding appointment and cancellation procedures, ID requirements, and information about the testing center location. In addition, you will receive a registration and payment confirmation letter. Exams can be scheduled weeks in advance or, in some cases, even as late as the same day.

After you have successfully passed the CWNA and CWAP exams, the CWNP program will award you a certification that is good for three years. To recertify, you will need to pass the current PW0-270 exam. If the information you provided the testing center is correct, you will receive an email from CWNP recognizing your accomplishment and providing you with a CWNP certification number. After you earn any CWNP certification, you can request a certification kit. The kit includes a congratulatory letter, a certificate, and a wallet-sized personalized ID card. You will need to log in to the CWNP tracking system, verify your contact information, and request your certification kit.

Who Should Buy This Book?

If you want to acquire a solid foundation in wireless analysis and your goal is to prepare for the exam, this book is for you. You will find clear explanations of the concepts you need to grasp and plenty of help to achieve the high level of professional competency you need in order to succeed.

If you want to become certified as a CWAP, this book is definitely what you need. However, if you just want to attempt to pass the exam without really understanding wireless, this *Study Guide* is not for you. It is written for people who want to acquire hands-on skills and in-depth knowledge of wireless networking.

How to Use This Book and the CD

We have included several testing features in the book and on the CD-ROM. These tools will help you retain vital exam content as well as prepare you to sit for the actual exam.

Before You Begin   At the beginning of the book (right after this introduction) is an assessment test that you can use to check your readiness for the exam. Take this test before you start reading the book; it will help you determine the areas you may need to brush up on. The answers to the assessment test appear on a separate page after the last question of the test. Each answer includes an explanation and a note telling you the chapter in which the material appears.

Chapter Review Questions   To test your knowledge as you progress through the book, there are review questions at the end of each chapter. As you finish each chapter, answer the review questions and then check your answers—the correct answers appear on the page following the last review question. You can go back and reread the section that deals with each question you answered wrong to ensure that you answer correctly the next time you are tested on the material.

Electronic Flashcards   You will find flashcard questions on the CD for on-the-go review. These are short questions and answers, just like the flashcards you probably used in school. You can answer them on your PC or download them onto a handheld device for quick and convenient reviewing.

Test Engine   The CD also contains the Sybex Test Engine. With this custom test engine, you can identify weak areas up front and then develop a solid studying strategy that includes each of the robust testing features described previously. The thorough readme file will walk you through the quick, easy installation process.

In addition to the assessment test and the chapter review questions, you will find three bonus exams. Use the test engine to take these practice exams just as if you were taking the actual exam (without any reference material). When you have finished the first exam, move on to the next one to solidify your test-taking skills. If you get more than 95 percent of the answers correct, you are ready to take the certification exam.

Labs and Exercises   Several chapters in this book have labs that use software, spreadsheets, and videos that are also provided on the CD-ROM that is included with this book. These labs and exercises will provide you with a broader learning experience by providing hands-on experience and step-by-step problem solving.

Exam Objectives

The CWAP exam measures your understanding of the fundamentals of RF behavior, your ability to describe the features and functions of wireless LAN components, and your knowledge of the skills needed to install, configure, and troubleshoot wireless LAN hardware peripherals and protocols.

The skills and knowledge measured by this examination were derived from a survey of wireless networking experts and professionals. The results of this survey were used in weighing the subject areas and ensuring that the weighting is representative of the relative importance of the content.

The following chart provides the breakdown of the exam, showing you the weight of each section:

Subject Area	% of Exam
802.11 Physical (PHY) Layer Frame Formats and Technologies	5%
802.11 MAC Layer Frame Formats and Technologies	20%
802.11 Operation and Frame Exchanges	40%
Spectrum Analysis and Troubleshooting	15%
Protocol Analysis and Troubleshooting	20%
Total	100%

802.11 Physical (PHY) Layer Frame Formats and Technologies: 5%

1.1 Understand the importance of each sublayer of the PHY Layer and differentiate between their functions:

    1.1.1. PMD

    1.1.2. PLCP

1.2 Describe PHY Layer terminology and understand PHY concepts found in the 802.11-2007 standard (as amended):

    1.2.1. PSDU

    1.2.2. PPDU

    1.2.3. Header

802.11 MAC Layer Frame Formats and Technologies: 20%

802.11 Operation and Frame Exchanges: 40%

3.3.3. Define Physical Carrier Sense (CCA), understand how it works, and differentiate between its two functional methods:

- Energy Detect
- Carrier Sense

3.3.4. Explain the purpose and detailed functionality of Virtual Carrier Sense (NAV).

3.3.5. Explain how Interframe Spacing (IFS) works, why it is used, and when each of the following IFS are used:

- SIFS
- PIFS
- DIFS
- EIFS
- AIFS
- RIFS

3.3.6. Describe the purpose, functionality, and selection of Contention Windows.

3.3.7. Describe how the Backoff Timer works and why it is used.

3.3.8. Define a Slot Time, calculate its value for each PHY specification, and understand how it is used.

3.3.9. Identify standards-based and non-standard methods used to manipulate 802.11 contention using EDCA Parameter Sets.

3.4 Illustrate the frame exchange processes involved in the following for both a QoS BSS and non-QoS BSS:

3.4.1. Active and Passive Scanning

3.4.2. Authentication, Association, and Reassociation

3.4.3. Disassociation and Deauthentication

3.4.4. Roaming within an ESS

3.4.5. Acknowledgements and Block Acknowledgements

3.4.6. Data frame forwarding

3.4.7. Data frame aggregation

3.4.8. Rate Selection

- Multirate support
- Basic rates
- Dynamic rate switching
- Modulation and Coding Schemes (MCSs)

3.5 Identify and illustrate the operation and frame exchange processes involved in 802.11 security:

3.5.1. 802.11 Authentication and Association

3.5.2. WEP

3.5.3. Shared Key Authentication

3.5.4. WPA-Personal and WPA2-Personal as described in 802.11-2007, Clause 8

3.5.5. 802.1X/EAP

3.5.6. 4-Way Handshake

3.5.7. Group Key Handshake

3.5.8. Robust Security Networks

3.5.9. 802.11n security requirements

3.5.10. 802.11w Protected Management Frames

3.5.11. WIPS rogue containment

3.6 Describe the methods and frame exchange processes used in 802.11 Fast/Secure Roaming within an RSN ESS:

3.6.1. Preauthentication

3.6.2. PMK Caching

3.6.3. Opportunistic Key Caching (OKC)

3.6.4. 802.11r Fast BSS Transition (FT)

- FT Initial Mobility Domain Association
- Over-the-Air Fast BSS Transition
- Over-the-DS Fast BSS Transition

3.6.5. Understand the basic functionality of common proprietary roaming mechanisms.

3.7 Understand and illustrate the following, related to 802.11 power management:

3.7.1. Understand how Active mode works as a basic 802.11 process.

3.7.2. Describe the processes and features of Legacy Power Save mode.

3.7.3. Illustrate a detailed knowledge of WMM Power Save and Unscheduled-Automatic Power Save Delivery (U-APSD), including:

- Effect on mobile device battery life and user experience
- Relationship with WMM QoS
- Power save behavior negotiation during association
- WMM AC transmit queue configuration using WMM-PS and legacy power save
- WMM-PS client initiation of queued data retrieval from QoS APs
- Downlink data frame transmission during an EDCA TXOP

- Application layer time sync functionality
- U-APSD/WMM operation
- The role of applications in specifying power save behavior

3.7.4. Identify and define the following terms and concepts related to 802.11 power management:

- APSD
- U-APSD
- S-APSD
- TIM
- DTIM
- ATIM
- AID

3.7.5. Demonstrate a thorough knowledge of 802.11n power save mechanisms, including:

- Power Save Multi-Poll (PSMP)
- Spatial Multiplexing Power Save (SMPS)

3.7.6. Compare and contrast each power save method, demonstrating a detailed knowledge of the following:

- Benefits and/or drawbacks of each, including efficiency and flexibility
- Operational differences between each process
- WMM-PS and Legacy Power-Save client compatibility and coexistence in a QoS BSS

3.8 Understand and explain the following, as related to 802.11 protection mechanisms:

3.8.1. Explain the frames and frame exchange processes included in mixed mode PHY environments.

3.8.2. Illustrate the operation of RTS/CTS and CTS-to-Self protection.

3.8.3. Describe the operation and uses for HT protection modes including:

- Mode 0 – Pure HT
- Mode 1 – HT non-Member Protection
- Mode 2 – HT 20 MHz Protection
- Mode 3 – non-HT Mixed Mode

3.8.4. Demonstrate an understanding of the functionality of HT protection/coexistence mechanisms and modes including:

- Dual-CTS
- L-Sig TXOP Protection

- Phased Coexistence Operation (PCO)
- 40 MHz Intolerant

3.8.5. Compare and contrast each type of protection mechanism and understand the benefits, drawbacks, and purpose for each.

3.9 Demonstrate a detailed understanding of the Wi-Fi Multimedia® (WMM®) certifications and QoS concepts, including the following:

3.9.1. Explain the terminology, purpose, and functionality of the WMM® certifications and how they relate to 802.11 QoS features:

- Use of Access Categories and User Priorities
- IEEE 802.1Q priority and DSCP tagging
- Relationship to 802.11 QoS features

3.9.2. Define QoS terminology and describe functionality relating to entities and coordination functions of QoS-enabled 802.11 networks:

- Quality of Service Station (QoS STA) and non-QoS STA
- Quality of Service Basic Service Set (QoS BSS) and non-QoS BSS
- Quality of Service Access Point (QoS AP) and non-QoS AP
- Service Period (SP), Scheduled Service Period, Unscheduled Service Period, and Service Interval (SI)
- Enhanced Distributed Channel Access (EDCA)
- Block Ack Procedures
- Controlled Access Phase (CAP)

3.9.3. Define 802.11 terminology relating to QoS features of QoS-enabled 802.11 networks:

- Access Category (AC)
- Traffic Specification (TSPEC)
- Traffic Classification (TCLAS)
- Differentiated Services Code Point (DSCP)
- Admission Control
- Automatic Power Save Delivery (APSD)
- Traffic Category (TC)
- User Priority (UP)
- Traffic Stream (TS)
- Traffic Identifier (TID)

- Traffic Stream Identifier (TSID)
- Transmission Opportunity (TXOP)
- TXOP Holder

3.9.4. Illustrate the use of end-to-end QoS in an enterprise network.

3.10 Describe mechanisms related to spectrum and transmit power management:

- Transmit Power Control (TPC) procedures and frame exchanges
- Dynamic Frequency Selection (DFS) procedures and frame exchanges

3.11 Define terms and concepts and illustrate procedures related to 802.11s mesh networks:

3.11.1. Mesh BSS

3.11.2. Mesh Coordination Function (MCF)

3.11.3. Simultaneous Authentication of Equals (SAE)

3.11.4. Abbreviated Handshake

3.12 Understand the basic differences between the frame exchange processes in a BSS and an IBSS.

Spectrum Analysis and Troubleshooting: 15%

4.1 Demonstrate appropriate use, features, and configuration of professional spectrum analysis tools, including the following:

4.1.1. Locate and identify RF sources

4.1.2. Interpret and quantify the results of a spectrum analyzer trace

4.1.3. Analyzer bandwidth resolution

4.1.4. Comparison of spectrum analyzer types

- Purpose-built spectrum analyzer chipsets
- Wi-Fi chipsets with spectrum capabilities

4.2 Identify common RF device signatures, their operating frequencies, behaviors, and impact on WLAN operations:

4.2.1. 802.11 PHYs

4.2.2. Microwave ovens

4.2.3. Analog transmitters (video, voice, etc.)

4.2.4. Cordless phones

4.2.5. Bluetooth and other frequency hopping devices

4.2.6. Baby monitors

4.2.7. Signal generators and antenna test tools

4.2.8. Telemetry and other healthcare RF devices

4.2.9. Radar

4.2.10. RF-producing lighting systems

4.3 Define and describe common terms and concepts related to RF spectrum analysis:

4.3.1. Signal strength

4.3.2. SNR

4.3.3. Channel utilization

4.3.4. Duty cycle

4.3.5. Sweep cycles

4.3.6. Narrow band interference

4.3.7. Wide band interference

4.3.8. Resolution Bandwidth

4.4 Identify the purpose and illustrate proper interpretation of common types of spectrum measurement:

4.4.1. Swept Spectrograph

4.4.2. Real Time FFT

4.4.3. Utilization

4.4.4. Duty Cycle

4.5 Describe the features, purpose, and deployment strategies of distributed spectrum analyzers.

4.6 Demonstrate effective use of spectrum analyzers for network troubleshooting.

Protocol Analysis and Troubleshooting: 20%

5.1 Demonstrate appropriate application, configuration, and basic use of an 802.11 protocol analyzer:

5.1.1. Install and configure an 802.11 protocol analyzer:

- Channel selection, scanning, or multichannel support

- Define and enable appropriate filters

5.1.2. Performance optimization

5.1.3. Advanced troubleshooting

5.1.4. Security protocol and intrusion analysis

5.2 Describe features common to most 802.11 protocol analyzers:

    5.2.1. Protocol decodes

    5.2.2. Peer map functions

    5.2.3. Conversation analysis

    5.2.4. Filtering: capture and display

    5.2.5. Expert functions

5.3 Demonstrate expert-level network troubleshooting using an 802.11 protocol analyzer:

    5.3.1. Understand the sequence of events for expected network behavior and identify aberrations.

    5.3.2. Understand the 802.11 WLAN frame structure and fields, and apply this knowledge to protocol analysis.

    5.3.3. Perform event correlation.

    5.3.4. Interpret and identify frame exchange processes.

    5.3.5. Interpret and understand data presented by a protocol analyzer and apply this knowledge to network troubleshooting.

5.4 Explain the benefits and interpret the results of multiple-channel protocol analysis using multiple adapters and aggregation software.

5.5 Perform roaming and VoWiFi analysis using a protocol analyzer.

5.6 Describe the features, purpose, and deployment strategies of distributed protocol analyzers.

5.7 Demonstrate appropriate use, configuration, and features of wired protocol analyzers for WLAN troubleshooting.

5.8 Perform end-to-end QoS troubleshooting and analysis for WLAN optimization.

5.9 Identify common challenges related to protocol analysis:

    5.9.1. PHY compatibility

    5.9.2. Roaming analysis

    5.9.3. Time synchronization with distributed analysis

    5.9.4. Location limitations with laptop-based tools

5.10 Describe the use of syslog messages in troubleshooting network problems.

5.11 Identify common client problems and use client logs and statistics to resolve connectivity problems.

CWAP Exam Terminology

The CWNP program uses specific terminology when phrasing the questions on any of the CWNP exams. The terminology used most often mirrors the same language that is used in the IEEE 802.11-2007 standard. Although technically correct, the terminology used in the exam questions often is not the same as the marketing terminology that is used by the Wi-Fi Alliance. The most current IEEE version of the 802.11 standard is the IEEE 802.11-2007 document, which includes all the amendments that have been ratified prior to the document's publication. Standards bodies such as the IEEE often create several amendments to a standard before "rolling up" the ratified amendments (finalized or approved versions) into a new standard.

For example, you might already be familiar with the term *802.11g*, which is a ratified amendment that has now been integrated into the IEEE 802.11-2007 standard. The technology that was originally defined by the 802.11g amendment is called Extended Rate Physical (ERP). Although the name 802.11g effectively remains the more commonly used marketing terminology, any exam questions will use the technical term ERP instead of 802.11g.

 To properly prepare for the CWAP exam, any test candidate should become 100 percent familiar with the terminology used by the CWNP program. This book defines and covers all terminology; however, the CWNP program maintains an updated current list of exam terms that can be downloaded from www.cwnp.com/exams/cwnp_exam_terms.pdf.

Tips for Taking the CWAP Exam

Here are some general tips for taking your exam successfully:

- Bring two forms of ID with you. One must be a photo ID, such as a driver's license. The other can be a major credit card or a passport. Both forms must include a signature.
- Arrive early at the exam center so you can relax and review your study materials, particularly tables and lists of exam-related information.
- Read the questions carefully. Do not be tempted to jump to an early conclusion. Make sure you know exactly what the question is asking.
- There will be questions with multiple correct responses. When there is more than one correct answer, a message at the bottom of the screen will prompt you to either "choose two" or "choose all that apply." Be sure to read the messages displayed to know how many correct answers you must choose.
- When answering multiple-choice questions you are not sure about, use a process of elimination to get rid of the obviously incorrect answers first. Doing so will improve your odds if you need to make an educated guess.
- Do not spend too much time on one question. This is a form-based test; however, you cannot move backward through the exam. You must answer the current question before you can move to the next question, and after you have moved to the next question, you cannot go back and change your answer on a previous question.

- Keep track of your time. Because this is a 120-minute test consisting of 60 questions, you have an average of 2 minutes to answer each question. You can spend as much or as little time on any one question, but when 120 minutes is up, the test is over. Check your progress. After 60 minutes, you should have answered at least 30 questions. If you have not, do not panic. You will simply need to answer the remaining questions at a faster pace. If on average you can answer each of the remaining 30 questions 4 seconds quicker, you will recover 2 minutes. Again, do not panic; just pace yourself.

- For the latest pricing on the exams and updates to the registration procedures, visit CWNP's website at www.cwnp.com.

Assessment Test

1. Which of the following are two terms that effectively describe the same item? (Choose two.)
   A. PPDU
   B. PSDU
   C. PLCP
   D. MPDU
   E. MSDU

2. When a packet is passed down from the Network layer to the Data-Link layer for transmission, what is the default maximum size of the MSDU?
   A. 2,308 bytes
   B. 1,500 bytes
   C. 1,518 bytes
   D. 2,304 bytes
   E. 2,346 bytes

3. A client STA is part of a BSS and is building an 802.11 frame to be transmitted to another client STA in the same BSS. When this frame is created and transmitted to the AP, how many address fields will it contain?
   A. 2
   B. 3
   C. 4
   D. The number of address fields cannot be determined. The number of fields will depend upon the network address of the final destination.

4. What data rate and modulation can be used to transmit the Short PLCP Header?
   A. 6 Mbps, BPSK
   B. 12 Mbps, QPSK
   C. 1 Mbps, DBPSK
   D. 2 Mbps, DQPSK
   E. 24 Mbps, 16-QAM

5. Although clause 19 devices support data rates of 6, 9, 12, 18, 24, 36, 48, and 54 Mbps, the standard requires them to support only three data rates. What are those three rates? (Choose three.)
   A. 6
   B. 9
   C. 12
   D. 18
   E. 24
   F. 36

6. Layer 2 retransmissions occur when frames become corrupted. What are some of the causes of layer 2 retries? (Choose all that apply.)

   A. Multipath

   B. Low SNR

   C. Co-channel interference

   D. RF interference

   E. Adjacent cell interference

7. How many different protocol versions of 802.11 technology are currently defined by the IEEE?

   A. Onem

   B. Two

   C. Three

   D. Four

   E. Many different protocols

8. Name the process by which 802.11 stations dynamically adjust their power level.

   A. DFS

   B. TPC

   C. BSS

   D. CFB

9. What is the name given to the period during which station traffic benefits from a negotiated QoS level with the AP?

   A. Service period

   B. Service interval

   C. TCLAS service

   D. TSPEC service

10. What is the name given to the information element that specifies the details of the type of encryption and authentication in use in a WPA/WPA2-compatible cell?

   A. RSN

   B. Privacy

   C. Cipher

   D. Security

11. What is the name of the field that provides information on the number of stations and current load on the AP?

   A. BSS Load Element

   B. Duty Cycle Element

   C. Station Count Element

   D. ERP Element

12. What is the name of the element used by APs to order stations to stop sending signals?

   A. Quiet

   B. Deauthentication

   C. Power Save

   D. DELTS

13. When an RTS frame is transmitted, the Duration value is set to include the duration of which of the following?

   A. 3 SIFS, CTS frame, Data frame, ACK frame

   B. 2 SIFS, Data frame, ACK frame

   C. 3 SIFS, RTS frame, CTS frame, Data frame, ACK frame

   D. 2 SIFS, Data frame, ACK frame

14. In which of the following frames does the Duration/ID field contain an AID as opposed to a Duration value?

   A. RTS

   B. CTS

   C. Block ACK Request

   D. PS-Poll

   E. ACK

15. When an ACK frame is generated, the receiver address (RA) field is copied from which address field of the frame that is being acknowledged?

   A. Address1

   B. Address2

   C. Address3

   D. Address4

16. In which of the following unicast scenarios would a non-QoS frame be transmitted instead of a QoS frame? (Choose all that apply.)

   A. A non-QoS station transmits a frame to a QoS station.

   B. A non-QoS station transmits a frame to a non-QoS station.

   C. A QoS station transmits a frame to a QoS station.

   D. A QoS station transmits a frame to a non-QoS station.

17. When capturing a packet with the TO DS field set to 1 and the FROM DS field set to 0, what address information does the Address1 field contain? (Choose all that apply.)

   A. RA

   B. DA

   C. TA

   D. SA

   E. BSSID

18. When A-MPDU is implemented, which of the following is true? (Choose all that apply.)

   A. The individual MPDUs within an A-MPDU must all have the same receiver address.

   B. The individual MPDUs must all be of the same 802.11e QoS category.

   C. A-MPDU requires the use of block acknowledgments.

   D. If encryption is enabled, all the MPDUs are encrypted together.

   E. The individual MPDUs within an A-MPDU must all have the same receiver address.

19. Name the interframe space that comes from the 802.11e amendment.

   A. AIFS

   B. DIFS

   C. EIFS

   D. PIFS

20. What is the name given to the quiet periods that make up the random backoff timer?

   A. Slot times

   B. Interframe spaces

   C. CCA idle periods

   D. NAV times

21. What is the name given to the series of frames sent by a QoS AP or station that has won arbitration?

   A. CFB

   B. MSDU

   C. NAV

   D. TXOP

22. Which of the following are power management methods specified in 802.11 amendments? (Choose three.)

   A. 802.11b Power Save Polling

   B. 802.11e Automatic Power Save Delivery

   C. 802.11n Power Save Multi-Poll

   D. 802.11n Spatial Multiplexing Power Save

23. When a station goes into Power Save mode, which of the following states may a station enter into? (Choose all that apply.)

   A. Doze

   B. Idle

   C. Receive

   D. Transmit

24. Which power management method involves the station notifying the AP of its changes from active mode to Power Save mode in order to retrieve buffered unicast frames?

   A. Power Save Polling

   B. APSD

   C. Scheduled PSMP

   D. SMPS

25. When Jane visits Aunt Marg's house and connects to her WEP-encrypted network, what is the maximum size of the MSDU frame?

   A. 1500

   B. 1512

   C. 2304

   D. 2312

   E. 2320

   F. 2324

26. At her office, Rita uses WPA-PSK with TKIP to connect to her corporate network. What is the maximum size of the MSDU frame?

   A. 1500

   B. 1512

   C. 2304

   D. 2312

   E. 2320

   F. 2324

27. WLAN protocol analyzers often display CCMP-encrypted data frames as a TKIP-encrypted data packet because the format of the 8-byte CCMP header is basically identical to the format of the 8-byte TKIP header. The RSN information element will identify which cipher is used. The RSN information element is *not* found in which of the following frames?

   A. Beacon frames

   B. Probe response frames

   C. Data frames

   D. Association request frames

   E. Reassociation request frames

28. What is the name of the additional MAC header field defined by the 802.11n amendment?

   A. HT Information field

   B. HT Control field

   C. HT Capabilities field

   D. HT Operations field

29. Which of the following is true regarding A-MSDUs?

   A. All MSDUs must be of the same QoS access category.

   B. The maximum size of an A-MSDU is greater than an A-MPDU.

   C. Encryption is applied to each MSDU separately.

   D. Only non-AP STAs can use A-MSDUs.

30. The Transmit Beamforming Capabilities field is part of which information element?

   A. HT information element

   B. HT 20/40 BSS Coexistence element

   C. HT Operation element

   D. HT Capabilities element

31. When purchasing a spectrum analyzer, which of the following are options or features that you would evaluate to differentiate between models? (Choose all that apply.)

   A. Frequency

   B. Form factor

   C. Resolution

   D. DFS/TPC support

   E. Supporting software

32. What is the name of the information that is added to the 802.11 frame that is taken from the RF to bit transition process, which includes date and time stamps, a channel stamp, a signal stamp, and a noise stamp?

   A. Receiver data

   B. Radio Header

   C. Radio Data field

   D. Radiotap Header

   E. RF Header

33. In RF monitor mode, how will a wireless network adapter operate?

   A. Can capture traffic from only the BSS to which it is associated

   B. Can capture traffic from all BSSs without affecting normal network operation

   C. Becomes a completely passive listening device, and normal network operation is disabled

   D. Uses time division multiplexing to split its time between listening and transmitting; network operation will be slower

34. What is the purpose of a network analyzer's expert system?

   A. Automatic detection of network events, errors, and problems

   B. Automatic configuration of access points' channel and power levels

   C. Packet replay for network testing and baselines

   D. Rogue device location

35. Which of the following metrics indicate the quality of a VoIP call? Choose all that apply.

   A. RTP response time

   B. MOS

   C. TTL

   D. R-Factor

Answers to Assessment Test

1. B, D. The PLCP Service Data Unit (PSDU) is a view of the MPDU from the other side. The MAC layer refers to an 802.11 frame as the MPDU, while the Physical layer refers to this same 802.11 frame as the PSDU. For more information, see Chapter 1.

2. D. 802.11 frames are capable of transporting frames with an MSDU payload of 2,304 bytes of upper-layer data as per the 802.11 standard. This maximum size can be configured and be reduced. For more information, see Chapter 1.

3. B. An 802.11 frame has up to four address fields. In most instances, only three address fields are actually needed. The fourth field is used when the frame is being transmitted across a wireless distribution system (WDS). For more information, see Chapter 1.

4. D. Like the Long PLCP Preamble, the Short PLCP Preamble is transmitted using DBPSK; however, the Short PLCP Header is transmitted using 2Mbps Differential Quadrature Phase Shift Keying (DQPSK). For more information, see Chapter 2.

5. A, C, E. The mandatory PHYs are ERP-OFDM and ERP-DSSS/CCK. To achieve the higher data rates, a PHY technology called Extended Rate Physical OFDM (ERP-OFDM) is mandated. Data rates of 6, 9, 12, 18, 24, 36, 48, and 54 Mbps are possible using this technology, although the IEEE requires only the data rates of 6, 12, and 24 Mbps. For more information, see Chapter 2.

6. A, B, D, E. If any portion of a unicast frame is corrupted, the cyclic redundancy check (CRC) will fail, and the receiving 802.11 radio will not return an ACK frame to the transmitting 802.11 radio. If an ACK frame is not received by the original transmitting radio, the unicast frame is not acknowledged and will have to be retransmitted. The MAC header of 802.11 frames contains a Retry field. If the Retry field is set to a value of 1 in either a management or data frame, the transmitting radio is indicating that the frame being sent is a retransmission. Multipath, RF interference, low SNR, hidden nodes, mismatched power settings, near/far problems, and adjacent cell interference may all cause layer 2 retransmissions. Co-channel interference usually does not cause retries but does add unnecessary medium contention overhead. For more information, see Chapter 3.

7. A. The MAC headers of all 802.11 frames contain a Protocol Version field. This field is simply used to indicate which protocol version of 802.11 technology is being used by the frame. Currently, all 802.11 frames have the value always set to 0 in the Protocol Version field. All other values are reserved. In other words, there is currently only one version of 802.11 technology. In the future, the IEEE could define another version of 802.11 technology that would not be backward compatible with the current version 0. For more information, see Chapter 3.

8. B. Transmit Power Control allows stations to reduce their power level so as not to disturb neighboring radars. For more information, see Chapter 4.

9. A. Stations requesting a QoS level for their traffic send an ADDTS request frame describing the traffic stream with TSPEC and optional TLCAS fields. When the QoS level is granted, the station traffic benefits from the negotiated QOS level for a given service period (SP). The SP can be repeated at regular intervals, called service intervals (SIs). For more information, see Chapter 4.

10. A. The RSN information element specifies the details of the encryption (WEP, TKIP, or CCMP) and authentication (PSK or 802.1X/EAP) in use in the WPA/WPA2-compatible cell. For more information, see Chapter 4.

11. A. The BSS Load Element, often called QBSS Load Element, provides information on the cell load from the AP point of view: station count and AP utilization (in%). For more information, see Chapter 4.

12. A. In an 802.11h-compliant deployment, APs can use the Quiet element in action frames or beacons to stop stations from sending signals on the current channel. For more information, see Chapter 4.

13. A. When an RTS frame is transmitted, the Duration value is set to include the following in order: SIFS ➢ CTS ➢ SIFS ➢ DATA ➢ SIFS ➢ ACK. For more information, see Chapter 5.

14. D. When a PS-Poll frame is transmitted, the Duration/ID field contains the station's AID, which is used by the AP to identify the station. For more information, see Chapter 5.

15. B. The Address2 field that contains the transmitter address is used by the acknowledging station to populate the receiver address (RA) field. For more information, see Chapter 5.

16. A, B, D. The only time when a QoS frame would be transmitted is when a QoS station is sending a frame to another QoS station. For more information, see Chapter 6.

17. A, E. Address1 always represents the receiver address. In this instance, the frame is being transmitted from a station to an access point, in which case Address1 also represents the BSSID. For more information, see Chapter 6.

18. A, B, C, E. If encryption is enabled, then each MPDU is encrypted individually. The MPDUs are then passed down to the PLCP sublayer where two or more MPDUs are placed in a single PPDU. The individual MPDUs within an A-MPDU must all have the same receiver address. Also, the individual MPDUs must all be of the same 802.11e QoS access category. A-MPDU also requires the use of block acknowledgments. For more information, see Chapter 6.

19. A. AIFS was introduced with the 802.11e amendment. DIFS, EIFS, and PIFS come from the 802.11 standard. For more information, see Chapter 7.

20. A. Slot times make up the random backoff timer. Interframe spaces precede the random backoff timer. CCA idle periods and NAV times are not quiet periods. For more information, see Chapter 7.

21. A. A contention-free burst (CFB) is a series of frames sent by a QoS AP or station that has won arbitration. The MSDU is a single frame of data. The NAV is the virtual carrier sense. The TXOP is a window of time where a CFB may be transmitted. For more information, see Chapter 7.

22. B, C, D. 802.11e APSD, 802.11n PSMP, and 802.11n SMPS are all power management methods from 802.11 amendments. There is no such thing as 802.11b PSP. For more information, see Chapter 8.

23. A, B, C, D. When a station is in Power Save mode, it can be in any power state. For more information, see Chapter 8.

24. B. APSD (specifically U-APSD) involves the station notifying the AP of changes in power management mode in order to retrieve buffered unicast frames.

Power save polling is not a power management method, but 802.11 power management does use PS-Poll frames to retrieve buffered data. 802.11 power management would not be a correct answer here because PS-Poll frames do not involve the changing of mode.

Scheduled PSMP is defined only for contention-free periods where APs control station activity.

SMPS involves stations not using spatial multiplexing as a way to limit power consumption. Power management modes are not affected. For more information, see Chapter 8.

25. D. Remember that WEP encrypts the MSDU upper-layer payload that is encapsulated in the frame body of an MPDU. The MSDU payload has a maximum size of 2,304 bytes. Because the IV adds 4 octets and the ICV also adds 4 octets, when WEP is enabled, the entire size of the body inside an 802.11 data frame is expanded by 8 bytes to a maximum of 2,312 bytes. In other words, WEP encryption adds 8 bytes of overhead to an 802.11 MPDU. For more information, see Chapter 9.

26. F. Because of the extra overhead from the IV (4 bytes), Extended IV (4 bytes), MIC (8 bytes), and ICV (4 bytes), a total of 20 bytes of overhead is added to the frame body of a TKIP-encrypted 802.11 data frame. When TKIP is enabled, the entire size of the frame body inside an MPDU is expanded by 20 bytes to a maximum of 2,324 bytes. In other words, TKIP encryption adds 20 bytes of overhead to an 802.11 MPDU. For more information, see Chapter 9.

27. C. The format of the 8-byte CCMP header is basically identical to the format of the 8-byte TKIP header (IV/Extended IV) used by TKIP. Therefore, most protocol analyzers cannot distinguish between TKIP-encrypted data frames and CCMP-encrypted data frames. However, you can always determine which cipher is being used by looking at a field called the RSN information element. The RSN information element is found in four different 802.11 management frames: beacon management frames, probe response frames, association request frames, and reassociation request frames. For more information, see Chapter 9.

28. B. The 802.11n amendment adds a new field to the 802.11 MAC header, called the HT Control field. The HT Control field is 4 octets long and follows the QoS Control field in the 802.11 MAC header. For more information, see Chapter 10.

29. A. An 802.11n access point using A-MSDU aggregation would receive multiple 802.3 frames, remove the 802.3 headers and trailers, and then wrap the multiple MSDU payloads into a single 802.11 frame for transmission. The size of an A-MSDU must not exceed a maximum length of 7935 bytes, which is much lower than the maximum length of an A-MPDU, which is 64 KB. The entire aggregated frame can be encrypted by using either TKIP or CCMP. It should be noted, however, that the individual MSDUs must all be of the same 802.11e QoS access category. For more information, see Chapter 10.

30. D. The HT Capabilities element has a Transmit Beamforming Capabilities field 4 octets in length that is used to advertise the beamforming capabilities of an HT STA. For more information, see Chapter 10.

31. A, B, C, E. In addition to these, other factors are price, hardware platform, and Wi-Fi integration. For more information, see Chapter 11.

32. D. The wireless NIC will use some of the specific information gleaned from the RF to bit transition process to actually add information to the wireless frame. This additional information is added at the receiving station and is in addition to the bits sent from the source. This added information is called the Radiotap Header. It includes date and time stamps, a channel stamp, a signal stamp, and a noise stamp. For more information, see Chapter 11.

33. C. A wireless network adapter is placed into a special mode called RF monitor mode by custom drivers written by network analyzer vendors. The wireless network adapter is placed into RF monitor mode during a packet capture, and the adapter becomes completely passive, allowing it to spend all its time capturing packets and thus ensuring it does not miss any. While in RF monitor mode, normal network operation is disabled. The custom driver should enable network operation once the analyzer has finished capturing packets. For more information, see Chapter 12.

34. A. Expert analysis is the automatic detection of network events, errors, and problems by the analyzer. The detected events can produce trigger notifications to alert the network administrator to a problem. For more information, see Chapter 12.

35. B, D. The mean opinion score (MOS) is a value from 1 to 5 that indicates the perceived quality of a call. The MOS scores displayed by your protocol analyzer are calculated from another quality metric that you will also see displayed in your protocol analyzer called R-Factor. R-Factor is calculated from measurable information such as jitter packet loss and latency. For more information, see Chapter 12.

Chapter

1

802.11 Overview

IN THIS CHAPTER, YOU WILL LEARN ABOUT THE FOLLOWING:

- ✓ **OSI model**

- ✓ **Packets, frames, and bits**

- ✓ **Data-Link layer**
    - MSDU
    - MPDU

- ✓ **Physical layer**
    - PSDU
    - PPDU

- ✓ **802.11 architecture**

- ✓ **802.11 services**
    - Station service
    - Distribution system service

- ✓ **802.11 frames**
    - Management frames
    - Control frames
    - Data frames

- ✓ **IEEE 802.11-2007 standard and amendments**
    - 802.11b
    - 802.11a
    - 802.11g
    - 802.11n-2009

- ✓ **Wi-Fi Alliance**

Before this book starts to get deep into the technical stuff, we want to take some time to discuss a little of the "what and why" of wireless LAN analysis. Since you are reading this book, it is likely that you have already read the CWNA and CWSP study guides. If you have not done so, do not worry. However, be prepared because after this overview chapter, this book is going to get very technical.

If you read the *CWNA: Certified Wireless Network Administrator Official Study Guide (Exam PW0-104),* by David D. Coleman and David A. Westcott (Sybex, 2009), you learned about the fundamentals of wireless LANs, the history of them, and the basic technologies relating to them. You should have a good understanding of how they work, in the same way that the typical person has an understanding of driving an automobile. Most drivers have a reasonable understanding of how a car accelerates, turns, and maneuvers. For the average person using the roads, a basic knowledge of how a car handles and maneuvers is adequate for driving on the roads. While traveling along various roads, congestion due to traffic and accidents will occasionally occur. When these problems occur occasionally, the additional time it takes for people to travel to their destinations is usually tolerated. However, when unusually heavy traffic occurs on the roads or excessive accidents happen, specialists are needed to analyze the situation to determine how to improve the traffic flow and to decrease the occurrences of accidents.

The people who analyze the roads and traffic need to have a much more in-depth knowledge of them than the individual who is driving on them. They need to understand the inertial forces that vehicles exert on the road so that they understand how well the road can handle the typical speeds at which the vehicles are traveling. They need to understand the type of traffic that is using the roads (cars, trucks, motorcycles, bicycles, and even pedestrians) so that they can optimize the flow of the traffic. They also need to understand outside factors that affect traffic such as weather, fog, and the location of the sun. These people need to monitor the roadway so that they can analyze and identify where and why bottlenecks and accidents are occurring and ideally come up with solutions to improve the flow of traffic.

Just as civil engineers need advanced training and experience to properly analyze and maintain roads, people who manage wireless LANs need specialized training and experience to properly design and maintain them. In this book, we hope to provide you with the advanced knowledge and skills needed to analyze and troubleshoot wireless LANs. To gain this knowledge and skill, you will need to learn and understand the underlying architecture and principles of wireless LANs and RF communications. This will include an understanding of the IEEE 802.11 standard along with RF signals.

In Chapter 1, we will provide some overview and fundamentals. You will learn about the OSI model and the two key layers that involve wireless network: Physical and Data-Link. You will learn about the different 802.11 services and the three types of frames that are used for 802.11 communications: management, control, and data. A review of many of the core 802.11 standard and amendments will make sure that you understand the key components of wireless 802.11 wireless networking. After that, the rest of the book is hard-core analysis and the principles and technologies needed to perform this level of analysis.

OSI Model

The *International Organization for Standardization (ISO)* is a global, nongovernmental organization that identifies business, government, and society needs and develops standards in partnership with the sectors that will put them to use. The ISO is responsible for creating the *Open Systems Interconnection (OSI) model*, which has been a standard reference for data communications between computers since the late 1970s.

Why Is It ISO and Not IOS?

ISO is not a mistyped acronym. It is a word derived from the Greek word *isos*, meaning equal. Because acronyms can vary among languages, the ISO decided to use a word instead of an acronym for its name. With this in mind, it is easy to see why a standards organization would give itself a name that means equal.

The OSI model is the cornerstone of data communications. The layers of the OSI model are as follows:

- Layer 7: Application
- Layer 6: Presentation
- Layer 5: Session
- Layer 4: Transport
- Layer 3: Network
- Layer 2: Data-Link
    - LLC sublayer
    - MAC sublayer
- Layer 1: Physical

The IEEE 802.11-2007 standard defines communication mechanisms only at the Physical layer and MAC sublayer of the Data-Link layer of the OSI model. By design, the 802.11 standard does not address the upper layers of the OSI model, although there are interactions between the 802.11 MAC sublayer and the upper layers for parameters such as quality of service (QoS).

It is important to have an understanding and knowledge of all layers of the OSI model when working with packet analyzers. When captured data is displayed in an analyzer, it is typically separated and grouped by the OSI layers that the data represents. When capturing wireless frames, if wireless encryption is implemented, all of the layer 3 through layer 7 information will be grouped and displayed as the encrypted payload.

You should have a working knowledge of the OSI model for both this book and the CWAP exam. Make sure you understand the seven layers of the OSI model and how communication takes place at the different layers. If you are not comfortable with the concepts of the OSI model, spend some time reviewing it on the Internet or from a good networking fundamentals book prior to taking the CWAP exam. You can find more information about the ISO at www.iso.org.

Packets, Frames, and Bits

When learning about any technology, it is important at times to step back and focus on the basics. If you have ever flown an airplane, it is important, when things get difficult, to refocus on the number-one priority— to fly the airplane. Navigation and communications are secondary to flying the airplane. When dealing with any complex technology, it is easy to forget the main objective; this is as true with 802.11 communications as it is with flying. With 802.11 communications, the main objective is to transfer user data from one computing device to another.

As data is processed in a computer and prepared to be transferred from one computer to another, it starts at the upper layers of the OSI model and moves down until it reaches the Physical layer, where it is ultimately transferred to the other devices. Initially, a user may want to transfer a word processing document from their computer to a shared network disk on another computer. This document will start at the Application layer and work its way down to the Physical layer, get transmitted to the other computer, and then work its way back up the layers of the OSI model to the Application layer on the other computer.

As data travels down the OSI model, for the purpose of being transmitted, each layer adds header information to that data. This enables the data to be reassembled when it is received by the other computer. At the Network layer, an IP header is added to the data that came from layers 4–7. A layer 3 IP *packet* or datagram encapsulates the data from the higher layers. At the Data-Link layer, a MAC header is added, and the IP packet is encapsulated inside a *frame*. Ultimately, when the frame reaches the Physical layer, a PHY header with more information is added to the frame.

Data is eventually transmitted as individual bits at the Physical layer. A *bit* is a binary digit, taking a value of either 0 or 1. Binary digits are a basic unit of communication in digital computing. A *byte* of information comprises 8 bits.

Data-Link Layer

The 802.11 *Data-Link layer* is divided into two sublayers:

- The upper portion is the IEEE 802.2 *Logical Link Control (LLC)* sublayer, which is identical for all 802-based networks, although not used by all IEEE 802 networks.

- The bottom portion of the Data-Link layer is the *Media Access Control (MAC)* sublayer, which is identical for all 802.11-based networks. The 802.11 standard defines operations at the MAC sublayer. The MAC sublayer acts as an interface between the lower layer PHY and the upper LLC sublayer.

Chapter 3 is dedicated to the MAC sublayer. In Chapter 3, the MAC sublayer frame format will be examined, along with an explanation of 802.11 MAC layer addressing.

MSDU

When the Network layer (layer 3) sends data to the Data-Link layer (layer 2), the data is handed off to the LLC and becomes known as the *MAC Service Data Unit (MSDU)*. The MSDU contains data from the LLC and layers 3–7. A simple definition of the MSDU is that it is the data payload that contains the IP packet plus some LLC data.

In Chapters 4, 5, and 6, you will learn about the three major 802.11 frame types:

- Management frames
- Control frames
- Data frames

802.11 management and control frames do not carry upper-layer information. Only 802.11 data frames carry an MSDU payload in the frame body. The 802.11-2007 standard states that the maximum size of the MSDU is 2,304 bytes. The maximum frame body size is determined by the maximum MSDU size (2,304 octets) plus any overhead from encryption.

MPDU

When the LLC sends the MSDU to the MAC sublayer, the MAC header information is added to the MSDU to identify it. The MSDU is now encapsulated in a *MAC Protocol Data Unit (MPDU)*. A simple definition of an MPDU is that it is an 802.11 frame. The 802.11 frame, as shown in Figure 1.1, contains a layer 2 MAC header, a variable-length frame body, and a trailer, which is a 32-bit CRC known as the *frame check sequence (FCS)*. The 802.11 MAC header is discussed in detail later in Chapter 3.

Once the layer 2 header, frame body, and trailer are assembled, the frame is ready to be passed onto the Physical layer, which will then further prepare the frame for transmission.

FIGURE 1.1   802.11 MPDU

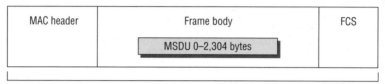

MPDU—802.11 data frame

Physical Layer

Similar to the way the Data-Link layer is divided into two sublayers, the *Physical layer (PHY)* is also divided into two sublayers. The upper portion of the Physical layer is known as the *Physical Layer Convergence Procedure (PLCP)* sublayer, and the lower portion is known as the *Physical Medium Dependent (PMD)* sublayer. The PLCP sublayer prepares the frame for transmission by taking the frame from the MAC sublayer and creating the *PLCP Protocol Data Unit (PPDU)*. The PMD sublayer then modulates and transmits the data as bits.

PSDU

When you are at a door, it could be the entrance or the exit. It depends on what side of the door you are on, but either way, it is the same door. The PLCP Service Data Unit (PSDU) is a view of the MPDU from the other side. The MAC layer refers to an 802.11 frame as the MPDU, while the Physical layer refers to this same exact 802.11 frame as the PSDU. The only difference is which side of the door you are on, or, in the OSI model, from which layer of the model you are looking at the frame.

PPDU

When the PLCP receives the PSDU, it then prepares the PSDU to be transmitted and creates the *PLCP Protocol Data Unit (PPDU)*. The PLCP sublayer adds a preamble and PHY header to the PSDU. The various PHY headers will be discussed in detail in Chapter 2. The preamble is used for synchronization between transmitting and receiving 802.11 radios. After the PPDU is created, the PMD sublayer takes the PPDU and modulates the data bits and begins transmitting.

Figure 1.2 depicts a flowchart that shows the upper-layer information moving between the Data-Link and Physical layers.

FIGURE 1.2   Data-Link and Physical layers

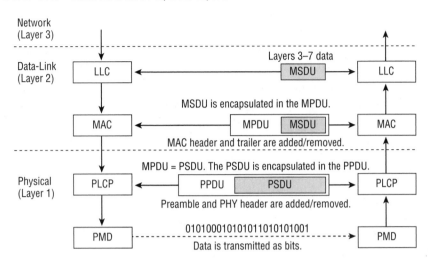

802.11 Architecture

Ideally, you are already familiar with most of the terminology that the IEEE uses to define 802.11 components. The following is a quick review of some of the basic components of WLAN architecture as defined by the IEEE 802.11-2007 standard:

station (STA)   Any device that contains 802.11-compliant MAC and PHY interface to the wireless medium (WM).

access point (AP)   Any entity that has station functionality and provides access to the distribution services, via the wireless medium for associated STAs.

basic service set (BSS)   A group of stations that are successfully synchronized for 802.11 communications. The communicating devices that make up a BSS are solely one AP with one or more client stations. Any stations that are members of a BSS have a layer 2 connection with the access point and are known as associated. All basic service sets can be identified by a 48-bit (6-octet) MAC address known as the *basic service set identifier (BSSID)*. The BSSID address is the layer 2 identifier of each individual basic service set. Most often the BSSID address is the MAC address of the access point.

distribution system (DS)   A system used to interconnect a set of basic service sets and integrated local area networks (LANs) to create an extended service set (ESS).

distribution system medium (DSM)   The logical physical medium used by a distribution system for communications between access points and portals of an extended service set. In most cases, the DSM is an 802.3 Ethernet LAN.

---

extended service set (ESS)   An extended service set is one or more basic service sets connected by a distribution system medium. Usually an extended service set is a collection of multiple access points and their associated clients, all united by a single distribution system medium. The logical network name of an ESS is often called an *extended service set identifier (ESSID)*, or, more simply, the *service set identifier (SSID)*.

independent basic service set (IBSS)   An IBSS consists solely of client stations that use peer-to-peer communications. An IBSS is a self-contained network that does not use an access point and has no access to a distribution system.

802.11 Services

An 802.11 *wireless local area network (WLAN)* normally serves as a portal to a preexisting wired network infrastructure. The distribution system (DS) that is used to interconnect the 802.11 basic service sets can be created from many different technologies. Usually the physical medium used by the DS is an 802.3 Ethernet LAN; however, there is no requirement that the DSM be Ethernet.

The 802.11-2007 standard also does not require the DS to use layer 3, Network layer communications. Normally TCP/IP communications are used on the wired network where the WLAN serves as a portal. Remember, all 802.11 communications occur at the Physical layer and the MAC sublayer of the Data-Link layer; therefore, there is no requirement that IP networking be used by the DS. Additionally, the 802.11-2007 standard does not "constrain a DS to be either centralized or distributed in nature." Because of this purposeful lack of constraints, commercial WLAN vendors offer many different types of architecture including autonomous access points, cooperative-control access points, and WLAN controller-based solutions.

Since the IEEE does not define detailed specifics of DS implementations, the 802.11-2007 standard defines 802.11 services. The 802.11 services are correlated with different components of the 802.11 architecture. The IEEE specifies two major categories of 802.11 services called the station service and the distribution system service, which both operate at the MAC sublayer.

Station Service

The *station service (SS)* is used by all 802.11 client stations including APs. Access points also use station services because they also have STA functionality. You should always remember that an access point is also a station. The majority of WLAN controller vendors implement what is known as a *split MAC architecture*. With this type of WLAN architecture, some of the MAC services are handled by the WLAN controller, and some are handled by the controller-based access point. Station services include the following:

- Authentication
- Deauthentication

- Data confidentiality (encryption)
- MSDU delivery
- Dynamic frequency selection (DFS)
- Transmit power control (TPC)
- Higher-layer timer synchronization (QoS facility only)
- QoS traffic scheduling (QoS facility only)

In later chapters of this book, you will learn about the MAC sublayer frame exchanges that are used to provide these station services.

Distribution System Service

The *distribution system service (DSS)* is comprised of MAC sublayer services that are provided by the distribution system. As mentioned earlier, because the IEEE does not define the specifics of DS implementation, the architecture that uses the distribution system services can be used by different types of WLAN architecture, including access points and WLAN controllers. The distribution system service provides the following:

- Association
- Reassociation
- Disassociation
- Distribution
- Integration
- QoS traffic scheduling (QoS facility only)

It should be noted that client STAs do not use any of the services of DSS and only use the capabilities of the 802.11 defined station service. Once again, these MAC sublayer distribution system services operate within access points and/or WLAN controllers.

The *integration service (IS)* enables delivery of MSDUs between the distribution system and a non-IEEE-802.11 local area network, via a portal. A simpler way of defining the integration service is to characterize it as a *frame format transfer method*. The portal is usually either an access point or a WLAN controller. As mentioned earlier, the payload of a wireless 802.11 data frame is the upper layer 3–7 information known as the MSDU. The eventual destination of this payload usually resides on a wired network infrastructure. Because the wired infrastructure is a different physical medium, an 802.11 data frame payload (MSDU) must be effectively transferred into an 802.3 Ethernet frame. For example, a VoWiFi phone transmits an 802.11 data frame to an autonomous access point. The MSDU payload of the frame is the VoIP packet with a final destination of a VoIP server residing on the wired network. The job of the integration service is to first remove the 802.11 header and trailer and then encase the MSDU VoIP payload inside an 802.3 Ethernet frame. Normally, the integration service transfers frame payloads between an 802.11 and 802.3 medium. However, the integration service could transfer an MSDU between the 802.11 medium and another MAC frame format such as 802.5 token ring.

All the IEEE 802 frame formats share similar characteristics, including the 802.11 frame. Because the frames are similar, it is easier to translate the frames as they move from the 802.11 wireless network to the 802.3 wired network, and vice versa.

One of the differences between 802.3 Ethernet and 802.11 wireless frames is the frame size. 802.3 frames have a maximum size of 1,518 bytes with a maximum data payload of 1,500 bytes. If the 802.3 frames are 802.1Q tagged for VLANs and user priority, the maximum size of the 802.3 frame is 1,522 bytes with data payload of 1,504 bytes. As you have just learned, 802.11 frames are capable of transporting frames with a MSDU payload of 2,304 bytes of *upper-layer* data. This means that as the data moves between the wireless and the wired network, the access point may receive a data frame that is too large for the wired network. This is rarely a problem thanks to the TCP/IP protocol suite. TCP/IP, the most common communications protocol used on networks, typically has an IP *maximum transmission unit (MTU)* size of 1,500 bytes. IP packets are usually 1,500 bytes based on the MTUs. When the IP packets are passed down to 802.11, even though the maximum size of the MSDU is 2,304 bytes, the size will be limited to the 1,500 bytes of the IP packets.

Another difference between 802.3 and 802.11 frames is the MAC addressing fields. 802.3 frames have only a source address (SA) and destination address (DA) in the layer 2 header. 802.11 frames have four address fields in the MAC header. 802.11 frames typically use only three of the MAC address fields. However, an 802.11 frame sent within a wireless distribution system (WDS) requires all four MAC addresses. The contents of these four fields can include the following MAC addresses: receiver address (RA), transmitter address (TA), basic service set identifier (BSSID), destination address (DA), and source address (SA). Certain frames may not contain some of the address fields. Even though the number of address fields is different, both 802.3 and 802.11 identify a source address and a destination address and use the same MAC address format. The first three octets are known as the *organizationally unique identifier (OUI)*, and the last three octets are known as the extension identifier. 802.11 MAC addressing will be discussed in further detail in Chapter 3.

802.11 Frames

802.11 frames are unlike many frames used by wired network standards such as IEEE 802.3, which uses a single data frame type. The IEEE 802.11 standard defines three major frame types: management, control, and data. These frame types are further subdivided into multiple subtypes.

Management Frames

802.11 *management frames* make up a majority of the frame types in a WLAN. Management frames are used by wireless stations to join and leave the basic service set. They are not necessary on wired networks, since physically connecting or disconnecting the network cable performs this function. However, because wireless networking is an unbounded medium, it is necessary for the wireless station to first find a compatible WLAN, then authenticate to the WLAN (assuming they are allowed to connect), and finally associate with the WLAN (typically with an access point) to gain access to the wired network (the distribution system).

Another name for an 802.11 management frame is a *Management MAC Protocol Data Unit (MMPDU)*. Management frames have a MAC header, a frame body, and a trailer; however, management frames do not carry any upper-layer information. There is no MSDU encapsulated in the MMPDU frame body, which carries only layer 2 information fields and information elements. *Information fields* are fixed-length mandatory fields in the body of a management frame. *Information elements* are variable in length and are optional.

The following is a list of all 12 management frame subtypes as defined by the 802.11-2007 standard:

- Association request
- Association response
- Reassociation request
- Reassociation response
- Probe request
- Probe response
- Beacon
- Announcement traffic indication message (ATIM)
- Disassociation
- Authentication
- Deauthentication
- Action

Chapter 4 will discuss the different subtypes of 802.11 management frames in great detail.

Control Frames

802.11 *control frames* assist with the delivery of the data frames. Under ideal conditions, control frames should be heard by all stations within a BBS; therefore, they must be transmitted at one of the basic rates. Control frames are also used to clear the channel, acquire the channel, and provide unicast frame acknowledgments. They contain only header information and a trailer. Control frames do not have a frame body.

The following is a list of all eight control frame subtypes as defined by the 802.11 standard:

- Power Save Poll (PS-Poll)
- Request to send (RTS)
- Clear to send (CTS)

- Acknowledgment (ACK)
- Contention Free-End (CF-End)
- CF-End + CF+ACK
- Block ACK Request (BlockAckReq)
- Block ACK (BlockAck)

Chapter 5 will discuss the different subtypes of 802.11 control frames in great detail. You will note that some of the control frames are indicated.

Data Frames

Most 802.11 *data frames* carry the actual MSDU data that is passed down from the higher-layer protocols. The layer 3–7 MSDU payload is normally encrypted for data privacy reasons. However, some 802.11 data frames carry no MSDU payload at all but do have a specific MAC control purpose within a basic service set. Any data frames that do not carry a MSDU payload are not encrypted because a layer 3–7 data payload does not exist. There are a total of 15 data frame subtypes. The data subtype is usually referred to as the *simple data frame*. The simple data frame has MSDU upper-layer information encapsulated in the frame body. The integration service that resides in autonomous APs and WLAN controllers takes the MSDU payload of a simple data frame and transfers the MSDU into 802.3 Ethernet frames. Null function frames are sometimes used by client stations to inform the access point of changes in Power Save status.

The following is a list of all 15 data frame subtypes as defined by the 802.11 standard:

- Data (simple data frame)
- Null function (no MSDU payload)
- Data + CF-ACK
- Data + CF-Poll
- Data + CF-ACK + CF-Poll
- CF-ACK (no MSDU payload)
- CF-Poll (no MSDU payload)
- CF-ACK + CF-Poll (no MSDU payload)
- QoS data
- QoS Null (no MSDU payload)
- QoS data + CF-ACK
- QoS data + CF-Poll
- QoS data + CF-ACK + CF-Poll
- QoS CF-Poll (no MSDU payload)
- QoS CF-ACK + CF-Poll (no MSDU payload)

Chapter 6 will discuss the different subtypes of 802.11 data frames in great detail. You will note that many of the data frames are collectively referred to as *QoS data frames*. 802.11 QoS will be discussed in detail in Chapter 8.

IEEE 802.11-2007 Standard and Amendments

The Institute of Electrical and Electronics Engineers (IEEE) is a global professional society with more than 395,000 members. The IEEE's mission is to "foster technological innovation and excellence for the benefit of humanity." To networking professionals, that means creating the standards that we use to communicate.

The IEEE is probably best known for its LAN standards, the IEEE 802 project. IEEE projects are subdivided into working groups to develop standards that address specific problems or needs. For instance, the IEEE 802.3 working group was responsible for creating a standard for Ethernet, and the IEEE 802.11 working group was responsible for creating the WLAN standard. The numbers are assigned as the groups are formed, so the *11* assigned to the wireless group indicates that it was the 11th working group formed under the IEEE 802 project. IEEE 802.11 technology, more commonly referred to as *Wi-Fi*, is a standard technology for providing LAN communications using radio frequencies (RF). The IEEE designates the 802.11-2007 standard as the most current guideline to provide operational parameters for WLANs.

As the need arises to revise existing standards created by the working groups, task groups are formed. These task groups are assigned a sequential single letter (multiple letters are assigned if all single letters have been used) that is added to the end of the standard number (for example, 802.11g, 802.11i, and 802.3af). Some letters are not assigned. For example, the letters *o* and *l* are not assigned, to prevent confusion with the numbers 0 and 1. Other letters may not be assigned to task groups to prevent confusion with other standards. For example, 802.11x has not been assigned because it can be easily confused with the 802.1X standard and because 802.11x has become a common casual reference to the 802.11 family of standards.

You can find more information about the IEEE at www.ieee.org. It is important to remember that the IEEE standards, like many other standards, are written documents describing how technical processes and equipment should function. Unfortunately, this often allows for different interpretations when the standard is being implemented, so it is common for early products to be incompatible between vendors, as was the case with the early 802.11 products.

The original 802.11 standard was published in June 1997 as IEEE Std. 802.11-1997, and it is often referred to as 802.11 Prime because it was the first WLAN standard. The standard was revised in 1999, reaffirmed in 2003, and published as IEEE Std. 802.11-1999 (R2003). On March 8, 2007, a new iteration of the standard was approved, IEEE Std. 802.11-2007. This new standard is an update of the IEEE Std. 802.11-1999 revision. The following documents have been rolled into this latest revision, providing users with a single document with all the amendments that have been published to date. The current 802.11-2007 standard includes the following:

- IEEE Std 802.11-1999 (R2003)
- IEEE Std 802.11a-1999
- IEEE Std 802.11b-1999
- IEEE Std 802.11d-2001
- IEEE Std 802.11g-2003
- IEEE Std 802.11h-2003
- IEEE Std 802.11i-2004
- IEEE Std 802.11j-2004
- IEEE Std 802.11e-2005

This revision also includes corrections, clarifications, and enhancements.

All CWNP exams are based on the most recently published version of the standard, 802.11-2007, and any 802.11 amendments that have been ratified after 2007. You can download the 802.11-2007 standard and amendments from http://standards.ieee.org/getieee802/802.11.html.

The IEEE specifically defines 802.11 technologies at the Physical layer and the MAC sublayer of the Data-Link layer. By design, the 802.11 standard does not address the upper layers of the OSI model, although there are interactions between the 802.11 MAC layer and the upper layers for parameters such as quality of service. The PHY Task Group worked in conjunction with the MAC Task Group to define the original 802.11 standard. The PHY Task Group defined three original Physical layer specifications:

Infrared (IR) Infrared technology uses a light-based medium. Although an infrared medium was indeed defined in the original 802.11 standard, the implementation is obsolete. You can find more information about modern implementations of infrared technology at the Infrared Data Association's website, www.irda.org. The scope of this book focuses on the 802.11 RF mediums. Infrared devices are known as clause 16 devices.

Frequency hopping spread spectrum (FHSS) Radio frequency signals can be defined as narrowband signals or as spread spectrum signals. An RF signal is considered spread spectrum when the bandwidth is wider than what is required to carry the data. FHSS is a spread spectrum technology that was first patented during World War II. Frequency hopping 802.11 radio cards are often called clause 14 devices because of the clause that referenced them in the original 802.11 standard. Although FHSS was popular when 802.11 Prime was first ratified, it is not compatible with the newer 802.11 PHY standards and amendments. Most, if not all, vendors have ceased production of clause 14 devices.

Direct sequence spread spectrum (DSSS)   Direct sequence spread spectrum is another spread spectrum technology that is frequently used and easiest to implement. DSSS 802.11 radio cards are often known as clause 15 devices.

What Is an IEEE Clause?

The IEEE standards are very organized, structured documents. A standards document is hierarchically structured, with each section numbered. The highest level (such as 7) is referred to as a clause, with the lower-level sections such as 7.3.2.4 referred to as subclauses. As amendments are created, the sections in the amendment are numbered relative to the original standard, even though the amendment is a separate document. When a standard and its amendments are rolled into a new version of the standard, as was recently done with IEEE Std. 802.11-2007, the clauses and subclauses of all the individual documents are unique, enabling the documents to be combined without having to change any of the section (clause/subclause) numbers or references.

As defined by 802.11 Prime, the frequency space in which either FHSS or DSSS radio cards can transmit is the license-free 2.4 GHz Industrial, Scientific, and Medical (ISM) band. DSSS 802.11 radio cards can transmit in channels subdivided from the entire 2.4 GHz to 2.4835 GHz ISM band. The IEEE is more restrictive for FHSS radio cards, which are permitted to transmit on 1 MHz subcarriers in the 2.402 GHz to 2.480 GHz range of the 2.4 GHz ISM band.

Chances are that you will not be working with older legacy 802.11 equipment because most WLAN deployments use technologies as defined by newer 802.11 amendments. WLAN companies had the choice of manufacturing either clause 14 FHSS radio cards or clause 15 DSSS radio cards. Because these spread spectrum technologies differ, they cannot communicate with each other and often have a hard time coexisting. These spread spectrum signals are analogous to oil and water in that they do not mix well. Therefore, it is important to understand that an 802.11 DSSS (clause 15) radio cannot communicate with an 802.11 FHSS (clause 14) radio. The majority of legacy 802.11 Prime WLAN deployments used frequency hopping, but some DSSS solutions were available as well.

What about the speeds? Data rates defined by the original 802.11 standard were 1 Mbps and 2 Mbps regardless of which spread spectrum technology was used. A data rate is the number of bits per second the Physical layer carries during a single-frame transmission, normally stated as a number of millions of bits per second (Mbps). Keep in mind that a data rate is the speed and not actual throughput. Because of medium access methods, aggregate throughput is typically one-half or less of the available data rate speed.

Understanding Exam Terminology

In 2007, the IEEE consolidated the majority of the ratified amendments with the original standard, creating a single document that is now published as the 802.11-2007 standard. The Wi-Fi Alliance and most WLAN professionals still refer to the ratified amendments by name.

However, the CWAP exam (PW0-270) rarely refers to any of the amendments by name. The exam will quiz you on the technologies used by each amendment. For example, 802.11b is a ratified amendment that has now been integrated into the 802.11-2007 standard. The technology that was originally defined by the 802.11b amendment is called High-Rate DSSS (HR-DSSS). Although the name 802.11b effectively remains the more commonly used marketing term, any exam questions will use the technical term HR-DSSS instead of 802.11b.

For the CWAP exam (PW0-270), you should understand the differences between technologies and how each one works. An understanding of which technologies are defined by each of the amendments will also be helpful for your career. Remember, the CWNP program maintains an updated current list of the exam terms that can be downloaded from the following URL: www.cwnp.com/exams/exam_terms.html.

802.11b

Although the Wi-Fi consumer market continues to grow at a tremendous rate, 802.11b-compatible WLAN equipment gave the industry the first needed huge shot in the arm. In 1999, the IEEE Task Group b (TGb) published the IEEE Std. 802.11b-1999, which was later amended and corrected as IEEE Std. 802.11b-1999/Cor1-2001. All aspects of the 802.11b ratified amendment can now be found in clause 18 of the 802.11- 2007 standard.

The Physical layer medium that is defined by 802.11b is High-Rate DSSS (HR-DSSS). The frequency space in which 802.11b radio cards can operate is the unlicensed 2.4 GHz to 2.4835 GHz ISM band.

Will 802.11b Devices Work with Legacy 802.11 Devices?

802.11b radio cards are known as clause 18 devices. The 802.11b amendment specifies the use of only a DSSS-type physical medium and does not specify FHSS. Because a good portion of the legacy 802.11 deployments used FHSS, 802.11b radio cards are not backward compatible with those systems and cannot be used. However, 802.11b clause 18 radio cards are backward compatible with the legacy 802.11 DSSS clause 15 devices. 802.11b HR-DSSS WLAN equipment should be able to communicate with legacy 802.11 DSSS WLAN equipment. The caveat to this is that, depending on the manufacturer, the legacy devices might not use the same interpretation of the IEEE standards. Many of the legacy devices did not undergo any compatibility testing such as that provided by the Wi-Fi Alliance.

The TGb's main goal was to achieve higher data rates within the 2.4 GHz ISM band. 802.11b radio devices accomplish this feat by using a different spreading/coding technique called Complementary Code Keying (CCK) and modulation methods using the phase properties of the RF signal. 802.11 devices used a spreading technique called the Barker code. The end result is that 802.11b radio devices support data rates of 1, 2, 5.5, and 11 Mbps. 802.11b systems are backward compatible with the 802.11 DSSS data rates of 1 Mbps and 2 Mbps. The transmission data rates of 5.5 Mbps and 11 Mbps are known as HR-DSSS. Once again, understand that the supported data rates refer to available bandwidth and not aggregate throughput. An optional technology called Packet Binary Convolutional Code (PBCC) is also defined under clause 18.

 Real World Scenario

Why Do You Need to Know About Legacy Technologies?

The authors of this book firmly believe that it is important to learn about legacy technologies. By understanding how legacy products functioned, it typically makes it easier to understand how current technologies work and their benefits when compared to the legacy technologies. Although this is a great answer, there is an even better answer. That answer is that these legacy technologies are still used. 802.11 Prime, defined in 1997, specified DSSS communications at 1 and 2 Mbps. 802.11b, 802.11g, and 802.11n are all backward compatible with these data rates. To maintain communications between devices that support different PHY standards, it is common for management frames to be transmitted at these slower data rates. So, when capturing and analyzing 802.11 frames, be prepared to see frames transmitted at these slower data rates.

802.11a

During the same year that the 802.11b amendment was approved, another important amendment was also ratified and published as IEEE Std. 802.11a-1999. The engineers in Task Group a (TGa) set out to define how 802.11 technologies would operate in the newly allocated Unlicensed National Information Infrastructure (UNII) frequency bands. 802.11a radio cards can transmit in three different 100 MHz unlicensed frequency bands in the 5 GHz range. A total of 12 channels are available in the three UNII bands. All aspects of the 802.11a ratified amendment can now be found in clause 17 of the 802.11-2007 standard.

The 2.4 GHz ISM band is a much more crowded frequency space than the 5 GHz UNII bands. Microwave ovens, Bluetooth devices, cordless phones, and numerous other devices all operate in the 2.4 GHz ISM band and are potential sources of interference. In addition, the sheer number of 2.4 GHz WLAN deployments has often been a problem in environments such as multitenant office buildings.

One big advantage of using 802.11a WLAN equipment is that it operates in the less-crowded 5 GHz UNII bands. Eventually, the three UNII bands will also become crowded.

Regulatory bodies such as the FCC are opening up more frequency space in the 5 GHz range, and the IEEE addressed this in the 802.11h amendment.

802.11a radio cards operating in the 5 GHz UNII bands are classified as clause 17 devices. As defined by the 802.11a amendment, these devices are required to support data rates of 6, 12, and 24 Mbps with a maximum of 54 Mbps. With the use of a spread spectrum technology called Orthogonal Frequency Division Multiplexing (OFDM), data rates of 6, 9, 12, 18, 24, 36, 48, and 54 Mbps are supported in most manufacturers' radio cards. It should be noted that an 802.11a radio does not have to support all these rates, and one vendor may have an implementation of data rates that is not compatible with another vendor.

It should also be noted that 802.11a radio cards cannot communicate with 802.11 legacy, 802.11b, or 802.11g radio cards for two reasons:

- 802.11a radio cards use a different spread spectrum technology than 802.11 legacy or 802.11b devices.

- 802.11a devices transmit in the 5 GHz UNII bands, while the 802.11/802.11b/802.11g devices operate in the 2.4 GHz ISM band.

The good news is that 802.11a can coexist in the same physical space with 802.11, 802.11b, or 802.11g devices because these devices transmit in separate frequency ranges.

The IEEE 802.11a amendment designated OFDM data transmissions within the frequency space of the 5 GHz UNII bands. The 802.11a amendment defined three groupings, or bands, of UNII frequencies, known as UNII-1 (lower), UNII-2 (middle), and UNII-3 (upper). All three of these bands are 100 MHz wide, and each has four channels. The IEEE 802.11h amendment introduced the capability for 802.11 radios to transmit in a new frequency band called UNII-2 Extended with 11 more channels. The 802.11h amendment effectively is an extension of the 802.11a amendment.

The UNII bands are as follows:

- UNII-1 (lower) is 5.15–5.25 GHz.

- UNII-2 (middle) is 5.25–5.35 GHz.

- UNII-2 Extended is 5.47–5.725 GHz.

- UNII-3 (upper) is 5.725–5.825 GHz.

The IEEE has defined multiple PHYs in these various amendments. You can find a more detailed discussion of all the 802.11 PHYs in Chapter 2.

802.11g

Another amendment that generated excitement in the Wi-Fi marketplace was published as IEEE Std. 802.11g-2003. The IEEE defines 802.11g cards as clause 19 devices, which transmit in the 2.4 GHz to 2.4835 GHz ISM frequency band. Clause 19 defines a technology called Extended Rate Physical (ERP). All aspects of the 802.11g ratified amendment can now be found in clause 19 of the 802.11-2007 standard.

The main goal of the Task Group g (TGg) was to enhance the 802.11b Physical layer to achieve greater bandwidth yet remain compatible with the 802.11 MAC. Two mandatory and two optional ERP PHYs are defined by the 802.11g amendment.

The mandatory PHYs are ERP-OFDM and ERP-DSSS/CCK. To achieve the higher data rates, a PHY technology called Extended Rate Physical OFDM (ERP-OFDM) is mandated. Data rates of 6, 9, 12, 18, 24, 36, 48, and 54 Mbps are possible using this technology, although once again the IEEE requires only the data rates of 6, 12, and 24 Mbps. To maintain backward compatibility with 802.11 (DSSS only) and 802.11b networks, a PHY technology called Extended Rate Physical DSSS (ERP-DSSS/CCK) is used with support for the data rates of 1, 2, 5.5, and 11 Mbps.

What Is the Difference Between ERP-DSSS/CCK, DSSS, and HR-DSSS?

From a technical viewpoint, there is no difference between ERP-DSSS/CCK and DSSS and HR-DSSS. A key point of the 802.11g amendment was to maintain backward compatibility with older 802.11 (DSSS only) and 802.11b radios while at the same time achieving higher data rates. 802.11g devices (clause 19 radios) use ERP-OFDM for the higher data rates. ERP-DSSS/CCK is effectively the same technology as the DSSS that is used by legacy 802.11 devices (clause 15 radios) and HR-DSSS that is used by 802.11b devices (clause 18 radios). Mandated support for ERP-DSSS/CCK allows for backward compatibility with older 802.11 (DSSS only) and 802.11b radios.

The 802.11g ratified amendment also defined two optional PHYs called ERP-PBCC and DSSS-OFDM. These optional technologies are beyond the scope of this book and rarely used by WLAN vendors.

What Is the Difference Between OFDM and ERP-OFDM?

From a technical viewpoint, there is no difference between OFDM and ERP-OFDM. The only difference is the transmit frequency. OFDM refers to 802.11a devices (clause 17 radios) that transmit in the 5 GHz UNII-1, UNII-2, and UNII-3 frequency bands. ERP-OFDM refers to 802.11g devices (clause 19 radios) that transmit in the 2.4 GHz ISM frequency band.

As you have learned, the 802.11g amendment requires support for both ERP-DSSS/CCK and ERP-OFDM. The good news is that an 802.11g AP can communicate with 802.11g client stations as well as 802.11 (DSSS only) or 802.11b stations. The ratification of the

802.11g amendment triggered monumental sales of Wi-Fi gear in the small office, home office (SOHO), and enterprise markets because of both the higher data rates and the backward compatibility with older equipment. As mentioned earlier in this chapter, different spread spectrum technologies cannot communicate with each other, yet the 802.11g amendment mandates support for both ERP-DSSS/CCK and ERP-OFDM. In other words, ERP-OFDM and ERP-DSSS/CCK technologies can coexist, yet they cannot speak to each other. Therefore, the 802.11g amendment calls for a protection mechanism that allows the two technologies to coexist. The goal of the protection mechanism is to prevent older 802.11b HR-DSSS or 802.11 DSSS radio cards from transmitting at the same time as 802.11g (ERP) radio cards.

802.11n-2009

The passage of the 802.11n-2009 amendment is having a major impact on the Wi-Fi marketplace. Since 2004, 802.11 Task Group n (TGn) had been working on improvements to the 802.11 standard to provide for greater throughput. Many of the past IEEE 802.11 amendments defined data bandwidth and data rates. 802.11n now defines data rates by using a modulation and coding scheme (MCS). The main objective of the 802.11n-2009 amendment was to increase the data rates and the throughput in both the 2.4 GHz and 5 GHz frequency bands. The 802.11n amendment defines a new operation known as *high throughput (HT)*, which provides PHY and MAC enhancements to provide for data rates potentially as high as 600 Mbps.

The mechanisms defined by the 802.11n-2009 amendment are vastly different from previous 802.11 technologies. However, clause 20 radios (HT) are required to be backward compatible with older clause 18 radios (HR-DSSS), clause 17 radios (OFDM), and clause 19 radios (ERP). Clause 18 HR-DSSS (802.11b) and clause 19 ERP (802.11g) radios can transmit in only the 2.4 GHz ISM band, while clause 17 OFDM (802.11a) radios transmit in the 5 GHz UNII bands. It should be noted that the technology defined for use by HT clause 20 radios is not frequency dependent. HT technology can be used in both the 2.4 GHz ISM band and the 5 GHz UNII bands.

HT clause 20 radios use *multiple-input multiple-output (MIMO)* technology in unison with OFDM technology. MIMO uses multiple receiving and transmitting antennas and actually capitalizes on the effects of multipath as opposed to compensating for or eliminating them. The beneficial consequences of using MIMO are increased throughput and even greater range.

It should be noted that many WLAN vendors offered pre-802.11n products in the SOHO marketplace. The majority of these products were not interoperable with other vendors' products and are not compatible with products based on the 802.11n Draft 2.0 amendment or the final 802.11n-2009 amendment. Because the 802.11n-2009 amendment introduced many new enhancements, protocol and spectrum analysis of 802.11n WLANs has become more complex. You can find a detailed discussion about 802.11n in Chapter 11.

Post-2007 Ratified Amendments

802.11a, 802.11b, and 802.11g are all considered to be part of the 802.11-2007 standard. The 802.11n amendment was ratified after 2007. Currently, the amendments that have been ratified post-2007 include the 802.11k-2008 amendment, the 802.11n-2009 amendment, the 802.11r-2008 amendment, the 802.11w-2009 amendment, and the 802.11y-2008 amendment. The technologies defined in these post-2007 amendments will be covered in various chapters of this book and on the CWAP exam.

Wi-Fi Alliance

The *Wi-Fi Alliance* is a global, nonprofit industry association of more than 300 member companies devoted to promoting the growth of WLANs. One of the primary tasks of the Wi-Fi Alliance is to market the Wi-Fi brand and raise consumer awareness of new 802.11 technologies as they become available. Because of the Wi-Fi Alliance's overwhelming marketing success, the majority of the more than 1 billion Wi-Fi users immediately recognize the Wi-Fi logo shown in Figure 1.3.

FIGURE 1.3   Wi-Fi logo

The Wi-Fi Alliance's main task is to ensure the interoperability of WLAN products by providing certification testing. During the early days of the 802.11 standard, the Wi-Fi Alliance further defined some of the ambiguous standards requirements and provided a set of guidelines to assure compatibility between different vendors. As shown in Figure 1.4, products that pass the Wi-Fi certification process receive a Wi-Fi Interoperability Certificate that provides detailed information about the individual product's Wi-Fi certifications. This certification not only includes radio interoperability such as 802.11a, 802.11b, 802.11g, and 802.11n but also certification of additional capabilities such as security, multimedia, convergence, and supported special features.

The Wi-Fi Alliance, originally named the Wireless Ethernet Compatibility Alliance (WECA), was founded in August 1999. The name was changed to the Wi-Fi Alliance in October 2002.

FIGURE 1.4   Wi-Fi interoperability certificate

The Wi-Fi Alliance has certified more than 7,000 Wi-Fi products for interoperability since testing began in April 2000. Multiple Wi-Fi CERTIFIED programs exist that cover basic connectivity, security, quality of service (QoS), and more. Testing of vendor Wi-Fi products is performed in 13 independent authorized test laboratories worldwide. The guidelines for interoperability for each Wi-Fi CERTIFIED program are usually based on key components and functions that are defined in the IEEE 802.11-2007 standard and various 802.11 amendments. In fact, many of the same engineers who belong to 802.11 task groups are also contributing members of the Wi-Fi Alliance. However, it is important to understand that the IEEE and the Wi-Fi Alliance are two separate organizations. The IEEE 802.11 task group defines the WLAN standards, and the Wi-Fi Alliance defines interoperability certification programs. The Wi-Fi CERTIFIED programs include the following:

802.11a, b, or g—IEEE 802.11 baseline   The baseline program certifies 802.11a, b, and/or g interoperability to ensure that the essential wireless data transmission works as expected. 802.11b and g utilize spectrum in the 2.4 GHz band. 802.11g has a higher data rate (54 Mbps) than 802.11b (11 Mbps). 802.11a utilizes frequencies in the 5 GHz band and has a maximum data rate of 54 Mbps. Each certified product is required to support one frequency band as a minimum, but it can support both. The CWAP exam will not use the terms 802.11 a/b/g; however, the a/b/g terminology is commonplace within the industry because of the Wi-Fi Alliance baseline certifications.

Wi-Fi CERTIFIED n—IEEE 802.11 baseline   This certification program is based on the 802.11n-2009 ratified amendment that defines an HT wireless network utilizing MIMO technology. HT provides PHY and MAC enhancements to support throughput of 100 Mbps and greater.

Wi-Fi Protected Access 2 (WPA2)—security   WPA2 is based on the security mechanisms that were originally defined in the IEEE 802.11i amendment that defines a *robust security network (RSN)*. Two versions of WPA2 exist: WPA2-Personal defines security for a SOHO environment, and WPA2-Enterprise defines stronger security for enterprise corporate networks. Each certified product is required to support WPA2-Personal or WPA2-Enterprise. You can find more detailed discussion of robust security networks in Chapter 10.

Wi-Fi Protected Setup—security   *Wi-Fi Protected Setup (WPS)* defines simplified and automatic WPA and WPA2 security configurations for home and small-business users. Users can easily configure a network with security protection by using a personal identification number (PIN) or a button located on the access point and the client device.

Wi-Fi Multimedia (WMM)—multimedia   WMM is based on the QoS mechanisms that were originally defined in the IEEE 802.11e amendment. WMM enables Wi-Fi networks to prioritize traffic generated by different applications. In a network where WMM is supported by both the access point and the client device, traffic generated by time-sensitive applications such as voice or video can be prioritized for transmission on the half-duplex RF medium.

WMM Power Save (WMM-PS)—multimedia   WMM-PS helps conserve battery power for devices using Wi-Fi radios by managing the time the client device spends in sleep mode. Conserving battery life is critical for handheld devices such as bar-code scanners and VoWiFi phones. To take advantage of power-saving capabilities, both the device and the access point must support WMM Power Save.

CWG-RF—multimedia   Converged Wireless Group-RF Profile (CWG-RF) was developed jointly by the Wi-Fi Alliance and the Cellular Telecommunications and Internet Association (CTIA), now known as the Wireless Association. CWG-RF defines performance metrics for Wi-Fi and cellular radios in a converged handset to help ensure that both technologies perform well in the presence of the other. All CTIA-certified handsets now include this certification.

Voice Personal—application   Voice Personal offers enhanced support for voice applications in residential and small-business Wi-Fi networks. These networks include one access point, mixed voice and data traffic from multiple devices (such as phones, PCs, printers, and other consumer electronic devices), and support for up to four concurrent phone calls. Both the access point and the client device must be certified to achieve performance matching the certification metrics.

As 802.11 technologies evolve, new Wi-Fi CERTIFIED programs will be detailed by the Wi-Fi Alliance. The next certification will probably be Voice Enterprise, which will define enhanced support for voice applications in the enterprise environment. Some aspects of the 802.11r-2008 (secure roaming) and 802.11k-2008 (resource management) amendments will probably be tested in Voice Enterprise.

Wi-Fi Alliance and Wi-Fi CERTIFIED

You can find more information about the Wi-Fi Alliance at www.wi-fi.org. The following five white papers from the Wi-Fi Alliance are also included on the CD that accompanies this book:

- "The State of Wi-Fi Security"

- "Wi-Fi CERTIFIED for WMM: Support for Multimedia Applications with Quality of Service in Wi-Fi Networks"

- "WMM Power Save for Mobile and Portable Wi-Fi CERTIFIED Devices"

- "Wi-Fi CERTIFIED n: Longer-Range, Faster-Throughput, Multimedia-Grade Wi-Fi Networks"

- "Wi-Fi CERTIFIED Voice-Personal: Delivering the Best End-User Experience for Voice over Wi-Fi "

Summary

To provide a basic understanding of data communications and components, we reviewed the OSI model, which has been a standard reference for data communications between computers since the late 1970s. We explained the relationship between bits, frames, and packets.

The Data-Link layer is divided into the upper portion known as the LLC, which is identical for all 802-based networks, and the bottom portion known as the MAC, which is identical for all 802.11-based networks and acts as an interface between the lower-layer PHY and the upper LLC sublayer.

We covered the MSDU and how it is the data payload containing the IP packet and some LLC data, along with the MPDU being the 802.11 frame. The physical is divided into the two sublayers, the upper portion known as the PLCP and the lower portion known as the PMD. The MAC layer refers to an 802.11 frame as the MPDU, while the Physical layer refers to it as the PSDU. The PLCP prepares the PSDU to be transmitted, creating the PPDU that the PMD modulates, and then begins transmitting.

When performing wireless analysis, a strong knowledge of the 802.11 architecture, services, and frame types is necessary. An overview of these topics was provided. In-depth coverage of these topics will be discussed in later chapters in the book.

This chapter also provided an overview and review of the 802.11 standards and amendments.

Exam Essentials

Explain the differences between a PPDU, PSDU, MPDU, and MSDU.   Understand at which layer of the OSI model each data unit operates and what comprises each data unit.

Know the differences between the station service and distribution station service.   Station services are used by client STAs as well as WLAN infrastructure devices. Client STAs do not use distribution station services.

Understand the similarities and differences of 802.11 frames and 802.3 frames.   The IEEE created both of these frame types. 802.11 and 802.3 frames share similar and different properties. Know how they compare to each other.

Know the three major 802.11 frame types.   Make sure you know the function of the management, control, and data frames. Know what makes the major frame types different. Data frames contain an MSDU, while management and control frames do not.

Know the frequency bands used by each PHY as defined by the 802.11-2007 standard.   OFDM equipment operates in the 5 GHz UNII bands. DSSS, FHSS, HR-DSSS, and ERP devices transmit and receive in the 2.4 GHz ISM band. Additionally, the 802.11-n-2009 amendment defines operation of HT radios in both the 2.4 and 5 GHz bands.

Explain all the Wi-Fi Alliance certifications.   Familiarize yourself with all the Wi-Fi Alliance certifications and how they relate to the various PHY and MAC mechanisms as defined by the IEEE-2007 standard.

Key Terms

Before you take the exam, be certain you are familiar with the following terms:

access point (AP)

basic service set (BSS)

basic service set identifier (BSSID)

bit

byte

control frames

data frames

Data-Link layer

distribution system (DS)

distribution system medium (DSM)

distribution system service (DSS)

extended service set (ESS)

extended service set identifier (ESSID)

frame

frame check sequence (FCS)

High Throughput (HT)

independent basic service set (IBSS)

Information elements

Information fields

Logical Link Control (LLC)

MAC Protocol Data Unit (MPDU)

MAC Service Data Unit (MSDU)

management frames

Management MAC Protocol Data Unit (MMPDU)

maximum transmission unit (MTU)

Media Access Control (MAC)

multiple-input multiple-output (MIMO)

Organizationally Unique Identifier (OUI)

packet

Physical layer (PHY)

Physical Layer Convergence Procedure (PLCP)

Physical Medium Dependent (PMD)

PLCP Protocol Data Unit (PPDU)

PLCP Service Data Unit (PSDU)

QoS data frames

robust security network (RSN)

service set identifier (SSID)

simple data frame

station (STA)

station service (SS)

Wi-Fi Alliance

Wi-Fi Protected Setup (WPS)

wireless local area network (WLAN)

Review Questions

1. The information found inside an IP packet is considered the main payload for which of the following?
   A. MPDU
   B. PPDU
   C. PSDU
   D. MSDU
   E. MMPDU

2. Which sublayer of the OSI model's Data-Link layer is used for communication between 802.11 radios?
   A. LLC
   B. WPA
   C. MAC
   D. FSK

3. Which of the following contains the same information found with an MPDU?
   A. APDU
   B. PPDU
   C. PSDU
   D. MSDU

4. What are the three main components of an 802.11 MPDU? (Choose the three best answers.)
   A. Frame body
   B. PPDU
   C. MSDU
   D. Trailer
   E. MAC header

5. Which 802.11 frames are usually encrypted for data privacy reasons?
   A. Management frames
   B. Control frames
   C. QoS data frames with MSDU payload
   D. Data frames without an MSDU payload
   E. MMPDU

6. Which OSI sublayer is responsible for modulation and transmission of data bits?

    A. PLCP

    B. PPTP

    C. MAC

    D. LLC

    E. PMD

7. In what type of WLAN devices can the distribution system services (DSSs) operate? (Choose all that apply.)

    A. Mesh Access point

    B. WLAN controller

    C. Autonomous access point

    D. Laptop client radio

    E. VoWiFi phone

8. Which service of the DSS is responsible for the transfer of upper layer 3–7 information from an 802.11 frame format to an 802.3 frame format?

    A. Association

    B. Integration

    C. Reassociation

    D. Disassociation

    E. QoS traffic scheduling

9. Which of these services can be characterized by the 802.11 station service (SS)? (Choose all that apply.)

    A. Association

    B. Authentication

    C. Disassociation

    D. Deauthentication

    E. Transmit power control

10. Which of these 802.11 frames carry a MAC sublayer payload inside the frame body? (Choose all that apply.)

    A. Beacon

    B. Data frame

    C. Reassociation request

    D. QoS data frame

    E. Probe response

    F. PS-Poll

11. In what type of WLAN devices can the stations service (SS) operate? (Choose all that apply.)

A. Mesh access point

B. WLAN controller

C. Autonomous access point

D. Laptop client radio

E. VoWiFi phone

12. The IEEE 802.11-2007 standard defines communication mechanisms at which layers of the OSI model? (Choose all that apply.)

A. Network

B. Physical

C. Transport

D. Application

E. Data-Link

F. Session

13. Which OSI sublayer is responsible for adding a preamble and PHY header to an MPDU?

A. PLCP

B. PPTP

C. MAC

D. LLC

E. PMD

14. Which of the following frequency spaces are supported by HT clause 20 radios? (Choose all that apply.)

A. UNII 5.15–5.25 GHz

B. UNII 5.25–5.35 GHz

C. UNII 5.47–5.715 GHz

D. UNII 5.725–5.825 GHz

E. ISM 2.4–2.4835 GHz

15. Which of the following devices are classified as 802.11 STA devices? (Choose all that apply.)

A. Autonomous AP

B. VoWiFi Telephone

C. Cellular Telephone

D. DSSS Barcode Scanner

16. Which Wi-Fi Alliance certification validates many of the robust security network (RSN) mechanisms that the IEEE has designated in the 802.11-2007 standard? (Choose all that apply.)

A. WMM

B. CWG-RF

C. 802.11k

D. WMM-PS

E. WPA2

17. HT clause 20 radios are backward compatible with which of the following type of 802.11 radios? (Choose all that apply.)

A. Clause 18 radios (HR-DSSS)

B. Clause 17 radios (OFDM)

C. Clause 14 radios (FHSS)

D. Clause 19 radios (ERP)

18. Which of these 802.11 frames are considered to be 802.11 control frames? (Choose all that apply.)

A. ATIM

B. ACK

C. CTS

D. Probe response

E. PS-Poll

19. What is the maximum size of the payload of a data frame as defined by the 802.11-2007 standard?

A. 1500 bytes

B. 2304 bytes

C. 1504 bytes

D. 1518

E. 1522

20. How many MAC address fields are found in the MAC header of an 802.11 frame? (Choose all that apply.)

A. Four

B. Three

C. Two

D. One

Answers to Review Questions

1. D. An IP packet comprises layer 3–7 information. The MAC Service Data Unit (MSDU) contains data from the LLC sublayer and/or any number of layers above the Data-Link layer. The MSDU is the payload found inside the body of 802.11 data frames.

2. C. The IEEE 802.11-2007 standard defines communication mechanisms at only the Physical layer and the MAC sublayer of the Data-Link layer of the OSI model. The Logical Link Control (LLC) sublayer of the Data-Link layer is not defined by the 802.11-2007 standard. WPA is a security certification. FSK is a modulation method.

3. C. The Data-Link layer refers to an 802.11 frame as the MPDU, while the Physical layer refers to this same 802.11 frame as the PLCP Service Data Unit (PSDU).

4. A, D, E. The 802.11 frame contains a layer 2 MAC header, a variable-length frame body, and a trailer, which is a 32-bit CRC known as the frame check sequence (FCS). The frame body contains the MSDU. The PPDU consists of a PSDU, preamble, and PHY header.

5. C. Most 802.11 data frames and QoS data frames carry the actual MSDU data that is passed down from the higher-layer protocols. The layer 3–7 MSDU payload is normally encrypted for data privacy reasons. However, some 802.11 data frames carry no MSDU payload at all but do have a specific MAC control purpose within a basic service set (BSS). Any data frames that do not carry an MSDU payload are not encrypted because a layer 3–7 data payload does not exist. Management frames do not carry any upper-layer information. 802.11 management frames have no MSDU encapsulated in the MMPDU frame body, which carries only layer 2 information fields and information elements. 802.11 control frames contain only header information and a trailer. Control frames do not have a frame body.

6. E. The PLCP and PMD are sublayers of layer 1, the Physical layer. The PLCP sublayer adds a preamble and PHY header to the PSDU to create a PPDU. The preamble is used for synchronization between transmitting and receiving 802.11 radios. After the PPDU is created, the PMD sublayer takes the PPDU and modulates the data bits and begins transmitting. The LLC and MAC are sublayers of the layer 2 Data-Link layer.

7. A, B, C. The IEEE does not define the specifics of DS implementation; the architecture that uses the distribution system services (DSSs) can be used by different types of WLAN architecture including access points and WLAN controllers. Client STAs do not use any of the services of DSS and only use the capabilities of the 802.11 defined station service (SS).

8. B. All the options are considered distribution system services (DSSs). The integration service (IS) enables delivery of MSDUs between the distribution system (DS) and a non-IEEE-802.11 local area network (LAN), via a portal. A simpler way of defining the integration service is to characterize it as a frame format transfer method. The portal is usually either an access point or a WLAN controller. The payload of a wireless 802.11 data frame is the upper layer 3–7 information known as the MSDU. The eventual destination of this payload usually resides on a wired network infrastructure. Because the wired infrastructure is a different physical medium, an 802.11 data frame payload (MSDU) must be effectively transferred into an 802.3 Ethernet frame.

9. B, D, E. Authentication, deauthentication, data confidentiality (encryption), MSDU delivery, dynamic frequency selection (DFS), transmit power control (TPC), higher layer timer synchronization (QoS facility only), and QoS traffic scheduling (QoS facility only) are all considered to be station services that are provided at the MAC sublayer. Association and disassociation are services that also operate at the MAC sublayer; however, they are classified as distribution system services.

10. A, C, E. Beacon, reassociation request, and probe response frames are all 802.11 management frames. Management frames have a MAC header, a frame body, and a trailer; however, management frames do not carry any upper-layer information. There is no MSDU encapsulated in the MMPDU frame body, which carries only layer 2 information fields and information elements. A PS-Poll frame is an 802.11 control frame. Control frames do not have a frame body. Data and QoS data frames are MPDUs whose frame body contains an MSDU upper-layer 3–7 payload.

11. A, B, C, D, E. The station service (SS) is used by all 802.11 client stations including APs. Access points also use station services because they also have STA functionality. The majority of WLAN controller vendors implement what is known as a split MAC architecture. With this type of WLAN architecture, some of the MAC services are handled by the WLAN controller, and some are handled by the controller-based access point. Therefore, the 802.11 station MAC services such as data privacy (encryption) are used by client STAs and other WLAN architecture. However, the distribution system MAC services such as the integration service do not operate with client STAs.

12. B, E. The IEEE 802.11-2007 standard only defines communication mechanisms at the Physical layer and MAC sublayer of the Data-Link layer of the OSI model.

13. A. The MAC layer refers to an 802.11 frame as the MPDU, while the Physical layer refers to this same exact 802.11 frame as the PSDU. The PLCP and PMD are sublayers of layer 1, the Physical layer. The PLCP sublayer adds a preamble and PHY header to the PSDU to create a PPDU. The preamble is used for synchronization between transmitting and receiving 802.11 radios. After the PPDU is created, the PMD sublayer takes the PPDU, modulates the data bits, and begins transmitting. The LLC and MAC are sublayers of the layer 2 Data-Link layer.

14. A, B, C, D, E. The 802.11n devices (HT clause 20) support the 4 UNII bands (UNII-1, UNII-2, UNII-3, and UNII-2 Extended).

15. A, B, D. The 802.11-2007 standard defines a station (STA) as any device that contains 802.11-compliant MAC and PHY interface to the wireless medium (WM). Although access points are typically specifically referred to as APs, since they contain an 802.11-compliant MAC and PHY interface to the wireless medium, they are technically stations, albeit a special type of station. Cellular telephones do not use 802.11 standards.

16. E. The Wi-Fi Alliance maintains the Wi-Fi Protected Access 2 (WPA2) certification. WPA2 is based on the robust security network (RSN) mechanisms that were originally defined in the IEEE 802.11i amendment that is now part of the 802.11-2007 standard. Two versions of WPA2 exist: WPA2-Personal defines security for a SOHO environment, and WPA2-Enterprise defines stronger security for enterprise corporate networks. Each certified product is required to support both WPA2-Personal and WPA2-Enterprise.

17. A, B, D. HT clause 20 radios are backward compatible with older clause 18 radios (HR-DSSS), clause 17 radios (OFDM), and clause 19 radios (ERP). In other words, 802.11n radios are backward compatible with 802.11b, 802.11a, and 802.11g radios. HT radios are not backward compatible with legacy frequency hopping radios.

18. B, C, E. The ACK, CTS and PS-Poll frames are all 802.11 control frames. The ATIM and probe response frame are 802.11 management frames. 802.11 control frames assist with the delivery of the data frames. Control frames are also used to clear the channel, acquire the channel, and provide unicast frame acknowledgments.

19. B. One of the differences between 802.3 Ethernet and 802.11 frames is the frame size. 802.3 frames have a maximum size of 1,518 bytes with a maximum data payload of 1,500 bytes. If the 802.3 frames are 802.1Q tagged for VLANs and user priority, the maximum size of the 802.3 frame is 1,522 bytes with data payload of 1,504 bytes. The payload of an 802.11 data frame is the layer 3–7 information found in the MAC Service Data Unit (MSDU). The 802.11-2007 standard states that the maximum size of the MSDU is 2,304 bytes. The maximum 802.11 frame body size is determined by the maximum MSDU size (2,304 octets) plus any overhead from encryption.

20. A. A huge difference between 802.3 and 802.11 frames is the MAC addressing fields. 802.3 frames have only a source address (SA) and destination address (DA) in the layer 2 header. 802.11 frames have four address fields in the MAC header. 802.11 frames typically use only three of the MAC address fields. However, an 802.11 frame sent within a wireless distribution system (WDS) requires four MAC addresses. The contents of these four fields can include the following MAC addresses: receiver address (RA), transmitter address (TA), basic service set identifier (BSSID), destination address (DA), and source address (SA). Certain frames may not contain some of the address fields.

Chapter

2

802.11 Physical (PHY) Layer Frame Format

IN THIS CHAPTER, YOU WILL LEARN ABOUT THE FOLLOWING:

- ✓ **Physical Layer Operations**
    - Carrier Sense/Clear Channel Assessment(CS/CCA)
    - Transmit (Tx)
    - Receive (Rx)
- ✓ **Physical Layer**
    - PLCP Service Data Unit
    - PLCP Protocol Data Unit
    - Physical Media Dependent
- ✓ **PLCP Protocol Data Unit**
    - PLCP Preamble
        - Long PPDU Preamble
        - Short PPDU Preamble
        - OFDM PLCP Preamble
    - PLCP Header
    - 802.11n PPDUs
        - Non-HT Legacy PPDU
        - HT Mixed PPDU
        - HT Greenfield PPDU
        - Data Field
- ✓ **2.4 GHz Communications**
    - 2.4 GHz Channels

✓ **5 GHz Communications**

- UNII-1 (Lower Band)
- UNII-2 (Middle Band)
- UNII-2 Extended
- UNII-3 (Upper Band)
- 5 GHz Channels

✓ **Adjacent, Nonadjacent, and Overlapping Channels**

✓ **Clause 14 FHSS PHY**

- Hopping Sequence
- Dwell Time
- Hop Time
- Modulation

✓ **Clause 15 DSSS PHY**

- DSSS Data Encoding
- Modulation

✓ **Clause 17 OFDM PHY**

- Convolutional Coding
- Modulation

✓ **Clause 18 HR-DSSS PHY**

- Modulation

✓ **Clause 19 ERP PHY**

✓ **Clause 20 HT PHY**

This chapter will introduce you to the Physical (PHY) layer frame format. The beginning of this chapter will provide a basic overview of the PHY layer and its functions. This overview will provide a foundation that will help you understand the components of the PHY layer and how they interact. This chapter will then provide details about each of the different 802.11 PHY layer implementations that are currently defined in the standard and ratified amendments.

Physical Layer Operations

No matter which PHY layer implementation is being used by the wireless station to transmit or receive data, there is a functional commonality between them all. Each STA must wait and listen to see whether there is data being sent that it must receive and process, or it must wait and listen to see whether the channel is clear so that it can transmit. The details of how these tasks are performed vary between the different PHY layer implementations and are beyond the scope of what is covered in this book. The following paragraphs describe these three modes or states that an STA will transition between:

Carrier Sense/Clear Channel Assessment (CS/CCA)

If the station is not currently transmitting or receiving, it listens and senses the channel either to detect the beginning of a network signal that can be received (carrier sense) or to identify whether the channel is unused and available prior to transmitting a packet (clear channel assessment).

Essentially, either a station is transmitting or it is idle. If it is idle, it could be listening and waiting for the channel to become available so that it can transmit a frame. It could also be listening, waiting to sense the beginning of a transmission from another station, or it could be listening and receiving a frame that is being transmitted by another station. This chapter covers the PHY frame format and how the different components of the frames are used in the communications process.

Transmit (Tx)

When a station needs to transmit a frame, it must first check to see whether the wireless medium is available. This is done by the CS/CCA process. After the medium is available and it is the station's turn to transmit, the station will transmit the frame and immediately switch back to receive mode. Since wireless stations cannot transmit and receive (or listen) at the same time, unlike Ethernet, it is not possible to listen for collisions. Therefore, after a frame is transmitted, if the frame is successfully received, the receiving station will reply to the transmitting station with an acknowledgment. The receiving station may send an acknowledgment (ACK) for a single frame or a block acknowledgment (BlockACK) for multiple frames. Both acknowledgments will be covered in chapter 5.

Receive (Rx)

If the CS/CCA identifies that the medium is busy, the station needs to be able to identify whether the medium is busy because of another device transmitting a frame. The transmitting station will precede that data portion of the frame with a preamble. This preamble contains a string of 0s and 1s that the receiving station can identify and synchronize with, essentially alerting the receiving station to the transmission. The preamble also includes a Start Frame Delimiter field, which the receiving station uses to identify the beginning of the frame. After the preamble, the length field in the frame header tells the receiving station how long the frame is. After the entire frame is received, if the frame is determined to be intact by the station it is addressed to, that station will reply to the transmitting station with an acknowledgment frame (ACK).

Physical Layer

The *Physical layer* is divided into two sublayers. The upper portion of the Physical layer is known as the *Physical Layer Convergence Procedure (PLCP) sublayer*, and the lower portion is known as the *Physical Medium Dependent (PMD) sublayer*. The PLCP prepares the frame for transmission by taking the frame from the MAC sublayer and creating the PLCP Protocol Data Unit (PPDU). The PMD sublayer then modulates and transmits the data as bits. When the *MAC Protocol Data Unit (MPDU)* is handed down to the physical layer, it is then referred to as a *PLCP Service Data Unit (PSDU)*. The PSDU is then prepared to be transported as part of a PPDU.

PLCP Service Data Unit

The PSDU is the data that the PHY transmits. The PSDU is equivalent to the MPDU that is passed down from the Data-Link layer. The PSDU and MPDU are like two sides of a door. When you are at a door, it could be the entrance or the exit. It depends on what side of the door you are on, but either way, it is the same door. The PSDU is a view of the MPDU from the other side. The MAC layer refers to the frame as the MPDU, while the Physical layer refers to this same frame as the PSDU. The difference is which side of the door you are on, or, in the OSI model, from which layer of the model you are looking at the frame.

PLCP Protocol Data Unit

When the PLCP receives the PSDU, it then prepares the PSDU to be transmitted and creates the *PLCP Protocol Data Unit (PPDU)*. The PLCP adds a preamble and PHY header to the PSDU. The preamble is used for synchronization between transmitting and receiving 802.11 radios. When the PPDU is created, the PMD sublayer takes the PPDU and modulates the data bits and begins transmitting.

Figure 2.1 shows the upper-layer information moving between the Data-Link and Physical layers.

FIGURE 2.1   Data-Link and Physical layers

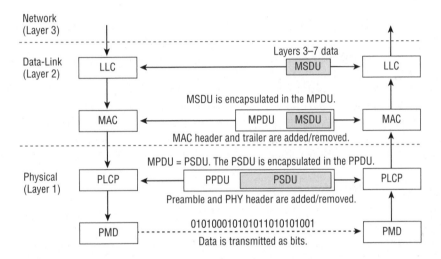

Physical Medium Dependent

When transmitting, the PMD receives the PPDU from the PLCP sublayer. The PMD is then responsible for transmitting the Physical layer data unit. The PMD transmits the data as RF modulated 1s and 0s. When receiving, the PMD listens to the RF, interpreting the modulated RF signal as 1s and 0s and then passing the received data up to the PLCP sublayer.

PLCP Protocol Data Unit

The PLCP Protocol Data Unit consists of three parts: PLCP Preamble, *PLCP Header*, and PSDU. When the PLCP layer receives the PSDU from the MAC layer, the appropriate PLCP Preamble and PLCP Header are added to the PSDU to create the PPDU.

Remember that the MPDU and PSDU are two names for the same thing. The MAC layer refers to the data that it passes to the Physical layer as the MPDU, while the Physical layer refers to it as the PSDU. Although this is the proper usage of these terms, they are often improperly interchanged. In fact, when referring to the different PHY implementations in the IEEE 802.11-2007 standard, one section of the standard shows the PPDU consisting of the PLCP Preamble, PLCP Header, and PSDU, while another section shows the PPDU consisting of the PLCP Preamble, PLCP Header, and MPDU.

PLCP Preamble

When transmitting data, the transmitting station alerts the receiving station of the transmission by sending a *PLCP Preamble* at the beginning of the transmission. The preamble is a string of 0 and 1 bits that are used to synchronize incoming transmissions. The IEEE 802.11-2007 standard defines three different preambles in the Long PPDU format, the Short PPDU format, and the OFDM PLCP preamble. The 802.11n amendment further defines three additional preambles in three different PPDUs: non-HT legacy PPDU, HT-mixed PPDU, and HT-Greenfield PPDU. The Long PLCP preamble, the Short PLCP preamble, and the OFDM PLCP preambles are described in the following sections, while the other three are discussed later in this chapter along with the rest of their PPDUs.

Long PLCP Preamble

The *Long PPDU* includes a 144-bit PLCP Preamble that consists of a 128-bit Sync field and a 16-bit *Start of Frame Delimiter (SFD)*, as shown in Figure 2.2. The purpose of the *Sync field* is to alert the receiver that the potentially receivable signal is present. A receiver (Rx) 802.11 station will then begin to synchronize with the incoming signal after detecting the Sync field. The Sync field is then followed by the SFD field, which consists of the following 16 bits (1111 0011 1010 0000). Synchronization between the Tx and Rx must occur before the SFD field. The SFD effectively is an indicator that the information found in the PLCP Header is coming next. The Long Preamble is transmitted using Differential Binary Phase Shift Keying (DBPSK) at the rate of 1 Mbps. The modulation used for the Long Preamble is fixed. The modulation of the PLCP Header is also fixed. The modulation of the PSDU (MPDU) is not necessarily the same as that used for the preamble or the header. When the Sync field is transmitted, receiving stations may not identify it immediately. It does not matter whether the entire Sync field is received, as long as the SFD is received and identified.

Short PLCP Preamble

The *Short PPDU* includes a 72-bit PLCP Preamble, which consists of a 56-bit Sync field and a 16-bit SFD, as shown in Figure 2.3. A 72-bit preamble used for synchronization effectively has half the PHY layer overhead of the legacy 144-bit Long Preamble. The SFD field consists of the following 16 bits (0000 0101 1100 1111), which is the reverse order of the SFD used in the Long PPDU. Like the Long PLCP Preamble, the Short PLCP Preamble is transmitted using DBPSK; however, the Short PLCP Header is transmitted using 2 Mbps Differential Quadrature Phase Shift Keying (DQPSK). The modulation used for the Short Preamble is fixed. In addition to the Short Preamble having a fixed modulation, the modulation of the PLCP Header is also fixed. Once again, keep in mind that this is not the same modulation used for data bit transmission of the PSDU (MPDU).

FIGURE 2.2 Long PPDU format

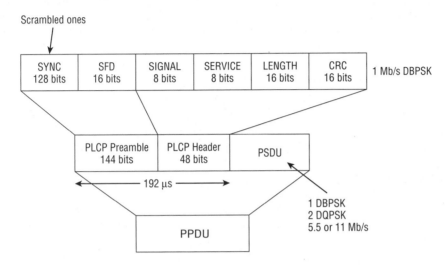

FIGURE 2.3 Short PPDU format

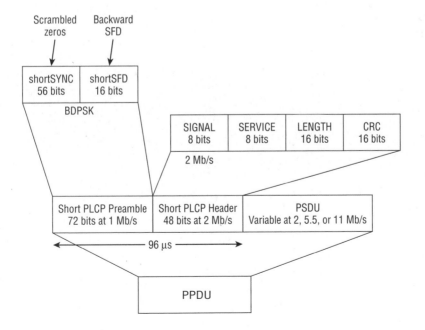

OFDM PLCP Preamble

The OFDM PLCP Preamble, also referred to as the OFDM training structure, consists of 10 short symbols and 2 long symbols, as shown in Figure 2.4. In the figure, t1 to t10 identify the short training symbols, GI2 is a long guard interval, and T1 and T2 identify the long training symbols. Following the PLCP preamble is the SIGNAL field and the DATA fields, each with a guard interval preceding them. The total training length is 16 µs. A short OFDM training symbol consists of 12 subcarriers while a long OFDM training symbol consists of 53 subcarriers.

FIGURE 2.4   The OFDM training structure (PLCP Preamble)

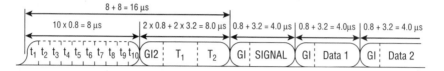

PLCP Header

Long and Short PLCP Headers are both 48 bits long and contain the following four fields, shown earlier: Signal (8 bits), Service (8 bits), Length (16 bits), and CRC (16 bits). The purpose of the *Signal field* is to indicate which modulation method will be used to transmit the PSDU portion of the PPDU. Remember that a PSDU is the same thing as an 802.11 MPDU; therefore, the Signal field is used to indicate what type of modulation is used for the transmission of the 802.11 MAC frame. When a Long PLCP Header is used, the PSDU can be transmitted at one of four transmission rates: 1 Mbps, 2 Mbps, 5.5 Mbps, and 11 Mbps. When a Short PLCP header is used, only three data rates are supported: 2 Mbps, 5.5 Mbps, and 11 Mbps.

The Service field has five of its eight bits defined in it. Bit 3 is used to indicate which modulation method is used. If it is set to 0, it indicates that complementary code keying is used. If it is set to 1, it indicates that the optional and seldom used modulation method packet binary convolutional code (PBCC) is used. Bit 2 is used to indicate that the transmit frequency and symbol clocks are derived from the same oscillator. Bits 5–7 are used to resolve data length field ambiguities for the optional and seldom used modulation methods ERP-PBCC-11 through ERP-PBCC-33 modes. The rightmost bit, b7, is also used to supplement the Length field, and resolve ambiguities for the CCK 11 Mbps mode.

The PLCP Length field indicates the number of microseconds that are required to transmit the PSDU. The last field that is part of the Long and Short PPDU is the CRC field. This 16-bit CRC provides protection for the other three fields in the PPDU: Signal, Service, and Length. This specific CRC is performed only on these three fields.

If the station is transmitting using clause 17 OFDM transmissions, the SIGNAL field is only 24 bits long. The first four bits (bits 0-3) indicate the data rate that will be used:

6, 9, 12, 18, 24, 36, 48, or 54 Mbps. The next bit (bit 4) is reserved for future use. The next 12 bits (bits 5–16) make up the PLCP Length field, which indicates the number of octets in the PSDU that will be transmitted. The following bit (bit 17) is a parity bit (even parity) for bits 0-16. The last 6 bits (bits 18–23) make up the SIGNAL TAIL, with all 6 bits set to 0.

802.11n PPDUs

When the 802.11n amendment was ratified, three new PPDUs were defined and introduced: non-HT legacy PPDU, HT-mixed PPDU, and HT-greenfield PPDU. The following sections provide an overview of each of them.

Non-HT Legacy PPDU

The *non-HT PPDU* is often also referred to as a legacy format because it was originally defined by clause 17 of the 802.11-2007 standard for OFDM transmissions. The packets are structured according to the clause 17 (OFDM) or clause 19 (ERP) specification. As pictured in Figure 2.5, the non-HT PPDU consists of a preamble that uses short and long training symbols, which are used for synchronization. The preamble consists of 10 short symbols and 2 long symbols.

FIGURE 2.5   802.11n PPDU formats

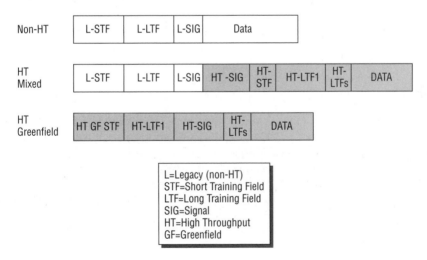

Support for the non-HT legacy format is mandatory for 802.11n radios, and transmissions can occur in only 20 MHz channels. The non-HT format effectively is the same format used by legacy 802.11a and 802.11g radios.

HT-Mixed PPDU

The first of the two new PPDU formats defined in the 802.11n amendment is the *HT-mixed* format. As shown in Figure 2.4, the beginning of the preamble contains the non-HT short and long training symbols that can be decoded by legacy 802.11a (clause 17 OFDM) or 802.11g (clause 19 ERP) radios, enabling them to detect the PPDU and acquire the carrier frequency and timing.

The rest of the HT-mixed preamble and header cannot be decoded by legacy 802.11 devices but can be decoded by HT devices, allowing them to also detect the PPDU and acquire the carrier frequency and timing. The HT portion of the preamble also enables estimation of the MIMO channel, providing HT STAs with the necessary information to demodulate the HT data.

The HT-mixed format will likely be the most commonly used format because it supports both HT and legacy 802.11a/g OFDM radios. Support of the HT-mixed format is also considered mandatory, and transmissions can occur in both 20 MHz and 40 MHz channels. When a 40 MHz channel is used, all broadcast traffic must be sent on a legacy 20 MHz channel so as to maintain interoperability with the 802.11a/g non-HT clients. Also, any transmissions to and from the non-HT clients will have to use a legacy 20 MHz channel.

HT-greenfield PPDU

The second of the two new PPDU formats defined by the 802.11n amendment is the *HT-greenfield* format. As pictured in Figure 2.4, the preamble is not compatible with legacy 802.11 radios, and only HT radios can communicate when using the HT-greenfield format. Support for the HT-greenfield format is optional, and the HT radios can transmit by using both 20 MHz and 40 MHz channels.

Data Field

The data field portion of the PPDU is the PSDU. In the Long and Short PPDUs, the data field is simply the MPDU passed down from the Data-Link layer. In layperson terms, the data field is the 802.11 MAC frame. The data field of the non-HT legacy, HT-mixed, and HT-greenfield PPDUs is displayed in Figure 2.6, and is the same as the data fields from clause 17 (OFDM) and 19 (ERP-OFDM). In these PPDUs, the Service field is prepended to the scrambled PSDU. Scrambling is used to randomize the PSDU, which could have long strings of 0s or 1s.

FIGURE 2.6   802.11n-defined PPDU Data field

SERVICE 16 bits	Scrambled PSDU	6-N_{ES} Tail bits	Pad bits

2.4 GHz Communications

The 2.4 GHz ISM band is the most common band used for wireless networking communications. The 2.4 GHz ISM band is 83.5 MHz wide and spans from 2.4000 GHz to 2.4835 GHz. Use of the 2.4 GHz ISM band for wireless LANs is defined by the IEEE in the 802.11-2007 standard. The bulk of Wi-Fi radios currently transmit in the 2.4 GHz ISM band, including radios that use the following technologies:

- 802.11 (FHSS clause 14 radios or DSSS clause 15 radios)
- 802.11b (HR-DSSS clause 18 radios)
- 802.11g (ERP clause 19 radios)
- 802.11n (HT clause 20 radios)

In addition to being used by wireless networking equipment, the 2.4 GHz ISM band is also used by microwave ovens, cordless home telephones, baby monitors, wireless video cameras, and many other devices. The 2.4 GHz ISM band is heavily used, and one of the big disadvantages of using 802.11b/g radios is the potential for interference.

Please keep in mind that not every country's RF regulatory body will allow for transmissions across the entire 2.4 to 2.4835 GHz ISM band. The IEEE 802.11-2007 standard allows for WLAN transmissions in this band across 14 channels. However, each country can determine which channels can be used.

2.4 GHz Channels

To better understand how legacy 802.11 (DSSS), 802.11b (HR-DSSS), and 802.11g (ERP) radios are used, it is important to understand how the IEEE 802.11-2007 standard divides the 2.4 GHz ISM band into 14 separate channels, as listed in Table 2.1. Although the 2.4 GHz ISM band is divided into 14 channels, the FCC or other local regulatory body designates which channels are allowed to be used. Table 2.1 also shows what channels are supported in a sample of a few countries. As you can see, the regulations can vary greatly between countries.

TABLE 2.1   2.4 GHz frequency channel plan

Channel ID	Center frequency (GHz)	U.S. (FCC)	Canada (IC)	Europe (ETSI)
1	2.412	X	X	X
2	2.417	X	X	X
3	2.422	X	X	X

TABLE 2.1   2.4 GHz frequency channel plan *(continued)*

Channel ID	Center frequency (GHz)	U.S. (FCC)	Canada (IC)	Europe (ETSI)
4	2.427	X	X	X
5	2.432	X	X	X
6	2.437	X	X	X
7	2.442	X	X	X
8	2.447	X	X	X
9	2.452	X	X	X
10	2.457	X	X	X
11	2.462	X	X	X
12	2.467			X
13	2.472			X
14	2.484			

X = supported channel

Channels are designated by their center frequency. Each channel is 22 MHz wide and is often referenced by the center frequency ±11 MHz. For example, channel 1 is 2.412 GHz ±11 MHz, which means that channel 1 spans from 2.401 GHz to 2.423 GHz. It should also be noted that within the 2.4 GHz ISM band, the distance between channel center frequencies is only 5 MHz, with the exception of channel 14. Because each channel is 22 MHz wide and because the separation between center frequencies of each channel is only 5 MHz, the channels will have overlapping frequency space.

Figure 2.7 shows an overlay of all the channels and how they overlap. Channels 1, 6, and 11 have been highlighted because, as you can see, they are separated from each other by enough frequencies that they do not overlap. For two channels to not overlap, they must be separated by at least five channels or 25 MHz. Channels, such as 2 and 9, do not overlap, but by selecting 2 and 9, there is no additional legal channel that can be chosen that does not overlap either 2 or 9. In the United States and Canada, the only three simultaneously nonoverlapping channels are 1, 6, and 11. In regions where channels 1 through 13 are allowed to be used, there are different combinations of three nonoverlapping channels, although channels 1, 6, and 11 are usually chosen.

FIGURE 2.7 2.4 GHz channel overlay diagram

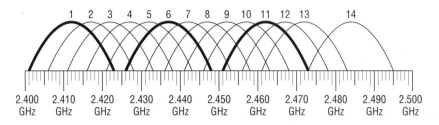

The IEEE 802.11-2007 definitions of nonoverlapping channels in the 2.4 GHz ISM band can be somewhat confusing if not properly explained. Legacy 802.11 (DSSS), 802.11b (HR-DSSS), and 802.11g (ERP) channels all use the same numbering schemes and have the same center frequencies. However, the individual channels' frequency space may overlap. Figure 2.8 shows channels 1, 6, and 11 with 25 MHz of spacing between the center frequencies. These are the most commonly used *nonoverlapping channels* in North America and most of the world for 802.11b/g networks.

FIGURE 2.8 HR-DSSS center frequencies

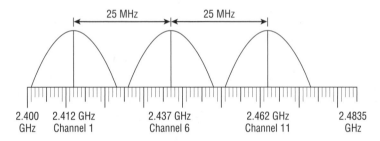

What exactly classifies DSSS or HR-DSSS channels as nonoverlapping? According to the original 802.11 standard, legacy DSSS channels had to have at least 30 MHz of spacing between the center frequencies to be considered nonoverlapping. In a deployment of legacy DSSS equipment using a channel pattern of 1, 6, and 11, the channels were considered overlapping because the center frequencies were only 25 MHz apart. Although DSSS channels 1, 6, and 11 were defined as overlapping, these were still the only three channels used in channel reuse patterns when legacy networks were deployed. This really is of little significance anymore because most 2.4 GHz deployments now use 802.11b/g/n technology.

HR-DSSS was introduced under the 802.11b amendment, which states that channels need a minimum of 25 MHz of separation between the center frequencies to be considered nonoverlapping. Therefore, when 802.11b was introduced, channels 1, 6, and 11 were considered nonoverlapping.

The 802.11g amendment, which allows for backward compatibility with 802.11b HR-DSSS, also requires 25 MHz of separation between the center frequencies to be considered nonoverlapping. Under the 802.11g amendment, channels 1, 6, and 11 are also considered nonoverlapping for both ERP-DSSS/CCK and ERP-OFDM.

Although it is very common to represent the RF signal of a particular channel with an arch-type line, this is not a true representation of the signal. To explain it simply, in addition to the main *carrier frequency*, or main frequency, sideband carrier frequencies are also generated, as shown in Figure 2.9. The IEEE defines a *transmit spectrum mask* for DSSS and HR-DSSS transmissions specifying that the first sideband frequency (–11 MHz to –22 MHz from the center frequency, and +11 MHz to +22 MHz from the center frequency) must be at least 30 dB less than the main frequency. The mask also specifies that any additional sideband carrier frequencies (–22 MHz from the center frequency and beyond, and +22 MHz from the center frequency and beyond) must be at least 50 dB less than the main frequency.

FIGURE 2.9   IEEE 802.11b transmit spectrum mask

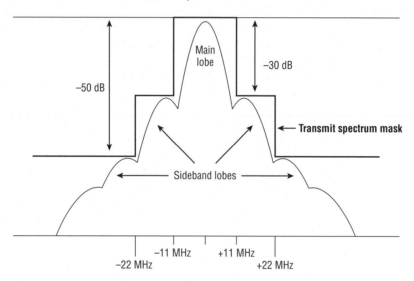

Figure 2.9 illustrates the transmit spectrum mask of an HR-DSSS channel at 2.4 GHz. The transmit spectrum mask is defined to minimize interference between devices on different frequencies. Even though the sideband carrier frequencies are mere whispers of signals compared to the main carrier frequency, even a whisper is noticeable when the person whispering is close to you. This is true for RF devices too.

Figure 2.10 represents RF signals on channels 1, 6, and 11. A signal-level line indicates an arbitrary level of reception by the access point on channel 6. At level 1, meaning the AP on channel 6 receives only the signals above the level 1 line, the signals from channel 1 and channel 11 do not intersect (interfere) with the signals on channel 6. However, at the level 2 line, the signals from channel 1 and channel 11 do intersect (interfere) slightly with the signals on channel 6. At the level 3 line, there is significant interference from the signals from channel 1 and channel 11. Because of the potential for this situation, it is important to separate access points (usually 5 to 10 feet is sufficient) so that interference from sideband frequencies does not occur. This is important both horizontally and vertically.

FIGURE 2.10   Sideband carrier frequency interference

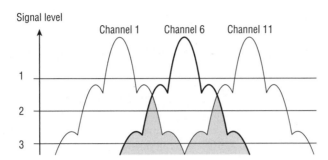

5 GHz Communications

The IEEE 802.11a amendment designated WLAN transmissions within the frequency space of the three 5 GHz bands, each with four channels. These frequency ranges are known as the *Unlicensed National Information Infrastructure (UNII) bands.* The 802.11a amendment defined three groupings, or bands, of UNII frequencies, often known as the lower, middle, and upper UNII bands. These three bands are typically designated as UNII-1 (lower), UNII-2 (middle), and UNII-3 (upper). All three of these bands are 100 MHz wide, which is a useful fact when trying to remember their frequency ranges.

When the 802.11h amendment was ratified, the IEEE had recently designated more frequency space for WLAN transmissions. This frequency space, which consists of 11 additional channels, is often referred to as UNII-2 Extended. Unlike the other three UNII bands that are 100 MHz wide, this new band is 255 MHz wide.

Although we use UNII as the abbreviation, many documents will show U-NII as the abbreviation. Both abbreviations are common and acceptable.

Wi-Fi radios that currently transmit in the 5 GHz UNII bands include radios that use the following protocols:

- 802.11a (OFDM clause 17 radios)
- 802.11h (TPC and DFS)
- 802.11n (HT clause 20 radios)

Please keep in mind that not every country's RF regulatory body will allow for transmissions in all these bands. The IEEE 802.11-2007 standard allows for WLAN transmissions in all four of the bands across 23 channels. However, each country may be different. A more detailed discussion of all the 5 GHz channels occurs later in this chapter.

UNII-1 (Lower Band)

UNII-1, the lower UNII band, is 100 MHz wide and spans from 5.150 GHz to 5.250 GHz. This band is typically used indoors with a maximum allowed output power of 50 mW at the intentional radiator (IR) as defined by the FCC. The IEEE has implemented a transmit power cap of 40 mW, which complies with the FCC maximum. Prior to 2004, the FCC required that all UNII-1–capable devices have permanently attached antennas. This meant that any 802.11a device that supported UNII-1 could not have a detachable antenna, even if the device supported other frequencies or standards.

In 2004, the FCC changed the regulations to allow detachable antennas, providing that the antenna connector is unique. This requirement is similar to the antenna requirements for the other UNII bands and the 2.4 GHz ISM band. Some access point manufacturers allow the ability to configure the device as a bridge and to work in the lower UNII band. Care must be taken to make sure you do not exceed the limitations of your local regulatory body.

UNII-2 (Middle Band)

UNII-2, the middle UNII band, is 100 MHz wide and spans from 5.250 GHz to 5.350 GHz. The FCC allows this band to be used for indoor or outdoor communications, with a maximum allowed output power of 250 mW. The IEEE has implemented a restriction on 802.11 devices of only 200 mW at the intentional radiator, which complies with the FCC maximum. Local regulatory agencies may impose other restrictions that you will need to comply with.

UNII-2 Extended

The UNII-2 Extended band is 255 MHz wide and spans from 5.470 GHz to 5.725 GHz. This band can be used for indoor or outdoor communications, with a maximum allowed output power of 250 mW as defined by the FCC. The IEEE has restricted that to 200 mW at the intentional radiator, which complies with the FCC maximum. Local regulatory agencies may impose other restrictions that you will need to comply with. Operations for WLAN communications were first allowed in this band with the ratification of the 802.11h amendment. Prior to the ratification of this amendment, 5 GHz WLAN communications were allowed in only UNII-1, UNII-2, and UNII-3.

The 802.11h amendment defined the use of transmit power control (TPC) and dynamic frequency selection (DFS) to avoid interference with other devices that use these bands, such as radar transmissions. Any 5 GHz WLAN products that ship in the United States or Canada on or after July 20, 2007, are required to support dynamic frequency selection. 802.11h was actually first implemented in Europe in 2005 and was driven by ETSI. FCC Rule # 15.407(h)(2) requires that WLAN products operating in the UNII-2 and UNII-2 Extended bands must support DFS, to protect WLAN communications from interfering with the other devices that use these bands, such as military or weather radar systems. As mentioned earlier, Europe also requires DFS safeguards. Once again, the local regulatory agencies determine how TPC and DFS restrictions are imposed in any of the UNII bands.

UNII-3 (Upper Band)

UNII-3, the upper UNII band, is 100 MHz wide and spans from 5.725 GHz to 5.825 GHz. This band is typically used for outdoor point-to-point communications but can also be used indoors in some countries, including the United States. Europe does not use the UNII-3 band for WLAN communications. The maximum allowed output power by the FCC is 1000 mW. The IEEE has implemented a power restriction of 800 mW at the intentional radiator, which complies with the FCC maximum. Table 2.2 shows a comparison between the four bands.

TABLE 2.2   The 5 GHz UNII bands

Band	Name	Frequency range	Channels
UNII-1	Lower	5.15 to 5.25 GHz	4 channels
UNII-2	Middle	5.25 to 5.35 GHz	4 channels
UNII-2 Extended	Extended	5.47 to 5.725 GHz	11 channels
UNII-3	Upper	5.725 to 5.825 GHz	4 channels

The CWAP exam will not test you on any power regulations because they vary from country to country. It is advisable to educate yourself about the maximum transmit power regulations of the country where you plan on deploying a WLAN so that no violations occur. The CWAP exam may test you on your knowledge of the frequency ranges of all the ISM and UNII bands or the power restrictions implemented by the IEEE.

5 GHz Channels

The 802.11-2007 standard specifies the channels defined in the 5 GHz UNII bands: UNII-1, UNII-2, UNII-2 Extended, and UNII-3. The centers of the outermost channels must be 30 MHz from the band's edge in the UNII-1 and UNII-2 bands and must be 20 MHz in the UNII-3 band. The original three UNII bands each have four nonoverlapping channels with 20 MHz separation between the center frequencies. The UNII-2 Extended band has 11 nonoverlapping channels with 20 MHz of separation between the center frequencies. The United States also allows for OFDM transmissions on ISM channel 165, whose center frequency is 5.825 GHz, which is at the upper edge of the UNII-3 band. Channel 165 resides squarely within the FCC's 5.725–5.875 GHz ISM band. With the addition of channel 165, there are potentially up to 24 usable 5 GHz channels.

Figure 2.11 shows the 8 UNII-1 and UNII-2 channels in the top graphic, the 11 UNII-2 Extended channels in the center graphic, and the 4 UNII-3 channels, along with ISM channel 165 in the bottom graphic. Channel 36 is highlighted so that it is easier to distinguish a single carrier and its sideband frequencies. The IEEE defines the center frequency of each channel as follows, where n_{ch} is all values from 0 through 200:

$$5{,}000 + 5 \times n_{ch} \text{ (MHz)}$$

FIGURE 2.11   UNII channel overview

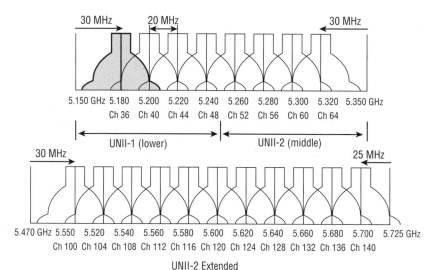

The IEEE does not specifically define a channel width; however, the spectral mask of an OFDM channel is approximately 20 MHz.

As shown in Figure 2.12 of the OFDM spectrum mask, the sideband carrier frequencies do not drop off very quickly, and therefore the sideband frequencies of two adjacent valid channels overlap and are more likely to cause interference. The 802.11a amendment, which originally defined the use of OFDM (clause 17), required only 20 MHz of separation between the center frequencies for channels to be considered nonoverlapping. All 23 channels in the 5 GHz UNII bands use OFDM and have 20 MHz of separation between the center frequencies. Therefore, all 5 GHz OFDM channels are considered nonoverlapping by the IEEE. In reality, there is some sideband carrier frequency overlap between any two adjacent 5 GHz channels. Luckily, because of the number of channels and the channel spacing of 802.11a, it is easier to separate adjacent channels and prevent interference.

FIGURE 2.12   OFDM spectrum mask

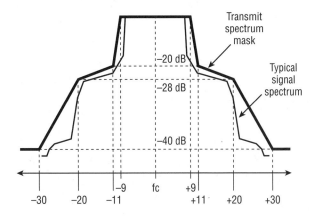

Adjacent, Nonadjacent, and Overlapping Channels

In the preceding paragraphs, you learned how the IEEE 802.11-2007 standard defines nonoverlapping channels. DSSS (legacy) channels require 30 MHz of separation between the center frequencies to be considered nonoverlapping. HR-DSSS (802.11b) and ERP (802.11g) channels require 25 MHz of separation between the center frequencies to be considered nonoverlapping. And finally, 5 GHz OFDM channels require 20 MHz of separation between the center frequencies to be considered nonoverlapping.

An often debated topic is what defines an *adjacent channel* and *nonadjacent channel*. The 802.11-2007 standard loosely defines an adjacent channel as any channel with nonoverlapping frequencies for the DSSS and HR-DSSS PHYs. With ERP and OFDM implementations, the standard loosely defines an adjacent channel as the first channel with a nonoverlapping frequency space. In other words, the IEEE's definition of adjacent channels is almost exactly the same as the definition of nonoverlapping channels that has been discussed earlier. Confused? Table 2.3 illustrates the CWNP program's interpretation of these concepts.

TABLE 2.3 Adjacent vs. nonadjacent

	DSSS clause 15	HR-DSSS clause 18	ERP clause 19	OFDM clause 17
Frequency band	2.4 GHz ISM	2.4 GHz ISM	2.4 GHz ISM	UNII bands
Adjacent	≥ 30 MHz	≥ 25 Mhz	= 25 MHz	= 20 MHz
Nonadjacent	N/A	N/A	> 25 MHz	> 20 MHz
Overlapping	< 30MHz	< 25 MHz	<25 MHz	N/A

Clause 14 FHSS PHY

Frequency hopping spread spectrum (FHSS) was used in the original 802.11 standard and provided 1 and 2 Mbps RF communications using the 2.4 GHz ISM band for legacy clause 14 radios. The majority of 802.11-compliant legacy FHSS radios were manufactured between 1997 and 1999. The IEEE specified that in North America, 802.11 FHSS would use 79 MHz of frequencies, from 2.402 GHz to 2.480 GHz.

Generally, the way FHSS works is that it transmits data by using a small frequency carrier space and then hops to another small frequency carrier space and transmits data, then to another frequency, and so on, as illustrated in Figure 2.13. More specifically, frequency hopping spread spectrum transmits data by using a specific frequency for a set period of time, known as the *dwell time*. When the dwell time expires, the system changes to another frequency and begins to transmit on that frequency for the duration of the dwell time. Each time the dwell time is reached, the system changes to another frequency and continues to transmit.

FIGURE 2.13 FHSS components

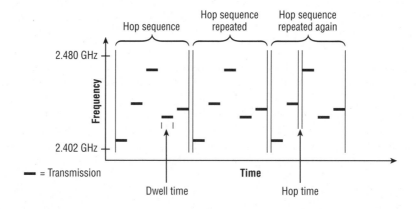

Hopping Sequence

FHSS radios use a predefined *hopping sequence* (also called a hopping pattern or hopping set) comprising a series of small carrier frequencies, or *hops*. Instead of transmitting on one set channel or finite frequency space, an FHSS radio card transmits on a sequence of subchannels called hops. Each time the hop sequence is completed, it is repeated. Figure 2.13 shows a make-believe hopping sequence that consists of five hops.

The original IEEE 802.11 standard mandates that each hop is 1 MHz in size. These individual hops are then arranged in predefined sequences. In North America and most of Europe, the hopping sequences contain at least 75 hops, but no greater than 79 hops. Other countries have different requirements; for example, France uses 35 hops, while Spain and Japan use 23 hops in a sequence. For successful transmissions to occur, all FHSS transmitters and receivers must be synchronized on the same carrier hop at the same time. The 802.11 standard defines hopping sequences that can be configured on an FHSS access point, and the hopping sequence information is delivered to client stations via the beacon management frame.

Dwell Time

Dwell time is a defined amount of time that the FHSS system transmits on a specific frequency before it switches to the next frequency in the hop set. The local regulatory body typically limits the amount of dwell time. For example, the FCC specifies a maximum dwell time of 400 milliseconds (ms) per carrier frequency during any 30-second period of time. Typical dwell times are around 100ms to 200ms. The IEEE 802.11 standard specifies that a hopping sequence must consist of at least 75 frequencies, 1 MHz wide. Because the standard specifies a maximum bandwidth of 79 MHz, the maximum number of hops possible for a hop set would be 79. With an FHSS hop sequence consisting of 75 hops and a dwell time of 400ms, it would take about 30 seconds to complete the hop sequence. After the hop sequence is complete, it is repeated.

Hop Time

Hop time is not a specified period of time but rather a measurement of the amount of time it takes for the transmitter to change from one frequency to another. Hop time is typically a fairly small number, often about 200 to 300 microseconds (µs). With typical dwell times of 100 ms to 200 ms, hop times of 200 µs to 300 µs are insignificant. Insignificant or not, the hop time is essentially wasted time, or overhead, and takes up the same amount of time regardless of the dwell time. The longer the dwell time, the less often the transmitter has to waste time hopping to another frequency, thus greater throughput. If the dwell time is shorter, the transmitter has to hop more frequently, thus decreasing throughput.

Modulation

FHSS uses Gaussian Frequency Shift Keying (GFSK) to encode the data. Two-level GFSK (2GFSK) uses two frequencies to represent a 0 bit or a 1 bit. Four-level GFSK (4GFSK) uses four frequencies, with each frequency representing 2 bits (00, 01, 10, or 11). Because it takes cycles before the frequency can be determined, the symbol rate (rate that the data is sent) is only about 1 or 2 million symbols per second, a fraction of the 2.4 GHz carrier frequency.

What Is the Significance of the Dwell Time?

Because FHSS transmissions jump inside a frequency range of 79 MHz, a narrowband signal or noise would disrupt only a small range of frequencies and would produce only a minimal amount of throughput loss. Decreasing the dwell time can further reduce the effect of interference. Conversely, because the radio card is transmitting data during the dwell time, the longer the dwell time and the greater the throughput.

Clause 15 DSSS PHY

Direct sequence spread spectrum (DSSS) was originally specified in the primary, or root, 802.11 standard and provides 1 Mbps and 2 Mbps RF communications using the 2.4 GHz ISM band. HR/DSSS was also specified in the 802.11b addendum and provides 5.5 Mbps and 11 Mbps RF communications using the same 2.4 GHz ISM band.

 DSSS 1 and 2 Mbps are specified in clause 15 of the 802.11-2007 standard. HR-DSSS 5.5 and 11 Mbps are specified in clause 18 of the 802.11-2007 standard.

Unlike FHSS, where the transmitter jumped between frequencies, DSSS is set to one channel. The data that is being transmitted is spread across the range of frequencies that make up the channel. The process of spreading the data across the channel is known as *data encoding*.

DSSS Data Encoding

RF signals can get altered or corrupted in many ways. Because 802.11 is an unbounded medium with a huge potential for RF interference, it had to be designed to be resilient enough that data corruption could be minimized. To achieve this, each bit of data is encoded and transmitted as multiple bits of data.

The task of adding additional, redundant information to the data is known as *processing gain*. In this day and age of data compression, it seems strange that we would use a technology that adds data to our transmission, but by doing so, the communication is more resistant to data corruption. The system converts the 1 bit of data into a series of bits that are referred to as *chips*. To create the chips, a Boolean XOR is performed on the data bit and a fixed-length bit sequence pseudo-random number (PN) code. Using a PN code known as the Barker code, the binary data 1 and 0 are represented by the following chip sequences:

Binary data 1 = 1 0 1 1 0 1 1 1 0 0 0

Binary data 0 = 0 1 0 0 1 0 0 0 1 1 1

This sequence of chips is then spread across a wider frequency space. Although 1 bit of data might need only 2 MHz of frequency space, the 11 chips will require 22 MHz of frequency carrier. This process of converting a single data bit into a sequence is often called *spreading* or *chipping*. The receiving radio card converts, or *de-spreads*, the chip sequence back into a single data bit. When the data is converted to multiple chips and some of the chips are not received properly, the radio will still be able to interpret the data by looking at the chips that were received properly. When the Barker code is used, as many as 9 of the 11 chips can be corrupted, yet the receiving radio card will still be able to interpret the sequence and convert them back into a single data bit. This chipping process also makes the communication less likely to be affected by intersymbol interference because it uses more bandwidth.

After the Barker code is applied to data, a series of 11 bits, referred to as chips, represent the original single bit of data. This series of encoded bits makes up 1 bit of data. To help prevent confusion, it is best to think of and refer to the encoded bits as *chips*.

Modulation

After the data has been encoded using a chipping method, the transmitter needs to modulate the signal to create a carrier signal containing the chips. *Differential Binary Phase Shift Keying (DBPSK)* utilizes two phase shifts, one that represents a 0 chip and another that represents a 1 chip. *Differential Quadrature Phase Shift Keying (DQPSK)* is an enhancement to DBPSK, utilizing four phase shifts, representing, allowing each phase shift to represent two chips; 00, 01, 10, or 11. Table 2.4 summarizes the data encoding and modulation techniques used by 802.11.

TABLE 2.4   DSSS encoding and modulation overview

Data rate (Mbps)	Encoding	Chip length	Bits encoded	Modulation
1	Barker coding	11	1	DBPSK
2	Barker coding	11	1	DQPSK

Clause 17 OFDM PHY

Orthogonal Frequency Division Multiplexing (OFDM) is one of the most popular communications technologies, used in both wired and wireless communications. The 802.11-2007 standard specifies the use of OFDM at 5 GHz and also specifies the use of ERP-OFDM at 2.4 GHZ. OFDM and ERP-OFDM are the same technology. OFDM is not a spread spectrum technology, even though it has similar properties to spread spectrum, such as low transmit power and using more bandwidth than is required to transmit data. Because of these similarities, OFDM is often referred to as a spread spectrum technology even though technically that reference is incorrect. OFDM actually transmits across 52 separate, closely and precisely spaced frequencies, often referred to as *subcarriers*, as illustrated in Figure 2.14.

The frequency width of each subcarrier is 312.5 KHz. The subcarriers are also transmitted at lower data rates, but because there are so many subcarriers, overall data rates are higher. Also, because of the lower subcarrier data rates, delay spread is a smaller percentage of the symbol period, which means that intersymbol interference (ISI) is less likely to occur. In other words, OFDM technology is more resistant to the negative effects of multipath than DSSS and FHSS spread spectrum technologies. Figure 2.15 represents four of the 52 subcarriers. One of the subcarriers is highlighted so that you can more easily understand the drawing. Notice that the frequency spacing of the subcarriers has been chosen so that the harmonics overlap and provide cancellation of most of the unwanted signals.

The 52 subcarriers are numbered from −26 to +26. Forty-eight of the subcarriers are used to transmit data. The other four, numbers −21, −7, +7, and +21, are known as *pilot carriers*. These four are used as references for phase and amplitude by the demodulator, allowing the receiver to compensate for distortion of the OFDM signal.

FIGURE 2.14   802.11 channels and OFDM subcarriers

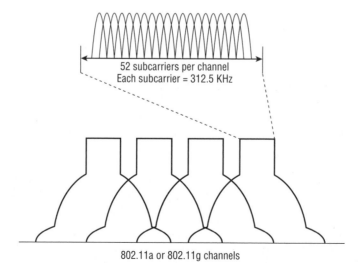

52 subcarriers per channel
Each subcarrier = 312.5 KHz

802.11a or 802.11g channels

FIGURE 2.15   Subcarrier signal overlay

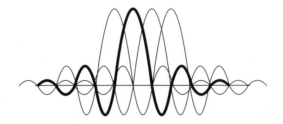

Convolutional Coding

To make OFDM more resistant to narrowband interference, a form of error correction known as *convolutional coding* is performed. The 802.11-2007 standard defines the use of convolutional coding as the error-correction method to be used with OFDM technology. It is a *forward error correction (FEC)* that allows the receiving system to detect and repair corrupted bits.

There are many levels of convolutional coding. Convolutional coding uses a ratio between the bits transmitted vs. the bits encoded to provide these different levels. The lower the ratio, the less resistant the signal is to interference and the greater the data rate will be. Table 2.5 displays a comparison between the technologies used to create the different data rates of both 802.11a and 802.11g. Notice that the data rates are grouped by pairs based on modulation technique and that the difference between the two speeds is caused by the different levels of convolutional coding. A detailed explanation of convolutional coding is extremely complex and even beyond the knowledge needed for the CWAP exam.

TABLE 2.5   802.11a and 802.11g data rate and modulation comparison chart

Data rates (Mbps)	Modulation method	Coded bits per subcarrier	Data bits per OFDM symbol	Coded bits per OFDM symbol	Coding rate (data bits/ coded bits)
6	BPSK	1	24	48	1/2
9	BPSK	1	36	48	3/4
12	QPSK	2	48	96	1/2
18	QPSK	2	72	96	3/4
24	16-QAM	4	96	192	1/2
36	16-QAM	4	144	192	3/4
48	64-QAM	6	192	288	2/3
54	64-QAM	6	216	288	3/4

Modulation

OFDM uses Binary Phase Shift Keying (BPSK) and Quadrature Phase Shift Keying (QPSK) phase modulation for the lower ODFM data rates. The higher OFDM data rates use 16-QAM and 64-QAM modulation. *Quadrature amplitude modulation (QAM)* is a hybrid of phase and amplitude modulation.

Clause 18 HR-DSSS PHY

Clause 18 devices were originally defined in the 802.11b amendment. The 802.11b 5.5 and 11 Mbps speeds are known as *High-Rate DSSS (HR-DSSS)*. 802.11b clause 18 devices are backward compatible with the legacy 802.11 DSSS clause 15 devices. This means that an 802.11b device can transmit using DSSS at 1 Mbps and 2 Mbps and using HR-DSSS at 5.5 Mbps and 11 Mbps. However, 802.11b devices are not capable of transmitting using FHSS; therefore, they are not backward compatible with 802.11 FHSS clause 14 devices.

To help provide the faster speeds of HR-DSSS, a more complex code, *Complementary Code Keying (CCK)*, is utilized instead of the Barker code that is used with DSSS transmissions. CCK uses an eight-chip pseudorandom number (PN), along with using different PNs for different bit sequences. CCK can encode 4 bits of data with 8 chips (5.5 Mbps) and can encode 8 bits of data with 8 chips (11 Mbps).

Modulation

As mentioned earlier in this chapter, after the data has been encoded using a chipping method, the transmitter needs to modulate the signal to create a carrier signal containing the chips. DSSS uses DBPSK and DQPSK to modulate the data at 1 Mbps and 2 Mbps. To provide the faster throughput for HR-DSSS, Complimentary Code Keying (CCK) is used to encode and modulate the data.

Table 2.6 summarizes the data encoding and modulation techniques used by 802.11b.

TABLE 2.6   HR-DSSS encoding and modulation overview

Data rate (Mbps)	Encoding	Chip length	Bits encoded	Modulation
5.5	CCK coding	8	4	CCK
11	CCK coding	8	8	CCK

Clause 19 ERP PHY

Another amendment that generated a lot of excitement in the Wi-Fi marketplace was published as IEEE Std. 802.11g-2003. The IEEE defines 802.11g cards as clause 19 devices, which transmit in the 2.4 GHz to 2.4835 GHz ISM frequency band. Clause 19 defines a technology called *Extended Rate Physical (ERP)*. All aspects of the 802.11g ratified amendment can now be found in clause 19 of the 802.11-2007 standard.

The main goal of the Task Group g (TGg) was to enhance the 802.11b Physical layer to achieve greater bandwidth yet remain compatible with the 802.11 MAC. Two mandatory and two optional ERP physical layers (PHYs) were defined by the 802.11g amendment.

The mandatory PHYs are ERP-OFDM and ERP-DSSS/CCK. To achieve the higher data rates, a PHY technology called *Extended Rate Physical OFDM (ERP-OFDM)* is mandated. Data rates of 6, 9, 12, 18, 24, 36, 48, and 54 Mbps are possible using this technology, although the IEEE requires only the data rates of 6, 12, and 24 Mbps. To maintain backward compatibility with 802.11 (DSSS only) and 802.11b networks, a PHY technology called *Extended Rate Physical DSSS (ERP-DSSS/CCK)* is used with support for the data rates of 1, 2, 5.5, and 11 Mbps.

 Real World Scenario

What Is the Difference Between ERP-DSSS/CCK, DSSS, and HR-DSSS?

From a technical viewpoint, there is no difference between ERP-DSSS/CCK and DSSS and HR-DSSS. A key point of the 802.11g amendment was to maintain backward compatibility with older 802.11 (DSSS only) and 802.11b radios while at the same time achieving higher data rates. 802.11g devices (clause 19 radios) use ERP-OFDM for the higher data rates. ERP-DSSS/CCK is effectively the same technology as the DSSS that is used by legacy 802.11 devices (clause 15 radios) and HR-DSSS that is used by 802.11b devices (clause 18 radios). Mandated support for ERP-DSSS/CCK allows for backward compatibility with older 802.11 (DSSS only) and 802.11b radios.

The 802.11g ratified amendment also defined two optional PHYs called *ERP-PBCC* and *DSSS-OFDM*. These optional technologies are rarely used by WLAN vendors.

As you have learned, the 802.11g amendment requires support for both ERP-DSSS/CCK and ERP-OFDM. The good news is that an 802.11g AP can communicate with 802.11g client stations as well as 802.11 (DSSS only) or 802.11b stations. The ratification of the 802.11g amendment triggered monumental sales of Wi-Fi gear in both the small office/home office (SOHO) and enterprise markets because of both the higher data rates and the backward compatibility with older equipment. As mentioned earlier in this chapter, different spread spectrum technologies cannot communicate with each other, yet the

802.11g amendment mandates support for both ERP-DSSS/CCK and ERP-OFDM. ERP-OFDM and ERP-DSSS/CCK technologies can coexist, yet they cannot speak to each other. Therefore, the 802.11g amendment calls for a *protection mechanism* that allows the two technologies to coexist. The goal of the protection mechanism is to prevent older 802.11b HR-DSSS or 802.11 DSSS radio cards from transmitting at the same time as 802.11g (ERP) radio cards. Table 2.7 shows a brief overview and comparison of 802.11, 802.11b, 802.11g, and 802.11a.

 Real World Scenario

What Is the Difference Between OFDM and ERP-OFDM?

From an 802.11 technical viewpoint, there is no difference between OFDM and ERP-OFDM. The only difference is the transmit frequency. OFDM refers to 802.11a devices (clause 17 radios) that transmit in the 5 GHz UNII-1, UNII-2, UNII-2E, and UNII-3 frequency bands. ERP-OFDM refers to 802.11g devices (clause 19 radios) that transmit in the 2.4 GHz ISM frequency band. The technology is explained further in Chapter 6.

TABLE 2.7   802.11 amendment comparison

	802.11 Legacy	**802.11b**	**802.11g**	**802.11a**
Frequency	2.4 GHz ISM band	2.4 GHz ISM band	2.4 GHz ISM band	5 GHz UNII-1, UNII-2, UNII-2 Extended, and UNII-3 bands.
Spread spectrum technology	FHSS or DSSS	HR-DSSS	ERP: ERP-OFDM and ERP-DSSS/CCK are mandatory	OFDM.
		PBCC is optional.	ERP-PBCC and DSSS-OFDM are optional.	

TABLE 2.7 802.11 amendment comparison *(continued)*

	802.11 Legacy	802.11b	802.11g	802.11a
Data rates	1, 2 Mbps	DSSS: 1, 2 Mbps	ERP-DSSS/CCK: 1, 2, 5.5, and 11 Mbps	6, 12, and 24 Mbps are mandatory.
		HR-DSSS: 5.5 and 11 Mbps	ERP-OFDM: 6, 12 and 24 Mbps are mandatory.	Also supported are 9, 18, 36, 48, and 54 Mbps.
			Also supported are 9, 18, 36, 48, and 54 Mbps.	
			ERP-PBCC: 22 and 33 Mbps	
Backward compatibility	N/A	802.11 DSSS only	802.11b HR-DSSS and 802.11 DSSS	None.
Ratified	1997	1999	2003	1999.

Clause 20 HT PHY

The 802.11a amendment defined the use of clause 17 radios using Orthogonal Frequency Division Multiplexing (OFDM) technology in the 5 GHz UNII bands. 802.11g defined the use of clause 19 radios using ERP-OFDM, which is effectively the same technology except that transmissions occur in the 2.4 GHz ISM band. The 802.11n amendment also defines the use of OFDM channels. However, key differences exist for HT clause 20 radios. The changes and additions introduced by the 802.11n amendment are so significant and important that there is an entire chapter designated to 802.11n. Chapter 10, "802.11n—HT Analysis," discusses in-depth analysis of 802.11n, along with a complete overview of its Physical layer implementation and components.

Summary

In this chapter, you looked at the Physical layer and the components that are used in taking the data from the Data-Link Layer and transmitting it into the air. You also looked at the 2.4 GHz and 5 GHz bands that are used by 802.11, along with the channel and power specifications defined by the IEEE. Each of the Physical layer standards were also reviewed, with exception of 802.11n defined in clause 20, which is reviewed later in a different chapter in this book.

Exam Essentials

Explain the differences between a PPDU, PSDU, MPDU, and MSDU.   Understand at which layer of the OSI model each data unit operates and what comprises each data unit. Although this chapter focuses on the Physical layer, it is important to understand the relationship between all four of the data units.

Know the different Physical layer implementations.   Know the differences and similarities of the Physical layer implementations. Understand how they interact with the upper layers and how they work to provide wireless communications.

Differentiate between adjacent, nonadjacent, and overlapping channels.   It is important to understand how channels relate to other channels and how they can interfere with each other.

Key Terms

adjacent channel

carrier frequency

chipping

chips

Complementary Code Keying (CCK)

convolutional coding

data encoding

de-spreads

Differential Binary Phase Shift Keying (DBPSK)

Differential Binary Phase Shift Keying (DBPSK)

Differential Quadrature Phase Shift Keying (DQPSK)

Direct sequence spread spectrum (DSSS)

DSSS-OFDM

dwell time

ERP-PBCC

Extended Rate Physical (ERP)

Extended Rate Physical DSSS (ERP-DSSS/CCK)

Extended Rate Physical OFDM (ERP-OFDM)

forward error correction (FEC)

Frequency hopping spread spectrum (FHSS)

High-Rate DSSS (HR-DSSS)

Hop time

hopping sequence

hops

HT-greenfield

HT-mixed

Long PPDU

MAC Protocol Data Unit (MPDU)

nonadjacent channel

non-HT PPDU

nonoverlapping channels

Orthogonal Frequency Division Multiplexing (OFDM)

Physical layer

Physical Layer Convergence Procedure (PLCP) sublayer

Physical Medium Dependent (PMD) sublayer

pilot carriers

PLCP Header

PLCP Preamble

PLCP Protocol Data Unit (PPDU)

PLCP Service Data Unit (PSDU)

processing gain

protection mechanism

Quadrature amplitude modulation (QAM)

Short PPDU

Signal field

spreading

Start of Frame Delimiter (SFD)

subcarriers

Sync field

transmit spectrum mask

Unlicensed National Information Infrastructure (UNII) bands

Review Questions

1. The 802.11-2007 standard requires how much separation between center frequencies for HR-DSSS (clause 18) channels to be considered nonoverlapping?

    A. 22 MHz

    B. 25 MHz

    C. 30 MHz

    D. 35 MHz

    E. 40 MHz

2. The upper portion of the Physical layer is known as the _____, and the lower portion is known as the _____ .

    A. PPDU

    B. PMD

    C. PSDU

    D. PLCP

    E. MSDU

3. What three parts make up the PPDU? (Choose all that apply.)

    A. PMD

    B. PLCP Preamble

    C. PLCP Header

    D. PSP

    E. PLCP Service Data Unit (PSDU)

4. The Long PPDU includes a _____ -bit PLCP Preamble, which consists of a _____ -bit Sync field.

    A. 144, 128

    B. 72, 56

    C. 256, 212

    D. 144, 72

    E. 128, 72

5. Both the Long and Short Preambles are transmitted using which modulation technique?

    A. DBPSK

    B. DQPSK

    C. 2GFSK

    D. 4GFSK

    E. 16-QAM

6. Which of the following fields are contained in the Long and Short PLCP Headers? (Choose all that apply.)

    A. Service

    B. Length

    C. Signal

    D. Preamble

    E. CRC

7. Which PPDUs were defined by the 802.11n amendment? (Choose all that apply.)

    A. Non-HT legacy PPDU

    B. HT PPDU

    C. HT-mixed PPDU

    D. Combined HT Legacy PPDU

    E. HT-greenfield PPDU

8. Which of the following define radios that can transmit in the 2.4 GHz ISM band? (Choose all that apply.)

    A. Clause 14

    B. Clause 15

    C. Clause 18

    D. Clause 19

    E. Clause 20

9. Clause 17 defines communications using which of the following modulation methods? (Choose all that apply.)

    A. DBPSK

    B. BPSK

    C. QPSK

    D. 16-QAM

    E. 64-QAM

10. According to the IEEE, clause 17 and clause 19 require which of the following data rates? (Choose all that apply.)

    A. 6

    B. 9

    C. 12

    D. 18

    E. 24

    F. 54

11. In descending order (moving from the Application layer toward the Physical), list the 4 sub-layers that make up the Data-Link and Physical layers.

   A. LLC, MAC, PSDU, PLCP

   B. MAC, LLC, PSDU, PLCP

   C. PMD, PLCP, MAC, LLC

   D. LLC, MAC, PLCP, PMD

   E. MAC, LLC, PLCP, PMD

12. When a Long PLCP Header is used, what speeds can be used for transmitting the PSDU? (Choose all that apply.)

   A. 1 Mbps

   B. 2 Mbps

   C. 5.5 Mbps

   D. 11 Mbps

   E. 54 mbps

13. According to the 802.11n amendment, which of the following PPDU formats is optional?

   A. Long PPDU

   B. Short PPDU

   C. Non-HT legacy PPDU

   D. HT-mixed PPDU

   E. HT-greenfield PPDU

14. How wide are the UNII-1, UNII-2, and UNII-3 bands?

   A. 20 MHz

   B. 22 MHz

   C. 11 MHz

   D. 100 MHz

   E. It varies depending upon the specific band.

15. What are the boundaries of the UNII-2 Extended bands?

   A. 5.470 GHz to 5.725 GHz

   B. 5.5 GHz to 5.75 GHz

   C. 2.4 GHz to 2.4835 GHz

   D. 902 MHz to 928 MHz

16. What is the frequency width of each clause 17 subcarrier?

   A. 20 KHz

   B. 22 KHz

   C. 100 KHz

   D. 312.5 KHz

   E. 350 KHz

17. Which terms are used to describe the error correction method used by clause 17 devices? (Choose all that apply.)

   A. Cyclic Redundancy Check

   B. Forward error correction

   C. Frame Check Sequence

   D. Convolutional coding

   E. Parity

18. Select the coding methods that are used by DSSS devices, along with the coding methods used by HR-DSSS devices. (Choose all that apply.)

   A. Barker code

   B. Convolutional coding

   C. Complementary Code Keying (CCK)

   D. Bitwise coding

19. From the perspective of the Physical layer, what are two terms that define the data portion of an 802.11 transmission? (Choose two.)

   A. PSDU

   B. PLCP

   C. MSDU

   D. MPDU

   E. PMD

20. When a Short PLCP Header is used, what speeds can be used for transmitting the PSDU? (Choose all that apply.)

   A. 1 Mbps

   B. 2 Mbps

   C. 5.5 Mbps

   D. 11 Mbps

   E. 54 Mbps

Answers to Review Questions

1. B.   HR-DSSS (clause 18) was introduced under the 802.11b amendment, which states that channels need a minimum of 25 MHz of separation between the center frequencies to be considered nonoverlapping.

2. D, B.   The upper portion of the Physical layer is known as the Physical Layer Convergence Procedure (PLCP) sublayer, and the lower portion is known as the Physical Medium Dependent (PMD) sublayer.

3. B, C, E.   The PLCP Protocol Data Unit (PPDU) consists of three parts: PLCP Preamble, PLCP Header, and PLCP Service Data Unit (PSDU). When the PLCP layer receives the PSDU from the MAC layer, the appropriate PLCP Preamble and PLCP header are added to the PSDU to create the PPDU.

4. A.   The Long PPDU includes a 144-bit PLCP Preamble, which consists of a 128-bit Sync field and a 16-bit Start of Frame Delimiter (SFD).

5. A.   The Long Preamble is transmitted using Differential Binary Phase Shift Keying (DBPSK) at the rate of 1 Mbps. Like the Long PLCP Preamble, the Short PLCP Preamble is also transmitted using DBPSK.

6. A, B, C, E.   Long and Short PLCP Headers are both 48 bits long and contain the following four fields: Signal (8 bits), Service (8 bits), Length (16 bits), and CRC (16 bits).

7. A, D, E.   When the 802.11n amendment was ratified, three new PPDUs were defined: non-HT legacy PPDU, HT-mixed PPDU, and HT-greenfield PPDU.

8. A, B, C, D, E.   The bulk of Wi-Fi radios currently transmit in the 2.4 GHz ISM band, including radios that use the following technologies:

    802.11 (FHSS clause 14 radios or DSSS clause 15 radios)

    802.11b (HR-DSSS clause 18 radios)

    802.11g (ERP clause 19 radios)

    802.11n (HT clause 20 radios)

9. B, C, D, E.   Clause 17 (802.11a) defines BPSK for 6 and 9 Mbps transmissions, QPSK for 12 and 18 Mbps transmissions, 16-QAM for 24 and 36 Mbps transmissions, and 64-QAM for 48 and 54 Mbps transmissions.

10. A, C, E.   Data rates of 6, 9, 12, 18, 24, 36, 48, and 54 Mbps are possible using 802.11a and 802.11g technology, although the IEEE requires only the data rates of 6, 12, and 24 Mbps.

11. D.   The Data-Link layer is divided into the upper LLC sublayer and the lower MAC sublayer. The Physical layer is divided into the upper Physical Layer Convergence Procedure (PLCP) sublayer and the lower Physical Medium Dependent (PMD) sublayer.

12. A, B, C, D.   When a Long PLCP Header is used, the PSDU can be transmitted at one of four transmission rates; 1 Mbps, 2 Mbps, 5.5 Mbps, and 11 Mbps.

13. E.   Support for the HT-greenfield format is optional, and the HT radios can transmit by using both 20 MHz and 40 MHz channels.

14. D.   These 3 UNII bands are 100 MHz wide, and UNII-2 extended is 255 MHz wide.

15. A.   The UNII-2 Extended band is 255 MHz wide and spans from 5.470 GHz to 5.725 GHz.

16. D. The frequency width of each OFDM subcarrier is 312.5 KHz. The subcarriers are also transmitted at lower data rates, but because there are so many subcarriers, overall data rates are higher.

17. B, D. To make OFDM more resistant to narrowband interference, a form of error correction known as convolutional coding is performed. The 802.11-2007 standard defines the use of convolutional coding as the error correction method to be used with OFDM technology. It is a forward error correction (FEC) that allows the receiving system to detect and repair corrupted bits.

18. A, C.   To help provide the faster speeds of HR-DSSS, a more complex code, Complementary Code Keying (CCK), is utilized instead of the Barker code that is used with DSSS transmissions.

19. A, D. The PLCP Service Data Unit (PSDU) is the data that the PHY transmits. The PSDU is equivalent to the MAC Protocol Data Unit (MPDU) that is passed down from the Data-Link layer.

20. B, C, D.   When a Short PLCP Header is used, only three data rates are supported: 2 Mbps, 5.5 Mbps, and 11 Mbps.

Chapter 3

802.11 MAC Sublayer Frame Format

IN THIS CHAPTER, YOU WILL LEARN ABOUT THE FOLLOWING:

- ✓ **General 802.11 frame format**
- ✓ **MAC header**
- ✓ **Frame control field**
  - ▪ Protocol Version field
  - ▪ Type and Sub-type fields
  - ▪ To DS and From DS fields
  - ▪ More Fragments field
  - ▪ Retry field
  - ▪ Power Management field
  - ▪ More Data field
  - ▪ Protected Frame field
  - ▪ Order field
- ✓ **Duration/ID field**
- ✓ **MAC layer addressing**
- ✓ **Sequence Control field**
- ✓ **QoS Control field**
- ✓ **Frame Body**
- ✓ **FCS field**

As you have already learned, the 802.11-2007 standard only defines operations at the Physical layer and the MAC sublayer of the Data-Link layer. In this chapter, we will discuss the MAC frame format that is the template for operations for all 802.11 frames. Although future chapters will focus on individual frame types and subtypes, this chapter will cover the entire structure of an 802.11 MPDU that provides the framework for all the complex MAC layer interactions between 802.11 client stations and access point stations.

The bulk of this chapter will focus on the components of the MAC header of an 802.11 frame. Some fields, such as the four MAC address fields used to forward 802.11 traffic, have a very specific purpose. However, other fields, such as the Duration/ID field, can have multiple purposes. Often various fields are used in conjunction; for example, fragmentation uses both the More Fragments field and the Sequence Control field. We will conclude this chapter with a discussion about the payloads found within the frame body and the importance of a data integrity check known as the frame check sequence (FCS).

General 802.11 MPDU Format

As we discussed in Chapter 1, the technical term for an 802.11 frame is an 802.11 MAC Protocol Data Unit (MPDU). As shown in Figure 3.1, an 802.11 MPDU consists of the following three basic components:

MAC Header   Contains frame control information, duration information, addressing, and sequence control information. Furthermore, QoS data frames contain specific QoS control information.

Frame Body   Can be variable in size and also contains information that is different depending on the frame type and frame subtype.

Frame Check Sequence (FCS)   Comprises 32-bit cyclic-redundancy check (CRC) that is used to validate the integrity of received frames.

The bulk of this chapter will focus on the individual fields of the MAC header that are used for frame control, duration, addressing, and sequencing. Some discussion of the frame body and the FCS will also be warranted.

FIGURE 3.1 802.11 MAC Protocol Data Unit (MPDU)

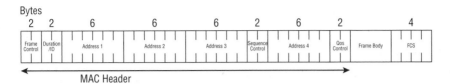

Bits, Bytes, Octets

A *bit* is a binary digit, taking a value of either 0 or 1. Binary digits are a basic unit of communication in digital computing. A byte of information comprises 8 bits. An *octet* is another name for a byte of data. The CWAP exam uses the terminology *octet* and *byte* interchangeably.

MAC Header

As was depicted in Figure 3.1, the 802.11 *MAC header* has eight major fields, four of which are used for addressing. The four address fields are each 6 bytes in length so that they can carry a standard IEEE 802 MAC address. The Frame Control field, the Duration/ID field, the Sequence Control field, and the QoS Control field are each 2 bytes in size. If all the fields are used, the maximum size of an 802.11 MAC header is 32 bytes. The 802.11n amendment adds a new field to the 802.11 MAC header, called the HT Control field. The HT Control field is 4 bytes long and follows the QoS Control field in the 802.11 MAC header. If the HT Control field is used, the maximum size of an 802.11 MAC header would be 36 bytes. The HT Control field is discussed in great detail in Chapter 10. However, the size of an 802.11 MAC header is not always the same for two reasons. First, the QoS Control field is used only in QoS Data frames. Second, not every frame uses all four address fields. Most 802.11 frames use only three addresses, and some 802.11 frames such as the acknowledgment (ACK) frame carry only a single address field. Figure 3.2 shows a frame capture of a MAC header with only three addresses and no QoS Control field. The sections that follow will cover all the MAC fields and their purposes.

FIGURE 3.2   802.11 MAC header

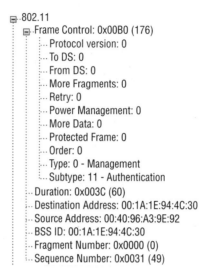

```
⊟· 802.11
  ⋮ ⊟· Frame Control: 0x00B0 (176)
  ⋮  ⋮  ⋮··· Protocol version: 0
  ⋮  ⋮  ···· To DS: 0
  ⋮  ⋮  ···· From DS: 0
  ⋮  ⋮  ···· More Fragments: 0
  ⋮  ⋮  ···· Retry: 0
  ⋮  ⋮  ···· Power Management: 0
  ⋮  ⋮  ···· More Data: 0
  ⋮  ⋮  ···· Protected Frame: 0
  ⋮  ⋮  ···· Order: 0
  ⋮  ⋮  ···· Type: 0 - Management
  ⋮  ⋮  ···· Subtype: 11 - Authentication
  ⋮ ···· Duration: 0x003C (60)
  ⋮ ···· Destination Address: 00:1A:1E:94:4C:30
  ⋮ ···· Source Address: 00:40:96:A3:9E:92
  ⋮ ···· BSS ID: 00:1A:1E:94:4C:30
  ⋮ ···· Fragment Number: 0x0000 (0)
  ⋮ ···· Sequence Number: 0x0031 (49)
```

Frame Control Field

The first two bytes of the MAC header consists of 11 subfields within the *Frame Control field*. These subfields include Protocol Version, Type, Subtype, To DS, From DS, More Fragments, Retry, Power Management, More Data, Protected Frame, and Order. Figure 3.3 illustrates the format of the Frame Control field.

FIGURE 3.3   Frame Control field

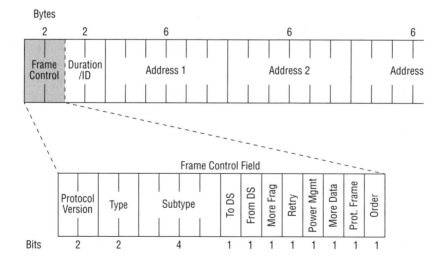

Each one of these subfields has very specific purposes for the layer 2 interactions between 802.11 stations.

Protocol Version Field

The *Protocol Version field* is a consistent 2-bit field that is always placed at the beginning of all 802.11 MAC headers, as shown in Figure 3.4.

FIGURE 3.4   Protocol field

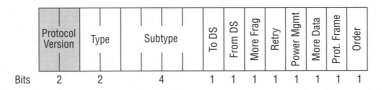

This field is simply used to indicate which protocol version of 802.11 technology is being used by the frame. As pictured in Figure 3.5, all 802.11 frames have the value of the Protocol Version field always set to 0. All other values are reserved. In other words, there is currently only one version of 802.11 technology. The IEEE could possibly in the future define another version of 802.11 technology that would not be backward compatible with the current version 0. There was talk about making 802.11n High Throughput (HT) technology a different protocol version of 802.11; however, that did not happen, and 802.11n ended up being an enhancement of 802.11 protocol version 0 and is backward compatible with older 802.11n radios.

FIGURE 3.5   Protocol Version field

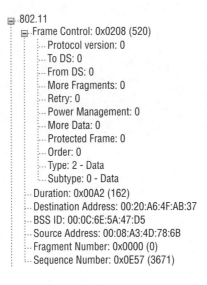

Type and Subtype Fields

After the protocol version of a frame has been indicated, the function of the frame must be announced. The *Type field* and *Subtype field* are used together to identify the function of the frame. The Type field is 2 bits in length, and the Subtype field is 4 bits in length. The three types of 802.11 frames are management, control, and data frames.

As shown in Table 3.1, the 2-bit Type field identifies whether the frame is a control, data, or management frame. A value of 00 means the type is a management frame, a value of 01 indicates a control frame, and a value of 10 indicates a data frame. The value of 11 is reserved for future use if needed. Who knows, in the future there might be the need for another major type of 802.11 frame.

TABLE 3.1   Type field

Bits	Frame type
0, 0	Management frame
0, 1	Control frame
1, 0	Data frame
1, 1	Reserved

There are many different kinds of management, control, and data frames, and therefore the 4-bit Subtype field is needed. For example, Figure 3.6 shows a frame capture of a management frame. The Subtype field indicates that the frame is a beacon management frame.

FIGURE 3.6   Type and Subtype fields

```
⊞-☌  802.11 MAC Header
  ┊┄☌ Version:   0 [0 Mask 0x03]
  ┊┄☌ Type:      %00 Management [0 Mask 0x0C]
  ┊┄☌ Subtype:   %1000 Beacon [0 Mask 0xF0]
```

Table 3.2 shows some of the various types and subtypes of all 802.11 frames.

TABLE 3.2   Valid Type and Subtype combinations

Type value b3 b2	Type description	Subtype value b7 b6 b5 b4	Subtype description
00	Management	0000	Association request
00	Management	0100	Probe request

TABLE 3.2   Valid Type and Subtype combinations *(continued)*

Type value b3 b2	Type description	Subtype value b7 b6 b5 b4	Subtype description
00	Management	1000	Beacon
00	Management	1010	Disassociation
01	Control	1010	Block ACK
01	Control	1011	RTS
01	Control	1101	ACK
10	Data	0000	Data
10	Data	0100	Null (no data)
10	Data	1000	QoS Data
10	Data	1100	QoS Null (no data)

In Chapter 6, you will learn that some data frames do not carry a frame body. In other words, some data frames actually do not carry data. Refer again to Table 3.2, and notice that when bit 6 of the Subtype field has a value of 1 in a data frame, no frame body is used. Also, notice that when bit 7 has a value of 1, a data frame becomes a QoS subtype. Bit 7 is considered the most significant bit for data frames and is defined as a QoS subfield. Figure 3.7 illustrates the position of the Type and Subtype fields in the 802.11 MAC header.

FIGURE 3.7   Type and Subtype fields

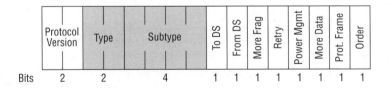

To DS and From DS Fields

The *To DS field* and *From DS field* are each 1 bit and are used in combination to change the meaning of the four MAC addresses in an 802.11 MPDU. These two bits also indicate the flow of the 802.11 data frames between a WLAN environment and the distribution system (DS). A more detailed discussion of how these bits are used is covered later in this chapter in the section called "MAC Layer Addressing." Figure 3.8 shows the position of these two subfields of the Frame Control field.

FIGURE 3.8   To DS and From DS fields

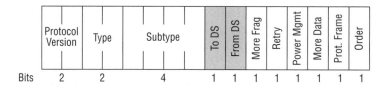

There are four possible combinations of these two bits. The first is as follows:

To DS = 0

From DS = 0

When both bits are set to 0, several different scenarios exist. The most common scenario is that these are management or control frames. Management and control frames do not have an MSDU payload, and therefore their final destination is never the distribution system (DS). Management and control exist only at the MAC sublayer and therefore have no need to be translated by the integration service (IS) and never are delivered to the distribution system service (DSS). Another scenario is a direct data frame transfer from one STA to another STA within an independent basic service set (IBSS) more commonly known as an ad hoc network. The third scenario involves what is known as a *station-to-station link (STSL)*, which involves a data frame being sent directly from one client station to another client station that belongs to the same BSS, thereby bypassing the AP. Although defined by the 802.11-2007 standard, widespread use of the STSL has yet to occur. The third scenario may become more relevant when the 802.11z draft amendment is ratified. 802.11z defines enhanced mechanisms for direct link setup (DLS) between two peer stations within a BSS.

To DS = 1

From DS = 0

When the To DS bit is set to 1 and the From DS bit is set to 0, it indicates that an 802.11 data frame is being sent upstream from a client station to an access point. In most cases, the final destination of the MSDU payload of the data frame is an address that exists on the distribution system medium (DSM). An example of the scenario would be a client station sending a DHCP request packet through an AP to a DHCP server that resides on the 802.3 network.

To DS = 0

From DS = 1

When the To DS bit is set to 0 and the From DS bit is set to 1, it indicates that an 802.11 data frame is being sent downstream from an access point to a client station. The original source of the MSDU payload of the 802.11 data frame is an address that exists on the distribution system medium (DSM). An example would be a DHCP server that resides on the 802.3 network forwarding a DHCP response packet through an AP with the final destination being an 802.11 client station.

To DS = 1

From DS = 1

When the To DS bit and the From DS bit are both set to 1, a data frame uses the four-address format. Although the standard does not define procedures for using this format, WLAN vendors often implement what is known as a wireless distribution system (WDS). Examples of a WDS include WLAN bridges and mesh networks.

A greater discussion of these two fields and how they relate to the meaning of the MAC addressing occurs later in the "MAC Layer Addressing" section of this chapter.

More Fragments Field

The *More Fragments field* is 1 bit in length and is set to 1 in all data or management type frames that have another fragment of the current MSDU or current MMPDU to follow. It is set to 0 in all other frames. Figure 3.9 shows the position of the More Fragments field in the MAC header.

FIGURE 3.9   More Fragments field

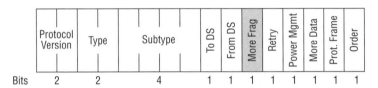

The single-bit More Fragments field is set to 1 if another fragment of the same MSDU follows in a subsequent frame. MAC layer services provide fragmentation service to support the division of MSDUs and MMPDUs into smaller elements for transmission.

The MAC layer fragments only those frames having a unicast receiver address (Address 1 in the MAC frame). It never fragments broadcast and multicast frames because frames sent to a multicast Address 1 are never acknowledged and retransmitted in any event. If the length of the resulting unencrypted MPDU needing transmission exceeds the FragmentationThreshold parameter located in the MAC's management information base (MIB), then the MAC protocol will fragment the MSDU. Each fragmented frame consists of a MAC header, frame body, and FCS, which comprise an MPDU. The unencrypted MPDU must not exceed the fragmentation threshold value, so the header and FCS must be taken into account when calculating the MSDU fragment size in each MPDU. Each fragment gets a fragment number (to be discussed later) indicating its ordered position in the sequence of fragments that carry the original MSDU. Each of the fragments is sent independently and requires separate acknowledgments (ACK frames) from the receiving station.

The More Fragment field in the Frame Control field indicates whether a frame is the last of a series of fragments and is always set to 0 for unfragmented MSDUs.

The receiving station will combine all fragments of the same sequence number in the correct order to reconstruct the corresponding MSDU. Based on the fragment numbers, the destination station will discard any duplicate fragments and then pass the MSDU up to the next highest layer for processing.

Retry Field

The *Retry field* comprises a single bit of the Frame Control field and is perhaps one of the most important fields in the MAC header. If the Retry bit has a value of 0, an original transmission of the frame is occurring. If the Retry bit is set to a value of 1 in either a management or data frame, the transmitting radio is indicating that the frame being sent is a retransmission. Figure 3.10 shows the position of the Retry field in the MAC header.

FIGURE 3.10 Retry field

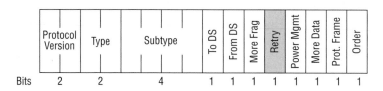

Every time an 802.11 radio transmits a unicast frame, if the frame is received properly and the cyclic redundancy check (CRC) of the FCS passes, the 802.11 radio that received the frame will reply with an acknowledgment (ACK) frame. If the ACK is received, the original station knows that the frame transfer was successful. Almost all unicast 802.11 frames must be acknowledged for delivery verification purposes. Broadcast and multicast frames do not require an acknowledgment.

If any portion of a unicast frame is corrupted, the CRC will fail, and the receiving 802.11 radio will not send an ACK frame to the transmitting 802.11 radio. If an ACK frame is not received by the original transmitting radio, the unicast frame is not acknowledged and will have to be retransmitted. There are some occasions when an ACK is not used. For instance in an RTS/CTS frame exchange, the CTS frame serves as the acknowledgement. Also a QoS No ACK policy might be used in some QoS Data frames. In most cases, unicast frames must be a acknowledged by an ACK or Block ACK frame.

The mortal enemy of WLAN performance is a layer 2 retransmission that occurs at the MAC sublayer. Excessive layer 2 retransmissions adversely affect the WLAN in two ways:

- Layer 2 retransmissions increase overhead and therefore decrease throughput. Many different factors can affect throughput, including a WLAN environment with abundant layer 2 retransmissions.

- If application data has to be retransmitted at layer 2, the timely delivery of application traffic becomes delayed or inconsistent.

Applications such as VoIP depend on the timely and consistent delivery of the IP packet. Excessive layer 2 retransmissions usually result in latency and jitter problems for time-sensitive applications such as voice and video. When discussing VoIP, latency and jitter often get confused. *Latency* is the time it takes to deliver a VoIP packet from the source device to the destination device. A delay in the delivery (increased latency) of a VoIP packet due to layer 2 retransmissions can result in echo problems. *Jitter* is a variation of latency. Jitter measures how much the latency of each packet varies from the average. If all packets travel at exactly the same speed through the network, jitter will be zero. A high variance in the latency (jitter) is the more common result of 802.11 layer 2 retransmissions. Jitter will result in choppy audio communications and reduced battery life for VoWiFi phones.

Most data applications in a Wi-Fi network can handle a layer 2 retransmission rate of up to 10 percent without any noticeable degradation in performance. However, time-sensitive applications such as VoIP require that higher-layer IP packet loss be no greater than 2 percent. Some vendors even recommend a higher-layer IP packet loss of less than 1 percent. Therefore, Voice over Wi-Fi (VoWiFi) networks need to limit layer 2 retransmissions to 5 percent or less to achieve the timely and consistent delivery of VoIP packets.

Any good 802.11 protocol analyzer can compile layer 2 retransmission rates by observing management and data frames that have the Retry field set to a value of 1. As shown in Figure 3.11, any good 802.11 protocol analyzer can track layer 2 retry statistics for the entire WLAN, and 802.11 protocol analyzers can also track retry statistics for each individual WLAN access point and client station.

FIGURE 3.11 Layer 2 retransmissions

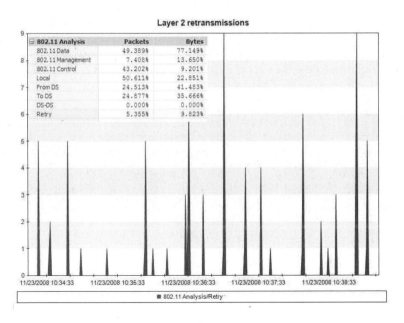

Unfortunately, layer 2 retransmissions are a result of many possible problems. Multipath, RF interference, and low SNR are problems that exist
at layer 1 yet result in layer 2 retransmissions. Other causes of layer 2
retransmissions include hidden node, near/far, mismatched power settings, and adjacent cell interference, which are all usually a symptom of
improper WLAN design. You can find a deep discussion about all these of
these causes of layer 2 retransmissions in Sybex's *CWNA Study Guide*.

Power Management Field

Legacy power management methods define an option mode called *Power Save mode* for
802.11 client stations. When a client station is set for Power Save mode, it will shut down
some of the transceiver components for a period of time to conserve power. The wireless
card basically takes a short nap. The station indicates that it is using Power Save mode by
changing the value of the Power Management bit to 1. When the Power Management bit is
set to 1, the access point is informed that the client station is using power management, and
the access point buffers all of that client's 802.11 frames.

If a station is part of a basic service set, it will notify the access point that it is enabling
Power Save mode by changing the Power Management field to 1. When the access point
receives a frame from a station with this bit set to 1, the access point knows that the station
is in Power Save mode. If the access point then receives any data that is destined for the station in Power Save mode, the AP will store the information in a buffer.

The *Power Management field* is used to indicate the power management mode of a client
STA. A value of 1 indicates that the client is using Power Save mode and that buffering of
the client traffic on the AP needs to occur. A value of 0 means that no power management
is being used, and therefore no buffering is needed. Figure 3.12 shows the position of the
Power Management field in the MAC header.

FIGURE 3.12   Power Management field

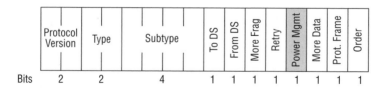

More Data Field

Any time a station associates to an access point, the station receives an *association identifier
(AID)*. The access point uses this AID to keep track of the stations that are associated and
the members of the BSS. If the access point is buffering data for a station in Power Save

mode, when the access point transmits its next beacon, the AID of the station will be seen in a field of the beacon frame known as the *traffic indication map (TIM)*. The TIM field is a list of all stations that have undelivered unicast data buffered on the access point waiting to be delivered. Every beacon will include the AID of the station until the data is delivered.

After the station notifies the access point that it is in Power Save mode, the station shuts down part of its transceiver to conserve energy. A station can be in one of two states, either awake or doze. During the awake state, the client station can receive frames and transmit frames.

As shown in Figure 3.13, when the station receives the beacon during the awake state, it checks to see whether its AID is set in the TIM, indicating that a buffered unicast frame waits. If so, the station will remain awake and will send a PS-Poll frame to the access point. When the access point receives the PS-Poll frame, it will send the buffered unicast frame to the station. The station will stay awake while the access point transmits the buffered unicast frame. When the access point sends the data to the station, the station needs to know when all of the buffered unicast data has been received so that it can go back to sleep. Each unicast frame contains a 1-bit field called the *More Data field*.

FIGURE 3.13   Power Save mode

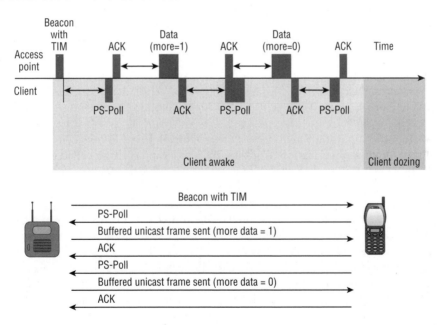

When the client station receives a buffered unicast frame with the More Data field set to 1, the station knows that it cannot go back to sleep yet because there is some more buffered data that it has not yet received. When the More Data field is set to 1, the station knows that it needs to send another PS-Poll frame and wait to receive the next buffered unicast frame. After all the buffered unicast frames have been sent, the More Data field in the last buffered frame will be set to 0, indicating that there is currently no more buffered data. The station is now free to go back into a doze state.

To summarize, the More Data field is used to inform Power Save mode clients that they still have buffered unicast traffic and that they should not go back into a doze state. Figure 3.14 shows the position of the More Data field in the MAC header.

FIGURE 3.14 More Data field

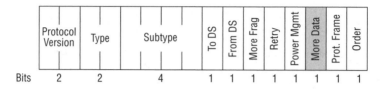

Protected Frame Field

The *Protected Frame field* is a single bit and is used to indicate whether the MSDU payload of a data frame is encrypted. Originally the field was called the WEP bit but was renamed to the protected frame bit when TKIP and CCMP encryption were introduced. When the Protected Frame field is set to a value of 1 in a data frame, the MSDU payload of the data frame is indeed encrypted. The Protected Frame field does not indicate which type of encryption is being used; it only indicates that in face the MSDU payload of the frame body is encrypted. The encryption can be either Wired Equivalent Privacy (WEP), Temporal Key Integrity Protocol (TKIP), or Counter Mode with Cipher Block Chaining Message Authentication Code Protocol (CCMP).

The Protected Frame field can also be set to a value of 1 within management frames with the subtype of Authentication. A legacy authentication method called *Shared Key authentication* uses WEP to authenticate client stations and requires that a static WEP key be configured on both the client STA and the access point. Shared Key authentication is a four-way authentication frame exchange where the AP sends a clear text challenge to a client and asks the client to encrypt the clear-text challenge with the WEP key and send it back to the AP. The encrypted clear text challenge is found in the body of the third authentication management frame sent during Shared Key authentication. Therefore, in the third authentication frame of the Shared Key authentication, the Protected Frame field is set to a value of 1.

The majority of management frames are never encrypted, therefore the Protected Frame field will be set to 0. The Shared Key authentication scenario just mentioned is a rare example of when a management frame is encrypted. The 802.11w-2009 amendment defines protection for unicast "robust management frames to prevent some layer 2 denial-of-service (DoS) attacks. The Protected Frame field is set to 1 only within data frames and within management frames of subtype Authentication, and unicast Robust Management frames. The Protected Frame field is set to 0 in all other frames. Some data frames such as Null Function frames do not have a frame body, and therefore the Protected Frame field will always to be set to 0.

The main purpose of the this field is to indicate that encryption is being used to provide data privacy for the MSDU payload found in the frame body of the majority of 802.11 data frames. If for some reason encryption is not being used, the field will also have a value of 0 in data frames. Figure 3.15 shows the position of the Protected Frame field in the MAC header.

FIGURE 3.15   Protected Frame field

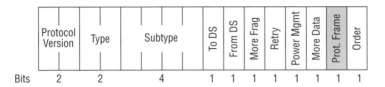

Order Field

The single-bit *Order field* is set to 1 in any non-QoS data frame when a higher layer has requested that the data be sent using a strictly ordered class of service, which tells the receiving station that frames must be processed in order. The field is set to 0 in all other frames. Figure 3.16 shows the location of the Order field within the Frame Control field of the MAC header. Although the Order field was originally intended to protect legacy protocols such as DEC LAT, the field is rarely used.

FIGURE 3.16   Order field

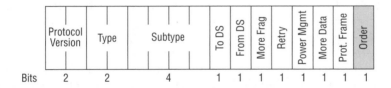

Duration/ID Field

The *Duration/ID field* is 16 bits in length. The Duration ID field can be used for three different reasons:

Virtual carrier-sense   The main purpose of this field is to reset the NAV timer of other stations.

Legacy power management   PS-Poll frames use the field as an association identifier (AID).

Contention-free period   The field is used as an indicator that a point coordination function (PCF) process has begun.

Figure 3.17 shows where the Duration/ID field is positioned in the MAC header.

FIGURE 3.17   Duration/ID field

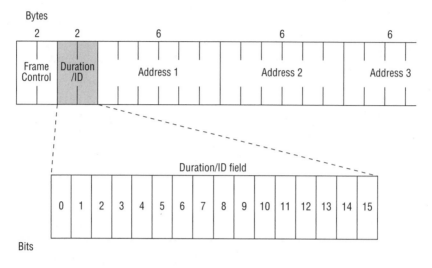

Without a doubt, the main purpose of the Duration/ID field is that it is used to reset the NAV timers of listening stations. 802.11 stations use a medium contention method known as *Carrier-Sense Multiple Access with Collision Avoidance (CSMA/CA)*. One aspect of CSMA/CA is virtual carrier-sense, which will be discussed in more detail in Chapter 7.

Virtual carrier-sense uses a timer mechanism known as the *network allocation vector (NAV)*. The NAV timer maintains a prediction of future traffic on the medium based on Duration value information seen in a previous frame transmission. When an 802.11 radio is not transmitting, it is listening. As depicted in Figure 3.18, when the listening radio hears a frame transmission from another station, it looks at the header of the frame and determines whether the Duration/ID field contains a Duration value or an ID value. If the field contains a Duration value, the listening station will set its NAV timer to this value. The listening station will then use the NAV as a countdown timer, knowing that the RF medium should be busy until the countdown reaches 0.

When a client transmits a unicast frame, the Duration/ID field uses bits 0–13 to represent a value from 0 to 32,767. The Duration/ID value represents the time, in microseconds, that is required to transmit the ACK plus one SIFS interval, as illustrated in Figure 3.18. The client that is transmitting the data frame calculates how long it will take to receive an ACK frame and includes that length of time in the Duration/ID field in the MAC header of the transmitted unicast data frame. The value of the Duration/ID field in the MAC header of the ACK frame that follows is 0 (zero). To summarize, the value of the Duration/ID field indicates how long the RF medium will be busy before another station can contend for the medium. The majority of the time, the main purpose of the Duration/ID field is to contain a Duration value that is used to reset other stations' network allocation vector (NAV) timers.

FIGURE 3.18   Virtual carrier-sense

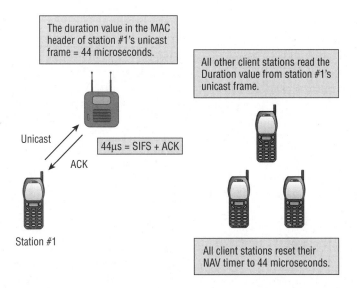

The duration value in the MAC header of station #1's unicast frame = 44 microseconds.

All other client stations read the Duration value from station #1's unicast frame.

Unicast

ACK

44μs = SIFS + ACK

Station #1

All client stations reset their NAV timer to 44 microseconds.

There is one exception when the Duration value of a transmitting station will not reset another station's timer. The NAV is not updated when the receiver address (RA) is the same as the receiving station's MAC address; in other words, the receiving station of a transmission station that does not reset the NAV timer. Refer to Figure 3.18, and you will notice that station #1's Duration/ID value of 44 microseconds was used to reset all the other client station NAV timers. The purpose was to ensure the transmission of the ACK frame by the AP. The AP radio did not reset its NAV timer because it was the receiving station and needed to send the ACK frame. Duration values are always about frame transmissions that are to follow; therefore, when the receiver address (RA) matches the receiving station's MAC address, the NAV timer is not updated by the receiving station. You should also understand that the Duration value of the transmitting station does not reset the trans-mitting station's NAV timer. The transmitter cannot hear its own transmitted frame. The transmitter's NAV will be zero after transmitting, just like it was zero before the transmitter gained control of the medium.

The second way in which the Duration/ID field is used is during the legacy power management process. As mention earlier in this chapter, any time a station associates to an access point, the station receives an association identifier (AID). The access point uses this AID to keep track of the stations that are associated and the members of the BSS. If the access point is buffering data for a station in Power Save mode, when the access point transmits its next beacon, the AID of the station will be seen in a field of the beacon frame known as the traffic indication map (TIM). The TIM field is a list of all stations that have undelivered unicast data buffered on the access point waiting to be delivered.

Power Save clients will send a PS-Poll frame to the access point to request that the AP sends the buffered unicast frame to the station. As shown in Figure 3.19, inside the PS-Poll frame the Duration/ID field will now be used as an AID value. In other words, the station will identify itself to the AP and request the buffered unicast frame. The Duration/ID field is now used strictly as an identifier and is not being used for duration or resetting NAV timers. Only power-save poll (PS-Poll) frames use this field as the AID. In PS-Poll frames, the AID is aligned in the least significant 14 bits of the field, and the most significant two bits of the field are both set to 1. The maximum allowable value for the AID is 2007.

FIGURE 3.19 AID

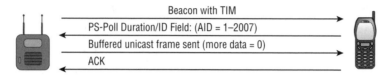

The final method in how the Duration/ID field can be used is when the field has a fixed value of 32,768 (that is, bit 15 is 1 and all other bits are 0) in all frames that are transmitted during a contention-free period (CFP). The 802.11-2007 standard defines two QoS mechanisms called point coordination function (PCF) and hybrid coordination function channel access (HCCA) that require the use of a contention-free period. WLAN vendors never implemented these functions; therefore, a discussion of how the Duration/ID field is used for the contention-free period is beyond the scope of the CWAP exam.

To summarize, as shown in Table 3.3, the main purpose of the Duration/ID field is to reset the NAV timer of other stations. When bit 15 of the field is 0, the value in bits 14–0 represent the duration of a frame exchange sequence remaining after the frame in which the Duration value is found. Bits 14–0 can have a Duration value of 0 to 32,767. The Duration value translates into microseconds when resetting NAV timers of other stations. The other common use of the Duration/ID field is as an AID in PS-Poll control frames. When bits 15 and 14 have a value of 1, bits 13–0 can be used to represent an AID in PS-Poll frames from 1 to 2007.

When bit 15 has a value of 1 and all the other bits are 0, a fixed value of 32,768 becomes the first indicator that a contention-free period has started. All other values are currently reserved for the Duration/ID field.

TABLE 3.3 Duration/ID values

Bit 15	Bit 14	Bits 13–0	Usage
0	0–32767		Duration
1	0	0	Fixed value of 32,768 used for CFP

TABLE 3.3   Duration/ID values *(continued)*

Bit 15	Bit 14	Bits 13–0	Usage
1	0	1–16383	Reserved
1	1	0	Reserved
1	1	1–2007	AID in PS-Poll frames
1	1	2008–16383	Reserved

MAC Layer Addressing

Much like in an 802.3 Ethernet frame, an 802.11 MAC sublayer address is one of the following two types:

Individual Address   Assigned to a unique station on the network (also known as a *unicast address*).

Group Address   A multiple-destination address, which could be used by one or more stations on a network. There are two kinds of group addresses:

> **Multicast-group Group Address**   An address used by an upper-layer entity to define a logical group of stations.

> **Broadcast Address**   A group address that indicates all stations that belong to the network. A broadcast address, all 1 bits, is received by all stations on a local area network. In hexadecimal, the broadcast address would be FF:FF:FF:FF:FF:FF.

However, 802.11 MAC addressing is much more complex than 802.3 addressing. 802.3 frames have only a source address (SA) and a destination address (DA) in the layer 2 header. 802.11 frames have up to four address fields in the MAC header. 802.11 frames typically use only three of the MAC address fields, but an 802.11 frame sent within a wireless distribution system (WDS) requires all four MAC addresses. The contents of these four fields can include the following MAC addresses: receiver address (RA), transmitter address (TA), basic service set identifier (BSSID), destination address (DA), and source address (SA). In other words, an 802.11 frame can contain as many as four MAC addresses with five different meanings. Certain frames may not contain some of the address fields. Even though the number of address fields is different, both 802.3 and 802.11 identify a source address and a destination address and use the same MAC address format. The first three octets are known as the *organizationally unique identifier (OUI),* and the last three octets are known as the extension identifier.

Definitions of MAC Address Fields

As shown in Figure 3.20, there are four 802.11 MAC address fields respectively called Address 1, Address 2, Address 3, and Address 4. Depending on how the To DS and From DS fields are used, the definition of each of the four MAC address fields will change. The five definitions are as follows:

Source Address (SA)   The MAC address of the original sending station. The source address either can originate from a wireless station or can originate from the wired network.

Destination Address (DA)   The MAC address that is the final destination of the frame. The final destination could be a wireless station or could be a destination on the wired network such as a server.

Transmitter Address (TA)   The MAC address of an 802.11 radio that is transmitting the frame onto the half-duplex 802.11 medium.

Receiver Address (RA)   The MAC address of the 802.11 radio that receives the incoming transmission from the transmitting station.

Basic Service Set Identifier (BSSID)   The MAC address that is the layer 2 identifier of the basic service set (BSS). The BSSID is the MAC address of the AP's radio or is derived from the MAC address of the AP's radio if multiple basic service sets exist.

FIGURE 3.20   802.11 MAC addressing

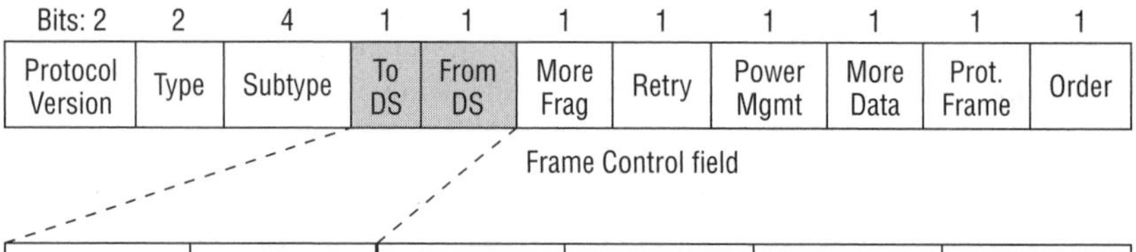

Bits: 2	2	4	1	1	1	1	1	1	1	1
Protocol Version	Type	Subtype	To DS	From DS	More Frag	Retry	Power Mgmt	More Data	Prot. Frame	Order

Frame Control field

To DS	From DS	Address 1	Address 2	Address 3	Address 4
0	0	RA = DA	TA = SA	BSSID	N/A
0	1	RA = DA	TA = BSSID	SA	N/A
1	0	RA = BSSID	TA = SA	DA	N/A
1	1	RA	TA	DA	SA

• SA = MAC address of the original sender (wired or wireless)
• DA = MAC address of the final destination (wired or wireless)
• TA = MAC address of the transmitting 802.11 radio
• RA = MAC address of the receiving 802.11 radio
• BSSID = L2 identifier of the basic service set (BSS)

As was already noted, depending on how the To DS and From DS fields are used together with the four MAC addresses, the definition of each field will change. One constant, however, is that the Address 1 field will always be the receiver address (RA) but may have a second definition as well. Address 2 will always be the transmitter address (TA) but also may have a second definition. Address 3 is normally used for additional MAC address information. Address 4 is used only in the case of a WDS.

Let's have a deeper discussion of how the To DS and From DS fields change the definition of the MAC address fields. As mentioned earlier in this chapter, when both the To DS and From DS fields are set to 0, several different scenarios exist. The most common scenario is that these are management or control frames. Management and control frames do not have an MSDU payload, and therefore their final destination is never the distribution system (DS). Management and control exist only at the MAC sublayer and therefore have no need to be translated by the integration service (IS) and never are delivered to the distribution system service (DSS). Figure 3.21 shows a frame capture and diagram of an association request management frame being sent by a client station. The address of the access point is 00:19:77:06:1D:90, and the address of the client station is D4:98:20:78:85:10. The Address 1 field is always the receiver address (RA), which is the access point, and it is also the final destination address (DA). The Address 2 field is always the transmitter address (TA) and in this case is the client station that was also the source address (SA). The Address 3 field carries additional information and is used to identify the BSSID. Address fields 1 and 3 have the same values because the access point is both the RA and BSSID.

FIGURE 3.21   Management frame sent by client

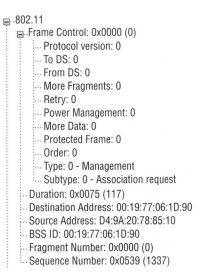

Figure 3.22 shows a frame capture and diagram of an association response management frame being sent by an access point. The address of the access point is 00:19:77:06:1D:90, and the address of the client station is D4:98:20:78:85:10. The first address field is always the receiver address (RA), which is the client station, and it is also the final destination address (DA). The second address field is always the transmitter address (TA), and which in this case is the access point that was also the source address (SA). The third address field carries additional information and is used to identify the BSSID. Address fields 2 and 3 have the same values because the access point is both the TA and BSSID.

FIGURE 3.22   Management frame sent by AP

```
□-802.11
  □-Frame Control: 0x0010 (16)
      ⋯ Protocol version: 0
      ⋯ To DS: 0
      ⋯ From DS: 0
      ⋯ More Fragments: 0
      ⋯ Retry: 0
      ⋯ Power Management: 0
      ⋯ More Data: 0
      ⋯ Protected Frame: 0
      ⋯ Order: 0
      ⋯ Type: 0 - Management
      ⋯ Subtype: 1 - Association response
    ⋯ Duration: 0x0085 (133)
    ⋯ Destination Address: D4:9A:20:78:85:10
    ⋯ Source Address: 00:19:77:06:1D:90
    ⋯ BSS ID: 00:19:77:06:1D:90
    ⋯ Fragment Number: 0x0000 (0)
    ⋯ Sequence Number: 0x0002 (2)
```

In some cases, the BSSID can be known as a *wildcard BSSID*. The value of a wildcard BSSID would be all 1s, making the address a broadcast address with a hexadecimal value of FF:FF:FF:FF:FF:FF. An example of this scenario would be a probe request sent by a client stations looking for APs to potentially roam to their BSS. In Figure 3.23, you will note that the first Address field, which is always the receiver address (RA), has a wildcard BSSID value. A broadcast address is used because clients typically do not know the BSSID address of APs to which the client is not already associated. Any AP that hears the probe request with a wildcard BSSID will answer back with a probe response with a BSSID unique to each AP.

FIGURE 3.23   Wildcard BSSID

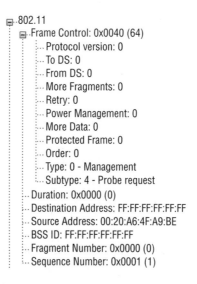

```
□-802.11
  □-Frame Control: 0x0040 (64)
      ⋯ Protocol version: 0
      ⋯ To DS: 0
      ⋯ From DS: 0
      ⋯ More Fragments: 0
      ⋯ Retry: 0
      ⋯ Power Management: 0
      ⋯ More Data: 0
      ⋯ Protected Frame: 0
      ⋯ Order: 0
      ⋯ Type: 0 - Management
      ⋯ Subtype: 4 - Probe request
    ⋯ Duration: 0x0000 (0)
    ⋯ Destination Address: FF:FF:FF:FF:FF:FF
    ⋯ Source Address: 00:20:A6:4F:A9:BE
    ⋯ BSS ID: FF:FF:FF:FF:FF:FF
    ⋯ Fragment Number: 0x0000 (0)
    ⋯ Sequence Number: 0x0001 (1)
```

Another scenario when both the To DS and From DS fields are set to 0 is a direct data frame transfer from one STA to another STA within an independent basic service set (IBSS), more commonly known as an ad hoc network. Figure 3.24 shows a frame capture of a data frame being sent from one IBSS station to another. The addresses of the ad hoc stations are D4:9A:20:78:85:10 and 00:15:00:24:77:3A. The Address 1 field is always the receiver address (RA), which is the station, and it is also the final destination address (DA). The Address 2 field is always the transmitter address (TA), and in the station that is also the source address (SA). The Address 3 field carries additional information and is used to identify the BSSID. How can there be a BSSID address if there is not an access point? The BSSID is the layer 2 identifier of the BSS, which in this case is an independent basic service set (IBSS). There has to be a layer 2 identifier of the IBSS in case other stations want to join for peer-to-peer communications. The BSSID address of an IBBS is a virtual address that is created by the first ad hoc station that begins transmitting. In this example, the virtual BSSID value of 02:15:00:00:02:44 is shown in Address 3 and the layer 2 identifier of the IBSS.

FIGURE 3.24   Ad hoc station data frame

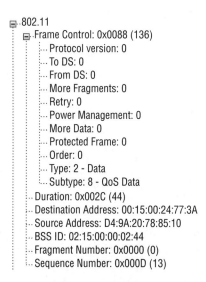

```
□ 802.11
    □ Frame Control: 0x0088 (136)
        Protocol version: 0
        To DS: 0
        From DS: 0
        More Fragments: 0
        Retry: 0
        Power Management: 0
        More Data: 0
        Protected Frame: 0
        Order: 0
        Type: 2 - Data
        Subtype: 8 - QoS Data
    Duration: 0x002C (44)
    Destination Address: 00:15:00:24:77:3A
    Source Address: D4:9A:20:78:85:10
    BSS ID: 02:15:00:00:02:44
    Fragment Number: 0x0000 (0)
    Sequence Number: 0x000D (13)
```

Indicating the Direction of Flow

So far, we have looked at MAC addressing for management and control frames and 802.11 data frames within an IBSS. Let's now look at how the To DS and From DS bits can be used to indicate the direction and flow of 802.11 data frames within a typical BSS. As shown in Figure 3.25, when the To DS bit is set to 1 and the From DS bit is set to 0, this indicates that an 802.11 data frame is being sent upstream from a client station to an access point. The final destination of the MSDU payload of the data frame is an address that exists on the distribution system medium (DSM). An example is a client station sending a DHCP request packet through an AP to a DHCP server that resides on the 802.3 network. The address of the access point is 00:19:77:06:1D:90, and the address of the client station is D4:9A:20:78:85:10. The address of the DHCP that resides on the distribution system (DS) is 00:0A:E4:DA:92:F7. The Address 1 field is always the receiver address (RA), which is the access point and the BSSID. The Address 2 field is always the transmitter address (TA) and is the client station that is also the source address (SA). The Address 3 field carries additional information and is used to identify the destination address (DA) of the DHCP server that exists on the 802.3 medium.

FIGURE 3.25   To DS 1, From DS 0

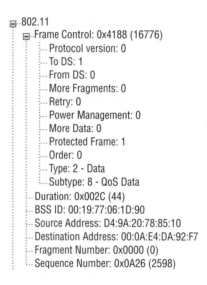

In this scenario, when the AP receives the frame from the client, the distribution system services (DSS) notice that the destination address (DA) is not an associated client. Therefore, the AP forwards the frame to the integration service (IS), which in turn strips off the 802.11 header and FCS. The MSDU payload is placed inside the body of an 802.3 Ethernet frame and is sent off to the final destination address, which is the DHCP server on the wired network.

As shown in Figure 3.26, when the To DS bit is set to 0 and the From DS bit is set to 1, this indicates that an 802.11 data frame is being sent downstream from an access point to a client station. The original source of the MSDU payload of the 802.11 data frame is an address that exists on the distribution system medium (DSM). An example is a DHCP server that resides on the 802.3 network and forwards a DHCP response packet through an AP, with the final destination being an 802.11 client station.

FIGURE 3.26   To DS 0, From DS 1

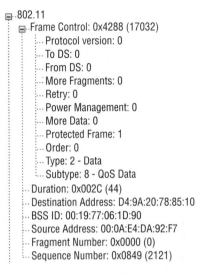

The address of the access point is 00:19:77:06:1D:90, and the address of the client station is D4:9A:20:78:85:10. The address of the DHCP that resides on 802.3 network is 00:0A:E4:DA:92:F7. The Address 1 field is always the receiver address (RA), which is the client station and the final destination address (DA). The Address 2 field is always the transmitter address (TA) and is the access point that is also the BSSID. The Address 3 field carries additional information and is used to identify the source address (SA) of the DHCP server that exists on the 802.3 medium.

In this scenario, when the AP receives the 802.3 frame from the DHCP server from the wired network, the AP's integration service strips the MSDU payload out of the 802.3 frame and creates a new 802.11 header and FCS. The distribution system services then forward the frame to the associated 802.11 client station.

Using All Four Address Fields

So far, we have looked only at examples of 802.11 frame transmissions when only three of the MAC address fields are needed. There are occasions when an 802.11 data frame needs to use all four address fields. Although the standard does not specifically define procedures for using this format, WLAN vendors often implement what is known as a wireless distribution system (WDS). Examples of a WDS include WLAN bridges, mesh networks, and wireless repeaters. In these WDS scenarios, a data frame is being sent across a second wireless medium before eventually being forwarded to a wired medium. When the To DS and From DS fields are both set to a value of 1, a WDS is being used, and four addresses are needed.

Figure 3.27 shows an example of an 802.11 point-to-point bridge link between two buildings. A frame needs to be sent from a wired server in building 1 to a wired desktop in building 2. The Address 1 field is always the receiver address (RA), which in this case is the WLAN bridge in building 2. The Address 2 field always is the transmitter address (TA), which in this example is the WLAN bridge from building 1. The Address 3 field holds the destination address (DA), which is the desktop in building 2, and the Address 4 field is the source address, which is the server from building 1. From this example, you can see why four addresses would be needed across the WLAN bridge link, which is the WDS.

FIGURE 3.27   WDS: WLAN bridging

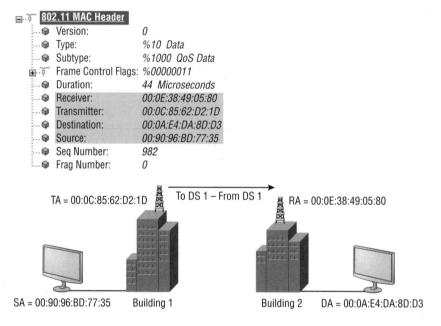

Figure 3.28 shows an example of an 802.11 mesh 5 GHz backhaul link between a mesh point and a mesh portal. A client station that is associated to the 2.4 GHz radio of the mesh point wants to send a frame to a server that resides on the 802.3 backbone. When the frame is forwarded over the 5 GHz wireless backhaul, the To DS and From DS bits are both set to 1, and four addresses are once again needed. The Address 1 field is always the receiver address (RA), which in this case is the 5 GHz radio of the mesh portal. The Address 2 field always is the transmitter address (TA), which in this example is the 5 GHz radio of the mesh point. The Address 3 field holds the destination address, (DA) which is the server on the wired network. The Address 4 field is the source address, which is the client station that is associated to the 2.4 GHz radio of the mesh point. From

this example, you can see why four addresses would be needed across the mesh backhaul, which is the WDS.

FIGURE 3.28   WDS: mesh backhaul

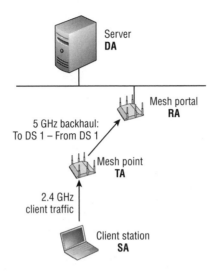

Multiple BSSIDS

Every WLAN has a logical name (SSID), and each WLAN BSS has a unique layer 2 identifier, the basic service set identifier (BSSID). The BSSID is typically the MAC address of the access point's radio card; however, access points have the capability of creating multiple virtual BSSIDs. WLAN vendors allow for the creation of virtual WLANs, each with a unique logical identifier (SSID) that is also assigned to a specific VLAN. Because the BSSID is the MAC address of the AP and because multiple virtual WLANs can be supported from the same physical AP, each virtual WLAN is typically linked with a unique *virtual BSSID*. Some vendors refer to this capability as multiple basic service set identifier (MBSSID). As shown in Figure 3.29, the MBSSIDs are usually increments of the original MAC address of the AP's radio. Within each AP's coverage area, multiple virtual WLANs can exist. Each virtual WLAN has a logical name (SSID) and a unique virtual layer 2 identifier (BSSID), and each WLAN is mapped to a unique layer 3 virtual local area network (VLAN). In other words, multiple layer 2/3 domains can exist within one layer 1 domain. Try to envision multiple basic service sets (BSSs) that are linked to multiple VLANs, yet they all exist within the same coverage area of a single access point.

FIGURE 3.29   Multiple BSSIDs

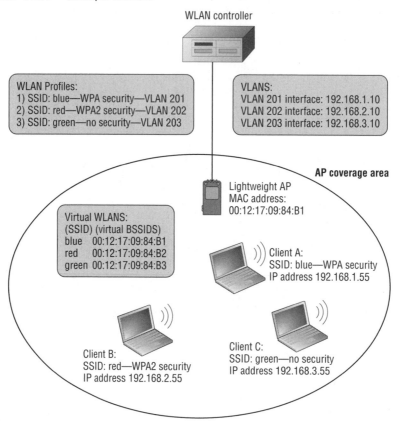

WLAN controller

WLAN Profiles:
1) SSID: blue—WPA security—VLAN 201
2) SSID: red—WPA2 security—VLAN 202
3) SSID: green—no security—VLAN 203

VLANS:
VLAN 201 interface: 192.168.1.10
VLAN 202 interface: 192.168.2.10
VLAN 203 interface: 192.168.3.10

AP coverage area

Lightweight AP
MAC address:
00:12:17:09:84:B1

Virtual WLANS:
(SSID) (virtual BSSIDS)
blue   00:12:17:09:84:B1
red   00:12:17:09:84:B2
green 00:12:17:09:84:B3

Client A:
SSID: blue—WPA security
IP address 192.168.1.55

Client B:
SSID: red—WPA2 security
IP address 192.168.2.55

Client C:
SSID: green—no security
IP address 192.168.3.55

 Real World Scenario

Will Multiple BSSIDS Affect the Performance of the WLAN?

The simple answer is yes if there are too many BSSIDs incrementing from the same source AP radio. Creating multiple virtual WLANs that use multiple SSIDs and BSSIDs creates excessive amounts of MAC layer overhead. Many WLAN vendors allow for the creation of as many as 16 WLANs that result in the creation of 16 BBSs. Each basic service set will have its own set of beacon, probe response, and other management and control frame overhead. If a single access point is transmitting 16 beacons at an interval of 100 ms each, a lot of extra MAC layer overhead is created and will have negative performance issues. Many management frames such as beacons are sent out at the lowest basic rates (required rates) of 1 and 2 Mbps. Excess management frames that are transmitted at lower data rates also create extra medium contention overhead. Some handheld Wi-Fi clients' association tables fill up when they see too many BSSIDs, and they have problems during the association process. Because of the potential degradation in performance, most WLAN vendors and Wi-Fi engineers recommend no more than four or five SSIDS and MBSSIDs.

Multiple SSIDs/BSSIDs are used to segment client stations. A common strategy is to separate traffic using one SSID for voice—one SSID for guest users and maybe another for other handheld devices such as WLAN bar-code scanners and finally the main SSID for laptops. Deploying three to five basic service sets is a common practice; however, exceeding that number affects performance. The best way to further segment client stations is to leverage returning RADIUS attributes to assign groups of users to unique VLANs and firewall policies even though the users are all associated to the same SSID/BSSID.

Sequence Control Field

The *Sequence Control field* is a 16-bit field comprising two subfields. The fields are a 4-bit fragment number and a 12-bit sequence number. As a whole, this field is used by a receiving station to eliminate duplicate received frames and to reassemble fragments. Figure 3.30 shows the positioning of the Sequence Control field in the MPDU.

FIGURE 3.30 Sequence Control field

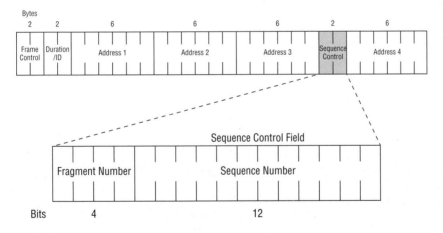

Sequence Control Subfields

The *Sequence Number subfield* contains a 12-bit number assigned sequentially by the sending station to each MSDU and MMPDU. The sequence number can have a value of 0 to 4095. This sequence number is incremented after each assignment and wraps back to 0 when incremented from 4095. The sequence number for a particular MSDU is transmitted in every data frame associated with the MSDU. It is constant over all transmissions and retransmissions of the MSDU. If the MSDU is fragmented, the sequence number of the MSDU is sent with each frame containing a fragment of the MSDU.

The *Fragment Number subfield* contains a 4-bit number assigned to each fragment of an MSDU. The first, or only, fragment of an MSDU is assigned a fragment number of 0. Each successive fragment is assigned a sequentially incremented fragment number. The fragment number is the same in a transmission or any retransmission of a particular frame or fragment.

The immediate receiver reassembles the fragments back into the original MSDU or MMPDU using sequence number and fragment numbers found in the MAC header of each frame. After ensuring the data unit is complete, the station hands it up to higher layers for processing.

Understanding the Fragmentation Threshold

All 802.11 stations can be configured with a *fragmentation threshold*. If the fragmentation threshold is set at 300 bytes, any MSDU larger than 300 bytes will be fragmented.

Let's take a look at how a station using a 300-byte fragmentation threshold (the minimum is 256 bytes) will fragment and sequence a 1,200-byte MSDU. Figure 3.31 shows the 1,200-byte MSDU with a sequence number of 542 and a fragmentation threshold of 300 bytes.

FIGURE 3.31   Fragmentation threshold

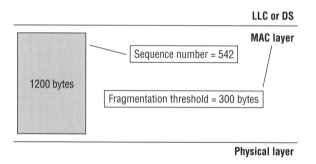

Figure 3.32 displays the fragmentation from the bottom upward because the fragments move down the OSI stack. The first fragment to be transmitted will be fragment #0, and the More Fragments bit in the Frame Control field will be set to 1. The More Fragments bit will stay set to 1 until the last fragment, at which time it will change to 0, indicating that there are no more fragments. The fragment number will increment by 1, starting at 0, until the last frame. The sequence number will remain unchanged throughout the fragment burst. Notice that the unencrypted MPDU, which includes the MAC header, frame body, and CRC, must not exceed the fragmentation threshold. Fragmentation does not take into account frame body expansion due to encryption; thus encrypted fragments may exceed the fragmentation threshold size. Since the unencrypted MPDU cannot exceed the fragmentation threshold, the size of the header and CRC must be taken into account when deciding how much of the original MSDU can be placed into the frame body of a fragment. In this

case, we're using a 24-byte non-QoS header (all header fields except address 4) and a 4-byte CRC. Since 300 − 28 = 272, the first four data fragments will carry 272 bytes of the original 1200-byte MSDU.

FIGURE 3.32   MSDU fragmentation

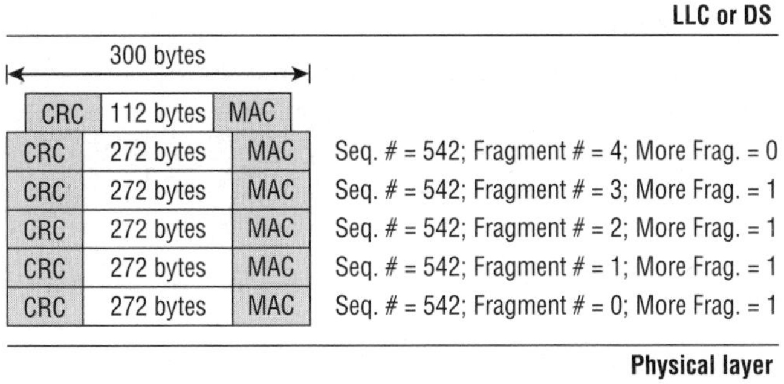

LLC or DS

	300 bytes		
CRC	112 bytes	MAC	
CRC	272 bytes	MAC	Seq. # = 542; Fragment # = 4; More Frag. = 0
CRC	272 bytes	MAC	Seq. # = 542; Fragment # = 3; More Frag. = 1
CRC	272 bytes	MAC	Seq. # = 542; Fragment # = 2; More Frag. = 1
CRC	272 bytes	MAC	Seq. # = 542; Fragment # = 1; More Frag. = 1
CRC	272 bytes	MAC	Seq. # = 542; Fragment # = 0; More Frag. = 1

Physical layer

Without encryption enabled, all fragments except the last fragment will be the size of the fragmentation threshold. The last fragment, not counting the MAC header and CRC, will be the size of whatever is left of the original MSDU. In this case, 1200 − 272 − 272 − 272 − 272 = 112. Once the receiving station receives all the fragments, they will be reassembled using the sequence number and all the fragment numbers.

Fragments are always sent in what is known as a *fragment burst*. Once the transmitting station gains control of the medium, it maintains control through two mechanisms: Duration values (which set other stations' NAVs) and SIFS. First, the value of the Duration field in the MAC header of data fragments and ACK frames is used to reserve the medium for the next fragment. As shown in Figure 3.33, as a backup mechanism, SIFS is used between data fragments and ACK frames in order to preempt those stations that are trying to gain control of the medium using DIFS.

FIGURE 3.33   Fragment burst

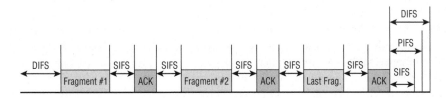

Because the transmitting station sends each fragment independently, the receiving station replies with a separate acknowledgment for each fragment. If a fragment is not acknowledged, then retries begin at the unacknowledged fragment (using DIFS), not at the beginning of the original MSDU. This functionality is the reason that using fragmentation in the presence of RF interference may increase throughput. The practical use of fragmentation is discussed further in Chapter 6.

QoS Control Field

The *QoS Control field* is a 16-bit field that identifies the quality-of-service (QoS) parameters of a data frame. It should be noted that not all data frames contain a QoS Control field. The 802.11-2007 standard states, "The QoS Control field is present in all data frames in which the QoS subfield of the Subtype field is set to 1." In other words, the QoS control field is only used in the MAC header of QoS data frames.

As shown in Table 3.4, the QoS Control field is comprised of five subfields called traffic identifier (TID) subfield, end of service period (ESOP) subfield, ACK policy subfield, and a reserved subfield. Depending on whether the QoS data frame is sent by an AP or a client station, the five subfield can represent four different types of information. The last 8 bits of the QoS Control field can be used as a TXOP Limit, TXOP Duration Requested, AP PS Buffer State, and Queue Size.

TABLE 3.4   QoS Control field

QoS Station	Bits 0-3	Bit 4	Bits 5-6	Bit 7	Bits 8-15
AP	TID/Access Class	EOSP	ACK Policy	Reserved	TXOP Limit
AP	TID/Access Class	EOSP	ACK Policy	Reserved	AP PS Buffer State
Client STA	TID/Access Class	0	ACK Policy	Reserved	TXOP Duration Requested
Client STA	TID/Access Class	1	ACK Policy	Reserved	Queue Size

On a wired 802.3 Ethernet network, different classes of service are available, represented in a 3-bit user priority field in an IEEE 802.1Q header added to an Ethernet frame. 802.1D enables priority queuing (enabling some Ethernet frames to be forwarded ahead of others within a switched Ethernet network). As shown in Table 3.5, these 802.1D service classes are mapped to 802.11 user priority levels.

Wi-Fi uses Enhanced Distributed Channel Access (EDCA), which is a wireless media access method that provides differentiated access for stations by using eight *user priority (UP)* levels. EDCA defines four QoS access categories (ACs), based on the UPs. The four access categories from lowest priority to highest priority are AC_BK (Background), AC_BE (Best Effort), AC_VI (Video), and AC_VO (Voice). Table 3.5 depicts the one-to-one mapping between the user priority levels and these QoS access categories. The Wi-Fi Alliance QoS certification is called Wireless Multimedia (WMM). Table 3.6 shows these same access categories as defined by the Wi-Fi Alliance. The QoS Control field is sometime referred to as the WMM QoS Control field.

TABLE 3.5 802.1D service classes and user priority (UP) levels

User Priority (UP)	802.1D class	QoS Access Category	Designation
1	BK	AC_BK	Background
2	—	AC_BK	Background
0	BE	AC_BE	Best Effort
3	EE	AC_BE	Best Effort
4	CL	AC_VI	Video
5	VI	AC_VI	Video
6	VO	AC_VO	Voice
7	NC	AC_VO	Voice

TABLE 3.6 Wi-Fi Multimedia (WMM) Access Categories

Access Category	Description	802.1D Tags
WMM Voice priority	This is the highest priority. It allows multiple and concurrent VoIP calls with low latency and toll voice quality.	7, 6
WMM Video priority	This supports prioritized video traffic before other data traffic. A single 802.11g or 802.11a channel can support three to four SDTV video streams or one HDTV video stream.	5, 4
WMM Best Effort priority	This is traffic from applications or devices that cannot provide QoS capabilities, such as legacy devices. This traffic is not as sensitive to latency but is affected by long delays, such as Internet browsing.	0, 3
WMM Background priority	This is low-priority traffic that does not have strict throughput or latency requirements. This traffic includes file transfers and print jobs.	2, 1

The first subfield of the QoS control field is the 4-bit TID subfield. The *traffic indicator (TID)* subfield is used to identify the user priority (UP) and traffic access category of the

QoS data frame. For example, a TID subfield could indicate a UP of 6, meaning that the access category would be for voice traffic.

802.11 WMM client stations use WMM Power-Save (WMM-PS) "trigger and delivery mechanisms" to indicate to an access point that the client STAs are awake and would like the AP to send their buffered traffic. Unlike clients that use legacy power management, WMM-Power Save clients can ask to receive more than one buffered frame while they are awake during what is known as the *service period (SP)*. When a WMM-PS client associates to an AP, the client STA must indicate the number of frames that can be received during a service period. The number of frames during the service period can be two, four, six, or all the frames.

The second subfield of the QoS Control field is the *end of service period (ESOP)*. The ESOP subfield is 1 bit in length and is used by the access point to indicate the end of the current service period (SP). The last frame sent during the service period will have the bit set to a value of 1 to tell the WMM-PS client station that either the service period is over or that the AP's buffer is empty. The WMM-PS client station can then go back asleep.

The third subfield of the QoS Control field is the 2-bit ACK policy subfield. The ACK Policy subfield defines which acknowledgement policy is used after the delivery of the QoS Data frame. The four ACK policies that can be used are ACK, No ACK, No Explicit ACK and Block ACK. Some WLAN vendors have an optional configurable setting that does not require ACK frames after the delivery of voice or video packets.

The fourth subfield of the QoS Control field is 1 bit and is currently reserved for future use.

The fifth subfield of the QoS Control field is 8 bits in length and can be used for a variety of purposes. The fifth subfield can be used as a TXOP Limit, an AP PS Buffer State, a TXOP Duration Requested, or a Queue Size.

When WMM-compliant radios contend for the RF medium, they receive from the access point an allotted amount of time to send frames. This allotted period of time is called a *transmit opportunity (TXOP)*. During this TXOP, an 802.11 radio may send multiple frames in what is called a *frame burst*. During the frame burst, a short interframe space (SIFS) is used between each frame to ensure that no other radios transmit during the frame burst. The IEEE defines default TXOP limit values for each QoS access category; however, these values can be configured on an access point. TXOP limits are set in intervals of 32 microseconds and are configurable for each of the four access categories. That means that if an AP has the voice AC configured for a TXOP limit of 47 (which happens to be the default value specified in 802.11e), then all traffic using the voice AC will be allocated a TXOP of up to 1,504 microseconds whenever access to the channel is won.

The 8-bit fifth subfield of the QoS Control field can be used as a *TXOP Limit* that indicates the duration of the transmit opportunity granted by the AP. The fifth subfield is used as a TXOP limit in frames sent by a WMM-compliant AP to WMM-compliant stations. The TXOP limit is defined in vales of 32 microseconds. If the TXOP limit has a value of 1, only a single MPDU can be transmitted during the TXOP.

The 8-bit fifth subfield of the QoS Control field can be also be used by client station as a *TXOP Duration Requested* field. The client station using the field tells the AP how much time the client station wants for its next TXOP. The AP may choose to assign a shorter TXOP duration than what was requested by the client station.

A client station may also use the 8-bit subfield of the QoS Control field to indicate *Queue Size*. The client station can use the Queue Size to tell the AP how much buffered traffic the client has for any given traffic category. The access point can then use this information to determine the length needed for the duration of the next TXOP for that client station.

One final use of the 8-bit fifth subfield of the QoS Control field is the *AP PS Buffer State*. The access point uses the subfield to indicate to a client station what the power-saving (PS) buffer state is for that client station. The 8 bits in the AP PS Buffer State which allows the AP to tell client station the access category (AC) traffic is still buffered for the client as well as the size of the buffer.

Frame Body

As you have already learned, there are three major 802.11 frame types: management, control, and data. It should be noted that not all three frame types carry the same type of payload in the *frame body*. As a matter of fact, control frames do not even have a body.

Another name for an 802.11 management frame is a Management MAC Protocol Data Unit (MMPDU). Management frames have a MAC header, a frame body, and a trailer; however, management frames do not carry any upper-layer information. There is no MSDU encapsulated in the MMPDU frame body, which carries only layer 2 information fields and information elements. Information fields are fixed-length mandatory fields in the body of a management frame. Information elements are variable in length and are optional. Chapter 4 will discuss the different subtypes of 802.11 management frames in great detail.

Control frames are used to clear the channel, acquire the channel, and provide unicast frame acknowledgments. They contain only header information and a trailer. Control frames do not have a frame body. Chapter 5 will discuss the different subtypes of 802.11 control frames in great detail.

Only 802.11 data frames carry an MSDU payload in the frame body. However, it should be noted that certain subtypes of data frames such as the null function frame do not have a frame body. Chapter 6 will discuss the different subtypes of 802.11 data frames in more detail.

Let's discuss further the upper load payload that is encased in most 802.11 data frames. When the Network layer (layer 3) sends data to the Data-Link layer, that data is handed off to the LLC and becomes known as the MAC Service Data Unit (MSDU). The MSDU contains data from the LLC and layers 3–7. A simple definition of the MSDU is that it is the data payload that contains the IP packet plus some LLC data. The 802.11-2007 standard states that the maximum size of the MSDU is 2,304 bytes.

The frame body is of variable size. As shown in Figure 3.35, the maximum frame body size is determined by the maximum MSDU size (2,304 octets) plus any overhead from encryption. The 802.11n-2009 HT amendment defines a frame aggregation method called *Aggregate MAC Service Data Unit (A-MSDU)*. An 802.11n station using this method of aggregation can have a frame body with a maximum A-MSDU size (3839 or 7935 octets, depending upon the STA's capability), plus any overhead from encryption.

FIGURE 3.34 Frame body

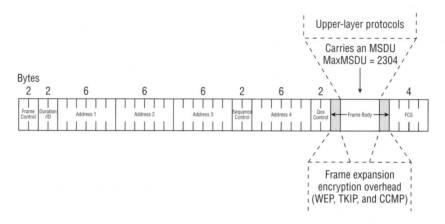

The majority of WLAN vendors do not use A-MSDU and instead have implemented a different method of frame aggregation called *Aggregate MAC Protocol Data Unit (A-MPDU)*, which does affect the individual frame body size. A-MSDU and A-MPDU will be discussed further in Chapter 10.

The 802.11-2007 standard defines three methods of encryption that can be used to provide data privacy for the MSDU payload within the frame body of an 802.11 data frame. The encryption can be either legacy Wired Equivalent Privacy (WEP), Temporal Key Integrity Protocol (TKIP), or Counter Mode with Cipher Block Chaining Message Authentication Code Protocol (CCMP).

Let's assume that WEP is used to encrypt the MSDU upper-layer payload that is encapsulated in the frame body of an 802.11 data frame. The MSDU payload has a maximum size of 2,304 bytes. The WEP initialization vector (IV) adds 4 octets, and the integrity check value (ICV) also adds 4 octets. When WEP is enabled, the entire size of the body inside an 802.11 data frame is expanded by 8 bytes to a maximum of 2312 bytes. In other words, WEP encryption adds 8 bytes of overhead to the frame body of an 802.11 data frame.

Let's assume that TKIP is used to encrypt the MSDU upper-layer payload that is encapsulated in the frame body of an 802.11 data frame. Because of the extra overhead from the IV (4 bytes), Extended IV (4 bytes), message integrity check (MIC) (8 bytes), and ICV

(4 bytes), a total of 20 bytes of overhead is added to the frame body of a TKIP encrypted 802.11 data frame. When TKIP is enabled, the entire size of the frame body inside an 802.11 data frame is expanded by 20 bytes to a maximum of 2,324 bytes. In other words, TKIP encryption adds 20 bytes of overhead to an 802.11 MPDU.

The overhead that results from CCMP encryption includes the CCMP header (8 bytes) and the MIC (8 bytes). When CCMP is enabled, the entire size of the frame body inside an MPDU is expanded by 16 bytes to a maximum of 2,320 bytes. In other words, CCMP encryption adds 16 bytes of overhead to an 802.11 data frame.

FCS Field

The *frame check sequence (FCS)* also known as the *FCS field* contains a 32-bit cyclic-redundancy check (CRC) that is used to validate the integrity of received frames. As shown in Figure 3.35, the FCS is calculated over all the fields of the MAC header and the Frame Body field. These are referred to as the *calculation fields*.

FIGURE 3.35   Frame check sequence

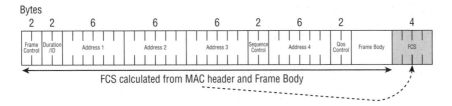

The FCS is calculated using the following standard generator polynomial of degree 32:

$$G(x) = x32 + x26 + x23 + x22 + x16 + x12 + x11 + x10 + x8 + x7 + x5 + x4 + x2 +$$

You will need to fully understand this formula for the CWAP exam. (Just kidding!) What you will absolutely need to understand for the exam is what happens if the CRC fails or passes when a unicast frame is received by an 802.11 station. As mentioned earlier in this chapter, every time an 802.11 radio transmits a unicast frame, if the frame is received properly and the cyclic redundancy check (CRC) of the FCS passes, the 802.11 radio that received the frame will reply with an acknowledgment (ACK) frame. If the ACK is received, the original station knows that the frame transfer was successful. All unicast 802.11 frames must be acknowledged. Broadcast and multicast frames do not require an acknowledgment.

If any portion of a unicast frame is corrupted, the CRC will fail, and the receiving 802.11 radio will not send an ACK frame to the transmitting 802.11 radio. If an ACK frame is not received by the original transmitting radio, the unicast frame is not acknowledged and will have to be retransmitted.

Summary

In this chapter, we discussed the three major components of an 802.11 MPDU: the MAC header, the frame body, and the frame check sequence. In a discussion about the MAC header, we learned about the Frame Control field and all of its subfields. You learned that currently there is only one protocol version of 802.11 technology, but three other versions are possible. We discussed how the Type and Subtype fields are used to identify the exact kind of 802.11 frame. We discussed the importance of the To DS and From DS fields and how they are used to change the meaning of the four MAC address fields.

We examined how the More Fragments field works together with the Sequence Control fields for fragmentation purposes. We discussed the importance of the frame check sequence (FCS), and how if it fails at the receiver, the transmitter will have to make use of the Retry field. A lot of discourse was given to the three purposes of the Duration/ID field. Finally, we covered the payload capabilities of the frame body.

Understanding the 802.11 MPDU framework is essential for a deeper understanding of 802.11 protocol analysis and is mandatory for successfully passing the CWAP exam.

Exam Essentials

Learn the entire 802.11 MPDU format.   Be able to explain all of the fields and subfields of the MAC header. Understand how the MAC header, frame body, and FCS comprise the entire MPDU.

Understand MAC addressing.   Be able to explain how the To DS and From DS fields can change the meanings of the four MAC address fields. Be able to identify this information with an 802.11 protocol analyzer.

Know three purposes of the Duration/ID field.   Understand how this field is used in the virtual carrier sense, in power management, and theoretically in a contention-free period.

Explain how the MAC header can be used for power management.   Understand how the Power Management field, the More Data field, and sometimes the Duration/ID field can all be used together for the legacy client STA power management process called Power Save mode.

Learn the basics of fragmentation.   Explain how the More Fragments field works with the Sequence Control fields for fragmentation purposes. Understand the concept of a fragment burst.

Explain the purpose of data integrity.   Understand why the frame check sequence (FCS) is needed for data integrity, and explain the negative effects of WLAN performance when the Retry bit is being used.

Know the payload capabilities of the frame body.   Understand the variable sizes of a frame body and the overhead created because of encryption.

Key Terms

Before you take the exam, be certain you are familiar with the following terms:

Aggregate MAC Protocol Data Unit (A-MPDU)

Aggregate MAC Service Data Unit (A-MSDU)

association identifier (AID)

basic service set identifier (BSSID)

Broadcast address

calculation fields

Carrier-Sense Multiple Access with Collision Avoidance (CSMA/CA)

destination address (DA)

Duration/ID field

end of service period (ESOP)

FCS field

fragment burst

Fragment Number subfield

fragmentation threshold

frame body

frame check sequence (FCS)

Frame Control field

From DS field

group address

individual address

jitter

latency

MAC header

More Data field

More Fragments field

multicast-group address

network allocation vector (NAV)

Order field

organizationally unique identifier (OUI)

Power Management field

Power Save mode

Protected Frame field

Protocol Version field

QoS Control field

receiver address (RA)

Retry field

Sequence Control field

Sequence Number subfield

Shared Key authentication

source address (SA)

station-to-station link (STSL)

Subtype field

To DS field

traffic identifier (TID)

traffic indication map (TIM)

transmission opportunity (TXOP)

transmitter address (TA)

Type field

unicast address

virtual carrier-sense

wildcard BSSID

Review Questions

1. Based on the 802.11 frame capture shown here, what type of networking communications are occurring?

```
╔═══════════════════════════╗
  ║ 802.11 MAC Header ║
  ⬡ Version:              0
  ⬡ Type:                 %10 Data
  ⬡ Subtype:              %1000 QoS Data
  ⬡ Frame Control Flags= %00000011
  ⬡ Duration:             44 Microseconds
  ⬛ Receiver:             00:0E:38:49:05:80
  ⬛ Transmitter:          00:0C:85:62:D2:1D
  ⬛ Destination:          00:0A:E4:DA:8D:DS
  ⬛ Source:               00:90:96:BD:77:35
  ⬡ Seq Number:           982
  ⬡ Frag Number:          0
```

   A. AP to client station

   B. Client station to server

   C. Client station to AP

   D. Server to client station

   E. Mesh backhaul

2. CCMP/AES encryption adds an extra _____ of overhead to the body of an 802.11 data frame.

   A. 16 bytes

   B. 12 bytes

   C. 20 bytes

   D. 10 bytes

   E. None of the above

3. Which of the following 802.11 frames carry an MSDU payload that may eventually be transferred by the integration service into an 802.3 Ethernet frame? (Choose all that apply.)

   A. 802.11 management frames

   B. 802.11 control frames

   C. 802.11 data frames

   D. 802.11 power-management frames

   E. 802.11 action frames

4. What would cause an 802.11 station to retransmit a unicast frame? (Choose all that apply.)

    A. The transmitted unicast frame was corrupted.

    B. The ACK frame from the receiver was corrupted.

    C. The receiver's buffer was full.

    D. The transmitting station sent a PS-Poll frame.

    E. The transmitting station sent a retransmit notification.

5. How does a client station indicate that it is using Power Save mode?

    A. It transmits a frame to the access point with the Sleep field set to 1.

    B. It transmits a frame to the access point with the Power Management field set to 1.

    C. Using DTIM, the access point determines when the client station uses Power Save mode.

    D. It doesn't need to, because Power Save mode is the default.

6. Which field in the MAC header of an 802.11 frame resets the NAV timer for all listening 802.11 stations?

    A. NAV

    B. Frame control

    C. Duration/ID

    D. Sequence number

    E. Strictly ordered bit

7. What are some the reasons for the existence of the Duration/ID field of the MAC header of an 802.11 MPDU? (Choose all that apply.)

    A. Physical carrier-sense

    B. Fragmentation

    C. Virtual carrier-sense

    D. Integrity check

    E. Power management

8. What is the maximum amount of microseconds that can be set on the NAV timers of listening stations that hear the transmission of another 802.11 station?

    A. 32,768 µs

    B. 2007 µs

    C. 16,383 µs

    D. 2008 µs

    E. 32,767 µs

9. What are some of the negative effects of layer 2 retransmissions? (Choose all that apply.)

   A. Decreased range

   B. Excessive MAC sublayer overhead

   C. Decreased latency

   D. Increased latency

   E. Jitter

10. When an AP sends a unicast frame to VoWiFi client station, which of the other stations will not update their NAV timers based on the Duration value represented in the Duration/ID field in the unicast frame sent by the AP? (Choose all that apply.)

   A. Transmitting access point

   B. Another access point nearby on the same channel

   C. All the other client stations

   D. The VoWiFi client

   E. Any other clients within listening range on the same channel

11. Which of these statements regarding the four MAC address fields in the header of a data MPDU are accurate? (Choose all that apply.)

   A. Address 2 is always the transmitter address (TA).

   B. Address 3 is always the transmitter address (TA).

   C. Address 1 is always the basic service set identifier (BSSID).

   D. Address 1 is always the receiver address (RA).

12. Which of the following is a possible scenario when the To DS field and the From DS field both have a value of 0? (Choose all that apply.)

   A. The frame transmission is a control frame.

   B. An ad hoc network exists.

   C. The frame transmission is a simple data frame.

   D. Fragmentation is not being used.

   E. The frame transmission is a management frame.

13. What can you conclude about this frame based on the frame capture graphic shown here? (Choose all that apply.)

```
802.11
  Frame Control: 0x0208 (520)
     Protocol version: 0
     To DS: 0
     From DS: 1
     More Fragments: 0
     Retry: 0
     Power Management: 0
     More Data: 0
     Protected Frame: 0
     Order: 0
     Type: 2 - Data
     Subtype: 0 - Data
  Duration: 0x002C (44)
  Destination Address: 00:90:96:8A:40:60
  BSS ID: 00:0C:6E:5A:47:DS
  Source Address: 00:04:5A:64:B7:2A
  Fragment Number: 0x0000 (2)
  Sequence Number: 0x0393 (915)
```

A. This is the second fragment of an MSDU.

B. This is the third fragment of an MSDU.

C. The AP is using fragmentation.

D. This is the last transmitted fragment of an MSDU.

E. The client station is using fragmentation.

14. What can you conclude about this frame based on the frame capture graphic shown here? (Choose all that apply.)

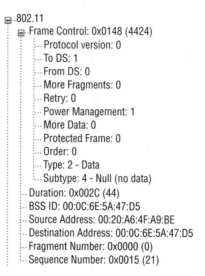

```
802.11
   Frame Control: 0x0148 (4424)
      Protocol version: 0
      To DS: 1
      From DS: 0
      More Fragments: 0
      Retry: 0
      Power Management: 1
      More Data: 0
      Protected Frame: 0
      Order: 0
      Type: 2 - Data
      Subtype: 4 - Null (no data)
   Duration: 0x002C (44)
   BSS ID: 00:0C:6E:5A:47:D5
   Source Address: 00:20:A6:4F:A9:BE
   Destination Address: 00:0C:6E:5A:47:D5
   Fragment Number: 0x0000 (0)
   Sequence Number: 0x0015 (21)
```

A. The Duration/ID field is an AID.

B. This is first fragment of a fragmented MSDU.

C. The AP is buffering the client station's traffic.

D. Fragmentation is not being used.

E. This is a PS-Poll frame.

15. What can you conclude about this frame based on the frame capture graphic shown here?

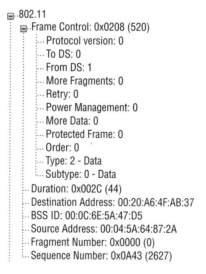

```
802.11
   Frame Control: 0x0208 (520)
      Protocol version: 0
      To DS: 0
      From DS: 1
      More Fragments: 0
      Retry: 0
      Power Management: 0
      More Data: 0
      Protected Frame: 0
      Order: 0
      Type: 2 - Data
      Subtype: 0 - Data
   Duration: 0x002C (44)
   Destination Address: 00:20:A6:4F:AB:37
   BSS ID: 00:0C:6E:5A:47:D5
   Source Address: 00:04:5A:64:87:2A
   Fragment Number: 0x0000 (0)
   Sequence Number: 0x0A43 (2627)
```

A. This data frame has no frame body.

B. CCMP encryption is being used.

C. This is an IBSS topology.

D. No data privacy is being provided.

E. The ACK frame was delivered successfully.

16. What can you conclude about this frame based on the frame capture graphic shown here? (Choose all that apply.)

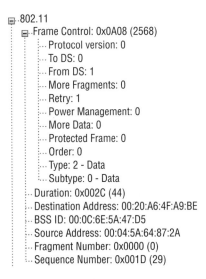

A. This is a unicast frame.

B. The frame check sequence (FCS) of the previous attempt of the same frame failed at the receiving station.

C. This is a multicast frame.

D. This is a mesh backhaul transmission.

E. The ACK frame was delivered successfully.

17. When the To DS field has a value of 0 and the From DS field has a value of 1, which of these statements possibly are accurate? (Choose all that apply.)

A. The frame transmission is a control frame.

B. This is a DHCP response packet.

C. The frame transmission is a data frame.

D. Client STA is transmitting.

E. The frame transmission is a management frame.

18. How many bytes is the frame body of an 802.11 MPDU?

    A.   0-2304

    B.   2304

    C.   2346

    D.   4095

    E.   Variable

19. How many MAC addresses are found in an 802.3 frame?

    A.   Four

    B.   Three

    C.   Two

    D.   One

    E.   Zero

20. How does a transmitting station maintain control of the medium during a fragment burst? (Choose all that apply.)

    A.   Random backoff algorithm

    B.   Duration

    C.   DIFS

    D.   Sequence Control

    E.   SIFS

Answers to Review Questions

1. E. The graphic displays four MAC addresses. Although 802.11 frames have four address fields in the MAC header, 802.11 frames typically use only three of the MAC address fields. An 802.11 frame sent within a wireless distribution system (WDS) requires all four MAC addresses. Although the standard does not specifically define procedures for using this format, WLAN vendors often implement WDS solutions. Examples of a WDS include WLAN bridges, mesh networks, and wireless repeaters.

2. A. CCMP/AES encryption will add an extra 16 bytes of overhead to the body of an 802.11 data frame. Eight bytes are added by the CCMP header, and 8 bytes are added by the MIC. WEP encryption will add an extra 8 bytes of overhead to the body of an 802.11 data frame. When TKIP is implemented, because of the extra overhead from the extended IV and the MIC, a total of 20 bytes of overhead is added to the body of an 802.11 data frame.

3. C. Only 802.11 data frames can carry an upper-layer payload (MSDU) within the body of the frame. The MSDU can be as large as 2,304 bytes and usually should be encrypted. 802.11 control frames do not have a body. 802.11 management frames have a body; however, the payload is strictly layer 2 information.

4. A, B. The receiving station may have received the data, but the returning ACK frame may have become corrupted, and the original unicast frame will have to be retransmitted. If the unicast frame becomes corrupted for any reason, the receiving station will not send an ACK.

5. B. When the client station transmits a frame with the Power Management field set to 1, it is enabling Power Save mode. The DTIM does not enable Power Save mode; it only notifies clients to stay awake in preparation for a multicast or broadcast.

6. C. When the listening radio hears a frame transmission from another station, it looks at the header of the frame and determines whether the Duration/ID field contains a Duration value or an ID value. If the field contains a Duration value, the listening station will set its NAV timer to this value.

7. C, E. The Duration/ID field has three possible purposes. The main purpose of this field is to reset the NAV timer of other stations, which is a virtual carrier-sense mechanism. PS-Poll frames use the Duration/ID field as an association identifier (AID) during legacy power management processes. Although never implemented by vendors, the Duration/ID field can also be used to signal that a contention-free period (CFP) process has begun.

8. E. The main purpose of the Duration/ID field is to reset the NAV timer of other stations. When bit 15 of the field is zero, the value in bits 14–0 represent the duration of a frame exchange sequence remaining after the frame in which the Duration value is found. Bits 14–0 can have a Duration value of 0 to 32,767. The Duration value translates into microseconds when resetting NAV timers of other stations. The other common use of the Duration/ID field is as an AID in PS-Poll control frames. When bits 15 and 14 have a value of 1, bits 13–0 can be used to represent an AID in PS-Poll frames from 1 to 2007.

9. B, D, E. Excessive layer 2 retransmissions adversely affect the WLAN in two ways. First, layer 2 retransmissions increase MAC overhead and therefore decrease throughput. Second, if application data has to be retransmitted at layer 2, the timely delivery of application traffic becomes delayed or inconsistent. Applications such as VoIP depend on the timely and consistent delivery of the IP packet. Excessive layer 2 retransmissions usually result in increased latency and jitter problems for time-sensitive applications such as voice and video.

10. A, D. The NAV is not updated when the receiver address (RA) is the same as the receiving station's MAC address. Therefore, in this scenario, the Duration value did not reset the VoWiFi client's NAV because it was the receiver. You should also understand that the Duration value of the transmitting station does not reset the transmitting stations NAV timer. The transmitter cannot hear its own transmitted frame. The transmitter's NAV will be zero after transmitting, just like it was zero before the transmitter gained control of the medium. The AP was the transmitter so the Duration value did not reset its NAV. Any other client or AP stations within hearing range on the same channel will reset their NAV, even if they are not members of the BSS.

11. A, D. Depending on how the To DS and From DS fields are used, the definition of the four MAC fields will change. One constant, however, is that the Address 1 field will always be the receiver address (RA) but may have a second definition as well. The Address 2 field will always be the transmitter address (TA) but also may have a second definition. Address 3 is normally used to additional MAC address information. Address 4 is used only in the case of a WDS.

12. A, B, E. When both bits are set to 0, several different scenarios exist. The most common scenario is that the frames are either management or control frames. Management and control frames do not have an MSDU payload, and therefore their final destination is never the distribution system (DS). Management and control exist only at the MAC sublayer and therefore have no need to be translated by the integration service (IS) and never are delivered to the distribution system service (DSS). Another scenario is a direct data frame transfer from one STA to another STA within an independent basic service set (IBSS), more commonly known as an ad hoc network. The third scenario involves what is known as a station-to-station link (STSL), which involves a data frame being sent directly from one client station to another client station that belongs to the same BSS, thereby bypassing the AP.

13. B, C, D. In the Sequence Control field, the Fragment Number subfield contains a 4-bit number assigned to each fragment of an MSDU. The first, or only, fragment of an MSDU is assigned a fragment number of 0. Each successive fragment is assigned a sequentially incremented fragment number. The graphic shows a fragment number of 2, which means it is the third fragment. The More Fragments field indicates a value of 0, which means it is the last transmitted fragment. The To DS field has a value of 0, and the From DS field has a value of 1, which means this is a downstream transmission from an AP to a client station.

14. C, D. The Power Management field indicates a value of 1, meaning that the client STA is in Power Save mode and that the AP must buffer the client STA's traffic. Fragmentation is not being used because the frag number in the Sequence Control field has a value of 0 and the More Fragments field also has a value of 0. The Subtype field indicates that this is a Null data frame and not a PS-Poll frame. PS-Poll frames are the only frames that use the Duration/ID field as an association identifier (AID).

15. D. The Protected Frame field has a value of 0, which indicates that the MSDU payload of this simple data frame is not encrypted.

16. A, B. The Retry field indicates a value of 1, meaning this is a retransmission. Every time an 802.11 radio transmits a unicast frame, if the frame is received properly and the cyclic redundancy check (CRC) of the FCS passes, the 802.11 radio that received the frame will reply with an acknowledgment (ACK) frame. If the ACK is received, the original station knows that the frame transfer was successful. All unicast 802.11 frames must be acknowledged. Broadcast and multicast frames do not require an acknowledgment.

    If any portion of a unicast frame is corrupted, the CRC will fail, and the receiving 802.11 radio will not send an ACK frame to the transmitting 802.11 radio. If an ACK frame is not received by the original transmitting radio, the unicast frame is not acknowledged and will have to be retransmitted.

17. B, C. When the To DS bit is set to 0 and the From DS bit is set to 1, this indicates that an 802.11 data frame is being sent downstream from an access point to a client station. The original source of the MSDU payload of the 802.11 data frame is an address that exists on the distribution system medium (DSM). An example is a DHCP server that resides on the 802.3 network forwarding a DHCP response packet through an AP with the final destination being an 802.11 client station.

18. E. The frame body is of variable size. The maximum frame body size is determined by the maximum MSDU size (2,304 octets) plus any overhead from encryption. The 802.11n-2009 HT amendment defines a frame aggregation method called Aggregate MAC Service Data Unit (A-MSDU). An 802.11n station using this method of aggregation can have a frame body with a maximum A-MSDU size (3839 or 7935 octets, depending upon the STA's capability), plus any overhead from encryption.

19. C. 802.3 Ethernet frames have only a source address (SA) and destination address (DA) in the layer 2 header. 802.11 frames have four address fields in the MAC header. The contents of these four fields can include the following MAC addresses: receiver address (RA), transmitter address (TA), basic service set identifier (BSSID), destination address (DA), and source address (SA). In other words, an 802.11 frame can contain as many as four MAC addresses with five different meanings.

20. B, E. Fragments are always sent in what is known as a fragment burst. Once the transmitting station gains control of the medium, it maintains control through two mechanisms: Duration values (which set other stations' NAVs) and SIFS. First, the value of the Duration field in the MAC header of data fragments and ACK frames is used to reserve the medium for the next fragment. As a backup mechanism, SIFS is used between data fragments and ACK frames in order to preempt those stations that are trying to gain control of the medium using DIFS.

Chapter 4

802.11 Management Frames

IN THIS CHAPTER, YOU WILL LEARN ABOUT THE FOLLOWING:

- ✓ Management Frame Types
- ✓ Beacons
- ✓ Probe Request / Response
- ✓ Authentication
- ✓ Association Request / Response
- ✓ Disassociation
- ✓ Deauthentication
- ✓ Reassociation Request / Response
- ✓ Management Frame body components
- ✓ Management Frame body main fields
- ✓ Management Frame body main Information Elements
- ✓ Action Frames
- ✓ Spectrum and Transmit Power Management (802.11h)
- ✓ Admission Control (802.11e)
- ✓ Fast BSS Transition (802.11r)
- ✓ Protected Management Frames (802.11w)

Management frames are often seen as the skeleton of wireless networks. They allow wireless devices to form a network and, as their name states, "manage" the connections. The original 802.11-1997 standard defined two types of management frames: the "notify" type and the "request and response" type. The "notify" type is a frame sent to the cell containing information to which no specific response is expected. The "request and response" type is an exchange between two stations or between an access point and a station.

In this chapter, we will examine each management frame. This task is complicated by the fact that the management frame body content is flexible, made of several elements where size is variable and presence is optional or mandatory, depending on the frame subtype and service provided to the cell. To help you get a clear understanding of these frames, we will show the structure of the main management frame types. We will then examine each field and information element, then by families. You will then take a closer look at a specific type of management frames, the action frames.

Management Frame Types

Figure 4.1 shows the structure of a management frame.

FIGURE 4.1 Management frame structure

			MAC header			Information elements and fixed fields	
2	2	6	6	6	2	0–2,312	4
Frame Control	Duration	DA	SA	BSS ID	Seq-ctl	Frame Body	FCS

Management frames always have a standard 24-byte-long MAC header with three addresses, followed by a body of variable size. When 802.11n is in use, the header is extended to show the HT Control section, as shown in Figure 4.2.

FIGURE 4.2 Management frame structure: 802.11n

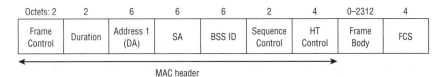

Octets: 2	2	6	6	6	2	4	0–2312	4
Frame Control	Duration	Address 1 (DA)	SA	BSS ID	Sequence Control	HT Control	Frame Body	FCS

MAC header

The DA field is the destination address of the frame. It can be broadcast or unicast depending on the frame subtype. The SA field is the MAC address of the station transmitting the frame. The BSSID can be the AP BSSID or a wildcard value (see the "Probe Request" section).

The size and content of the body depend on the management frame subtype. Table 4.1 lists all 12 management frame subtypes, as defined by the 802.11-2007 standard.

TABLE 4.1 Management frame subtypes

Subtype bits	Subtype description
0000	Association request
0001	Association response
0010	Reassociation request
0011	Reassociation response
0100	Probe request
0101	Probe response
1000	Beacon
1001	Announcement traffic indication message (ATIM)
1010	Disassociation
1011	Authentication
1100	Deauthentication
1101	Action
1110	Action no ack

Type is always 00 (management). Some subtypes are "reserved" and currently unused (0110, 0111, and 1111).

Management frames are sourced and dealt with at the MAC layer and never forwarded to the upper layers. Management frames are always limited to the cell space; they are never relayed through an access point to the DS, from the DS, or from a station to another station. For this reason, management frames sent by access points always have the To DS and From DS fields set to 0.

Beacon Frame

Connecting to a wired network is often as simple as locating a connector on a switch or a wall, attaching the right cable, and plugging in your computer. Connecting to a wireless network presents more challenges. The AP may be hidden from view, in the ceiling, or in another room. You do not know which channel it uses and which modulations are supported. One way to learn about possible wireless connection points is to use passive scanning. With passive scanning, the wireless client tunes its radio to each possible channel in turn and listens for signals from access points. The speed and duration of dwelling time on each channel depends on the wireless client vendor driver and is defined in each driver MIB by the MaxChannelTime parameter.

Beacon frames are used by the access points (and stations in an IBSS) to communicate throughout the serviced area the characteristics of the connection offered to the cell members. Notice that this information is not only used by potential clients during passive scanning but also by clients that are already associated to the BSS.

Beacon frames are sent periodically, at a time called target beacon transmission time (TBTT) and at a rate defined by the dot11BeaconPeriod parameter in the AP MIB. All 802.11 device clocks count time by units of 1 kilomicrosecond each (in a world driven by powers of 2, this unit is 1,024 microseconds, not 1,000 microseconds). The dot11BeaconPeriod parameter is by default 100 time units (TUs), that is, 102,400 microseconds, which is a little over 102 milliseconds. This interval can be configured on some access points.

The access point tries to send the beacon at each defined TU interval and announces when the next beacon is expected to be sent. Nevertheless, access points are just like any wireless device in the cell. They cannot send if the network is busy. When the time comes for an AP to send a beacon, if the network is busy, the AP will delay its beacon transmission until it can gain access to the media. Although the beacon is slightly delayed, the AP will still try to send the next beacon at the originally planned interval. For example, suppose that a beacon is to be sent every 102.4 milliseconds, at times 0, 102.4, and 204.8. The first beacon is sent on time, but suppose the network is busy at time 102.4. The second beacon has to be delayed and can then be sent, for example, at time 103.2 millisecond and therefore 0.8 millisecond late. The AP will still try to send the third beacon at time 204.8 and will not delay that third beacon even if the previous one was late. Figure 4.3 illustrates this mechanism.

FIGURE 4.3   Beacon in busy network

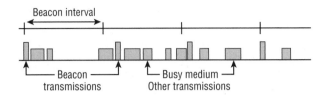

All stations in the cell use the AP beacon as a time reference. Each beacon contains a time stamp and also an indication about when the next beacon will be sent. Each station uses the time stamp with what the 802.11 standard calls the timing synchronization function (TSF) to make sure that their clock uses the same tempo as the access point.

In an IBSS, stations use beacon frames for time synchronization and to maintain a common set of parameters for the IBSS. Because there is no central access point taking care of the beacon generation, the process is distributed. The first station to create the ad hoc network defines the *beacon interval* and announces it in the subsequent probe requests and responses. All stations joining the IBSS learn this interval. When the time comes for the next beacon, each station treats the beacon as the next packet to send. This means that each station of the IBSS does the following:

1. Interrupts its countdown for the next packet to send or wakes up if it was in Power Save mode.

2. Picks up a random number between zero and twice CWmin and 2× aSlotTime.

3. Counts down to zero from that number.

4. The first station to reach zero sends the beacon.

5. Hearing the beacon, the other stations remove the beacon from their network stack and resume their previous activity.

Figure 4.4 shows an example of a beacon capture. A beacon contains mandatory elements but also optional and vendor-specific elements. The size of the beacon body can therefore vary depending on the type of information carried by the beacon.

Table 4.2 lists the elements and fields you can expect to find (mandatory or optional) in a beacon frame body (see Figure 4.5). Most elements are defined in the 802.11-2007 standard. Some of them are introduced by specific amendments (and therefore used only by vendors implementing those amendments). The 802.11k amendment introduces processes for Radio Resource Management to help dynamically assign APs channels and power levels. The 802.11w amendment introduces the Management Frame Protection. The 802.11r amendment introduces Fast Basic Service Set transition (fast roaming between APs). The 802.11y amendment introduces the usage of a new band, 3650 to 3700, in the United States.

FIGURE 4.4   Beacon capture

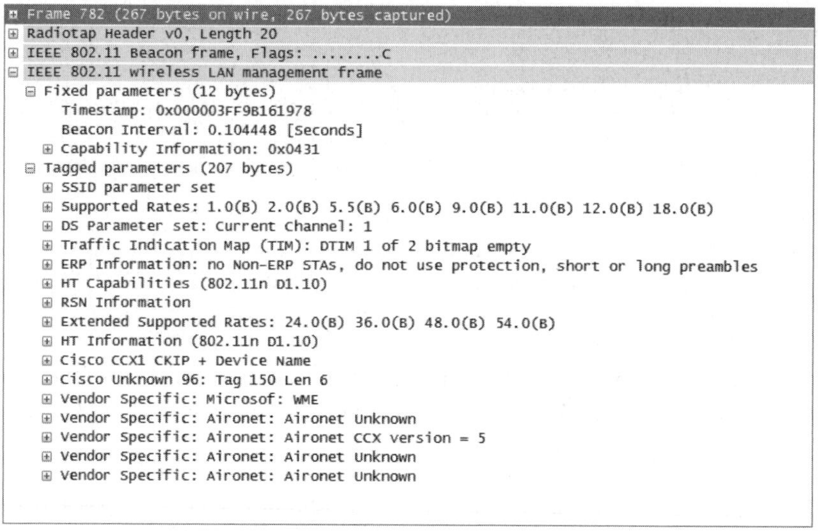

```
⊞ Frame 782 (267 bytes on wire, 267 bytes captured)
⊞ Radiotap Header v0, Length 20
⊞ IEEE 802.11 Beacon frame, Flags: ........C
⊟ IEEE 802.11 wireless LAN management frame
  ⊟ Fixed parameters (12 bytes)
      Timestamp: 0x000003FF9B161978
      Beacon Interval: 0.104448 [Seconds]
    ⊞ Capability Information: 0x0431
  ⊟ Tagged parameters (207 bytes)
    ⊞ SSID parameter set
    ⊞ Supported Rates: 1.0(B) 2.0(B) 5.5(B) 6.0(B) 9.0(B) 11.0(B) 12.0(B) 18.0(B)
    ⊞ DS Parameter set: Current Channel: 1
    ⊞ Traffic Indication Map (TIM): DTIM 1 of 2 bitmap empty
    ⊞ ERP Information: no Non-ERP STAs, do not use protection, short or long preambles
    ⊞ HT Capabilities (802.11n D1.10)
    ⊞ RSN Information
    ⊞ Extended Supported Rates: 24.0(B) 36.0(B) 48.0(B) 54.0(B)
    ⊞ HT Information (802.11n D1.10)
    ⊞ Cisco CCX1 CKIP + Device Name
    ⊞ Cisco Unknown 96: Tag 150 Len 6
    ⊞ Vendor Specific: Microsof: WME
    ⊞ Vendor Specific: Aironet: Aironet Unknown
    ⊞ Vendor Specific: Aironet: Aironet CCX version = 5
    ⊞ Vendor Specific: Aironet: Aironet Unknown
    ⊞ Vendor Specific: Aironet: Aironet Unknown
```

FIGURE 4.5   Beacon frame structure

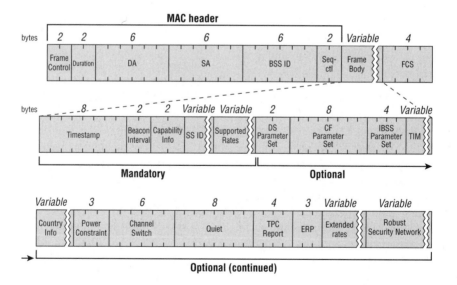

TABLE 4.2 Elements and fields in a beacon frame body

Order	Information	Note
1	Timestamp	
2	Beacon interval	
3	Capability	
4	Service Set Identifier (SSID)	
5	Supported rates	
6	Frequency-Hopping (FH) Parameter Set	Used by legacy FH stations.
7	DS Parameter Set	Present within beacon frames generated by STAs using clause 15, clause 18, and clause 19 PHYs or if the beacon is sent using one of the rates defined by one of these clauses.
8	CF Parameter Set	Used with PCF; unused in real networks.
9	IBSS Parameter Set	Present only within beacon frames generated by STAs in an IBSS.
10	Traffic indication map (TIM)	Present only within beacon frames generated by APs.
11	Country	Used with 802.11d and with 802.11.
12	FH Parameters	Used by legacy FH stations.
13	FH Pattern Table	Used by legacy FH stations.
14	Power Constraint	Used with 802.11h.
15	Channel Switch Announcement	Used with 802.11h.
16	Quiet	Used with 802.11h.
17	IBSS DFS	Used with 802.11h in IBSS.
18	TPC Report	Used with 802.11h.

TABLE 4.2   Elements and fields in a beacon frame body *(continued)*

Order	Information	Note
19	ERP Information	Present in 802.11g networks; optional in other cases.
20	Extended Supported Rates	The Extended Supported Rates element is present whenever there are more than eight supported rates; it is optional otherwise.
21	RSN	Used with 802.11i.
22	BSS Load	Used with 802.11e QoS.
23	EDCA Parameter Set	Used with 802.11e QoS when the QoS Capability element is not present.
24	QoS Capability	Used with 802.11e QoS when EDCA Parameter Set element is not present.
25–32, 34–36	Vendor Specific	One or more vendor-specific information elements may appear in this frame. This information element follows all other information elements.
33	Mobility Domain	Used with 802.11r Fast BSS Transition.
37	HT Capabilities	Used with 802.11n.
38	HT Operation	Used with 802.11n.
39	20/40 BSS Coexistence	Used with 802.11n.
40	Overlapping BSS Scan Parameters	Used with 802.11n.
41	Extended Capabilities	The Extended Capabilities element may be present if any of the fields in this element are nonzero.

As a wireless LAN analysis professional, you should know each of these elements and understand their purpose. We will cover each of them later in this chapter.

Probe Request Frame

Discovering the network by scanning all possible channels and listening to beacons is not considered to be very efficient. At the scale of a wireless NIC, this process is seen as slow. To enhance this discovery process, stations often use what is called active scanning. In this mode, stations still go through each channel in turn, but instead of passively listening to the signals on that frequency, stations send a *probe request* management frame aimed at asking what network is available on this channel. If any AP or active station in an IBSS is present on that frequency, they should answer with the requested information. The probe request frame body contains the element and fields listed in Table 4.3.

TABLE 4.3   Elements and fields in a probe request frame body

Order	Information	Note
1	Service Set Identifier (SSID)	
2	Supported Rates	
3	Request Information	Used with 802.11d.
4	Extended Supported Rates	The Extended Supported Rates element is present whenever there are more than eight supported rates; it is optional otherwise.
5	Vendor Specific	One or more vendor-specific information elements may appear in this frame. This information element follows all other information elements.

The probe requests are usually sent to the broadcast DA address (ff:ff:ff:ff:ff:ff). The frame is sent using the common CSMA/CA procedure. Once the probe is sent, the emitting station starts a ProbeTimer countdown and waits for answers. This ProbeTimer value is decided by each vendor, but it is usually a lot shorter than a beacon interval. Common values are in the 10 millisecond range. At the end of the timer, the station processes the answers it has received. If no answer was received, the station moves to the next channel and repeats the discovery process.

Stations sending probe requests may specify the SSID they are looking for (in that case the probe request is called a *directed probe request*). Only those IBSS stations or APs supporting the requested SSID will answer. The SSID value can also be set to 0 (that is, the SSID field is present but empty). This is called a wildcard SSID, and the frame is a null probe request. In that case, an IBSS station or AP on the probed channel should send a probe response indicating the SSID it supports and the characteristics of the cell (see the next section).

The purpose of a probe request is typically to discover APs and their supported networks (SSIDs and/or BSSIDs). The station performing the discovery indicates the rates it supports so that the AP or IBSS station answering the probe request can determine the best data rate to use for the answer. The requesting station may also use the probe request to discover specific elements about the network (for example, "What are the local country parameters?"). To allow for this additional information discovery, the probe request can contain a Request Information element, shown in Figure 4.6, that can request one or several additional parameters.

FIGURE 4.6   Request Information element

Element ID	Length
Requested element ID 1	Requested element ID 2
. . .	
Requested element ID N–1	Requested element ID N

This Request Information element is optional. The probe request may also contain additional, vendor-specific requests to exchange information specific to a vendor implementation of features that are optional or not described in the 802.11 standard.

Probe Response Frame

Upon receiving a probe request frame, a station in an IBSS or an AP will respond with a *probe response* frame, which contains information about itself and the cell (see Figure 4.7). The format of the probe response is very close to the format of a beacon, because both frames essentially answer the same question: what are the specs of the cell?

FIGURE 4.7   Probe response capture

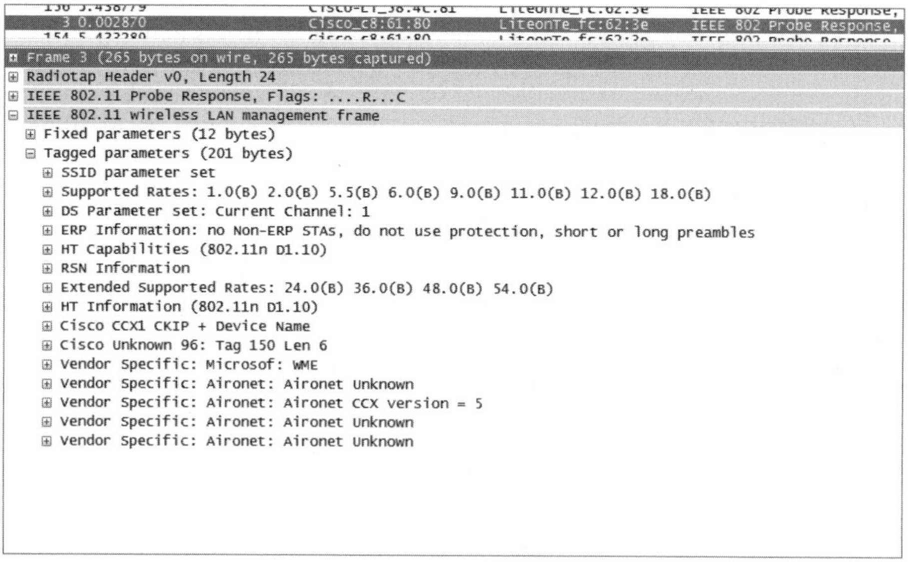

Table 4.4 lists the elements and fields you can expect to find (mandatory or optional) in a probe response frame body.

TABLE 4.4 Elements and fields in a probe response frame body

Order	Information	Note
1	Timestamp	
2	Beacon interval	
3	Capability	
4	Service Set Identifier (SSID)	
5	Supported rates	
6	Frequency-Hopping (FH) Parameter Set	Used by legacy FH stations.
7	DS Parameter Set	The DS Parameter Set information element is present within beacon frames generated by STAs using clause 15, clause 18, and clause 19 PHYs.
8	CF Parameter Set	Used for PCF. Unused in real world.
9	IBSS Parameter Set	Used within beacon frames generated by STAs in an IBSS.
10	Country	Used with 802.11d and used with 802.11h.
11	FH Parameters	Used by legacy FH stations.
12	FH Pattern Table	Used by legacy FH stations.
13	Power Constraint	Used with 802.11h.
14	Channel Switch Announcement	Used with 802.11h.
15	Quiet	Used with 802.11h.
16	IBSS DFS	Used with 802.11h in an IBSS.
17	TPC Report	Used with 802.11h.

TABLE 4.4   Elements and fields in a probe response frame body *(continued)*

Order	Information	Note
18	ERP Information	Used in 802.11g networks and optionally present in other cases.
19	Extended Supported Rates	The Extended Supported Rates element is present whenever there are more than eight supported rates; it is optional otherwise.
20	RSN	Used with 802.11i.
21	BSS Load	Used with 802.11e QoS.
22	EDCA Parameter Set	Used with 802.11e QoS when the QoS Capability element is not present.
23	Measurement Pilot Transmission Information	Used with 802.11k
24	Multiple BSSID	Used with 802.11k.
25	RRM Enabled Capabilities	Used with 802.11k.
26	AP Channel Report	Used with 802.11k.
27	BSS Average Access Delay	Used with 802.11k.
28–30		Reserved/unused.
31	Mobility Domain	Used with 802.11r.
32	DSE Registered Location	Used with 802.11w.
33	Extended Channel Switch Announcement	Used with 802.11y.
34	Supported Regulatory Classes	Used with 802.11y.
35	HT Capabilities	Used with 802.11n.
36	HT Operation	Used with 802.11n.
37	20/40 BSS Coexistence	Used with 802.11n.
38	Overlapping BSS Scan Parameters	Used with 802.11n.

TABLE 4.4   Elements and fields in a probe response frame body *(continued)*

Order	Information	Note
39	Extended Capabilities	The Extended Capabilities element may be present if any of the fields in this element are nonzero.
Last-1	Vendor Specific	One or more vendor-specific information elements may appear in this frame. This information element follows all other information elements.
Last-n	Requested information elements	Elements requested by the request information element of the probe request frame.

The probe response is sent as a unicast frame. The DA field is the MAC address of the station from which the probe request was sent. The probe response is sent at the lowest common rate supported by both the station sending the probe request and the answering AP (or IBSS station). The probe response should be acknowledged by the receiving station, just like any other unicast frame.

If you compare this list to the beacon frame body component list, you will see that both frame bodies are very similar, with the following differences:

- The beacon frame contains a TIM field; the probe response does not.

- The beacon frame can contain a QoS Capability Information element that announces basic QoS support to the cell.

- The probe response also contains the Requested Information elements that may have been requested by the probing station.

Authentication Frame

Discovery is the first step a station should perform before trying to join the cell. The next step is the join phase, which is an exchange comprised of at least four frames: authentication request, authentication response, association request, and association response. You will learn in Chapter 9 that the process can be more complex and may include specific frame exchanges that provide authentication and data protection mechanisms. These mechanisms add frames to the standard 802.11 four frame authentication and association exchange mentioned earlier.

In all cases, after having performed a network discovery through the probe request/ probe response exchange or by listening to beacons, a station wanting to join a cell goes through an authentication process, exchanging authentication frames with the access point. Unlike the probe and association phases, which use a different frame for the request and the response, there is only one type of authentication frame. Figure 4.8 shows its format.

FIGURE 4.8 Authentication frame format

				MAC header				Frame body				
bytes	2	2	6	6	6	2	2	2	2	Variable	4
	Frame Control	Duration	DA	SA	BSS ID	Seq-ctl	Authentication Algorithm Number	Authentication Transaction Seq. No.	Status Code	Challenge Text	FCS

The answer to an authentication frame is an acknowledgment frame. This is because authentication frames are always an exchange between a requesting station and a granting AP or IBSS station and are therefore always unicast frames. Unicast frames should be acknowledged to confirm proper delivery.

The initial purpose of the *authentication frame* is to validate the device type, in other words, verify that the requesting station has proper 802.11 capabilities to join the cell. This exchange is based on a simple two-frame dialogue (authentication request, authentication response) called the Open System. A possibility for a WEP shared key exchange was also included in the original 802.11-1997 standard. This shared key exchange adds two frames to the default Open System authentication, resulting in a four-frame exchange. This latter method is called Shared Key authentication, requires the use of WEP encryption, and is not widely used (or recommended) today.

The *Authentication Algorithm number* field value describes which authentication system is used (0 for Open System and 1 for Shared Key).

Notice that when more complex authentication is in place (such as with modern WPA and WPA2 security), Open System is used first, and then the more complex mechanism follows the 802.11 association.

In the authentication exchange, the 2-byte *Authentication Transaction Sequence Number* field indicates the current state of progress through the multistep transaction.

Depending on the exchange, the result of the authentication phase can be a successful authentication or a failure. The last frame of the authentication sequence contains the status code. 0 is Success, 1 is unspecified failure, and 2–9 are reserved values (they are used when the status field is present in the frame, but there is no status to report, for example because the frame is an authentication request). When the result is a failure (excluding unspecified failures), the code indicates the reason for the failure. The possible reasons are listed later in this chapter.

The 802.11 standard distinguishes the Reason Code field from the Status Code field. When a station negotiates a parameter, like authentication, the result of the negotiation is the status (success or failure). The AP or client can also suddenly send messages (such as a deauthentication or disassociation) interrupting the station communication without any negotiation. In that case, the AP justifies its action using the Reason Code field.

Table 4.5 summarizes the authentication frame field values and usage.

TABLE 4.5   Summary of authentication frame fields values and usage

Authentication algorithm	Authentication transaction sequence no.	Status code	Challenge text
Open System	1	Reserved	Not present
Open System	2	Status	Not present
Shared Key	1	Reserved	Not present
Shared Key	2	Status	Present
Shared Key	3	Reserved	Present
Shared Key	4	Status	Not present

Association Request Frame

If the 802.11 authentication phase completes with a Success result, the station moves to the association phase. The purpose of this exchange is for the station to join the cell and obtain a cell member identifier (called an association ID [*AID*]).

> When a security authentication mechanism is in place, with WPA or WPA2, a second "authentication" phase occurs after the association phase. For this reason, the first authentication phase described earlier is called the 802.11 authentication phase to distinguish it from the later PSK or 802.1X authentication phase used with WPA or WPA2. It is important to note that the 802.11 authentication does not provide any security whatsoever. It is merely a formality. Notice that the WEP challenge uses the term *shared key*, whereas WPA/WPA2 refer to *preshared key*. Many vendors mix both terms or use other terms, such as *passphrase*, *secret key*, and so on.

The first frame sent in the association phase is from the requesting station to the AP (or a station in an IBSS). This frame is the *association request* frame and is shown in Figure 4.9. It is a unicast management frame and is always acknowledged. The SA is the requesting station MAC address, and the DA is the AP or IBSS station MAC address that was used for the authentication phase.

The association request body contains the elements and fields shown in Table 4.6.

FIGURE 4.9   Association request frame format

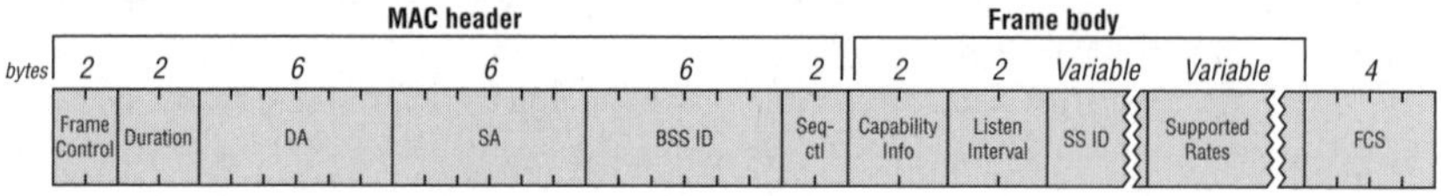

TABLE 4.6   Elements and fields in the association request body

Order	Information	Notes
1	Capability Information	
2	Listen interval	
3	SSID	
4	Supported rates	
5	Extended Supported Rates	Present whenever there are more than eight supported rates; it is optional otherwise.
6	Power Capability	Used with 802.11h.
7	Supported Channels	Used with 802.11h.
8	RSN	Used with 802.11i.
9	QoS Capability	Used with 802.11e QoS.
10	RRM Enabled Capabilities	Used with 802.11k.
11	Mobility Domain	Used with 802.11r.
12	Supported Regulatory Classes	Used with 802.11r.
13	HT Capabilities	Used with 802.11n.
14	20/40 BSS Coexistence	Used with 802.11n.
15	Extended Capabilities	The Extended Capabilities element may be present if any of the fields in this element are nonzero.
Last	Vendor Specific	One or more vendor-specific information elements may appear in this frame. This information element follows all other information elements.

The details of each information element listed in this table will be covered later in this chapter. You can see that in the association request frame, the station communicates its characteristics and capabilities to the AP so that the AP can take note of how to communicate properly with this station.

Association Response Frame

After acknowledging reception of the association request frame, the AP examines each field of the request and verifies whether they all match its own 802.11 parameters (see Figure 4.10). If there is a mismatch, the AP decides whether this difference is a blocking (to the association) factor. If the difference is not blocking, the AP takes note of the limitations of the station parameters and grants access to the cell, indicating its own parameters in the *association response*. If the difference is blocking, the AP rejects the association.

FIGURE 4.10 Association response frame format

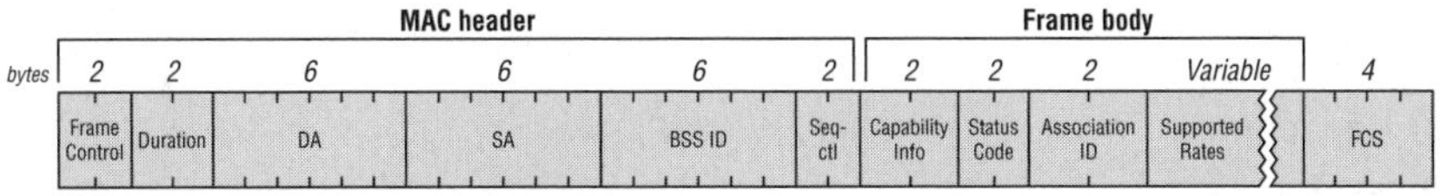

The rejected station is not associated to the cell. It can examine the answer from the AP, determine the reasons for the rejection, and correct its own parameters if possible before trying again. To allow for this mechanism, the association response frame contains the AP 802.11 parameters, as described in Table 4.7.

TABLE 4.7 The association response frame

Order	Information	Notes
1	Capability Information	
2	Status Code	
3	Association ID	
4	Supported rates	
5	Extended Supported Rates	The Extended Supported Rates element is present whenever there are more than eight supported rates; it is optional otherwise.
6	EDCA Parameter Set	

TABLE 4.7   The association response frame *(continued)*

Order	Information	Notes
7	RCPI	Used with 802.11k.
8	RSNI	Used with 802.11k.
9	RRM Enabled Capabilities	Used with 802.11k.
10	Mobility Domain	Used with 802.11r.
11	Fast BSS Transition	Used with 802.11r.
12	DSE Registered Location	Used with 802.11y.
13	Timeout Interval (association comeback time)	Used with 802.11w.
14	HT Capabilities	Used with 802.11n.
15	HT Operation	Used with 802.11n.
16	20/40 BSS Coexistence	Used with 802.11n.
17	Overlapping BSS Scan Parameters	Used with 802.11n.
18	Extended Capabilities	The Extended Capabilities element may be present if any of the fields in this element are nonzero.
Last	Vendor Specific	One or more vendor-specific information elements may appear in this frame. This information element follows all other information elements.

The AP also returns a status code informing the station whether the association is successful. If the result is Success (0), the AP communicates an association ID, which is the station identifier on the access point. The AID value is an integer between 1 and 2007. Although the field is 2 bytes long, only the 14 less significant bits are used (the others are set to 1). In reality, you would probably never see 2,007 stations associated to a single AP. The overhead required to maintain the cell state with so many stations would create so many collisions that the associations could never reach this number.

Once the station receives its association ID, it is associated to the cell and can start to communicate, sending data or moving to a second layer of authentication (see Chapter 9 for more details). If the association fails, the station receives in the status code the reason for the failure. Based on the status code and the parameters returned by the AP, it can modify its parameters and send a new association request frame, if the AP parameters are compatible with its own, or drop the association process and start looking for another AP, if the parameters are incompatible.

Disassociation Frame

Once a station is associated to an AP, either side can terminate the association at any time by sending a disassociation frame (see Figure 4.11). A station would send such a frame, for example, because it leaves the cell to roam to another AP. An AP could send this frame for example because the station tries to use invalid parameters or for reasons related to the AP itself (configuration change, and so on).

FIGURE 4.11 Disassociation frame format

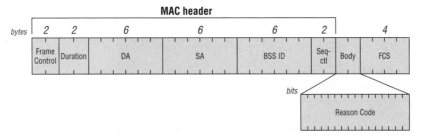

The *disassociation frame* DA can be the unicast MAC address of the station to disassociate or a broadcast address if the AP needs to disassociate all the stations in its cell. When the disassociation frame is unicast, it is acknowledged by the receiving station. Broadcast frames are not acknowledged. The disassociation frame is quite small and contains the following elements:

Order	Notes
1	Reason code.
2 – (Last – 1)	One or more vendor-specific information elements may appear in this frame.
Last	Used with 802.11w.

A disassociated station is still authenticated. It can try to reassociate by sending a new association request frame, keeping its authenticated status. For this reason, disassociation frames are typically used when parameters change and the station or the AP needs to renegotiate the communications parameters. A station roaming to another cell may also choose to use a disassociation frame, to be able to keep its authenticated status and accelerate the process when roaming back to the same cell before its authentication timeout expires.

Deauthentication Frame

The station or AP can also send a *deauthentication frame*. This frame is used when all communications are terminated, for example, because the AP has to reboot or because the station stops its Wi-Fi communications. It is also used when a frame is received before authentication has completed. For example, a station trying to send an association request or a data frame before having performed the authentication sequence will receive a deauthentication frame from the AP, indicating that authentication must be performed first.

The format of the deauthentication frame is the same as the disassociation frame, containing the following elements:

Order	Notes
1	Reason code.
2 – (Last – 1)	One or more vendor-specific information elements may appear in this frame.
Last	Used with 802.11w.

Stations or APs receiving either of these frames recognize them by their type and subtype (00-1010 for the disassociation frame and 00-1100 for the deauthentication frame).

Reassociation Request Frame

This type of frame can be sent only by a station to an access point (never from an AP to a station or from a station to a station in an IBSS) and is used when the station is already associated to the ESS and wants to associate to another access point connecting to the same ESS. This frame (Figure 4.12) can also be used if the station left the cell for a short duration and wants to rejoin the cell again. This can occur while the station authentication is still valid on the AP or after the expiration of the authentication timer. In that case, the station first starts with an authentication phase, followed by the reassociation phase. A station already associated to an AP can also use the *reassociation request* message to renegotiate some parameters exchanged in the Association Request/Response dialog box.

The reassociation request frame is a unicast and acknowledged frame, just like the association request frame. It contains the elements shown in Table 4.8.

FIGURE 4.12   Reassociation request frame format

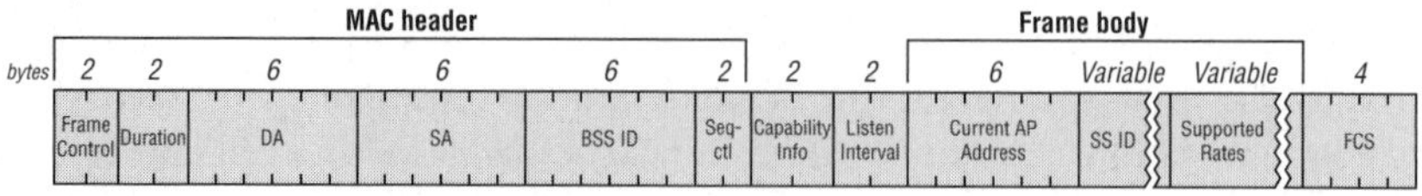

TABLE 4.8   Elements of the reassociation request frame

Order	Information	Notes
1	Capability Information	
2	Listen interval	
3	Current AP address	
4	SSID	
5	Supported rates	
6	Extended Supported Rates	The Extended Supported Rates element is present whenever there are more than eight supported rates, and it is optional otherwise.
7	Power Capability	Used with 802.11h.
8	Supported Channels	Used with 802.11h.
9	RSN	Used with 802.11i and 802.11y.
10	QoS Capability	Used with 802.11e QoS.
11	RRM Enabled Capabilities	Used with 802.11k.
12	Mobility Domain	Used with 802.11r.
13	Fast Transition	Used with 802.11r.
14	Resource Information Container	Used with 802.11r.
15	Supported Regulatory Classes	Used with 802.11y.
16	HT Capabilities	Used with 802.11n.
17	20/40 BSS Coexistence	Used with 802.11n.
18	Extended Capabilities	Used with 802.11n.
Last	Vendor Specific	One or more vendor-specific information elements may appear in this frame. This information element follows all other information elements.

The logic of the reassociation request was linked to roaming. In this logic, the station leaves the coverage area of an access point and needs to associate to another access point offering the same SSID. This roaming station goes through the authentication phase with the new access point, then sends a reassociation request mentioning the old AP MAC address, and finally joins the cell on the new AP, getting a new AID.

Why not proceed with a simple association request frame? It's because the logic is that the new access point should contact the old access point and move the parameters for the station from the old AP to the new one. A station can be associated to only one AP at a time. It is therefore the responsibility of the new AP to inform the old AP about the roam and disassociate the station from the old AP.

A station can be authenticated to several access points, as long as it is associated to only one of them.

Reassociation Response Frame

An AP uses the *reassociation response* frame in response to a reassociation request frame. The reassociation response contains the elements shown in Table 4.9.

TABLE 4.9   Elements of the reassociation response frame

Order	Information	Notes
1	Capability Information	
2	Status Code	
3	Association ID	
4	Supported rates	
5	Extended Supported Rates	The Extended Supported Rates element is present whenever there are more than eight supported rates, and it is optional otherwise.
6	EDCA Parameter Set	Used with 802.11e QoS.
7	RCPI	Used with 802.11k.
8	RSNI	Used with 802.11k.
9	RRM Enabled Capabilities	Used with 802.11k.
10	RSN	Used with 802.11i and 802.11r.
11	Mobility Domain	Used with 802.11r.

TABLE 4.9   Elements of the reassociation response frame *(continued)*

Order	Information	Notes
12	Fast BSS Transition	Used with 802.11r.
13	RIC	Used with 802.11r.
14	DSE Registered Location	Used with 802.11y.
15	Timeout Interval (Association Comeback time)	Used with 802.11w.
16	HT Capabilities	Used with 802.11n.
17	HT Operation	Used with 802.11n.
18	20/40 BSS Coexistence	Used with 802.11n.
19	Overlapping BSS Scan Parameters	Used with 802.11n.
20	Extended Capabilities	The Extended Capabilities element may be present if any of the fields in this element are nonzero.
Last	Vendor Specific	One or more vendor-specific information elements may appear in this frame. This information element follows all other information elements.

As you can see, its format is exactly the same as the association response frame. The only difference is its position in the exchange (it has to be preceded with a reassociation request frame) and the consequence of the exchange. With association request/response, the station gets an AID on the local AP. With reassociation request/response, the station details have to be moved from the old AP to the new AP.

EXERCISE 4.1

Viewing an Association Sequence

In this exercise, you will use a protocol analyzer to view a complete 802.11 association sequence. The following directions should assist you with the installation and use of Wireshark Packet capture software. If you have already installed Wireshark, you can skip steps 1–2.

1. Open the CD provided with this book.

2. Under Product Evals, choose Wireshark, double-click to start the installation process, and follow the installation prompt.

3. In Windows, choose Start ➤ Programs ➤ Wireshark. The Wireshark application should appear.

4. Click the Open Capture File icon, and browse the book's CD. Open the packet capture file called ch04_capture1.PCAP.

5. When you click a packet, its details appear in the lower window. You can use the + sign to expand each element.

6. Navigate to frame 703, and examine frames 703 and 705. They are the probe request/exchange that precedes the authentication phase.

7. Examine frames 715 to 718. They are the authentication phase, using Open System.

8. Examine frames 719 to 722. They are the final association phase.

ATIM Frame

The *ATIM frame* is specific to IBSS networks and used for distribution of buffered frames to stations in sleep mode in the ad hoc network.

Beacons in IBSS are sent by any participating station. There is an ATIM window in the beacon to indicate that participating stations should not fall back to doze mode. During the ATIM window, the ATIM frame is used to distribute broadcast and multicast packets, just like the DTIM in infrastructure networks, and also when new stations want to join the ad hoc network. You will learn more about ATIM in Chapter 8.

Action Frame

Action frames form the 12th and last type of management frame. They are used to trigger specific actions in the cell. Figure 4.13 shows their format.

FIGURE 4.13 Action frame format

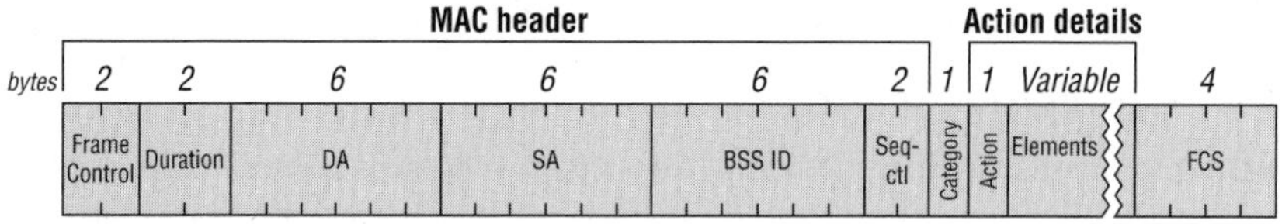

We will cover them in more detail later in this chapter.

Information Elements and Fields

Management frame bodies consist of fields and information elements. A field is a section of the frame body that is always present for a given type of frame and has a static size. An information element is a section of the frame body that can be of fixed or variable size, depending on its content, and may be present or not, depending on the features supported by the AP or station sending the frame.

For example, beacon frames contain a Beacon Interval field. This section of the beacon is a field because it is always present and always has the same size. Beacon frames also contain a Supported Rate element. This is an element, because although it is always present, its size may vary from 1 to 8 octets. Similarly, the SSID section of the beacon is also called an element, because its size is variable. Beacon frames also contain a QoS Capability element, the size of which is fixed (1 octet). This is an element, because it is present only if the emitting station or AP supports QoS.

As a wireless analysis professional, you should know the various possible fields and elements you may see in a frame capture to be able to determine whether all elements are present, whether unexpected elements are present, and whether each field or element encountered presents abnormal values.

We will first cover the fields and then the main possible information elements, starting with those that you will see in most frames, before focusing on the more uncommon types. Notice that the management frames can contain some information elements not described in this chapter. We focus on the main elements found in most packet captures.

Management Frame Fields

Management frame fields are usually found at the beginning of the frame body.

Timestamp Field

The *timestamp* field is 8 bytes long, as represented in Figure 4.14. It can be found in beacons and probe responses.

FIGURE 4.14 Timestamp field

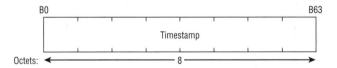

You know now that the timestamp is a value representing the time on the access point, which is the number of microseconds the AP has been active. When that timestamp reaches its maximum value, the counter is simply reset and restarts from zero. Nevertheless, because the Timestamp field is 8 bytes long, the AP would need to be running for more than 580,000 years before this field reaches its maximum value! Of course, no one expects any AP to be running that long. The logic was that this field should need to have a length that would be a power of two: 2, 4, or 8 bytes. Four bytes would allow for only 71 minutes before the field would reach its maximum, which was too short. This is why the next logical value, 8 bytes, was chosen.

The stations in the cell use that timestamp value to adjust their own clock (using their Time Synchronization Function).

Beacon Interval Field

The Beacon Interval field represents the number of time units between target beacon transmission times (TBTTs). The length of the Beacon Interval field is 2 octets. Figure 4.15 illustrates the Beacon Interval field.

FIGURE 4.15   Beacon Interval field

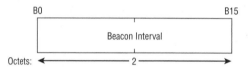

The default value is 100 TUs (0.102400 seconds), but the field size allows for any value between 1 and more than 67 seconds! Nevertheless, most stations' drivers allow only a small variation from the default value. If the interval between beacons is too short, stations using Power Save mode might not be able to doze and wake up fast enough, creating collisions in the cell and disconnections. If the interval is too long, stations using the beacon as a sign that the network is still available may disconnect because the interval exceeds their waiting capacity. This long interval also creates traffic issues because more traffic is buffered at the AP while non-QoS stations are sleeping between beacons.

Capability Information Field

The *Capability Information field* is more complex than the other fields, because it contains a number of subfields that are used to indicate requested or advertised optional capabilities.

The length of the Capability Information field is 2 octets. The format of the Capability Information field is defined in Figure 4.16.

Notice that this Capability Information field exists in several management frames (beacons, probe response, association request, association response, reassociation request, and reassociation response). For this reason, each Capability Information subfield is interpreted according to the management frame subtype.

Many of these fields show optional features that can be implemented or not. This section shows only the main items.

FIGURE 4.16 Capability Information field

B0	B1	B2	B3	B4	B5	B6	B7
ESS	IBSS	CF Pollable	CF-Poll Request	Privacy	Short Preamble	PBCC	Channel Agility

B8	B9	B10	B11	B12	B13	B14	B15
Spectrum Mgmt	QoS	Short Slot Time	APSD	Radio Measurement	DSSS-OFDM	Delayed Block Ack	Immediate Block Ack

ESS/IBSS Subfields

The ESS bit indicates whether the beacon is coming from an AP (1) or not (0). The IBSS bit indicates whether the beacon is coming from an IBSS station (1) or not (0).

Privacy Subfield

APs set the Privacy subfield to 1 if data confidentiality is required for all data frames exchanged within the BSS. If data confidentiality is not required, the Privacy subfield is set to 0. Data confidentiality means any type of encryption (AES, TKIP, or WEP). The mechanism by which the encryption type is decided is determined by the presence of other fields in the beacon, in particular field 21, RSN. The Privacy field only shows the requirement (or not) for encryption when sending data frames.

Short Preamble Subfield

You learned about the short and long preamble in Chapter 2. The short preamble is set to 1 in beacons when short preambles are allowed (therefore, stations can use short or long preambles). This field is set to 0 when short preambles are not allowed, and only long preambles should be used.

Channel Agility Subfield

Channel Agility was an optional feature introduced when the 802.11b protocol was released. Its aim was to offer the possibility for the center channel to shift periodically slightly up and down, in the hopes of avoiding interferences. The Channel Agility feature was never widely implemented. It is still present as a possibility in the Capability field, but only for HR/DSSS stations (OFDM does not implement this feature).

Spectrum Management Subfield

This subfield is linked to the 802.11h amendment. When APs and clients operate on the affected section of 5 GHz in countries where 802.11h compliance is mandatory, they must set their Spectrum Management field to 1 to reflect that they implement DFS and TPC.

The Spectrum Management subfield is set to 0 when the cell operates on a channel unaffected by the 802.11h amendment or in a country where 802.11 compliance is not required.

QoS Subfield

As its name states, this field shows whether the AP supports QoS. Do not get confused by the many QoS fields in 802.11 management frames! In a beacon frame, field 24, QoS Capability, provides more details about how QoS is supported in the cell. In frame headers, the QoS Control field also provides details about that particular frame's QoS characteristics. The QoS subfield in the Capability Information field simply tells the cell "I can do QoS; look for other QoS fields in my frames."

Short Slot Time Subfield

Slot time and SIFS are the two values from which all other interframe spaces and count-down values are defined. Standard slot time used to be 20 μs with 802.11 and 802.11b and was reduced to 9 μs with 802.11g (802.11a also uses 9 μs slot times). This subfield deter-mines whether short slot time is allowed in the cell (the Short Slot Time subfield set to 1), which is a clear sign that the AP is not supporting 802.11b. There are a few details you need to remember:

- If at least one station joins the cell and cannot support short slot time (the station is 802.11b only), then short slot time should be disabled entirely in the cell, and this sub-field will be set to 0 in the subsequent beacons, until the 802.11b station disconnects.

- The rule is a bit different for 802.11a networks! The 802.11a specification describes three slot times, depending on the interchannel spacing (9 μs for 20 MHz spacing, 13 μs for 10 MHz spacing, or 21 μs for 5 MHz spacing). Because 20 MHz spacing is in use in standard networks, 9 μs should be the standard slot time, and there is no short slot time (because there is no long slot time!). The Short Slot Time should therefore be disabled and set to 0 for 802.11a networks, but this implementation is vendor-depen-dant, so you might find both 0 and 1 values.

- For IBSS networks, short slot time should always be set to 0, which means that IBSS networks never support short slot times.

APSD Subfield

Automatic Power Save Delivery (APSD) is an enhancement introduced by the 802.11e speci-fication. When this APSD bit is set to 1, the AP supports the 802.11e APSD feature. When the bit is set to 0, the AP only supports the legacy Power Save mode. Notice that stations sending capability information to the cell (in association or reassociation requests) always set that subfield to 0, because this feature is a function of the entire cell, not individual sta-tion decisions.

DSSS-OFDM Subfield

This subfield name is self-explanatory. DSSS-OFDM provides 54 Mbps speeds in 802.11b/g-compatible networks. When this bit is set to 1, the DSSS-OFDM mode is allowed in the cell. When the bit is set to 0, this mode is not allowed. This rule is also valid for an IBSS.

This bit is always set to 0 for 802.11a networks.

This bit set to 0 does not mean that 802.11g is not allowed but simply that the hybrid DSSS-OFDM mode, allowing frames with a DSSS preamble and header followed by an OFDM PPDU as its PSDU, is not allowed. Stations may still be able to perform at 802.11g speeds, using protection when 802.11b stations are detected. The Supported Rates and Extended Supported Rates field of the beacon frame body will inform the stations about which rates and which modulations are allowed.

Listen Interval Field

In frames sent from stations to access points (association request, reassociation request), the *Listen Interval* field is used to indicate to the AP how often a station in Power Save mode wakes to listen to beacon management frames. This value is an integer expressed in beacon interval units (for example, a value of 3 indicates that the station wakes up every three beacons). This field is 2 bytes long, which means that the maximum interval could be 65,535.

All other values of authentication number are reserved.

Status Code Field

The *Status Code* field is used in a response management frame to indicate the success or failure of a requested operation. You will find this field in the authentication response frame, the association response frame, and the reassociation response frame. This field is 2 bytes long. If an operation is successful, then the status code is set to 0. If an operation results in failure, the status code indicates a failure cause. However, status code 1 indicates an unspecified failure.

Association ID Field

The AID field is a value assigned by an AP during association that represents the 16-bit ID of an STA. The length of the AID field is 2 octets. The value assigned as the AID is in the range 1–2007 and is placed in the 14 low-weight bits of the AID field, with the two high-weight bits of the AID field each set to 1.

Reason Code Field

This *Reason Code* field is used to indicate the reason that an unsolicited notification management frame of type disassociation, deauthentication, DELTS, DELBA, or DLS teardown was generated. Don't confuse this field with the Status Code field! The Status Code field indicates if a request is successful and details the cause of the failure. The Reason Code field is present only when the frames listed earlier are sent to a station without the station asking for any negotiation of any parameter.

Action Frame–Related Fields

There are several other fields that are found only in action frames and their related responses. These fields will be covered in the "Action Frames" section of this chapter.

EXERCISE 4.2

Viewing Beacon Frame Fields

In this exercise, you will use a protocol analyzer to view the 802.11 beacon. The following directions should assist you with the installation and use of the Wireshark Packet capture software. If you have already installed Wireshark, you can skip steps 1–2.

1. Open the CD provided with this book.

2. Under Product Evals, choose Wireshark, double-click to start the installation process, and follow the installation prompt.

3. In Windows, choose Start ➤ Programs ➤ Wireshark. The Wireshark application should appear.

4. Click the Open Capture File icon, and browse the book's CD. Open the packet capture file called ch04_capture2.PCAP.

5. When you click a packet, its details appear in the lower window. You can use the + sign to expand each element.

6. Compare the structure of packet 6 and packet 7. You should see two differences in the fields of each beacon:

   - The beacon interval is different. It uses the default TBTT for frame 7 but a longer interval for frame 6.

   - Frame 6 allows short preambles, while frame 7 does not.

   - All other fields indicate the same values.

As a wireless professional, you should also be able to read the Radiotap Header section to verify on which channel and at what speed the frames were received.

Management Frame Information Elements

All the other fields present in the management frames are called information elements (IEs). Remember that they are called this because they may or may not be present or their size may vary. All information elements have the same structure: at least three subfields, the first one being an element ID (defined by the 802.11 standard), the second defining the length of the element, and the remaining fields being the element itself, as shown in Figure 4.17.

FIGURE 4.17   Generic information element format

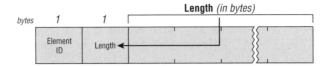

Extended Capabilities Element

The Extended Capabilities element is an extension of the Capability Information field; it adds capabilities that would not be covered by the Capability Information field. As such, it is present in the same types of frames: beacons, probe responses, association requests, association responses, reassociation requests, and reassociation responses. Figure 4.18 shows the format of the Extended Capabilities element.

FIGURE 4.18   Extended Capabilities element

Element ID	Length	Capabilities
1	1	n

Octets:

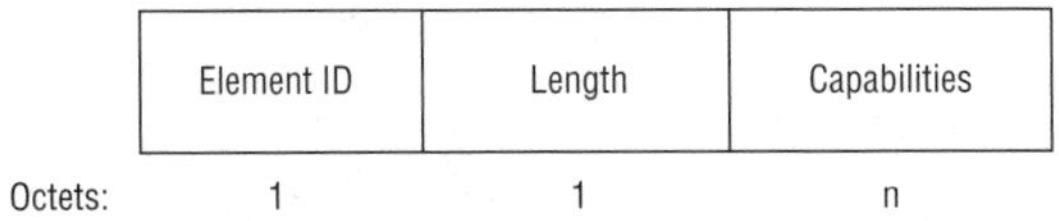

Several amendments use this element. Among them, 802.11y describes the 3650-3700 band operations in the United States and uses the Extended Capabilities element with an option identifier 2 for a feature called extended channel switch announcement (ECSA). This feature is close to the 802.11h amendment channel switch announcement feature. The AP scans the available channels and informs the stations about the next, better channel they should all jump to. The 802.11n amendment also uses the Extended Capabilities elements. You will learn more about 802.11n in Chapter 10.

SSID Element

The *SSID element* is present in all beacons, probe requests, probe responses, association requests, and reassociation requests. Figure 4.19 shows the format of the SSID field.

FIGURE 4.19   SSID element

The element ID is 0. The length section defines the length of the SSID string, in octets. The SSID string is a text string, with each character being coded over one octet. It contains as many octets as it has characters, with a maximum of 32 characters.

Notice that some APs support Multiple Basic Service Set Identifier (MBSSID) features, by which an AP can offer several SSIDs on the same radio. In this case, most vendors simply send as many beacons as they support SSIDs. If your AP is expected to send a beacon every 100 TUs and your AP supports 5 SSIDs, the AP will send one beacon every 20 TU, advertising its capabilities for each SSID in turn.

Supported Rates Element

The *Supported Rates* element is present in beacons, probe requests, probe responses, and all association frames (association request, response, reassociation request/response). This element specifies up to eight rates. This was more than enough for the legacy 802.11 rates and is still perfectly fine for 802.11b. Since the introduction of OFDM rates, this field became too small, and a second field was added at the end of the beacon to list the additional supported rates. In the Supported Rates field, the length field is encoded as 1 to 8 octets, where each octet describes a single supported rate. When both Supported Rates and Extended Supported Rates fields are used, which particular individual rate appears in which field is of no importance, as long as all rates are mentioned. Most vendors just list them in order.

Figure 4.20 defines the format of the Supported Rates field.

FIGURE 4.20   Supported Rates element

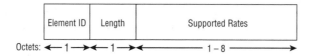

Each rate is listed over one octet, with the following logic:

- The last bit (bit 7) is set to 1 if the rate is a basic rate (or mandatory rate) and set to 0 if the rate is simply supported.

- The other seven bits (bits 0 to 6) are set to the data rate, if necessary rounded up to the next 500 Kbps, in units of 500 Kbps.

  For example, a 5.5 Mbps rate contained in the BSSBasicRateSet parameter is encoded as 10001011 (10000000 because it is set to Basic Rate, and binary 1011 for decimal 11, because 5.5 Mbps are 11 times 500 kbps); 2 Mbps supported would be 00000100.

Any station wanting to join the cell must support all mandatory/basic rates. The 802.11 standard defines, by default, several basic rates, which represent each possible modulation of the protocol. Leaving these defaults ensures that all stations joining the cell understand all the modulations in use in the cell. This is the reason why, for example, you will find 6, 12, and 24 Mbps as default mandatory rates for 802.11a networks, ensuring that joining stations understand BPSK (6, 9 Mbps), QPSK (12, 18 Mbps), and QAM (24 Mbps and higher). This parameter can usually be configured on an access point, but at least one mandatory rate must be set, because this first mandatory rate is going to be used to determine the "common rate" understood by all stations, at which many broadcast frames will be sent. As explained earlier, the first mandatory rate is usually the lowest supported rate so that the footprint reached by frames such as probes and beacons matches the footprint of the cell itself.

Extended Supported Rates Element

The Extended Supported Rates element specifies the supported rates not carried in the Supported Rates element. It is present in beacons, probe requests and probe responses, and all association frames (association request/response, reassociation request/response). The information element is encoded as 1 to 255 octets where each octet describes a single supported rate. Figure 4.21 defines the format of the Extended Supported Rates field.

FIGURE 4.21   Extended Supported Rates element

The rate structure is the same in this field as in the Supported Rates field. The first 7 bits (bits 0 to 6) express the rate in units of 500 Kbps. The last bit (bit 7) is set to 1 if the rate is configured as Basic (or mandatory) and set to 0 otherwise.

The Extended Supported Rates field is of course necessary only if there are more than eight supported rates. If there are eight or fewer supported rates, only the Supported Rates field is used.

Extended Rate PHY (ERP) Element

The ERP element is present only on 2.4 GHz networks supporting 802.11g and is present in beacons and probe responses. Figure 4.22 shows the format of the Extended Supported Rates element.

FIGURE 4.22   ERP element

This field is essential to the operation of 802.11b/g/n networks.

You probably remember from your CWNA the protection mechanisms in place in 802.11b/g networks when 802.11b clients are detected. The ERP field regulates how the presence (or absence) of 802.11b devices is transmitted to the cell.

The NonERP_Present bit is set to 1 if at least one of the following conditions occurs:

- A nonERP station (legacy 802.11 or 802.11b) associates to the cell.

- A neighboring cell (BSS or IBSS) is detected, allowing only nonERP data rates. This detection is expected to occur by receiving a beacon from the neighboring cell.

- Any other management frame (except probe requests) is received from a neighboring cell supporting only nonERP data rates.

Notice the word *associates* in the first condition. This means that, as per the 802.11-2007 protocol, the NonERP_Present bit should be set to 1 only when the association phase completes for a nonERP station (the legacy 802.11 or 802.11b station is completely associated to the cell). Nevertheless, many vendors have a broader understanding of the association process and consider that a probe request is the first step toward a complete association. This is why many vendors implement the nonERP_Present bit as soon as an 802.11 or 802.11b station is detected, even if this detection is limited to probes. This is an extension to the protocol but is a common and valid behavior.

The UseProtection bit is set to 1 as soon as a nonERP client is associated to the cell. This bit informs ERP clients that they have to use a protection mechanism (RTS/CTS or CTS to self) before sending. The UseProtection bit is also linked to the concept of "association," at least in the 802.11-2007 protocol. The same protocol defines a larger use case for this bit in an IBSS. Because there is no concept of "association" per se in an IBSS, any station detecting a member of the IBSS supporting only nonERP rates can set the UseProtection bit warning message in its frames. The UseProtection bit is heard and repeated by the other members of the IBSS so that all IBSS ERP members get informed. This behavior was extended by many vendors to standard BSSs. This means that most of the time, the simple detection of a management frame, even coming from a neighboring cell, displaying the UseProtection bit set to 1 will trigger the local AP to set its UseProtection bit to 1.

This behavior makes a lot of sense. The nonERP present bit is set to 1 only if the AP detects a non-ERP station in the cell. If the AP detects a beacon from a neighboring AP having the UseProtection bit set to 1, there may be a nonERP station in the neighboring cell that can impact the traffic of the local cell clients in the direction of this neighbor, even if the local AP does not hear the nonERP client directly. Figure 4.23 illustrates this case.

FIGURE 4.23   UseProtection ripple

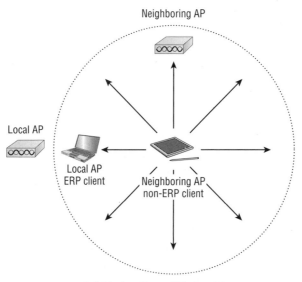

Neighboring AP

Local AP

Local AP
ERP client

Neighboring AP
non-ERP client

Neighboring AP non-ERP client RF footprint

Asking the local cell clients to use protection anyway is a good way to avoid that this hidden nonERP client (hidden from the local AP standpoint) disrupts the cell communications.

In the same ERP field, the Barker Preamble Mode subfield is set to determine whether, when using protection, short preambles are allowed (Barker Preamble Mode set to 0) or whether only long preambles should be used (Barker Preamble Mode set to 1).

Bits r3 to r7 are unused and ignored. They were set as padding and for possible future expansion of the ERP Element. This expansion hasn't occurred so far. There is a protection mechanism for 802.11n, but it uses another field called the HT Protection field.

Robust Security Network (RSN) Information Element

This element is crucial when using WPA/WPA2 to determine the authentication and encryption mechanisms in place in the cell. The Privacy subfield in the Capability Information field was enough when the only choice was WEP or Open. Now that several mechanisms are in place, a more complete communication is needed between the AP and its potential clients to specify how to authenticate to the cell and encrypt traffic. You will learn more about this element component in Chapter 9.

The RSN element has an element ID of 48 and is present in beacons, probe responses, association responses, and reassociation responses. Figure 4.24 shows the structure of the RSN element.

FIGURE 4.24   RSN element

Element ID	Length	Version	Group Cipher Suite	Pairwise Cipher Suite Count	Pairwise Cipher Suite List	AKM Suite Count	AKM Suite List	RSN Capabilities	PMKID Count	PMKID List
Octets: 1	1	2	4	2	4–*m*	2	4–*n*	2	2	16–*s*

The element size is flexible and depends on how many authentication and encryption mechanisms are allowed.

Beyond the usual element ID and length, the first field, Version, is always set to 1. It is 2 bytes long, which leaves some room for future versions!

Just after the Group Cipher Suite descriptor, individual ciphers are listed to protect unicast frames. As several ciphers may be allowed, the Pairwise Cipher Suite Count field is here to state how many ciphers are allowed. Then, each cipher is listed in an individual Pairwise Cipher Suite List field. Each field is of course 4 bytes long, because each cipher is represented over 4 bytes. There is no limitation in the number of ciphers listed, except that the entire RSN element should not exceed 255 bytes.

When a station supports several ciphers, it always chooses the strongest one first (in order: CCMP, TKIP, WEP 104, WEP 40).

Now that the ciphers allowed in the cell are defined, you still need to inform potential cell clients about how they are supposed to authenticate in order to join the cell. This is done with the Authentication and Key Management (AKM) section. The AKM Suite count defines the number of methods allowed, and the AKM Suite list displays each individual method. Just like for the cipher, each method is coded over 4 bytes: the first 3 bytes are an OUI, and the last byte is one of the methods supported by the vendor matching the OUI. The 802.11i committee defined two methods—00-0F-AC-1 for 802.1X or PMK caching and 00-0F-AC-2 for PSK—but any vendor-specific method is possible, provided that clients and APs support it.

Basic Service Set (BSS) Load Element

This element is used only when QoS is supported (when the QoS subfield in the Capability Information element is set to Enabled). It is often called QBSS Load element. It provides information on the cell load, from the AP point of view. It is typically sent by the AP (although the 802.11 standard does not restrict it to APs only) and used by the receiving stations to decide how to roam.

Figure 4.25 defines the format of the *BSS Load element*.

FIGURE 4.25   BSS Load element

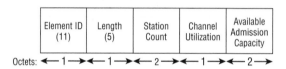

The station count is a simple number, showing how many stations are currently associated to the cell. The term *associated* is understood to apply to stations completely associated, not to probing stations.

The Channel Utilization field is defined as the percentage of time, normalized to 255, that the AP sensed the medium was busy, as indicated by either the physical or virtual carrier sense mechanism.

The AP senses the medium, just like any other station, every slot time. At regular intervals (every 50 beacons by default, which represents 5.12 seconds if the beacons are sent at 100 TU intervals), the AP looks over the last period and counts how many times the network was seen as busy and how many times the network was seen as idle. The AP then calculates a simple percentage and translates it into a 0 to 255 range.

This information is used by QoS stations to gauge the space available on several APs in range.

Enhanced Distributed Channel Access (EDCA) Parameter Element

This element is used only when QoS is supported. You will learn more about QoS detailed mechanisms in Chapter 7. This section is a summary. In most QoS-enabled networks, this field is not used, and the same information is provided through the WMM or the WME vendor-specific element.

QoS Capability Element

This element is used only when QoS is supported. It is used as a replacement to the EDCA Parameter element when EDCA Parameter is not present. It is also used by the AP to communicate to the cell the QoS information. It is a shorter version of the EDCA Parameter Set element and contains only the QoS information section. In most QoS-enabled networks, this field is not used, and the same information is provided through the WMM or the WME vendor-specific element.

Direct Sequence Parameter Set Element

This element is used by both the DSSS and OFDM systems, on both 2.4 GHz and 5 GHz spectrums. It is a very important field that simply indicates the current channel. Figure 4.26 shows the format of the *DS Parameter Set* element.

FIGURE 4.26   DS Parameter Set element

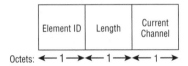

This element is key for proper operation of 802.11 networks, because 802.11 signals spread across several channels. This tells the receiving station on which channel the emitter is centering its signal. The value is simply the channel number.

When using 802.11n and channel bonding, this element focuses on the primary channel. The secondary channel information is displayed in several 802.11n-specific fields, such as the Secondary Channel information element or the 20/40 BSS Coexistence element. You will learn more about these elements in Chapter 10.

Traffic Indication Map (TIM) Element

This element is present only in beacons. The *TIM* element contains information useful for stations in low-power mode. Figure 4.27 shows the format of the TIM field.

FIGURE 4.27   TIM element

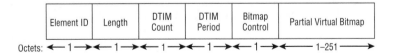

Besides the classical element ID and length, the TIM contains two types of elements: the virtual bitmap and the *DTIM* information.

The DTIM is not present in all beacons and all TIMs. At regular intervals (usually configurable on the AP), the beacon will contain a TIM that will also be a DTIM. The DTIM purpose is easy to understand. The AP uses the beacon frames Delivery Traffic Indication Message (DTIM) information to inform the cell if it has broadcasts or multicasts frames buffered. Stations in low power mode should wake up at least for every beacon that is a DTIM. The DTIM does not have to be in every beacon but can, for example, occur every two to five beacons. The DTIM is contained in the TIM, so in that case it is said that the TIM is also a DTIM.

In the TIM field, the DTIM period element indicates the number of beacon intervals between successive DTIMs (for example, 3 means every third beacon is a DTIM). The DTIM Count field indicates how many beacon frames (including the current frame) appear before the next DTIM. A DTIM Count field of 0 indicates that the current TIM is a DTIM. A DTIM count of 1 indicates that the next beacon is a DTIM.

When a DTIM shows that there is broadcast or multicast traffic buffered at the AP level, all stations stay awake. Just after sending the beacon announcing that buffered broadcast or multicasts the AP contends for the medium and then forwards the buffered broadcast or multicast to the cell. All stations receive it and then can go back to sleep if needed. Multicast and broadcast traffic is of course never acknowledged.

The first bit of the bitmap control field is used to announce the presence of multicast or broadcast traffic buffered on the AP. Figure 4.28 illustrates this case.

FIGURE 4.28 DTIM multicast present

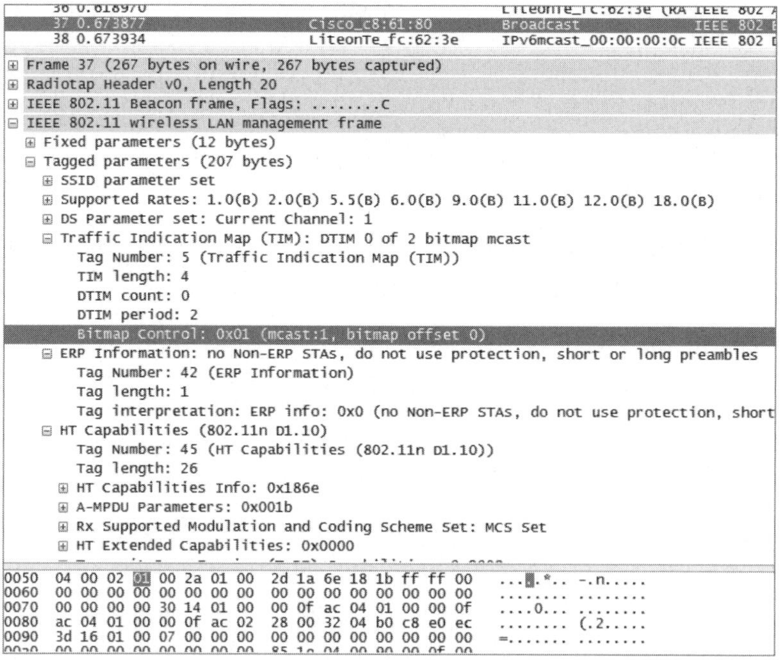

When the first bit of the Bitmap Control field is set to 1, the AP has multicast or broadcast buffered. When this first bit is set to 0, there is no buffered broadcast or multicast. Notice that this analyzer (Wireshark) displays mcast, for multicast, but there is no way of knowing from the DTIM information whether the buffered traffic is broadcast or multicast. Some analyzers will display multicast, some others broadcast, and some others broadcast/multicast.

The next 7 bits of the Bitmap Control field, along with the virtual bitmap, represent the stations in low power mode for which the AP has traffic buffered. You will learn more about this process in Chapter 8.

IBSS Parameter Set Element

This element is present only on probe responses and beacons of stations in an IBSS. Figure 4.29 shows the format of the IBSS Parameter Set element.

FIGURE 4.29   IBSS Parameter Set element

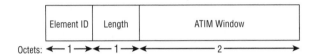

Just like the TIM, the Announcement Traffic Indication Message (ATIM) window displayed in the IBSS Parameter Set element is used for power save (see Figure 4.30).

FIGURE 4.30   IBSS DFS element

Element ID	Length	DFS Owner	DFS Recovery Interval	Channel Map
1	1	6	1	2*n

Octets:

A lot of people get confused about the TIM, DTIM and ATIM acronyms expansion, calling them wrongly traffic indication message, delivery traffic indication map, or ad hoc traffic indication map (or message). The right expansions are as follows:

TIM is Traffic Indication Map.

DTIM is Delivery Traffic Indication Message.

ATIM is Announcement Traffic Indication Message.

So, there is only one map, and there are two messages. In ATIM, *A* is Announcement, even if it is used for ad hoc networks.

You will learn more about ATIM in Chapter 8.

The first station to start the IBSS is determined as being the DFS owner. It determines the 802.11h operations in the cell. The DFS Owner MAC address is mentioned in the IBSS DFS Field, although it is present as the SA of the frame. If the DFS owner disappears or is lost during a jump, the IBSS DFS field defines a DFS Recovery Interval (expressed in TBTTs or beacon intervals), which is a form of timeout. A station not hearing from the DFS owner for longer than the DFS recovery interval will select its own channel and assume the role of DFS owner.

The last field of the IBSS DFS element is a list of possible channels.

Country Element

Each country has regulatory bodies that can limit the channels or power levels allowed in their regulatory domain. Instead of having to update all drivers of all wireless devices every time regulations change in a country, the 802.11 standard introduced the idea, via the amendment 802.11d, to send the local regulatory values from the AP. The Country field defines the country of operation, along with the allowed channels and maximum transmit power. It is not a mandatory field and is typically found on APs that can support several country settings.

Figure 4.31 shows an example of a capture with a country code.

FIGURE 4.31   Capture with Country element

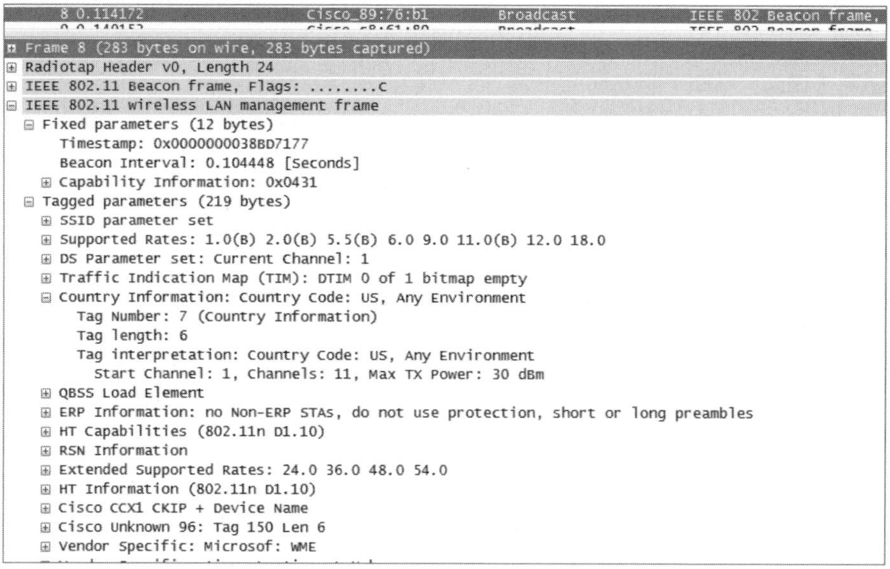

```
    8 0.114172              Cisco_89:76:b1        Broadcast         IEEE 802 Beacon frame,
    0 0 114152              Cisco c8:61:80        Broadcast         IEEE 802 Beacon frame
□ Frame 8 (283 bytes on wire, 283 bytes captured)
⊞ Radiotap Header v0, Length 24
⊞ IEEE 802.11 Beacon frame, Flags: ........C
⊟ IEEE 802.11 wireless LAN management frame
  ⊟ Fixed parameters (12 bytes)
      Timestamp: 0x0000000038BD7177
      Beacon Interval: 0.104448 [Seconds]
    ⊞ Capability Information: 0x0431
  ⊟ Tagged parameters (219 bytes)
    ⊞ SSID parameter set
    ⊞ Supported Rates: 1.0(B) 2.0(B) 5.5(B) 6.0 9.0 11.0(B) 12.0 18.0
    ⊞ DS Parameter set: Current Channel: 1
    ⊞ Traffic Indication Map (TIM): DTIM 0 of 1 bitmap empty
    ⊟ Country Information: Country Code: US, Any Environment
        Tag Number: 7 (Country Information)
        Tag length: 6
        Tag interpretation: Country Code: US, Any Environment
          Start Channel: 1, Channels: 11, Max TX Power: 30 dBm
    ⊞ QBSS Load Element
    ⊞ ERP Information: no Non-ERP STAs, do not use protection, short or long preambles
    ⊞ HT Capabilities (802.11n D1.10)
    ⊞ RSN Information
    ⊞ Extended Supported Rates: 24.0 36.0 48.0 54.0
    ⊞ HT Information (802.11n D1.10)
    ⊞ Cisco CCX1 CKIP + Device Name
    ⊞ Cisco Unknown 96: Tag 150 Len 6
    ⊞ Vendor Specific: Microsof: WME
```

Refer to Figure 4.4 earlier in this chapter for an example of a capture on an access point not implementing the Country field. That AP was of SOHO type and built for only one country of operation. The AP used for Figure 4.31 is of Enterprise type and offers options to enable or disable the Country field.

Power Constraint Element

This element is related to 802.11h. In countries where compliance with 802.11h is implemented, stations operating in the 5 GHz bands should reduce their power level so as not to disturb with too powerful emissions other devices using the same spectrum. This limitation is called satellite services, although it is so far implemented only to avoid interference with civilian airport radars in the UNII-2 and UNII-2 extended bands. The mechanism is that each country has a maximum power value that can be known from the wireless device or learned from the AP via the Country field. In the Power Constraint field, the AP indicates how much lower than this maximum power participants should try to go.

TPC Report Element

This element is also related to 802.11h. The TPC Report element contains transmit power and link margin information, usually sent in response to a TPC Request element. We will look at this element more closely at the end of this chapter.

Channel Switch Announcement Element

This element is also related to 802.11h. When a radar blast is detected, all stations must leave the affected channel. The AP can be set to announce to the cell which is the next channel. We will look at this element more closely in the "Spectrum and Transmit Power Management" section of this chapter.

Quiet Element

This element is also related to 802.11h. An AP can request a quiet time during which no stations should transmit in order to test the channel for the presence of radars. We will look at this element more closely in the "Spectrum and Transmit Power Management" section of this chapter.

The following elements are also present in 802.11n networks: HT Capabilities Element, HT Operation Element, 20/40 BSS Coexistence Element, Overlapping BSS Scan Parameters Element. You will learn more about their content and detailed roles in Chapter 10.

Vendor-Specific Elements

Beyond all the options defined by the standard or any of its amendments, each vendor can define proprietary options and add them to any management frames' supporting elements (beacon, probe request, probe response, association request, association response, reassociation request, and reassociation response frames), depending on the option. Figure 4.32 shows the format of the vendor-specific element.

FIGURE 4.32 Vendor-specific element

	Element ID	Length	OUI	Vendor-specific content
Octets:	1	1	3	n–3

Each vendor wanting to implement vendor-specific elements needs to obtain an OUI for this purpose from the IEEE. The vendor will display this OUI in the element header, along with the element ID 221, which identifies a vendor-specific element. The element itself will then depend on the vendor. There is no limitation in the number of elements that can be sent in a management frame, except only the maximum frame size.

Figure 4.33 shows an example of a vendor-specific capture.

FIGURE 4.33 Vendor-specific capture

```
⊞ Frame 3 (265 bytes on wire, 265 bytes captured)
⊞ Radiotap Header v0, Length 24
⊞ IEEE 802.11
⊟ IEEE 802.11 wireless LAN management frame
  ⊞ Fixed parameters (12 bytes)
  ⊟ Tagged parameters (201 bytes)
    ⊞ SSID parameter set: "Honeypot"
    ⊞ Supported Rates: 1.0(B) 2.0(B) 5.5(B) 6.0(B) 9.0(B) 11.0(B) 12.0(B) 18.0(B)
    ⊞ DS Parameter set: Current Channel: 1
    ⊞ ERP Information: no Non-ERP STAs, do not use protection, short or long preambles
    ⊞ Reserved tag number: Tag 45 Len 26
    ⊞ RSN Information
    ⊞ Extended Supported Rates: 24.0(B) 36.0(B) 48.0(B) 54.0(B)
    ⊞ Reserved tag number: Tag 61 Len 22
    ⊞ Cisco Unknown 1 + Device Name
    ⊞ Reserved tag number: Tag 150 Len 6
    ⊟ Vendor Specific: WME
        Tag Number: 221 (Vendor Specific)
        Tag length: 24
        Tag interpretation: WME PE: type 2, subtype 1, version 1, parameter set 129
        Tag interpretation: WME AC Parameters: ACI 0 (Best Effort), Admission Control not Mandatory, AIFSN 3, ECWmin 4, ECWmax 4, TXOP 0
        Tag interpretation: WME AC Parameters: ACI 1 (Background), Admission Control not Mandatory, AIFSN 7, ECWmin 4, ECWmax 4, TXOP 0
        Tag interpretation: WME AC Parameters: ACI 2 (Video), Admission Control not Mandatory, AIFSN 2, ECWmin 3, ECWmax 3, TXOP 94
        Tag interpretation: WME AC Parameters: ACI 3 (Voice), Admission Control not Mandatory, AIFSN 2, ECWmin 2, ECWmax 2, TXOP 47
    ⊟ Vendor Specific: Aironet Unknown
        Tag Number: 221 (Vendor Specific)
        Tag length: 6
        Aironet IE type: Unknown (1)
        Aironet IE data: 0100
    ⊟ Vendor Specific: Aironet CCX version = 5
        Tag Number: 221 (Vendor Specific)
        Tag length: 5
        Aironet IE type: CCX version (3)
        Aironet IE CCX version?: 5
    ⊞ Vendor Specific: Aironet Unknown
    ⊞ Vendor Specific: Aironet Unknown
```

An interesting aspect of the vendor-specific element is that "vendor specific" does not mean "secret." In Figure 4.33, some vendor-specific elements are well known and understood by many analyzers. This is the case of the Cisco Compatible Extension (CCX). Some other options are not understood and are displayed as "unknown." Some options are allocated to a vendor but used by another one! In Figure 4.33, consider the vendor-specific element WME. WME was a consortium with Microsoft, Cisco, and others working on the precursor of WMM. The WME vendor-specific OUI was attributed to Microsoft for the WME consortium. This Cisco access point is using the WME vendor-specific element to communicate 802.11e parameters that could very well be displayed using a standardized EDCA Parameter Set element. But as long as all clients can read and understand this WME element (and all Cisco compatible clients can), using one or the other does not matter.

Action Frames

Action frames are a type of management frame used to trigger an action in the cell. They first appeared in 2003 with the 802.11h amendment, and their number increased with each later amendment released between 2005 and today. They are somehow special, because they allow a form of added control to the cell, where a station can tell the AP, or the AP can tell one or several stations, "I need you to do this or that" or "This is what is going to happen."

Their format is always built on the same model. Figure 4.34 shows their structure.

FIGURE 4.34   Action frame structure

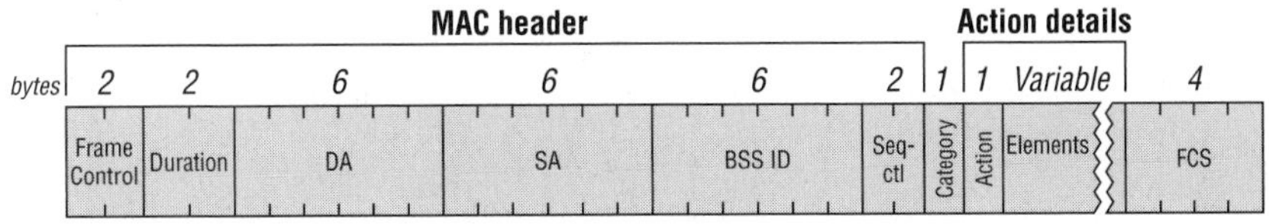

The frame body contains three sections:

Category   Describes the action frame type. Category allows you to know which family the action frame belongs to and which protocol introduced it.

Action   The action to perform. It is usually a number. You need to know the category to understand which action is called.

Element   Adds additional information specific to the action.

As you can guess, the action frame content makes sense when examined against the features it allows. Table 4.10 lists the different types.

TABLE 4.10   Action frame types

Category	Meaning	Action	Action description
0	Spectrum management	0	Measurement request
0	Spectrum management	1	Measurement report
0	Spectrum management	2	TPC request
0	Spectrum management	3	TPC report
0	Spectrum management	4	Channel switch announcement
0	Spectrum management	5–255	Unused/reserved

TABLE 4.10   Action frame types *(continued)*

Category	Meaning	Action	Action description
1	QoS	0	ADDTS request
1	QoS	1	ADDTS response
1	QoS	2	DELTS
1	QoS	3	Schedule
1	QoS	4–255	Unused/reserved
2	DLS	0	DLS request
2	DLS	1	DLS response
2	DLS	2	DLS teardown
2	DLS	3–255	Unused/reserved
3	Block ack	0	ADDBA request
3	Block ack	1	ADDBA response
3	Block ack	2	DELBA
3	Block ack	3–255	Unused/reserved
4	Public	0	Reserved
4	Public	1	DSE enablement
4	Public	2	DSE deenablement
4	Public	3	DSE registered location announcement
4	Public	4	Extended channel switch announcement
4	Public	5	DSE measurement request
4	Public	6	DSE measurement report

TABLE 4.10   Action frame types *(continued)*

Category	Meaning	Action	Action description
4	Public	7	Measurement pilot
4	Public	8	DSE power constraint
4	Public	9	Vendor specific
4	Public	10–255	Unused/reserved
5	Radio measurement	0	Radio measurement request
5	Radio measurement	1	Radio measurement report
5	Radio measurement	2	Link measurement request
5	Radio measurement	3	Link measurement report
5	Radio measurement	4	Neighbor report request
5	Radio measurement	5	Neighbor report response
5	Radio measurement	6–255	Unused/reserved
6	Fast BSS transition	0	Reserved
6	Fast BSS transition	1	FT request
6	Fast BSS transition	2	FT response
6	Fast BSS transition	3	FT confirm
6	Fast BSS transition	4	FT ack
6	Fast BSS transition	5–255	Unused/reserved
7		0–255	Unused/reserved
8	SA query	0	SA query
8	SA query	1	SA response
8	SA query	2–255	Unused/reserved

TABLE 4.10   Action frame types *(continued)*

Category	Meaning	Action	Action description
9	Protected dual of public action	0	Reserved
9	Protected dual of public action	1	Protected DSE enablement
9	Protected dual of public action	2	Protected DSE deenablement
9	Protected dual of public action	3	Reserved
9	Protected dual of public action	4	Protected extended channel switch announcement
9	Protected dual of public action	5	Protected DSE measurement request
9	Protected dual of public action	6	Protected DSE measurement report
9	Protected dual of public action	7	Reserved
9	Protected dual of public action	8	Protected DSE power constraint
9	Protected dual of public action	9–255	Unused/reserved
10–125			Unused/reserved
126	Vendor-specific protected	0–255	Vendor dependent
127	Vendor specific	0–255	Vendor dependent
128–255	Error	0–255	Unused, returns an error message

The 802.11h-2003 amendment introduced category 0. The 802.11e-2005 amendment introduced categories 1 (QoS), 2 (Direct Link setup between stations, which will be replaced by the future 802.11z), and 3 (Block Acknowledgment). The 802.11k-2008 amendment introduced category 4 and 5, Radio Measurement (used for Radio Resource management and dynamic power level and channel allocation). The 802.11r-2008 amendment introduced category 6 (Fast BSS Transition). The 802.11w-2009 amendment introduced categories 8 and 9 (related to Management Frame Protection and creating a Dependant Station Enablement [DSE] scheme) and the vendor-specific possible categories 127 (when DSE is not used) and 126 (when DSE is used). 802.11r and 802.11w will also be briefly described in this section.

Spectrum and Transmit Power Management

The 802.11h-2003 amendment defines how stations and APs must control their power and channel assignments to avoid disturbing other devices already using the 5 GHz spectrum. As mentioned earlier, practically speaking this amendment protects civilian airport radars operating in the UNII-2 and UNII-2 extended bands. When a radar blast is detected, all stations must leave the affected frequency. This capability is a part of Dynamic Frequency Selection (*DFS*). In countries where compliance with 802.11h is implemented, stations operating on UNII-2 and UNII-2 extended bands must also comply with transmit power regulations. This is called Transmit Power Control (*TPC*).

 Real World Scenario

Can 802.11a/n Access Points Really Disturb Airport Operations?

The perspective of disturbing civilian airport radars is frightening...one would soon imagine how terrorists would use an 802.11a access point to jam an airport radar and crash planes! Luckily, the reality is far from this nightmare scenario. Civilian airport radars use multiple frequencies for multiple purposes. The UNII-2 and UNII-2 extended bands are so close to an ISM band located in the UNII-3 area that the decision has long been taken by most civilian national regulatory bodies not to use them for any other purpose than weather reporting.

Can an airport radar still be disturbed by an 802.11a/n access point? Oh, yes! As a matter of fact, one of the first large outdoor mesh networks was deployed not long after the 802.11a amendment was published, not far from a major international airport of northern Europe. Because it was a mesh network, the backhaul link between access points was built on a common 802.11 frequency, creating a large web of several tens of access points on the same channel over several square miles. When the neighboring airport radar was scanning the affected frequency, what was displayed was a large snow cloud—not a big surprise in winter but a bit more disturbing when the outside temperature was reported as being close to 90 degrees Fahrenheit (30 degrees Celsius) in mid-summer!

Because snow is a perfectly valid type of report, it was not possible to modify airport radars to ignore 802.11a networks. Instead, each 802.11a access point that implemented in its code the 802.11h amendment had to be programmed to recognize radar blasts. The IEEE 802.11h working group distinguished eight types or radar signals, each having its own pattern. They are typically very short in duration (300 to 800 milliseconds) and very "spiky" and intense. Some of them are so short that an access point with a standard 802.11a/n radio module has a hard time recognizing or even detecting it! To help in the discovery process, the 802.11h committee had to design a "quiet period," during which the AP can silence all the cell stations to listen carefully and determine whether that weak and short signal it just heard was a radar or something else.

Channel Switch Announcement

We saw how the *Channel Switch Announcement* element was used for the AP to inform the cell that all stations had to move to another channel because a radar was detected on the current frequency. This Channel Switch Announcement element is present in beacons and probe responses and announces a future switch.

Figure 4.35 describes the format of this element.

FIGURE 4.35   Channel Switch Announcement element

Element ID	Length	Channel Switch Mode	New Channel Number	Channel Switch Count
1	1	1	1	1

Octets:

This element is not mandatory, but you can imagine what happens when it is not present in beacons and probe responses: the AP detects a radar blast and then suddenly disappears from the channel! Stations suddenly have to scan all channels to find where the AP went, which may disrupt communications. With this feature, the AP informs the cell about the next channel (New Channel Number). It also tells the cell when the switch is going to occur. The Channel Switch Count segment can be set to 0 to indicate that the change will occur any time after the present beacon was sent. It can be set to 1 to show that the jump will occur just before the next beacon.

The Channel Switch Announcement element is also associated with an action frame of the same name that can be sent by the AP between beacons to announce the channel switch. Figure 4.36 shows the format of this action frame.

FIGURE 4.36   Channel Switch Announcement action frame

Category	Action Value	Channel Switch Announcement element
1	1	5

Octets:

Refer to Table 4.10 for a list of the various action frame categories and action types. The Category field for the Channel Switch Announcement action frame is set to 0, representing spectrum management. All action frames related to 802.11h are category 0. The Action Value field is set to 4 (representing a Channel Switch Announcement frame). Why design a special frame if the information element is already present in beacons and probe responses? The AP can send the Channel Switch Action frame between beacons to any station that may not have received the beacon or to instruct a station that it should not send traffic until the switch occurs.

Measurement Request Frame and Measurement Report Frame

The AP must have good reasons to jump to another channel. It will do so because it detected a radar blast or because a station detected a radar blast. The 802.11h amendment allows for action frames to measure the radar activity in the channel. There is a measurement request action frame, by which a station (typically an AP) asks another station to listen to a particular channel, and a measurement report action frame, by which a station (AP or not) informs the emitter of the measurement request action frame of the results of the measurements. This frame can also be broadcast to the cell by the AP to inform its members about measurement results.

Both frames belong to category 0 (spectrum management). Measurement request is indicated by a 1 in the Action Value field, and measurement report is indicated by a 2 in the Action Value field.

Figure 4.37 shows the structure of the measurement request frame.

FIGURE 4.37   Measurement request frame structure

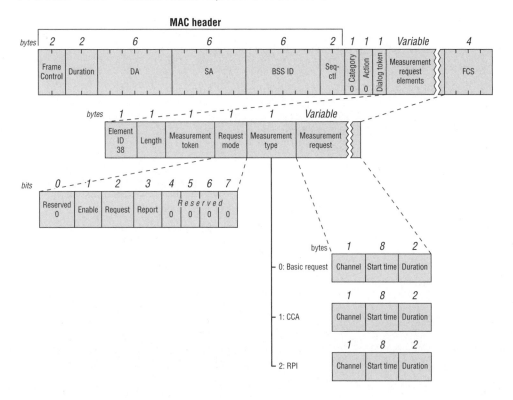

The measurement request frame contains a token, which acts as a sequence number when several requests and reports are exchanged. The frame then contains one or several measurement request elements. The element ID is always 38. The token is used to uniquely identify the request (when several requests are sent). The measurement request mode bitmap is used to show whether the station accepts autonomous (nonsolicited) reports. Measurement type shows whether the requested measurement is basic (0), a clear channel assessment (type 1), or a Receive Power Indicator (RPI) histogram (type 2), showing a measurement value over time.

Once the measurement was performed, the measuring station can send the result over a measurement report action frame. It is built on the same structure as the measurement request frame, as shown in Figure 4.38.

FIGURE 4.38 Measurement report frame structure

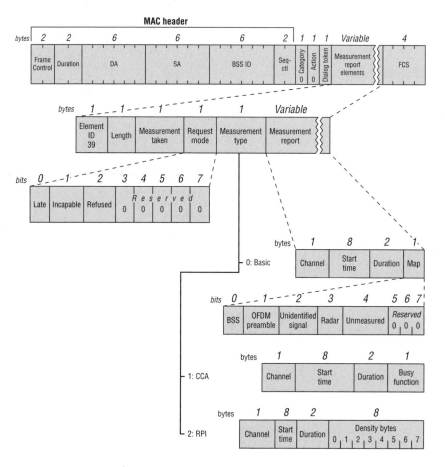

Most elements are the same as in the measurement request frame. The additional or different elements are as follows:

- The measurement report mode bitmap still contains three useful bits, but they are used this time to specify whether the request arrived too late (late bit), for example after the time frame requested by the request, if the station cannot perform the measurement (incapable bit), or if the station does not want to perform the measurement (refused bit).

- The measurement report contains the result for each measurement performed. The basic report can identify other neighboring cells (BSS), OFDM signals, unidentified signals, or recognized radar signatures (in the sense that a radar matches a specific pattern, which 802.11h compliant stations must recognize). The CCA measurement simply reports the RF activity in the cell, that is, for what percentage of the measurement period RF activity was detected. The RPI histogram returns a measurement of the detected 802.11 activity on the channel over time, coded over 8 bytes.

TPC Request Frame and TPC Report Frame

The 802.11h amendment also specifies that stations should be able to reduce their power level dynamically. This helps in reducing the impact of the cell on neighboring devices using the same frequency by reducing each device's RF footprint. Determining the right power level requires a dynamic dialogue between communicating stations, because each of them hears the other but does not know how the others hear it. The TPC request and report frames allow the exchange of this information, by which one station asks, "How do you hear me?" thus allowing the other station to provide feedback on the quality of the radio link.

Figure 4.39 shows the TPC request and TPC report frames.

FIGURE 4.39   TPC request frame and TPC report frame structure

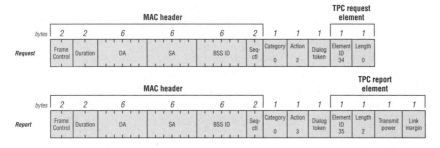

The TPC request frame is action type 2 in action frame category 0. The length of the action element is set to 0, because the request is a simple question, identified by the frame type and subtype.

The TPC report frame provides two descriptive statistics, Transmit Power and Link Margin. To better understand them, suppose station A sends the TPC request and station B sends the TPC report. First, the report indicates at which power level station B sends the TPC report frame. This will allow station A to establish the link margin, that is, the attenuation of the signal when the frame travels from station B to station A. The report also contains the station B link margin, which is the quality of the link station B expects. This concept is better understood with an example. Suppose stations can only read signals received at -85 dBm or better. If station B indicates that it wants a link margin of 10 dB, it tells station A, "After calculating from my answer how many dBs are lost on the path between us, make sure that when you reduce your power level, you keep a safety margin of 10 dB." This prevents stations from decreasing their power so much that the slightest variation of RF conditions on the link makes the frame get lost in the surrounding noise or interference. The desired link margin is vendor dependant.

Quiet Element

Remember that an AP can request a quiet time during which no stations should transmit in order to test the channel for the presence of radars. They do not request this quiet time directly with an action frame, but by adding the Quiet element in probe responses and beacons.

Figure 4.40 shows the format of the Quiet element.

FIGURE 4.40   Quiet element

		Quiet Count	Quiet Period	Quiet Duration	Quiet Offset
Element ID	Length				

Octets: 1   1   1   1   2   2

The Quiet Count field is set to the number of TBTTs until the quiet interval starts. A value of 1 indicates that the quiet interval will start after the next beacon. A value of 0 is reserved.

If the quiet interval should not start just after a beacon but slightly later, you can use the Quiet Offset field to indicate the offset of the start of the quiet interval from the TBTT specified by the Quiet Count field, expressed in TUs. The value of the Quiet Offset field should be less than one beacon interval. For example, if the Quiet Count field is set to 2 and the Quiet Offset to 10, you are indicating that the next Quiet Interval should start 10 TUs (therefore 10.24 milliseconds) after the second beacon to come.

The quiet period can occur once or at regular intervals. The Quiet Period field represents the number of beacon intervals between the start of regularly scheduled quiet intervals defined by this Quiet element. A value of 0 indicates that no periodic quiet interval is defined.

The Quiet Duration field is set to the duration of the quiet interval, expressed in TUs.

The Quiet feature is often use in combination with channel jump (and channel announcement) to test the new channel before resuming operations. The test lasts typically 60 seconds. This improves the stability of the cell but also creates slots of time when stations cannot transmit, which may disrupt communications (especially if you run VoWLAN!). Its support is mandatory, but its implementation is optional, just like TPC and channel announcement.

Admission Control

Managing QoS in wireless cells is complex. The 802.11 standard was built on the concept that all stations would have an equal and fair access to the medium. With the emergence of VoWLAN and video applications, these rules needed to be adapted to prioritize time-sensitive traffic. The first step is of course to recognize which traffic has to receive which level of priority. This is done by marking frames and packets with a priority value. This marking can be done at layer 2 or at layer 3.

In wired networks, the *802.1p protocol* determined eight levels of priority for 802.3 wired frames, from 0 (untagged) to 7 (highest priority). This priority level is coded over 3 bits and integrated in a 4-byte field called 802.1Q tag, added to 802.3 frame headers on trunk links (between switches). This tag is a layer 2 tag, which means it is stripped off when routers process the packet to move it from one interface to the other. For the QoS marking to survive routing, another mechanism was created to mark QoS in the IP header. The most common variant of this mechanism is Differentiated Service Code Point (*DSCP*). DSCP still uses the eight priority levels as main markers but also adds three other bits to determine, within each priority level, subpriorities called drop precedences. DSCP allows for more values than 802.1p and more refined QoS tuning with this possibility to create subpriorities within each main priority category. When the subpriority value is set to 0, the main priority value can be seen as the equivalent to the same 802.1p value. This allows you to partially map 802.1p (Layer 2) QoS values into DSCP values, and vice versa.

When the 802.11e working group decided to create QoS values for the wireless space, it was clear that DSCP was not adapted, because it had too many subcategories that could never be implemented in a wireless space where all stations have equal access to the medium. The 802.11e working group took the eight 802.1p values, and mapped them to eight equivalent wireless User Priorities (UP). These eight UPs were grouped 2 by 2 into four access categories (AC), called Voice, Video, Best Effort, and Background.

To regulate the traffic in the cell, access points supporting QoS use TXOP, Transmit Opportunities, to grant to stations the possibility to send one or more frames of a given QoS level. You will learn more about these mechanisms in Chapter 7.

For this mechanism to be efficient, stations needing to introduce a new traffic stream (or TS, a flow of data) into the cell need to negotiate the stream parameters with the AP. The underlying logic is that the TS should be set up only if the corresponding QoS level can be provisioned. If the access point accepts the TS, it should then provide the expected QoS level by scheduling Service Periods (SP), contiguous periods of times scheduled at regular intervals, during which one or more downlink unicast frames can be sent to the station, and/or one or several unicast uplink frames can be polled from the station.

The TS operation uses four action frames: ADDTS request, ADDTS response, DELTS, and schedule frames. Just like category 0 identified spectrum and transmit management action frames, category 1 identifies all QoS-related action frames. Refer to Table 4.10 for a list of the various action frame categories and action types.

ADDTS Request and ADDTS Response Frames

The *ADDTS* request is always sent by a station (that is, never by an access point) wanting to add a new TS to the cell. As an action frame, it has the usual structure: Category, Action, Element.

Category is set to 1, to identify the QoS action frame. The ADDTS request frame is identified as action type 0. The element is composed of the following fields:

A Dialog Token   This field, just like for 802.11h related frames, acts as sequence number reference when several frames of the same types are sent.

TSPEC   Traffic specification. The *TSPEC* element contains the set of parameters defining in detail the characteristics and QoS expectations of a traffic flow, such as packet size, quantity, expected rate, and so on.

TCLAS   Traffic class definition (optional; there can be several consecutive TCLAS fields). The TCLAS defines the traffic in simpler terms than TSPEC and is used in implementations where TSPEC is not supported.

TCLAS Processing   Present only when more than one TCLAS fields are present in the frame.

Once the ADDTS request has been received, the AP processes it and replies with an ADDTS response action frame. The structure of the response frame is very close to the request. Category is set to 1 to identify the QoS action frame. The ADDTS response action is 1. The element is composed of the following fields:

A Dialog Token   This field, just like for 802.11h-related frames, acts as sequence number reference when several frames of the same type are sent.

Status Code   Accepts or rejects the stream and specifies why. The reasons can range from a lack of bandwidth to wrong parameters.

TS Delay   When the TS is denied, TS Delay announces when the TS can be retried.

TSPEC   Traffic specification.

TCLAS   Traffic class definition (optional; there can be several consecutive TCLAS fields).

TCLAS Processing   Present only when more than one TCLAS fields are present in the frame.

Schedule   Describes how the accepted TS is scheduled.

If the admission is granted, the AP has to schedule *service periods* for this traffic, not allowing more traffic than it has space (in EDCA mode), or switching from EDCA to a centralized mode called HCCA but not used by any vendor today (see Chapter 7 for more details on QoS). If the admission is refused, the requesting station can always retry, hoping that some other traffic using the same QoS level has been deleted in between. The requesting station can also choose to try another QoS level for the same traffic. The AP can also reject the TS but suggest an alternate configuration (in the logic "I cannot do what you asked, but I can do this..."). The station can then accept or reject the suggestion.

DELTS Frames

Once a TS is admitted, a station receives the predetermined QoS level negotiated in the ADDTS exchange. After a while, the TS can be removed to free resources from the cell. The deletion can be initiated by the station or the AP, because the TS is completed (no more frames of that category to send), because the station is leaving the cell, because the TS times out, or because the station tries to send an unrecognized TS.

This TS deletion is communicated by a *DELTS* action frame, sent from the station or the AP. The structure of the DELTS frame follows the now familiar structure. Category is set to 1 to identify the QoS action frame. The DELTS action is 2. The element is composed of the following fields:

TS Info   This is the same TS Info field as in the ADDTS frame.

Reason Code   This specifies why the TS is deleted. Reasons can range from ACKs are not received, timeout, TS refused by receiving station, station leaving the cell, and so on. Notice that because this is a deletion, we have here a Reason Code field. In the ADDTS response, we had a status code (showing the result of the request).

Schedule Frames

When a TS is admitted, the schedule frame is transmitted by the AP to the station to announce the schedule of delivery of data and polls (when the station also uses power save). This simple frame contains the usual Category, Action, and Element fields. Category is set to 1 to identify the QoS action frame. The schedule action is 3. The element is composed of the Schedule element, which specifies the service start time, service interval, TSID, and TS direction. The station can then send its traffic in a burst. The standard also allows the AP to switch from the distributed EDCA mode to the more centralized HCCA mode to take control of the cell and allocate the rights to transmit only to those stations that were granted today, but no vendor implements HCCA yet.

You will learn more about QoS in Chapter 7, but you will also read about scheduling in Chapter 8.

802.11r and 802.11w

Several other amendments introduce new action frames. Examining them all in detail is beyond the scope of this book, but providing a quick view of some main types may help you better understand complex frames in new wireless deployments. Refer to Table 4.10 for a list of the various action frame categories and action types.

Fast BSS Transition

The 802.11r amendment defines how fast secure roaming can be handled between access points.

Four action frame formats are defined to support fast BSS transitions over the DS, which are initiated through the currently associated AP. The Fast Transition (FT) action frames are sent over the air between the station and its current AP. The action frame is used as a transport mechanism for data that are destined for the new AP. The four action frames are FT request, FT response, FT confirm, and FT ack. These action frames have the usual structure: Category (FT is category 6), Action (to identify which action frame is being used), followed by one or several elements determining how the Fast Transition is planned.

These elements can describe the security model being used, the time frame of the transition, and what resources are being requested.

Protected Management Frames

Management frames are not encrypted, even when WEP, TKIP, or AES encryption is in place to protect the data stream. This limitation allows for numerous attacks in which the AP is impersonated by the attacker. Some vendors have implemented proprietary counter-measures to protect their network from these attacks. In 2009, the 802.11w amendment was published to provide a way to protect management frames. The 802.11w amendment defines 5 types of new action frames, for a total of 14 action frames. These frames are used to negotiate security parameters between stations and access points to sign with hash management frames. As several categories are defined, the Category field can take several values (4, 8, 9, 126, or 127). This management frame protection is complex, because it requires security parameter exchanges between AP and connecting stations, while still not preventing new stations from associating. At regular intervals, these security parameters need to be renewed. They must be unique to the AP and its client and be shared with the AP clients, while still be secure enough not to be compromised. The details of each of these frames is beyond the scope of this book.

Summary

Well done for getting though this chapter. Management frames are an essential part of wireless networks, and understanding their structure and components will allow you to have a very precise view on what the cell is capable of and also understand the changes occurring in the BSS. By observing the differences between what stations negotiate and what access points allow, you will be able to determine why some stations get disconnected or do not get the same level of throughput as the others.

After having reviewed each type of management frame and its expected components, mandatory or optional, we examined in detail the possible fields and information elements that make the body of a management frame. We then had a closer look at the action frames, which are a specific type in that they are associated to changes in the cell activity.

Going through all these fields and information elements for the first time may seem over-whelming. If you keep practicing the exercises suggested in this chapter, capturing frames and observing their content, you will soon come to see that each component, each field, and each information element is a part of the story the cell has to tell. By looking at each of them, you will see the overall picture of what the cell is and what its stations can achieve, and they will become the natural members of the staff that makes the cell possible. During this learning phase, do refer to this chapter every time a component looks out of place or redundant. Understanding their purpose is as important as learning their structure.

Exam Essentials

Know the different management frame subtypes. Identify which frames are management frames. You should be able to recognize their subtype from a capture by looking at their components.

Describe a beacon. You should be able to describe the structure of beacon frame, how often it is sent, and the main elements it carries.

Explain the network discovery process. Explain how a station discovers the network, with passive or active scanning. You should be able to list the main elements involved in each frame needed for this discovery process.

Explain the authentication/association process. You will learn more details about the authentication process in Chapter 9. Related to the current chapter, you should be able to describe the authentication frame and the frames used for the association phase.

Understand reassociation and deauthentication. You should be able to explain why reassociation, disassociation, and deauthentication frames are sent. You should also be able to explain the role of these frames by describing their content and differentiate the Status Code field from the Reason Code field.

Know the different management frame subtypes. Identify which frames are management frames. You should be able to recognize their subtype from a capture by looking at their components.

Understand your information elements. At a minimum, you should be able to recognize an information element from its content and explain its purpose.

Know the different management frame subtypes. Identify which frames are management frames. You should be able to recognize their subtype from a capture by looking at their components.

Explain priority and tagging. Chapter 7 will give you information on QoS. Based on this chapter, you should be able to explain the tagging principles involved in QoS implementation in wireless cells.

Explain admission control. You should also be able to explain how admission control can be put in place to regulate the bandwidth consumption in the cell.

Understand spectrum and transmit power management. Know what 802.11h is and which action frames are involved in its support, for both DFS and TPC.

Know the different action frames. Identify which action frames can be in use in a wireless network, to implement management frame protection, fast BSS transition, or HT. Chapter 11 will give you more details about HT implementation.

Key Terms

Before you take the exam, be certain you are familiar with the following terms:

802.1p protocol	DS Parameter Set
action frames	DSCP
ADDTS	DTIM
AID	Listen Interval
association request	probe request
association response	probe response
ATIM frame	Reason Code
Authentication Algorithm number	reassociation request
authentication frame	reassociation response
Authentication Transaction Sequence Number	service period
beacon frames	SSID element
beacon interval	Status Code
BSS Load element	Supported Rates
Capability Information field	Extended Supported Rates
channel switch announcement	TIM
deauthentication frame	time stamp
DELTS	TPC
DFS	TSPEC
disassociation frame	

Review Questions

1. How many management frame types are described by the 802.11-2007 standard?

    A. 4

    B. 11

    C. 12

    D. 13

2. In which frame would you find a timestamp field?

    A. Beacon

    B. Association request

    C. Association response

    D. Authentication

3. What is the purpose of the Listen Interval field?

    A. To determine the next QoS service period

    B. To organize the detection of radar blasts

    C. To optimize BSS Fast Roaming transition times

    D. To specify when stations in low power mode would wake up

4. In which case would a station send a reassociation frame?

    A. To rejoin an IBSS after a member disconnected

    B. To join a new AP on the same ESS

    C. To rejoin an AP after deauthentication occurred

    D. To reenter the cell after the AP jumped to a new channel

5. How does a QoS station request a quality of service commitment from its AP?

    A. By using the ADDTS frame

    B. By using the TSPEC request frame

    C. By using the QoS BSS Load action frame

    D. By sending the Schedule Request frame

6. How long do stations have before leaving a channel affected by a radar blast?

    A. 260 milliseconds

    B. 10 seconds

    C. 30 seconds

    D. 60 seconds

7. Which of the following is true about the Privacy subfield?

   A. When its value is 1, WEP encryption is in place.

   B. When its value is 1, any encryption may be in place.

   C. Its values can be 0 for no encryption, 1 for WEP, 2 for WPA, and 3 for WPA2.

   D. When its value is 1, the station is in low power mode and not listening to the cell frames.

8. What is the beacon default interval?

   A. 100 milliseconds

   B. 102.4 TUs

   C. 102.4 milliseconds

   D. 100 TBTTs

9. Which of the following is the OUI used by the IEEE in the RSN information element?

   A. 00-00-00

   B. 0E-EE-00

   C. 11-11-11

   D. 00-0F-AC

10. Which amendment uses FT frames?

   A. 802.11i

   B. 802.11n

   C. 802.11r

   D. 802.11w

11. What should a station where an ADDTS request has been refused do next?

   A. Retry the same or a lower TSPEC

   B. Revert back to PCF

   C. Roam to the next AP

   D. Drop the current TS and negotiate the next TS

12. What information is sent in a TPC report sent from station A to station B?

   A. Link margin as measured by A

   B. Link margin as measured by B

   C. A to B attenuation value

   D. B to A attenuation value

13. What is the category number allocated to QoS-related action frames?

    A. 0

    B. 1

    C. 4

    D. 5

14. What does ATIM stand for?

    A. Ad Hoc Traffic Indication Message

    B. Announcement Traffic Indication Message

    C. Announcement Traffic Indication Map

    D. Ad Hoc Traffic Indication Map

15. Which information element is a summary of the AP QoS capabilities?

    A. EDCA Parameter Set

    B. TSPEC

    C. QoS Subfield

    D. QoS Capabilities

16. How does an AP hide its SSID (SSID not broadcasted in beacons)?

    A. By not sending the SSID information element

    B. By sending an empty SSID information element

    C. By stopping beacon broadcasts

    D. By moving the SSID information element to the vendor-specific section of the beacon

17. For which specific conditions does the 802.11 standard describe that the NonERPPresent bit should be set in AP beacons?

    A. 802.11g station associated to the AP

    B. 802.11/802.11b station detected by the AP

    C. 802.11/802.11b station associated to the AP

    D. 802.11/802.11b station authenticated by the AP

18. How do the Supported Rates and Extended Supported Rates information elements specify which rates are mandatory (basic)?

    A. By setting bit 7 to 1 when basic and 0 when supported

    B. By setting mandatory rates in the Supported Rates IE and Supported Rates in the Extended Supported Rates information element

    C. By displaying the six basic rates first and then the supported rates

    D. The distinction between mandatory and supported is set by the 802.11 standard, not by the information elements

19. Which information element describes support for 40 MHz wide channels?

   A. The Channel Bonding information element

   B. The HT Extended Channel information element

   C. The HT Frequency Slicing information element

   D. The HT Operation element

20. Which of the following can be identified in an 802.11h measurement report frame?

   A. DSSS signals

   B. OFDM signals

   C. FHSS stations

   D. NonERP stations

Answers to Review Questions

1. C. The 802.11-2007 standard describes 12 management frame types: beacon, probe request, probe response, authentication, association request, association response, reassociation request, reassociation response, disassociation, deauthentication, ATIM, and action frame.

2. A. The timestamp is present in beacons and is used by stations associated to the cell as a clock reference. The time synchronization function uses the timestamp to align the stations' cell clock to the AP clock.

3. D. In frames sent from stations to access points (association request, reassociation request), the Listen Interval field is used to indicate to the AP how often a station in Power Save mode wakes to listen to beacon management frames.

4. B. This type of frame can be sent only by a station to an access point and is used when the station is already associated to the ESS and wants to associate to another access point connecting to the same ESS.

5. A. QoS station use the ADDTS frame to ask the AP to add a traffic stream to the cell. The ADDTS contains a TSPEC element describing the traffic specifications. There is no such thing as a TSPEC request frame. The QBSS Load Element is present in the beacon to inform potential client stations about the current load in the cell. Schedule is a frame sent by the AP to determine when the service period will start.

6. B. Stations detecting a radar blast have 10 seconds from the moment of detection to leave the affected frequency. During this interval, they have the right to still send up to 260 milliseconds worth of frames. Upon getting to a new channel, they can respect a quiet interval to listen for radar blasts on the new frequency. This quiet interval is commonly 60 seconds. Stations cannot return to the affected channel for 30 minutes.

7. B. Although originally designed for WEP, the Privacy subfield today indicates that some form of encryption is in place, WEP, TKIP, or AES.

8. C. A beacon is sent by default every 102.4 milliseconds or 100 TUs (one time unit is 1.024 millisecond). The time at which the next beacon should be sent is the target beacon transmission time (TBTT). The AP tries to send the beacon at each planned TBTT.

9. D. The RSN element uses a cipher suite to describe what encryption should be used for unicast or broadcast/multicast frames. The element is composed of an organization unique identifier representing the cipher vendor and of a cipher number for this vendor. The IEEE uses the OUI 00-0F-AC.

10. C. FT frames are action frames defined by the BSS Fast Transition amendment 802.11r and are used for fast and secure roaming between APs part of the same ESS.

11. A. When an ADDTS is denied by an AP, the station cannot get the QoS level it requested, usually because there was not enough space to accept this TS as requested in the cell. The station can retry, hoping that other TSPEC of the same level got terminated and that space becomes available, or it can revert its ADDTS to a lower QoS level and retry. A station would not leave the cell by default, because roaming takes longer than retry, and would not drop its queued traffic. PCF was never implemented by any vendor.

12. A. Station A sends its link margin, that is to say what margin it wants B to take when reducing its power. If station A link margin is 5 dB and B calculates that it can send with its power down to 6 dBm, B will send at 11 dBm to respect station A's link margin request.

13. B. The 802.11e amendment defines several action frames. QoS-related frames are Category 1. Category 0 is allocated to spectrum management frames introduced by the 802.11h amendment. Category 4 is used by public action frames introduced by the 802.11w amendment. Category 5 is used by radio measurement action frames introduced by the 802.11k amendment.

14. B. ATIM stands for Announcement Traffic Indication Message. Don't confuse this acronym with Traffic Indication Map (TIM) or Delivery Traffic Indication Message (DTIM).

15. D. The QoS Capabilities IE summarizes the AP QoS Capabilities. A more extensive support description is given in the EDCA parameter set. TSPEC element is used by stations (not APs) requesting QoS level through ADDTS Request frames. It can be found in the AP answers but only to describe the original station request, not the AP capabilities. The QoS subfield simply informs whether the AP supports QoS, without details about its capabilities.

16. B. An AP cannot stop broadcasting beacons (most clients would disconnect). The SSID information element has to be present, but its size is not fixed. APs hide the SSID by sending an empty SSID IE. Moving the SSID IE to the vendor-specific section would mean removing the SSID IE from its standard position (order 4 in beacons), which is not allowed by the 802.11 standard.

17. C. The standard describes that the NonERPPresent bit should be set by the AP if a non 802.11g station (that is, 802.11 or 802.11b) is associated to the AP. Many vendors implement this bit as soon as the station is detected by the AP, thus extending the standard requirements.

18. A. Each rate is coded over 8 bits (bits 0 to 7), representing a multiple of 500 Kbps. Bit 7 is set to 1 when the rate is mandatory and to 0 when the rate is supported. Disabled rates are not listed.

19. D. The HT Operation element describes how 40 MHz channel support is set. The Channel Bonding information element, HT Extended Channel information element, and HT Frequency Slicing information element do not exist.

20. B. The basic measurement report can identify other neighboring cells (BSS), OFDM signals, unidentified signals, or recognized radar signatures (in the sense that a radar matches a specific pattern, which 802.11h-compliant stations must recognize). The CCA measurement can also simply report the RF activity in the cell.

Chapter 5

802.11 Control Frames

IN THIS CHAPTER, YOU WILL LEARN ABOUT THE FOLLOWING:

✓ **Understanding Control Frames**

✓ **Carrier Sense**
- Virtual Carrier Sense
- Physical Carrier Sense

✓ **RTS/CTS Frames**

✓ **CTS-to-self**

✓ **Protection Mechanism**
- Preventing Collisions
- ERP Information Element
- Triggering Protection Mechanism

✓ **Acknowledgement Frame**

✓ **Block Acknowledgement Request**

✓ **Block Acknowledgement**

✓ **PS-Poll**

✓ **Control Wrapper**

✓ **Contention Free**

In this chapter, we will take a detailed look at the different control frames and discuss the purpose of each of the frames. *Control frames* are the traffic cops of the 802.11 network, assisting with the delivery of data and management frames.

Understanding Control Frames

In addition to defining frames that are used to transport data from one station to another, the 802.11 standard defines frames for managing the wireless communications and assisting with the delivery of data frames. To provide dependable communications, the 802.11 standard defines three different *frame types* and an assortment of *frame subtypes*. The three frame types are control, data, and management. Each of these frame types is subdivided into multiple frame subtypes, with each subtype providing a different function and having a different frame structure.

Control frames assist with the delivery of data and management frames. Unlike management and data frames, control frames do not have a frame body. In addition to the PHY and preamble, control frames contain only a layer 2 header and trailer. Control frames perform many different functions; therefore, they can be transmitted at different data rates. In a mixed PHY environment, control frames are typically transmitted at one of the defined basic rates. This helps assure that all stations can receive the control frames. Section 9.6 Multirate Support of the 802.11-2007 standard defines a set of transmission rules that must be followed by all stations.

Every 802.11 frame has a *Frame Control field* (Figure 5.1), which specifies information about the frame. The Type and Subtype subfields of the Frame Control field are used to identify the function of the frame. The Type field is 2 bits long, and the Subtype field is 4 bits long, and they are used to identify the function of the frame. As shown in Figure 5.1, many of the values of the other fields of a control frame are fixed, such as the type value of 01, which identifies the frame as a control frame. Table 5.1 displays the Type and Subtype values for control frames, along with a subtype description of each frame.

FIGURE 5.1 Control frame: Frame Control fields

B0										B15
Protocol version	Type	Subtype	To DS	From DS	More frag	Retry	Pwr mgt	More data	Protected frame	Order
Protocol version	Control	Subtype	0	0	0	0	Pwr mgt	0	0	0
Bits : 2	2	4	1	1	1	1	1	1	1	1

TABLE 5.1   Control frames: valid Type and Subtype combinations

Type value b3 b2	Type description	Subtype value b7 b6 b5 b4	Subtype description
01	Control	0000–0110	Reserved
01	Control	0111	Control wrapper
01	Control	1000	Block ack request (BlockAckReq)
01	Control	1001	Block ack (BlockAck)
01	Control	1010	PS-Poll
01	Control	1011	RTS
01	Control	1100	CTS
01	Control	1101	ACK
01	Control	1110	CF-End
01	Control	1111	CF-End and CF-Ack

Carrier Sense

The first step that an 802.11 CSMA/CA device takes to begin transmitting is to perform a *carrier sense*. This is a check to see whether the medium is busy. Think of it like listening for a busy signal when you call someone on the phone. A carrier sense is performed in two ways: *virtual carrier sense* and *physical carrier sense*. Both methods will be covered in greater detail in Chapter 7; however, a brief overview of virtual carrier sense is needed prior to learning details about control frames.

Virtual Carrier Sense

Virtual carrier sense uses a timer mechanism known as the *network allocation vector (NAV)*. The NAV timer maintains a prediction of future traffic on the medium, based on the Duration value information seen in a previous frame transmission. When an 802.11 radio is not transmitting, it is listening. As depicted in Figure 5.2, when the listening radio hears a frame transmission from another station, it looks at the header of the frame and determines whether the *Duration/ID field* contains a Duration value or an ID value. If the transmitted frame is a PS-Poll frame (PS-Poll frames are discussed later in this chapter), then the Duration/ID field contains the *association identifier (AID)* of the station that transmitted the frame. In all other frames, the Duration/ID field contains a Duration value. If the field does contain a Duration value, the listening station will set its NAV timer to this value. The listening station will then use the NAV as a countdown timer, knowing that the RF medium should be busy until the NAV countdown reaches 0.

FIGURE 5.2 Virtual carrier sense

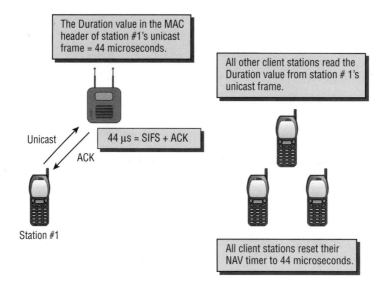

This process essentially allows the transmitting 802.11 radio to notify the other stations that the medium will be busy for a period of time (Duration/ID value). The stations that are not transmitting listen and hear the Duration/ID, set a countdown timer (NAV), and wait until their timer hits 0 before they can contend for the medium and eventually transmit on the medium. A station cannot contend for the medium until its NAV timer is 0, nor can a station transmit on the medium if the NAV timer is set to a nonzero value.

Physical Carrier Sense

The virtual carrier sense is one method of keeping other stations from transmitting while another radio has control of the RF medium. However, it is possible that a station did not hear the other radio transmitting so was unable to read the Duration/ID field and set its NAV timer. There could be numerous reasons why, but that is irrelevant at the moment. CSMA/CA utilizes another line of defense to ensure that a station does not transmit while another is already transmitting: the 802.11 standard defines a *physical carrier sense*.

Physical carrier sensing is performed constantly by all stations that are not transmitting or receiving. When a station performs a physical carrier sense, it is actually listening to the channel to see whether any other transmitters are taking up the channel.

Physical carrier sense has two purposes. The first purpose is to determine whether a frame transmission is inbound for a station to receive. If the medium is busy, the radio will attempt to synchronize with the transmission. The second purpose is to determine whether the medium is busy before transmitting. This is known as the *clear channel assessment (CCA)*. The CCA involves listening for 802.11 RF transmissions at the Physical layer. The medium must be clear before a station can transmit.

It is important to understand that both virtual carrier sense and the physical carrier sense are always happening at the same time. Virtual carrier sense is a layer 2 line of defense, while physical carrier sense is a layer 1 line of defense. If one line of defense fails, ideally the other will prevent collisions from occurring.

RTS/CTS Frames

Request to send (RTS) and *clear to send (CTS)* frames are used to enhance the virtual carrier sense process. For a client station to participate in a basic service set, it must be able to communicate with the access point. This is straightforward and logical; however, it is possible for the client station to be able to communicate with the access point but not be able to hear or be heard by any of the other client stations. This can be a problem because a station performs collision avoidance by setting its NAV when it hears another station transmitting (virtual carrier sense) and by listening for RF (physical carrier sense). If a station cannot hear the other stations or cannot be heard by the other stations, there is a greater likelihood that a collision can occur.

Request to send/clear to send (RTS/CTS) is a mechanism that performs a NAV distribution and helps prevent collisions from occurring. The NAV distribution reserves the medium prior to the transmission of the data frame. When RTS/CTS is enabled on a station, every time the station wants to transmit a frame, it must perform an RTS/CTS exchange prior to the normal data transmission. When the transmitting station begins to transmit data, it first sends a 20-octet RTS control frame (Figure 5.3). The Duration value of the RTS frame includes the time needed for the subsequent frames in the transmit operation to be transmitted. This value is in microseconds. All listening stations will set their NAV timers to this value and cannot contend for the medium or transmit data until their NAV counts down to 0. After the RTS frame is transmitted, the receiving station responds by sending a 14-octet CTS control frame (Figure 5.4). The Duration value of the CTS frame includes the time needed for the subsequent frames in the transmit operation to be transmitted.

FIGURE 5.3 RTS frame

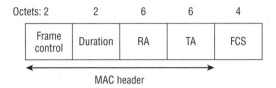

FIGURE 5.4 CTS frame

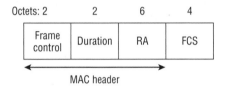

When the RTS frame is created, the *receiver address (RA)* is the address of the intended receiver of the pending data or management frame. The *transmitter address (TA)* of the station is transmitting the RTS frame and pending data or management frame. When the CTS frame is created, the RA field is copied from the TA field of the RTS to which it is responding. Figure 5.5 displays the RTS/CTS duration periods and frames that are transmitted if the NAV reservation is being provided prior to the transmission of a single data frame.

Figure 5.6 depicts an RTS/CTS exchange between a client station and an access point, along with displaying how two nontransmitting stations may use these frames to reset their NAV.

CTS-to-Self

The phrase RTS/CTS not only refers to two types of control frames but also to a method of performing NAV distribution. *CTS-to-self* is simply another method of performing NAV distribution that solely uses CTS control frames. CTS-to-self is used strictly as a protection mechanism for mixed-mode environments. When a station is using CTS-to-self, prior to transmitting a data frame, it performs a NAV distribution by sending a CTS frame. This CTS frame notifies all other stations that they must wait until the DATA and ACK have been transmitted, as shown in Figure 5.7. Any station that hears the CTS-to-self will set their NAV to the value provided. The CTS-to-self NAV distribution mechanism requires less network overhead than the RTS/CTS NAV distribution mechanism; however, it is also less robust against hidden nodes and collisions than RTS/CTS.

FIGURE 5.5   RTS/CTS Duration values

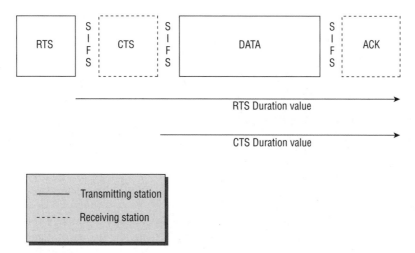

FIGURE 5.6   RTS/CTS frame exchange

Station 3

Station 3 does not hear the RTS
but does hear the CTS and resets
the NAV timer for the Data/ACK
exchange.

RTS duration = CTS/Data/ACK exchange
CTS duration = Data/ACK exchange
Data duration = ACK
ACK duration = 0 (exchange is over)

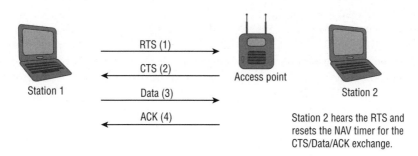

Station 1

RTS (1)

CTS (2)

Data (3)

ACK (4)

Access point

Station 2

Station 2 hears the RTS and
resets the NAV timer for the
CTS/Data/ACK exchange.

FIGURE 5.7   CTS-to-self frame Duration values

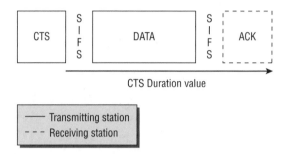

CTS Duration value

Transmitting station
Receiving station

 CTS-to-self is better suited for use by an access point. It is important that all stations hear the CTS to reserve the medium, and this is most likely to occur if it is being sent by an access point. If a client station were to use CTS-to-self as a protection mechanism, there is a chance that another client station on the opposite side of the BSS might be too far away from the CTS and would not realize the medium is busy. Even though this is true, from our experience, it appears that most use CTS-to-self on client stations to reserve the medium instead of RTS/CTS. CTS-to-self is used because of the decreased overhead when compared with RTS/CTS. Some vendors allow the user to select whether the client station uses RTS/CTS or CTS-to-self when in Protected mode.

Protection Mechanism

The 802.11-2007 standard mandates support for both *direct sequence spread spectrum* (DSSS) and *orthogonal frequency division multiplexing* (OFDM) technologies for clause 19 ERP radios (802.11g). When clause 18 HR-DSSS (802.11b) client stations need to communicate in a basic service set with an ERP (802.11g) access point and ERP (802.11g) client stations, the 802.11g devices need to provide compatibility for the slower 802.11b devices. ERP access points must also be backward compatible with legacy clause 15 DSSS (802.11) client stations. This environment is often referred to as mixed-mode. Contrary to what some people believe, the 802.11g devices do not simply switch to 802.11b mode and communicate using 802.11b data rates. For 802.11g, 802.11b stations, and legacy 802.11 DSSS stations to coexist within the same BSS, the 802.11g devices enable what is referred to as the *protection mechanism*, also known as *802.11g Protected mode*.

Many access point vendors offer three configuration modes for an 802.11g access point:

802.11b-Only Mode   When an 802.11g AP is running in this operational mode, support for DSSS technology is solely enabled. Effectively, the access point has been configured to be an 802.11b access point. Legacy 802.11 DSSS clients, 802.11b HR-DSSS clients, and 802.11g clients using ERP-DSSS will all be able to communicate with the AP at data rates of 1 and 2 Mbps, and 802.11b HR-DSSS clients and 802.11g clients using ERP-DSSS will also be able to communicate with the AP at data rates of 5.5 and 11 Mbps. Aggregate throughput will be the same as achieved in an 802.11b network.

Protection mechanisms are used to provide coexistence between ERP (802.11g) radios and non-ERP legacy radios, such as DSSS (802.11) and HR-DSSS (802.11b). Higher-speed HT clause 20 radios have to deal with some of the same issues, providing backward compatibility with earlier 802.11a/b/g radios. In Chapter 10, you will learn about the four different 802.11n protection modes.

802.11g-Only Mode   APs configured as g-only will communicate with only 802.11g client stations using ERP-OFDM technology at data rates of 6, 9, 12, 18, 24, 36, 48, and 54 Mbps. Support for DSSS and HR-DSSS is disabled; therefore, 802.11b HR-DSSS clients and legacy 802.11 DSSS clients will not be able to associate with the access point. Ideally, aggregate throughput will be equivalent to what can be achieved in an 802.11a network. The aggregate throughput of an AP with a data rate of 54 Mbps might be about 19 to 20 Mbps; however, you will learn later in this chapter that this is often not the case. G-only wireless LANs are sometimes referred to as a *pure G* networks.

802.11b/g Mode   This is the default operational mode of most 802.11g access points and is often called mixed-mode. Support for both DSSS and OFDM is enabled. Legacy 802.11 DSSS clients and 802.11b HR-DSSS clients will be able to communicate with the AP at data rates of 1, 2, 5.5, or 11 Mbps, depending upon the capability of the client. The ERP (802.11g) clients will communicate with the AP by using the ERP-OFDM data rates of 6, 9, 12, 18, 24, 36, 48, and 54 Mbps.

You need to understand that these vendor configurations are not part of the 802.11-2007 standard. Although most vendors do indeed support these configurations, the standard mandates support for 802.11b clause 18 devices and 802.11g clause 19 devices within the ERP basic service set.

 Real World Scenario

How Can You Make Sure That 802.11g Networks Are Transmitting at 802.11g Speeds?

Even if all the wireless devices in your company support 802.11g, your WLAN will enable the protection mechanism if it sees even one 802.11b device. This 802.11b device could be a visitor to your company, someone driving past your building with an 802.11b wireless adapter enabled in their laptop, or a nearby business or home that also has a wireless network. If you want your network to always use the higher ERP-OFDM rates, you must configure the access points to support 802.11g clients only. Remember that if you do this, any 802.11b and legacy 802.11 DSSS devices will not be able to connect to your network, and these clients will not be recognized as 802.11 devices. Any signals that they transmit will be recognized as RF interference. So, even though you may think that you are ignoring these legacy devices, you are not; you are just identifying them differently.

Preventing Collisions

As mentioned earlier in this chapter, one of the ways of preventing collisions is for the stations to set a countdown timer known as the network allocation vector (NAV). This notification is known as NAV distribution. NAV distribution is done through the Duration/ID field that is part of the data frame. When a data frame is transmitted by a station, the Duration/ID field is used by the listening stations to set their NAV timers. Unfortunately, this is not inherently possible in a mixed-mode environment. If an 802.11g device were to transmit a data frame, 802.11b devices would not be able to interpret the data frame or the Duration/ID value because the 802.11b HR-DSSS devices are not capable of understanding 802.11g ERP-OFDM transmissions. The 802.11b devices would not set their NAV timers and could incorrectly believe that the medium is available. To prevent this from happening, the 802.11g ERP stations switch into what is known as Protected mode.

In a mixed-mode environment, when an 802.11g device wants to transmit data, it will first perform a NAV distribution by transmitting a request to send/clear to send (RTS/CTS) or a CTS-to-self using a data rate and modulation method that the 802.11b HR-DSSS stations can understand. The RTS/CTS or CTS-to-self will be heard and understood by all the 802.11b and 802.11g stations. The RTS/CTS or CTS-to-self will contain a Duration/ID value that will be used by all the listening stations to set their NAV timers. To put it simply, using a slow transmission that all stations can understand, the ERP (802.11g) device notifies all the stations to reset their NAV values. After the RTS/CTS or CTS-to-self has been used to reserve the medium, the 802.11g station can transmit a data frame by using OFDM modulation without worrying about collisions with 802.11b HR-DSSS or legacy 802.11 DSSS stations.

Within an ERP basic service set, the HR-DSSS (802.11b) and legacy 802.11 DSSS stations are known as non-ERP stations. The purpose of the protection mechanism is that ERP stations (802.11g) can coexist with non-ERP stations (802.11b and 802.11 legacy) within the same BSS. This allows the ERP stations to use the higher ERP-OFDM data rates to transmit and receive data yet still maintain backward compatibility with the older legacy non-ERP stations.

ERP Information Element

The ERP information element (IE) contains information about clause 15 (802.11) or clause 18 (802.11b) stations in the basic service set that are not capable of communicating using clause 19 (ERP-OFDM) data rates. It also identifies whether the AP should use protection mechanisms to optimize performance in the BSS and whether to use long or short preambles. The ERP information element, as shown in Figure 5.8, is 3 octets long; however, the length is flexible and can be expanded in the future. The element ID field contains the value 42, which identifies the IE as an ERP IE, and the length field contains the value 3. The fields r3 through r7 are reserved and set to 0 by default.

FIGURE 5.8   ERP information element

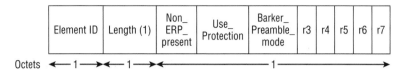

Octets ←— 1 —→←— 1 —→←———————————— 1 ———————————————→

The remaining three fields are NonERP_Present, Use_Protection, and Barker_Preamble_Mode. When a non-ERP station is associated to the BSS, the Non-ERP_Present bit is set to 1. If one or more associated non-ERP stations are not capable of using short preambles, then the Barker_Preamble_Modebit is set to 1.

> Included on the CD of this book is a white paper titled "Protection Ripple in ERP 802.11 WLANs" by Devin Akin. This white paper goes into much greater detail about the protection mechanism and is highly recommended extra reading for preparing for the CWAP exam.

Triggering Protection Mechanism

So, what exactly triggers the protection mechanism? When an ERP access point decides to enable the use of a protection mechanism, it needs to notify all the ERP (802.11g) stations in the BSS that protection is required. It accomplishes this by setting the NonERP_Present bit in the ERP information element in the beacon frame. Every time the access point transmits a beacon, any ERP station that hears the beacon will see the NonERP_Present bit and will know that Protected mode is required. There are an assortment of reasons why Protected mode may be enabled. The following are three scenarios that can trigger protection in an ERP basic service set:

- If a non-ERP STA associates with an ERP AP, the ERP AP will enable the NonERP_Present bit in its own beacons, enabling protection mechanisms in its BSS. In other words, an HR-DSSS (802.11b) client association will trigger protection.

- If an ERP AP hears a beacon from an AP where the supported data rates contain only 802.11b or 802.11 DSSS rates, it will enable the NonERP_Present bit in its own beacons, enabling protection mechanisms in its BSS. In simpler terms, if an 802.11g AP hears a beacon frame from an 802.11 or 802.11b access point or ad hoc client, the protection mechanism will be triggered.

- If an ERP AP hears a management frame (other than a probe request) where the supported rate includes only 802.11 or 802.11b rates, the NonERP_Present bit may be set to 1.

How Does 802.11b Affect 802.11g Throughput?

A common misconception is that 802.11g radios revert to 802.11b data rates when the protection mechanism is used. In reality, ERP (802.11g) radios still transmit data at the higher ERP-OFDM rates. However, when an HR-DSSS (802.11b) station causes an ERP (802.11g) BSS to enable the protection mechanism, a large amount of RTS/CTS or CTS-to-self overhead is added prior to every ERP-OFDM data transmission. The aggregate data throughput loss is caused by the extra overhead and not by using slower 802.11b rates. A data rate of 54 Mbps usually will provide about 18–20 Mbps of aggregate throughput when protection is not enabled. After protection is enabled, even though the ERP STA may be transmitting frames at ERP rates, the overhead of protection will likely reduce the aggregate data throughput to below 13 Mbps and possibly as low as 9 Mbps.

Acknowledgement Frame

Since 802.11 stations are not able to transmit and receive at the same time, while a station is transmitting a frame, it is not able to determine whether the frame was received or whether there was a collision. Therefore, every time an 802.11 radio transmits a unicast frame, if the frame is received properly, the 802.11 radio that received the frame will reply with a 14-octet *acknowledgement (ACK)* frame. Figure 5.9 illustrates this frame exchange along with the NAV reservation set by the Duration value of the data frame. 802.11 is also capable of sending a single acknowledgement for multiple unicast frames. This is known as block acknowledgements and is discussed later in this chapter.

FIGURE 5.9   Data frame and acknowledgement

If the ACK is received, the original station knows that the frame transfer was successful. All unicast 802.11 frames must be acknowledged. Broadcast and multicast frames do not require an acknowledgement. If any portion of a unicast frame is corrupted, the cyclic redundancy check (CRC) will fail, and the receiving 802.11 radio will not send an ACK frame to the transmitting 802.11 radio. If an ACK frame is not received by the original transmitting radio, the unicast frame is not acknowledged and will have to be retransmitted.

This process does not specifically determine whether a collision occurs; in other words, there is no collision detection. However, if an ACK frame is not received by the original radio, there is collision assumption. Think of the ACK frame as a method of delivery verification. If no proof of delivery is provided, the original radio card assumes there was a delivery failure and retransmits the frame.

Another environment where delivery failure and retransmits may occur is when using long-distance bridges. When a frame is transmitted, because of the distance, a delay can occur in generating and receiving the ACK. By the time the ACK is received, the ACKtimeout of the transmitting station may have already expired, leading the transmitting station to believe that the frame was not received. In reality, it was just delayed. Many bridge and mesh vendors provide easy techniques to modify the ACKtimeout value to help prevent this problem from occurring.

Figure 5.10 displays the frame format for the ACK frame. The receiver address (RA) field is copied from the address 2 field of the frame that is being acknowledged.

FIGURE 5.10 ACK frame

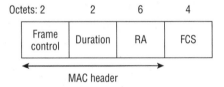

The mortal enemy of WLAN performance is layer 2 retransmissions that occur at the MAC sublayer. As you have learned, all unicast 802.11 frames must be acknowledged. If a collision occurs or any portion of a unicast frame is corrupted, the *cyclic redundancy check (CRC)* will fail, and the receiving 802.11 radio will not return an ACK frame to the transmitting 802.11 radio. If an ACK frame is not received by the original transmitting radio, the unicast frame is not acknowledged and will have to be retransmitted.

Excessive layer 2 retransmissions adversely affect the WLAN in two ways:

- Layer 2 retransmissions increase overhead and therefore decrease throughput. Many different factors can affect throughput, including a WLAN environment with abundant layer 2 retransmissions.

- If application data has to be retransmitted at layer 2, the timely delivery of application traffic becomes delayed or inconsistent.

Applications such as VoIP depend on the timely and consistent delivery of the IP packet. Excessive layer 2 retransmissions usually result in latency and jitter problems for time-sensitive applications such as voice and video. When discussing VoIP, latency and jitter often get confused. *Latency* is the time it takes to deliver a VoIP packet from the source device to the destination device. A delay in the delivery (increased latency) of a VoIP packet because of layer 2 retransmissions can result in echo problems and can even cause the VoIP connection to be dropped. *Jitter* is a variation of latency. Jitter measures how much the latency of each packet varies from the average. If all packets travel at exactly the same speed through the network, jitter will be zero. A high variance in the latency (jitter) is the more common result of 802.11 layer 2 retransmissions. Jitter will result in choppy audio communications and reduced battery life for VoWiFi phones.

Most data applications in a Wi-Fi network can handle a layer 2 retransmission rate of up to 10 percent without any noticeable degradation in performance. However, time-sensitive applications such as VoIP require that higher-layer IP packet loss be no greater than 2 percent. Therefore, Voice over Wi-Fi (VoWiFi) networks need to limit layer 2 retransmissions to 5 percent or less to guarantee the timely and consistent delivery of VoIP packets. How can you measure layer 2 retransmissions?

A good 802.11 protocol analyzer can track layer 2 retry statistics for the entire WLAN. 802.11 protocol analyzers can also track retry statistics for each individual WLAN access point and client station. Unfortunately, layer 2 retransmissions are a result of many possible problems. Multipath, RF interference, and low SNR are problems that exist at layer 1 yet result in layer 2 retransmissions. Other causes of layer 2 retransmissions include hidden node, near/far, mismatched power settings, and adjacent cell interference, which are all usually symptoms of improper WLAN design.

Block Acknowledgement Request

The 802.11e amendment introduced a *block acknowledgement (BA)* mechanism that is now also defined by the 802.11-2007 standard. A Block ACK improves channel efficiency by aggregating several acknowledgements into one single acknowledgement frame. When a station intends to use the Block ACK mechanism to transmit QoS data, it first checks to see whether the peer station is capable of performing the Block ACK mechanism. As shown in Figure 5.11, an originator station sends a block of QoS data frames to a recipient station. During this transmission, a NAV reservation is performed so that the block of frames can be sent without risk of the other stations trying to transmit. Each of the frames has the Ack Policy subfield in the QoS Control field set to Block ACK. The originator requests acknowledgement of all the outstanding QoS data frames by sending a *block acknowledgement request (BlockAckReq)* frame. Figure 5.12 shows the BlockAckReq. The RA field is the address of the recipient station, and the TA field is the address of the station transmitting the frame. The Multi-TID and Compressed Bitmap subfields determine whether this is a basic Block ACK request, a compressed Block ACK request, or a multi-TID Block ACK request.

Instead of acknowledging each unicast frame independently, the block of QoS data frames are all acknowledged by a single Block ACK.

FIGURE 5.11   Immediate block acknowledgement process

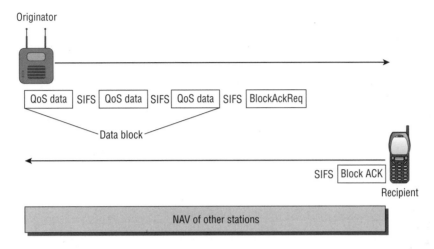

FIGURE 5.12   BlockAckReq frame

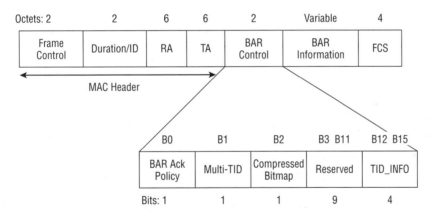

Block Acknowledgement

Figure 5.13 shows the BlockAck frame. It is used to acknowledge a block of QoS data frames, instead of acknowledging each unicast frame independently. A bitmap in the BlockAck frame is used to indicate the status of each of the received data frames. The RA field is the address of the station that requested the BlockAck frame. The TA field is the address of the station transmitting the BlockAck frame.

FIGURE 5.13   BlockAck frame

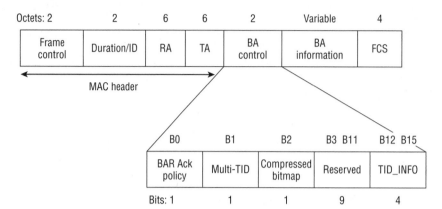

PS-Poll

When a client station is set for *Power Save mode*, it will shut down some of the transceiver components for a period of time to conserve power. The wireless card basically takes a short nap. The station indicates that it is using Power Save mode by changing the value of the Power Management bit to 1. When the station sends a frame to the AP with the Power Management bit set to 1, the access point is informed that the client station is using power management, and the access point buffers all of that client's 802.11 frames.

Any time a station associates to an access point, the station receives an association identifier (AID). The access point uses this AID to keep track of the stations that are associated and the members of the BSS. If the access point is buffering data for a station in Power Save mode, when the access point transmits its next beacon, the AID of the station will be seen in a field of the beacon frame known as the traffic indication map (TIM). The TIM field is a list of all stations that have undelivered data buffered on the access point waiting to be delivered. Every beacon will include the AID of the station until the data is delivered.

After the station notifies the access point that it is in Power Save mode, the station shuts down part of its transceiver to conserve energy. A station can be in one of two states, either awake or doze:

- During the awake state, the client station can receive frames and transmit frames.
- During the doze state, the client station cannot receive or transmit any frames and operates in a very low power state to conserve power.

Because beacons are transmitted at a consistent predetermined interval known as the *target beacon transmission time (TBTT)*, all stations know when beacons will occur. The station will remain asleep for a short period of time and awaken in time to hear a beacon frame. The station does not have to awaken for every beacon. To conserve more power, the station can sleep for a longer period of time and then awaken in time to hear an upcoming beacon. How often the client station awakens is based on a variable called the *listen interval* and is usually vendor specific.

When the station receives the beacon, it checks to see whether its AID is set in the TIM, indicating that a buffered unicast frame waits. If so, the station will remain awake and will send a 20-octect *PS-Poll frame* to the access point. When the access point receives the PS-Poll frame, it will send the buffered unicast frame to the station. The station will stay awake while the access point transmits the buffered unicast frame. When the access point sends the data to the station, the station needs to know when all the buffered unicast data has been received so that it can go back to sleep. Each unicast frame contains a 1-bit field called the More Data field. When the station receives a buffered unicast frame with the More Data field set to 1, the station knows that it cannot go back to sleep yet because there is some more buffered data that it has not yet received. When the More Data field is set to 1, the station knows that it needs to send another PS-Poll frame and wait to receive the next buffered unicast frame.

As shown in Figure 5.14, the PS-Poll frame consists of five fields. The BSSID (receiver address) is the MAC address of the AP that the client is associated with. The transmitter address (TA) is the MAC address of the station that is generating the PS-Poll frame. The AID is the association ID that was assigned to the station by the access point. In most frames, this field is actually the Duration value; however, in the PS_Poll frame, it is used to identify the ID of the station making the PS-Poll request.

FIGURE 5.14   PS-Poll frame

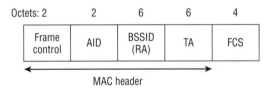

The IEEE 802.11e amendment introduced an enhanced power management method called *automatic power save delivery (APSD)*. Two APSD methods are defined: *scheduled automatic power save delivery (S-APSD)* and *unscheduled automatic power save delivery (U-APSD)*. These power management methods are discussed in Chapter 8. The Wi-Fi Alliance's *WMM Power Save (WMM-PS)* certification is based on U-APSD. WMM-PS is an enhancement over the legacy power-saving mechanisms discussed earlier in this section. The goal of WMM-PS is to have client devices spend more time in a doze state and consume less power. WMM-PS also is designed to minimize latency for time-sensitive applications such as voice during the power-management process.

The legacy power-management methods have several limitations. As pictured in Figure 5.15, a client using legacy power management must first wait for a beacon with a TIM before the client can request buffered unicast frames. The client must also send a unique PS-Poll frame to the AP to request every single buffered unicast frame. This ping-pong power-management method increases the latency of time-sensitive applications such as voice. The clients must also stay awake during the ping-pong process, which results in reduced battery life. In addition, the amount of time that the clients spend dozing is determined by the vendor's driver and not by the application traffic.

FIGURE 5.15 Legacy power management

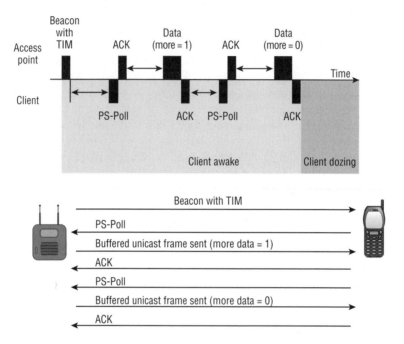

Control Wrapper

The Control Wrapper frame was defined by the 802.11n amendment, which defined high throughput (HT) transmissions. The Control Wrapper is used to carry any other control frame, other than another Control Wrapper frame, together with an additional HT Control field. Figure 5.16 shows the Control Wrapper frame. The values of the Duration/ID field, Address 1 field, and Carried Frame Control fields are copied from the corresponding fields of the carried frame and used in the Control Wrapper frame.

The Carried Frame field contains the fields that follow the Address 1 field for the control frame that is being carried, with the exception of the FCS field. The FCS files of the Control Wrapper frame is a typical FCS field containing a 32-bit CRC, calculated over all the fields of the MAC header and the frame body, in this case the Carried Frame field.

FIGURE 5.16   Control Wrapper frame format

Octets: 2   2   6   2   4   variable   4

| Frame Control | Duration/ID | Address 1 | Carried Frame Control | HT Control | Carried Frame | FCS |

Contention Free

Two additional control frames are defined by the 802.11-2007 standard: *CF-End* and *CF-End+CF-ACK*. The CF-End frame, as shown in Figure 5.17, is a 20-octet frame that is used to indicate the end of a contention-free period.

FIGURE 5.17   CF-End frame format

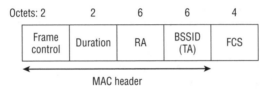

Octets: 2   2   6   6   4

| Frame control | Duration | RA | BSSID (TA) | FCS |

MAC header

The CF-End+CF-ACK frame, as shown in Figure 5.18, is also a 20-octet frame that is used to indicate the end of a contention-free period and acknowledge receipt of a frame. The CF-End+CF-ACK is structurally identical to the CF-End frame.

FIGURE 5.18   CF-End+CF-Ack frame format

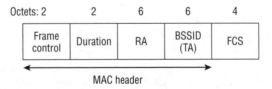

Octets: 2   2   6   6   4

| Frame control | Duration | RA | BSSID (TA) | FCS |

MAC header

Both of these control frames are defined for use with an optional medium access method known as *Point Coordination Function (PCF)*. This access method is a form of polling. The access point performs the function of the point coordinator (PC). Because an access point is taking the role of the point coordinator, the PCF medium access method will work in only a basic service set (BSS). PCF cannot be utilized in an ad hoc network because no access point exists in an independent basic service set (IBSS). Because polling is performed from a central device, PCF provides managed access to the medium.

For PCF to be used, both the access point and the station must support it. If PCF is enabled, DCF will still function. The access point will alternate between PCF mode and DCF mode. When the access point is functioning in PCF mode, it is known as the contention-free period (CFP). During the contention-free period, the access point polls only clients in PCF mode about their intention to send data. This is a method of prioritizing clients. When the access point is functioning in DCF mode, it is known as the contention period (CP).

If you want to learn more about PCF, we suggest that you read the 802.11-2007 standard document. As we stated earlier, PCF is an optional access method, and as this book is being written, we do not know of any vendor that has implemented it.

If there are no vendors that have implemented PCF, how is it possible to receive CF-End or CF-End+CF-ACK frames? Technically, it is not. However, when a packet analyzer identifies a frame, it reads the contents of the Type and Subtype fields from the frame that is received, looks them up in a table, and displays the frame description from this lookup. Wireless transmissions are subject to many outside influences, and as such, sometimes frames become corrupted between when they are transmitted and when they are received. Stations will identify corrupted frames and retransmissions should enable the communication to be success. Packet analyzers are designed to listen and report what they hear, even if what they hear is corrupt. So, if any packet analysis or network analysis software indicates that you have received a contention-free frame, what you have actually received is a corrupted frame.

Summary

In this chapter, we discussed the purpose of control frames, the different types of control frames, and the tasks that each type of control frame performed. RTS/CTS and CTS-to-self frames are used to perform NAV reservation and to provide protection mechanism in mixed-mode environments. The ACK frame is one of the most commonly transmitted frames and is used to provide delivery verification by acknowledging the successful receipt of unicast frames. Block Acknowledgement Request frames and Block Acknowledgement frames improve channel efficiency by aggregating several acknowledgements into one single acknowledgement. PS-Poll frames aid with power conservation and the delivery of buffered unicast frames. Although defined by the 802.11 standard, contention-free PCF is optional and, to our knowledge, has not been implemented by any vendors.

Exam Essentials

Know the different control frame subtypes.   Identify which frames are control frames vs. data or management frames. You should also be able to identify data and management frames; however, those frame types are covered in other chapters.

Describe carrier sense.   You should be able to describe carrier sense and virtual carrier sense. You need to know how the Duration/ID field is used to perform NAV reservation.

Explain how and why protection mechanism is performed.   Explain how, in a mixed-mode environment, RTS/CTS and CTS-to-self is used to allow different PHYs to coexist, along with how these techniques affect network performance.

Understand the use of acknowledgements and block acknowledgements.   Understand how ACKs, BlockAckReqs, and BlockAcks are used to confirm the successful receipt of unicast frames.

Understand the use of PS-Poll frames.   You should know how PS-Poll frames are used by stations that have Power Save mode enabled.

Know the different contention-free control frames.   Know the two types of contention-free control frames, along with the optional medium access method known as Point Coordination Function (PCF).

Key Terms

802.11g Protected mode

acknowledgement (ACK)

association identifier (AID)

block acknowledgement (BA)

block acknowledgement request (BlockAckReq)

carrier sense

CF-End

CF-End+CF-ACK

clear to send (CTS)

Control frames

CTS-to-self

Duration/ID field

frame subtypes

frame types

mixed-mode

network allocation vector (NAV)

physical carrier sense

Point Coordination Function (PCF)

Power Save mode

protection mechanism

PS-Poll frame

receiver address (RA)

Request to send (RTS)

transmitter address (TA)

virtual carrier sense

Review Questions

1. ACK and CTS frames follow which interframe space?
   A. EIFS
   B. DIFS
   C. PIFS
   D. SIFS
   E. LIFS

2. 802.11 collision detection is handled using which technology?
   A. Network allocation vector (NAV)
   B. Clear channel assessment (CCA)
   C. Duration/ID value
   D. Receiving an ACK from the destination station
   E. Positive collision detection cannot be determined

3. What would cause an 802.11 station to retransmit a unicast frame? (Choose all that apply.)
   A. The transmitted unicast frame was corrupted.
   B. The ACK frame from the receiver was corrupted.
   C. The receiving station was set to PCF mode.
   D. The transmitting station will attempt to retransmit the data frame.
   E. The transmitting station will send a retransmit notification.

4. A station has enabled protection mechanism and has to enable RTS/CTS to provide NAV reservation. During this process, which of the following frames are transmitted by the station? (Choose all that apply.)
   A. RTS
   B. CTS
   C. DATA
   D. SIFS
   E. ACK

5. When Power Save mode is enabled, the station uses the TBTT to determine when to awaken so that it can listen for the _____ frame, specifically looking to see whether its _____ is set in the _____ field.

   A. Data, AID, TIM

   B. Data, AID, ATIM

   C. Beacon, AID, TIM

   D. Beacon, AID, ATIM

   E. Beacon, SID, TIM

   F. Data, SID, TIM

6. While performing a packet analysis, you periodically see some CF-End frames along with some CF-End+CF-ACK frames. Why are these frames occurring? (Choose all that apply.)

   A. These are corrupted frames.

   B. You are running an IBSS network that has PCF enabled.

   C. You are running a BSS network that has DCF enabled.

   D. These are normal frames in a contention network.

7. Which of the following are protection mechanisms? (Choose all that apply.)

   A. NAV back-off

   B. RTS/CTS

   C. RTS-to-self

   D. CTS-to-self

   E. WEP encryption

8. Control frames contain which of the following components? (Choose all that apply.)

   A. Layer 2 header

   B. Layer 3 header

   C. Layer 2 trailer

   D. Layer 3 trailer

   E. Frame body

   F. Data

9. The Type and Subtype fields are used to identify the function of the frame. The Type field is _____ bits long, and the Subtype field is _____ bits long.

   A. 2, 2

   B. 2, 4

   C. 4, 4

   D. 4, 8

   E. 8, 8

10. During a packet capture, you see that the Barker_Preamble_Mode bit of the ERP information element is set to 1. What is the likely cause?

   A. All nodes support ERP.

   B. A station is not capable of using short preambles.

   C. This is a setting that was manually configured on the AP.

   D. A station is only capable of complementary code keying.

   E. This is the default setting.

11. Which field in the MAC header of an 802.11 frame resets the NAV timer for all listening 802.11 stations?

   A. NAV

   B. Frame control

   C. Duration/ID

   D. Sequence number

   E. Strictly ordered bit

12. Prior to using the Block ACK mechanism to transmit QoS data, which of the following is true? (Choose all that apply.)

   A. The station must first check to see whether the peer station is capable of performing the Block ACK mechanism.

   B. All stations are capable of performing Block ACK, so no validation is required.

   C. Notify the station of the QoS mode being used.

   D. Block ACK cannot be used with QoS data.

13. A station is operating in a mixed-mode environment and is using RTS/CTS to perform NAV distribution. Assuming that the station is not using block acknowledgements, when the station transmits the RTS frame, the Duration field will include the time necessary for which of the following to occur? (Choose all that apply.)

   A. One SIFS

   B. Two SIFS

   C. Three SIFS

   D. RTS transmission

   E. CTS transmission

   F. ACK transmission

   G. Data transmission

14. What are the two reasons that 802.11 radios use physical carrier sense? (Choose two.)

   A. Synchronize incoming transmissions

   B. Synchronize outgoing transmissions

   C. Reset the NAV

   D. Start the random back-off timer

   E. Assess the RF medium

15. The presence of what type of transmissions can trigger the protection mechanism within an ERP basic service set? (Choose all that apply.)

    A. Association of an HR-DSSS client

    B. Association of an ERP-OFDM client

    C. HR-DSSS beacon frame

    D. ERP beacon frame with the NonERP Present bit set to 1

    E. Association of an FHSS client

16. Which of the following frames will receive an acknowledgment if the transmission is successful? (Choose all that apply.)

    A. Simulcast frames

    B. Multicast frames

    C. Broadcast frames

    D. Unicast frames

17. While performing a packet analysis, after the data transfer is complete, you notice that you captured three data frames and two ACKs. Which of the following can explain this capture? (Choose all that apply.)

    A. One of the ACKs is providing a block acknowledgment for two data frames.

    B. One of the frames was not received properly, so there was no ACK.

    C. All frames were received properly; however, for some reason the packet analyzer did not hear the third ACK.

    D. There is not enough information to explain this occurrence.

    E. This is a normal packet capture.

18. A station is participating in a mixed-mode network and wants to transmit data. The station is configured to use CTS-to-self as its protection mechanism. Which of the following frames are transmitted by the station? (Choose all that apply.)

    A. RTS

    B. CTS

    C. Data

    D. ACK

    E. SIFs

19. ACKs are required for which of the following frames?

    A. Unicast

    B. Broadcast

    C. Multicast

    D. Simulcast

20. During a basic RTS/CTS transmission, when a station sends. an RTS, the Duration/ID field notifies the other stations that they must set their NAV timers to which of the following values?

A. 213 microseconds

B. The time necessary to transmit the DATA and ACK frames, along with one SIFS

C. The time necessary to transmit the CTS frame

D. The time necessary to transmit the CTS, DATA, and ACK frames, along with three SIFS

Answers to Review Questions

1. D. ACK frames and CTS frames may follow a SIFS. LIFS do not exist.

2. E. 802.11 technology does not use collision detection. If an ACK frame is not received by the original transmitting radio, the unicast frame is not acknowledged and will have to be retransmitted. This process does not specifically determine whether a collision occurs. Failure to receive an ACK frame from the receiver means that either a unicast frame was not received by the destination station or the ACK frame was not received, but it cannot positively determine the cause. It may be because of collision or other reasons such as a high noise level. All of the other options are used to help avoid collisions.

3. A, B. The receiving station may have received the data, but the returning ACK frame may have become corrupted, and the original unicast frame will have to be retransmitted. If the unicast frame becomes corrupted for any reason, the receiving station will not send an ACK.

4. A, C. During the RTS/CTS process, the transmitting station will first transmit the RTS. After a SIFS, the intended recipient of the frame will transmit a CTS. After another SIFS, the station will transmit the data frame, and then following another SIFS, the intended recipient will transmit an ACK if the frame was received correctly.

5. C. When Power Save mode is enabled, the station uses the Target Beacon Transmission Time along with the Beacon frame's time stamp to know when to awaken prior to the transmission of a Beacon. If the AP has cached frames for the station, it will notify the station by indicating the station's Association ID (AID) in the Traffic Indication Map (TIM) field.

6. A. Contention-free (CF) frames occur if a Point Coordination Function (PCF) network is configured; however, to our knowledge, no manufacturers have implemented PCF. If PCF were implemented, it would require an AP to operate as the point coordinator, so PCF could not operate on an IBSS or ad hoc network. Since no manufacturers have implemented PCF, the only way these frames could be displaying in the packet analyzer is if other frames are corrupted and are being misidentified as PCF frames.

7. B, D. RTS/CTS and CTS-to-Self provide 802.11g protection mechanisms, sometimes referred to as mixed-mode support. NAV back-off and RTS-to-Self do not exist. WEP encryption provides data security.

8. A, C. Unlike management and data frames, control frames contain only a layer 2 header and trailer.

9. B. In any frame, the Type field is 2 bits long and identifies whether the frame is a data frame, management frame, or control frame. The Subtype field is 4 bits long.

10. B, C. If one or more associated NonERP stations are not capable of using short preambles, then the Barker_Preamble_Mode bit is set to 1. This is a setting that can also be manually set on many access points.

11. C. When the listening radio hears a frame transmission from another station, it looks at the header of the frame and determines whether the Duration/ID field contains a Duration value or an ID value. If the field contains a Duration value, the listening station will set its NAV timer to this value.

12. A, D. When a station intends to use the Block ACK mechanism, it must first check to see whether the peer station is capable of performing the Block ACK mechanism.

13. C, E, F, G. When RTS/CTS is enabled, the RTS frame performs a NAV distribution by setting its Duration field to the time it will take for the following to occur, in this order: SIFS, CTS transmission, SIFS, Data transmission, SIFS, ACK transmission.

14. A, E. The first purpose is to determine whether a frame transmission is inbound for a station to receive. If the medium is busy, the radio will attempt to synchronize with the transmission. The second purpose is to determine whether the medium is busy before transmitting. This is known as the clear channel assessment (CCA). The CCA involves listening for 802.11 RF transmissions at the Physical layer. The medium must be clear before a station can transmit.

15. A, C, D. An ERP access point signals for the use of the protection mechanism in the ERP information element in the beacon frame. Three scenarios can trigger protection in an ERP basic service set. If a non-ERP STA associates to an ERP AP, the ERP AP will enable the NonERP_Present bit in its own beacons, enabling protection mechanisms in its BSS. In other words, an HR-DSSS (802.11b) client association will trigger protection. If an ERP AP hears a beacon with an 802.11b or 802.11 supported rate set from another AP or an IBSS STA, it will enable the NonERP_Present bit in its own beacons, enabling protection mechanisms in its BSS. If an ERP AP hears a beacon from another ERP access point with the NonERP_Present bit set to 1, it also will enable protection mechanisms in its BSS.

16. D. Only Unicast frames will be acknowledged.

17. B, C. Every data frame needs to receive an ACK to acknowledge that the data was received properly. Since there are three data frames, there should be three ACKs. One possible reason is the one of these data frames was not successfully received by the intended recipient; therefore, there is no ACK. The other possible reason is that all of the data frames were successfully received and acknowledged. However, the station that was performing the packet analysis did not hear one of the ACKs.

18. B, C. When CTS-to-self is enabled, the transmitting station will transmit a CTS, wait for a SIFS, and then transmit the data frame. If the frame is received correctly, after another SIFS, the receiving station will transmit an ACK.

19. A. All unicast 802.11 frames must be acknowledged. Broadcast and multicast frames do not require an acknowledgement. Simulcast frames do not exist.

20. D. When the RTS frame is sent, the value of the Duration/ID field is equal to the time necessary for the CTS, DATA, and ACK frames to be transmitted, along with a SIFS before each of these frames.

Chapter

6

Data Frames

IN THIS CHAPTER, YOU WILL LEARN ABOUT THE FOLLOWING:

- ✓ **Data Subtypes**

- ✓ **QoS and Non-QoS Data Frames**

- ✓ **Data-carrying versus non-data-carrying frames**

- ✓ **Simple data frames**

- ✓ **Data frame address fields**

- ✓ **Fragmentation**

- ✓ **Data frame aggregation**

- ✓ **Rate Selection**

  - ▪ Multirate support

  - ▪ Basic rates

  - ▪ Dynamic rate selection

In this chapter, we will take a detailed look at the different data frames and discuss the purpose of each frame. Data frames transport the information across the network in the wireless portion of the user network.

Data Subtypes

The 802.11 standard defines 15 different data frames, as displayed in Table 6.1. Each *data frame* is represented by a *Type* value of 10 and a different group of 4 *Subtype* bits. These Type and Subtype fields are part of the Frame Control field (Figure 6.1). The 15 different combinations of Subtype fields are displayed in the type description column of Table 6.1. The basic data frame is represented by a Subtype of 0 (bits b7–b4 = 0000). By changing any of these Subtype bits, a modification is made to the basic data frame. Most people are not aware that there is actually a pattern or system to the Subtype bits, with each of the individual bits having a specific meaning. By changing bit 4 (b4) from a 0 to a 1, the data subtype includes +CF-Ack. Changing bit 5 (b5) from a 0 to a 1 will include +CF-Poll. Changing bit 6 (b6) from a 0 to a 1 will indicate that the frame contains no data, specifically, that it contains no Frame Body field. The most significant bit (MSB) of the Subtype field (bit b7) is defined as the quality of service (QoS) subfield, specifying that the frame is a QoS data frame. This pattern or system applies to all subtypes except for 1101, which is Reserved.

TABLE 6.1 Data frames: valid Type and Subtype combinations

Type value b3 b2	Type description	Subtype value b7 b6 b5 b4	Subtype description
10	Data	0000	Data
10	Data	0001	Data + CF-Ack [PCF only]
10	Data	0010	Data + CF-Poll [PCF only]
10	Data	0011	Data + CF-Ack + CF-Poll [PCF only]
10	Data	0100	Null (no data)

TABLE 6.1   Data frames: valid Type and Subtype combinations *(continued)*

Type value b3 b2	Type description	Subtype value b7 b6 b5 b4	Subtype description
10	Data	0101	CF-Ack (no data) [PCF only]
10	Data	0110	CF-Poll (no data) [PCF only]
10	Data	0111	CF-Ack + CF-Poll (no data) [PCF only]
10	Data	1000	QoS Data [HCF]
10	Data	1001	QoS Data + CF-Ack [HCF]
10	Data	1010	QoS Data + CF-Poll [HCF]
10	Data	1011	QoS Data + CF-Ack + CF-Poll [HCF]
10	Data	1100	QoS Null (no data) [HCF]
10	Data	1101	Reserved
10	Data	1110	QoS CF-Poll (no data) [HCF]
10	Data	1111	QoS CF-Ack + CF-Poll (no data) [HCF]

FIGURE 6.1   Frame Control field

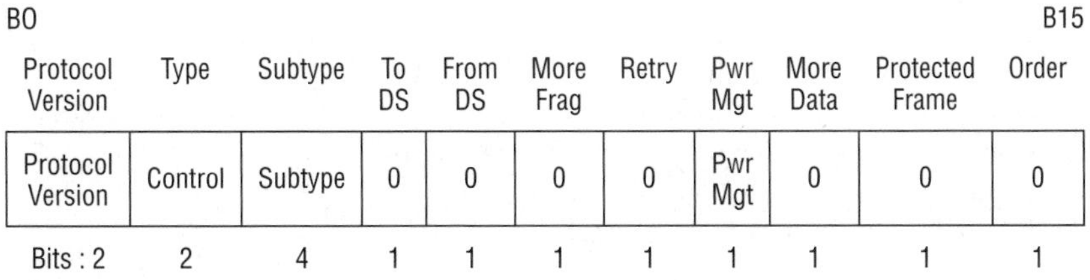

Protocol Version	Type	Subtype	To DS	From DS	More Frag	Retry	Pwr Mgt	More Data	Protected Frame	Order
Protocol Version	Control	Subtype	0	0	0	0	Pwr Mgt	0	0	0
Bits: 2	2	4	1	1	1	1	1	1	1	1

B0 ... B15

QoS and Non-QoS Data Frames

Quality of service stations are capable of transmitting both QoS and non-QoS data frames. It is not uncommon to have a wireless network that consists of both QoS and non-QoS stations. In this type of mixed environment, it is likely that QoS devices will transmit both QoS data frames and non-QoS data frames depending upon the capabilities of the receiving station. When a QoS data frame is transmitted, the QoS subfield (the b7 bit) contains a value of 1, and the frame contains a QoS Control field in the MAC header, as shown in Figure 6.2. When a non-QoS data frame is transmitted, the QoS subfield (the b7 bit) contains a value of 0, and the QoS Control field is not present in the MAC header.

FIGURE 6.2 Data Frame format

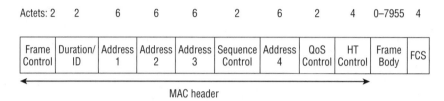

This paragraph will explain when QoS and non-QoS data frames are transmitted in a QoS mixed environment (Table 6.2 provides a summary). When a QoS station transmits to another QoS station, a QoS data frame is used, since both devices are capable of understanding the frame format. Whenever a non-QoS device is involved in the communication, either as the transmitting or as the receiving station, a non-QoS data frame must be used. Broadcast frames are transmitted by default as non-QoS frames, unless the transmitting station knows that all the stations in the *basic service set* (BSS) are QoS capable, in which case the broadcast frame will be a QoS frame. Like the broadcast frames, multicast frames are transmitted by default as non-QoS frames, unless the transmitting station knows that all the stations in the basic service set that are members of the multicast group are QoS capable, in which case the multicast frame will be a QoS frame.

TABLE 6.2 QoS and non-QoS transmissions

Transmitting station	Receiving station	Data frame subtype used
Non-QoS station	Non-QoS station	Non-QoS frame
Non-QoS station	QoS station	Non-QoS frame
QoS station	QoS station	QoS frame
QoS station	Non-QoS station	Non-QoS frame
All	Broadcast	Non-QoS frame, unless the transmitting station knows that all stations in the BSS are QoS capable, in which case a QoS frame would be used
All	Multicast	Non-QoS frame, unless the transmitting station knows that all stations in the BSS that are members of the multicast group are QoS capable, in which case a QoS frame would be used

Data-Carrying vs. Non-Data-Carrying Frames

As strange as it may sound, some data frames do not actually carry any data. In fact, almost half of the data frames defined do not carry any data. The frames that do carry data are as follows:

- Data (simple data frame)
- Data + CF-Ack
- Data + CF-Poll
- Data + CF-Ack + CF-Poll
- QoS Data
- QoS Data + CF-Ack
- QoS Data + CF-Poll
- QoS Data + CF-Ack + CF-Poll

And the frames that do not carry any data are as follows:

- Null
- CF-Ack
- CF-Poll
- CF-Ack + CF-Poll
- Qos Null
- QoS CF-Poll
- QoS CF-Ack + CF-Poll

So, why have a data frame that does not carry data? Sometimes a station needs to transmit special control information to an access point or another station, without actually transmitting any data. Client stations sometimes use Null data frames to enable or disable power save mode, which is indicated by a bit in the frame control field. Using the Null data frame allows a station to communicate with another device without requiring it to transmit data.

Simple Data Frame

Most 802.11 data frames that are transmitted carry actual data that is passed down from the higher-layer protocols. The data subtype, often referred to as the *simple data frame*, is the most commonly transmitted data frame. The simple data frame has MSDU upper-layer information encapsulated in the frame body. When the simple data frame is received by an autonomous AP or WLAN controller, the MSDU payload of the simple data frame is transferred into an 802.3 Ethernet frame (this is assuming that Ethernet is the networking platform used by the distribution system).

Data Frame Address Fields

If you refer to the format of the 802.11 data frame (Figure 6.2), you will see that the 802.11 data frame defines four address fields, named Address 1, Address 2, Address 3, and Address 4. If you are familiar with 802.3, where data frames simply contain a source address and a destination address, having four address fields is likely new territory for you. Even though the 802.11 data frame defines four address fields, in most instances only three of the address fields are used to represent four addresses, and the fourth address is simply omitted from the frame. Do not worry—it is not as bad as it seems.

The first step to understanding the addressing scheme of an 802.11 frame is to identify the logical addresses that are used. The following are the five addresses that are potentially used in a data frame:

Source Address (SA)   This is the address where the frame is sent from.

Destination Address (DA)   This is the address where the frame is being sent to.

Transmitter Address (TA)   This is the address of the station that is transmitting the RF frame.

Receiver Address (RA)   This is the address of the station that is receiving the RF frame.

Basic Service Set Identifier (BSSID)   This is the basic service set ID of the AP.

Now we will look at a scenario. In Figure 6.3, there are two stations and two access points. Ultimately, STA1 wants to send data to STA2. STA1 and AP1 form a basic service set known as BSS1. STA2 and AP1 form a BSS known as BSS2. AP1 and AP2 can bridge data between the two BSSs using a wireless distribution system (WDS). For STA1 to send data to STA2, the following three steps occur:

1. STA1 must send the frame to AP1.

2. AP1 must forward that frame to AP2.

3. AP2 must forward that frame to STA2.

FIGURE 6.3   802.11 addressing example

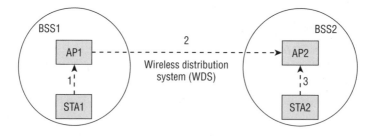

At this stage, we will now identify the addressing of each of these transmissions (as you read through the steps, look at Table 6.3 to see the addressing):

1. In the first transmission, STA1 is the source of the data (SA), and STA2 is the destination of the data (DA). STA1 must transmit the data (TA) to its access point, AP1 (RA).

   Notice that STA1 is both the SA and the TA, which means that we actually have only three unique addresses, therefore only requiring three address fields.

2. In the second transmission, STA1 is still the source of the data (SA), and STA2 is still the destination (DA). In this transmission, AP1 is transmitting the frame (TA) to AP2, which is receiving the frame (RA).

   In this instance, there are four unique addresses, so all four address fields will be used.

3. In the third transmission, STA1 is still the source of the data (SA), and STA2 is still the destination (DA). In this transmission, AP2 is transmitting the frame (TA) to STA2, which is receiving the frame (RA).

   Notice again that in this instance, STA2 is both the DA and the RA, which again means that we have only three unique addresses and will require three address fields.

TABLE 6.3   802.11 addressing

Step #	SA	DA	TA	RA	To DS	From DS
1	STA1	STA2	STA1	AP1	1	0
2	STA1	STA2	AP1	AP2	1	1
3	STA1	STA2	AP2	STA2	0	1

In Table 6.3 there are two columns that have not been discussed yet, the *To DS* and *From DS* columns. These are two 1-bit fields that are part of the Frame Control field. These subfields represent whether the frame is going to or from the distribution system. In the first step, the frame is going from the station to the DS, so the bits are 10. In the second step, the frame is going to and from the DS, so the bits are 11. In the last step, the frame is going from the DS to the stations, so the bits are 01. Although not discussed here, in an IBSS (ad hoc) network, since there is no DS, the bits would be 00.

Ideally you now have a better understanding of addressing. Figure 6.4 shows the exact address contents as defined in the 802.11n-2009 amendment to the 802.11-2007 standard. Address 1 is always the RA, and Address 2 is always the TA. The only time the fourth address field is used is when the To DS and From DS bits are both 1. If the frame contains an aggregate MAC service data unit (A-MSDU), then Address 3 and Address 4 (if used) are set to the BSSID address.

FIGURE 6.4   Address field contents and usage

To DS	From DS	Address 1	Address 2	Address 3		Address 4	
				MSDU case	A-MSDU case	MSDU case	A-MSDU case
0	0	RA = DA	TA = SA	BSSID	BSSID	N/A	N/A
0	1	RA = DA	TA = BSSID	SA	BSSID	N/A	N/A
1	0	RA = BSSID	TA = SA	DA	BSSID	N/A	N/A
1	1	RA	TA	DA	BSSID	SA	BSSID

Addressing and Packet Analyzers

As technology gets more complex, it is difficult to remember all the components in a wireless network. Fortunately, packet analyzers help you so that you do not have to remember everything. When a packet analyzer captures a frame, it processes the frame, converts the addressing information, and displays it not as the address fields but as the logical address. Packet analyzers cannot tell you everything about a frame but can simplify some of the information.

Fragmentation

The 802.11-2007 standard allows for the fragmentation of unicast addressed frames. *Fragmentation* breaks an 802.11 frame into smaller pieces known as *fragments*, adds header information to each fragment, and transmits each fragment individually. Figure 6.5 shows an MSDU that has been fragmented into four fragments. Although the same amount of actual data is being transmitted, each fragment requires its own header, and the transmission of each fragment is followed by a SIFS and an ACK. In a properly functioning 802.11 network, smaller fragments will actually decrease data throughput because of the MAC sublayer overhead of the additional header, SIFS, and ACK of each fragment. On the other hand, if the network is experiencing a large amount of data corruption, lowering the 802.11 fragmentation setting may improve data throughput.

If an 802.11 frame is corrupted and needs to be retransmitted, the entire frame must be sent again. When the 802.11 frame is broken into multiple fragments, each fragment is smaller and transmits for a shorter period. If interference occurs, instead of an entire large frame becoming corrupted, it is likely that only one of the small fragments will become corrupted, and therefore only this one fragment will need to be retransmitted. Retransmitting the small fragment will take much less time than retransmitting the larger frame. If fragmentation is implemented, retransmission overhead may be reduced.

FIGURE 6.5   Fragmentation of an MSDU

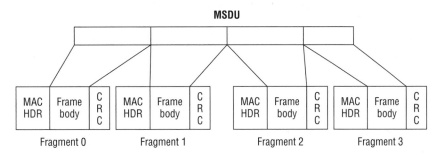

Each fragment is transmitted and acknowledged individually. This provides the ability to transmit a small fragment as opposed to the entire MSDU or MMPDU. Unless they are interrupted because of medium occupancy limitations, the fragments of a single MSDU or MMPDU are transmitted as a sequential burst, allowing the receiving station adequate time after each fragment to transmit the corresponding acknowledgment before transmitting the next fragment.

For the MSDU or MMPDU fragments to be reassembled, the header must contain the following information:

- Frame type

- Address of the sender (obtained from the Address 2 field)

- Destination address

- Sequence Control field: The 12-bit sequence number remains the same for all fragments from the same MSDU or MMPDU, while the 4 bit fragment number within this field is incremented for each individual fragment.

- More Fragments indicator: This is a subfield of the Frame Control field and is set to 0 for the last fragment, indicating that there are no more fragments. For all other fragments, this field is set to 1.

Figure 6.6 illustrates how smaller fragments can reduce retransmission overhead. (Please note that this is a representation and not drawn to scale. Additionally, to simplify the illustration, ACKs were not included.) This illustration shows the transmission and retransmission of a large 1,500-byte frame above and the transmission and the retransmission of smaller 500-byte fragments below. If there was no RF interference, only the solid-lined rectangles would need to be transmitted. Because of the additional headers (H) and the time between the fragments for each SIFS and ACK, the smaller fragments would take longer to transmit. However, if RF interference occurred, it would take less time to retransmit the smaller fragment than it would to retransmit the larger frame.

FIGURE 6.6   Frame fragmentation

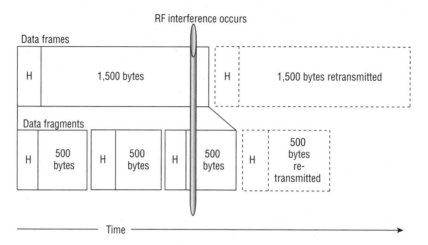

Not all wireless LAN adapters allow you to adjust the fragmentation settings. If you do set your wireless LAN adapter to use a smaller fragment size, you must realize that as you roam between access points and as you move between networks, all of your 802.11 frames will be fragmented using the setting you have configured. This means that if you roam to a location where there is no interference, your station will still be using the smaller frame fragments and will actually perform worse than if you had left the fragmentation value at its largest setting.

Will fragmentation increase throughput? Fragmentation may reduce retransmission overhead in an environment with a lot of data corruption. However, fragmentation always introduces more MAC sublayer overhead to the network. Usually, if fragmentation is used within a BSS, the additional MAC overhead will cause the network throughput to decrease. In some rare cases, the fragmentation threshold settings on an access point may be tweaked to improve throughput by reducing retransmission overhead caused by data corruption. Fragmentation is usually a temporary fix, and the better solution is to find the cause of the data corruption and permanently fix the problem.

Data Frame Aggregation

With the ratification of the 802.11n amendment, two types of *frame aggregation* were added to 802.11, *aggregate MAC service data unit (A-MSDU)* and *aggregate MAC protocol data unit (A-MPDU)*. When a frame of data is transmitted, no matter how big or small the data is, each frame requires a certain amount of overhead to transmit that frame, such as header information, acknowledgments, and interframe spacing. Whether the frame is a big or small frame, the overhead is a necessary part of transmitting that frame. Frame aggregation allows multiple smaller MSDUs or MPDUs to be grouped together into a single frame, reducing the amount of overhead that would have been necessary for each individual frame. As an example, if you needed to rent a truck to move three armoires from one location to another, it would be more efficient to use a single truck that was capable of transporting all three armoires instead of three trucks that are each capable of transporting only one. As shown in Figure 6.7, the difference between the sizes of the trucks is the cargo area needed to hold the armoires. Of course, there is a practical size limit, since it is not likely that we could build or rent a truck that was capable of carrying 100 armoires, and if we did, it would probably be too long to be able to turn around a corner or even a slight bend in the road. Just as using a single truck is more efficient and faster to transport your armoires, using a single frame is more efficient and faster to transmit your wireless data.

FIGURE 6.7 Efficiency of aggregation

A-MSDU is an aggregation process that combines multiple MSDUs within a single MPDU, as shown in Figure 6.8. The network layer passes the MSDUs down to the MAC layer. Normally at this point each MSDU would be packaged with its own MPDU. With A-MSDU, two or more MSDUs are placed in an MPDU, and a single MAC and PHY layer header is added to the group of MSDUs. If encryption is enabled, then all the MSDUs are encrypted together as a single payload. There are some restrictions for aggregating multiple MSDUs into a single MPDU. The MPDU can only contain MSDUs where the DA and SA values map to the same RA and TA values. All of the MSDUs must also have the same priority value.

FIGURE 6.8 A-MSDU frame aggregation

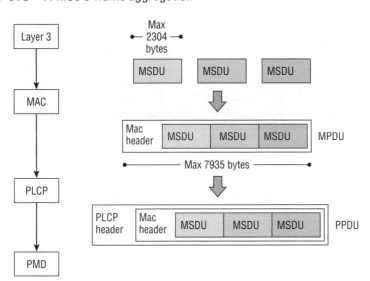

A-MPDU is an aggregation process that combines multiple MPDUs within a single PPDU (see Figure 6.9). The network layer passes the MSDUs down to the MAC layer, where an MPDU is created for each MSDU. If encryption is enabled, then each MPDU is encrypted individually. The MPDUs are then passed down to the PLCP sublayer where two or more MPDUs are placed in a single PPDU. The individual MPDUs within an A-MPDU must all have the same receiver address. Also, the individual MPDUs must all be of the same 802.11e QoS access category. A-MPDU also requires the use of block acknowledgments.

FIGURE 6.9 A-MPDU frame aggregation

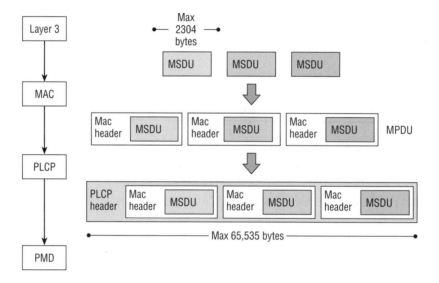

Rate Selection

One of the key objectives of wireless communications is to transmit information or data accurately and quickly. This is especially true in a multinode environment, such as in an 802.11 network. In this section, we will describe some of the different methods that 802.11 uses to perform rate selection.

Multirate Support

Since 1997, when 802.11 was originally introduced, multiple data rates have been supported. Each new PHY has provided faster speeds along with a larger selection of data rates. Multiple data rates provide 802.11 stations with the ability to communicate at the highest possible speed, dependent upon the current RF conditions. Every wireless adapter has defined minimum received signal and minimum SNR levels. Some vendors release tables or charts that display these values, as shown in Table 6.4, while other vendors release just a few of the values, as shown in the following list of receiver sensitivity values released by a vendor:

300 Mbps: -68 dBm, 54 Mbps: -74 dBm, 6 Mbps: -90 dBm

TABLE 6.4   WLAN data cell: vendor recommendations

Data rate	Minimum received signal	Minimum signal-to-noise ratio
54 Mbps	–71 dBm	25 dB
36 Mbps	–73 dBm	18 dB
24 Mbps	–77 dBm	12 dB
12/11 Mbps	–82 dBm	10 dB
6/5.5 Mbps	–89 dBm	8 dB
2 Mbps	–91 dBm	6 dB
1 Mbps	–94 dBm	4 dB

Basic and Supported Rates

As you learned in earlier chapters, the 802.11-2007 standard defines supported rates for various RF technologies. For example, HR-DSSS (clause 18) radios are capable of supporting data rates of 1, 2, 5.5, and 11 Mbps. ERP (clause 19) radios are capable of supporting the HR-DSSS data rates but are also capable of supporting ERP-OFDM rates of 6, 9, 12, 18, 24, 36, 48, and 54 Mbps.

On any autonomous AP or WLAN controller, specific data rates can be configured as required rates. The 802.11-2007 standard defines required rates as *basic rates*. For a client station to successfully associate with an AP, the station must be capable of communicating by using the configured basic rates that the access point requires.

In addition to the basic rates, the access point defines a set of *supported rates*. This set of supported rates is advertised by the access point in the beacon frame and is also in some of the other management frames. The supported rates are the group data rates that the access point will use when communicating with a station. After a station associates with an access point, it will use one of the advertised supported rates to communicate with the access point.

Dynamic Rate Selection

As client station radios move away from an access point, they will shift down to lower-bandwidth capabilities by using a process known as *dynamic rate switching (DRS)*. Access points can support multiple data rates depending on the spread spectrum technology used by the AP's radio card. For example, an HR-DSSS (802.11b) radio supports data rates of 11, 5.5, 2, and 1 Mbps. Data rate transmissions between the access point and the client stations will shift down or up depending on the quality of the signal between the two radio cards, as pictured in Figure 6.10. There is a correlation between signal quality and distance from the AP. As a result, transmissions between two 802.11b radio cards may be at 11 Mbps at 30 feet but at 2 Mbps at 150 feet.

FIGURE 6.10   Dynamic rate switching

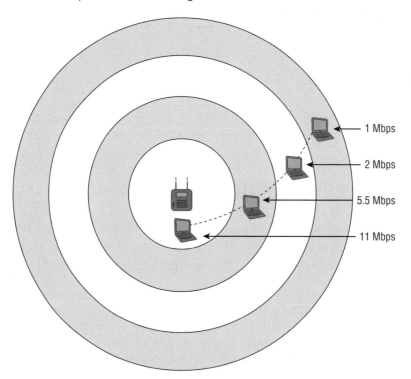

DRS is also referred to as *dynamic rate shifting*, *adaptive rate selection*, and *automatic rate selection*. All these terms refer to a method of speed fallback on a wireless LAN client as signal quality from the access point decreases. The objective of DRS is upshifting and downshifting for rate optimization and improved performance. Effectively, the lower data rates will have larger concentric zones of coverage than the higher data rates, as pictured in Figure 6.11.

The algorithms used for dynamic rate switching are proprietary and are defined by radio card manufacturers. Most vendors base DRS on receive signal strength indicator (RSSI) thresholds, packet error rates, and retransmissions. RSSI metrics are usually based on signal strength and signal quality. In other words, a station might shift up or down between data rates based both on received signal strength in dBm and possibly on a signal-to-noise ratio (SNR) value. Because vendors implement DRS differently, you may have two different vendor client cards at the same location, while one is communicating with the access point at 11 Mbps and the other is communicating at 2 Mbps. For example, one vendor might shift down from data rate 11 Mbps to 5 Mbps at –70 dBm while another vendor might shift between the same two rates at –75 dBm. Keep in mind that DRS works with all 802.11 PHYs. For example, the same shifting of rates will also occur with 802.11n radios shifting between 130, 117, 104, 78, 52, 39, 26, and 13 Mbps data rates. As a result, there is a correlation between signal quality and distance from the AP.

FIGURE 6.11   Data rate coverage zones

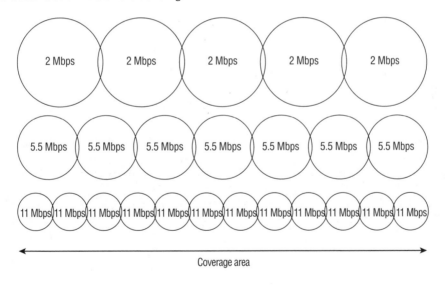

Summary

In this chapter, we discussed the different types, actually subtypes, of data frames. Data frames subtypes include QoS and non-QoS data frames, data-carrying and non-data-carrying frames, and simple data frames. We explained when and how the four different address fields are used. Data frame fragmentation and aggregation were explained. We reviewed the support for multiple communication rates and how they are chosen using dynamic rate selection, along with basic and supported rates. PCF and contention-free communications were briefly reviewed.

Exam Essentials

Know the different data frame subtypes.   Identify which frames are data frames vs. control or management frames. You should also be able to identify control and management frames; however, those frame types are covered in other chapters.

Describe fragmentation.   Describe fragmentation, why it is used, and how it is used, along with its benefits. Describe how fragment burst is performed.

Understand what data frame subtypes are used for the transmission of QoS and non-QoS data frames.   QoS capable and non-QoS capable devices will transmit different types of data frames depending upon the capability of the device they are communicating with. Understand when QoS and non-QoS data frames are used.

Know which data frame subtypes carry data and which do not.   There are 15 different data frame subtypes, 8 of which carry data and 7 of which do not. Know the different subtypes and whether they carry data.

Explain the different data frame address fields.   Explain the functions of the four address fields. Know the contents of each of the address fields based upon the four different To DS and From DS scenarios. Be able to look at the To DS and From DS fields and identify where the frame is coming from and going to.

Explain the two types of data frame aggregation.   Explain what data frame aggregation is. Know the differences between A-MSDU and A-MPDU.

Understand data rates.   802.11 supports many different transmission rates. Know the difference between basic rates and supported rates. Understand why different rates are used, and explain the difference between general and functional policies.

Key Terms

adaptive rate selection

aggregate MAC protocol data unit
(A-MPDU)

aggregate MAC service data unit (A-MSDU)

automatic rate selection

basic rates

contention free (CF)

contention-free period (CFP)

DA (Destination Address)

data frame

dynamic rate shifting

dynamic rate switching (DRS)

frame aggregation

From DS

Point Coordination Function (PCF)

point coordinator (PC)

Quality of service (QoS)

RA (Receiver Address)

SA (Source Address)

simple data frame

Subtype

supported rates

TA (Transmitter Address)

To DS

Type

Review Questions

1. In the data subtype field, by changing the bits b7–b4 from a binary 0 to a binary 1, which of the following will be added to the basic data frame? (Choose all that apply.)

   A. +CF-Ack

   B. (no data)

   C. +CF-Poll

   D. +ToS

   E. QoS

2. When a station transmits a multicast frame, what type of data frame subtype is used?

   A. Non-QoS frame always

   B. QoS frame always

   C. Non-Qos frame unless the transmitting station knows that all stations in the BSS are QoS capable, in which case a QoS frame would be used

   D. Two multicast frames are transmitted, one QoS and one non-QoS

   E. QoS frame unless the transmitting station knows that all stations in the BSS that are members of the multicast group are QoS capable, in which case a QoS Frame would be used.

3. Which of the following data frames carry data?

   A. Data

   B. CF-Ack

   C. CF-Ack + CF-Poll

   D. QoS Null

   E. QoS CF-Ack + CF-Poll

4. When transmitting a data frame, the values of the To DS and From DS fields designate the contents of the address fields. During a packet capture of a wireless bridge, what are the values of these fields?

   A. To DS = 0, From DS = 0

   B. To DS = 0, From DS = 1

   C. To DS = 1, From DS = 0

   D. To DS = 1, From DS = 1

   E. Not enough information to determine the values

5. When looking at a packet capture, which of the following address field statements is false?

   A. The receiver address is always Address 1.

   B. The transmission address is always Address 2.

   C. Address 3 is always the BSSID when the frame is an A-MSDU frame.

   D. Address 4 is the source address when both the To DS and From DS fields are 1.

   E. The source address is always Address 4.

6. Frame aggregation allows multiple smaller pieces of data to be grouped together into a single frame, reducing the amount of overhead. With the 802.11n amendment, two types of frame aggregation were added. What are the two types? (Choose all that apply.)

   A. A-PPDU

   B. A-PLCP

   C. A-MSDU

   D. A-MPDU

   E. A-MMDU

7. When A-MSDU is used to aggregate frames, which of the following is true about encryption?

   A. All of the MSDUs are encrypted together as a single payload.

   B. All of the MPDUs are encrypted together as a single payload.

   C. The MSDUs are encrypted individually, prior to aggregation.

   D. The MPDUs are encrypted individually, prior to aggregation.

   E. A-MSDU does not affect the encryption process.

8. A 2.4 GHz access point is configured with basic rates of 5.5 and 11 Mbps. Which of the following stations could connect to this AP? (Choose all that apply.)

   A. 802.11 station

   B. 802.11b station

   C. 802.11g station

   D. 802.11a station

   E. 802.11n station

9. When referring strictly to the Point Coordination Function (PCF) media access method, which of the following terms do not apply? (Choose all that apply.)

   A. Polling

   B. Contention-free period (CFP)

   C. Contention free (CF)

   D. CSMA/CD

10. A-MSDU is being used for frame aggregation. Which of the following statements is true for this process? (Choose all that apply.)

    A. Two or more MSDUs are placed in an MPDU.

    B. The MPDU can only contain MSDUs that have DA and SA values that map to the same RA and TA values.

    C. If encryption is enabled, the MSDUs are encrypted together as a single payload.

    D. A single MAC and PHY layer header is added to the group of MSDUs.

    E. The MSDUs can have different priority values.

11. Which of the following statements is false regarding quality of service (QoS) stations?

    A. When a QoS data frame is transmitted, the frame contains a QoS Control field in the MAC header.

    B. When a non-QoS data frame is transmitted, the QoS Control field in the MAC header is empty.

    C. When a QoS data frame is transmitted, the QoS subfield contains a value of 1.

    D. QoS stations are capable of transmitting both QoS and non-QoS data frames.

    E. It is likely that QoS devices will transmit both QoS and non-QoS data frames in a mixed environment.

12. A wireless 802.11g adapter supports multiple data rates, with the manufacturer specifications showing a minimum received signal of -73 dBm for the 36 Mbps data rate and a minimum signal-to-noise ratio of 18 dB. For the 54 Mbps data rate, which of the following are likely values? (Choose all that apply.)

    A. -71 dBm minimum received signal

    B. -77 dBm minimum received signal

    C. 12 dB minimum signal-to-noise ratio

    D. 25 dB minimum signal-to-noise ratio

13. Which of the following are other terms used for dynamic rate selection? (Choose all that apply.)

    A. Dynamic rate shifting

    B. Fast rate selection

    C. Adaptive rate selection

    D. Automatic rate selection

14. During the packet capture of a frame from an AP to a station, which of the following statements about the frame header are true if the frame payload originated from a wired-side server? (Choose all that apply.)

    A. To DS = 1, From DS = 0

    B. Address 1 = RA = DA

    C. Address 2 = TA = BSSID

    D. Address 3 = SA

    E. Address 4 = BSSID

15. Which of the following is true regarding dynamic rate switching? (Choose all that apply.)

    A. The algorithms used are proprietary and defined by the radio card manufacturers.

    B. The 802.11 standard defines limits for when to switch between different rates.

    C. Most vendors base switching upon RSSI thresholds, packet error rates, and retransmissions.

    D. Strict adherence to the 802.11 rate selection algorithms provides consistent roaming across devices.

16. A-MSDU is being used for frame aggregation. Which of the following statements is true for this process? (Choose all that apply.)

    A. Two or more MPDUs are placed in a single PPDU.

    B. An MPDU is created for each MSDU.

    C. If encryption is enabled, each MPDU is encrypted individually.

    D. The individual MPDUs must all be of the same 802.11e QoS access category.

    E. Each A-MPDU will receive an ACK.

17. When A-MSDU is used to aggregate frames, which of the following is true about encryption?

    A. All of the MSDUs are encrypted together as a single payload.

    B. All of the MPDUs are encrypted together as a single payload.

    C. The MSDUs are encrypted individually, prior to aggregation.

    D. The MPDUs are encrypted individually, prior to aggregation.

    E. A-MSDU does not affect the encryption process.

18. For the MSDU or MMPDU fragments to be reassembled, which of the following must be contained in the header of the fragmented frames? (Choose all that apply.)

    A. Frame type

    B. Address of the sender

    C. Destination address

    D. Sequence Control field

    E. More Fragments indicator

19. During a packet capture, you notice that there is a series of fragmented frames. These frame fragments can contain what type of frames?

   A. Broadcast

   B. Multicast

   C. Anycast

   D. Unicast

   E. All of the above

20. When the To DS bit is 1 and the From DS bit is 0, what is the value of the Address 1 field? (Choose all that apply.)

   A. Receiver address

   B. Transmitter address

   C. Destination address

   D. Source address

   E. BSSID

Answers to Review Questions

1. A, B, C, E. The basic data frame is represented by a Subtype of 0 (bits b7–b4 = 0000). By changing any of these Subtype bits, a modification is made to the basic data frame. Most people are not aware that there is actually a pattern or system to the Subtype bits, with each of the individual bits having a specific meaning. By changing bit 4 (b4) from a 0 to a 1, the data subtype includes +CF-Ack. Changing bit 5 (b5) from a 0 to a 1 will include +CF-Poll. Changing bit 6 (b6) from a 0 to a 1 will indicate that the frame contains no data, specifically, that it contains no Frame Body field. The most significant bit (MSB) of the Subtype field (bit b7) is defined as the quality of service (QoS) subfield, specifying that the frame is a QoS data frame. This pattern or system applies to all subtypes except for 1101, which is Reserved. +ToS does not exist.

2. E. If the transmitting station knows that all stations in the BSS that are members of the multicast group are QoS capable, it will send a QoS frame. If the transmitting station were sending a broadcast frame, then it would send a QoS frame if it knew all stations in the BSS are QoS capable. A QoS station would send a unicast frame only to another QoS station. All other transmissions would be non-QoS.

3. A. The only one of these frames that actually carries data is the data frame, also commonly referred to as the simple data frame. The names of all the frames that carry data begin with either Data or QoS Data.

4. D. A wireless bridge connection is also referred to as a wireless distribution system. In this case, both the To DS and From DS bits are set to 1.

5. E. Address 4 is used only when the To DS and From DS bits are 1. Address 1 is always the receiver address, and Address 2 is always the transmission address.

6. C, D. With the ratification of the 802.11n amendment, two types of frame aggregation were added to 802.11: aggregate MAC service data unit (A-MSDU) and aggregate MAC protocol data unit (A-MPDU). Frame aggregation allows multiple smaller MSDUs or MPDUs to be grouped together into a single frame, reducing the amount of overhead that would have been necessary for each individual frame.

7. A. A-MSDU is an aggregation process that combines multiple MSDUs within a single MPDU. The network layer passes the MSDUs down to the MAC layer. Normally at this point each MSDU would be packaged with its own MPDU. With A-MSDU, two or more MSDUs are placed in an MPDU, and a single MAC and PHY layer header is added to the group of MSDUs. If encryption is enabled, then all the MSDUs are encrypted together as a single payload.

8. B, C, E. Since the AP is a 2.4 GHz device, the 802.11a station could not connect. Since 802.11 supports only 1 and 2 Mbps, that station could not connect. The basic rate is required in order to connect to the network. Since 802.11b, 802.11g, and 802.11n are all capable of transmitting at 5.5 and 11 Mbps, they can connect.

9. D. PCF is a central polling method that provides contention-free access. CSMA/CD is a contention method used by wired Ethernet.

10. A, B, C, D. With A-MSDU, two or more MSDUs are placed in an MPDU, and a single MAC and PHY layer header is added to the group of MSDUs. If encryption is enabled, then all the MSDUs are encrypted together as a single payload. There are some restrictions for aggregating multiple MSDUs into a single MPDU. The MPDU can only contain MSDUs that have DA and SA values that map to the same RA and TA values. All of the MSDUs must also have the same priority value.

11. B. Quality of service (QoS) stations are capable of transmitting both QoS and non-QoS data frames. It is not uncommon to have a wireless network that consists of both QoS and non-QoS stations. In this type of mixed environment, it is likely that QoS devices will transmit both QoS data frames and non-QoS data frames depending upon the capabilities of the receiving station. When a QoS data frame is transmitted, the QoS subfield (the b7 bit) contains a value of 1, and the frame contains a QoS Control field in the MAC header. When a non-QoS data frame is transmitted, the QoS subfield (the b7 bit) contains a value of 0, and the QoS Control field is not present in the MAC header.

12. A,D. Since 54 Mbps is a faster data rate than the 36 Mbps, then the minimum received signal needs to be stronger, and the difference between the signal and the noise needs to be greater.

13. A, C, D. DRS is also referred to as dynamic rate shifting, adaptive rate selection, and automatic rate selection. All these terms refer to a method of speed fallback on a wireless LAN client as signal quality from the access point decreases.

14. B, C, D. To begin with, Address 1 is always the receiver address, and Address 2 is always the transmitter address. When the frame is transmitted from an AP to a station, the To DS and From DS bits are 01. In this case, the transmitter address is also the address of the BSSID, so Address 2 is also the BSSID address. Since the source of this frame is the AP, then the receiver address and the destination address are the same in Address 1. Address 3 is thus set to the source address, and Address 4 is not used.

15. A, C. Since the 802.11-2007 standard does not define any specific rate selection algorithm, the algorithms used for dynamic rate switching are proprietary and are defined by radio card manufacturers. Most vendors base DRS on receive signal strength indicator (RSSI) thresholds, packet error rates, and retransmissions. RSSI metrics are usually based on signal strength and signal quality. In other words, a station might shift up or down between data rates based both on received signal strength in dBm and possibly on a signal-to-noise ratio (SNR) value. Because vendors implement DRS differently, you may have two different vendor client cards at the same location, while one is communicating with the access point at 65 Mbps and the other is communicating at 6 Mbps.

16. A, B, C, D. A-MPDU is an aggregation process that combines multiple MPDUs within a single PPDU. The network layer passes the MSDUs down to the MAC layer, where an MPDU is created for each MSDU. If encryption is enabled, then each MPDU is encrypted individually. The MPDUs are then passed down to the PLCP sublayer where two or more MPDUs are placed in a single PPDU. The individual MPDUs within an A-MPDU

must all have the same receiver address. Also, the individual MPDUs must all be of the same 802.11e quality-of-service access category. A-MPDU also requires the use of block acknowledgments.

17. A. A-MPDU is an aggregation process that combines multiple MPDUs within a single PPDU. The network layer passes the MSDUs down to the MAC layer, where an MPDU is created for each MSDU. If encryption is enabled, then each MPDU is encrypted individually.

18. A, B, C, D, E. The header must contain all this information. The Sequence Control field is actually made up of two pieces, the sequence number and the fragment number. The sequence number within this field remains the same for all fragments from the same MSDU or MPDU, while the fragment number within this field is incremented for each individual fragment.

19. D. The 802.11-2007 standard allows for the fragmentation of unicast addressed frames.

20. A, E. To begin with, Address 1 is always the receiver address, and Address 2 is always the transmitter address. When the To DS and From DS bits are 10, then the frame is being sent from a station to the distribution system. In this case, the receiver address is also the address of the BSSID, so Address 1 is also the BSSID address. Since the source of this frame is the station, then the transmitter address and the source address are the same in Address 2. Address 3 is thus set to the destination address, and Address 4 is not used.

Chapter

7

802.11 Medium Contention

IN THIS CHAPTER, YOU WILL LEARN ABOUT THE FOLLOWING:

✓ **802.11 Channel Access**

- Describe the operation of CSMA/CA

- Describe the essential components of the DCF

- Describe the steps taken before a frame transmission

That 802.11 devices are resilient is no secret. Anyone who has ever managed a WLAN in a crowded space such as a trade show or office complex can attest to that. The secret is how it all works. The IEEE 802.11 standard was blessed with an elegant mosaic of medium contention protocols that allow a large number of devices to effectively share a wireless channel. Medium contention means that all 802.11 devices—access points (APs) and base stations—with frames ready to be transmitted onto a given channel will contend with each other for access to that channel. In this chapter, we'll discuss these protocols that govern access to the wireless medium.

We will discuss the overall design of 802.11 medium contention, as well as additional medium contention protocols that are unique to the 802.11e and 802.11n amendments.

CSMA/CA

802.11 stations, including both AP stations and non-AP stations, use *carrier sense multiple access with collision avoidance* (CSMA/CA) to contend for the wireless channel. If the acronym CSMA looks familiar to you as a network professional, that's because it should: 802.3 Ethernet LANs use *carrier sense multiple access with collision detection* (CSMA/CD) to contend for the wired channel. That means both wired and wireless LANs use carrier sense (observing the communication medium) for multiple access (more than one device at the same time), but they just do it differently.

The difference between CSMA/CA and CSMA/CD is as simple as examining the last two letters of each acronym: wireless devices must avoid collisions (defined as failed transmissions because of multiple devices transmitting simultaneously over a shared medium), while wired stations can detection collisions. The reason? Simply that wireless stations operate in a half-duplex, wireless medium. Any entity operating in a half-duplex, wireless medium is going to be unable to detect collisions. A half-duplex communications device is one that cannot transmit and receive at the same time. Imagine what would happen, then, if a person's ears were to shut off as soon as they started talking (thus making the person's audio capabilities the equivalent of half-duplex). Would such a person be able to tell whether a loud noise caused their spoken words to go unheard? No. The half-duplex human would be unable to detect collisions when speaking.

The analogy of a person hearing can be expanded to better understand the differences between CSMA/CD and CSMA/CA. Since human beings can detect audio collisions, they are able to repeat their words if a loud noise is detected during speech. If humans lacked the ability to detect loud noises while they were speaking, they'd have to avoid collisions. How? One method could be by raising their hands, as in a grade-school classroom. The first person with a hand up would be allowed to talk. That analogy bears some relation to the design of CSMA/CA.

It is important to understand that collision detection is more efficient than collision avoidance. This is because any type of collision handling takes precious time on the channel. Time spent on collision handling could be more efficiently spent on transmitting data. Collision detection means that collision handling has to happen only after a collision occurs. Collision avoidance means that collision handling has to happen before any data is transmitted. The end result is that CSMA/CA causes WLANs to have a much lower throughput-to-data rate ratio than wired LANs.

Distributed Coordination Function

CSMA/CA involves use of the *distributed coordination function* (DCF) for non-QoS WLANs and the *hybrid coordination function* (HCF) using *enhanced distributed channel access* (EDCA) for QoS WLANs (DCF, HCF, and EDCA will be explained later in the chapter). EDCA has a design that is very similar to the design of DCF, only with added parameters that differentiate priority levels. This prioritization of traffic makes EDCA the spine of *Wi-Fi Multimedia* (WMM), which is a *Wi-Fi Alliance* certification for APs and stations that support *IEEE 802.11e* QoS protocols.

What Happened to the Point Coordination Function?

The *point coordination function* (PCF), as defined in the original 802.11 standard, and the HCF using HCF-controlled channel access (HCCA), as defined in 802.11e, are also protocols that use CSMA/CA. Neither one, however, is used in real-world WLAN devices. Both the PCF and HCCA involve the AP taking control of the wireless channel and dictating which stations are allowed to send through the use of polling.

DCF and EDCA involve a series of protocols designed to keep the wireless channel clear so that collisions are avoided. These protocols are numerous, and they can be a bit difficult to comprehend. As these protocols are discussed, always remember that the most basic goal of 802.11 medium contention is similar to the goal of having students raise their hands in class: to keep the channel clear so that collisions are avoided.

An Example of 802.11 Medium Contention

A good way to begin learning about the protocols that make up 802.11 medium contention is by examining an example of WLAN devices using the DCF. Then once you understand DCF, we'll discuss the minor adjustments that make up EDCA.

The basic concept of DCF and EDCA is that all WLAN devices must complete an arbitration process before transmitting a frame. Arbitration entails all APs and stations staying quiet for a variable amount of time before attempting to transmit. Whichever device finishes arbitration first gains access to the channel.

In the example, there are three total 802.11 devices: one AP and two non-AP stations. Both stations are associated to the AP, which means that all three devices must contend for access to the same channel. To simplify the medium contention process as much as possible, we will stipulate that all devices are not using 802.11e QoS.

By not using 802.11e, the AP and stations become non-QoS devices. Non-QoS APs must not include any QoS information elements in their beacon frames. This includes the EDCA parameter set and the QBSS load. Both non-QoS APs and non-QoS stations must use DCF rather than EDCA for medium contention. Both non-QoS APs and non-QoS stations must also use data and null frames rather than QoS data and QoS null frames. Data and null frames are encapsulated with a header that lacks the QoS Control field.

In this example, both stations have data to send, while the AP does not have data to send. Figure 7.1 illustrates this scenario. It should be remembered that if an AP does have data to send, it uses the exact same DCF or EDCA protocols that are used by stations.

FIGURE 7.1   Whose turn is it?

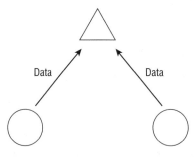

A significant aspect of the DCF and EDCA protocols that govern 802.11 medium contention is the ability of APs and stations to identify when a channel is busy. There are two *carrier sense* protocols used by stations to indicate whether a channel is busy or idle:

- Physical carrier sense, also known as the *clear channel assessment* (CCA)
- Virtual carrier sense, also known as the *network allocation vector* (NAV)

Both QoS and non-QoS devices use the CCA and the NAV in the same way. So, before either station in this example attempts to transmit data, both the CCA and the NAV must be checked in order to verify that the channel is idle.

Physical Carrier Sense

The clear channel assessment is the physical carrier sense mechanism for 802.11 APs and stations. The CCA simply involves listening to the channel. If the channel is considered occupied, then the CCA indicates a state of busy. If the channel is considered clear, then the CCA indicates a state of idle.

The CCA is set to busy if a high enough level of energy is detected coming from valid, modulated 802.11 bits. The *energy detection* level varies by transmit power according to the chart shown in Figure 7.2.

FIGURE 7.2   CCA energy detection

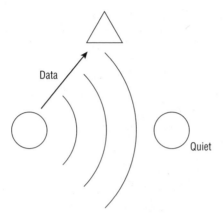

If modulated bits are detected at those energy levels, the CCA will go busy for 15 micro-seconds if DSSS modulation is being used or for 4 microseconds if OFDM modulation is being used. If at the end of that period modulated bits continue to be detected on the channel at the requisite energy levels, the CCA will continue to stay busy, and 802.11 devices—both APs and stations—will continue to stay quiet.

There are two important points to remember about the CCA. The first point is that it applies only to 802.11 modulation. Interference from non-802.11 devices does not cause the CCA to go into a busy state. The other important point is that the CCA may not keep all devices within a BSS quiet. If an AP or station is too far away to detect data transmissions at the requisite energy level, the CCA may go into the idle state even though the channel is still occupied.

If an AP or station sees the CCA as idle while the channel is still occupied, it could lead to collisions. That's why 802.11 WLANs have the NAV, which acts as a virtual alternative to the CCA.

Virtual Carrier Sense

The network allocation vector is the virtual carrier sense mechanism for 802.11 APs and stations. The NAV is a timer that counts down toward zero. When a device has a NAV value greater than zero, the device stays quiet. Once the NAV value reaches zero, the wireless medium is considered clear.

The design of the NAV is that it keeps APs and stations quiet even if the CCA cannot be used to clear the channel. There are several reasons why the CCA may fail to keep other devices on the channel quiet, including the following:

- Too far from the transmitting device

- Obstructions blocking the RF path from the transmitting device

- Interference in the RF path to the transmitting device

APs and stations set their NAV values according to the Duration value inside the 802.11 header. The Duration value is contained within the Duration/ID field of all 802.11 frames except the power save poll. The Duration value will set the NAV only if the AP or station viewing the header is not the receiver of the frame.

It is important to remember that APs and stations must be within RSSI data range in order to successfully demodulate a transmitted frame so that the *Duration/ID* field in the header can be read. If an 802.11 device lacks the ability to receive a high-quality signal from another device on the channel because of distance, obstructions, or interference, the two devices will not be able to read each other's Duration/ID fields and therefore will not have their NAV values set properly.

Interframe Spaces

In the example shown in Figure 7.1, both wireless stations begin the 802.11 medium contention process by staying quiet when the channel is busy because of either the CCA or the NAV. Once the channel becomes idle, the stations will look to transmit data. The problem is that if both stations begin transmitting data immediately, there will be a collision. Therefore, 802.11 devices must have additional medium contention protocols beyond the CCA and the NAV. These additional protocols must be both similar and dissimilar to the CCA and NAV. They should be similar in that they will keep APs and stations quiet in order to avoid collisions. They should be dissimilar in that channel access will be differentiated so that one device can begin transmitting while all other devices stay quiet.

The first 802.11 protocol that differentiates medium access is the *interframe space* (IFS). The IFS is a quiet period that APs and stations must wait before any 802.11 frame transmission. There are several different IFS times. Shorter IFS times are used before transmissions with higher priority to the channel. The idea is that if APs and stations wait for a shorter quiet period before transmitting, they will gain access to the channel while other devices are still staying quiet. Once the device that used the shorter IFS begins transmitting, all other APs and stations on the channel will hear the frame transmission and stay quiet because of the CCA.

There are six different IFS values in 802.11 networks. The specific timing and parameters of those six values will be discussed shortly. Before getting into specifics, it's best to understand when each IFS value is used. Here are four quick rules that define which IFS will be used before a frame transmission:

- If the arbitration has been completed, then a reduced IFS (*RIFS*) or short IFS (*SIFS*) will be used. In most cases, the SIFS is used. The RIFS is only used between consecutive frames transmitted by the same 802.11n device.

- If arbitration has not been determined, then an arbitration IFS (*AIFS*) or DCF IFS (*DIFS*) will be used. The AIFS is used for WLANs that support 802.11e QoS, and the DIFS is used for WLANs that do not support 802.11e QoS.

- If an AP or station has received a corrupted frame—as defined by having an incorrect *frame check sequence* (FCS)—then an extended IFS (*EIFS*) will be used.

- The PCF IFS (*PIFS*) is part of PCF and therefore not used in the real world.

   In the example discussed earlier, two stations both have data to send at the same time. That means both stations will have to wait an IFS before transmitting a data frame over the wireless channel. In this example, the IFS used by both stations will be the DIFS because neither station has completed the random backoff and 802.11e QoS is not in use. Figure 7.3 shows a timeline illustrating the use of the DIFS for this example.

FIGURE 7.3   DIFS

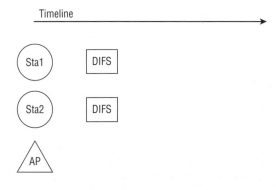

   Both stations are staying quiet for the same amount of time because of the DIFS. That means that in this particular example, neither station has gained priority over the other in the IFS.

   It is important to understand the details of all types of IFS. Here is an overview of each type of IFS.

SIFS

The SIFS is designed as a foundation for all IFSs. It is set to a static length, and its length is used to determine the length of other IFSs.

Depending on the type of WLAN, the SIFS may be either 10 microseconds or 16 microseconds long. The SIFS will be 10 microseconds for 802.11b/g/n devices operating in the 2.4 GHz band and 16 microseconds for 802.11a/n devices operating in the 5 GHz band.

SIFS is a commonly used IFS. With one exception, it is used whenever arbitration has been completed. The exception is that if an 802.11n AP or station is using multiple input/multiple output (MIMO) to transmit frames. If an 802.11n device is transmitting multiple frames as part of a contention-free burst (CFB), then the RIFS will be used between those frames instead of a SIFS.

RIFS

The RIFS is the simplest IFS to understand. The length is always the same: 2 microseconds. Only one type of device uses it: 802.11n devices using MIMO. It precedes only one type of frame: data.

The RIFS is used only between frames of a CFB. It also is used only between frames sent by a single device. It cannot be used, for example, between a data/acknowledgment pair because those frames are transmitted by two different devices.

DIFS

The DIFS is designed to force APs and stations with ordinary data in the queue to stay quiet for enough time to allow higher-priority frames to have access to the channel. It is used when the arbitration process has yet to be completed. The DIFS is made long—equal to the length of an SIFS plus two slot times.

Slot times are quiet periods, just like IFSs. Slot times are 9 microseconds in length for 802.11a/n devices operating in the 5 GHz band. The same slot time length is used for 802.11g/n devices operating in the 2.4 GHz band, but only when HT or ERP is used with the short preamble. When 802.11b/g/n devices operate in the 2.4 GHz band using DSSS, a 20-microsecond slot time is used instead. The 20-microsecond slot time is also used if HT or ERP is used with the long preamble. The short preamble is the default setting when HT or ERP is used.

There is a third slot time. 802.11 FHSS networks use a 50-microsecond slot time. Very, very few 802.11 FHSS APs or stations were ever produced in real life, but knowing the length of the FHSS slot time is a CWAP exam objective.

The DIFS is used only by APs and stations that do not use 802.11e QoS. For 802.11e QoS devices, the AIFS is used. The AIFS will be described in the "Quality of Service" section of this chapter.

EIFS

The EIFS is designed to give APs and stations a chance to retransmit after a failed frame. It takes a complicated design to make that happen.

A failed frame happens when an AP or station fails to receive an acknowledgment after a transmission. But how do APs and stations identify failed frames that are not their own? Each 802.11 AP and station is something of an island unto itself. Each device sees the wireless channel differently because each device is located in a different location. Since each device sees the channel differently, the identification of a failed frame cannot be perfect. APs and stations must simply do the best they can to identify frame failures. The way they do this is by looking for corrupted frames.

A corrupted frame is identified by having an incorrect FCS. The FCS is a 32-bit cyclic redundancy check that is both encapsulated with the header to form the MPDU and calculated after the reception of the frame. If the calculated FCS fails to match the encapsulated FCS, then the frame is regarded as corrupt. When APs and stations hear a corrupt frame on the channel, they stay quiet for an EIFS. The EIFS length is kept long so that the channel will stay quiet long enough for the assumed failed frame to be retransmitted.

The length of the EIFS is equal to an SIFS plus a DIFS plus the time it takes an acknowledgment frame to transmit. For 802.11b/g/n devices using DSSS in the 2.4 GHz band, that works out to 364 microseconds by default. For 802.11a/n devices operating in the 5 GHz band and 802a11g/n devices operating in the 2.4 GHz band using OFDM, that works out to 160 microseconds by default. Either way, the EIFS is by far the longest of the IFSs.

PIFS

The PIFS is equal to one slot time plus one SIFS, and it is designed to give APs the chance to send a beacon in order to begin a CFP. The design of the PIFS is that it has a shorter length than the DIFS, thus giving it a higher priority.

In real-world 802.11 devices, the PIFS is only used with the Channel Switch Announcement frame, which is one of the Action frames from 802.11h. When stations have a Channel Switch Announcement to transmit, the PIFS gives them priority over all other frame types that must be sent after arbitration.

Random Backoff

In the example of two stations having data to send, the IFS is not enough to determine which device will have access to the channel. Both devices stay quiet because of the CCA and the NAV while the channel is busy, and then both devices stay quiet for the length of a DIFS once the channel becomes idle. The problem then becomes making sure that both devices don't start transmitting data simultaneously, thereby causing a collision.

The mechanism that prevents collisions by differentiating 802.11 channel access is the *random backoff*. The random backoff is a quiet period before a frame transmission, similar to the IFS. Unlike the IFS, the random backoff is not static. It is a period of time that changes based on a random number chosen by each AP or station.

APs and stations stay quiet during the random backoff by randomly choosing a number of *slot times* and then counting down until the number of slot times equals zero. Once the number of slot times hits zero, an AP or station is allowed to transmit a frame.

If all APs and station begin contending at the same time and choose differing numbers of slot times, then collisions should be prevented assuming all STAs begin contending at the same time. As soon as one device exhausts its slot times, it will transmit, thus turning the CCA to a busy state in all other devices on the channel. In our example, one station randomly chooses three slot times, while the other station randomly chooses eleven slot times, as depicted in Figure 7.4.

FIGURE 7.4   Random backoff

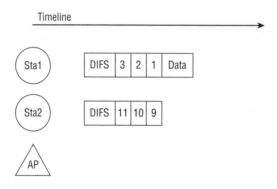

For the random backoff to work, there must be an upper and lower limit to the number of slot times that can be chosen. The lower limit for the random backoff is always 0. The upper limit for the random backoff is always equal to the *contention window* (CW).

The CW is derived from the equation $2^x - 1$, where x is a value that increments with each failed frame. For DSSS-based networks, x starts at 5, which results in a CW of 31. For OFDM-based networks, x starts at 4, which results in a CW value of 15. For both DSSS and OFDM-based networks, the x value stops incrementing at 10, which results in a CW value of 1023. It should be noted that in the real world many APs and stations will give up retransmitting the frame before it ever reaches an x value of 10. That Retry limit is defined separately, however. There is no requirement in the 802.11 standard that stations and APs endure a specific number of retries before they give up.

The design of the CW gives OFDM-based WLANs a major boost in efficiency compared to DSSS-based networks. Not only is the slot time shorter (9 microseconds compared to 20), but the random sample is half as large.

This random backoff design should also illuminate why it is so important to monitor retransmissions on a WLAN. As stated earlier, failed frames cause the CW to grow exponentially because of incrementing x values. A larger CW results in more quiet time on the channel because of larger numbers of slot times being chosen on average when APs and stations have frames to transmit. More quiet time means a less efficient channel, thus resulting in lower throughput.

Frame Transmission

Once a station or AP counts down all slot times, it is given access to the channel. The original 802.11 standard specifies that the station or AP is allowed to transmit one frame during this time. That means if an 802.11 device has a large amount of data to transmit (say, an AP sending a web page containing multimedia content to a smartphone), it will have to go through the arbitration process multiple times before the full package of data reaches its destination.

 Always remember that the transmission of frames is unrelated to data rates. Whether a station or AP transmits at 6.5 Mbps or 450 Mbps, it always gets the same level of access to the wireless channel.

After a station or AP transmits data, an acknowledgment frame must be received in order for the transmission to be considered successful. Just as with data frames, an acknowledgment frame must be preceded by an IFS. But which IFS? If you look at the IFS rules that were articulated earlier in the "Interframe Spaces" section of this chapter, you see that when a nondata frame is about to be transmitted with arbitration having already been decided, an SIFS is used. Figure 7.5 shows this process.

FIGURE 7.5   SIFS and acknowledgment

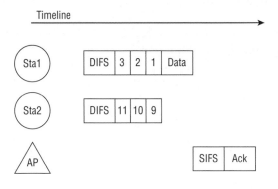

Once the acknowledgment has been received, the data transmission process is finished. The CCA will be set to IDLE because there will be no frame transmissions on the channel. The NAV will be at 0 because Duration values are designed to be exactly large enough to allow the NAV countdown to expire by the time the acknowledgment frame finishes. At this point, stations and APs go back to the beginning of the arbitration process and start over again. Stations and APs that have already begun the random backoff timer will keep the number of slot times they chose during the previous arbitration sequence.

In some cases, the arbitration process described to this point in the chapter will be altered. Corrupted frames, QoS, and 802.11n all may change the traditional 802.11 arbitration process.

Corrupted Frames

Corrupted frames cause the 802.11 arbitration process to change only slightly. The only difference is that when APs or stations demodulate a frame transmission with an incorrect frame check sequence (FCS) value, the frame is considered corrupt, and an EIFS is used in place of a DIFS during the arbitration process.

Figure 7.6 shows the 802.11 arbitration process after the receipt of a corrupted frame.

FIGURE 7.6   EIFS

When APs and stations are forced to stay quiet for an EIFS instead of a DIFS, it gives the device that transmitted the corrupted frame an opportunity to retransmit. The spirit of this design is that 802.11 devices should retransmit failed frames as soon as possible in order to avoid delays that could affect time-sensitive applications.

Near/Far

An unfortunate side effect of the EIFS is that it can lead to a *Near/Far* problem. Near/Far is a nickname given to the problem of stations that are close to an AP causing problems for stations that are further from an AP. When data is sent between the AP and the near station, it may be transmitted at a data rate that is too high for the far station to correctly demodulate. (This is why stations dynamically switch their data rates downward when moving away from APs.) The frame therefore will appear to be corrupt even though it was transmitted successfully between the AP and the near station. The far station will then have to stay quiet for an EIFS at the beginning of the arbitration process, while the near station will be allowed to use the shorter DIFS. The use of the DIFS will give the near station higher priority, thus giving the near station two or more consecutive opportunities to transmit while the far station remains quiet. If this scenario perpetuates, it can lead to far stations having an adequate signal strength to join the basic service set (BSS), but little or no opportunity to transmit data on the channel.

 Real World Scenario

Near/Far, iPhone Problem

Anyone own an iPhone 4? Great, isn't it? Anyone remember the iPhone 4 unveiling? Not so great.

For those who may have missed it, the unflappable Steve Jobs was flapped during the iPhone 4 unveiling by a poor Wi-Fi connection to his demo phone. Mr. Jobs and many of the people covering the event described the problem as "interference," and as a layman explanation, that works.

The technical explanation for the Wi-Fi difficulties at the iPhone 4 unveiling is the aforementioned Near/Far problem. When multiple APs operate on the same channel in the same area, you run into a situation where a high rate data sent to and from one AP cannot be successfully demodulated by the stations associated to the other AP. The stations from the other AP may be close enough to receive a signal but not a signal high enough to read a high rate frame. When high rate frames are received and demodulated unsuccessfully, that is seen as corrupted data. Once corrupted data is seen, stations will then start using the EIFS. At that point, it becomes a vicious cycle whereby the journalists in the crowd successfully send and receive data to the near APs set up at their seats while Mr. Jobs' iPhone 4 continually sees those frames as corrupted and therefore continually keeps quiet.

A solution at the iPhone 4 unveiling would have been the classic solution to the Near/Far problem: try to set up the wireless network so that only one AP operates on each channel in any given area. In that specific case, offering free Wi-Fi to the journalists covering the event may have done the trick.

Quality of Service

The 802.11e amendment introduced QoS to 802.11 networks, and most of the protocols that define 802.11e affect 802.11 channel access. 802.11e defines the hybrid coordination function as a new method for channel access that improves upon both the DCF and the PCF.

HCF involves two channel access methods:

HCF controlled channel access   Designed to be an improvement for contention-free access (specifically, PCF)

Enhanced distributed channel access   Designed to be an improvement for contention-based access (specifically, DCF)

Both are designed to make more efficient use of the wireless channel while also prioritizing time-sensitive traffic such as voice and video.

HCCA: Same Fate as PCF Mode

As with PCF from the original 802.11 standard, HCCA from 802.11e is not used in real-world APs and stations, probably because the theoretical efficiency of the design does not hold up in the real world when other WLANs are around. The design of HCCA makes a lot of sense in that it allows the AP to create service periods. These service periods would be negotiated as traffic specifications (TSPECs), which would define what type of channel access is needed by a station in order for its applications to run successfully. The AP would then allocate service periods to each station. Stations would be allowed to sleep between service periods, thus creating the most theoretically efficient usage of both the wireless channel and the wireless stations' power resources.

APs and stations that support 802.11e QoS protocols are called QoS APs and QoS stations, respectively. When QoS stations associate to a QoS AP, they join a QoS BSS. A QoS AP or QoS station can be identified by the Wi-Fi Multimedia certification from the Wi-Fi Alliance. For a device to gain WMM certification, it must support all EDCA protocols that are described in the "Quality of Service" section of this chapter. HCCA protocols are not required for WMM certification.

When a QoS AP and QoS stations form a QoS BSS, channel access is altered. Instead of having channel access being equal for all devices, as is the case in a non-QoS BSS, a QoS BSS has four access categories (ACs) with varying levels of channel access. The four ACs, ordered from highest priority to lowest, are *voice*, *video*, *best effort*, and *background*.

EDCA prioritizes the four ACs by altering the traditional 802.11 medium contention protocols that were originally defined as part of the DCF. The three areas of 802.11 medium contention that are altered are as follows:

IFS   An AIFS is used instead of a DIFS.

CW   Different access categories are assigned different CW values.

Frame transmission   A *transmit opportunity* (TXOP) is allocated rather than allowing a single frame.

The cumulative result of these changes is that traffic in higher-priority ACs gets more access to the channel, and traffic in any access category has a lower likelihood of being slowed down by low-speed traffic on the channel. The following section describes how.

AIFS

The AIFS is the 802.11e *QoS* replacement for the DIFS. Like the DIFS, the AIFS is used when arbitration has yet to be completed. Unlike the DIFS, the AIFS is not a static value equal to the length of an SIFS plus two slot times.

Slot times are used to determine the length of an AIFS. The AIFS is equal to a SIFS plus a varying number of slot times. The design of the AIFS is to vary based on the priority level of the data, as based on 802.11e QoS. By default, higher-priority data uses an AIFS with fewer slot times, thus making the length of the AIFS shorter. The number of slot times used in the AIFS is called the arbitration interframe space number (AIFSN).

802.11e QoS specifies four access categories (ACs) for WLAN traffic, and each AC uses a different number of slot times.

The highest- and second-highest priority ACs are voice and video, respectively. Both voice and video use two slot times by default.

The third-highest priority AC is best effort, which uses three slot times by default.

The lowest-priority AC is background. Background uses seven slot times by default.

The end result of the AIFS is that traffic in higher priority ACs has a greater chance of gaining immediate access to the channel.

QoS-Based Random Backoff Timer

The AIFS adds a degree of prioritization to QoS-based traffic, but it is not the only mechanism that prioritizes traffic by access category. The random backoff timer is a second way that EDCA differentiates channel access.

In the DCF that is part of the original 802.11 standard, the random backoff timer has a primary purpose of keeping the channel free of collisions. It also has a secondary purpose of giving all devices equal access to the channel over time.

The 802.11e amendment keeps the primary purpose of the random backoff timer while changing the secondary purpose. In EDCA, the random backoff timer still keeps the channel free of collisions, but instead of giving equal access to *all traffic*, it only gives equal access to *all traffic in a given AC*. That may seem like a minor difference, but it is a significant one. If data from two stations or APs is part of the same AC, then EDCA operates the same as the DCF. If different ACs are operating on the same channel, however, then channel access will not be equal.

The way that tiered access is given to different ACs is by manipulation of the CW. Each AC has a *minimum* CW (CWmin) and *maximum* CW (CWmax) value defined by the AP. Like in the DCF, the CW in EDCA is equal to $2^x - 1$. The difference with EDCA is that the minimum and maximum values are different for each AC. These values can be configured on the AP, but the 802.11e amendment does define default x values. These default x values and their corresponding default CWmin and CWmax values are shown in Table 7.1.

TABLE 7.1 AIFS

Access category	Min x	CW Min	Max x	CW Max
Voice	2	3	3	7
Video	3	7	4	15
Best effort	4	15	10	1023
Background	4	15	10	1023

In the example shown earlier in this chapter where two stations are attempting to send data, the CW could work one of two different ways with EDCA. If the two stations are in the same AC, then channel access will work similarly to the way it worked with the DCF, only with different times.

If the two stations in the example shown earlier are sending traffic in different ACs, then channel access will work differently than with the DCF. Figure 7.7 shows an example of how channel access would work if one station is using the voice AC and the other station is using the video AC.

FIGURE 7.7 EDCA-based channel access: different ACs

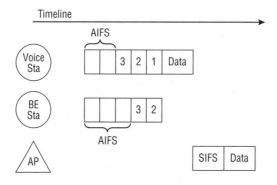

It should be noted that transmitting data in a higher-priority AC does not guarantee that channel access will be acquired before data that is transmitted in a lower-priority AC. All ACs still use a random backoff timer. The randomness is necessary to avoid collisions, but it also introduces enough unpredictability that it is possible that traffic from a low-priority AC could gain immediate channel access. Figure 7.8 shows an example of how this could happen:

FIGURE 7.8 Best-effort AC usurping the voice AC

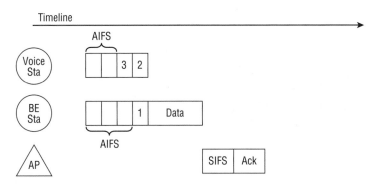

TXOP

EDCA introduces one more change to 802.11 channel access that applies to traffic in all ACs. A *TXOP limit* is allocated for frame transmission when stations or APs gain access to the channel. The *TXOP* is just a time period where one device, called the *TXOP holder*, has unfettered access to the channel for data frame transmissions. The data frame transmissions within a TXOP are called a contention-free burst. No DIFS or AIFS may happen, and no random backoff time may interrupt the CFB as long as the TXOP has not expired. During a TXOP, only the data that makes up a CFB and the acknowledgments for that data may access the channel.

The benefit of the TXOP is that it theoretically prevents low-speed frames from taking up disproportionately large amounts of channel time. In a DCF-based WLAN, the wireless channel is sort of like an intersection governed by a four-way stop sign. When a low rate frame is transmitted, it's like having a car at the intersection that crosses at five miles per hour. The offending car ends up taking more time at the intersection, but so does every other car. With an EDCA-based WLAN, the wireless channel effectively becomes an intersection with a stop light. When the light turns green, cars will get a given amount of time to access the intersection. If drivers proceed through the intersection slowly, it has less of an effect on other cars that are going in a perpendicular direction.

The 802.11e amendment defines default TXOP limit values for each AC, but these values can be configured on APs. TXOP limits are set in intervals of 32 microseconds, and they are configured individually for each AC. That means that if an AP has the voice AC configured for a TXOP limit of 47 (which happens to be the default value specified in 802.11e), then all traffic using the voice AC will be allocated a TXOP of up to 1,504 microseconds whenever access to the channel is won. If the TXOP limit is lower than the time it would take one data/acknowledgment cycle to complete, then a single data frame is transmitted.

Figure 7.9 shows an example of how the channel would be allocated when TXOPs are used.

FIGURE 7.9   TXOP

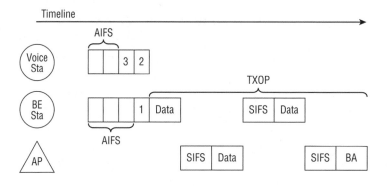

> **NOTE**   Notice how multiple frames are transmitted without having arbitration before each frame. This is a fundamental way that TXOPs make the wireless channel more efficient.

Table 7.2 shows a list of default TXOP limit values for each AC.

TABLE 7.2   Default TXOP limits

Access category	DSSS (b,g,n)	OFDM (a,g,n) TXOP
Voice	3264	1504
Video	6016	3008
Best effort	0	0
Background	0	0

Notice how the default TXOP limit for the best-effort AC is equal to 0. A TXOP limit value of 0 means that best-effort traffic will be sent one frame at a time, just like non-QoS traffic. That is by design, because traffic in the best-effort AC is supposed to be equivalent to non-QoS traffic.

802.11n

The 802.11n amendment does not affect arbitration. 802.11n stations and APs must stay quiet when the CCA or the NAV indicates that the channel is busy, just like 802.11a/b/g stations and APs. 802.11n devices use the DIFS or AIFS, just like legacy devices. And 802.11n devices use the same slot times and random backoff timer that are used by legacy devices. Why, then, would 802.11n need to be mentioned during a discussion of channels access? 802.11n needs to be mentioned in the channel access discussion because it affects channel access *after* arbitration has been completed. After the CCA, NAV, IFS, and random backoff timer have had their say in which AP or station has rights to the channel, the data frame transmission and acknowledgment process gets affected by 802.11n.

802.11n adds two features to channel access that improve the efficiency of the data/acknowledgment process: the RIFS and the *block acknowledgment*.

Block Acknowledgments

Block acknowledgments are designed to make the acknowledgment process more efficient. They were originally introduced in the 802.11e amendment, but they were made optional, and no real-world 802.11a/b/g APs or stations that support 802.11e use them. Block acknowledgments are mandatory in 802.11n and therefore are used in the real world by every 802.11n AP and station.

The block acknowledgment process is designed to make TXOPs more efficient. The basic design of the TXOP aids overall channel efficiency as described earlier in this chapter, but it does nothing to assuage the inefficiencies of acknowledgments. Even in a standard TXOP, the normal data-acknowledgment pattern must be adhered to. When block acknowledgments are used, the data frames of a CFB may be sent consecutively, without interruption by acknowledgments. At the end of the CFB, the data-transmitting station will simply send a block acknowledgment request frame and receive a single block acknowledgment frame in return.

By adding the block acknowledgment, 802.11n stations are able to transmit larger numbers of data frames within a TXOP. For instance, a station with eight data frames to transmit could transmit all eight frames consecutively instead of having valuable TXOP time taken up by waiting to receive individual acknowledgment frames after each data frame.

In the real world, the block acknowledgment is used in a different way. Real world WLAN devices rarely, if ever, use the CFB. Once reason is that the TXOP is almost never used and another reason is that when the TXOP is used, stations and APs almost never have more than one frame ready for transmission at any given moment. 802.11n devices, therefore, use the block acknowledgment for another purpose: to acknowledge aggregated frames. As discussed in the 802.11n chapter, HT stations and APs support frame aggregation (A-MPDU in the real world; A-MSDU as well in the standard). When multiple frames are aggregated by an 802.11n station or AP into an A-MPDU, a block acknowledgment can be used to acknowledge those frames more efficiently.

RIFS

A further 802.11n enhancement that is interwoven with the block acknowledgments is the RIFS. The RIFS is a two-microsecond IFS that is used in place of the longer SIFS when a TXOP, CFB, and block acknowledgment are all in use.

The RIFS was designed for the sole purpose of improving efficiency. Two microseconds is shorter than the 10 or 16 microseconds of the SIFS, which means that the RIFS takes up less channel time.

The RIFS is used only when block acknowledgments are enabled. While block acknowledgments are an optional part of 802.11e that could be used without the RIFS, the RIFS is defined only in 802.11n.

Figure 7.10 shows the use of the RIFS.

FIGURE 7.10   RIFS

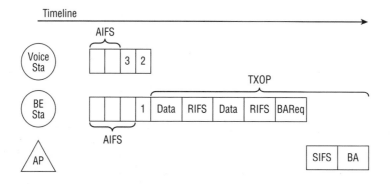

Exam Essentials

Know CSMA/CA and the DCF.   That includes the CCA, the NAV, IFS, and the random backoff timer.

Understand the carrier sense mechanisms.   You should know how both the CCA and the NAV keep APs and stations quiet when the channel is busy.

Know all of the different IFSs and when they are used.   This includes DIFS, PIFS, SIFS, EIFS, AIFS, and RIFS.

Understand the random backoff timer.   You should know what slot times are and how the CW works.

Be familiar with EDCA.   QoS changes the 802.11 medium contention process, and you should know how that works. That includes the AIFS, changes to the CW, and the use of TXOPs.

Understand how 802.11n affects medium contention.   You should understand RIFS and the block acknowledgment process.

Key Terms

AIFS	IFS
background	NAV
best effort	Near/Far
Block acknowledgments	QoS
CCA	random backoff
CFB	RIFS
contention window	SIFS
CSMA/CA	slot times
DCF	TXOP
DIFS	TXOP holder
Duration/ID	TXOP limit
EDCA	video
EIFS	voice
energy detection	Wi-Fi Alliance
HCF	WMM
IEEE 802.11e	

Summary

The 802.11 medium contention process may initially seem complicated, but in some ways it is quite simple. If APs and stations hear a busy channel when listening, then they stay quiet. If APs and stations cannot hear a busy channel, there is a backup way that they stay quiet. Once the channel becomes idle, APs and stations must wait some more so that there is a space between frames. And in order to avoid collisions, a randomized countdown precedes frame transmissions. Listen, wait, count, and send—that's all there is to it.

Review Questions

1. Which coordination function is an optional method that is not used in real-world 802.11 APs?

    A. ACF mode

    B. DCF mode

    C. ECF mode

    D. PCF mode

2. Which of the following will cause a 2.4 GHz 802.11n station to stay quiet even though it has data ready to be transmitted?

    A. An 802.11b station from a nearby BSS is transmitting a data frame, and the received signal is above the ED threshold.

    B. An 802.11b station associated to the same BSS is transmitting a data frame, and the received signal is below the ED threshold.

    C. A Bluetooth pairing has been made and detected on the channel by the AP.

    D. The 2.4 GHz 802.11n station has just chosen zero slot times in the random backoff timer.

3. Which IFS is used only in between frame transmissions by the same AP or station?

    A. AIFS

    B. EIFS

    C. RIFS

    D. SIFS

4. When an 802.11n station begins the arbitration process after a failed frame transmission, which IFS is used?

    A. AIFS

    B. DIFS

    C. EIFS

    D. SIFS

5. Which two access categories use the same default AIFSN values by default? (Choose two.)

    A. Voice

    B. Video

    C. Best effort

    D. Background

6. Which two access categories use the same default CW values by default?

   A. Voice

   B. Video

   C. Best effort

   D. Background

7. An AP without RTS/CTS enabled, a station with an RTS/CTS enabled, and a station with RTS/CTS disabled all have a data frame ready to be transmitted as part of the same BSS. Which device will transmit first?

   A. The station with RTS/CTS enabled will always transmit first.

   B. The AP will always transmit first.

   C. The station without RTS/CTS enabled will be allowed to transmit first only if it chooses the lowest slot time during the random backoff timer.

   D. The station with RTS/CTS enabled will be allowed to transmit first only if it chooses the highest number of slot times during the random backoff timer.

8. In a mixed mode 5 GHz WLAN, which of the following devices would transmit first?

   A. An 802.11n AP with a beacon frame to transmit after choosing two slot times

   B. An 802.11n station with a data frame to transmit after choosing one slot time

   C. An 802.11n station with a data frame to send and RTS/CTS enabled, no matter what number of slot times are chosen

   D. An 802.11a station with a data frame to transmit after choosing zero slot times

9. What is the minimum CWmin value for an 802.11b AP?

   A. 15

   B. 16

   C. 31

   D. 32

10. What is the non-QOS CW value for an 802.11g station when it is about to transmit its second retry frame to an 802.11n AP?

   A. 63

   B. 64

   C. 127

   D. 128

11. When will an EIFS be used prior to a frame transmission?

   A. When a corrupted frame has been received

   B. When a station is about to send a retransmitted frame

   C. When an 802.11n station is about to transmit on a mixed mode 802.11b/g/n or 802.11a/n BSS

   D. When an 802.11a/b/g station is about to transmit on a mixed mode 802.11b/g/n or 802.11a/n BSS

12. Which well-known problem is EIFS known to cause?

   A. Hidden node

   B. Mixed mode

   C. Near/Far

   D. Protection mechanism

13. Which 802.11e QoS channel access method requires the QoS AP to take control of the wireless channel and manage service periods for associated stations?

   A. DCF mode

   B. PCF mode

   C. HCF mode using EDCA

   D. HCF mode using HCCA

14. Which IFS is used prior to the random backoff timer when a QoS AP or station is about to transmit a frame and a corrupted frame has just been received?

   A. AIFS

   B. DIFS

   C. EIFS

   D. PIFS

15. By default, what is the AIFSN value for the background access category?

   A. 2

   B. 3

   C. 5

   D. 7

16. By default, what is the minimum CW value for the video access category?

   A. 3

   B. 7

   C. 15

   D. 31

17. If an AP is configured with the TXOP limit for the voice access category left to the default value of 47, how many microseconds will the maximum TXOP be for traffic that uses the voice access category?

   A. 47

   B. 188

   C. 470

   D. 1504

18. What protocols are required in 802.11n to make TXOPs more efficient that are not required in 802.11e? (Choose two.)

    A. Block acknowledgments

    B. CFB

    C. CWmax

    D. RIFS

19. How many frames will be transmitted within a TXOP if the transmitting AP has four frames to send and block acknowledgments are not used?

    A. 4

    B. 6

    C. 8

    D. 10

20. How long is the RIFS?

    A. 2 microseconds

    B. 10 microseconds

    C. 16 microseconds

    D. 32 microseconds

Answers to Review Questions

1. D. PCF mode is the coordination function that involves the AP taking control of the BSS at regular intervals in order to regulate channel access. It is optional in the 802.11 standard and unavailable in APs. DCF mode is the coordination function that involves all 802.11 devices—APs and stations—arbitrating equally for channel access. It is required in the 802.11 standard. ACF mode and ECF mode are not 802.11 coordination functions.

2. A. APs and stations stay quiet because of the CCA being set to Busy whenever another 802.11 transmission is detected above the ED threshold. In the case of a 2.4 GHz 802.11n station, that means an 802.11b, 802.11g, or 802.11n frame transmission received above the ED threshold will cause the CCA to be set to Busy, no matter which BSS the frame emanates from. If frames are received at a signal below the ED threshold, then stations set the CCA to Idle and frames may be transmitted. Bluetooth transmissions will not set the CCA to Idle in 802.11 stations. When zero slot times have been chosen in the random backoff timer, an 802.11 device immediately transmits a frame.

3. C. The RIFS, which was introduced with 802.11n, is used exclusively between frames transmitted during a single CFB. A single CFB is always transmitted by a single station. The AIFS and EIFS are used exclusively between frames transmitted by different stations. The SIFS may be used during a CFB, but it may also be used prior to an acknowledgment, which would place it between frames transmitted by different stations.

4. A. Even if the previous frame transmission failed, 802.11n stations will always use the AIFS during arbitration. DIFS is used during the arbitration process for 802.11a/b/g stations that are not using 802.11e QoS if the previous frame seen on the channel was not corrupted. EIFS is used only if the previous frame transmission on the channel was received as corrupted. This is the case for all 802.11a/b/g/n stations. SIFS is never used during arbitration.

5. A, B. The voice and video access categories both have default AIFSN values of 2. The best-effort access category has a default AIFSN value of 3. The background access category has a default AIFSN value of 7.

6. C, D. The best-effort and background access categories both have default CWmin values of 15 and default CWmax values of 1023. The voice access category has a default CWmin value of 3 and a default CWmax value of 7. The video access category has a default CWmin value of 7 and a default CWmax value of 15.

7. C. The station or AP that has the lowest amount of time from the combination of the IFS and the random backoff timer will always transmit first. That means a low number of slot times allows a station to transmit first. RTS/CTS settings do not affect which station or AP will gain access to the channel first when multiple devices have data ready to transmit. APs do not have priority over stations when accessing the wireless channel.

8. D. The station or AP that chooses the lowest number of slot times during the random backoff timer will always transmit first. Frame type, 802.11a/b/g/n standards support, and RTS/CTS do not affect which station will transmit first when multiple stations have data ready to be transmitted.

9. C. The default CWmin value for 802.11b devices is 31. That is the default CWmin value whenever DSSS frame transmissions are ready to be sent. The default CWmin value for 802.11a/g/n devices is 15. Finally, 16 and 32 are not default CWmin values under any circumstance.

10. A. An 802.11g station associated to an 802.11n AP will have a default CWmin value of 15. The CW will increase exponentially with each retry. On the first retry, the CW value will be 31, and on the second retry the CW value will be 63. On the third retry from an 802.11g station that is about to transmit to an 802.11n AP, a CW value of 127 will be used. Finally, 64 and 128 are not CW values under any circumstances.

11. A. The EIFS is used only after a corrupted frame has been received. When a station has failed to receive an acknowledgment after a frame transmission, it sends a retransmitted frame. The retransmitted frame will be sent after either DIFS (non-QoS) or AIFS (QoS). Distinctions between 802.11a/b/g/n do not affect whether the EIFS is used prior to a frame transmission.

12. C. Near/Far may be caused by EIFS because successful frame transmissions may be seen as corrupted if stations are too far from the AP. The hidden node problem is caused by two stations or APs that cover the same transmission area but cannot hear each other's transmissions. Mixed mode and protection mechanism are not problems.

13. D. HCF mode using HCCA is a QoS-based channel access method that involves the AP taking control of the wireless channel in order to manage station service periods. DCF mode and HCF mode using EDCA do not involve the AP taking control of the wireless channel. PCF mode does involve the AP taking control of the wireless channel, but it comes from the original 802.11 standard, not the 80211e QoS amendment.

14. C. The EIFS is used prior to frame transmission any time a corrupted frame has just been received. The AIFS is used prior to frame transmission when data frames are about to be sent by QoS devices. The DIFS is used prior to frame transmission when data frames are about to be sent by non-QoS devices. The PIFS is used by APs to take control of the wireless channel before a contention-free period when in PCF mode.

15. D. The background AC has a default AIFSN value of 7. Higher AIFSN values give traffic a lower priority, and background is designed to be the lowest-priority AC. Voice and video traffic uses an AIFSN value of 2 by default, and best-effort traffic uses a default AIFSN value of 3. There is no AC with a default AIFSN value of 5.

16. B. The default CWmin value for the video AC is 7. That gives video traffic a lower priority level than voice traffic (which has a default CWmin value of 3) and higher priority than best-effort and background traffic (which both have default CWmin values of 15). 802.11b stations and APs that do not support QoS use the default CWmin value of 31.

17. D. The TXOP limit value is multiplied by 32 to determine the maximum number of microseconds in a TXOP. Therefore, a TXOP limit value of 47 would result in a maximum TXOP of 1504 microseconds.

18. A, D. Block acknowledgments are optional in 802.11e but required in 802.11n. Block acknowledgments make the channel more efficient by reducing the number of acknowledgment frames on the channel. The RIFS is not part of 802.11e and is required in 802.11n. The RIFS is an interframe space of 2 microseconds, allowing the channel to be more efficient than when the SIFS of 10 or 16 microseconds is used. CFBs were introduced in 802.11e and are required. CFBs do make the channel more efficient by allowing multiple data frames to be transmitted without going through arbitration for each frame. CWmax was part of the 802.11 standard. A low CWmax value could make the wireless channel more efficient because large CW values can cause stations to spend a large amount of time in the random backoff timer before transmitting a frame.

19. C. If block acknowledgments are not used, then one acknowledgment must be received for every data frame sent. That means a total of eight frame transmissions during a TXOP that includes a four-frame CFB. If block acknowledgments were used, a four-frame CFB would result in six total frames being sent during the TXOP.

20. A. RIFS is 2 microseconds. SIFS is 10 microseconds for 2.4 GHz 802.11b/g/n devices and 16 microseconds for 5 GHz 802.11a/n devices.

Chapter

8

Power Management

IN THIS CHAPTER, YOU WILL LEARN ABOUT THE FOLLOWING:

✓ **802.11 Power Management**

- Describe the operation of 802.11 Power Management

- Describe the use of Power Save Poll frames

- Describe the operation of 802.11e Unscheduled Automatic Power Save Delivery

- Describe the purpose of Null data frames as it relates to power management.

- Describe the operation of 802.11n Power Save Multi-Poll

Ask five power users to describe their dream wireless gadget, and you will probably get five different answers. Should it have a nice, spacious screen, or should it fit in your pocket? Should you be able to tap out emails on a keyboard, or is a touch screen a more efficient use of space? Do you want full multitasking, or would you rather have apps stop using the processor once they are closed? The gadget industry is quite subjective in just about every area, save one: battery life. Everyone wants more of it.

A lot of factors affect the battery life of 802.11 devices. Screen size, brightness, multi-tasking capabilities, and wireless transmitter power are some. And in this chapter, none of those will be discussed. This chapter covers the one area of power management that is covered in the 802.11 standard: how *802.11 power management* protocols allow wireless radios go to sleep.

 Keep in mind that wireless radios going to sleep and computers going to sleep are two different things. 802.11 power management protocols are not relevant to what happens when a wireless device goes to sleep. Only the wireless radio inside an awake wireless device is affected by the protocols discussed in this chapter.

Wireless Radios and Battery Life

To understand the need for power management of wireless radios and its effect on battery life, you must first understand the different activities a wireless radio can perform and their varying effects on battery life. A wireless radio can perform one of four activities. It can be

- Asleep
- *Idle* and awake
- Receiving
- Transmitting

The power consumed by each activity increases from the former to the latter. The goal of 802.11 power management, then, is to have wireless radios perform low-power activities, such as sleeping, as much as possible while performing high-power activities, such as trans-mitting, as little as possible. Of course, the reason a wireless radio exists is to *transmit* and receive frames. The idea of power management is to allow receiving and transmitting activities to happen as needed but to make them as efficient as possible.

Power Save Modes

There are two Power Save modes in 802.11 stations, *active mode* and *Power Save mode*:

Active Mode   Stations and APs operate with the assumption that the station is always available to transmit and *receive* data.

Power Save Mode   The AP operates under the assumption that a station radio is sleeping and therefore unable to receive frame transmissions.

The active mode is simple to understand, but there is sometimes confusion over Power Save mode. Power Save mode does not mean that the station's wireless radio is always saving power by staying asleep. It just means that the AP has to assume that the station's wireless radio is asleep unless otherwise notified. The AP buffers all data destined to a station in Power Save mode unless the AP receives a frame transmission from the station while the station requests a frame from the AP's buffer (more on that later in this chapter).

Power States

When a station is in Power Save mode, it vacillates between one of two power states, the *doze* state and the *awake* state:

Doze State   The station is saving the most battery life.

Awake State   The station may either be idle, receiving, or transmitting.

This chapter will go into full detail of which power state is used at various times by stations. There are three 802.11 power management protocols, and each one will be covered in detail. Although each power management protocol is unique, they all share one overarching goal: to maximize doze time and minimize awake/idle time. 802.11 station radios are always going to have to receive and transmit frames because that is their primary purpose. Power management really is just the management of the time when a station is not transmitting or receiving frames. If more of that time is spent in the doze state rather than the awake/idle state, then the battery life of the station will improve.

Every power management method that is used in the real world works from the same basic power management structure, as illustrated in the following steps and figures:

1. Before a station goes into the doze state, it sends a frame, usually a *null data* frame, to the AP indicating that power management is enabled (see Figure 8.1).

FIGURE 8.1   Station sends a null data frame

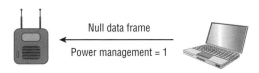

Null data frame

Power management = 1

2.   Once the station indicates that it is in Power Save mode, the AP begins to *buffer* all frames destined to that station (see Figure 8.2).

FIGURE 8.2   AP buffers data

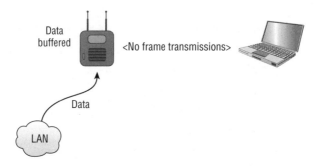

3.   When the station goes into the awake state (more on that later), it sends a frame to the AP in order to begin the data retrieval process (see Figure 8.3).

FIGURE 8.3   Station retrieves data

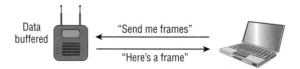

4.   When the AP has finished sending all buffered data to the station, the station goes back into the doze state (see Figure 8.4).

FIGURE 8.4   Station returns to the doze state

The basic structure is quite simple. Stations doze, APs buffer data, stations wake, and then APs send data. Once that basic structure is understood, you can begin to dive deeper into analyzing exactly what frames are sent as part of the power management process and exactly what those frames do to trigger the steps of this basic structure.

Power Management Structure

There are three methods of power management that are used today in the 802.11 family:

- 802.11 power management
- Unscheduled automatic power save delivery (*U-APSD*) from the *802.11e* amendment
- Power save multi-poll (*PSMP*) from the *802.11n* amendment.

The first method of power management for WLANs is called 802.11 power management, and it was introduced with the original 802.11 standard.

 Though the standard uses the term *802.11 power management*, many client utilities use different names. Power Save Polling (PSP) was a term used by Cisco for years, and many Broadcom-based mini-PCI and mini-PCIe adapters call it Enabled (as opposed to Fast) power management.

Association Identifier

Every 802.11 power management method begins when the station associates to the BSS. When the AP sends the association response frame to the station during the last step of 802.11 association, an association identifier (*AID*) value is present in the AID fixed field. The AID is a 16-bit value (meaning a range between 1 and 2007) where the AID value of 0 is not assigned to stations. The 0 value is used as an indicator for broadcast/multicast traffic.

Once an AID value has been assigned to a station, the station is allowed to enter Power Save mode. The station will notify the AP that it is entering Power Save mode by sending a frame—almost always a null data frame—with the power management subfield in the 802.11 header set to 1. Once the AP receives a frame with the Power Management field set to 1, it begins buffering data for the station that sent that frame. At this point, the station is in Power Save mode.

 Only the association request and reassociation request frames contain the AID fixed field. The beacon contains an indicator whether stations with a given AID have data buffered at the AP, but that information is carried in the traffic indication map (*TIM*) information element.

Stations are allowed to enter the doze state after the AP has been notified that the station is about to enter Power Save mode. At that point, the behavior of stations will vary. Stations with no need to receive broadcast or multicast data frames may wake at set intervals, regardless of the behavior of the AP. Stations that may need to receive broadcast/multicast traffic have to wake from the doze state under more rigid guidelines. Unfortunately, the power management behavior of stations is often unavailable from vendors.

Stations will wake from the doze state for one of three reasons. The first reason is if the station has a frame to send. In that case, it will wake up immediately and send its frame. When the station does this, it may stay in Power Save mode or move to active mode when sending the frame. The decision on which mode to continue in will be indicated in the Power Management subfield of the 802.11 header.

Traffic Indication Map

The second reason stations may wake up is based on some kind of internal timing mechanism. Stations will still have a defined set of steps when using this method of waking up, but the decision on how long to doze and how often to wake will be solely in the hands of the station.

When stations make the choice to wake up based on an internal timing mechanism, they will time their awakening to occur just before a beacon frame is transmitted. This is because the beacon frame carries a traffic indication map that lists which stations need to request frames from the AP's buffer.

The TIM is an information element, and it has five subfields that give information about buffered frames on the AP. Figure 8.5 shows the format of the TIM.

FIGURE 8.5 TIM format

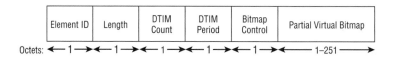

As shown in Figure 8.5, the TIM has four information-carrying fields that follow the Element ID and Length fields that are present in every information element:

- DTIM Count
- DTIM Period
- Bitmap Control
- Partial Virtual Bitmap

The Element ID field for the TIM is 5, and the Length field does its usual job of indicating how many combined bytes long the information-carrying fields are.

The *DTIM Count* field indicates the number of incremental beacon frames until the next *DTIM beacon*. (The DTIM beacon will be discussed shortly.) For example, if the next beacon is a DTIM beacon, then the DTIM Count field will be 1. If the current beacon is a DTIM beacon, then the DTIM Count field will be 0. The maximum DTIM Count value is always one less than the *DTIM Period* value. That means if you configure your AP to have a DTIM Period field of 5, the DTIM Count value in your AP's beacon frames will always be somewhere between 0 and 4.

The DTIM Period field indicates the number of beacon frames between DTIM beacons. For example, if the DTIM Period field is 2, then every other beacon will be a DTIM beacon. If the DTIM Period field is 1, then every beacon will be a DTIM beacon. The maximum DTIM Period value is 255, and the minimum value is 1. These values will become important later when we discuss optimizing your AP configurations to enhance battery life or latency.

The Bitmap Control field is one byte that has two purposes. The first bit of the byte is used only in a DTIM beacon, and its purpose is to indicate whether broadcast/multicast frames are buffered at the AP. The remaining seven bits are the *Bitmap Offset*, which may have any value between 0 and 127, and are used as a space saver. The way it works is if any of the bytes at the start of the *Partial Virtual Bitmap* (to be discussed shortly) are all zeros, then the Bitmap Offset indicates that those bytes can be skipped. The Bitmap Offset value is multiplied by 2, and then the resulting number of bytes in the Partial Virtual Bitmap are assumed to be all zeros. For example, if stations with AIDs between 1 and 43 all do not have buffered *unicast* frames at the AP, then the Bitmap Offset value would be 2. That way, instead of forcing the AP to have five bytes of zeros (indicating AIDs 1–39) at the start of the Partial Virtual Bitmap value, there can be just one byte of zeros, and the first four bytes can be assumed to be all zeros.

The Partial Virtual Bitmap value is just a series of flags (bits set to either a 1 or a 0) indicating whether each associated station has unicast frames buffered at the AP. Each station is assigned an AID value in the association response or reassociation response frame when they associate. Each bit in the Partial Virtual Bitmap value corresponds to one of those AID values. The idea is that if a station that has recently woken up from the doze state sees a TIM with a 1 in the space in the Partial Virtual Bitmap that corresponds to their AID, then the station will begin the process of retrieving those buffered unicast data frames.

The TIM information element is an important part of 802.11 power management; it is something that allows stations to wake up whenever they want to find out whether their unicast frames might be buffered at the AP. The TIM does not, however, do anything about buffered broadcast or multicast frames.

Broadcast and multicast frames are a tricky thing when dealing with power management because all stations must be awake for a broadcast or multicast to be successful. The 802.11 standard has a mechanism to support this, and it is the delivery traffic indication message (DTIM). The DTIM is a version of the TIM that indicates whether broadcast/multicast frames are buffered at the AP. All stations must be awake for beacon frames that carry a DTIM (typically called *DTIM beacon frames*) unless the Receive *DTIMs* setting (which is not configurable by the user) in the station is set to false.

Delivery Traffic Indication Message

The DTIM beacon is identical in structure to the ordinary beacon. The only difference is that the contents of the TIM information element will give information about broadcast/multicast traffic that is buffered at the AP in addition to the typical information about buffered unicast frames that is always present in the TIM.

When a beacon is a DTIM beacon, two fields of the TIM information element are affected:

DTIM Count   This will always be set to 0.

Bitmap Control   The first bit will be used. If broadcast and/or multicast frames are buffered at the AP, then the first bit will be 1. If no broadcast and/or multicast frames are buffered at the AP, then the first bit will be 0.

The rest of the TIM information element remains the same in a DTIM beacon. That includes the DTIM Period value and the Partial Virtual Bitmap value.

Real World Scenario

To Wake or Not to Wake?

Standard operating procedure when configuring an AP states that you raise the DTIM Period setting when you want to allow stations to conserve more battery life and you lower the DTIM Period setting when your APs experience buffer overflows or when broadcast/multicast traffic needs to be sent with low latency. But what about stations with the Receive DTIMs setting set to false? How do you know if your station has Receive DTIMs set to false, and how should that affect your DTIM Period settings?

To see whether your stations have the Receive DTIMs setting set to false, configure a low DTIM Period setting on your AP and then start capturing frames in a protocol analyzer. When your station is both associated and idle, it will start transmitting null data frames as part of the 802.11 power management process. Make a filter so that only null data frames are captured, and then check out the *delta time* between those frames. If null data frames are being sent at larger intervals than the product of the *Beacon Interval* and DTIM Period settings on the AP, then there's a good chance that Receive DTIMs is set to false on your station.

If you do have a station with Receive DTIMs set to false, your next move should be to lower the DTIM Period setting on the AP to 1, the lowest possible value. If Receive DTIMs is set to false on your station, then that means your station is allowed to sleep through DTIM beacons. In that case, the only effect that a high DTIM Period setting has on your network is introducing a larger potential buffer period to your broadcast/multicast traffic.

802.11 Power Management

802.11 power management is the power management method from the original 802.11 standard. As mentioned earlier, all power management methods that are used in the real world have the same basic structure, and stations using any of the three power management methods will wake from the doze state for the same reasons; however, there are a few areas where 802.11 power management is unique:

Stations Stay in Power Save Mode   In U-APSD, stations alternate between Power Save mode and active mode. This affects the third and fourth steps of the basic power management structure detailed earlier in this chapter.

> **Third Step**   When 802.11 power management is used, the station never sends a frame with the *power management flag* in the header set to 0. As shown in Figure 8.6, frames sent by the station when retrieving buffered unicast frames have the power management flag set to 1.

FIGURE 8.6   Station enters Power Save mode

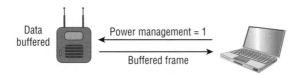

Fourth Step   When 802.11 power management is used, stations return to the doze state without having to notify the AP. As shown in Figure 8.7, since the station stays in Power Save mode, the AP must always buffer all frames intended for the station until the station actively requests those frames. Therefore, the station does not have to tell the AP that it needs to start buffering frames again after the buffer has been emptied.

FIGURE 8.7   Station returns to the doze state

Power Save Poll (*PS-Poll*) Frames Are Used   U-APSD typically relies on the use of null data frames. This affects the third step of the basic power management structure detailed earlier in this chapter:

As shown in Figure 8.8, when 802.11 power management is used, the station uses a PS-Poll frame instead of a null data frame when retrieving buffered unicast frames from the AP. The PS-Poll frame retrieves frames one frame at a time from the AP.

FIGURE 8.8   Station retrieves data

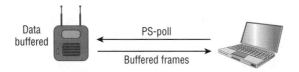

The station will know whether more frames are buffered at the AP by viewing the *More Data flag* in the header. If the AP sends a frame with More Data = 1, then the station will send another PS-Poll. If the AP sends a frame with More Data = 0, then the station will return to the doze state.

Stations Transmit Frames While in Power Save Mode   In U-APSD, stations change to active mode before transmitting any frames. This affects the third step of the basic power management structure, as shown in Figure 8.6. In that figure, frames are being sent by the station with the power management flag set to 1. When the power management flag is set to 1, stations are in Power Save mode.

802.11 power management has two major limitations. One is that overhead is added to the wireless channel. PS-Poll frames do not contain data, and therefore when those frames are transmitted, it lessens the maximum throughput of the channel. 802.11 power management requires the transmission of a PS-Poll frame before each retrieved data frame from the AP's buffer.

The other major limitation of 802.11 power management is that stations must spend too much time in the transmitting state. Remember from way back at the start of the chapter that the most amount of power a wireless radio can consume is in the transmitting state. Those PS-Poll frames that precede each retrieved frame from the AP's buffer must be transmitted by the station. That is an onerous drain on the station's battery life, and it is a big reason why 802.11 power management is rarely used in the real world.

802.11e Unscheduled Automatic Power Save Delivery

U-APSD is the power management method from the 802.11e amendment. It is part of the WMM-Power Save certification from the Wi-Fi Alliance and is also required for 802.11n stations.

U-APSD uses the same basic power management structure that is employed by 802.11 power management but has the following differences:

Stations Vacillate Between Active Mode and Power Save Mode In 802.11 power management, stations stay in Power Save mode and then change their power state between awake and doze. When U-APSD is used, the third and fourth steps of the basic power management structure would look like this:

> **Third Step** When U-APSD is used, the station typically sends null data frames in order to retrieve buffered unicast frames from the AP. As shown in Figure 8.9, frames sent by the station when retrieving buffered unicast frames have the power management flag set to 0.

FIGURE 8.9 Station retrieves data

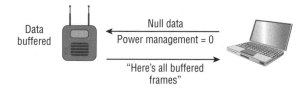

Data buffered

Null data
Power management = 0

"Here's all buffered frames"

> **Fourth Step** When U-APSD is used, stations must notify the AP that they are going back into Power Save mode by sending a frame. As shown in Figure 8.10, since the station goes into active mode when retrieving buffered unicast frames, the AP will resume

buffering frames only if the station sends a frame indicating that it is going back into Power Save mode. Therefore, the station does have to tell the AP that it needs to start buffering frames again after the buffer has been emptied.

FIGURE 8.10   Station returns to the doze state

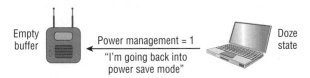

PS-Poll Frames Are Not Used   Null data frames are typically used. This affects the third step of the basic power management structure.

As shown in Figure 8.11, when U-APSD is used, the station uses a null data frame when retrieving buffered unicast frames from the AP. The null data frame retrieves all buffered unicast frames from the AP at once.

FIGURE 8.11   Station retrieves data

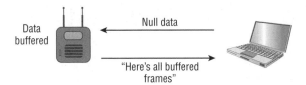

These differences compared to 802.11 power management solve the two big problems that were prevalent with older stations. With 802.11 power management, there was excessive protocol overhead because each retrieved unicast frame from the AP's buffer had to be preceded by a PS-Poll frame. With U-APSD, a single null data frame is capable of retrieving a limitless number of unicast frames from the AP's buffer. That causes much less overhead on the channel.

The even more important improvement in U-APSD compared to 802.11 power management is that less power is consumed by the station's radio. That is because the station is required to transmit fewer frames when in Power Save mode. With 802.11 power management, a PS-Poll had to be transmitted by the station prior to each retrieved frame from the AP's buffer. U-APSD improves upon that by having the station transmit a single frame (a null data frame with the power management flag set to 0) prior to retrieving all unicast frames from the AP's buffer.

The bottom line is that U-APSD is a superior power management method to 802.11 power management, and it should be chosen whenever there is an option to enable either method.

As mentioned earlier in the chapter, U-APSD was introduced by the 802.11e amendment. A lot of stations are being used in the real world that do not support 802.11e, but that does not mean those stations are stuck using the old 802.11 power management method. Many non-802.11e stations support a U-APSD-esque method of power management.

The difference between 802.11e U-APSD and the non-802.11e power management method that is similar to U-APSD is what happens when the station sends that null data frame to retrieve all unicast frames from the AP's buffer. When U-APSD is employed, those formerly buffered frames are transmitted by the AP using a TXOP, which means that a little SIFS or RIFS (for 802.11n devices only) may be used between frames. When the non-802.11e power management method that is similar to U-APSD is employed, the formerly buffered frames are transmitted by the AP without using a TXOP. That means a full DIFS and random backoff timer must precede each frame as the AP's buffer empties.

> In the real world, U-APSD and the non-802.11e power management method that is similar to U-APSD may offer identical power savings. The default settings for Best Effort traffic is to use a TXOP limit of 0, which means that only one frame is allowed per TXOP. Since most applications (even voice and video applications) use the Best Effort access category for their traffic, in most cases it makes no difference whether a device is certified WMM Power Save as long as it uses null data frames in place of PS-Poll frames.

802.11n Power Management

802.11n power management must be mentioned because the CWAP exam covers it, but really there is nothing to see here. 802.11n stations use U-APSD in real life, and that is all that you need to know for practical analysis.

The CWAP certification does require that candidates understand 802.11n power management, however, and therefore power save multi-poll (PSMP) and spatial multiplexing power save (*SMPS*) must be briefly mentioned here.

PSMP

PSMP is a power management method that builds on scheduled automatic power save delivery (*S-APSD*). S-APSD comes from the 802.11e amendment. It is the power management method primarily defined for networks that use hybrid coordination function (HCF) controlled channel access (*HCCA*), which is a method of channel access that involves the AP negotiating or assigning service periods for stations to transmit and receive frames. With S-APSD, stations are allowed to doze in between their service periods.

PSMP also allows stations to doze in between their service periods. There are differences in the frames sent when using PSMP and S-APSD (for example, PSMP involves the use of the PSMP field and the identification of frames as "PSMP frames"), but the basic structure is the same.

Unscheduled PSMP is also defined by 802.11n, and it has the same structure as U-APSD with different messages being used. There is more detail on PSMP in the 802.11n chapter.

SMPS

SMPS is similar to PSMP in that it is simple to describe, but it is different in that it might actually be seen in real-world products. SMPS involves stations reducing the number of data streams used during spatial multiplexing. 802.11n stations may be able to transmit multiple data streams at once by using spatial multiplexing in order to increase throughput or extend range, but that causes a drain in battery life. SMPS just involves disabling spatial multiplexing temporarily so that battery life can be extended.

SMPS is described in more detail in Chapter 10.

IBSS Power Management

Independent basic service sets (IBSS) may also use power management, though it is different from the power management methods described so far in this chapter. The basic structure is the same: stations send a notification before dozing, and then frames get buffered, and finally the dozing stations wake up in order to retrieve their frames. The difference is that there is no central AP to buffer the frames, and there is no need for a TIM or DTIM.

In an IBSS, all communication is direct. Therefore, if a station has gone into the doze state, there may be multiple associated stations that have to buffer data.

To accommodate the fact that multiple devices may be buffering frames for one dozing station, IBSS power management introduces the use of the announcement traffic indication message (*ATIM*) frame. The ATIM is a management frame that has no frame body. When a station receives an ATIM frame, that formerly dozing station must begin the process of retrieving buffered frames from the station that transmitted the ATIM.

ATIM frames may be transmitted within the ATIM window. The ATIM window is a period of time—starting with the time that a beacon is expected to be received—where ATIM frames may be transmitted by stations that are buffering frames that are destined for dozing stations. The length of the ATIM window is set in the IBSS Parameter Set information element that is transmitted in beacon frames by stations that are members of an IBSS. Stations are not allowed to doze during the ATIM window, similar to the way that stations in a BSS are not allowed to doze when a DTIM beacon frame is transmitted.

As far as the process of retrieving frames in an IBSS from a station's buffer after waking from the doze state goes, when the station that is buffering frames transmits an ATIM, the sleeping station must transmit an acknowledgment in response. After that acknowledgment is received, the buffered frames will be transmitted using the normal contention rules.

Exam Essentials

Know the different power management types. That includes 802.11 power management, 802.11e U-APSD, 802.11n PSMP, and 802.11n SMPS.

Understand the effect of the different power states. Doze, idle, transmit, and receive power states each consume different amounts of power.

Know what each power management mode entails. Power Save mode allows stations to doze, while active mode means that a station always must be awake.

Understand the frame types and information elements used for power management. That includes PS-Poll frames, null data frames, and the TIM information element in beacon frames.

Be familiar with the basic structure of power management. You should understand the activity of both stations and APs.

Key Terms

802.11 power management	idle
802.11e	information element
802.11n	More Data
active mode	More Data flag
AID	Null data
ATIM	Partial Virtual Bitmap
Beacon Interval	power management flag
Bitmap Control	Power Save mode
Bitmap Offset	PSMP
buffer	PS-Poll
delta time	receive
doze	Receive DTIMs
DTIM beacon	S-APSD
DTIM Count	SMPS
DTIM Period	TIM
DTIMs	transmit
HCCA	U-APSD
	unicast

Summary

The 802.11 power management process involves allowing stations to spend as much time in the power-saving doze state as possible and as little time in power-draining idle state as possible. When a station is not transmitting or receiving frames, it needs the AP to buffer those frames while the station dozes. Then when the station goes back to transmitting and receiving, it needs a method of retrieving those frames from the buffer. That is it. How that is accomplished is where things get tricky. The original 802.11 standard specified 802.11 power management, 802.11e specified APSD, and 802.11n specified PSMP as ways to make that happen. Each one works, but the amount of battery life that gets saved will vary.

Review Questions

1. Which one of the following 802.11 amendments defined new power management methods, involving stations entering the doze state, that are used in real-world devices? (Choose all that apply.)

   A. 802.11b

   B. 802.11e

   C. 802.11h

   D. 802.11n

2. Which of the following frame types is typically used by stations to notify an AP of a change in power management mode?

   A. Acknowledgment

   B. Null data

   C. PS-Poll

   D. RTS

3. Which of the following states drains the most battery life?

   A. Doze

   B. Idle

   C. Receive

   D. Transmit

4. Which of the following states drains the least battery life?

   A. Doze

   B. Idle

   C. Receive

   D. Transmit

5. Which power management method uses the PS-Poll frame?

   A. 802.11 power management

   B. 802.11 power save polling

   C. 802.11e automatic power save delivery

   D. 802.11n power save multi-poll

6. If the only station that has buffered unicast frames at the AP was assigned an AID of 27, what will be the value of the Bitmap Offset in the TIM information element?

   A. 1

   B. 2

   C. 3

   D. 4

7. What is the minimum value of the Length field of the TIM information element?
   A. 4
   B. 5
   C. 6
   D. 7

8. What is the element ID of the TIM information element?
   A. 4
   B. 5
   C. 6
   D. 7

9. Which of the following is false?
   A. Stations must use the PS-Poll frame to retrieve buffered unicast frames from the AP when 802.11 power management is used.
   B. Stations use the DTIM beacon to view information about unicast, multicast, and broadcast frames that are buffered at the AP.
   C. Stations must always be awake when DTIM beacon frames are sent by the AP.
   D. Stations using 802.11e U-APSD will never transmit a PS-Poll frame.

10. Which additional fields are added to the TIM information element in a DTIM beacon frame?
    A. DTIM Count
    B. DTIM Period
    C. Both A and B
    D. Neither A nor B

11. Which type of power management frame is used only in an IBSS?
    A. ATIM
    B. DTIM
    C. CF-Poll
    D. PS-Poll

12. Which type of frame used during power management is a control frame?
    A. ATIM
    B. Beacon
    C. PS-Poll
    D. Null

13. When a station sends a PS-Poll frame to the AP, how many frames of buffered unicast data are retrieved?

   A. 0

   B. 1

   C. Enough to fill a single TXOP

   D. All unicast frames in the AP's buffer

14. When an AP is sending a unicast frame to a station in response to a PS-Poll, which flag in the 802.11 header lets the station know whether there are more frames in the AP's buffer for the station to retrieve?

   A. From DS

   B. More data

   C. Order

   D. Power management

15. Which field in the TIM information element is used to indicate whether broadcast and/or multicast frames are buffered at the AP?

   A. DTIM Count

   B. DTIM Period

   C. Bitmap Control

   D. Partial Virtual Bitmap

16. Which of the following are reasons that stations might wake up from the doze state? (Choose two.)

   A. The station has received a frame from the AP.

   B. The station's NAV timer expires.

   C. The station has a frame ready to be transmitted.

   D. The station expects a DTIM beacon frame to be transmitted by the AP.

17. If a station has sent a frame to the AP with the power management flag set to 1, which of the following states may the station go into? (Choose all that apply.)

   A. Doze

   B. Idle

   C. Receive

   D. Transmit

18. If a station has sent a frame to the AP with the power management flag set to 0, which of the following states may the station go into? (Choose all that apply.)

   A. Doze

   B. Idle

   C. Receive

   D. Transmit

19. Name two reasons why 802.11 power management is considered inefficient.

   A. All buffered unicast frames sent by the AP must be followed by an acknowledgment frame.

   B. All buffered unicast frames sent by the AP must be preceded by a PS-Poll frame.

   C. Too much protocol overhead is caused by the acknowledgment frames that follow retrieved unicast frames from the AP's buffer.

   D. Too much protocol overhead is caused by the PS-Poll frames that precede retrieved unicast frames from the AP's buffer.

20. You perform a frame capture on a BSS that has a WMM Power Save–certified AP. You notice in the beacon frames that the Beacon Interval is 100 and the DTIM Period is 3. You also notice that when your station is idle, null data frames are transmitted once every second and that the power management flag alternates between 0 and 1 in those null data frames. What does this mean? (Choose two.)

   A. The Receive DTIMs setting in your station is set to false.

   B. The Receive DTIMs setting in your station is set to true.

   C. The station supports U-APSD.

   D. The station does not support U-APSD.

Answers to Review Questions

1. B, D. 802.11e defined U-APSD and 802.11n defined unscheduled PSMP, which are used in real-world stations and APs that are WMM Power Save certified. 802.11b and 802.11h amendments did not define new power management methods.

2. B. Null data frames use the power management flag in the 802.11 header to change between active mode and Power Save mode. Acknowledgment and RTS frames do not play a role in power management. PS-Poll frames are used in power management, but they are typically used to retrieve buffered unicast frames from the AP, not to notify the AP of a change in power state.

3. D. The transmit state drains the most battery life. The receive state drains the second-most battery life, idle drains the third most, and doze drains the least battery life.

4. A. The doze state drains the least battery life. The idle state drains the second-least battery life, receive drains the third most, and transmit drains the most battery life.

5. A. 802.11 power management is the only power management method that uses the PS-Poll frame. 802.11 power save polling is not a power management method. 802.11e APSD uses null data frames to alternate between power management modes. 802.11n PSMP does not use PS-Poll frames.

6. A. The Bitmap Offset defines how many 8-bit sequences (octets) may be eliminated from the Partial Virtual Bitmap field because of the stations not having unicast frames buffered at the AP. Each station is assigned an AID, and if the station does not have any unicast frames buffered at the AP, then the value for that station's AID in the Partial Virtual Bitmap is 0. If an entire byte of AIDs at the start of the bitmap are 0s (AIDs 0–7, 8–15, 16–24, and so on), then a Bitmap Offset value can be set. If the station with an AID of 27 is the first AID with unicast frames buffered at the AP, then a Bitmap Offset value of 1 (meaning that AIDs 0–7 and 8–15 are all set to 0) would be used.

   If the Bitmap Offset were set to 2, then AIDs 0–7, 8–15, 16–23, and 24–31 would all be equal to 0. Since AID 27 is equal to 1 in the Partial Virtual Bitmap, 2 is incorrect.

7. A. The Length field defines how many bytes are used by information carrying fields in the TIM information element. The DTIM Count, DTIM Period, Bitmap Control, and Partial Virtual Bitmap are the fields of the TIM, and each field has a minimum length of 1 byte. Therefore, 4 is the lowest possible value for the Length field.

   5, 6, and 7 are all possible values for the Length field, but 4 is the lowest possible value.

8. B. 5 is the element ID for the TIM information element.

9. C. Stations with the Receive DTIMs setting set to false will not wake up for DTIM beacon frames from the AP. 802.11 power management does involve stations retrieving unicast frames from the AP using PS-Poll frames. DTIM beacon frames do carry information about unicast, multicast, and broadcast frames buffered at the AP. U-APSD does not support the use of PS-Poll frames.

10. D. The DTIM Count and DTIM Period fields are present in all TIM information elements of beacon frames. If a beacon is a DTIM beacon, then the DTIM Count field will be set to 0. The DTIM Period field plays no role in identifying whether a beacon is a DTIM beacon.

11. A. The ATIM is a frame used in IBSS networks to allow a station with frames in its buffer to notify a sleeping station that the frames are ready to be retrieved. DTIM is not a type of frame. CF-Poll and PS-Poll frames are not unique to IBSS networks.

12. C. The PS-Poll is a control frame. The ATIM and beacon frames are management frames. The null frame is a data frame.

13. B. A PS-Poll frame retrieves one unicast frame buffered at the AP. Null data frames retrieve all unicast frames in the AP's buffer. Frames that are not PS-Poll frames and that have the power management flag in the 802.11 header set to 1 retrieve 0 unicast frames from the AP's buffer. There is no type of frame that retrieves only a single TXOP's worth of unicast frames from the AP's buffer.

14. B. The More Data flag in the 802.11 header is set to 1 by the AP when additional unicast frames are still in the AP's buffer. The From DS and Order flags have nothing to do with power management. The Power Management flag is set to 1 by stations as a way of indicating to the AP that frames should be held in the AP's buffer.

15. C. When broadcast and/or multicast frames are buffered at the AP, the first bit of the Bitmap Control field (which corresponds to AID 0) will be set to 1.

The DTIM Count, DTIM Period, and Partial Virtual Bitmap fields are all present in DTIM beacon frames, but none of them carries the indicator to stations that broadcast and/or multicast frames that are buffered at the AP.

16. C, D. Stations may wake from the doze state when a frame is ready to be transmitted, if the station expects a DTIM beacon frame or if the station has an internal timer that tells it when to wake up. Receiving a frame from the AP would not affect a dozing station because a station's radio cannot receive frames when dozing. The NAV timer has nothing to do with power management.

17. A, B, C, D. All states may be used by stations that are in Power Save mode. When a station goes into Power Save mode, it causes the AP to buffer frames, but it does not prevent the station from transmitting, receiving, or staying awake and in the idle state.

18. B, C, D. The doze state may not be used by a station that is in active mode, because APs will not buffer frames if all stations are in active mode.

19. B, D. 802.11 power management is inefficient because the transmission of a PS-Poll frame by stations in advance of retrieving buffered unicast frames from the AP causes the station to drain too much battery life and causes too much overhead to be added to the channel. Acknowledgment frames are not added to the network when 802.11 power management is used.

20. **A, D.** If the Beacon Interval field is 100 and the DTIM Period field is 3, then a DTIM beacon frame is transmitted by the AP every 300 kilomicroseconds (approximately every 300 milliseconds). If the delta time between a station's transmitted null data frames alternating the power management mode is 1 second (1,000 milliseconds), then that means the station is dozing while DTIM beacon frames are being transmitted by the AP. The only way a station may doze while DTIM beacon frames are being transmitted by the AP is if the Receive DTIMs setting on the station is set to false.

If the Receive DTIMs setting on the station were set to true, then a station would show a delta time of no more than three tenths of a second if the Beacon Interval is 100 and the DTIM Period is 3.

The use of null data frames rather than QoS null data frames indicates that the station is not using U-APSD, but rather the non-802.11e power management method that is similar to U-APSD.

Chapter

9

802.11 Security

IN THIS CHAPTER, YOU WILL LEARN ABOUT THE FOLLOWING:

- ✓ **Authentication**
  - ▪ Open System Authentication
  - ▪ Shared Key Authentication
- ✓ **WLAN Encryption Methods**
  - ▪ WEP
  - ▪ TKIP
  - ▪ CCMP
- ✓ **WPA/WPA2**
- ✓ **Robust Security Networks (RSN)**
- ✓ **RSN Information Element**
- ✓ **802.1X**
  - ▪ Supplicant
  - ▪ Authenticator
  - ▪ Authentication Server
- ✓ **EAP**
  - ▪ Strong EAP Protocols
  - ▪ EAP-PEAP
- ✓ **4-Way Handshake**
- ✓ **Group Key Handshake**
- ✓ **FastBSS Transition (FT)**
  - ▪ Information Elements
  - ▪ FT Initial Mobility Domain Association
  - ▪ Over-the-air Fast BSS Transition
  - ▪ Over-the-DS Fast BSS Transition
- ✓ **802.11w Protected Management Frames**

In this chapter, we will cover 802.11 security, highlighting some of the frame exchanges and changes to frames when security is enabled. The focus of this book is 802.11 analysis and not security. If you would like to learn more about 802.11 security, you should consider reading *CWSP Certified Wireless Security Professional Official Study Guide: Exam PW0-204* (Sybex, 2010).

Authentication

Authentication is the first of two steps required to connect to the 802.11 basic service set. Both authentication and association must occur, in that order, before an 802.11 client can pass traffic through the access point to another device on the network. Authentication is a process that is often misunderstood. When many people hear *authentication*, they think of what is commonly referred to as network authentication, in other words, entering a username and password in order to get access to the network. In this chapter, we are referring to 802.11 authentication that occurs at layer 2 of the OSI model. When an 802.3 device needs to communicate with other devices, the first step is to plug the Ethernet cable into a wall jack. When this cable is plugged in, the client creates a physical link to the wired switch and is now able to start transmitting frames. When an 802.11 device needs to communicate, it must first authenticate with the access point. This authentication is not much more of a task than plugging the Ethernet cable into the wall jack. The 802.11 authentication merely establishes an initial connection between the client and the access point, basically validating or authenticating that the STA is a valid 802.11 device. The 802.11-2007 standard specifies two different methods of authentication: Open System authentication and Shared Key authentication.

Open System Authentication

Within a basic service set (BSS), Open System authentication occurs with an exchange of frames between the client station and the access point station. Open System authentication utilizes a two-message authentication transaction sequence. The client that is looking to join the BSS sends the first message, which in itself is essentially asserting its 802.11 identity and requesting authentication to the BSS. The second message returns the authentication result. If the result is "successful," the STAs will be declared mutually authenticated, both identified as 802.11 devices. Open System authentication is also used by STAs in an independent basic service set (IBSS), which is more commonly known as an ad hoc WLAN.

Open System authentication occurs after a client STA knows about the existence of an access point (AP) by either passive or active scanning. The client STA can passively find out about the parameters of the BSS from the AP's beacon management frame or extract the same information during the active probing process from the AP's probe response frame. An Open System authentication frame exchange process then begins with the goal of eventually joining the BSS. As shown in Figure 9.1, the client STA must first become authenticated before exchanging two more association frames. Once Open System authentication and association occurs, the client STA establishes a layer 2 connection to the AP and is a member of the BSS.

FIGURE 9.1   Open System authentication

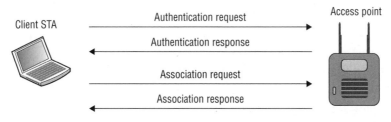

Exchange complete–client STA joins the BSS

WEP encryption is optional with Open System authentication. For data privacy, Wired Equivalent Privacy encryption can be used with Open System authentication, but WEP is used only to encrypt the layers 3–7 MAC Service Data Unit (MSDU) payload of 802.11 data frames and only after the client station is authenticated and associated. In other words, WEP is not used as part of the Open System authentication process, but WEP encryption can be used to provide data privacy after authentication and association occur. So, if Open System authentication is so simple and basic—providing no verification of identity—then why is it still used when security is so important? The answer to this question is simple. It doesn't need to be secure, because other more advanced overlay security authentication methods such as 802.1X/EAP are now being implemented. As you can see in Figure 9.2, Open System authentication and association between the client STA and AP still occurs prior to the 802.1X/EAP authentication exchange between the client STA and a RADIUS server. In Exercise 9.1, you will look at a packet capture containing Open System authentication frames.

The 802.11-2007 standard now defines more advanced authentication methods. A more detailed discussion about 802.1X/EAP can be found later in this chapter and in *CWSP Certified Wireless Security Professional Official Study Guide: Exam PW0-204.*

FIGURE 9.2   Open System and 802.1X/EAP authentication

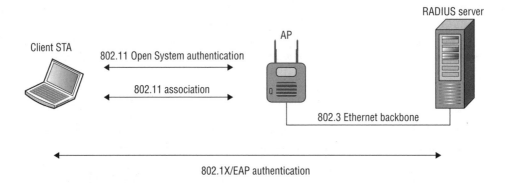

Shared Key Authentication

Shared Key authentication is a four-way authentication frame exchange, as shown in Figure 9.3. Shared Key authentication requires WEP to authenticate the client station. The client station sends an authentication request to the AP, and the AP sends a clear-text challenge to the client station in an authentication response. The client station then encrypts the clear-text challenge and sends it back to the AP in the body of another authentication request frame. The AP decrypts the station's response and compares it to the challenge text. If they match, the AP will respond by sending a fourth and final authentication frame, an authentication response frame to the station, confirming successful authentication. If they do not match, the AP will respond negatively. If the WEP ICV check fails or if the AP cannot decrypt the challenge, it will also respond negatively. If Shared Key authentication is successful, the same static WEP key that was used during the Shared Key authentication process will also be used to encrypt the 802.11 data frames.

When WEP is enabled, it might seem that Shared Key authentication is a more secure solution than Open System authentication, in reality Shared Key could be the bigger security risk. Anyone who captures the clear-text challenge phrase and then captures the encrypted challenge phrase in the response frame could potentially derive the static WEP key. If the static WEP key is compromised, a whole new can of worms has been opened because now all the data frames can be decrypted.

Do not confuse the Shared Key authentication with Preshared Key (PSK) authentication. Shared Key authentication is a legacy method defined as a pre-RSNA security method. The 802.11-2007 standard defines robust security that requires either 802.1X/EAP authentication or PSK authentication. PSK authentication methods are discussed later in this chapter and in *CWSP Certified Wireless Security Professional Official Study Guide: Exam PW0-204*.

FIGURE 9.3   Shared Key authentication exchange

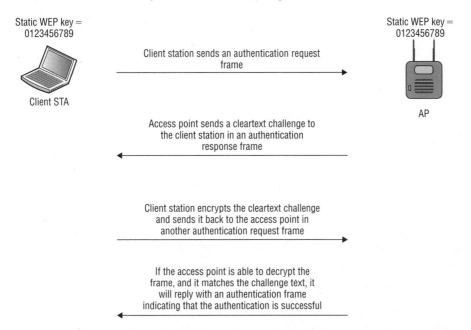

In Exercise 9.1, you will look at packet captures containing encrypted and decrypted Shared Key authentication frames.

EXERCISE 9.1

Viewing Open System and Shared Key Authentication Frames

In this exercise, you will use a protocol analyzer to view the 802.11 frame exchanges used to authenticate a client to the access point. To perform the exercises in this chapter, we will walk you through using Wireshark. The following directions should assist you with locating, downloading, and installing Wireshark. If you are familiar with another protocol

Continued

analyzing software, feel free to use it to perform this lab. If you have already installed Wireshark, you can skip steps 1–4.

1. In your web browser, go to the Wireshark website: www.wireshark.org.

2. Click the Download Wireshark button to locate the installation file, and download the file that is appropriate for your operating system.

3. After downloading the file, double-click it to proceed with the installation, and follow the installation directions.

4. The exercise will use frame captures that are on the book's companion CD. If you would like to use Wireshark for live wireless captures (and you are running Windows), you will have to purchase an AirPcap adapter from Cace Technologies (www.cacetech.com).

5. In Windows, choose Start ➢ All Programs, and then click the Wireshark icon. The Wireshark application should appear.

6. In the center section, click the Open icon, and browse to the book's CD.

7. Open the packet capture file called OPEN_SYSTEM_AUTHENTICATION.PCAP.

    The file will open, and Wireshark will display three sections:

    ▪   The top section is called the *packet list*, displaying a list of the individual packets.

    ▪   The middle section is called the *packet detail*, displaying as much detail about each packet as possible.

    ▪   The bottom section shows the bytes in the current packet.

    When you click packet 1 in the packet list, Wireshark will display the packet detail in the middle section of the window.

8. Click the + next to IEEE 802.11 Wireless LAN Management Frame to expand that section, and then click the + to expand the Fixed Parameters (6 Bytes) section.

    If you look in this section, you will see Authentication Algorithm is Open System and Authentication Seq Num is 1. This indicates it is an Open System authentication request frame.

    In the packet list section, if you click the third packet, in the packet detail section you will see Authentication Algorithm is Open System and Authentication Seq Num is 2. This indicates it is an Open System authentication reply frame. You can also see that Status Code indicates that the authentication was successful.

9. Go to the File menu, and select Close. This will bring you back to the initial Wireshark screen.

10. In the center section, click the Open icon, and browse the book's CD.

11. Open the packet capture file called SHARED_KEY_AUTHENTICATION_ENCRYPTED.PCAP.

    The two packets of most interest are packets 3 and 5. In packet 3, the access point is responding to the authentication request and including the challenge text unencrypted.

12. Expand the IEEE 802.11 Wireless LAN Management Frame section, and you will see the challenge text.

13. Select packet 5. This frame is the response from the client to the access point. The client has taken the challenge text and encrypted it. If you expand the IEEE 802.11 Authentication section, you will see the WEP parameters, and if you expand the Data section, you will see 136 bytes of encrypted data.

14. Go to the File menu, and select Close.

15. In the center section, click the Open File icon, and browse to the book's CD.

16. Open the packet capture file called SHARED_KEY_AUTHENTICATION_DECRYPTED.PCAP.

17. This file is a decrypted version of the file you were just looking at. Repeat steps 12 and 13 using the decrypted file.

WLAN Encryption Methods

The 802.11-2007 standard defines three encryption methods that operate at layer 2 of the OSI model: Wired Equivalent Privacy (WEP), Temporal Key Integrity Protocol (TKIP), and CTR with CBC-MAC Protocol (CCMP). The information that is being protected by these layer 2 encryption methods is data found in the upper layers of 3–7. Layer 2 encryption methods are used to provide data privacy for 802.11 data frames.

The 802.11 data frame, or *MAC Protocol Data Unit (MPDU)*, as shown in Figure 9.4, contains a layer 2 MAC header, a frame body, and a trailer, which is a 32-bit CRC known as the *frame check sequence (FCS)*. The layer 2 header contains MAC addresses and the Duration value. Encapsulated inside the frame body of an 802.11 data frame is the upper-layer payload, the *MAC Service Data Unit (MSDU)*. The MSDU contains data from the Logical Link Control (LLC) and layers 3–7. The MSDU is the data payload that contains an IP packet plus some LLC data. The 802.11-2007 standard states that the MSDU payload can be anywhere from 0 to 2,304 bytes. The frame body may actually be larger because of encryption overhead.

WEP, TKIP, CCMP, and other proprietary layer 2 encryption methods are used to encrypt the MSDU payload of an 802.11 data frame. Therefore, the information that is being protected is the upper layers of 3–7, more commonly known as the IP packet. The current 802.11-2007 standard defines WEP as a legacy encryption method for prerobust security network association (pre-RSNA) security. TKIP and CCMP are considered to be compliant *robust security network (RSN)* encryption protocols.

FIGURE 9.4   802.11 MAC Protocol Data Unit

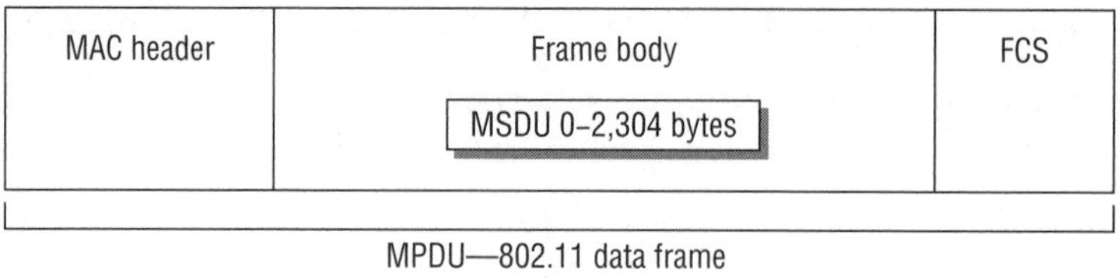

MAC header	Frame body	FCS
	MSDU 0–2,304 bytes	

MPDU—802.11 data frame

WEP

Wired Equivalent Privacy is a layer 2 security protocol that uses the RC4 streaming cipher. The original 802.11 standard defined both 64-bit WEP and 128-bit WEP as supported encryption methods. The current 802.11-2007 standard still defines WEP as a legacy encryption method for pre-RSNA security. The Wi-Fi Alliance has been certifying 802.11 radios using WEP encryption since 2000.

64-bit WEP uses a secret 40-bit static key, which is combined with a 24-bit number selected by the card's device drivers. This 24-bit number, known as the initialization vector (IV), is sent in clear text and is different on every frame. Although the IV is said to be different on every frame, there are only 16,777,216 different IV combinations; therefore, you are forced to reuse the IV values. 128-bit WEP encryption uses a 104-bit secret static key that is also combined with a 24-bit IV. Because of the 24-bit IV that is added to the WEP key by the device driver, the 802.11-2007 standard refers to 64-bit WEP as WEP-40 and 128-bit WEP as WEP-104.

As shown in Figure 9.5, the static key and the IV are used as WEP seeding material through the pseudorandom RC4 algorithm that generates the keystream. The pseudorandom bits in the keystream are then combined with the plain-text data bits by using a Boolean XOR process. The end result is the WEP cipher text, which is the encrypted data. WEP also runs a *cyclic redundancy check (CRC)* on the plain-text data that is to be encrypted and then appends the *integrity check value (ICV)* to the end of the plain-text data. The ICV is used for data integrity and should not be confused with the IV, which is part of the seeding material for the RC4 cipher.

If You Thought WEP Used RC4 Encryption, You Are Right and Wrong!

RC4 is also known as ARC4 or Arcfour. ARC4 is short for Alleged RC4. RC4 was created in 1987 by Ron Rivest of RSA Security. It is known as either Rivest Cipher 4 or Ron's Code 4. RC4 was initially a trade secret; however, in 1994, a description of it was leaked onto the Internet. Comparison testing confirmed that the leaked code was genuine. RSA has never officially released the algorithm, and the name RC4 is trademarked, which is why it's called Arcfour or ARC4.

FIGURE 9.5   WEP encryption process

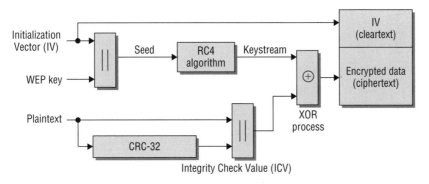

The encryption and decryption process for WEP is the same whether you are using WEP-40 or WEP-104. Figure 9.6 shows the WEP frame body, which contains an encrypted MSDU. To create the WEP-encrypted MSDU, WEP runs a cyclic redundancy check on the plain-text data that is to be encrypted and then appends the ICV to the end of the plain-text data. The ICV adds 32 bits (4 octets) of overhead to an 802.11 data frame. The data and ICV are then encrypted. WEP can be configured with up to four different keys. A Key ID identifies which WEP key was combined with the system-generated 24-bit IV to perform the encryption. This 24-bit IV is combined with the Key ID and 6 bits of padding to create a 32-bit IV. The IV adds 32 bits (4 octets) of overhead to the frame body of an 802.11 data frame. The IV is not encrypted and is appended to the front of the encrypted MSDU payload.

Bits, Bytes, Octets

A *bit* is a binary digit, taking a value of either 0 or 1. Binary digits are a basic unit of communication in digital computing. A byte of information comprises 8 bits. An *octet* is another name for one byte of data. The CWAP exam uses the terminology of octet and byte interchangeably.

Remember that WEP encrypts the MSDU upper-layer payload that is encapsulated in the frame body of an MPDU. The MSDU payload has a maximum size of 2,304 bytes. Because the IV adds 4 octets and the ICV also adds 4 octets, when WEP is enabled, the entire size of the body inside an 802.11 data frame is expanded by 8 bytes to a maximum of 2312 bytes. In other words, WEP encryption adds 8 bytes of overhead to an 802.11 MPDU.

FIGURE 9.6 WEP MPDU format

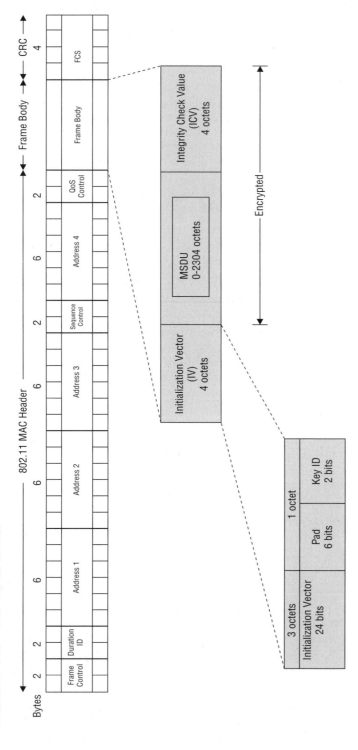

TKIP

TKIP is an enhancement of WEP. Like WEP, TKIP uses the ARC4 algorithm for performing its encryption and decryption processes. The TKIP enhancements were also intended to address the many known weaknesses of WEP. TKIP uses dynamically created encryption keys as opposed to the static keys. Any two radios use a *4-Way Handshake* process to create dynamic unicast keys that are unique to those two radios.

Figure 9.7 shows the TKIP encryption and data integrity process. It will be helpful to refer to this figure as you read about the steps TKIP performs.

TKIP starts with a 128-bit temporal key. An often-asked question is "Where does the 128-bit temporal key come from?" The answer is that the 128-bit temporal key is a dynamically generated key that comes from a 4-Way Handshake creation process. This key is identical on the AP and client pair. The 128-bit temporal key can either be a *pairwise transient key (PTK)* used to encrypt unicast traffic or a *group temporal key (GTK)* used to encrypt broadcast and multicast traffic.

After the appropriate 128-bit temporal key (pairwise or group) is created, the two-phase key-mixing process begins. A 48-bit TKIP sequence counter (TSC) is generated and broken into 6 octets labeled TSC0 (least significant octet) through TSC5 (most significant octet). Phase 1 key mixing combines the 128-bit temporal key (TK) with the TSC2 through TSC5 octets of the TSC as well as the *transmit address (TA)*. The TA is the MAC address of the transmitting 802.11 radio. The output of the Phase 1 key mixing is the creation of the *TKIP-mixed transmit address and key (TTAK)*.

After the TTAK is generated, the Phase 2 key mixing can begin. Phase 2 key mixing combines the TTAK with the TSC0 and TSC1 octets of the TSC with the 128-bit TK. The output of the Phase 2 key mixing is referred to as the *WEP seed*. This WEP seed is then run through the ARC4 algorithm, and the keystream is created. The WEP seed is represented as a WEP IV and 104-bit WEP key when fed into the ARC4 algorithm. You may often hear TKIP referenced as using a 48-bit IV. During the Phase 2 key mixing process, TKIP encodes the TSC value from the sender as a WEP IV and an extended IV. The encoding of the 48-bit TSC effectively creates a 48-bit IV.

The two-phase key-mixing process can be summarized as follows:

- TTAK = Phase 1 (TK, TA, TSC)

- WEP seed = Phase 2 (TTAK, TK, TSC)

TKIP uses a stronger data integrity check known as the message integrity code (MIC) to mitigate known forgery attacks against WEP. The MIC is often referred to by its nickname of Michael. The MIC can be used to defeat bit-flipping attacks, fragmentation attacks, redirection, and impersonation attacks. The MIC is computed using the destination address (DA), the source address (SA), the MSDU priority, and the entire unencrypted MSDU plaintext data. After the MIC is generated, it is appended the end of the MSDU payload. The MIC is 8 octets in size and is labeled individually as M0 through M7. The MIC contains only 20 bits of effective security strength, making it somewhat vulnerable to brute-force attacks. Because the MIC only provides weak protection against active attacks, the 802.11-2007 standard defines *TKIP countermeasures* procedures. The TKIP countermeasures include the following.

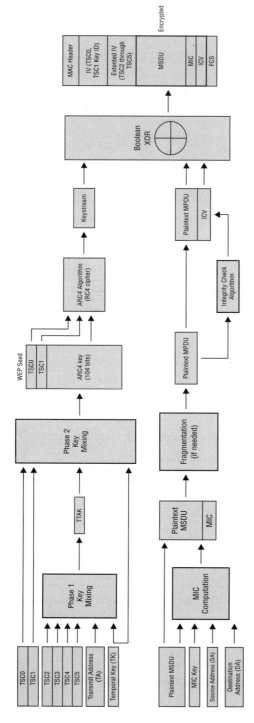

FIGURE 9.7 TKIP encryption and data integrity process

The TKIP MIC augments, but does not replace, the WEP ICV. TKIP protects the MIC with encryption, which makes TKIP MIC forgeries more difficult. The WEP ICV helps prevent false detection of MIC failures that would cause the countermeasures to be invoked.

After the MIC is created and appended to the plain-text MSDU, the 802.11 MAC performs its normal processing on this MSDU. If fragmentation is enabled, it is possible that this could be broken up into one or more MPDUs. It is even possible for the MIC to wind up split between two MPDUs. To keep things simple, we will assume that only one MPDU is created. An integrity check is performed on the plain-text MPDU, and the WEP ICV is then appended to the MPDU. A Boolean XOR is then performed on the keystream and the MPDU/ICV to generate the encrypted payload. A frame check sequence is calculated over all the fields of the header and entire frame body. The resulting 32-bit CRC is then placed in the FCS field.

Before verifying the MIC, a receiving 802.11 STA will check the FCS, ICV, and TSC of all MPDUs. Any MPDU that has an invalid FCS, an incorrect ICV, or a TSC value that is less than or equal to the TSC replay counter is dropped before checking the MIC. This avoids unnecessary MIC failure events. Checking the TSC before the MIC makes countermeasure-based DoS attacks harder to perform. Checking the TSC also protects against replay/injection attacks. Although considered weak for data integrity protection, the ICV also offers some error detection. If the MPDU is corrupted by multipath interference or collisions, the FCS fails, and the entire MPDU must be retransmitted. After the FCS, ICV, and TSC are checked, the MIC is used for verification of data integrity.

Figure 9.8 shows the TKIP MPDU. The first 32 bytes are the 802.11 MAC header, which does not change. The encrypted frame body consists of five key pieces:

- IV/Key ID
- Extended IV
- MSDU payload
- MIC
- ICV

It begins with the IV/Key ID combination. This is 4 octets in size and is similar to the IV/Key ID that is found in WEP. TSC0 and TSC1, the first two octets of the 48-bit TKIP sequence counter (TSC0 and TSC1), make up part of the IV/Key ID. If TKIP is being used, which is the case in this example, the Extended IV field is set to 1, indicating that an extended IV of 4 octets will follow the original IV. The Extended IV is 4 octets and is made up of the other 4 octets of the 48-bit TKIP sequence counter (TSC2 through TSC5). Both the original IV and the Extended IV are not encrypted. The 8 bytes that comprise the IV/Key ID and Extended IV could be considered a TKIP header.

FIGURE 9.8 TKIP MPDU

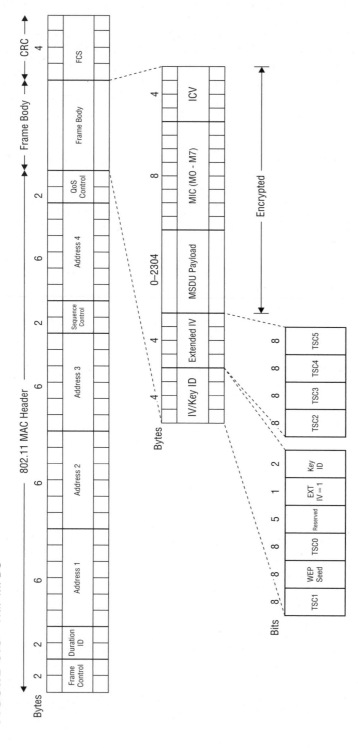

After the original IV and the Extended IV comes the MSDU payload, followed by the 8 MIC octets, which is then followed by the 32-bit ICV that was calculated on the MPDU. The MSDU upper-layer payload as well as the MIC and ICV are all encrypted. The frame is then completed by adding the 32-bit frame check sequence (FCS) that is calculated over all the fields of the header and frame body.

Because of the extra overhead from the IV (4 bytes), Extended IV (4 bytes), MIC (8 bytes), and ICV (4 bytes), a total of 20 bytes of overhead is added to the frame body of a TKIP-encrypted 802.11 data frame. When TKIP is enabled, the entire size of the frame body inside an MPDU is expanded by 20 bytes to a maximum of 2,324 bytes. In other words, TKIP encryption adds 20 bytes of overhead to an 802.11 MPDU.

EXERCISE 9.2

TKIP-Encrypted Frames

In this exercise, you will use a protocol analyzer to view 802.11 data frames encrypted with TKIP. The following directions should assist you with locating, downloading, and installing Wireshark. If you are familiar with another protocol analyzing software, feel free to use it to perform this lab. If you have already installed Wireshark, you can skip steps 1–4.

1. In your web browser, go to the Wireshark website: www.wireshark.org.

2. Click the Download Wireshark button to locate the installation file, and download the file that is appropriate for your operating system.

3. After downloading the file, double-click it to proceed with the installation, and follow the installation directions.

   The exercise will use frame captures that are on the CD that came with this book. If you would like to use Wireshark for live wireless captures (and you are running Windows), you will have to purchase an AirPcap adapter from Cace Technologies (www.cacetech.com).

4. In Windows, choose Start ➢ All Programs, and then click the Wireshark icon. The Wireshark application should appear.

5. In the center section, click the Open icon, and browse the book's CD.

6. Open the packet capture file called TKIP_FRAMES.PCAP.

7. The file will open, and Wireshark will display its three sections. If you click one of the 802.11 TKIP data packets (listed in the Info column), Wireshark will display the details of the frame in the middle section.

8. If you click one of the beacons with the source address of 00:1A:1E:94:4C:31, Wireshark will display the details of the beacon frame in the middle section. If you expand the frame and scroll down, you will see the cipher TKIP is listed.

CCMP

CCMP consists of many components that provide different functions. Before going any further in this section, there are numerous acronyms and abbreviations relating to CCMP to which you need to be introduced. These acronyms and abbreviations are commonly used in the wireless industry and in the IEEE 802.11-2007 standard. Since CCMP consists of many different components, it is common to reference the components individually. Counter mode is often represented as CTR. CTR is used to provide data confidentiality. The acronym for cipher-block chaining is CBC. You should also be familiar with CBC-MAC, which is the acronym for cipher-block chaining message authentication code (CBC-MAC). The CBC-MAC is used for authentication and integrity.

The full phrase of counter mode with the Cipher-Block Chaining Message Authentication Code protocol is represented by the acronym of CCMP. However, the shorter phrase of CTR with CBC-MAC is also sometimes represented by the CCMP acronym.

Some references to CCMP leave off the letter *P* and use the term *CCM* when referencing the block cipher and not the actual protocol. CCMP is based on the CCM of the AES encryption algorithm. CCM combines CTR to provide data confidentiality and CBC-MAC for authentication and integrity. In much simpler words, the CCM process uses the same key for encrypting the MSDU payload and provides for a cryptographic integrity check. The integrity check is used to provide data integrity for both the MSDU data and portions of the MAC header of the MPDU.

CCM is used with the AES block cipher. Although it is capable of using different key sizes, when implemented as part of the CCMP encryption method, AES uses a 128-bit key and encrypts the data in 128-bit blocks.

Figure 9.9 shows the CCMP encryption and data integrity process. It will be helpful to refer to this figure as you read about the steps CCMP performs.

CCMP encrypts the payload of a plain-text MPDU using the following steps:

1. A 48-bit packet number (PN) is created. Packet numbers increment with each individual MPDU, although they remain the same for retransmissions.

2. As shown in Figure 9.10, certain fields in the MPDU header are used to construct the additional authentication data (AAD). Additional authentication data is constructed from portions of the MPDU header. This information is used for data integrity of portions of the MAC header. Receiving stations can then validate the integrity of these MAC header fields.

FIGURE 9.9 CCMP encryption and data integrity process

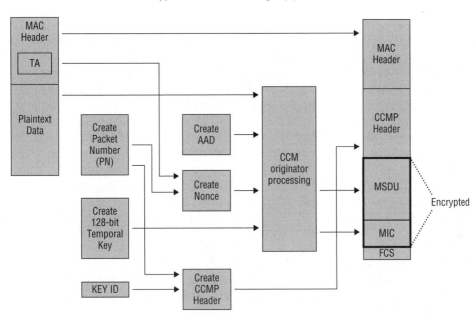

FIGURE 9.10 Additional authentication data (AAD)

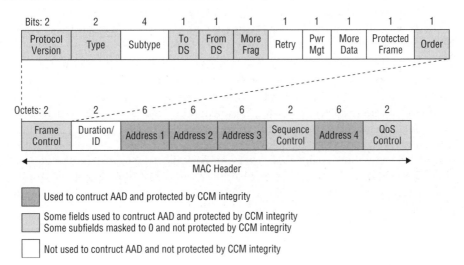

The MIC provides integrity protection for these fields in the MAC header as well as for the frame body. All of the MAC addresses, including the BSSID, are protected. Portions of the other fields of the MAC header are also protected. Receiving stations will validate the integrity of these protected portions of the MAC header. For example, the frame type and the distribution bits that are subfields of the Frame Control field are protected. Receiving stations will validate the integrity of these protected portions of the MAC header. The AAD does not include the header Duration field, because the Duration field value can change because of normal IEEE 802.11 operation. For similar reasons, several subfields in the Frame Control field, the Sequence Control field, and the QoS Control field are masked to 0 and therefore are not protected. For example, the Retry bit and Power Management bits are also masked and are not protected by CCM integrity.

3.   A nonce is created from the packet number (PN), transmitter address (TA), and priority data used in QoS.

4.   The 8-octet CCMP header is constructed. The CCMP header includes the Key ID and the packet (PN), which is divided into 6 octets. You will notice that the construction of the CCMP header is basically identical to the 8-octet TKIP header.

5.   The CCM module, which uses the AES clock cipher, will now be used to create a data integrity check and encrypt the upper-layer data. The 128-bit temporal key, the nonce, the AAD, and the plain-text data are then processed to create an 8-byte MIC. The MSDU payload of the frame body and the MIC are then encrypted in 128-bit blocks. This process is known as CCM originator processing.

6.   The original MAC header is appended to the CCMP header, the encrypted MSDU, and the encrypted MIC. A frame check sequence is calculated over all of the fields of the header and entire frame body. The resulting 32-bit CRC is then placed in the FCS field.

Figure 9.11 shows the CCMP MPDU. The first 32 bytes are the 802.11 MAC header, which does not change. The frame body consists of the CCMP header, the MSDU upper-layer payload, and the MIC. The CCMP header includes the one octet Key ID and the 48-bit packet (PN), which is spread across 6 octets. You will notice that the format of the CCMP header is basically identical to the format of the 8-octet TKIP header (IV/Extended IV). The CCMP header is not encrypted. The MSDU payload and the 8-byte MIC are encrypted.

The overhead that results from CCMP encryption includes the CCMP header (8 bytes) and the MIC (8 bytes). When CCMP is enabled, the entire size of the frame body inside an MPDU is expanded by 16 bytes to a maximum of 2,320 bytes. In other words, CCMP encryption adds 16 bytes of overhead to an 802.11 MPDU.

FIGURE 9.11 CCMP MPDU

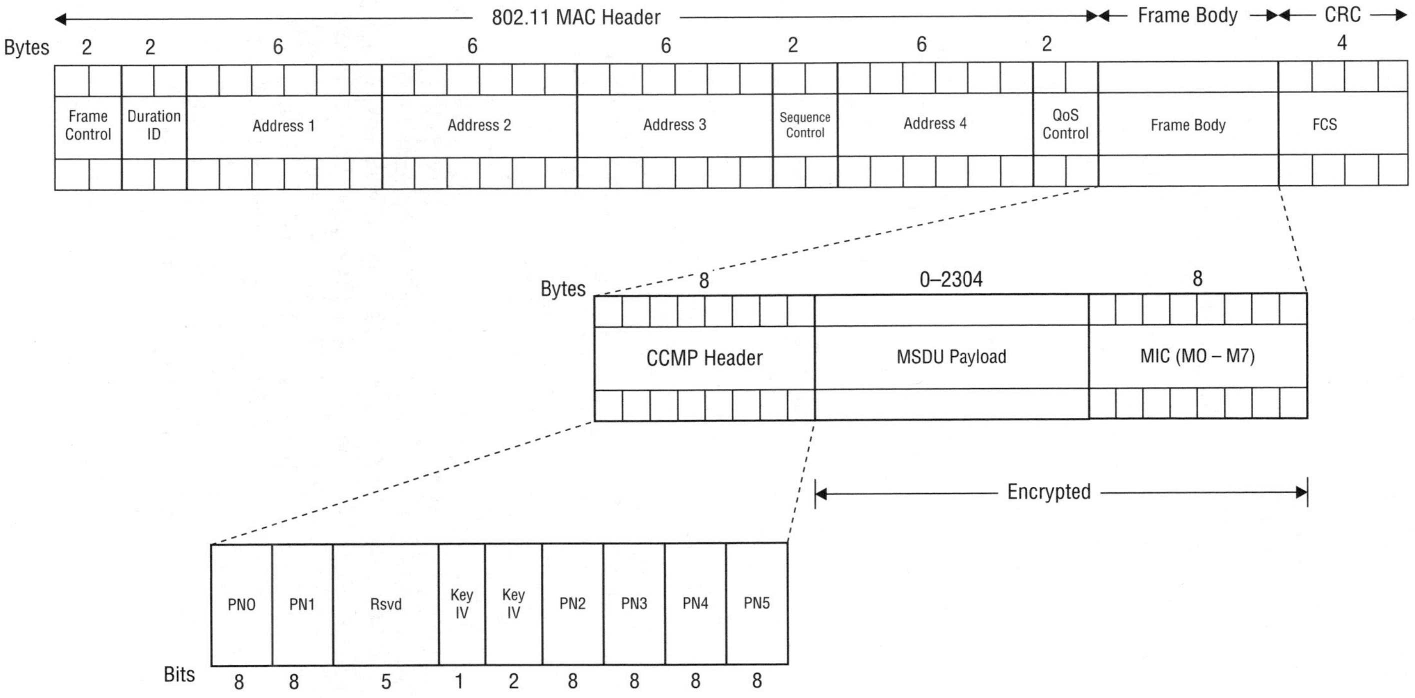

EXERCISE 9.3

CCMP-Encrypted Frames

In this exercise, you will use a protocol analyzer to view 802.11 data frames encrypted with CCMP. The following directions should assist you with locating, downloading, and installing Wireshark. If you are familiar with another protocol analyzing software, feel free to use it to perform this lab. If you have already installed Wireshark, you can skip steps 1–4.

1. In your web browser, go to the Wireshark website: www.wireshark.org.

2. Click the Download Wireshark button to locate the installation file, and download the file that is appropriate for your operating system.

3. After downloading the file, double-click it to proceed with the installation, and follow the installation directions.

4. The exercise will use frame captures that are on the CD that came with this book. If you would like to use Wireshark for live wireless captures (and are running Windows), you will have to purchase an AirPcap adapter from Cace Technologies (www.cacetech.com).

5. In Windows, choose Start ≻ All Programs, and then click the Wireshark icon. The Wireshark application should appear.

6. In the center section, click the Open icon, and browse to the book's CD. Open the packet capture file called CCMP_FRAMES.PCAP.

7. The file will open, and Wireshark will display its three sections. If you click one of the beacons with the source address of 00:1A:1E:94:4C:32, Wireshark will display the details of the frame in the middle section. If you expand the frame and scroll down to the RSN section, you will see the cipher AES (CCM) listed.

Why does the WLAN protocol analyzer display CCMP-encrypted data frames as TKIP-encrypted data packets? As you have already learned, the format of the 8-byte CCMP header is basically identical to the format of the 8-byte TKIP header (IV/Extended IV) used by TKIP. Therefore, most protocol analyzers cannot distinguish between TKIP-encrypted data frames and CCMP-encrypted data frames. However, you can always determine which cipher is being used by looking at a field called the *RSN information element*. The RSN information element is found in four different 802.11 management frames: beacon management frames, probe response frames, association request frames, and reassociation request frames.

WPA/WPA2

Prior to the ratification of the 802.11i amendment, the Wi-Fi Alliance introduced the *Wi-Fi Protected Access (WPA)* certification. WPA was a snapshot of the not-yet-released 802.11i amendment, but the WPA certification only required support for TKIP/RC4 dynamic encryption key generation. 802.1X/EAP authentication was required in the enterprise, and passphrase authentication was required in a SOHO environment. TKIP was designed as a stopgap measure, with a limited life span (five years), until 802.11i was finalized. Recently, numerous publicly announced attacks have shown that there are flaws in TKIP and that it is able to be exploited. The Beck-Tews attack can recover plain text from an encrypted short packet, recover the MIC key, and inject forged frames. However, the attack has a limitation in that the targets are restricted to WPA implementations that support WMM QoS features. The Ohiagi/Morii attack further enhances the Beck-Tews attack with a man-in-the-middle-approach. It should be noted that these attacks do not recover the encryption key but instead are used to recover the MIC checksum used for packet integrity.

These exploits can usually be prevented by changing TKIP settings as keying intervals on a WLAN controller or AP. The better solution is to stop using TKIP and upgrade to CCMP with AES. TKIP has begun to show its flaws, and more will certainly be exposed in the future. TKIP has provided WLAN data privacy for more than the five years for which it was intended. WLANs should now be protected with CCMP to provide the necessary data privacy and data integrity.

In June 2004, the IEEE 802.11 TGi working group formally ratified 802.11i, which added support for CCMP/AES encryption. The Wi-Fi Alliance therefore revised the previous WPA specification to WPA2, incorporating the CCMP/AES cipher. Therefore, the only practical difference between WPA and WPA2 has to do with the encryption cipher. WPA-Personal and WPA2-Personal both use the PSK authentication method; however, WPA-Personal specifies TKIP/RC4 encryption, and *WPA2-Personal* specifies CCMP/AES.

WPA2 is a Wi-Fi Alliance certification that is a mirror of the IEEE 802.11i security amendment. Testing of WPA2 interoperability certification began in September 2004. WPA2 incorporates the AES algorithm in CCMP, providing government-grade security based on the NIST FIPS 140-2 compliant AES encryption algorithm. WPA2 supports 802.1X/EAP authentication or preshared keys and is backward compatible with WPA.

The further migration from TKIP to CCMP can be seen in the IEEE 802.11n amendment, which states that high throughput (HT) stations cannot use WEP or TKIP when communicating with other stations that support stronger ciphers. The IEEE states that an HT station cannot use pre-RSNA security methods to protect unicast frames if the receiver address (RA) or address 1 of the frame corresponds to another HT station. The Wi-Fi Alliance also began requiring that all HT radios not use TKIP when using HT data rates. Starting on September 1, 2009, the Wi-Fi Alliance began testing 802.11n APs and client STAs for compliance with this requirement. Most likely, the WLAN vendors will still offer support for TKIP and WEP with HT rates, but the use of TKIP and WEP will not be a default setting.

Robust Security Network (RSN)

The 802.11i amendment, which was ratified and published as IEEE Std. 802.11i-2004, defined stronger encryption and better authentication methods. The 802.11i security amendment is now part of the 802.11-2007 standard. The 802.11-2007 standard defines what is known as a robust security network (RSN) and robust security network associations (RSNAs).

A security association is a set of policies and keys used to protect information. A *robust security network association (RSNA)* requires two 802.11 stations (STAs) to establish procedures to authenticate and associate with each other as well as create dynamic encryption keys through a process known as the *4-Way Handshake*. This association between two stations is referred to as an RSNA. In other words, any two radios must share dynamic encryption keys that are unique between those two radios. CCMP/AES encryption is the mandated encryption method, while TKIP/RC4 is an optional encryption method.

Anyone who has passed the CWNA certification exam is familiar with the WLAN topologies of a basic service set and an independent basic service set. *The basic service set* is the cornerstone topology of an 802.11 network. The communicating devices that make up a BSS are solely one AP with one or more client stations. Client stations join the AP's wireless domain and begin communicating through the AP. Stations that are members of a BSS have a layer 2 connection and are called *associated*. The 48-bit (6-octet) MAC address of an access point's radio card is known as the *basic service set identifier (BSSID)*. The BSSID address is the layer 2 identifier of each individual BSS. Most often, the BSSID is the MAC address of the access point. Do not confuse the BSSID address with the SSID. The *service set identifier (SSID)* is the logical WLAN name that is user configurable, while the BSSID is the layer 2 MAC address of an AP provided by the hardware manufacturer.

When RSN security associations are used within a BSS, all the client station radios have unique encryption keys that are shared with the radio of the access point. As shown in Figure 9.12, all the client stations have undergone a unique RSNA process called the 4-Way Handshake where the access point and each client radio has either a unique dynamic TKIP/RC4 or CCMP/AES key that is shared between the client radio and the access point radio. This key is called the pairwise transient key and is used to encrypt/decrypt unicast traffic. All the stations share a broadcast key called the group temporal key (GTK), which is used to encrypt/decrypt all broadcast and multicast traffic. You will learn more about the PTK and GTK keys later in this chapter in the section "4-Way Handshake."

The 802.11 standard also defines a WLAN topology called an *independent basic service set*. The radio cards that make up an IBSS network consist solely of client stations (STAs), and no access point is deployed. An IBSS network that consists of just two STAs is analogous to a wired crossover cable. An IBSS can, however, have multiple client stations in one physical area communicating in an ad hoc fashion. As you can see in Figure 9.13, all the stations within an IBSS have undergone a unique RSNA process (called the 4-Way Handshake) with each other, because all unicast communications are peer to peer. Each station has either a unique dynamic TKIP/RC4 or a CCMP/AES pairwise transient key that is shared with any other station within the IBSS. In an IBSS, each STA defines its own group temporal key, which is used for its broadcast/multicast transmissions. Each IBSS station will use either the 4-Way Handshake or the Group Key Handshake to distribute its transmit GTK to its peer stations. PSK authentication is used within the IBSS to seed the 4-Way Handshake. Therefore, every time a client joins an IBSS with a peer station, the client must reauthenticate and create new keys.

FIGURE 9.12   RSNA within a BSS

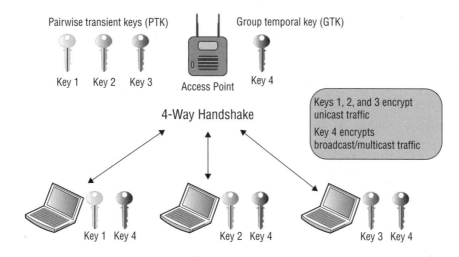

FIGURE 9.13   RSNA within an IBSS

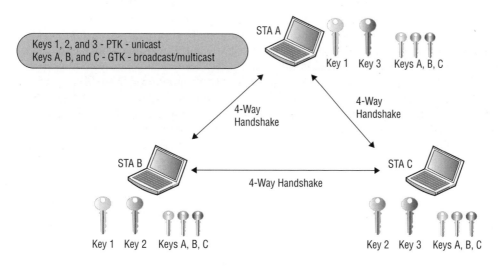

A *robust security network (RSN)* is a network that allows for the creation of only robust security network associations. In other words, a basic service set or independent basic service set where all the stations are using only TKIP/RC4 or CCMP/AES dynamic keys for encryption would be considered an RSN. Robust security exists only when all devices in the service set use RSNAs. As shown in Figure 9.14, all the stations within the BSS have established an RSNA that resulted in either TKIP/RC4 or CCMP/AES unique dynamic keys. Because only RSNA security is in use, the pictured BSS would be considered a robust security network.

FIGURE 9.14 Robust security network

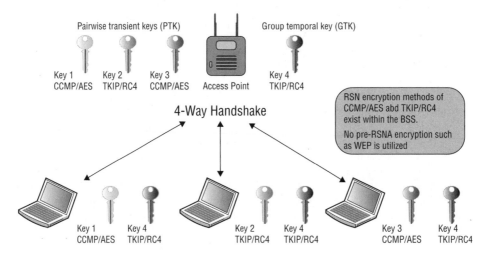

A pre-RSN security network uses static WEP encryption and legacy authentication methods. A WLAN that uses dynamic WEP encryption keys would also be considered as using pre-RSN security, but the use of dynamic WEP was never defined by either the IEEE or the Wi-Fi Alliance. The 802.11-2007 standard does allow for the creation of *pre-robust security network associations (pre-RSNAs)* as well as RSNAs. In other words, legacy security measures can be supported in the same basic service set along with RSN-security-defined mechanisms. A *transition security network (TSN)* supports RSN-defined security as well as legacy security, such as WEP, within the same BSS. As you can see in Figure 9.15, some of the stations within the BSS have established an RSNA that resulted in either TKIP/RC4 or CCMP/AES unique dynamic keys. However, some of the stations are using static WEP keys for encryption. Because both RSNAs and pre-RSNAs are in use, the pictured BSS would be considered a transition security network.

FIGURE 9.15   Transition security network

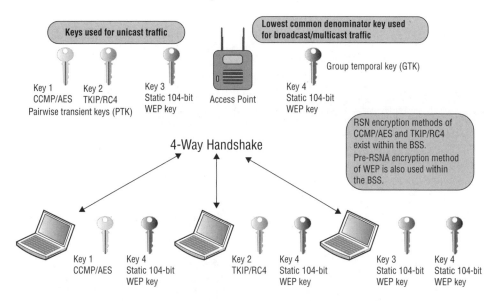

Keys used for unicast traffic

Lowest common denominator key used for broadcast/multicast traffic

Group temporal key (GTK)

Key 1
CCMP/AES

Key 2
TKIP/RC4

Key 3
Static 104-bit
WEP key

Pairwise transient keys (PTK)

Access Point

Key 4
Static 104-bit
WEP key

RSN encryption methods of CCMP/AES and TKIP/RC4 exist within the BSS.
Pre-RSNA encryption method of WEP is also used within the BSS.

4-Way Handshake

Key 1
CCMP/AES

Key 4
Static 104-bit
WEP key

Key 2
TKIP/RC4

Key 4
Static 104-bit
WEP key

Key 3
Static 104-bit
WEP key

Key 4
Static 104-bit
WEP key

As you learned earlier in this chapter, each WLAN has a logical name (SSID), and each WLAN BSS has a unique layer 2 identifier, the BSSID. The BSSID is typically the MAC address of the access point's radio card. Most WLAN devices have the capability of creating multiple virtual BSSIDs. This allows for the creation of virtual WLANs, each with a unique logical identifier (SSID) that can also be assigned to a specific VLAN. Because the BSSID is the MAC address of the AP and because the WLAN controller can support many virtual WLANs on the same physical AP, each virtual WLAN is typically linked with a unique virtual BSSID. Each virtual WLAN has a logical name (SSID) and a unique virtual layer 2 identifier (BSSID), and each WLAN can be mapped to a unique layer 3 virtual local area network (VLAN). Each WLAN can also require different types of security associations. Effectively, multiple basic service sets exist within the same coverage cell area of the access point. As shown in Figure 9.16, because multiple virtual BSSIDs exist with different security requirements, an RSN WLAN, a pre-RSNA WLAN, and a TSN WLAN can also exist within the same coverage area of an access point.

FIGURE 9.16   RSN, pre-RSN, and TSN within the same AP cell

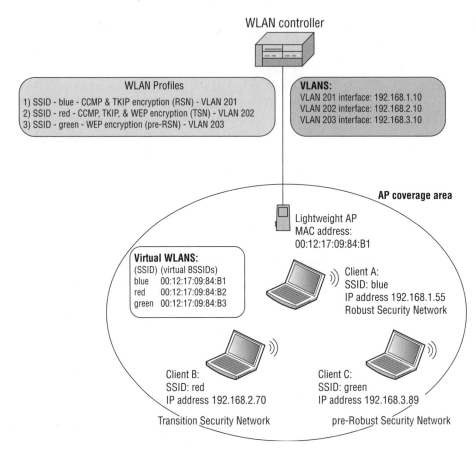

RSN Information Element

Within a BSS, how can client stations and an access point notify each other about their RSN capabilities? RSN security can be identified by a field found in certain 802.11 management frames. This field is known as the *robust security network information element (RSNIE)* and is often referred to simply as the *RSN information element.* An information element is an optional field of variable length that can be found in 802.11 management frames. The RSN information element can identify the encryption capabilities of each station. The RSN information element will also indicate whether 802.1X/EAP authentication or preshared key (PSK) authentication is being used.

The RSN information element field is found in four different 802.11 management frames: beacon management frames, probe response frames, association request frames, and reassociation request frames. Within a basic service set, an access point and client stations use the RSN information element within these four management frames to communicate with each other about their security capabilities prior to establishing association. As shown in Figure 9.17, access points will use beacons and probe response frames to inform client stations of the AP security capabilities.

FIGURE 9.17   Access point RSN security capabilities

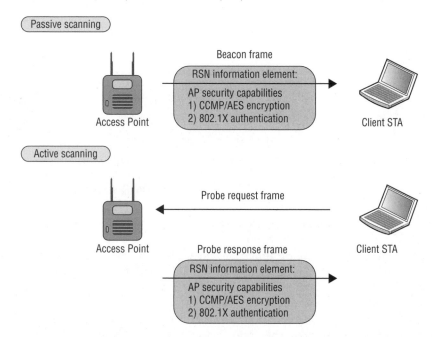

As you can see in Figure 9.18, client stations use the association request frame to inform the access point of the client station security capabilities. When stations roam from one access point to another access point, they use the reassociation request frame to inform the new access point of the roaming client station's security capabilities. The security capabilities include supported encryption cipher suites and supported authentication methods.

All 802.11 radios will use one cipher suite for unicast encryption and another cipher suite for encrypting multicast and broadcast traffic. Pairwise unicast encryption keys are created that are unique between two stations—the AP and a single client station. The pairwise cipher suite of the RSN information element contains the cipher suite information used by stations for unicast traffic. The cipher suite selector 00-0F-AC-04 (CCMP) is the default cipher suite value. The cipher suite selector 00-0F-AC-02 (TKIP) is optional. A group key is also created that is shared by all stations for broadcast and multicast traffic. The Group Cipher Suite field of the RSN information element contains the cipher suite information used by the BSS to protect broadcast/multicast traffic.

FIGURE 9.18 Client station RSN security capabilities

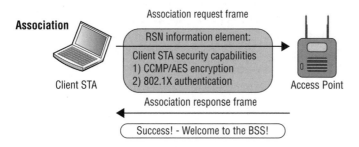

FIGURE 9.19 RSN Information element—CCMP pairwise and CCMP group cipher

Figure 9.19 shows a capture of a beacon frame from an access point configured to use only CCMP/AES encryption. The RSN information element indicates that CCMP/AES encryption is being used for both the group cipher suite and the pairwise cipher suite. The access point is using the RSN information element to inform all client stations that the AP will be using CCMP encryption for all broadcast/multicast and will also be using CCMP/AES encryption for any unicast traffic. Any client station must support those exact ciphers for the client stations to be able to establish a robust secure network association (RSNA) with the AP and to create dynamic encryption keys. In other words, the client stations must support CCMP/AES encryption to be allowed to join the AP's basic service set.

FIGURE 9.19 RSN Information element—CCMP pairwise and CCMP group cipher

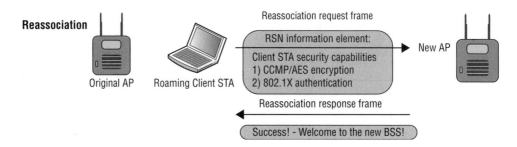

Figure 9.20 shows a beacon frame from an access point configured to support both CCMP/AES and TKIP/RC4 encryption. The RSN information element indicates that TKIP encryption is being used for the group cipher suite. CCMP/AES is the default cipher for the pairwise cipher suite. The access point is using the RSN information element to inform all client stations that the AP will support either CCMP/AES or TKIP/RC4 encryption for any unicast traffic. However, only TKIP/RC4 encryption can be used for broadcast/multicast traffic. In this situation, the client stations must support either CCMP or TKIP to be allowed to join the AP's basic service set. Because all the stations share a single group encryption key for broadcast and multicast traffic, the lowest common denominator must be used for the group cipher. In this case, the group cipher is TKIP.

FIGURE 9.20   RSN information element—CCMP pairwise and TKIP group cipher

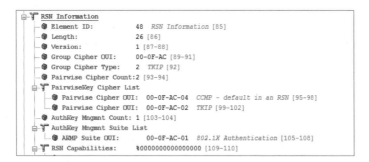

The cipher suite selectors 00-0F-AC-01 (WEP-40) and 00-0F-AC-05 (WEP-104) are used as a group cipher suite in a transition security network (TSN) to allow pre-RSNA devices to join a BSS. For example, an access point might support CCMP, TKIP, and WEP encryption. WPA2-capable clients will use CCMP encryption for unicast traffic between the client STA and the AP. WPA capable clients will use TKIP encryption for unicast traffic between the client STAs and the AP. Legacy clients will use WEP encryption for unicast traffic between the client STAs and the AP. All the clients will use WEP encryption for the broadcast and multicast traffic. Because all the stations share a single group encryption key for broadcast and multicast traffic, the lowest common denominator must be used for the group cipher. In the case of a TSN, the group cipher is WEP.

Figure 9.21 shows a capture of a beacon frame from an access point configured to support CCMP/AES, TKIP/RC4, or static WEP encryption using a 40-bit static key. The RSN information element indicates that WEP-40 encryption is being used for the group cipher suite. CCMP/AES is the default cipher for the pairwise cipher suite. The access point is using the RSN information element to inform all client stations that the AP can support CCMP/AES, TKIP/RC4 encryption, or WEP-40 for any unicast traffic. However, only WEP-40 encryption can be used for broadcast/multicast traffic. In this situation, the client stations can support CCMP/AES, TKIP, or WEP-40 and be allowed to join the AP's basic service set.

FIGURE 9.21 RSN information element—CCMP pairwise and WEP-40 group cipher

```
RSN Information
    Element ID:              48   RSN Information [66]
    Length:                  20 [67]
    Version:                 1 [68—69]
    Group Cipher OUI:        00—0F—AC {70—72}
    Group Cipher Type:       1  WEP-40 [73]
    Pairwise Cipher Count:1 [74—75]
    PairwiseKey Cipher List
        Pairwise Cipher OUI:   00—0F—AC—04   CCMP — default in an RSN [76—79]
    AuthKey Mngmnt Count: 1 [80—81]
    AuthKey Mngmnt Suite List
        AKMP Suite OUI:        00—0F—AC—02 None [82—85]
    RSN Capabilities=%000000000101000
```

The RSN information element can also be used to indicate what authentication methods are supported. The authentication key management (AKM) suite field in the RSN information element indicates whether the station supports either *802.1X* authentication or PSK authentication. If the AKM suite value is 00-0F-AC-01, authentication is negotiated over an 802.1X infrastructure using an EAP protocol. If the AKM suite value is 00-0F-AC-02 (PSK), then PSK is the authentication method being used.

Figure 9.22 shows a capture of an association request frame from a client station configured to 802.1X/EAP. The AKM suite field in the RSN information element indicates that 802.1X is the chosen authentication method.

FIGURE 9.22 RSN information element—AKM suite field: 802.1X

```
RSN Information
    Element ID:              48   RSN Information [52]
    Length:                  20 [53]
    Version:                 1 [54—55]
    Group Cipher OUI:        00—0F—AC [56—58]
    Group Cipher Type:       4 CCMP — default in an RSN [59]
    Pairwise Cipher Count:1 [60—61]
    Pairwise Cipher List Pairwise Cipher OUI=00—0F—AC—04
    AuthKey Mngmnt Count: 1 [66—67]
    AuthKey Mngmnt Suite List AKMP Suite OUI=00—0F—AC—01 802.1X Authentication
    RSN Capabilities=%000000000101000
```

802.1X

The IEEE 802.1X-2004 standard is not specifically a wireless standard and is often mistakenly referred to as 802.11x. The 802.1X standard is a port-based access control standard. 802.1X provides an authorization framework that allows or disallows traffic to pass through a port and thereby access network resources. An 802.1X framework may be implemented in either a wireless or wired environment. The 802.1X authorization framework consists of three main components, each with a specific role. These three 802.1X components work together to make sure only properly validated users and devices are authorized to access network resources. The layer 2 authentication protocol called *Extensible Authentication Protocol (EAP)* is used within the 802.1X framework to validate users at layer 2. The three major components of an 802.1X framework are as follows:

Supplicant   A host with software that is requesting authentication and access to network resources. Each supplicant has unique authentication credentials that are verified by the authentication server. In a WLAN, the supplicant is often the laptop or wireless handheld device trying to access the network.

Authenticator   A device that blocks or allows traffic to pass through its port entity. Authentication traffic is normally allowed to pass through the *authenticator*, while all other traffic is blocked until the identity of the supplicant has been verified. The authenticator maintains two virtual ports: an *uncontrolled port* and a *controlled port*. The uncontrolled port is used for EAP traffic, and the controlled port is used for all other traffic. Initially, the uncontrolled port is the only port that is open and passing traffic. A successful 802.1X authentication will trigger the controller port to be opened, allowing other traffic to traverse the network. In a WLAN, the authenticator is usually either an AP or a WLAN controller.

Authentication Server   A server that validates the credentials of the supplicant that is requesting access and notifies the authenticator that the supplicant has been authorized. The authentication server will maintain a user database or may proxy with one or more external user databases to authenticate supplicant credentials.

You will see this terminology repeatedly over the course of your reading and hands-on work in WLAN security both inside this study guide and throughout industry publications. Each of these 802.1X components will now be briefly discussed in the sections that follow.

Supplicant

The *supplicant* is the device that will need to be validated by the authentication server before being allowed access to network resources. The supplicant will use an EAP protocol to communicate with the authentication server at layer 2. The supplicant will not be allowed to communicate at the upper layers of 3–7 until the supplicant's identity has been validated at layer 2 by the authentication server

Think of the supplicant as the client software on a Wi-Fi device where the WLAN client security is configured. This is not to be confused with the *driver* for the 802.11 radio of the device. The supplicant is a software application that performs the 802.1X endpoint services on a client device such as a laptop. Fully featured enterprise supplicants can offer support for the wired Ethernet adapter and perhaps multiple 802.11 network adapters if necessary.

Authenticator

From the context of EAP authentication, the role of the authenticator is quite simple. The authenticator plays the role of the intermediary, passing messages between the supplicant and the authentication server. These messages travel via an EAP authentication protocol. Remember that authenticator is an 802.1X term. Also remember that 802.1X was described as a port-based access control standard. 802.1X essentially blocks traffic until a successful Layer 2 authentication occurs. When 802.1X is implemented on a Wi-Fi network, EAP is the authentication method that is used. As mentioned earlier, the authenticator maintains two virtual ports: an uncontrolled port and a controlled port. The uncontrolled port allows EAP authentication traffic to pass through, while the controlled port blocks all other traffic until the supplicant has been authenticated.

As shown in Figure 9.23, the authenticator is the AP when an autonomous access point solution is deployed, and the authentication server is typically a RADIUS server. Figure 9.23 also shows that when an 802.1X security solution is used with a WLAN controller solution, the WLAN controller is the authenticator—and not the controller-based access points.

FIGURE 9.23   802.1X comparison-autonomous access point and WLAN controller

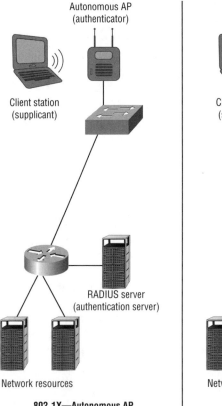
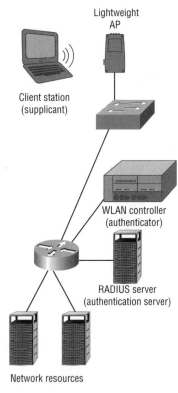

802.1X—Autonomous AP   **802.1X—WLAN Controller**

The term authenticator is a misnomer because the authenticator does not validate the supplicant's credentials. The authenticator's job is simply to let traffic either pass through or not pass through. What the authenticator needs to know is essentially who is going to provide the guest list services, which is the role of the authentication server. Therefore, when configuring a WLAN controller or AP as an authenticator, you would need to be able to point the authenticator in the direction of an authentication server. As shown in Figure 9.24, the authenticator would need to be configured with the RADIUS server's IP address and UDP port along with a shared secret in order to communicate with the server. The shared secret is only for the authenticator-to-authentication server communication link. It should also be noted that the authenticator will be configured to "require" EAP authentication, but a specific EAP type is not chosen. Remember that the authenticator is essentially a pass-through device that either allows or disallows traffic to flow through the authenticator's virtual ports.

FIGURE 9.24   Authenticator configuration

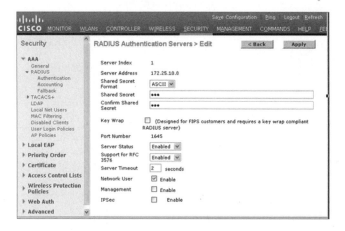

Authentication Server

The *authentication server (AS)* validates the credentials of a supplicant that is requesting access and notifies the authenticator that the supplicant has been authorized. The authentication server will maintain a user database or may proxy with an external user database to authenticate user credentials. The authentication server and the supplicant communicate using a layer 2 EAP authentication protocol.

The 802.1X standard defines the authentication server as a RADIUS server. Although RADIUS is what is officially defined in the standard, EAP is flexible, allowing other authentication servers such as a Lightweight Directory Access Protocol (LDAP)–compliant database to be used for authentication.

When configuring a RADIUS server, you need to be able to point the authentication server back in the direction of the authenticator. Typically the authenticator is a WLAN controller or autonomous AP. As shown in Figure 9.25, the AS would need to be configured with the authenticator's IP address and shared secret in order to communicate with the authenticator.

FIGURE 9.25   Authentication server configuration

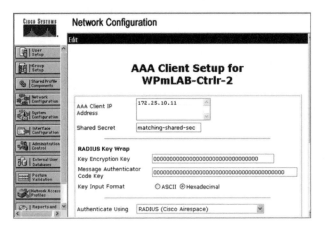

Configuration Gotchas

When configuring authenticators (APs or WLAN controllers) and RADIUS servers, there are usually two configuration problems that people regularly encounter: nonmatching shared secrets and wrong UDP ports. Ensure these values are correct before attempting any supplicant authentication attempts. RADIUS uses UDP ports 1812 for RADIUS authentication and 1813 for RADIUS accounting. These ports were officially assigned by the Internet Assigned Number Authority (IANA). However, prior to IANA allocation of UDP ports 1812 and 1813, the UDP ports of 1645 and 1646 (authentication and accounting, respectively) were used as the default ports by many RADIUS server vendors.

EAP

Extensible Authentication Protocol (EAP), as defined in IETF RFC 2284, provides support for many authentication methods. EAP was originally adopted for use with PPP. EAP has since been redefined in the IETF RFC 3748 for use with 802.1X port-based access control.

As noted earlier, EAP stands for Extensible Authentication Protocol. The key word in EAP is *extensible*. EAP is a layer 2 protocol that is very flexible, and many different flavors of EAP exist. Some are proprietary, while others are considered standards based. Some may provide for only one-way authentication, while others provide two-way authentication more commonly called *mutual authentication*. Mutual authentication not only requires that the authentication server validate the client credentials but also that the supplicant authenticate the validity of the authentication server. Most types of EAP that require mutual authentication use a server-side digital certificate to validate the authentication server.

As you learned earlier in this chapter, 802.1X is an authorization framework with the three components of the supplicant, authenticator, and authentication server. The main purpose of an 802.1X solution is to authorize the supplicant to use network resources. The supplicant will not be allowed to communicate at the upper layers of 3–7 until the supplicant's identity has been validated at layer 2. EAP is the layer 2 protocol used within an 802.1X framework.

As mentioned earlier, the EAP messages are encapsulated in EAP over LAN (EAPOL) frames. EAPOL is used between the supplicant and the authenticator, but the EAPOL encapsulation is translated to EAP in RADIUS between the authenticator and the authentication server. There are five major types of EAPOL messages, as shown in Table 9.1.

Let's review a generic EAP exchange. The two workhorses are the supplicant and the authentication server because they both use the EAP protocol to communicate with each other at layer 2. The authenticator sits between the two devices. As you have already learned, the authenticator maintains two virtual ports: an uncontrolled port and a controlled port. When open, the uncontrolled port allows EAP authentication traffic to pass through. The controlled port blocks all other traffic until the supplicant has been authenticated. When the controlled port is open, upper layers 3–7 traffic can pass through. Dynamic IP addressing with DHCP is performed once the controlled port is opened.

As shown in Figure 9.26, 802.1X/EAP authentication works together with standard 802.11 Open System authentication and association. An 802.11 client station will actually establish a layer 2 connection with the AP by associating and joining the basic service set. However, if 802.1X/EAP is implemented, layer 2 is as far as the 802.11 station gets until the client also goes through the entire 802.1X/EAP process.

TABLE 9.1   EAPOL messages

Packet type	Name	Description
0000 0000	EAP-Packet	This is an encapsulated EAP frame. The majority of EAP frames are EAP-Packet frames.
0000 0001	EAPOL-Start	This is an optional frame that the supplicant can use to start the EAP process.
0000 0010	EAPOL-Logoff	This frame terminates an EAP session and shuts down the virtual ports. Hackers sometimes use this frame for DoS attacks.
0000 0011	EAPOL-Key	This frame is used to exchange dynamic keying information. For example, it is used during the 4-Way Handshake.
0000 0100	EAPOL- Encapsulated - ASF-Alert	This frame is used to send alerts, such as SNMP traps to the virtual ports.

FIGURE 9.26   802.11 association and 802.1X/EAP

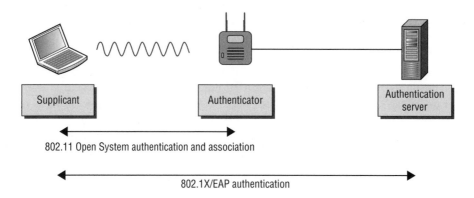

Figure 9.27 displays all the steps in a generic EAP exchange. The authenticator in this example is an autonomous AP. Please refer to the figure as you read each step.

FIGURE 9.27   Generic EAP exchange

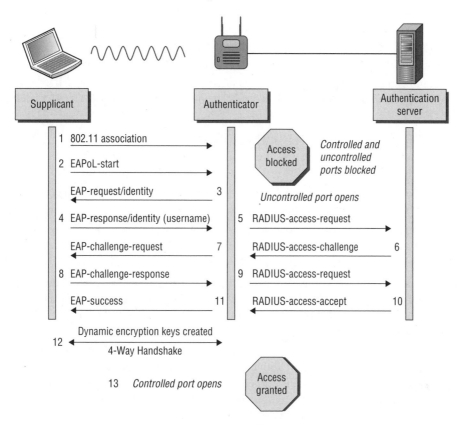

1. The 802.11 client (supplicant) associates with the AP and joins the BSS. Both the controlled and uncontrolled ports are blocked on the authenticator.

2. The supplicant initiates the EAP authentication process by sending an 802.11 EAPOL-Start frame to the authenticator. This is an optional frame and may or may not be used by different types of EAP.

3. The authenticator sends an 802.11 EAP-Request frame requesting the identity of the supplicant. The EAP-Request Identity frame is always a required frame.

4. The supplicant sends an EAP response frame with the supplicant's identity in clear text. The username is always in clear text in the EAP-Response Identity frame. At this point, the uncontrolled port opens to allow EAP traffic through. All other traffic remains blocked by the controlled port.

5. The authenticator encapsulates the EAP response frame in a RADIUS packet and forwards it to the authentication server.

6. The AS looks at the supplicant's name and checks the database of users and passwords. The AS will then send a password challenge to the supplicant encapsulated in a RADIUS packet.

7. The authenticator forwards the password challenge to the supplicant in an 802.11 EAP frame.

8. The supplicant takes the password and hashes it with a hash algorithm such as MD-5 or MS-CHAPv2. The supplicant then sends the hash response in an EAP from back to the AS.

9. The authenticator forwards the challenge response in a RADIUS packet to the AS.

10. The AS runs an identical hash and checks to see whether the response is correct. The AS will then send either a success or failure message back to the supplicant.

11. The authenticator forwards the AS message to the supplicant in an EAP-Success frame. The supplicant has now been authenticated.

12. The final step is the 4-Way Handshake negotiation between the authenticator and the supplicant. This is a complex process used to generate dynamic encryption keys. This process is discussed in great detail in Chapter 5.

13. Once the supplicant has completed layer 2 EAP authentication and created dynamic encryption keys, the controlled port is unblocked. The supplicant is then authorized to use network resources. If using IP, the next step the supplicant will take is to obtain an IP address either statically or by using DHCP.

You should notice that in step 4 the supplicant's username is seen in clear text. You might say that is a security risk—and you would be correct. You should also notice that in steps 6–9, the supplicant's password credentials are validated using a weak challenge/hash response. This frame exchange can be captured using a WLAN protocol analyzer. This is a security risk because the hash algorithms have been cracked and they are susceptible to offline dictionary attacks. In other words, the presentation of supplicant identity and validation of supplicant credentials is a security risk. Wouldn't it be better if steps 4–9 were protected in an encrypted tunnel? Since its original adoption, a number of weaknesses were discovered with some EAP authentication methods. The most secure EAP methods used today employ *tunneled authentication* to pass identity credentials (usernames and passwords) similar to what you find with web-based ecommerce transactions.

We will now discuss the more commonly used strong EAP protocols that typically use tunneled authentication.

Strong EAP Protocols

The stronger and more commonly deployed methods of EAP use *Transport Layer Security (TLS)*–based authentication and/or TLS-tunneled authentication. In this section, we will cover some of these EAP types and their inner workings in detail.

Unlike some of the weaker EAP types, such as EAP-MD5 and EAP-LEAP, which have only one supplicant identity, EAP methods that use tunneled authentication have two supplicant identities. These two supplicant identities are often called the *outer identity* and *inner identity*. The outer identity is effectively a bogus username, and the inner identity is the true identity of the supplicant. The outer identity is seen in clear text outside the encrypted TLS tunnel, while the inner identity is protected within the TLS tunnel.

As you can see in Figure 9.28, the original EAP standard requires that there always be a clear-text value in the initial EAP-Response frame sent by the supplicant to the authentication server. This clear-text value is the outer identity that travels outside the TLS tunnel. The default value used by most supplicants is "anonymous."

FIGURE 9.28   Outer identity

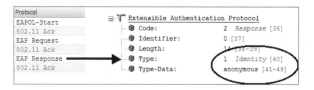

Although the default value used by most supplicants for the outer identity is "anonymous," the outer identity is usually a configurable setting. Keep in mind that this is not the real username. Some WLAN administrators use funny names such as Donald Duck or Mickey Mouse. Other WLAN administrators use a facility code identifying a group of supplicants. The facility code could be used for troubleshooting efforts of 802.1X supplicant failures and can help you quickly narrow down the facility where the problem is occurring. Other WLAN administrators use the outer identity as a social engineering honeypot.

Do not confuse the encryption used by the TLS tunnel with layer 2 encryption that is used to protect the payload of 802.11 data frames. The encrypted TLS tunnel is created and exists only for a few milliseconds. The whole purpose of tunneled authentication is to provide a secure channel to protect the user identity credentials. The user credentials are encrypted inside the TLS tunnel. The TLS tunnel is *not* used to encrypt 802.11 data frames. We will now discuss versions of EAP that support tunneled authentication.

Tunnelled EAP and a Social Engineering Honeypot

In computer terminology, a *honeypot* is a trap set for potential hackers to detect and possibly counteract unauthorized access of a computer network. EAP methods, such as EAP-PEAP or EAP-TTLS, that use tunnelled authentication will always have an outer identity that can be seen in clear text with a WLAN protocol analyzer. A common strategy is to set a social engineering honeypot using the outer identity. The WLAN administrator configures all the company's supplicants with the same value for the outer identity. The value could be Jane Barrett, when there is no user by that name who works at the company. Employees at the company are trained to alert security if anyone ever inquires about an employee named Jane Barrett. If someone inquires about the imaginary Jane Barrett, a social engineering attack is occurring and can be further investigated.

EAP-PEAP

EAP-Protected Extensible Authentication Protocol (EAP-PEAP), also known simply as PEAP, creates an encrypted TLS tunnel within which the supplicant's inner identity is validated. Thus, the term *protected* is used because the supplicant's identity and credentials are always encrypted inside the TLS tunnel that is established.

PEAP is probably the most common and most widely supported EAP method used in WLAN security. That is, it is the most popular EAP type that is considered highly secure. The confusion regarding PEAP usually revolves around the fact that there are multiple flavors of PEAP, including these three major versions:

- EAP-PEAPv0 (EAP-MSCHAPv2)

- EAP-PEAPv0 (*EAP-TLS*)

- EAP-PEAPv1 (EAP-GTC)

PEAP is often referred to as "EAP inside EAP" authentication because the inner authentication protocol used inside the TLS tunnel is also another type of EAP. PEAPv0 and PEAPv1 both refer to the outer authentication method and are the mechanisms that create the secure TLS tunnel to protect subsequent authentication transactions. The EAP protocol enclosed within parentheses is the inner EAP protocol used with each of these three flavors of EAP-PEAP. The main difference between these three major flavors of EAP is simply the inner EAP protocol that is used within the TLS tunnel.

Let's discuss how all flavors of PEAP operate. A key point is that in order to establish the TLS tunnel, a server-side certificate is required for all flavors of PEAP. As shown in Figure 9.29, the EAP-PEAP process involves two phases. Please refer to the figure as we discuss the two phases of EAP-PEAP. We will use EAP-PEAPv0 (EAP-MSCHAPv2), as shown in Figure 9.29.

Phase 1

This first phase of EAP-PEAP establishes a secure tunnel using EAP-TTLS with server authentication.

1. The authenticator sends an EAP frame requesting the identity of the supplicant.

2. The supplicant responds with an EAP response frame with the clear-text outer identity that is not the real username and is a bogus username.

3. At this point, the uncontrolled port opens on the authenticator to allow EAP traffic through. All other traffic remains blocked by the controlled port. The authenticator forwards the outer identity response to the AS.

4. The outer identity response cannot inform the AS about the actual identity of the supplicant. It simply informs the AS that a supplicant wants to be validated.

5. The AS sends the server certificate down to the supplicant. The supplicant validates the server-side certificate and therefore authenticates the authentication server.

6. An encrypted point-to-point TLS tunnel is created between the supplicant and the authentication server. Once the TLS tunnel is established, Phase 2 can begin.

FIGURE 9.29   EAP-PEAP process

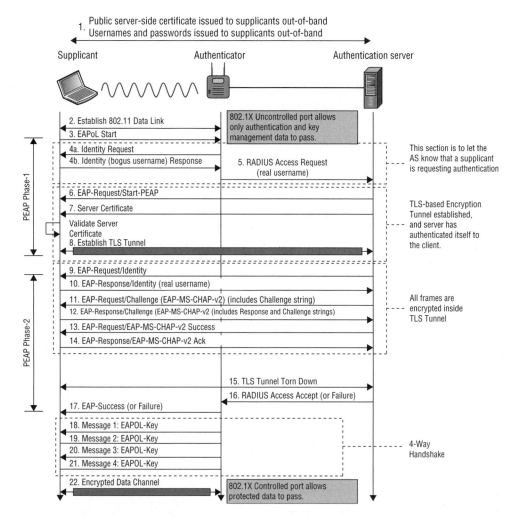

Phase 2

The second phase of EAP-PEAP implements the client authentication process.

1. The AS requests the real identity of the supplicant.

2. The supplicant responds with the inner identity, which is the real username. The real username is now hidden because it is encrypted inside the TLS tunnel.

3. The remaining steps in Phase 2 involve a password challenge from the AS and a hashed response from the supplicant using an authentication protocol within the tunnel. The supplicant credentials are validated by the authentication server. The entire exchange is encrypted within the TLS tunnel.

The whole point of Phase 2 is to validate the supplicant credentials while encrypted within the TLS tunnel. The inner identity, or real username, is protected and therefore hidden. Whatever authentication method is used inside the tunnel is also protected; therefore, any offline dictionary attacks are ineffective in obtaining the password.

PEAP has an interesting history. It began as a joint proposal by Cisco, Microsoft, and RSA Security. It was reported that Microsoft and Cisco did not completely agree on every detail, and subsequently Microsoft implemented PEAPv0 using MS-CHAPv2 as the inner authentication method. MS-CHAPv2 is Microsoft's own version of CHAP. Because Microsoft is the dominant player in both client and server operating systems providing built-in support, this has led to the success of EAP-PEAPv0 (EAP-MS-CHAPv2). Cisco split from the original specification and created PEAPv1, which predominantly uses EAP-GTC as the inner authentication method.

PEAP is often referred to as "EAP inside EAP" authentication because the inner authentication protocol used inside the TLS tunnel is also another type of EAP. The only real difference is the inner EAP protocol that is used within the TLS tunnel. PEAPv0 and PEAPv1 both refer to the outer authentication method and are the mechanisms that create the secure TLS tunnel to protect subsequent authentication transactions. PEAPv0 supports inner EAP methods of EAP-MSCHAPv2 and EAP-TLS while PEAPv1 supports the inner EAP method of EAP-GTC. All versions of PEAP require a server-side certificate, and all versions of PEAP operate using the two phases described earlier.

EXERCISE 9.4

802.1X/EAP Frame Exchanges

In this exercise, you will use a protocol analyzer to view the 802.11 frame exchanges used during an 802.1X/EAP authentication process. The following directions should assist you with locating, downloading, and installing Wireshark. If you are familiar with another protocol analyzing software, feel free to use it to perform this lab. If you have already installed Wireshark, you can skip steps 1–4.

1. In your web browser, go to the Wireshark website: www.wireshark.org.

2. Click the Download Wireshark button to locate the installation file, and download the file that is appropriate for your operating system.

3. After downloading the file, double-click it to proceed with the installation, and follow the installation directions.

    The exercise will use frame captures that are on the book's companion CD. If you would like to use Wireshark for live wireless captures (and you are running Windows), you will have to purchase an AirPcap adapter from Cace Technologies (www.cacetech.com).

4. In Windows, choose Start ➤ All Programs, and then click the Wireshark icon. The Wireshark application should appear.

5. In the center section, click the Open icon, and browse to the book's CD.

6. Open the packet capture file called EAP_MD5.PCAP.

 The file will open and Wireshark will display three sections:

- The top section is called the *packet list*, displaying a list of the individual packets.

- The middle section is called the *packet detail*, displaying as much detail about each packet as possible.

- The bottom section shows the bytes in the current packet.

7. In the packet list, scroll down so that you can see packets 15–25. These packets are using EPA-MD5. Notice that there is only one EAPOL-key frame. This is because EAP-MD5 uses one-way authentication and dynamic encryption keys are not created. Notice in frames 7–13 that Open System authentication and association occurs prior to the EAP exchange.

8. Select packet 15 to observe the frame details. Notice that this is an EAPOL-Start frame.

9. Select packet 17 to observe the frame details. In the details section, scroll down to the 802.1X Authentication field. Observe that the packet type is an EAP packet.

10. Go to the File menu, and select Close. This will bring you back to the initial Wireshark screen.

11. In the center section, click the Open icon, and browse to the book's CD.

12. Open the packet capture file called EAP_LEAP.PCAP.

13. Select packet 7 to observe the frame details. Notice that this is an EAP-Response frame. If you scroll down to the Extensible Authentication Protocol section, you will see the identity is airspy. The real username is always seen in clear text when LEAP is used.

14. Go to the File menu, and select Close. This will bring you back to the initial Wireshark screen.

15. In the center section, click the Open icon, and browse to the book's CD.

16. Open the packet capture file called EAP_PEAP.PCAP.

17. Select packet 13. Scroll down to the field called Extensible Authentication Protocol. Observe that this is a response frame and that the identity is administrator. This is the outer identity that is always seen in clear text when PEAP is used. This is a bogus username. The real username is hidden inside the encrypted TLS tunnel.

18. Scroll down to display packets 47–53. These are the frames used to create dynamic encryption keys following the authentication process. Once the supplicant gets validated and the keys are created, the controlled port becomes unblocked.

19. Go to the File menu, and select Close.

20. In the center section, click the Open File icon, and browse to the book's CD.

21. Open the packet capture file called EAP_TTLS.PCAP. Observe the EAP-TTLS frame exchange. Notice the similarity to PEAP.

22. Go to the File menu, and select Close.

23. In the center section, click the Open File icon, and browse to the book's CD.

24. Open the packet capture file called EAP_TTLS.PCAP. Observe the EAP-TLS frame exchange.

4-Way Handshake

The 802.11-2007 standard requires EAPOL-Key frames be used to exchange cryptographic information between the client STA supplicants and the authenticator, which is usually an access point. EAPOL-Key frames are used for the implementation of three different frame exchanges:

- 4-Way Handshake
- Group Key Handshake
- PeerKey Handshake

The 4-Way Handshake is a final process used to generate pairwise transient keys for encryption of unicast transmissions and a group temporal key for encryption of broadcast/multicast transmissions.

The 4-Way Handshake uses four EAPOL-Key frame messages between the authenticator and the supplicant for six major purposes:

- Confirm the existence of the PMK at the peer station
- Ensure that the PMK is current
- Derive a new pairwise transient key from the PMK
- Install the PTK on the supplicant and the authenticator
- Transfer the GTK from the authenticator to the supplicant and install the GTK on the supplicant and, if necessary, the authenticator
- Confirm the selection of the cipher suites

802.1X/EAP authentication is completed when the access point sends an EAP-Success frame and the AP can now initiate the 4-Way Handshake. Keep in mind that the authentication process has already generated the master keys (PMK and GMK), which will be used by the 4-Way Handshake to derive the temporal keys.

Before we explain the 4-Way Handshake process, it is necessary to define several key terms. The 4-Way Handshake uses pseudorandom functions. A *pseudorandom function (PRF)* hashes various inputs to derive a pseudorandom value. The PMK is one of the inputs combined with other inputs to create the pairwise transient key. Some of the other inputs used by the pseudorandom function are called nonces. A *nonce* is a random numerical value that is generated one time only. A nonce is used in cryptographic operations and is associated with a given cryptographic key. In the case of the 4-Way Handshake, a nonce is associated with the PMK. A nonce is used only once and is never used again with the PMK. Two nonces are created by the 4-Way Handshake: the *authenticator nonce (ANonce)* and the *supplicant nonce (SNonce)*.

To create the pairwise transient key, the 4-Way Handshake uses a pseudorandom function that combines the pairwise master key, a numerical authenticator nonce, a supplicant nonce, the authenticator's MAC address (AA), and the supplicant's MAC address (SPA).

The following is a simplified depiction of the formula used by the pseudorandom function (PRF) to derive a pairwise transient key:

PTK = PRF (PMK + ANonce + SNonce + AA + SPA)

As Figure 9.30 shows, the 4-Way Handshake consists of the following steps:

1. **4-Way Handshake Message 1**

    The authenticator and supplicant each randomly create their respective nonces. The authenticator sends an EAPOL-Key frame containing an ANonce to the supplicant. The supplicant now has all the necessary inputs for the pseudorandom function. The supplicant derives a PTK from the PMK, ANonce, SNonce, and MAC addresses. The supplicant is now in possession of a pairwise transient key that can be used to encrypt unicast traffic.

2. **4-Way Handshake Message 2**

    The supplicant sends an EAPOL-Key frame containing an SNonce to the authenticator. The authenticator now has all the necessary inputs for the pseudorandom function. The supplicant also sends its RSN information element capabilities to the authenticator and a message integrity code (MIC). The authenticator derives a PTK from the PMK, ANonce, SNonce, and MAC addresses. The authenticator also validates the MIC. The authenticator is now in possession of a pairwise transient key that can be used to encrypt unicast traffic.

FIGURE 9.30   The 4-Way Handshake

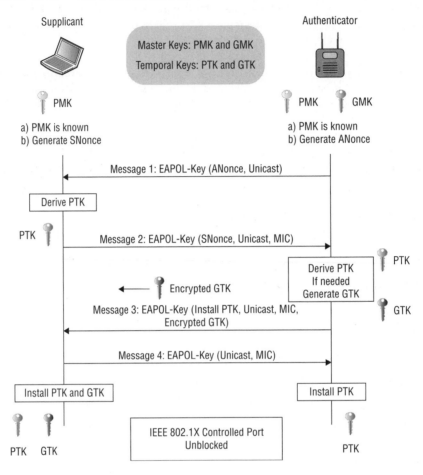

3.   4-Way Handshake Message 3

If necessary, the authenticator derives a GTK from the GMK. The authenticator sends an EAPOL-Key frame to the supplicant containing the ANonce, the authenticator's RSN information element capabilities, and an MIC. The EAPOL-Key frame may also contain a message to the supplicant to install the temporal keys. Finally, the GTK will be delivered inside this unicast EAPOL-Key frame to the supplicant. The confidentiality of the GTK is protected because it will be encrypted with the PTK.

4.   4-Way Handshake Message 4

The supplicant sends the final EAPOL-Key frame to the authenticator to confirm that the temporal keys have been installed.

5.   Controlled Port Unlocked

The virtual controlled port opens on the authenticator, and now, encrypted 802.11 data frames from the supplicant can pass through the authenticator and on to their final destination. All unicast traffic will now be encrypted with the PTK, and all multicast and broadcast traffic will now be encrypted with the GTK.

EXERCISE 9.5

The 4-Way Handshake

In this exercise, you will use a protocol analyzer to view the 4-Way Handshake EAPOL-Key frames that are used to generate the temporal keys used for encryption. The following directions should assist you with locating, downloading, and installing Wireshark. If you are familiar with another protocol analyzing software, feel free to use it to perform this lab. If you have already installed Wireshark, you can skip steps 1–4.

1. In your web browser, go to the Wireshark website: www.wireshark.org.

2. Click the Download Wireshark button to locate the installation file, and download the file that is appropriate for your operating system.

3. After downloading the file, double-click it to proceed with the installation, and follow the installation directions.

   The exercise will use frame captures that are on the CD that came with this book. If you would like to use Wireshark for live wireless captures (and you are running Windows), you will have to purchase an AirPcap adapter from Cace Technologies (www.cacetech.com).

4. In Windows, choose Start ➢ All Programs, and then click the Wireshark icon. The Wireshark application should appear.

5. In the center section, click the Open icon, and browse to the book's CD.

6. Open the packet capture file called 4WAY_HANDSHAKE.PCAP.

   The file will open and Wireshark will display three sections:

   ▪ The top section is called the *packet list*, displaying a list of the individual packets.

   ▪ The middle section is called the *packet detail*, displaying as much detail about each packet as possible.

   ▪ The bottom section shows the bytes in the current packet. Observe the EAP-Success frame at packet 66.

   At this point, 802.1X/EAP authentication is completed, and the AP can now initiate the 4-Way Handshake. The access point (authenticator) MAC address is 00:12:43:CB:0F:30. The client station (supplicant) MAC address is 00:40:96:A3:0C:45.

   Continued

7. Observe the EAPOL-Key frames of the 4-Way Handshake in packets 68, 70, 72, and 74. Open the first EAPOL-Key frame in packet 68. Notice that the AP is sending the client station an ANonce.

8. Open the second EAPOL-Key frame in packet 70. Notice that the client station is sending the AP an SNonce, an RSN information element, and a MIC.

9. Open the third EAPOL-Key frame in packet 72. Notice the AP is sending the supplicant an MIC and instructions to install the temporal keys.

10. Open the fourth EAPOL-Key frame in packet 74. The supplicant is now sending a message to the authenticator that the temporal keys are installed.

Group Key Handshake

The 802.11-2007 standard also defines a two-frame handshake that is used to distribute a new group temporal key to client stations that have already obtained a PTK and GTK in a previous 4-Way Handshake exchange. The *Group Key Handshake* is used only to issue a new group temporal key to client stations that have previously formed security associations. Effectively, the Group Key Handshake is identical to the last two frames of the 4-Way Handshake. Once again, the purpose of the Group Key Handshake is to deliver a new GTK to all client stations that already have an original GTK generated by an earlier 4-Way Handshake.

The authenticator can update the GTK for a number of reasons. For example, the authenticator may change the GTK on disassociation or deauthentication of a client station. WLAN vendors may also offer a configuration setting to trigger the creation of a new GTK based on a timed interval.

As shown in Figure 9.31, the Group Key Handshake consists of the following steps:

1. Group Key Handshake Message 1

   The authenticator derives a new GTK from the GMK. The new GTK is sent in a unicast EAPOL-Key frame to the supplicant. The confidentiality of the new GTK is protected because it will be encrypted with the original PTK from the initial 4-Way Handshake. The authenticator also sends a message integrity code. The supplicant validates the MIC when it receives the EAPOL-Key frame. The supplicant decrypts and installs the new GTK.

2. Group Key Handshake Message 2

   The supplicant sends an EAPOL-Key frame to the authenticator to confirm that the GTK has been installed. The supplicant also sends a message integrity code. The authenticator validates the MIC when it receives the EAPOL-Key frame.

FIGURE 9.31 The Group Key Handshake

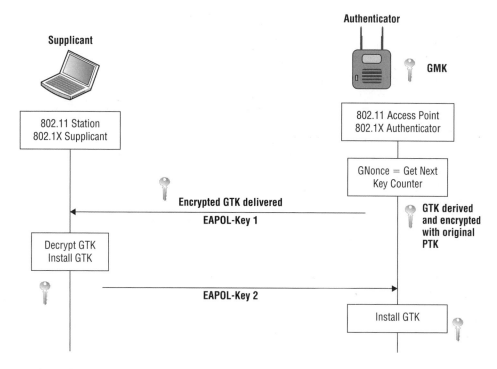

Please do not confuse Group Key Handshake with the two EAPOL-Key frame exchange that is used to distribute dynamic WEP keys. Although both handshakes use a two EAPOL-Key frame exchange, each handshake has an entirely different purpose.

Fast BSS Transition (FT)

The recently ratified 802.11r-2008 amendment is known as the *fast basic service set transition (FT)* amendment. Think of the term *fast BSS transition* as the technical name for standardized fast secure roaming. The main difference between OKC and FT is that the 802.11r-2008 amendment fully defines the key hierarchy used when creating cached keys.

802.11r mechanisms can be used in an autonomous AP environment; however, an intelligent, or coordinated enterprise WLAN solution is best suited for an FT solution. Therefore, we will discuss 802.11r within the context of a WLAN controller architecture. 802.11r mechanisms operate within a mobility domain. A *mobility domain* is a set of basic service sets, within the same extended service set (ESS), that supports fast BSS transitions between themselves. In simpler words, a mobility domain is a group of APs that belong to the same ESS where client stations can roam in a fast and secure manner. Some WLAN vendors even refer to their WLAN controllers as the *mobility domain controller (MDC)*. The first time a client station enters a mobility domain, the client will associate with an AP and perform an initial 802.1X authentication. From that point forward, as the client station roams between APs, the client will be using FT BSS transitions. FT BSS transition can be over-the-air or over-the-DS.

Information Elements

To achieve successful fast secure roaming, FT mechanisms require the use of the RSN information element to indicate the specific authentication key management (AKM) suites and pairwise cipher suites that are being used between the AP and the client station. The 802.11r-2008 amendment also adds four new information elements. However, we are going to focus on just two of them.

The *mobility domain information element (MDIE)* is used to indicate the existence of a mobility domain as well as the method of fast BSS transition. As shown in Figure 9.32, the *mobility domain identifier (MDID)* field is the unique identifier of the group of APs that constitute a mobility domain. The FT capability and policy field is used to indicate whether over-the-air or over-the-DS fast BSS transition is to be performed. We will discuss the difference between over-the-air and over-the-DS fast BSS transition later in this chapter.

FIGURE 9.32 Mobility domain information element

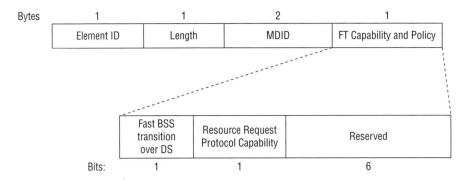

The *fast BSS transition information element (FTIE)* includes information needed to perform the FT authentication sequence during a fast BSS transition. As shown in Figure 9.33, some of the fields look very similar to the information used during a typical 4-Way Handshake exchange. In the next section, you will see how this information is used in a similar manner during the various FT processes.

FIGURE 9.33 Fast BSS transition information element

Element ID	Length	MIC Control	MIC	ANonce	SNonce	Optional Parameter(s)
1	1	2	16	32	32	Variable

Octets:

FT Initial Mobility Domain Association

The *FT initial mobility domain association* is the first association in the mobility domain. As shown in Figure 9.34, the client station first exchanges the standard 802.11 Open System authentication request/response frames with the first AP. The client station and AP then use the MDIE and FTIE information in the association request/response frames to indicate future use of the FT procedures. An original 802.1X/EAP exchange between the client station and the RADIUS server must then occur so seeding material is established for a *FT 4-Way Handshake* that occurs only during the first association. The PTK and GTK encryption keys are created during the FT 4-Way Handshake and the 802.1X controlled port is unblocked. The original 802.1X/EAP exchange also creates the master session key (MSK) that is used for the FT key hierarchy. As you can see, the FT initial mobility domain association is not much different from any initial association used by pre-802.11r clients. The main difference is that extra information, such as the MDIE and FTIE, is communicated during an FT initial mobility domain association.

FIGURE 9.34 FT initial mobility domain association

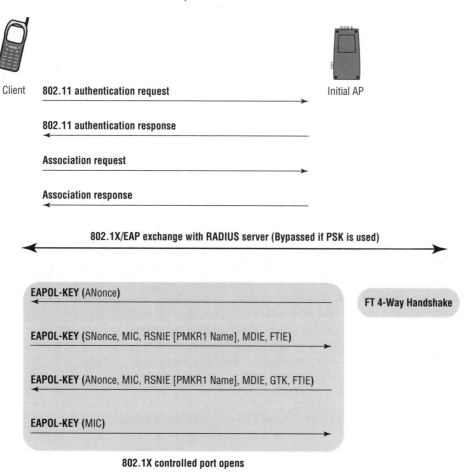

After the initial association, two new methods are defined for a client station to roam from the original AP to a target AP. We will now discuss these two methods of fast BSS transition.

Over-the-Air Fast BSS Transition

Let's consider all the frames that need to be exchanged between a client station and an AP. First, a client has to exchange Open System authentication frames and association frames, as was shown in Figure 9.32. This is a total of four frames, not including the ACKs. Next, a successful 802.1X/EAP exchange between the supplicant and the RADIUS server is needed. The 802.1X/EAP exchange requires many frames. Finally, a 4-Way Handshake exchange is needed between the AP and the client station to create the final dynamic encryption keys. We already know that the purpose of FT and other fast secure roaming mechanisms is to eliminate the need for a new 802.1X/EAP frame exchange every time a client roams. However, the initial four frames of Open System authentication and reassociation are still needed as well as the four frames used during the 4-Way Handshake.

The FT process defines a more efficient method that effectively combines the initial Open System authentication and reassociation frames with the 4-Way Handshake frames. In other words, four less frames are needed when a client roams, thus speeding up the roaming process. As shown in Figure 9.33, an FT protocol frame exchange is used to initiate the roaming exchange and create dynamic encryption keys. Note that the authentication request/response frames and reassociation request/response frames carry an FT authentication algorithm (FTAA) along with nonces and other information needed to create the final dynamic keys. The process shown in Figure 9.35 is known as *over-the-air fast BSS transition*. The client station communicates directly with the target AP using standard 802.11 authentication with the FT authentication algorithm. The PMK-R1 key is the seeding material for the over-the-air fast BSS transition process that creates the final pairwise transient key.

Over-the-DS Fast BSS Transition

An alternative to the FT method is *over-the-DS fast BSS transition,* which requires the use of *FT Action frames* to complete the PTK creation process. The over-the-DS process uses the FT Action frames over the wired 802.3 infrastructure. As shown in Figure 9.36, the client station sends an FT Action request frame to the original AP. The FT Action request frame is forwarded over the distribution system (DS), which is the wired infrastructure. The target AP responds to the client station over the DS with an FT Action response frame. The reassociation request and response frames are then sent from the client station to the target AP over the air. The PMK-R1 key is the seeding material for the over-the-DS fast BSS transition exchange that creates the final pairwise transient key (PTK).

FIGURE 9.35   Over-the-air fast BSS transition

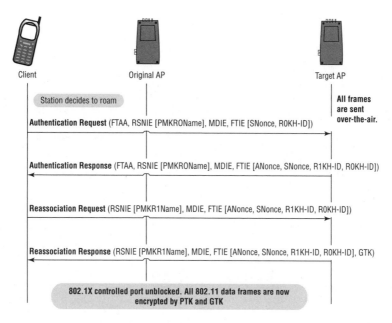

FIGURE 9.36   Over-the-DS fast BSS transition

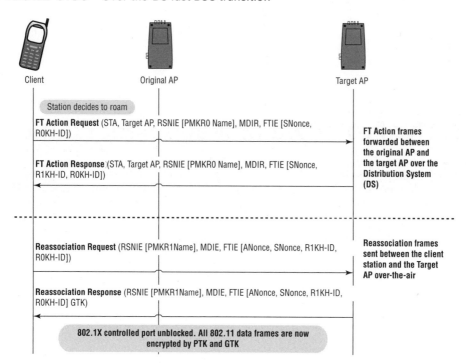

Figure 9.37 shows the multiple steps of the complex fast BSS transition process that has been discussed in this chapter. The process begins with an initial mobility domain association and finally ends with creation of the pairwise transient keys needed for encryption and decryption.

FIGURE 9.37   802.11r fast BSS transition summary

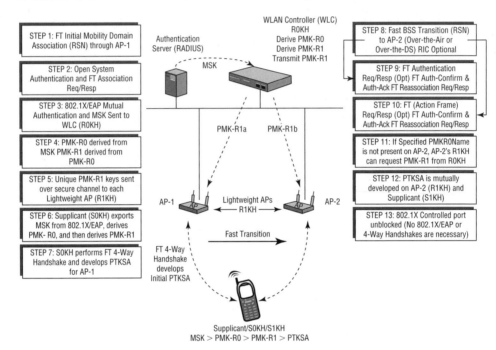

802.11w Protected Management Frames

The 802.11i amendment was created to provide robust security to wireless LANs; however, 802.11i was designed only to provide security for data frames. A common type of attack on an 802.11 WLAN is a denial-of-service attack (DoS attack). There are a multitude of DoS attacks that can be launched against a wireless network; however, a very common DoS attack occurs at layer 2 using spoofed 802.11 management frames. It is fairly simple for an attacker to edit deauthentication or disassociation frames and then retransmit the frames into the air and effectively shut down the wireless network.

The goal of the IEEE Task Group w (TGw) was to provide a way of delivering management frames in a secure manner, therefore preventing the management frames from being able to be spoofed. Figure 9.38 shows the RSN capabilities field format. Bit 6 is the

Management Frame Protection Required (MFPR) bit, which an STA uses to advertise that it requires the use of protected management frames. Bit 7 is the *Management Frame Protection Capable (MFPC)* bit, which an STA uses to advertise that it is capable of using protected management frames but does not require them.

FIGURE 9.38 RSN capabilities field format

b0	b1	b2–b3	b4–b5	b6	b7	b8	b9	b10–15
Pre-Auth	No Pairwise	PTKSA Replay Counter	GTKSA Replay Counter	Management Frame Protection Required (MFPR)	Management Frame Protection Capable (MFPC)	Reserved	Peer Key Enabled	Reserved

802.11w provides protection for unicast, broadcast, and multicast management frames. These 802.11w frames are referred to as *robust management frames*. Robust management frames can be protected by the management frame protection service and include disassociation, deauthentication, and robust action frames. Action frames are used to request a station to take action on behalf of another station, and not all action frames are robust.

When unicast management frames are protected, frame protection is achieved by using CCMP. Broadcast and multicast frames are protected using broadcast/multicast integrity protocol (BIP). BIP provides data integrity and replay protection using AES-128 encryption in Cipher Based Message Authentication Code (CMAC) mode.

Summary

In this chapter, we discussed many of the different methods to provide wireless security. Different types of encryption were reviewed along with advanced wireless authentication methods. We also looked at many of the security frame formats and exchanges.

Exam Essentials

Understand 802.11 authentication.　There are two types of 802.11 authentication: Open System and Shared Key. Know the differences between them along with the frame exchange that is used to establish each. Also understand why Shared Key authentication is considered to be less secure.

Know the WLAN encryption methods.　Understand WLAN encryption and know the differences between WEP, TKIP, and CCMP. Know the different encryption processes along with how the frames are modified during these processes.

Explain WPA and WPA2.　Explain the background of WPA and WPA2 along with their similarities and differences. Know how the Personal and Enterprise versions differ.

Define robust security network.　Define what a robust security network is and how it provides security for both BSS and IBSS wireless networks. Understand its differences from a transition security network.

Understand RSN information elements.　Understand how the RSN information element can identify the encryption capabilities of each station.

Explain 802.1X components.　Explain the different components of an 802.1X network: supplicant, authenticator, and authentication server. Understand their relationship between each other and each of their roles.

Understand the function of EAP.　Understand the EAP process from a basic overview to a more advanced and secure version such as EAP-PEAP.

Understand the 4-Way and Group Key handshake processes.　Understand the communications processes involved with these handshake methods.

Know fast BSS transition.　Know the 802.11r-2008 amendment defined FT, also known as fast secure roaming. Know how RSN information elements are used with it, along with the FT initial mobility domain association. Know how over-the-air fast BSS transition and over-the-DS fast BSS transition is performed.

Explain 802.11w protected management frames.　Explain why 802.11w was created and how it achieves what it was designed to perform.

Key Terms

Before you take the exam, be certain you are familiar with the following terms:

4-Way Handshake

802.1X

associated

authentication server (AS)

authenticator

authenticator nonce (ANonce)

basic service set identifier (BSSID)

EAP-TLS

EAP-TTLS

Group Key Handshake

independent basic service set (IBSS)

Management Frame Protection Capable (MFPC)

Management Frame Protection Required (MFPR)

nonce

pre-robust security network associations (pre-RSNAs)

pseudo-random function (PRF)

robust security network (RSN)

robust security network association (RSNA)

robust security network information element (RSNIE)

RSN information element

service set identifier (SSID)

supplicant nonce (SNonce)

The basic service set (BSS)

transition security network (TSN)

Transport Layer Security (TLS)

Wi-Fi Protected Access (WPA)

Review Questions

1. Laura is attempting to diagnose a WLAN by using a packet analyzer to capture the exchange of frames and packets between a wireless client and the AP. In the process of analyzing the packets, she sees two 802.11 authentication frames, two 802.11 association frames, and DHCP requests and responses, and then she begins to see encrypted data. Which of the following could the client be using? (Choose all that apply.)

   A. Open System authentication

   B. Shared Key authentication

   C. 802.1X/EAP

   D. WEP

   E. PPTP

   F. L2TP/IPsec

2. This graphic shows a packet capture of a successful 802.11 authentication. In which of the following types of client connections could this authentication not occur? (Choose all that apply.)

Source	Destination	BSSID	Protocol
Aironet Wireles...	Cisco:0D:4B:6A	Cisco:0D:4B:6A	802.11 Auth
Cisco:0D:4B:6A	Aironet Wireless Comm:A3:9E:92		802.11 Ack
Cisco:0D:4B:6A	Aironet Wireless Comm:A3:9E:92	Cisco:0D:4B:6A	802.11 Auth
Aironet Wireles...	Cisco:0D:4B:6A		802.11 Ack
Aironet Wireles...	Cisco:0D:4B:6A	Cisco:0D:4B:6A	802.11 Auth
Cisco:0D:4B:6A	Aironet Wireless Comm:A3:9E:92		802.11 Ack
Cisco:0D:4B:6A	Aironet Wireless Comm:A3:9E:92	Cisco:0D:4B:6A	802.11 Auth
Aironet Wireles...	Cisco:0D:4B:6A		802.11 Ack

   A. 802.1X/EAP

   B. VPN

   C. WEP with Shared Key authentication

   D. WEP with Open System authentication

   E. Open System authentication with WEP

3. The graphic shows a packet capture of a successful 802.11 authentication. In which of the following types of client connections could this not occur?

Source	Destination	BSSID	Protocol
Aironet Wireles...	00:1A:1E:94:4C:30	00:1A:1E:94:4C:30	802.11 Auth
00:1A:1E:94:4C:30	Aironet Wireless Comm:A3:9...		802.11 Ack
00:1A:1E:94:4C:30	Aironet Wireless Comm:A3:9...	00:1A:1E:94:4C:30	802.11 Auth
Aironet Wireles...	00:1A:1E:94:4C:30		802.11 Ack

    A. 802.1X/EAP

    B. VPN

    C. WEP with Shared Key authentication

    D. WEP with Open System authentication

    E. Unencrypted

4. Given that CCMP uses a MIC for data integrity to protect the frame body and portions of the MAC header, what information needs to be constructed to protect certain fields in the MAC header?

    A. Nonce

    B. Extended IV

    C. ICV

    D. AAD

    E. PN

    F. IV

5. How many extra bytes of overhead does TKIP/RC4 encryption add to the body of an 802.11 MPDU?

    A. 16 bytes

    B. 12 bytes

    C. 20 bytes

    D. 10 bytes

    E. None of the above

6. The TKIP MIC is used for data integrity. Which portions of an 802.11 MPDU does the TKIP MIC protect from being altered? (Choose all that apply.)

    A. MSDU

    B. SA

    C. DA

    D. TA

    E. Frame Control field

    F. MSDU priority bit

7. What does 802.1X/EAP provide when implemented for WLAN security? (Choose all that apply.)

    A. Access to network resources

    B. Verification of access point credentials

    C. Dynamic authentication

    D. Dynamic encryption-key generation

    E. Verification of user credentials

8. View the frame capture of the 4-Way Handshake in the graphic shown here. Which EAPOL-Key message frame is displayed?

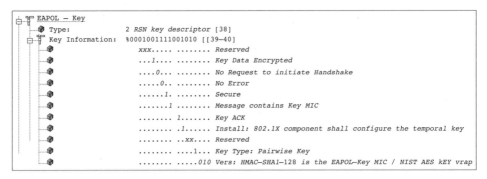

```
⊟ ⯈ EAPOL — Key
  ├─ ⯈ Type:            2 RSN key descriptor [38]
  ├─ ⯈ Key Information: %0001001111001010 [[39—40]
  │   ├─⯈               xxx..... ........ Reserved
  │   ├─⯈               ...1.... ........ Key Data Encrypted
  │   ├─⯈               ....0... ........ No Request to initiate Handshake
  │   ├─⯈               .....0.. ........ No Error
  │   ├─⯈               ......1. ........ Secure
  │   ├─⯈               .......1 ........ Message contains Key MIC
  │   ├─⯈               ........ 1....... Key ACK
  │   ├─⯈               ........ .1...... Install: 802.1X component shall configure the temporal key
  │   ├─⯈               ........ ..xx.... Reserved
  │   ├─⯈               ........ ....1... Key Type: Pairwise Key
  │   └─⯈               ........ .....010 Vers: HMAC—SHA1—128 is the EAPOL—Key MIC / NIST AES kEY vrap
```

    A. 4-Way Handshake message 1

    B. 4-Way Handshake message 2

    C. 4-Way Handshake message 3

    D. 4-Way Handshake message 4

9. What are some of the frames that carry the security capabilities found in the RSN information element? (Choose all that apply.)

    A. Beacon management frame

    B. Probe request frame

    C. Probe response frame

    D. Association request frame

    E. EAPOL-Key frame

    F. Request-to-Send frame

10. In a robust security network (RSN), which 802.11 management frames are used by client stations to inform an access point about the RSNA security capabilities of the client STAs? (Choose all that apply.)

    A. Beacon management frame

    B. Probe request frame

    C. Probe response frame

    D. Association request frame

    E. Reassociation response frame

    F. Reassociation request frame

    G. Association response frame

11. After viewing the frame capture shown here, identify the type of authentication method being used.

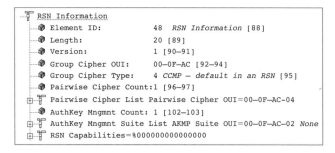

```
⊤ RSN Information
   ⬤ Element ID:          48  RSN Information [88]
   ⬤ Length:              20 [89]
   ⬤ Version:             1 [90–91]
   ⬤ Group Cipher OUI:    00–0F–AC [92–94]
   ⬤ Group Cipher Type:   4 CCMP – default in an RSN [95]
   ⬤ Pairwise Cipher Count:1 [96–97]
 ⊞ ⊤ Pairwise Cipher List Pairwise Cipher OUI=00–0F–AC–04
   ⬤ AuthKey Mngmnt Count: 1 [102–103]
 ⊞ ⊤ AuthKey Mngmnt Suite List AKMP Suite OUI=00–0F–AC–02 None
 ⊞ ⊤ RSN Capabilities=%0000000000000000
```

A. EAP-TTLS

B. Open System

C. PSK

D. EAP-TLS

E. PEAP

12. Which of these roaming methods requires the use of FT Action frames?

A. Over-the-air fast BSS transition

B. Over-the-WDS fast BSS transition

C. Over-the-DS fast BSS transition

D. Over-the-WLS fast BSS transition

13. Before an 802.11 client STA can pass traffic through the AP, which two of the following must occur? (Choose two answers.)

A. 802.1X

B. EAP

C. Association

D. Authentication

E. WEP keys must match

14. How many extra bytes of overhead does CCMP/AES encryption add to the body of an 802.11 data frame?

A. 16 bytes

B. 12 bytes

C. 20 bytes

D. 10 bytes

E. None of the above

15. A data integrity check known as message integrity code (MIC) is used by which of the following? (Choose all that apply.)

    A. WEP

    B. TKIP

    C. CCMP

    D. AES

    E. DES

16. How does a RADIUS server communicate with an authenticator? (Choose all that apply.)

    A. UDP ports 1812 and 1813

    B. TCP ports 1645 and 1646

    C. Encrypted TLS tunnel

    D. Encrypted IPsec tunnel

    E. RADIUS IP packets

    F. EAPOL frames

17. What must occur in order for dynamic TKIP/RC4 or CCMP/AES encryption keys to be generated? (Choose all that apply.)

    A. Shared Key authentication and 4-Way Handshake

    B. 802.1X/EAP authentication and 4-Way Handshake

    C. Open System authentication and 3-Way Handshake

    D. Open System authentication and 4-Way Handshake

    E. 802.1X/EAP authentication and 3-Way Handshake

18. After viewing the frame capture in the graphic shown here, identify which type of security network is being used.

```
⊤⊤ RSN Information
  ⊕ Element ID:              48   RSN Information [66]
  ⊕ Length:                  20 [67]
  ⊕ Version:                 1 [68–69]
  ⊕ Group Cipher OUI:        00–0F–AC [70–72]
  ⊕ Group Cipher Type:       5  WEP – 104 [73]
  ⊕ Pairwise Cipher Count:1 [74–75]
⊞⊤⊤ Pairwise Cipher List Pairwise Cipher OUI=00–0F–AC–04
  ⊕ AuthKey Mngmnt Count: 1 [80–81]
⊞⊤⊤ AuthKey Mngmnt Suite List AKMP Suite OUI=00–0F–AC–02 None
⊞⊤⊤ RSN Capabilities=%000000000101000
```

    A. Robust Security Network

    B. Rotund Security Network

    C. Transition Security Network

    D. WPA Security Network

    E. WPA

19. 802.11w provides protection for which of the following types of frames? (Choose all that apply.)

   A. Unicast

   B. Broadcast

   C. Anycast

   D. Simulcast

   E. Multicast

20. 802.11w Protected Management Frames was created to prevent which of the following types of attacks? (Choose all that apply.)

   A. Denial of service

   B. Deauthentication attack

   C. Disassociation attack

   D. Impersonation attack

   E. Bit-flipping attack

Answers to Review Questions

1. **A, E, F.** Since there are only two 802.11 authentication frames, Open System authentication is being used. Shared Key authentication would generate four 802.11 authentication frames. If 802.1X/EAP or WEP were being used, then the client would be doing L2 encryption, and the DHCP frames would be encrypted and not visible. Therefore, 802.1X/EAP and WEP are not being used. Both PPTP and L2TP/IPsec perform layer 3 encryption that would allow Laura to see the DHCP exchange and any other IP traffic.

2. **A, D, E.** The graphic shows an 802.11 Shared Key authentication that consists of four authentication frames: an authentication request followed by a clear-text challenge frame, followed by a challenge response with the clear-text data encrypted, and then followed by an authentication response. 802.1X/EAP works together with Open System authentication but cannot be deployed when WEP is used. To use Shared Key authentication, WEP must be enabled. A VPN can be used with Shared Key or Open System authentication. Companies would use a VPN for data privacy because WEP has been cracked, but they often would still use WEP as an added layer of security. Shared Key authentication is optional with WEP, although not recommended.

3. **C.** The graphic shows a two-frame Open System authentication. 802.1X/EAP works together with Open System authentication. VPN can be configured with either Open System or Shared Key authentication. An unencrypted session uses Open System authentication.

4. **D.** Additional authentication data (AAD) is constructed from portions of the MPDU header. This information is used for data integrity of portions of the MAC header. Receiving stations can then validate the integrity of these MAC header fields. The MIC protects the AAD information and the frame body for data integrity.

5. **C.** When TKIP is implemented, because of the extra overhead from the extended IV and the MIC, a total of 20 bytes of overhead is added to the body of an 802.11 MPDU. CCMP/AES encryption will add an extra 16 bytes of overhead to the body of an 802.11 MPDU. WEP encryption will add an extra 8 bytes of overhead to the body of an 802.11 MPDU.

6. **A, B, C.** TKIP uses a stronger data integrity check known as the message integrity code (MIC) to mitigate known forgery attacks against WEP. The MIC is often referred to by its nickname of Michael. The MIC can be used to defeat bit-flipping attacks, fragmentation attacks, redirection, and impersonation attacks. The MIC is computed using the destination address (DA), source address (SA), MSDU Priority, and the entire unencrypted MSDU plaintext data. After the MIC is generated, it is appended to the end of the MSDU payload.

7. **A, D, E.** The purpose of 802.1X/EAP is authentication of user credentials and authorization to access network resources. Although the 802.1X framework does not require encryption, it highly suggests the use of encryption. A by-product of 802.1X/EAP is the generation and distribution of dynamic encryption keys. Although the encryption process is actually a byproduct of the authentication process, the goals of authentication and encryption are very different. Authentication provides mechanisms for validating user identity while encryption provides mechanisms for data privacy or confidentiality.

8. C. The third EAPOL-Key frame of the 4-Way Handshake may also contain a message to the supplicant to install the temporal keys. The frame capture indicates that the temporal key is to be installed. The third EAPOL-Key frame also sends the supplicant the ANonce, the authenticator's RSN information element capabilities, and a MIC. If a GTK has been generated, the GTK will be inside the third EAPOL-Key frame. The GTK confidentiality is protected because it will be encrypted with the PTK.

9. A, C, D, E. The RSN information element field is found in four different 802.11 management frames: beacon management frames, probe response frames, association request frames, and reassociation request frames. The RSN information element can also be found in the second and third EAPOL-Key frames of the 4-Way Handshake.

10. D, F. The RSN information element field is found in four different 802.11 management frames: beacon management frames, probe response frames, association request frames, and reassociation request frames. Within a basic service set, an access point and client stations use the RSN information element within these four management frames to communicate with each other about their security capabilities prior to establishing association. Client stations use the association request frame to inform the access point of the client station security capabilities. When stations roam from one access point to another access point, they use the reassociation request frame to inform the new access point of the roaming client station's security capabilities. The security capabilities include supported encryption cipher suites and supported authentication methods.

11. C. The RSN information element can also be used to indicate what authentication methods are supported. The authentication key management (AKM) suite field in the RSN information element indicates whether the station supports either 802.1X authentication or PSK authentication. If the AKM suite value is 00-0F-AC-01, authentication is negotiated over an 802.1X infrastructure using an EAP protocol. If the AKM suite value is 00-0F-AC-02, then PSK is the authentication method that is being used.

12. C. The pairwise transient key (PTK) is the third-level key of the FT key hierarchy. The PTK is the final key used to encrypt 802.11 data frames. The PTK is created during either an over-the-air fast BSS transition frame exchange or over-the-DS fast BSS transition frame exchange. In any 802.11 robust security network (RSN), the PTK is used to encrypt the MSDU payload of an 802.11 unicast data frame.

13. C, D. For a client to connect to the WLAN and pass data, the client must authenticate and associate. The other three choices could occur but do not have to do so.

14. A. CCMP/AES encryption will add an extra 16 bytes of overhead to the body of an 802.11 data frame. Eight bytes are added by the CCMP header and 8 bytes are added by the MIC. WEP encryption will add an extra 8 bytes of overhead to the body of an 802.11 data frame. When TKIP is implemented, because of the extra overhead from the extended IV and the MIC, a total of 20 bytes of overhead is added to the body of an 802.11 data frame.

15. B, C. A stronger data integrity check known as a message integrity code (MIC), or by its common name, Michael, was introduced with TKIP to correct some of the weaknesses in WEP. CCMP also uses a MIC. AES and DES are encryption algorithms and are not concerned with message integrity.

16. A, E. The RADIUS protocol uses UDP ports 1812 for RADIUS authentication and 1813 for RADIUS accounting. These ports were officially assigned by the Internet Assigned Number Authority (IANA). However, prior to IANA allocation of UDP ports 1812 and 1813, the UDP ports of 1645 and 1646 (authentication and accounting, respectively) were used as the default ports by many RADIUS server vendors. TCP is not used. All Layer 2 EAP traffic sent between the RADIUS server and the authenticator is encapsulated in RADIUS IP packets. The encrypted TLS tunnel communications are between the supplicant and the authentication server. IPsec is not used.

17. B, D. Open System and Shared Key authentication are legacy authentication methods that do not provide seeding material to generate dynamic encryption keys. However, a four-way Open System authentication must occur prior to the EAP exchange. A robust security network association requires a four-frame EAP exchange known as the 4-Way Handshake that is used to generate dynamic TKIP or CCMP keys.

18. C. The frame capture shows an RSN information element field that can be found in a management frame. The RSN information element shows that the group cipher that is being used is WEP. A transition security network (TSN) supports RSN-defined security as well as legacy security such as WEP within the same BSS. Within a TSN, some client stations will use RSNA security using TKIP/RC4 or CCMP/AES for encrypting unicast traffic. However, some legacy stations are still using static WEP keys for unicast encryption. All of the clients will use WEP encryption for the broadcast and multicast traffic. Because all the stations share a single group encryption key for broadcast and multicast traffic, the lowest common denominator must be used for the group cipher.

19. A, B, E. 802.11w provides protection for unicast, broadcast, and multicast management frames. These 802.11w frames are referred to as robust management frames. Anycast and simulcast frames do not exist.

20. A, B, C. 802.11w was developed to provide security for management frames. This prevents denial-of-service attacks, such as deauthentication attacks and disassociation attacks. It will not prevent bit-flipping attacks. Some impersonation attacks use denial of service prior to performing the impersonation; however, since some do not use DoS attacks, this answer is not always correct.

Chapter

10

802.11n HT Analysis

IN THIS CHAPTER, YOU WILL LEARN ABOUT THE FOLLOWING:

✓ **Introduction to 802.11n**

✓ **802.11n Fields, Information Elements, and Frames**

- HT Control Field

- HT Control Wrapper Frame

- HT Capabilities Element

- HT Operation Element

✓ **Physical Layer Enhancements**

- Spatial Multiplexing

- Transmit Beamforming

- Space Time Block Coding (STBC)

- Antenna Selection

- 40 MHz Channels

- Short Guard Interval

- Modulation and Coding Schemes (MCSs)

✓ **MAC Layer Enhancements**

- A-MSDU

- A-MPDU

- Delayed BlockAcks

- RIFS

✓ **802.11n Protection Mechanisms**

- Mode 0 – Green Field
- Mode 1 – HT non-Member Protection
- Mode 2 – HT 20 MHz Protections
- Mode 3 – Non-HT Mixed Mode
- Dual CTS
- L-Sig TXOP Protection
- Phased Co-Existence Operation
- 40-MHz Intolerant

The 802.11n amendment Enhancements for Higher Throughput (HT) specifies a number of improvements to the 802.11 physical (PHY) layer and Medium Access Control (MAC) layer to support throughput of 100 Mbps or greater. With the promise of data rates up to 600 Mbps, increased range, and more robust connections, 802.11n HT technology is certainly an attractive prospect.

Many of the PHY layer enhancements are due to a new PHY layer technology called multiple-input multiple-output (MIMO), which utilizes multiple antennas and radios. The Physical layer enhancements are spatial multiplexing (SM), transmit beamforming (TxBF), space-time block coding (STBC), low-density parity check (LDPC), antenna selection (ASEL), and channel bonding (where throughput is increased by extending the channel width from 20 MHz to 40 MHz, effectively bonding two channels together as one).

Another PHY layer enhancement implemented by many MIMO access points is Maximal Ratio Combining (MRC). MRC processes the signals received on multiple antennas into one stronger signal. This is achieved through an advanced digital signal processing technique that brings all the receive signals in phase with each other and then combines them together into one signal. Although implemented by vendors, MRC is not defined in the 802.11n amendment and is not a technology that can be easily analyzed and therefore will not be discussed within this chapter.

For each 20 MHz and 40 MHz channel, the 802.11n amendment introduces 77 new modulation and coding schemes (MCSs). This, in turn, introduces a whole array of new data rates. Each MCS is given an index to provide easy reference. Two new PPDU headers are also defined, giving HT stations the choice of legacy non-HT format, HT mixed format, and HT Greenfield format.

MAC layer enhancements improve efficiency by reducing the overhead required for standard frame exchanges. The MAC layer enhancements are frame aggregation, block acknowledgments, power save multi-poll (PSMP), and Reverse Direction (RD) protocol. MAC layer protection mechanisms for supporting the coexistence with non-HT STAs are also introduced.

 The number and combination of these 802.11n enhancements that a vendor decides to implement will govern the theoretical maximum data rate possible. Environmental conditions of an installed access point will then dictate the actual throughput achieved.

The 802.11n-2009 amendment is a 536-page document, and this chapter does not attempt to discuss all the details within its pages. This chapter will instead focus on the information that is of use when performing wireless network analyses. After an introduction to the 802.11n amendment, this chapter will focus on three main areas: the HT Control field, the HT Capabilities Element, and the HT Operation Element. Within these three elements and their associated frames are more than 100 fields and subfields to be discussed.

As we explore the wealth of information available to the wireless analyst in these three areas, we'll also discuss the protocol exchanges and frames that support them. We will outline how the different enhancements affect wireless network analysis and what we can expect to see in a protocol analyzer.

As we take a ride through the 802.11n amendment looking at all the new frames, fields, and flags that are needed to support the vast array of enhancements, you must be prepared for some hard study.

Introduction to 802.11n

Before we delve into the details of 802.11n wireless analysis, it is essential to have a general overview of the HT amendment. The 802.11n-2009 amendment was ratified on September 11, 2009, six years to the day after the IEEE-SA New Standards Committee approved the request to create the 802.11 Task Group n (TGn). This group was responsible for the development of the 802.11n amendment. The amendment is essentially a list of enhancements to the current 802.11 standard that answer the following question: "What can we do to improve the performance and throughput of current 802.11 wireless networks?" We get answers like the following: "If we transmit data over two channels instead of one, we can double our throughput." "If we don't have to acknowledge every data packet, we can make data transfer more efficient." "If we reduce the amount of time we have to wait between sending packets, we increase our efficiency."

This section will provide a high-level overview of the technologies defined by the 802.11n amendment. For CWNAs, this section should act as an 802.11n refresher, providing you with the prerequisite 802.11n knowledge required for the rest of this chapter. The different enhancements added by the 802.11n amendment will be defined in this section, and then you'll look at the parts of the amendment that the Wi-Fi Alliance tests and certifies products against.

Frequency Spectrum

HT (clause 20) technology defined by the 802.11n amendment is backward compatible with existing HR-DSSS (clause 18), ERP (clause 19), and OFDM (clause 17) technology. Because HR-DSSS and ERP radios operate in the 2.4 GHz ISM band and OFDM radios operate in the 5 GHz UNII band, HT technology is not frequency dependant and can be used in both the 2.4 GHz and 5 GHz bands.

MIMO

The heart and soul of the 802.11n amendment exists at the PHY layer with the use of a technology known as *multiple-input multiple-output* (MIMO). MIMO requires the use of multiple radios and antennas, called *radio chains*. MIMO systems use multiple antennas to provide for better antenna diversity, which can increase range. Transmitting multiple streams of data with spatial multiplexing provides for greater throughput and takes advantage of the old enemy known as multipath. Transmit beamforming is an optional smart antenna technology that can be used in MIMO systems to "steer" beams and provide for greater range and throughput.

Radio Chains

Conventional 802.11 radios transmit and receive RF signals by using a *single-input single-output* (SISO) system. SISO systems use a single radio chain. A radio chain is defined as a single radio and all of its supporting architecture, including mixers, amplifiers, and analog/digital converters.

A MIMO system consists of multiple radio chains, with each radio chain having its own antenna. A MIMO system is characterized by the number of transmitters and receivers used by the multiple radio chains. For example, a 2×3 MIMO system would consist of three radio chains with two transmitters and three receivers. A 3×3 MIMO system would use three radio chains with three transmitters and three receivers. In a MIMO system, the first number always references the transmitters (TX), and the second number references the receivers (RX).

Figure 10.1 illustrates both 2×3 and 3×3 MIMO systems. Please note that both systems utilize three radio chains; however, the 3×3 system has three transmitters, whereas the 2×3 system has only two transmitters.

FIGURE 10.1   2×3 and 3×3 MIMO

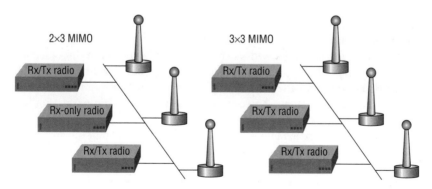

Using multiple transmitters in a MIMO system provides for the transmission of more data via spatial multiplexing. Using multiple receivers increases signal-to-noise ratio (SNR) because of advanced MIMO antenna diversity. The 802.11n standard allows for MIMO systems up to 4×4 using four radio chains. Each radio chain requires power. A 2×2 MIMO system would require much less of a power draw than a 4×4 MIMO system.

MIMO Enhancements

The enhancements provided by MIMO technology are summarized here:

Transmit Beamforming (TxBF)   This is a method that allows a MIMO transmitter using multiple antennas to "focus" the transmissions in the best direction of a receiver (RX).

Spatial Multiplexing (SM)   MIMO radios transmit multiple radio signals at the same time. Each independent signal is known as a spatial stream, and each unique stream can contain different data. SM increases our overall throughput.

Space-Time Block Coding (STBC)   This is a method to improve the reliability of data transfer by transmitting different copies of the data stream from different antennas. This adds a level of redundancy to our data communication. By increasing the signal quality, the range is also increased.

Antenna Selection (ASEL)   This is a method to increase signal diversity by dynamically selecting which antennas to use when a STA has more antennas than radio chains.

The details of how TxBF and ASEL work and their protocols will be discussed later in this chapter when exploring the fields of the HT Capabilities Element. TxBF operation will be explained in the section "Transmit Beamforming Capabilities," and ASEL operation will be discussed in the section "ASEL Capabilities." You can find more information on STBC in the section "HT Capabilities Element," covering the TX STBC and RX STBC subfields, as well as the section "HT Operation Element," covering dual beacons, dual CTS, and STBC beacons. A more detailed description of spatial multiplexing will be discussed next. Many of the topics in this chapter require you to have a basic understanding of SM. However, the basic operation of SM is not manifested in the packets and is therefore hard to analyze.

Spatial Multiplexing

In traditional 802.11 environments, the phenomenon of multipath has long caused problems. Multipath is a propagation phenomenon that results in two or more paths of the same signal arriving at a receiving antenna at the same time or within nanoseconds of each other. Because of the natural broadening of the waves, the propagation behaviors of reflection, scattering, diffraction, and refraction will occur. A signal may reflect off an object or may scatter, refract, or diffract. These propagation behaviors can each result in multiple paths of the same signal. The negative effects of multipath can include loss of amplitude and data corruption. 802.11n MIMO systems, however, take advantage of multipath, and, believe it or not, multipath then becomes our friend.

MIMO radios transmit multiple radio signals at the same time and take advantage of multipath. Each individual radio signal is transmitted by a unique radio and antenna of the MIMO system. Each independent signal is known as a spatial stream, and each unique stream can contain different data than the other streams transmitted by one or more of the other radios. Each stream will also travel a different path, because there is at least a half-wavelength of space between the multiple transmitting antennas. The fact that the multiple streams follow different paths to the receiver because of the space between the transmitting antennas is known as spatial diversity. Sending multiple independent streams of unique data using spatial diversity is often also referred to as *spatial multiplexing* (SM) or spatial diversity multiplexing (SDM).

When using spatial multiplexing, both the transmitter and the receiver must participate. In other words, both the transmitter and the receiver must be MIMO systems. A simplistic description of spatial multiplexing would be to envision multiple unique data streams being transmitted via unidirectional antennas to multiple receiving unidirectional antennas. Spatial multiplexing can also be accomplished with omnidirectional antennas because of the advanced digital signal processing (DSP) techniques used by MIMO systems. The benefit of sending multiple unique data streams is that throughput is drastically increased. If a MIMO access point sends two unique data streams to a MIMO client station that receives both streams, the throughput is effectively doubled. If a MIMO access point sends three unique data streams to a MIMO client station that receives all three streams, the throughput is effectively tripled. Figure 10.2 depicts a 3×3 MIMO AP transmitting three independent streams of unique data to a 3×3 MIMO client. Currently, most 802.11n radios deploy 2×3 or 3×3 MIMO systems. The 802.11n amendment allows for up to a 4×4 MIMO system.

Throughput is theoretically doubled when moving from one to two spatial streams, but because of other considerations within the signal transmission, this gain does not follow a linear progression as the spatial streams increase. The cost of increasing the number of spatial streams beyond the four specified by the 802.11n amendment would have to be carefully considered against the gain that would be achieved.

FIGURE 10.2   Multiple spatial streams

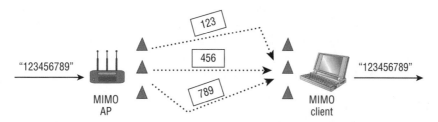

For simplicity, Figure 10.2 shows the different transmit streams all taking just one unique path; however, in reality, each individual stream will be affected by multipath and take many different paths to the receiver. Each receiving antenna will then receive several copies of each transmitted signal combined together. As is pictured in Figure 10.3, the receiver will then perform some advanced DSP on the combination of all signals received at each receive antenna. The result of this DSP will be the individual bit streams that were transmitted, which will then be merged together, back into the original data.

FIGURE 10.3   SM process

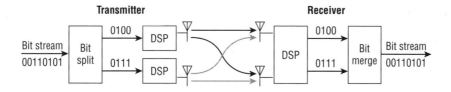

HT Channels

HT radios use 20 MHz Orthogonal Frequency Division Multiplexing (OFDM) channels and may optionally use larger 40 MHz channels. The OFDM channels used by 802.11n radios are larger in size and bandwidth than legacy 802.11a/g radios. The greater frequency bandwidth provided by the OFDM channels used by HT clause 20 radios also provides for greater eventual throughput.

20 MHz Non-HT and HT Channels

802.11a and 802.11g radios use 20 MHz OFDM channels. Each 20 MHz OFDM channel contains 62 subcarriers. Each subcarrier is 312.5 KHz wide and can be separately modulated with part of the data stream. The first six and last five subcarriers are null because they act as a guard band for the channel. As well as the 11 guard band subcarriers, the center subcarrier is also null and is called the direct conversation (DC) subcarrier. This leaves 52 subcarriers, as pictured in Figure 10.4. Forty-eight of these subcarriers transmit data, while four of the subcarriers are used as pilot tones for dynamic calibration between the transmitter and receiver. OFDM technology also employs the use of convolutional coding and forward error correction.

HT clause 20 radios also use the same OFDM technology and have the capability of using either 20 MHz channels or 40 MHz channels. The 20 MHz channels used by HT radios use four extra subcarriers to carry data and subsequently have a smaller guard bands. Therefore, HT channels can carry a little more data than a non-HT OFDM channel. As a result, the HT 20 MHz channel can provide greater aggregate throughput for the same frequency space. As pictured in Figure 10.5, an HT 20 MHz OFDM channel has 56 subcarriers. Fifty-two of the subcarriers transmit data, while four of the subcarriers are used as pilot tones for dynamic calibration between the transmitter and receiver.

40 MHz Channels

HT clause 20 radios also have the capability of using 40 MHz OFDM channels. As pictured in Figure 10.6, the 40 MHz HT channels use 114 OFDM subcarriers. One hundred and eight of the subcarriers transmit data, while six of the subcarriers are used as pilot tones for dynamic calibration between the transmitter and receiver. A 40 MHz channel more than doubles the frequency bandwidth available for data transmissions, which is because the 20 MHz guard bands in the center of the 40 MHz channel can now be used for data.

The 40 MHz channels used by HT radios are essentially two 20 MHz OFDM channels that are bonded together. Each 40 MHz channel consists of a primary and secondary 20 MHz channel. The primary and secondary 20 MHz channels must be adjacent 20 MHz channels for the frequencies across which they operate. As pictured in Figure 10.7, the two 20 MHz channels used to form a 40 MHz channel are designated as primary and secondary and are indicated by two fields in the body of certain 802.11 management frames. The primary field indicates the number of the primary channel. A positive or negative offset indicates whether the secondary channel is one channel above or one channel below the primary channel.

FIGURE 10.4   20 MHz non-HT (802.11a/g) channel

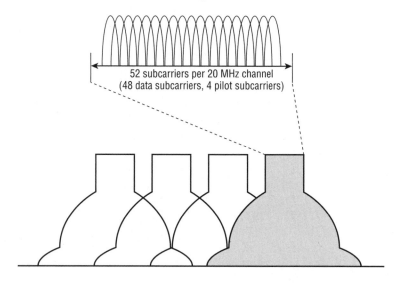

FIGURE 10.5   20 MHz HT (802.11n) channel

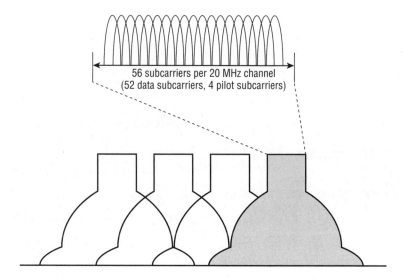

FIGURE 10.6   40 MHz HT (802.11n) channel

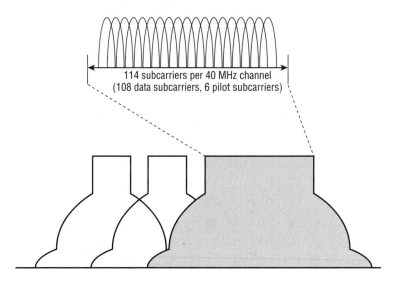

114 subcarriers per 40 MHz channel
(108 data subcarriers, 6 pilot subcarriers)

FIGURE 10.7   Channel bonding

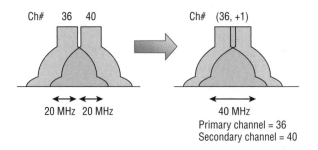

Ch#   36   40   Ch#   (36, +1)

20 MHz   20 MHz   40 MHz
                                     Primary channel = 36
                                     Secondary channel = 40

Additional HT Information
- Element ID: *61 Additional HT Information*
- Length: *22*
- Primary Channel: *36*
- Srvc Int Granularity: *%000 5ms*
- PSMP STAs Only: *%0 Association Requests are Accepted Regardless of PSMP Capability*
- RIFS Mode: *%0 Use of RIFS Prohibited*
- STA Channel Width: *%1 Use Any Channel Width Enabled Under Supported Channel Width Set*
- 2nd Channel Offset: *%01 Above the Primary Channel*

A standard 20 MHz HT channel reserves some frequency bandwidth at the top and bottom of the channel to avoid interference with adjacent 20 MHz HT channels. When two 20 MHz HT channels are bonded together, there is no need to reserve this bandwidth at the bottom of the higher channel and at the top end of the lower channel. Therefore, an HT (802.11n) 40 MHz channel uses this spectral space to add two more subcarriers, giving a total of 114 subcarriers instead of 112.

Modulation and Coding Scheme

The 802.11n amendment defines data rates with a *modulation and coding scheme* (MCS). Non-HT radios that used OFDM technology (802.11a/g) defined data rates of 6 Mbps to 54 Mbps based on the modulation that was used. HT radios, however, define data rates based on numerous factors including modulation, the number of spatial streams, channel size, and guard interval. Each modulation coding scheme is a combination of these multiple factors. Seventy-seven modulation coding schemes exist for both 20 MHz HT channels and 40 MHz HT channels. There are eight mandatory modulation and coding schemes for 20 MHz HT channels, as shown in Table 10.1. The eight mandatory MCSs for 20 MHz channels are comparable to basic (required) rates.

TABLE 10.1   Mandatory modulation and coding schemes—20 MHz channel

MCS index	Modulation	Spatial streams	Data rates 800 ns GI	Data rates 400 ns GI
0	BPSK	1	6.5 Mbps	7.2 Mbps
1	QPSK	1	13.0 Mbps	14.4 Mbps
2	QPSK	1	19.5 Mbps	21.7 Mbps
3	16-QAM	1	26.0 Mbps	28.9 Mbps
4	16-QAM	1	39.0 Mbps	43.3 Mbps
5	64-QAM	1	52.0 Mbps	57.8 Mbps
6	64-QAM	1	58.5 Mbps	65.0 Mbps
7	64-QAM	1	65.0 Mbps	72.2 Mbps

As you can see from Table 10.1, the modulation type, the guard interval, and the number of spatial streams all determine the eventual data rate. The guard interval (GI) and its two alternative lengths will be explained in the "HT Capabilities Element" section of this chapter. Table 10.2 depicts the modulation and coding schemes for a 20 MHz channel using four spatial streams.

TABLE 10.2 MCS—20 MHz channel, four spatial streams

MCS index	Modulation	Spatial streams	Data rates	
			800 ns GI	400 ns GI
24	BPSK	4	26.0 Mbps	28.9 Mbps
25	QPSK	4	52.0 Mbps	57.8 Mbps
26	QPSK	4	78.0 Mbps	86.7 Mbps
27	16-QAM	4	104.0 Mbps	115.6 Mbps
28	16-QAM	4	156.0 Mbps	173.3 Mbps
29	64-QAM	4	208.0 Mbps	231.1 Mbps
30	64-QAM	4	234.0 Mbps	260.0 Mbps
31	64-QAM	4	260.0 Mbps	288.9 Mbps

Table 10.3 depicts the modulation and coding schemes for a 40 MHz channel using one spatial stream.

TABLE 10.3 MCS—40 MHz channel, one spatial stream

MCS index	Modulation	Spatial streams	Data rates	
			800 ns GI	400 ns GI
0	BPSK	1	13.5 Mbps	15.0 Mbps
1	QPSK	1	27.0 Mbps	30.0 Mbps
2	QPSK	1	40.5 Mbps	45.0 Mbps
3	16-QAM	1	54.0 Mbps	60.0 Mbps
4	16-QAM	1	81.0 Mbps	90.0 Mbps
5	64-QAM	1	108.0 Mbps	120.0 Mbps
6	64-QAM	1	121.5 Mbps	135.0 Mbps
7	64-QAM	1	135.0 Mbps	150.0 Mbps

Table 10.4 depicts the modulation and coding schemes for a 40 MHz channel using four spatial streams.

TABLE 10.4   MCS—40 MHz channel, four spatial streams

MCS index	Modulation	Spatial streams	Data rates 800 ns GI	400 ns GI
24	BPSK	4	54.0 Mbps	60.0 Mbps
25	QPSK	4	108.0 Mbps	120.0 Mbps
26	QPSK	4	162.0 Mbps	180.0 Mbps
27	16-QAM	4	216.0 Mbps	240.0 Mbps
28	16-QAM	4	324.0 Mbps	360.0 Mbps
29	64-QAM	4	432.0 Mbps	480.0 Mbps
30	64-QAM	4	486.0 Mbps	540.0 Mbps
31	64-QAM	4	540.0 Mbps	600.0 Mbps

Other factors such as the use of unequal modulation can also determine the final data rate. As depicted in Table 10.5, different spatial streams may use different modulation methods.

TABLE 10.5   MCS—40 MHz channel, four spatial streams, unequal modulation

MCS index	Modulation Stream 1	Stream 2	Stream 3	Stream 4	Data Rates 800 ns GI	400 ns GI
67	16-QAM	16-QAM	16-QAM	QPSK	283.4 Mbps	315.0 Mbps
68	64-QAM	QPSK	QPSK	QPSK	243.0 Mbps	270.0 Mbps

HT PHY

When an MPDU (802.11 frame) is sent down from layer 2 to the Physical layer, a preamble and PHY header are added to the MPDU. This creates what is called a PLCP Protocol Data Unit (PPDU). The main purpose of the preamble is to use bits to synchronize transmissions at the Physical layer between two 802.11 radios. The main purpose of the PHY header is to use a signal field to indicate how long it will take to transmit or receive the 802.11 frame (MPDU). The 802.11n amendment defines the use of three PPDU structures that use three different preambles. One of the preambles is a legacy format, and two are newly defined HT preamble formats.

Non-HT Legacy

The first PPDU format is called non-HT and is often also referred to as a legacy format because it was originally defined by the 802.11a amendment for OFDM transmissions. As pictured in Figure 10.8, the non-HT PPDU consists of a preamble that uses short and long training symbols, which are used for synchronization. An OFDM symbol consists of 12 bits. The header contains the signal field, which indicates the time needed to transmit the payload of the non-HT PPDU, which of course is the MPDU (802.11 frame).

FIGURE 10.8 802.11n PPDU formats

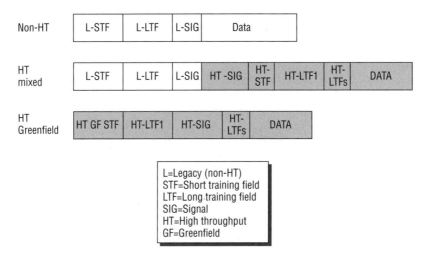

Support for the non-HT legacy format is mandatory for 802.11n radios, and transmissions can occur only in 20 MHz channels. The non-HT format effectively is the same format used by legacy 802.11a and 802.11g radios.

HT Mixed

The first of the two new PPDU formats defined in the 802.11n amendment is the HT mixed format. As shown in Figure 10.8, the beginning of the preamble contains the non-HT short and long training symbols along with the L-SIG field that can be decoded by legacy 802.11a and 802.11g radios. The rest of the HT mixed preamble and header cannot be decoded by legacy 802.11a/g devices. Non-802.11n receivers will not be able to read the frame, but the length field in the legacy section of the header will allow them to know how long the medium is going to be busy for, and they will therefore stay silent without having to do an energy detect at each cycle. The HT mixed format will likely be the most commonly used format because it supports both HT and legacy 802.11a/g OFDM radios. The HT mixed format is also considered mandatory, and transmissions can occur in both 20 MHz and 40 MHz channels. When a 40 MHz channel is used, all broadcast traffic must be sent on a legacy 20 MHz channel so as to maintain interoperability with the 802.11a/g non-HT clients. Also, any transmissions to and from the non-HT clients will have to use a legacy 20 MHz channel.

HT Greenfield

The second of the two new PPDU formats defined by the 802.11n amendment is the HT Greenfield format. As pictured in Figure 10.8, the preamble is not compatible with legacy 802.11a/g radios, and only HT radios can communicate when using the HT Greenfield format. Support for the HT Greenfield format is optional, and the HT radios can transmit by using both 20 MHz and 40 MHz channels.

Analysis of PPDUs

PLCP headers cannot be seen in a protocol analyzer because an 802.11 network interface card (NIC) will strip off the PLCP header and pass only the MPDU up to the MAC layer. NIC cards do, however, pass some packet information up along with every frame. Figure 10.9 shows typical packet information statistics that you can obtain when using a protocol analyzer. Some of these statistics come from information held within the PLCP header.

FIGURE 10.9 Packet information

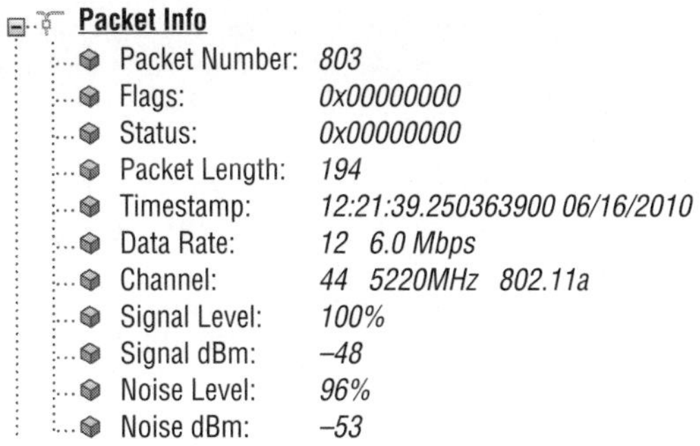

```
⊟ ⊤  Packet Info
   ⊢⬡ Packet Number:  803
   ⊢⬡ Flags:          0x00000000
   ⊢⬡ Status:         0x00000000
   ⊢⬡ Packet Length:  194
   ⊢⬡ Timestamp:      12:21:39.250363900 06/16/2010
   ⊢⬡ Data Rate:      12  6.0 Mbps
   ⊢⬡ Channel:        44  5220MHz  802.11a
   ⊢⬡ Signal Level:   100%
   ⊢⬡ Signal dBm:     −48
   ⊢⬡ Noise Level:    96%
   ⊢⬡ Noise dBm:      −53
```

HT MAC

So far, we have defined enhancements to the Physical layer that 802.11n radios use to achieve greater bandwidth and throughput. The 802.1n amendment also addresses new enhancements to the MAC sublayer of the Data-Link layer to increase throughput and improve power management. Medium contention overhead is addressed by using two new methods of frame aggregation. Reduced interframe spacing and block acknowledgments are also used to limit the amount of fixed MAC overhead. Finally, two new methods of power management are defined for HT clause 20 radios.

These MAC layer enhancements and their frame exchanges will be discussed in more detail, and we will discuss their relevant fields throughout this chapter.

Wi-Fi Alliance

Before the 802.11n amendment was ratified, HT technology was already being developed, certified, and sold. The Wi-Fi Alliance had developed a vendor certification program called Wi-Fi CERTIFIED 802.11n draft 2.0. This certification program, as the name suggests, certified products against draft 2.0 of the 802.11n amendment. Draft 2.0–certified equipment supports a maximum data rate of 300 Mbps, which is half the maximum data rate specified in the ratified amendment. Since the publication of the 802.11n amendment, the Wi-Fi alliance has replaced this certification program with the more simply named Wi-Fi CERTIFIED n. This new certification program has some mandatory requirements and optional capabilities that can be tested if implemented, as shown in Table 10.6. All certified products must also support both Wi-Fi Multimedia (WMM) QoS mechanisms and WPA2 security mechanisms.

TABLE 10.6   Wi-Fi CERTIFIED n features

Feature	Description	Type
Two spatial streams*	Can transmit and receive two spatial streams for double the throughput.	Mandatory
A-MSDU and A-MPDU in receive mode	Frame aggregation: Increases the maximum frame size, making the data transfer more efficient.	Mandatory
Block acknowledgment	Stations can acknowledge several frames at once, reducing the overhead of acknowledging every data frame.	Mandatory
Three spatial streams**	Increases throughput by sending data over three spatial streams as opposed to two.	Tested if implemented

TABLE 10.6   Wi-Fi CERTIFIED n features *(continued)*

Feature	Description	Type
2.4 GHz operation***	2.4 GHz ISM band operation; must be backward compatible with HR-DSSS and ERP equipment.	Tested if implemented
5 GHz operations***	5 GHz UNII band operation, must be backward compatible with OFDM equipment.	Tested if implemented
40 MHz channels in the 5 GHz band	Bonding two channels together to double throughput. 40 MHz operation is supported by the Wi-Fi Alliance in the 5 GHz band. Vendors are free to implement 40 MHz channels in the 2.4 GHz band, but 40 MHz 2.4 GHz operation will not be tested by the Wi-Fi Alliance.	Tested if implemented
20/40 MHz coexistence mechanicals in the 2.4 GHz band**	Access points sense nearby legacy 802.11 wireless equipment operating on the same frequency and enable 20 MHz protection mechanisms.	Tested if implemented
Greenfield preamble	The Greenfield preamble improves efficiency of the 802.11n networks in the absence of legacy devices.	Tested if implemented
SGI, 20 MHz and 40 MHz channels	The GI is the time that a transmitter waits between sending symbols. Short GI is 400 nanoseconds vs. the traditional GI of 800 nanoseconds.	Tested if implemented
STBC**	A data stream is distributed in blocks across multiple transmit streams. These transmission streams are then received by the multiple antennas, and the original data stream is reconstructed in the optimal way.	Tested if implemented
HT Duplicate Mode (MCS 32)	The same packet is transmitted simultaneously on both the primary and secondary 20 MHz channel of a 40 MHz bonded pair.	Tested if implemented
A-MPDU (Transmit Mode)**	Aggregating several MPDUs together into one packet increases overall throughput.	Tested if implemented

*Client devices are only required to transmit and receive at least one spatial stream.

** Optional features added in the updated 802.11n program.

***Access points that can operate in both the 2.4 GHz and 5 GHz bands are certified as "concurrent dual-band."

It should be noted that prior to the Wi-Fi CERTIFIED 802.11n draft 2.0 certification program, many WLAN vendors offered *pre-802.11n* products in the SOHO marketplace. The majority of these products were not interoperable with other vendors' products and are not compatible with certified Wi-Fi Alliance products.

 A white paper from the Wi-Fi Alliance, called "Wi-Fi CERTIFIED n: Longer-Range, Faster-Throughput, Multimedia-Grade Wi-Fi Networks," is included on the CD of this book.

HT Control Field

The 802.11n amendment adds a new field to the 802.11 MAC header, called the *HT Control field*. The HT Control field is 4 octets long and follows the QoS Control field in the 802.11 MAC header, as shown in Figure 10.10.

FIGURE 10.10 802.11 MAC header

Frame Control	Duration ID	Address 1	Address 2	Address 3	Sequence Control	Address 4	QoS Control	HT Control	Frame Body	FCS
2	2	6	6	6	2	2	2	4	0–7955	4

 Notice how the maximum length for the Frame Body is now 7955. This might at first seem strange because the maximum 802.11 MSDU size is 2304; however, 802.11n introduces frame aggregation, and the maximum A-MSDU is 3839 or 7035 depending upon the STA capabilities plus any security/encryption overhead.

Any MPDU that contains an HT Control field is referred to as a +HTC MPDU.

This section will detail the format of the HT Control field and discuss its different sub-fields. However, before going into detail, we will discuss how the order bit present in the MAC header of all 802.11 frames is used by 802.11n STAs to indicate that an HT Control field is also present in the MAC header, and we will discuss how a new frame called the Control Wrapper frame adds an HT Control field to existing control frames.

The Order Bit

The 802.11n amendment uses the existing but relatively unused order bit in the Frame Control field of the MAC header (see Figure 10.11) to indicate the presence of an HT Control field in QoS data and management frames.

The original purpose of this bit, as defined in the original 802.11 standard, was to indicate that data must be sent using a strictly ordered class of service. When set to 1, it tells the receiving station that frames must be processed in order. This is still the correct interpretation of the order bit in non-QoS frames, but it is rarely used, and you are unlikely to see it set to anything but 0. The introduction of QoS into the 802.11 standard through the 802.11e amendment negated the need for an order bit, and it was always set to 0 in QoS frames. However, with the 802.11n amendment, this unused bit now has a purpose again. When set to 1 in QoS data and management frames, it indicates that they contain an HT Control field. The HT Control field is only present in one type of control frame, the Control Wrapper frame, which is described next.

FIGURE 10.11   Order bit of the Frame Control field

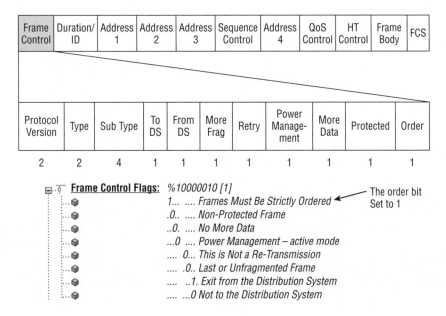

Control Wrapper Frame

The *Control Wrapper frame* is a new control frame introduced by the 802.11n amendment. Its purpose is to carry other control frames along with an HT Control field. Figure 10.12 shows the format of the Control Wrapper frame. The Subtype value for this control frame is 0111, as highlighted in Figure 10.12.

FIGURE 10.12   Control Wrapper frame

Frame Control	Duration ID	Address 1	Carried Frame Control	HT Control	Carried Frame	FCS
2	2	6	2	4	Variable	4

Protocol Version	Type = 01	Sub Type = 0111	To DS	From DS	More Frag	Retry	Power Man	More Data	Protected	Order

The Duration ID and Address 1 fields are generated using the same rules as would be used for the carried frame. The Carried Frame Control field is set to the same value as the Frame Control field of the carried frame.

Control Wrapper frames are described by using their carried frame name +HTC, for example RTS+HTC or CTS+HTC.

HT Control Field Format

Figure 10.13 shows the format of the HT Control field. This control field is used for link adaptation, TxBF, ASEL, and the RD protocol. Figure 10.14 shows a protocol decode of the HT Control field. A brief description of each field will follow, although when appropriate, a more detailed description of how and when each field is used will be described in context later in this chapter when discussing the relevant 802.11n enhancement.

FIGURE 10.13   HT Control field format

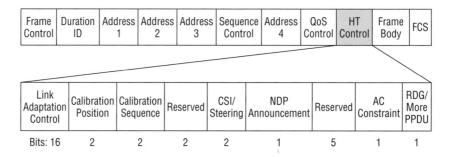

Frame Control	Duration ID	Address 1	Address 2	Address 3	Sequence Control	Address 4	QoS Control	HT Control	Frame Body	FCS

Link Adaptation Control	Calibration Position	Calibration Sequence	Reserved	CSI/ Steering	NDP Announcement	Reserved	AC Constraint	RDG/ More PPDU
Bits: 16	2	2	2	2	1	5	1	1

Link Adaptation Control

The Link Adaptation Control subfield is further subdivided into five more subfields, as shown in Figure 10.15.

FIGURE 10.14   HT Control field decode

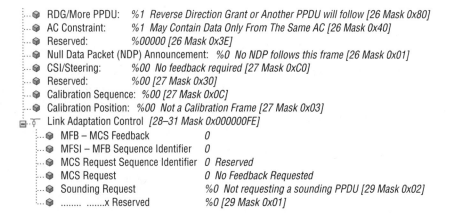

⬡ RDG/More PPDU: %1 Reverse Direction Grant or Another PPDU will follow [26 Mask 0x80]
⬡ AC Constraint: %1 May Contain Data Only From The Same AC [26 Mask 0x40]
⬡ Reserved: %00000 [26 Mask 0x3E]
⬡ Null Data Packet (NDP) Announcement: %0 No NDP follows this frame [26 Mask 0x01]
⬡ CSI/Steering: %00 No feedback required [27 Mask 0xC0]
⬡ Reserved: %00 [27 Mask 0x30]
⬡ Calibration Sequence: %00 [27 Mask 0x0C]
⬡ Calibration Position: %00 Not a Calibration Frame [27 Mask 0x03]
⊟ Link Adaptation Control [28–31 Mask 0x000000FE]
  ⬡ MFB – MCS Feedback   0
  ⬡ MFSI – MFB Sequence Identifier 0
  ⬡ MCS Request Sequence Identifier 0 Reserved
  ⬡ MCS Request   0 No Feedback Requested
  ⬡ Sounding Request   %0 Not requesting a sounding PPDU [29 Mask 0x02]
  ⬡ ....x Reserved   %0 [29 Mask 0x01]

FIGURE 10.15   Link Adaptation Control subfield format

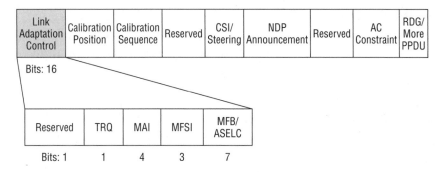

The subfields of the Link Adaptation Control subfield are as follows:

TRQ (Training request)   When set to 1, the training request (TRQ) field acts as a request to the receiver of the frame to respond with a sounding PPDU. Sounding PPDUs are used in beamforming to perform over-the-air calibration of a STA's radios and as a feedback mechanism allowing a STA to estimate the channel in order to calculate a steering matrix. A steering matrix is required for a station to perform transmit beamforming, which will be discussed in greater detail in the "Transmit Beamforming Capabilities" section.

MAI (MCS request (MRQ) or ASEL indicator)   The MAI subfield has two interpretations. When set to 14, it is an ASEL indicator, which indicates that you would interpret the MFB/ASELC subfield as an ASEL command (ASELC). Any other value for the subfield is interpreted as an MCS request (MRQ), which is used for link adaptation to dynamically select the best modulation and coding scheme. The value of this subfield indicates the type of request.

MFSI (MCS feedback sequence identifier)   An MCS feedback (MFB) frame is sent in response to an MCS request. The MCS feedback sequence identifier (MFSI) subfield in an MCS feedback (MFB) frame is set to the value of the MCS request field from the frame that contained the request.

MFB/ASELC (MCS Feedback/Antenna Selection Command)   When an ASEL indicator is present, the MCS Feedback/Antenna Selection Command (MFB/ASELC) subfield is interpreted as an ASEL command subfield. This subfield will be described in more detail in the "ASEL Capabilities" section of this chapter. Otherwise, it is interpreted at the MFB subfield and contains the feedback response to an MCS request.

Calibration Position

An STA that supports transmit beamforming can perform an over-the-air calibration process in order to correct differences between its transmit and receive chains. This process involves the exchange of four sounding PPDUs. The Calibration Position subfield is set to a value of 0, 1, 2, or 3 in calibration frames to indicate their position within the calibration exchange.

Calibration Sequence

The Calibration Sequence number identifies a calibration sounding exchange. Each of the four packets within the calibration exchange will have the same sequence number.

CSI/Steering

When using sounding frames to transmit feedback about the channel, the Channel State Information (CSI)/Steering subfield identifies the type of feedback being used.

NDP Announcement

A null data packet (NDP) is a PPDU that contains no MPDU. The NDP Announcement subfield indicates that an NDP will follow the current frame. NDPs are used to send sounding PPDUs when no other data needs to be transmitted. If a frame is transmitted that requires an immediate response and also has the TRQ subfield = 1 (request for a sound PPDU), then the receiver can either transmit the MPDU response within a sounding PPDU or send the response MPDU with the NDP Announcement bit set to 1, indicating that an NDP will be transmitted following the current PPDU.

AC Constraint and RDG/More PPDU

The AC Constraint and RDG/More PPDU subfields are used by the *Reverse Direction (RD) protocol*. A description of this protocol and the use of these subfields follow.

The Reverse Direction Protocol

The RD protocol was introduced in the 802.11n amendment and improves the efficiency of data transfer between STAs. Legacy devices must contend for access to the medium before initiating a data transfer. When using the RD protocol, a STA, having obtained a transmit opportunity (TXOP), may grant other STAs the opportunity to transmit data back within the same TXOP, without requiring the responding STA to contend for the medium before transmission.

The RD protocol defines two STA roles: the RD initiator and RD responder. The RD initiator is the STA that has contended for and obtained the TXOP. The RD initiator will give the RD responder permission to transmit, by sending a reverse direction grant (RDG). The RD initiator will set the RDG/More PPDU subfield to 1, indicating it is an RDG. The Duration ID within an RDP is set to the length of the TXOP remaining.

Upon receipt of an RDG, the RD responder may send one or more PPDUs within a burst. During a response burst, only the RD responder is allowed to transmit. All PPDUs within a burst must be destined to the RD initiator and will be separated by SIFS or RIFS. In all but the last PPDU within a response burst, the RDG/More PPDU subfield is set to 1, which indicates that more PPDUs will follow. The last PPDU in a response burst has the RDG/More subfield set to 0. The transmission of all PPDUs and any expected responses must fit within the remaining TXOP, as indicated by the Duration ID in the RDG. Figure 10.16 shows an example RD protocol exchange.

The RD protocol exchange is summarized as follows:

1. The RD initiator (the TXOP holder) sends a PPDU that requires an immediate response. This PPDU contains an RDG.

2. The RD responder will respond with one or more PPDUs. The first or only PPDU will contain one or more ACKs or BlockAckframes.

3. The last or only PPDU transmitted by the RD responder in the burst will contain any packets that require an immediate ACK or BlockAck response. The last PPDU will also have the RDP/More PPDU subfield set to 0.

Although the 802.11 standard does define another optional QoS channel access mechanism, HCCA, it is not currently implemented, and the Wi-Fi Alliance WMM certification only tests EDCA. All HT STAs are required to be QoS STAs. This means that currently all 802.11n devices are going to be using EDCA and therefore will be required to set the RD Initiator bit to 1, requiring all traffic within a TXOP to be of the same access category.

This means that when looking at an RDG in a protocol analyzer, you should always see both the RDG/More PPDU and AC Constraint subfields set to 1.

FIGURE 10.16 Reverse Direction protocol exchange example

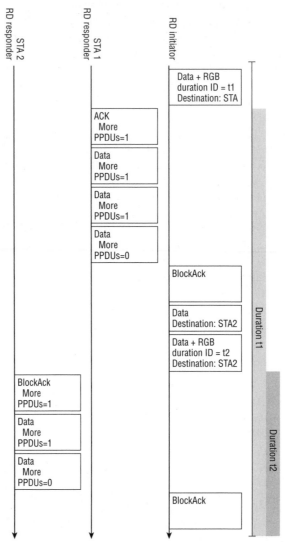

If an RD initiator sets the AC Constraint subfield to 1 in an RDG, then the RD responder must only transmit frames that have the same QoS access category (AC) as the last frame it received from the RD initiator. The AC can be determined by looking in the Traffic Identifier (TID) field within the QoS Control field in the MAC header. If the RD initiator obtained its TXOP from the EDCA mechanism, then it must set the RD initiator to 1. If the TXOP has been obtained from any other access mechanism, then it must be set to 0.

HT Action Frames and Information Elements

The 802.11n amendment introduces many new action frames and information elements. These will be summarized in the following sections. When looking at HT protocol decodes, the two most common information elements you are likely to see will be the HT Capabilities Element and HT Operation Element. Later we'll detail each of these two information elements and their fields and relevant operations.

Action Frames

The 802.11n amendment introduces several new action frames. Figure 10.17 shows the protocol decode for a HT action. The category field in all HT action frames is set to 7 indicating it is an HT action frame. Table 10.7 shows the different HT action frames and how they are categorized by the Action field value.

FIGURE 10.17   HT action frame decode

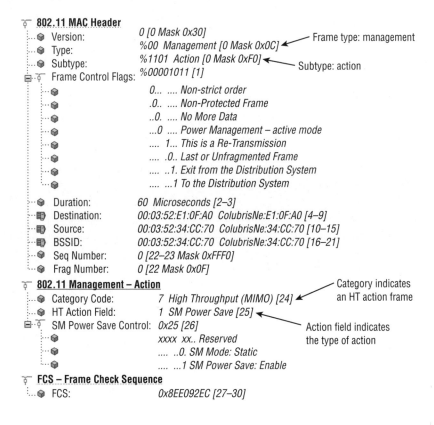

TABLE 10.7   HT action frame, action fields

HT action field value	Meaning
0	Notify channel width
1	SM power save
2	PSMP
3	Set PCO phase
4	CSI
5	Noncompressed beamforming
6	Compressed beamforming
7	ASEL indices feedback
8–255	Reserved

Information Elements

If looking at 802.11 a/b/g beacon frames in a protocol analyzer is something you are already familiar with but you have not yet seen an 802.11n beacon decode, then be prepared for a whole wealth of new information displayed in your beacons. The 802.11n amendment greatly expands the 802.11 beacon with the option of up to four new information elements. Table 10.8 shows these new information elements.

TABLE 10.8   HT beacon information elements

Information Element	Element ID	Length (Octets)	Description
HT Capabilities	54	28	Advertises optional HT capabilities of an HT STA
HT Operations	61	24	Controls the operation of an HT station within a BSS

TABLE 10.8 HT beacon information elements *(continued)*

Information Element	Element ID	Length (Octets)	Description
20/40 BSS Coexistence	72	3	Exchanges information that affects how 20 MHz and 40 MHz STAs coexist in the same frequency space
Overlapping BSS Scan Parameters	74	16	Advertises values to be used by BSS members when performing overlapping BSS (OBSS) scan operations

An HTML document containing a full decode of an 802.11n beacon showing both the HT Capabilities Element and HT Operations Element is included on the book's CD.

In draft 2.0 of the 802.11n amendment, the HT Operations Element was called the HT Information Element and is still decoded as such by many wireless analyzers.

HT Capabilities Element

HT STAs declare themselves as HT STAs by the transmission of the *HT Capabilities Element* in Beacon, Probe Request, Probe Response, Association Request, Association Response, Reassociation Request, and Reassociation Response frames. Figure 10.18 shows the format of the HT Capabilities Element. The HT Capabilities Element is 28 octets long and contains 8 fields used by the HT STA to advertise the optional HT capabilities it supports.

FIGURE 10.18 HT Capabilities Element format

Element ID	Length	HT Capabilities Info	A-MPDU Parameters	Supported MCS Set	HT Extended Capabilities	Transmit Beamforming Capabilities	ASEL Capabilities
Bytes: 1	1	2	1	16	2	4	1

The Element ID for the HT Capabilities element is set to 45, and the length field is set to 26, indicating that another 26 octets follow the length field. The remaining fields of the HT Capabilities element and their subfields will be described in the following sections.

HT Capabilities Info Field

The HT Capabilities Info field is 2 octets long and contains HT capability information bits. Figure 10.19 shows the format of this field. Figure 10.20 shows a decode of the HT Capabilities field.

FIGURE 10.19 HT Capabilities Info field format

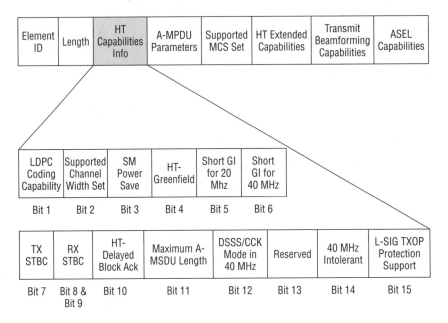

FIGURE 10.20 HT Capabilities Info field decode

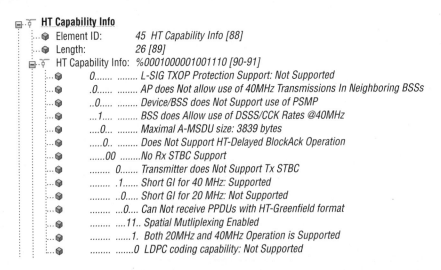

The subfields of the HT Capabilities Information field are described in the following sections.

LDPC Coding Capability

Low-density parity check (LDPC) is a coding method for transmitting data in a noisy environment and provides excellent error correction and performance. An STA indicates it is capable of receiving LDPC-coded packets by setting the LDPC coding bit to 1.

Supported Channel Width Set

The Supported Channel Width Set bit indicates the channel widths supported by a STA.

If an HT station can support only 20 MHz channels, it advertises this by setting the Support Channel Width Set bit to 0. Configuring your 802.11n wireless network to only support 20 MHz channels might be something you do by design in the 2.4 GHz band. This is because deploying 40 MHz HT channels at 2.4 GHz does not scale well in multiple channel architectures. Although we have up to either 13 (Europe) or 11 (North America) channels available in the 2.4 GHz ISM band, there are only three nonoverlapping 20 MHz channels available in North America. When the 20 MHz channels are bonded together to form 40 MHz channels in the 2.4 GHz ISM band, any two 40 MHz channels will overlap, as pictured in Figure 10.21. In other words, only one 40 MHz channel can be used at 2.4 GHz, and the possibility of a channel reuse pattern is essentially impossible.

Channel reuse patterns using 40 MHz channels at 5 GHz are feasible because there are many possible combinations within the UNII bands. The use of 40 MHz HT channels in the 5 GHz UNII bands makes perfect sense because there are up to twenty-four (including channel 165,the 5.8GHz ISM channel available in the U.S.) 20 MHz channels that can be bonded together in various pairs, as pictured in Figure 10.22. When a STA can support both 20 MHz and 40 MHz channels, it sets the Support Channel Width Set bit to 1.

FIGURE 10.21   Channel bonding—2.4 GHz ISM band

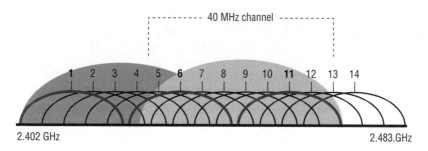

FIGURE 10.22 Channel bonding—5 GHz UNII bands

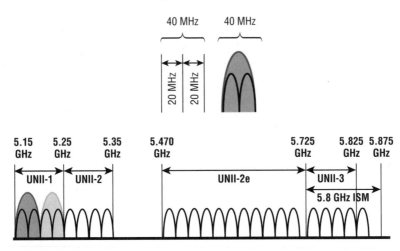

SM Power Save

Mobility is one of the main benefits that wireless networks provide. Battery-powered mobile devices no longer need to be tethered to a wired connection and can even transfer data while moving. Unfortunately, RF radios have a big drain on battery resources and can significantly reduce the battery life of the mobile device. It is for this reason that power-save mechanisms have been included in the 802.11 standard from its conception.

HT STAs include multiple radios to support MIMO features such as spatial multiplexing, which transmit multiple streams of data simultaneously. The more radios we use, the more power we require and the faster we drain our batteries. In an attempt to try to combat this problem, a new power-save method that powers down the extra radios when not needed has been included in the 802.11n amendment. This new power save method is called *SM Power Save*.

Both static and dynamic methods of SM Power Save are defined by the 802.11n amendment. The SM Power Save subfield of the HT Capabilities field of the HT Capabilities Element indicates a STA's support for the SM Power Save, as indicated in Table 10.9.

Draft 2.0 of the 802.11n amendment interprets an SM Power Save subfield value of 3 as SM Enabled. This might at first seem like a completely different interpretation, but it is not. If SM is enabled, the STA is capable of receiving multiple streams and cannot therefore be in SM Power Save mode. Do not be surprised if you see protocol analyzers reporting an SM Power Save subfield value of 3 as SM Enable instead of SM Power Save disabled until the decodes are updated.

⊕ **Real World Scenario**

The DFS Gremlin

A large UK manufacturing company recently upgraded its old 802.11g wireless network to an 802.11n 20/40 MHz wireless network in the 5 GHz band, in the hope that 802.11n would provide the throughput and reliability to provide all the company's mobility needs, including VoIP handsets and real-time control systems. One of the deciding factors when choosing 802.11n was that in the 5 GHz band there were so many nonoverlapping channels, and a 40 MHz multichannel environment was easily obtainable. Shortly after the installation, complaints started to be logged about dropped VoIP calls and intermittent control system lag. After investigation of the wireless network log files, it was noticed that there were Dynamic Frequency Selection (DFS) events causing the access points to change frequencies at the same time as the logged issues. Having consulted the vendor, the company was advised it should disable the DFS channels. However, by doing this, the company was left with only the first four 20 MHz channels in the UNII-1 band, leaving just two 40 MHz HT bonded channels, which is not enough for a multichannel architecture deployment. The company had to reconfigure its access points for 20 MHz HT channels and was not able to experience the full potential of 40 MHz 802.11n operation.

Static SM Power Save

While in static SM Power Save mode, an HT STA maintains only one active receive radio chain. An STA may indicate it is in static SM Power Save in one of two ways: by setting the SM Power Save subfield in the HT Capabilities field of the HT Capabilities Element to 2 in the STA's Association request frame or by sending an SM Power Save action frame. Figure 10.23 shows the format of a Power Save action frame. An STA will set the SM Power Save Enable bit to 1 and the SM Mode bit to 0 to indicate it is now in static SM Power Save mode. Figure 10.24 shows the decode of an SM Power Save action frame with these settings.

TABLE 10.9 SM Power Save subfield values

SM Power Save subfield value	Interpretation
0	Static SM Power Save mode
1	Dynamic SM Power mode
2	Reserved
3	SM Power Save disabled

FIGURE 10.23   SM Power Save action frame format

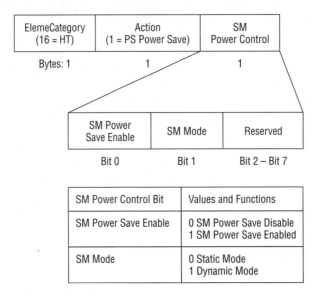

FIGURE 10.24   Static SM Power Save action frame decode

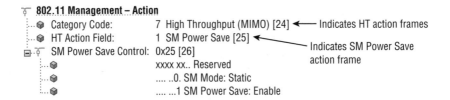

When a STA operating in static SM Power Save mode wants to receive multiple spatial streams, it must send an SM Power Save action frame to the access point, indicating it is no longer in SM Power Save mode. Figure 10.25 shows the process of enable and disabling static SM Power Save mode using action frames.

FIGURE 10.25   SM static Power Save

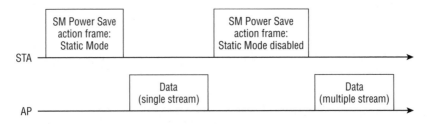

Dynamic SM Power Save

In dynamic SM Power Save, a STA will also turn off all but one receive radio chain; however, the STA may quickly reenable its multiple radio chains upon receipt of a frame addressed to it.

Figure 10.26 shows the dynamic SM Power save process. An access point will typically send an RTS frame using only one spatial stream to wake up a STA's dozing receive radio chains. An STA will then respond with a CTS frame indicating that multiple spatial streams may now be used for the rest of the current frame sequence. The STA immediately switches back to just having one receive chain enabled when the frame sequence has finished.

FIGURE 10.26   Dynamic SM Power Save

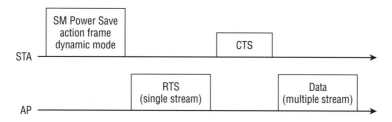

HT Greenfield

The HT Greenfield PPDU format is one of the two new PPDU formats introduced by the 802.11n amendment, as shown earlier in Figure 10.8. When set to 1, the HT Greenfield bit in the HT Capabilities Element (see Figure 10.19) indicate that a STA is capable of receiving HT Greenfield PPDUs.

Support for the HT Greenfield format is optional. As of this writing, many 802.11n chip manufacturers have not implemented the HT Greenfield format.

Short GI for 20 MHz and Short GI for 40 MHz

For digital signals, data is modulated onto the carrier signal in bits, or collections of bits, called symbols. All the data bits of an OFDM symbol are transmitted across the 48 data subcarriers of a 20 MHz non-HT channel.

802.11a/g radios use an 800-nanosecond guard interval between OFDM symbols. The guard interval is a period of time between symbols that accommodates the late arrival of symbols over long paths. In a multipath environment, symbols travel along different physical paths, and therefore some symbols arrive later or earlier than others. A "new" symbol may arrive at a receiver before a "late" symbol has been completely received. This is known as intersymbol interference (ISI) and usually results in data corruption.

The delay spread is the time differential between multiple paths of the same signal. Normal delay spread is 50–100 nanoseconds, and a maximum delay spread is about 200 nanoseconds. The guard interval should be two to four times the length of the delay spread. Think of the guard interval as a buffer for the delay spread. The normal guard interval is an 800-nanosecond buffer between symbol transmissions. As pictured in Figure 10.27, a guard interval will compensate for the delay spread and help prevent intersymbol interference. If the guard interval is too short, intersymbol interference may still occur.

FIGURE 10.27 Guard interval

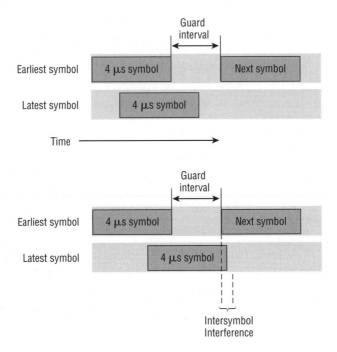

802.11n also uses an 800-nanosecond guard interval; however, a shorter 400-nanosecond guard interval is optional. A shorter guard interval results in a shorter symbol time, which has the effect of increasing data rates by about 10 percent. If the optional, *short guard interval* of 400 nanoseconds is used with an 802.11n radio, throughput will increase, but the odds of an intersymbol interference occurrence increases. If intersymbol interference does indeed occur because of the shorter GI, the result is data corruption. If data corruption occurs, layer 2 retransmissions will increase, and the throughput will be adversely affected. Retransmissions can be seen in a protocol analyzer by examining the retry flag in the Frame Control field of the 802.11 MAC header. Many protocol analyzers report the number of retransmissions as a statistic and can trigger a notification if this statistic goes beyond a configured threshold. A 400-nanosecond guard interval should be used only in good RF environments. If throughput goes down because of a shorter GI setting, the default guard interval setting of 800 nanoseconds should be used instead.

The short GI for 20 MHz and short GI for 40 MHz bits in the HT Capabilities field of the HT Capabilities Element indicate a STA's capability to receive packets transmitted with a short GI for 20 MHz and 40 MHz channels, respectively. Table 10.10 shows the encoding for these bits.

TABLE 10.10   Encoding for short GI for 20 MHz and 40 MHz bits

Subfield	Encoding
Short GI for 20 MHz	0 = Short GI not supported 1 = Short GI support
Short GI for 40 MHz	0 = Short GI not supported 1 = Short GI support

TX STBC and RX STBC

Space Time Block Coding (STBC) is a MIMO diversity technique used to improve the reliability of data transfer. STBC adds redundancy into the transmission by transmitting different copies of the data stream from different antennas. The effect multipath has on the received signals means that some of them are received with better quality than the others. Because of redundancy gained from receiving multiple copies of the same data stream, there is a higher chance that the receiving STA will be able to correctly decode the signal.

The TX STBC subfields indicate whether a STA is capable of transmitting PPDUs using STBC, and the RX STBC subfield indicates a STA's capabilities to receive PPDUs transmitted using STBC. Table 10.11 lists the encoding for these two frames.

TABLE 10.11   Encoding for RX STBC and TX STBC subfields

Subfield	Encoding
TX STBC	0 = TX STBC is disabled. 1 = TX STBC is enabled.
RX STBC	0 = RX STBC is disabled. 1 = RX STBC is supported for one spatial stream. 2 = RX STBC is supported for two spatial streams. 3 = RX STBC is supported for three spatial streams.

HT-Delayed BlockAck

As you already know from Chapter 5, BlockAcks were originally introduced to the 802.11 standard by the 802.11e amendment to improve the efficiency of MAC operations by removing the requirement that a STA must send an immediate acknowledgment (ACK) for every unicast data or management frame. Instead, a STA could send one BlockAck message that effectively includes many ACKs for different frames it has received. The 802.11n amendment makes support for BlockAcks compulsory for all HT STAs.

The 802.11e amendment extended the capabilities of the information field found in many management frames by adding the Immediate BlockAck and Delayed BlockAck bits to indicate a STA's support for these two BlockAck methods. The 802.11n amendment further extends these two methods and defines HT-Immediate BlockAcks and HT-Delayed BlockAcks.

The HT-Delayed BlockAck subfield of the HT Capabilities Info field indicates a STA's support for the 802.11n extensions to the Delayed BlockAck method. The HT-Delayed BlockAck subfield is set to 1 when a STA is able to receive an ADDBA request for an HT-delayed BlockAck.

Supporting the HT-Delayed BlockAck is optional, but when implemented, it simplifies the use of delayed BlockAcks. One way it does this is by not requiring an ACK frame to be sent in response to BlockAckReq and BlockAck frames. Figure 10.28 shows the difference between a Delayed BlockAck protocol exchange and an HT-Delayed BlockAck protocol exchange. ACK frames are overhead, and by not requiring these two ACK frames to be transmitted, the medium is freed up for other frame exchanges.

To implement the no ACK policy and indicate that no acknowledgment is expected in response, a STA sets the BAR Ack Policy subfield of the BAR Control field to 1 in a BlockAckRequest and sets the BA ACK Policy subfield of the BA Control field to 1 in a BlockAck. These two subfields are highlighted in Figure 10.29, showing the frame format for both BlockAckRequest and BlockAck frames.

FIGURE 10.28   Delayed BlockAck protocol exchanges

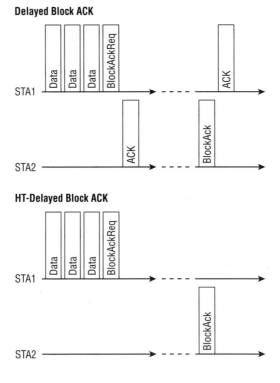

FIGURE 10.29   BAR and BA ACK subfields

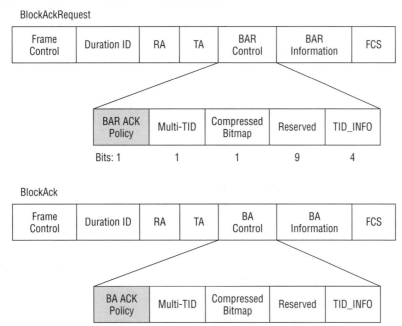

Maximum A-MSDU Length

As pictured in Figure 10.30, every time a unicast 802.11 frame is transmitted, a certain amount of fixed overhead exists as a result of the PHY header, MAC header, MAC trailer, interframe spacing, and acknowledgment frame. Medium contention overhead also exists because of the time required when each frame must contend for the medium.

FIGURE 10.30   802.11 unicast frame overhead

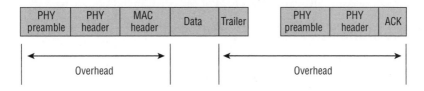

The 802.11n amendment introduces two new methods of *frame aggregation* to help reduce the overhead. Frame aggregation is a method of combining multiple frames into a single frame transmission. The fixed MAC layer overhead is reduced, and the overhead caused by the random back-off timer during medium contention is also minimized.

The first method of frame aggregation is known as aggregate MAC Service Data Unit (A-MSDU). As you learned in earlier chapters, the MSDU is the layer 3–7 payload of a data frame with a Logical Link Control (LLC) header. As pictured in Figure 10.31, multiple MSDUs can be aggregated into a single frame transmission.

FIGURE 10.31 A-MSDU

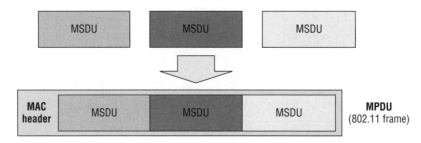

An 802.11n access point using A-MSDU would receive multiple 802.3 frames, remove the 802.3 headers and trailers, and then wrap the multiple MSDU payloads into a single 802.11 frame for transmission. The aggregated MSDUs will have a single destination when wrapped together in a single frame.

The size of an A-MSDU must not exceed the maximum A-MSDU size that a STA is capable of receiving; this is defined in the Maximum A-MSDU Length subfield of the HT Capabilities Info field. An STA can support one of two maximum lengths:

0 = 3839 bytes

1 = 7935 bytes

The entire aggregated frame can be encrypted by using either TKIP or CCMP. It should be noted, however, that the individual MSDUs must all be of the same 802.11e QoS access category. Voice MSDUs cannot be mixed with best-effort or video MSDUs inside the same aggregated frame.

The second type of frame aggregation introduced by the 802.11n amendment is Aggregate MAC Protocol Data Unit (A-MPDU); this method will be discussed shortly when we look at the A-MPDU Parameters field of the HT Capabilities Element.

DSSS/CCK Mode in 40 MHz

Table 10.12 shows the encoding for the DSSS/CCK Mode in the 40 MHz subfield. This sub-field indicates an HT 20/40 MHz–capable STA's ability to support Direct Sequence Spread Spectrum (DSSS) and Complementary Code Keying (CCK), which are the modulation and coding methods use by legacy clause 15 (DSSS 802.11 original) and clause 18 (HR 802.11b) radios. The purpose of this is not to enable DSSS/CCK communication between 20/40 MHz HT STAs but to allow 22 MHz BSS/CCK STAs to transmit within a 20/40 MHz BSS.

TABLE 10.12 DSSS/CCK mode in the 40 MHz subfield encoding

Encoding	Values
Access points encoding	0 = BSS does not allow DSSS/CCK in 40 MHz.
	1 = BSS does allow DSSS/CCK in 40 MHz.
Client STA encoding	0 = Client STA does not use DSSS/CCK in 40 MHz.
	1 = Client STA does use DaSS/CCK in 40 MHz.

HT 40 MHz–capable client STAs advertise their ability to support DSS/CCK transmissions when associating to an access point (AP) by setting the DSSS/CCK mode in the 40 MHz subfield to 1 in Association and Reassociation response/request frames.

An AP can set the DSSS/CCK mode in 40 MHz subfield to 1 in Beacons and Probe Response frames to indicate that the BSS supports DSSS/CCK transmissions. When an AP sets the DSSS/CCK mode in the 40 MHz subfield to 0, an associated STA cannot send DSSS/CCK transmissions even if the STA has advertised its own ability to do so during association. APs not supporting DSSS/CCK must not include an ERP Information Element in Beacon and Probe response frames and as such not advertise any DSSS/CCK supported rates.

Forty MHz Intolerant

As you have already learned earlier in this chapter, we only have one nonoverlapping 40 MHz channel in the 2.4 GHz ISM band; therefore, using 2.4 GHz 40 MHz channels in multichannel architectures does not scale well. Essentially, 40 MHz channels in the 2.4GHz band are really feasible only when deploying a single-channel architecture (SCA) or a single access point. However, implementing 40 MHz channels in an SCA or on a solitary access point works well only when you are transmitting in a clean RF environment, isolated from other overlapping 2.4 GHz wireless networks.

Even when implementing an HT 2.4 GHz wireless network using only 20 MHz channels, you might still have a problem from neighboring networks that have implemented a 40 MHz BSS. Figure 10.32 illustrates a 40 MHz channel in the center of the 2.4 GHz band—leaving no room for a nonoverlapping 20 MHz channel. It is for scenarios like this that the *Forty MHz Intolerant* operation of the 802.11n amendment was devised.

FIGURE 10.32 40 MHz channel in the 2.4 GHz band

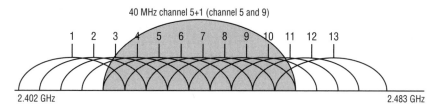

When the Forty MHz Intolerant subfield is set to 1, it prohibits the use of 40 MHz channels. An access point that receives frames with the Forty MHz Intolerant bit set, or reports it, is not allowed to operate a 20/40 MHz BSS.

Advertising Forty MHz Intolerant is allowed only by HT 2.4GHz STAs. HT 5GHz STAs will always set the Forty MHz Intolerant subfield to 0, indicating that 20/40 BSSs are permissible.

L-SIG TXOP Protection Support

The 802.11g amendment introduced protection mechanisms into the 802.11 standard to prevent HR (802.11b) STAs from transmitting at the same time as ERP (802.11g) STAs. Because an HR station does not understand an ERP STA's OFDM transmissions, the ERP STAs need some method to reserve the medium before transmitting frames that use OFDM. This is done through either RST/CTS or CTS-to-self. In an HT BSS, the HT STAs must also protect their transmission from legacy STAs (802.11 a/b/g). The 802.11n amendment defines many different protection mechanisms, of which L-SIG TXOP protection is one.

The L-SIG TXOP Protection Support subfield in the HT Capabilities Info field is set to 1 to indicate that a STA supports the L-SIG protection mechanism. The L-SIG protection mechanism reserves the medium using the L-SIG (Legacy Signal) field in the HT Mixed PPDU Format header pictured earlier in Figure 10.8. Because this field is in the legacy part of the PPDU header, all STAs should hear it and reserve the medium accordingly. A more detailed description of this and other protection mechanisms will be discussed in the "Protection Mechanisms" section when investigating the HT Operations Element, because many of the fields supporting these protection mechanisms include this information element.

A-MPDU Parameters

You have already learned about one of the two frame aggregation methods, A-MSDU, described earlier in the chapter. The second method of frame aggregation is Aggregate MAC Protocol Data Unit (A-MPDU). As you learned in earlier chapters, the MPDU is an entire 802.11 frame including the MAC header, body, and trailer. As pictured in Figure 10.33, multiple MPDUs can be aggregated into a single frame transmission.

The individual MPDUs within an A-MPDU must all have the same receiver address. Also, the data payload of each MPDU is encrypted separately by using either TKIP or CCMP. Much like MSDU aggregation, individual MPDUs must all be of the same 802.11e QoS access category. Voice MPDUs cannot be mixed with best-effort or video MPDUs inside the same aggregated frame. Please note that MPDU aggregation has more overhead than MSDU aggregation because each MPDU has an individual MAC header and trailer.

The maximum size for an MPDU carried with in an A-MPDU is 4095 bytes. Therefore, when an A-MPDU carries an A-MSDU, it is limited to 4065 bytes plus 30 bytes for the QoS Data overhead (4,095 total). Any A-MSDU longer than 4,065 bytes cannot be included in the A-MPDU.

FIGURE 10.33 A-MPDU

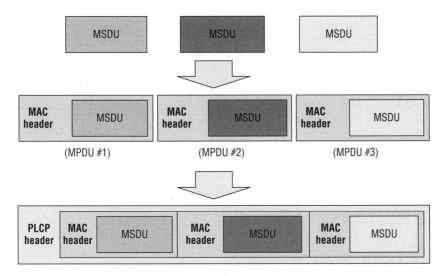

Figure 10.34 shows the format of the A-MPDU Parameters field of the HT Capabilities Element. This field has two subfields: Maximum A-MPDU Length Exponent and the Minimum MPDU Start Spacing.

FIGURE 10.34 A-MPDU Parameters Field format

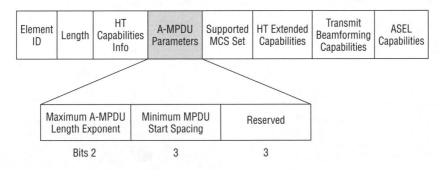

Maximum A-MPDU Length Exponent

The first of these two subfields, the Maximum A-MPDU Length Exponent, is used by a STA during association to define the maximum A-MPDU length that the STA can receive. The value for this subfield is an integer between 0 and 3 from which the length in bytes is calculated using the following formula:

$$2^{(13 + \text{Maximum A-MPDU Length Exponent})} - 1$$

Most protocol analyzers will do this calculation for you and display the result in the packet decode as pictured in Figure 10.35. The decode shows the A-MPDU Length Exponent subfield set to 3; this is decoded as 64k. The following are the possible values for this field:

0 = 8K

1 = 16K

2 = 36K

3 = 64K

FIGURE 10.35   A-MPDU Parameters decode

```
A-MPDU Parameters:  %00000011 [92]
                    xxx..... Reserved [92 Mask 0xE0]
                    ...000.. Minimum MPDU Start Spacing: No Restriction [92 Mask 0x1C]
                    ......11 Maximum Rx A-MPDU Size: 64K [92 Mask 0x03]
```

Minimum MPDU Start Spacing

The second subfield in the A-MPDU parameters field is the Minimum MPDU Start Spacing subfield, which specifies the minimum amount of time that must elapse between starting the transmission of one MPDU and starting to transmit the next one. Within an A-MPDU, the number of octets between the start of one MPDU and the start of the next must be counted to make sure that the required amount of time will elapse. If needed, padding bits may be added between MPDUs. The following list shows the encoding for this subfield:

0 = no restriction

1 = 1/4 μs

2 = 1/2 μs

3 = 1 μs

4 = 2 μs

5 = 4 μs

6 = 8 μs

7 = 16 μs

Upon receipt of an A-MPDU, a wireless NIC removes the PPDU header and passes each MPDU up to the MAC layer separately. Therefore, in a protocol analyzer, you will see each MPDU separately. Wireless NIC cards do tell the MAC layer that the MPDU was part of an A-MPDU, and therefore this information can be displayed in a protocol analyzer, as shown in Figures 10.36 and 10.37.

Each A-MPDU must be acknowledged by a BlockAck containing an acknowledgment for each MPDU within the A-MPDU, as shown in Figure 10.37, which shows several frames with the aggregation flag set followed by a BlockAck.

FIGURE 10.36   A-MPDU packet information flag

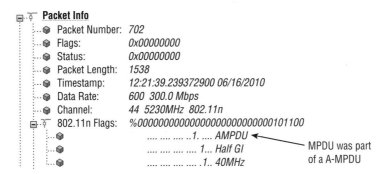

Packet Info
- Packet Number: *702*
- Flags: *0x00000000*
- Status: *0x00000000*
- Packet Length: *1538*
- Timestamp: *12:21:39.239372900 06/16/2010*
- Data Rate: *600 300.0 Mbps*
- Channel: *44 5230MHz 802.11n*
- 802.11n Flags: *%0000000000000000000000000101100*
  - *.... ....1. .... AMPDU* ◄——— MPDU was part of a A-MPDU
  - *.... .... 1... Half GI*
  - *.... .... .1.. 40MHz*

FIGURE 10.37   A-MPDU packets

Flag indicating MPDU was part of a A-MPDU

Packet	Source	Destination	Flags	Channel	Signal dBm	Data Rate	Size	Protocol
1	10.10.0.2	10.10.5.100	A	36	−48	2.0	1538	PING Req
2	10.10.0.2	10.10.5.100	A	36	−48	2.0	1538	IP Fragment
3	10.10.0.2	10.10.5.100	A	36	−48	2.0	1538	IP Fragment
4	10.10.0.2	10.10.5.100	A	36	−48	2.0	1538	IP Fragment
5	10.10.0.2	10.10.5.100	A	36	−48	2.0	1538	IP Fragment
6	10.10.0.2	10.10.5.100	A	36	−48	2.0	1538	IP Fragment
7	10.10.0.2	10.10.5.100	A	36	−48	2.0	1186	IP Fragment
8	AtherosCom: 0B:A4:0E	Intelorate: 04:A5:37	#	36	−48	24.0	46	802.11 BA

Supported MCS Set

A station uses the Supported MCS field to advertise which MCSs it supports. Figure 10.38 shows the structure of the Supported MCS Set field.

FIGURE 10.38   Supported MCS Set format

Element ID	Length	HT Capabilities Info	A-MPDU Parameters	Supported MCS Set	HT Extended Capabilities	Transmit Beamforming Capabilities	ASEL Capabilities

RX MSC Bitmask	Reserved	RX Highest Supported Data Rate	Reserved	TX MCS Set Defined	TX RX MCS Set Not Equal	TX Maximun Number of Spatial Streams Supported	TX Unequal Modulation Supported	Reserved
Bits 77	3	1	6	1	1	2	1	27

The 802.11n amendment defines 77 MCSs that are represented by an MCS index from 0–76. The RX MCS Bitmask subfield has one bit for each of the 77 MCSs. If the first bit of this subfield is set to 1, then the STA supports MCS index 0; if the second bit of the subfields is set to 1, then the STA support MCS index 1; and so on. An example decode of this field in Figure 10.39 shows a STA that supports the first 16 MCSs.

The RX Highest Supported Data Rate subfield defines the highest data rate that the STA supports; however, a STA is not required to provide this information and may set this subfield to 0.

FIGURE 10.39 Supported MCS decode

```
⊟ ⏚ Supported MCS Set
  ⊟ ⏚ One Spatial Stream:   %11111111 [93]
    ⦿ MCS Index 0 Supported – BPSK. Coding Rate: 1/2
    ⦿ MCS Index 1 Supported – QPSK. Coding Rate: 1/2
    ⦿ MCS Index 2 Supported – QPSK. Coding Rate: 3/4
    ⦿ MCS Index 3 Supported – 16 QAM. Coding Rate: 1/2
    ⦿ MCS Index 4 Supported – 16 QAM. Coding Rate: 3/4
    ⦿ MCS Index 5 Supported – 64 QAM. Coding Rate: 2/3
    ⦿ MCS Index 6 Supported – 64 QAM. Coding Rate: 3/4
    ⦿ MCS Index 7 Supported – 64 QAM. Coding Rate: 5/6
  ⊟ ⏚ Two Spatial Streams:   %11111111 [94]
    ⦿ MCS Index 8 Supported – BPSK. Coding Rate: 1/2
    ⦿ MCS Index 9 Supported – QPSK. Coding Rate: 1/2
    ⦿ MCS Index 10 Supported – QPSK. Coding Rate: 3/4
    ⦿ MCS Index 11 Supported – 16 QAM. Coding Rate: 1/2
    ⦿ MCS Index 12 Supported – 16 QAM. Coding Rate: 3/4
    ⦿ MCS Index 13 Supported – 64 QAM. Coding Rate: 2/3
    ⦿ MCS Index 14 Supported – 64 QAM. Coding Rate: 3/4
    ⦿ MCS Index 15 Supported – 64 QAM. Coding Rate: 5/6
  ⦿ Rx Bitmask b16–b23:   %00000000 [95]
  ⦿ Rx Bitmask b24–b31:   %00000000 [96]
  ⦿ Rx Bitmask b32–b39:   %00000000 [97]
  ⦿ Rx Bitmask b40–b47:   %00000000 [98]
  ⦿ Rx Bitmask b48–b55:   %00000000 [99]
  ⦿ Rx Bitmask b56–b63:   %00000000 [100]
  ⦿ Rx Bitmask b64–b76:   %0000000000000 [101–102 Mask 0xFFF8]
  ⦿ Reserved:   %000 [102 Mask 0x07]
  ⦿ Highest Supported Rate:0 Mbps [103–104 Mask 0xFFC0]
  ⦿ Reserved:   %000000 [104 Mask 0x3F]
  ⦿ Tx Supported MCS Set:  %0 Not Defined [105 Mask 0x80]
  ⦿ Tx and Rx MCS Set:   %0 Equal [105 Mask 0x40]
  ⦿ Tx Maximum Number Spatial Streams Supported: %00 1 Spatial Stream [105 Mask 0x30]
  ⦿ Tx Unequal Modulation: %0 Not Supported [105 Mask 0x08]
  ⦿ Reserved: %0000000000000000000000000000  b101–b127 [105–108 Mask 0x07FFFFFF]
```

The last four subfields define the TX MCS scheme used. Table 10.13 shows the encoding for these subfields. When the TX MCS Set Defined subfield is set to 1, it indicates that the remaining three subfields will define the TX MCS set. If the TX MCS Set Defined subfield is set to 0, as shown in the decode in Figure 10.36, it indicates the STA is not specifying a TX MCS set and all remaining subfields should also be set to 0. When the TX MCS Set Defined subfield is set to 1 and the TX RX MCS Set Not Equal subfield is set to 0, the STA is indicating it will use the same MCS set defined by the RX MCS Bitmask subfield. When both the TX MCS Set Defined subfield and the TX RX MCS Set Not Equal subfields are set to 1, the remaining two subfields define the TX MCS set in terms of the number of spatial streams and support for unequal modulation (UEQM), as defined in Table 10.13.

TABLE 10.13   TX modulation set encoding

Condition	TX MCS set defined	TX RX MCS set not equal	TX maximum spatial streams supported	TX unequal modulation supported
No TX MCS set is defined.	0	0	0	0
The TX MCS set is defined to be equal to the RX MCS set.	1	0	0	0
The TX MCS set may differ from the RX MCS set.	1	1	0 = 1 spatial stream 1 = 2 spatial streams 2 = 3 spatial streams 3 = 4 spatial streams	0 = UEQM not supported 1 = UEQM supported

HT Extended Capabilities Field

Do I hear you say, "HT Extended Capabilities Field? Surely there cannot be any more HT capabilities left to be define?" Unfortunately, there are more, and although at this point it might seem like a never-ending list of fields and features, we encourage you to keep going as you start to make sense of the information shown in the 802.11 protocol decodes, because without this information, the wireless network analyst can get complete lost in all the detail when troubleshooting 802.11n networks.

Figure 10.40 shows the format of the HT Extended Capabilities field. The first subfield indicates a station's support for phased coexistence operation (PCO), which is a new protection mechanism introduced by the 802.11n amendment. The various protection mechanisms and their operations are going to be discussed in the "Protection Mechanisms" section when looking at the fields of the HT Operations Element. A full discussion of the PCO subfield and the PCO Transmission Time subfield will be left for later in the chapter.

FIGURE 10.40   HT Extended Capabilities field format

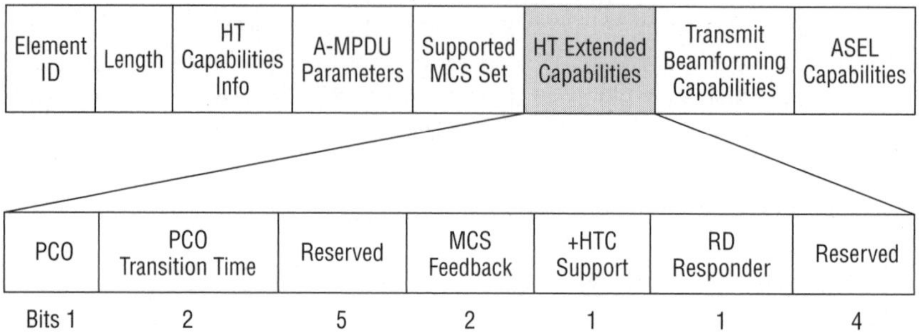

Element ID	Length	HT Capabilities Info	A-MPDU Parameters	Supported MCS Set	HT Extended Capabilities	Transmit Beamforming Capabilities	ASEL Capabilities

PCO	PCO Transition Time	Reserved	MCS Feedback	+HTC Support	RD Responder	Reserved
Bits 1	2	5	2	1	1	4

MCS Feedback

The MCS feedback subfield indicates a STA's ability to provide MCS feedback used during link adaptation. Link adaptation allows an 802.11n wireless network to make use of MIMO channel variations and transmit beamforming to dynamically assign an MCS. This is achieved through the transmission of sounding PPDUs. The link adaptation protocol uses subfields of the HT Control field in the MAC header, which were defined earlier in this chapter. An STA can request another station to send a sounding PPDU containing an MFB by sending an MCS request using the MRQ subfield of the HT Control field in the MAC header. The receiving STA may send either an immediate or delayed response to the requester. An STA may also send unsolicited MFBs. The following list shows the encoding of the MCS Feedback field, including which type of MFB response a STA supports:

> 0 = MFB not supported
>
> 1 = Reserved
>
> 2 = Only unsolicited MFB supported
>
> 3 = STA can respond to an MRQ and send unsolicited MFBs

A full description of link adaptation operations is beyond the scope of this chapter.

+HTC Support

The +HTC Support subfield indicates a STA's support for receiving frames that include the HT Control field in the MAC header. STAs advertise their ability to receive +HTC frames by setting the +HTC Support subfield to 1.

When a STA that does not support +HTC frames receives a +HTC frame destined for another STA, it must still read the duration ID and calculate the CRC.

RD Responder

You have already looked at the Reverse Direction (RD) protocol in this chapter when describing the HT Control Field in the MAC header. The RD Responder subfield of the HT Extended Capabilities field indicates a STA's ability to act as an RD responder. An STA indicates its ability to send data to an RD initiator in response to an RDG by setting the RD Responder subfield to 1.

Transmit Beamforming Capabilities

The 802.11n amendment proposes an optional PHY capability called *transmit beamforming (TxBF)*. Beamforming technology, which has been used in radar systems for many years, is also known as a phased-array antenna system and is often referred to as smart antenna technology.

The two major types of smart antenna array systems include a switched array and an adaptive array. As pictured in Figure 10.41, a switched antenna array uses a number of fixed beam patterns, while an adaptive antenna array maneuvers the beam in the direction of a targeted receiver. 802.11n performs chip-based TxBF and does not require special antennas. By manipulation of the transmitted signal through the use of multiple antennas the signal is optimized at specific locations.

FIGURE 10.41　Antenna arrays and beamforming

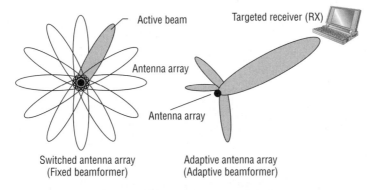

Switched antenna array
(Fixed beamformer)

Adaptive antenna array
(Adaptive beamformer)

Transmit beamforming is a method that allows a MIMO transmitter using multiple antennas to "focus" the transmissions in a coordinated method much like an adaptive antenna array. The focused transmissions are sent in the best direction of a receiver (RX). When multiple copies of the same signal are sent to a receiver, the signals will usually arrive out of phase with each other. If the transmitter (TX) knows about the receiver's location, the phase of the multiple signals sent by a MIMO transmitter can be adjusted. When the multiple signals arrive at the receiver, they are in-phase, resulting in constructive multipath instead of the destructive multipath caused by out-of-phase signals. Carefully controlling the phase of the signals transmitted from multiple antennas has the effect of emulating a high-gain unidirectional antenna or "steering" the beams.

Because transmit beamforming results in constructive multipath communication, the result is a higher signal-to-noise ratio and greater received amplitude. Therefore, transmit beamforming will result in greater range for individual clients communicating with an access point. Transmit beamforming will also result in higher throughput because of the higher SNR, which allows for the use of more-complex modulation methods that can encode more data bits. The higher SNR also results in fewer layer 2 retransmissions.

The HT Capabilities Element has a Transmit Beamforming Capabilities field 4 octets in length, which is used to advertise the beamforming capabilities of an HT STA. Figure 10.42 shows the structure of the Transmit Beamforming Capabilities field. As we take a look at the operation of TxBF, some of these subfields will be discussed. Table 10.14 provides a summary and encoding for all the subfields within the Transmit Beamforming Capabilities field.

FIGURE 10.42 Transmit Beamforming Capabilities field format

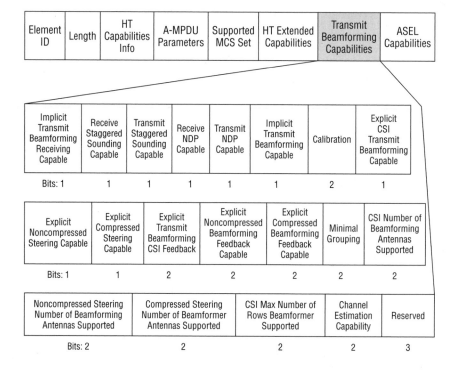

TABLE 10.14 Transmit Beamforming Capabilities subfields

Subfield	Description	Encoding
Implicit Transmit Beamforming Receiving Capable	Indicates a STA's capability to receive TxBF frames using implicit feedback	0 = Not supported 1 = Supported
Receive Staggered Sounding Capable	Indicates a STA's capability to receive staggered sounding frames	0 = Not supported 1 = Supported

TABLE 10.14   Transmit Beamforming Capabilities subfields *(continued)*

Subfield	Description	Encoding
Transmit Staggered Sounding Capable	Indicates a STA's capability to transmit staggered sounding frames	0 = Not supported 1 = Supported
Receive NDP (Null Data Packet) Capable	Indicates a STA's capability to interpret received NDPs and sounding frames	0 = Not supported 1 = Supported
Transmit NDP Capable	Indicates a STA's capability to transmit NDPs as sounding frames	0 = Not supported 1 = Supported
Implicit Transmit Beam-forming Capable	Indicates a STA's capability to implement implicit transmit beamforming	0 = Not supported 1 = Supported
Calibration	Indicates a STA's capability to perform calibration	0 = Not supported 1 = Can respond to a calibration request 2 = Reserved 3 = Can both initiate and respond to a calibration request
Explicit CSI Transmit Beamforming Capable	Indicates a STA's capability to perform TxBF using CSI (Channel State Information) explicit feedback	0 = Not supported 1 = Supported
Explicit Noncompressed Steering Capable	Indicates a STA's capability to perform TxBM using explicit noncompressed beamforming feedback	0 = Not supported 1 = Supported
Explicit Compressed Steering Capable	Indicates a STA's capability to perform TxBF using explicit compressed beamforming feedback	0 = Not supported 1 = Supported
Explicit Transmit Beam-forming CSI Feedback	Indicates a STA's capability to provide CSI explicit feedback	0 = Not supported 1 = Delayed feedback 2 = Immediate feedback 3 = Both delayed and immediate feedback

TABLE 10.14 Transmit Beamforming Capabilities subfields *(continued)*

Subfield	Description	Encoding
Explicit Noncompressed Beamforming Feedback Capable	Indicates a STA's capability to provide noncompressed beamforming explicit feedback	0 = Not supported 1 = Delayed feedback 2 = Immediate feedback 3 = Both delayed and immediate feedback
Explicit Compressed Beamforming Feedback Capable	Indicates a STA's capability to provide compressed beamforming explicit feedback	0 = Not supported 1 = Delayed feedback 2 = Immediate feedback 3 = Both delayed and immediate feedback
Minimal Grouping	Indicates the minimal grouping a STA supports for explicit feedback reports	0 = No Grouping 1 = Groups of 1 or 2 2 = Groups of 1 or 4 3 = Groups of 1, 2 or 4
CSI Number of Beamforming Antennas Supported	Indicates the maximum number of beamformer antennas a beamformee can support when CSI feedback is required	0 = 1 TX antenna 1 = 2 TX antennas 2 = 3 TX antennas 3 = 4 TX antennas
Noncompressed Steering Number of Beamforming Antennas Supported	Indicates the maximum number of beamformer antennas a beamformee can support when noncompressed beamforming feedback is required	0 = 1 TX antenna 1 = 2 TX antennas 2 = 3 TX antennas 3 = 4 TX antennas
Compressed Steering Number of Beamformer Antennas Supported	Indicates the maximum number of beamformer antennas a beamformee can support when compressed beamforming feedback is required	0 = 1 TX antenna 1 = 2 TX antennas 2 = 3 TX antennas 3 = 4 TX antennas
CSI Max Number of Rows Beamformer Supported	Indicates the maximum number of CSI explicit feedback rows a beamformer, calibration initiator, or transmit ASEL initiator can support	0 = 1 CSI row 1 = 2 CSI rows 2 = 3 CSI rows 3 = 4 CSI rows

TABLE 10.14   Transmit Beamforming Capabilities subfields *(continued)*

Subfield	Description	Encoding
Channel Estimation Capability	Indicates the maximum number of space time streams for which a channel can be estimated when receiving sounding PPDUs	0 = 1 space-time steam 1 = 2 space-time streams 2 = 3 space-time streams 3 = 4 space-time streams

Transmit beamforming relies on the transmitter understanding the characteristics of the MIMO channel in order to calculate a steering matrix needed to be able to steer a beam in the direction of the receiver. In order to characterize the channel correctly, the transmitter must receive some feedback from the receiver. 802.11n beamforming transmitters will try to adjust the phase of the signals based on this feedback. The transmitter is considered the beamformer, while the receiver is considered the beamformee. Two feedback methods are provided by the 802.11n amendment:

Implicit Feedback   The beamformer estimates the channel characteristics from the High Throughput Long Training Fields (HT_LTF) in PPDUs it receives from the beamformee.

Explicit Feedback   The beamformee estimates the channel characteristics from the High Throughput Long Training Fields (HT_LTF) in PPDUs it receives from the beamformer. The beamformee then sends this information to the beamformer to use in calculating its steering matrix.

Implicit Feedback

Implicit feedback can operate in one of two modes, unidirectional or bidirectional. In unidirectional mode, only one STA is capable of steering beams; in bidirectional, both STAs can steer beams and take on both the beamformer and beamformee roles. Two subfields within the Transmit Beamforming Capabilities field in the HT Capabilities element are used to indicate that a STA supports implicit feedback:

Implicit Transmit Beamforming Capable subfield   Indicates that the STA is capable of implementing implicit feedback

Implicit Transmit Beamforming Receiving Capable   Indicates that the STA can receive TxBF steered frames using implicit feedback

The beamformer must set both subfields to 1, but the beamformee is only required to set the Implicit Transmit Beamforming Receiving Capable subfield to 1.

The feedback needed to estimate the MIMO channel characteristics is transmitted in sounding PPDUs. A PPDU is identified as sounding by setting the Not Sounding field of the HT Signal field (HT-SIG) in the PPDU header to 0. Many HT-LTFs are needed in order to correctly estimate the channel. Standard PPDUs only contain Data HT-LTFs, but in sounding PPDUs, the Data HT-LTFs can be followed by Extension HT-LTFs.

A beamformer can send a request to the beamformee to transmit sounding PPDUs by setting the Training Request (TRQ) subfield to 1 of the Link Adaptation Control subfield of the HT Control field, shown earlier in Figure 10.15. Sounding frames are used to calibrate the beamformer to improve the performance of TxBF.

Any frame can be used as a sounding frame. NDPs can be used as sounding frames if another frame is not used. If an MPDU that has the TRQ subfield set to 1 requires an immediate response, the beamformee may include the response in a sounding PPDU or set the NDP Announcement subfield of the HT Control field in the MAC header of the response to 1 and then send a sounding NDP after waiting a SIFS. Figure 10.43 shows an NDP announcement frame, and Figure 10.44 shows the NDP announcement frame exchange.

FIGURE 10.43   NDP announcement

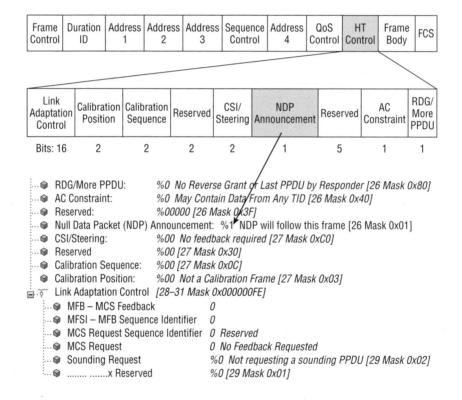

Frame Control	Duration ID	Address 1	Address 2	Address 3	Sequence Control	Address 4	QoS Control	HT Control	Frame Body	FCS

Link Adaptation Control	Calibration Position	Calibration Sequence	Reserved	CSI/ Steering	NDP Announcement	Reserved	AC Constraint	RDG/ More PPDU
Bits: 16	2	2	2	2	1	5	1	1

- RDG/More PPDU: %0 No Reverse Grant or Last PPDU by Responder [26 Mask 0x80]
- AC Constraint: %0 May Contain Data From Any TID [26 Mask 0x40]
- Reserved: %00000 [26 Mask 0x3F]
- Null Data Packet (NDP) Announcement: %1 NDP will follow this frame [26 Mask 0x01]
- CSI/Steering: %00 No feedback required [27 Mask 0xC0]
- Reserved   %00 [27 Mask 0x30]
- Calibration Sequence: %00 [27 Mask 0x0C]
- Calibration Position: %00 Not a Calibration Frame [27 Mask 0x03]
- Link Adaptation Control   [28–31 Mask 0x000000FE]
    - MFB – MCS Feedback   0
    - MFSI – MFB Sequence Identifier   0
    - MCS Request Sequence Identifier   0 Reserved
    - MCS Request   0 No Feedback Requested
    - Sounding Request   %0 Not requesting a sounding PPDU [29 Mask 0x02]
    - ....x Reserved   %0 [29 Mask 0x01]

FIGURE 10.44   NDP announcement frame exchange

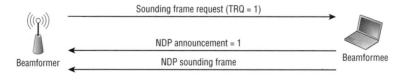

Because NDPs are PPDUs that do not contain an MPDU, you will not see them in a protocol analyzer. By examining the TRQ and NDP Announcement subfields of the HT Control field in the MAC header, you might be able to conclude that NDPs are in fact being transmitted even though you do not see them.

Figure 10.45 summarizes the PPDU protocol exchange for unidirectional implicit feedback, and Figure 10.46 summarizes the PPDU protocol exchange for bidirectional implicit feedback.

FIGURE 10.45   Unidirectional implicit feedback PPDU protocol exchange

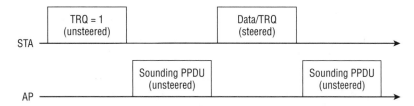

FIGURE 10.46   Bidirectional implicit feedback PPDU protocol exchange

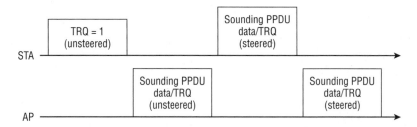

Calibration

Differences between transmit and receive chains in a STA degrade the performance of implicit beamforming. Through over-the-air calibration, a set of correction matrices can be calculated that reduces the differences between a STA's transmit and receive chains. STAs acting as the beamformer are required to be calibrated before they can use the HT-LTFs to correctly estimate the channel. In this chapter, we will just look at the fields and frames used in the calibration procedure and not worry too much about what information is being transferred and what calculations are being made by the STAs.

The ability for a STA to partake in this over-the-air calibration process is indicated in the Calibration subfield of the Transmit Beamforming Capabilities field of the HT Capabilities element. Table 10.15 shows the encoding for this subfield.

TABLE 10.15   Calibration subfield encoding

Value	Interpretation
0	Is not supported.
1	An STA can respond to a calibration request but not initiate one.
2	Reserved.
3	An STA can initiate and respond to a calibration request.

The calibration procedure consists of two steps:

1. The first step of the calibration process involves the exchange of sounding PPDUs between the calibration initiator and the calibration responder.

2. The second step of the calibration process involves the transmission of a CSI report, which includes the resulting information gained from the PPDU exchange in step 1.

Figure 10.47 shows the calibration protocol exchange and is outlined next. The Calibration Sequence control subfield of the HT Control field is incremented every time a new calibration procedure is started.

FIGURE 10.47   Calibration protocol exchange

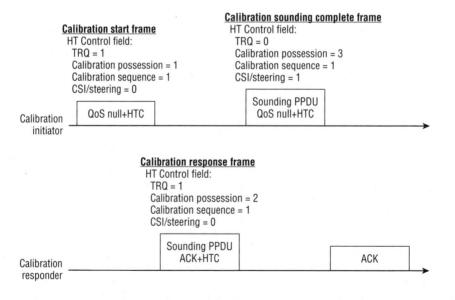

1. The calibration initiator sends a calibration start frame that is a QoS Null+HTC data frame.

The TRQ subfield of the HT Control field is set to 1 to request a sounding PPDU, and the Calibration Position subfield is set to 1 to indicate that this is the first frame in the calibration procedure. Figure 10.48 shows an HT Control field decode for a calibration start frame.

FIGURE 10.48 Calibration start frame decode

```
 ⋯⬡ RDG/More PPDU:          %0  No Reverse Grant or Last PPDU by Responder [26 Mask 0x80]
 ⋯⬡ AC Constraint:          %0  May Contain Data From Any TID [26 Mask 0x40]
 ⋯⬡ Reserved:               %00000 [26 Mask 0x3E]
 ⋯⬡ Null Data Packet (NDP) Announcement:  %0  No NDP follows this frame [26 Mask 0x01]
 ⋯⬡ CSI/Steering:           %00  No feedback required [27 Mask 0xC0]
 ⋯⬡ Reserved                %00 [27 Mask 0x30]
 ⋯⬡ Calibration Sequence:   %01 [27 Mask 0x0C]
 ⋯⬡ Calibration Position:   %01  Calibration Start [27 Mask 0x03]
 ⊟⋯ Link Adaptation Control [28–31 Mask 0x000000FE]
   ⋯⬡ MFB – MCS Feedback             0
   ⋯⬡ MFSI – MFB Sequence Identifier 0
   ⋯⬡ MCS Request Sequence Identifier 0  Reserved
   ⋯⬡ MCS Request                    0  No Feedback Requested
   ⋯⬡ Sounding Request               %1  Requesting a sounding PPDU [29 Mask 0x02]
   ⋯⬡ ........ .......x Reserved      %0 [29 Mask 0x01]
```

2. After waiting a SIFS, the calibration responder will reply with a sounding PPDU carrying an ACK+HTC control wrapper MPDU.

    The Calibration Position subfield is set to 2 to indicate that this is the second frame in the calibration procedure. The Calibration Sequence subfield will be set to the same value as was set in the calibration start frame. Upon receipt of this sounding PPDU, the calibration responder can estimate the MIMO channel. This calibration response frame also contains the TRQ subfield set to 1, requesting the calibration initiator to send a sounding PPDU.

3. The calibration initiator will transmit a Calibration Sounding Complete frame, which is a sounding PPDU containing a QoS Null+HTC data MPDU.

    This frame has a Calibration Position value of 3 and upon receipt allows the calibration responder to estimate the MIMO channel. This third frame of the HTC calibration procedure also sets the CSI/Steering subfield of the HT Control field to 1 to request a CSI feedback frame.

4. The calibration responder will send an ACK to acknowledge receipt of the Calibration Sounding Complete frame.

    Having successfully exchanged sounding PPDUs, stage 1 of the calibration procedure is now complete.

5. In stage 2 of the calibration procedure, the calibration responder must transmit one or more CSI frames that include a CSI report.

The CSI frame is a new type of action frame introduced by the 802.11n amendment. Figure 10.49 shows the frame format for a CSI action frame. A full description of the CSI action frame is beyond the scope of this chapter.

FIGURE 10.49 CSI action frame format

Category (16 = HT)	Action (4 = CSI)	MIMO Control	CSI Report
1	1	6	Variable

Stage 1 of the calibration procedure can be performed by sending the sounding PPDUs in NDPs, in this case any data, management, or control frame can be the calibration start frame (indicated by a calibration position number of 1), which will have the NDP Announcement subfield set to 1. If the calibration initiator does not have any frames to send to the calibration responder, it may set the NDP Announcement subfield using an RTS/CTS exchange.

Explicit Feedback

The advantage of explicit feedback over implicit feedback is that the beamformer does not need to be calibrated; however, explicit feedback does put additional load on the beamformee and increases the transmission overhead. In explicit feedback, the beamformer receives beamforming feedback from the beamformee. This feedback can take one of three forms:

Channel State Information   This CSI frame contains MIMO channel coefficients that the beamformer can use to calculate its steering matrix.

Noncompressed beamforming   The beamformee calculates the steering matrix and sends it back to the beamformer.

Compressed beamforming   The beamformee calculates the steering matrix, compresses it, and sends it back to the beamformer.

An STA shall indicate which feedback methods they support through the use of the Explicit CSI Transmit Beamforming Capable, Explicit Noncompressed Steering Capable, and Explicit Compressed Steering Capable subfields of the Transmit Beamforming Capabilities field in the HT Capabilities Element.

A Beamformee sends beamforming feedback in response to receiving a sounding PPDU from which it can estimate the channel. A beamformee capable of providing explicit feedback must also indicate how soon after receiving a sounding PPDU it will respond with feedback. The options are as follows:

Immediate   The feedback response will be sent a SIFS after the sounding PPDU.

Delayed   The feedback is sent sometime before the end of the beamformer's TXOP.

Immediate and Delayed   The beamformee is capable of sending immediate or delayed feedback.

The beamformee's feedback response capabilities are advertised in the Explicit Transmit Beamforming CSI Feedback, Explicit Noncompressed Beamforming Feedback Capable, and Explicit Compressed Beamforming Feedback Capable subfields of the Transmit Beamforming Capabilities field in the HT Capabilities Element. These subfields set a value of 1 to indicate delayed, 2 to indicate immediate, and 3 to indicate support for both.

A detailed description of the information contained within the TxBF feedback message is beyond the scope of this chapter. If you do require more detailed information about the 802.11n amendment, you can always download a copy from the IEEE website at `http://standards.ieee.org/getieee802/802.11.html`.

Beamforming Summary

Transmit beamforming will work best between 802.11n STAs that have similar capabilities, because the technology depends heavily on feedback from the receiving radio. 802.11 a/b/g radios cannot provide the implicit/explicit feedback used by HT radios that are capable of transmit beamforming. Access points using beamforming can target multiple clients, but only for unicast transmissions. Transmit beamforming is not used for broadcast or multicast transmissions. 802.11n TxBF is not currently tested by the Wi-Fi Alliance. As of this writing, chipset vendors are just starting to release next-generation chipsets that support 802.11n TxBF. However, it will be some time before we start to see products implementing these chipsets and even longer before we see 802.11n TxBF products tested for interoperability. Currently Cisco and Ruckus have their own propriety implementations of beamforming, although it should be said that their beamforming implementations are very different from how TxBF is specified in the 802.11n amendment.

ASEL Capabilities

Antenna selection (ASEL) is a MIMO antenna diversity method used when a STA has more antennas than radio chains. An STA uses ASEL to dynamically create a time-variant mapping of antennas to radio chains, picking the combination of antennas that will yield the best signal-to-noise ratio. This mapping is created based upon CSI. To correctly create this mapping, a STA must carry out an ASEL training frame exchange by sending or receiving a series of sounding PPDUs over all antennas. These sounding PPDUs must all be transmitted within one TXOP.

The training information is transmitted using the ASEL Control subfield of the HT Control field in the MAC header. Figure 10.50 shows the format for this subfield. When the MAI subfield of the Link Adaptation Control subfield of the HT Control field in the MAC header is set to 14, it acts as an ASEL indicator. This indicates that the MFB/ASELC subfield is to be interpreted as an ASEL command (ASELC). The ASELC has two subfields, the ASEL command and ASEL data. Table 10.16 shows the different commands of the ASEL Command subfield. The ASEL Data subfield carries data relating to the command being sent.

FIGURE 10.50 ASEL Control format

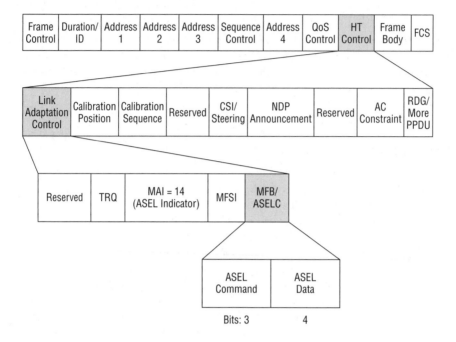

TABLE 10:16 ASEL commands

Command	Interpretation
0	Transmit antenna selection sounding indication (TXASSI)
1	Transmit antenna selection sounding request (TXASSR) or transmit ASEL sounding resumption
2	Receive antenna selection sounding indication (RXASSI)
3	Receive antenna selection sounding request (RXASSR)
4	Sounding Label
5	No feedback due to ASEL training failure or stale feedback
6	Transmit antenna selection sounding indication requesting feedback of explicit CSI (TXASSI-CSI)
7	Reserved

An STA advertises its ASEL capabilities through the ASEL Capabilities field of the HT Capabilities Element. Figure 10.51 shows the format of the ASEL Capabilities field. Each of the subfields within the ASEL Capabilities field can be set to 1, indicating that the specified capability is supported or set to 0 when not supported. An ASEL-capable STA will set the Antenna Selection Capable subfield to 1 and then set the other subfields accordingly.

FIGURE 10.51   ASEL Capabilities format

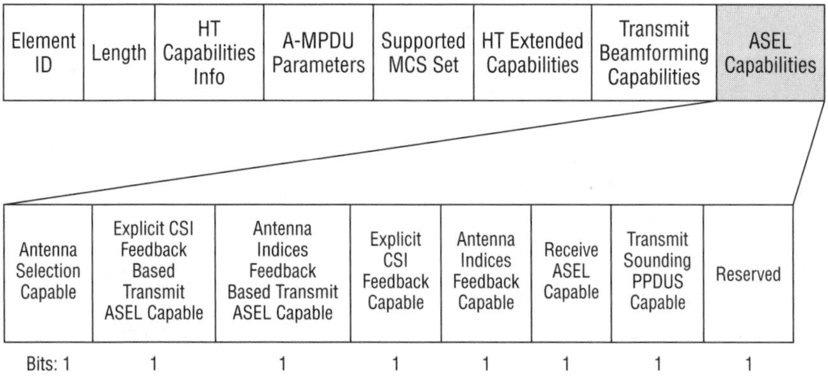

Transmit ASEL

ASEL supports both transmit and receive diversity methods. Transmit diversity is achieved through the transmit ASEL procedure. Figure 10.52 shows the transmit ASEL procedure. The STA that is responsible for conducting the transmit ASEL procedure is referred to as the ASEL transmitter. The STA that provides the ASEL feedback is defined as the transmit ASEL responder. The following are the steps for transmit ASEL.

1. The transmit ASEL responder may optionally initiate the transmit ASEL procedure by sending an +HTC frame with the ASEL Command subfield set to 1, indicating a transmit antenna selection sounding request (TXASSR).

2. The ASEL transmitter will send sounding PPDUs on each antenna.

    These sounding PPDUs may be sounding +HTC frames or sounding NDPs. The +HTC frames have the ASEL command subfield set to 0, indicating transmit antenna selection sounding indication (TXASSI), or set to 6, indicating TXASSI requesting feedback of explicit CSI (TXASSI-CSI). If using sounding NDPs, the ASEL transmitter will first send a TXASSI or TXASSI-CSI frame but with the NDP Announcement flag set, indicating consecutive sounding NDPs will follow.

FIGURE 10.52 Transmit ASEL procedure

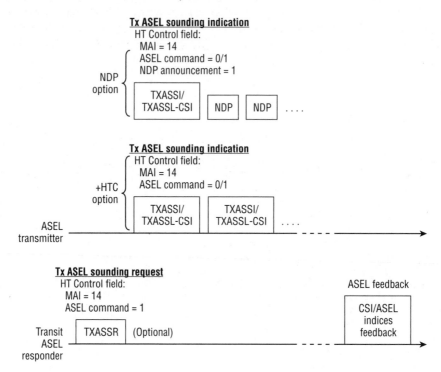

3. The transmit ASEL responder will use the received sounding PPDUs to estimate the MIMO channel.

4. Next in a separate TXOP, the transmit ASEL responder will then send ASEL feedback using one of two action frames:

   ▪ If the ASEL transmitter sent a TXASSI-CSI ASEL command, the ASEL feedback will be sent within a CSI action frame (as shown in Figure 10.49).

   ▪ If the ASEL transmitter sent a TXASSI ASEL command, the ASEL responder can provide feedback using either a CSI action frame or an ASEL Indices Feedback action frame.

Figure 10.53 shows the format of an ASEL Indices Feedback action frame; a full explanation of this frame is beyond the scope of this chapter.

FIGURE 10.53 ASEL Indices Feedback action frame format

Category (16 = HT)	Action (7 = ASEL Indices Feedback)	Antenna Selection Indices
Bytes: 1	1	1

Receive ASEL

Figure 10.54 shows the receive ASEL procedure, used for received diversity. The STA, which is conducting the receive ASEL, is referred to as the ASEL receiver, and the STA sending the required sounding PPDUs to the ASEL receiver is defined as the ASEL sounding-capable transmitter.

FIGURE 10.54   Receive ASEL procedure

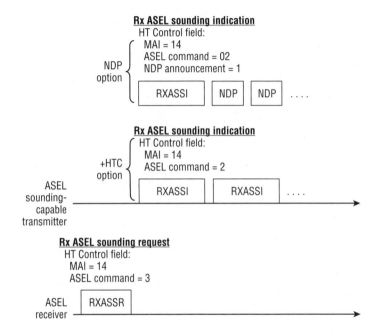

The following steps outline the receive ASEL procedure:

1. The ASEL receiver initiates the receive ASEL procedure by transmitting an +HTC frame with the ASEL command set to 3, indicating a receive antenna selection sounding request (RXASSR).

2. Upon receipt of an RXASSR frame, the ASEL sounding-capable transmitter will begin transmission of the consecutive sounding PPDUs.

    The sounding PPDUs can either be +HTC frames or NDPs. The +HTC frames will have the ASEL command set to 2, indicating receive antenna selection sounding indication (RXASSI). When using NDPs, the ASEL sounding-capable transmitter will send an RXASSI frame first with the NDP announcement bit set to 1, indicating sounding NDPs will follow.

3. The ASEL receiver uses different antenna sets to receive the sounding PPDUs and calculates its ASEL mapping.

HT Operation Element

An STA operation within an HT BSS is controlled by the *HT Operation Element.* Figure 10.55 shows the format of the HT Operation Element. The HT Operation Element is found in Beacon, Reassociation Response, and Probe Response frames transmitted by an AP.

FIGURE 10.55   HT Operation Element

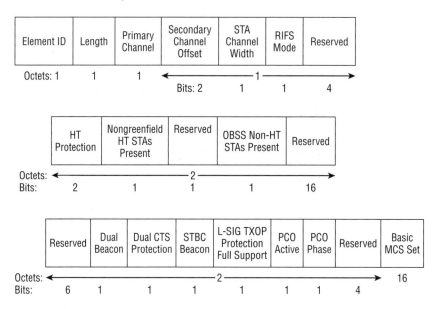

The HT Operation Element ID is 61, and the Length field is set to 22, indicating that another 22 octets will follow the Element ID and Length fields. The reaming fields of the HT Operation Element and their subfields will be described in the following sections.

Primary Channel, Secondary Channel Offset, and STA Channel Width

As you have already seen in this chapter, 802.11n STAs can use either 20 MHz channels or 40 MHz channels. An AP STA uses the Supported Channel Width Set subfield in the HT Capabilities Element to indicate whether it is a 20 MHz BSS or 20/40 MHz BSS. If the Supported Channel Width Set subfield is set to 0, indicating a 20 MHz BSS, then the Primary Channel field of the HT Operation Element indicates the 20 MHz channel number the BSS is operating on.

40 MHz channels consist of two consecutive 20 MHz channels bonded together:

Primary Channel One of the two bonded channels is selected as the primary channel and is used by the access point to communicate with legacy and HT 20 MHz-only STAs, which are associated to the BSS. When the Supported Channel Width Set subfield is equal to 1, indicating a 20/40 MHz BSS, then the Primary Channel field indicates the primary channel number.

Secondary Channel The secondary channel must be one channel directly above or below the primary. The Secondary Channel Offset field in the HT Operation Element indicates whether the primary channel is bonded with the channel above or below.

Table 10.17 shows the encoding for the Secondary Channel Offset field.

TABLE 10.17 Secondary channel offset encoding

Value	Interpretation
0	No secondary channel (20 MHz BSS)
1	Secondary channel is above the primary channel
2	Reserved
3	Secondary channel is below the primary channel

If the Secondary Channel Offset field is set to 1 or 3, indicating a secondary channel above or below the primary channel, the AP will set the STA Channel Width field in the HT Operation Element to 1, indicating that 40 MHz channels may be used to transmit to an associated STA. If that Secondary Channel Offset field is set to 0, then the STA Channel Width field is also set to 0, indicating that only 20 MHz channels may be used.

RIFS Mode

The 802.11e QoS amendment introduced the capability for a transmitting radio to send a burst of frames during a transmit opportunity (TXOP). During the frame burst, a Short Interframe Space (SIFS) was used between each frame to ensure that no other radios transmitted during the frame burst. The 802.11n amendment defines a new interframe space that is even shorter in time, called a *Reduced Interframe Space (RIFS)*. A SIFS interval is 16 µs for OFDM (10 µs for DSSS), whereas a RIFS interval is only 2 µs. A RIFS interval can be used in place of a SIFS interval, resulting in less overhead during a frame burst. It should be noted that RIFS intervals can be used only when a HT Greenfield network is in place. RIFS can be used only between HT radios, and no legacy devices can belong to the basic service set.

The RIFS Mode field of the HT Operation Element indicates whether the use of RIFS is allowed within the BSS. A value of 1 allows RIFS to be used, and a value of 0 prohibits the use of RIFS.

Protection Mechanisms

The majority of the remaining fields within the HT Operation Element support the operation of various protection mechanisms defined by the 802.11n amendment. These protection mechanisms and their relevant fields will be described next.

In Chapter 5, you have already learned how ERP (802.11g) STAs must use either RTS/CTS or CTS-Self to protect their transmissions from non-ERP (802.11b) STAs. ERP STAs must prevent non-ERP stations who do not understand their OFDM modulation from transmitting at the same time as them. They do this by reserving the medium for the length of their transmission.

The 802.11n amendment requires backward compatibility with 802.11a and 802.1b/g radios. Therefore, the 802.11n amendment defines HT protection modes that enable HT clause 20 radios to be backward compatible with older clause 18 radios (HR-DSSS), clause 17 radios (OFDM), and clause 19 radios (ERP). In additional to RTS/CTS and CTS-to-self, the 802.11n amendment defines some new protection mechanisms, namely, Dual CTS and L-SIG TXOP.

As well as protecting HT transmission against legacy 20 MHz radios, an HT 20/40 MHz–capable STA will have to protect its 40 MHz transmissions against HT STAs that are only 20 MHz capable. The 802.11n amendment defines an optional mode of operation called phased coexistence operation that divides time and alternates between 20 MHz and 40 MHz transmissions.

HT Protection Modes

To ensure backward compatibility with older 802.11 a/b/g radios, an HT access point will operate in one of four *protection modes*. Much like an ERP access point, the protection modes may change dynamically depending on devices that are nearby or associated to the HT access point. The protection mechanisms used are RTS/CTS, CTS-to-Self, Dual-CTS, or other protection methods. The four modes are as follows:

Mode 0—Greenfield Mode   This mode is referred to as Greenfield because only HT radios are in use. All the HT client stations must also have the same operational capabilities. If the HT basic service set is a 20/40 MHz BBS, all the stations must be 20/40 capable. If these conditions are met, there is no need for protection.

Mode 1—HT Nonmember Protection Mode   In this mode, all the stations in the BSS must be HT stations. Protection mechanisms kick in when a non-HT client station or non-HT access point is heard that is not a member of the BSS. For example, an HT AP and stations may be transmitting on a 40 MHz HT channel when a non-HT 802.11a access point or client station is detected to be transmitting in a 20 MHz space that interferes with either the primary or secondary channel of the 40 MHz HT channel.

Mode 2—HT 20 MHz Protection Mode   In this mode, all the stations in the BSS must be HT stations and are associated to a 20/40 MHz access point. If a 20 MHz–only HT station associates to the 20/40 MHz AP, protection must be used. In other words, the 20/40–capable HT stations must use protection when transmitting on a 40 MHz channel in order to prevent the 20 MHz-only HT stations from transmitting at the same time.

Mode 3—non-HT Mixed Mode   This protection mode is used when one or more non-HT stations are associated to the HT access point. The HT basic service set can be either 20 MHz or 20/40 MHz capable. If any clause 18 radios (HR-DSSS), clause 17 radios (OFDM), or clause 19 radios (ERP) associate to the BSS, protection will be used. For the foreseeable future, mode 3 will probably be the most commonly used protection mode because most basic service sets will most likely have legacy devices as members.

HT access points advertise which one of the four HT protection modes an associated HT STA should use through the HT Protection field. Table 10.18 shows the encoding for the HT Operations Element.

TABLE 10.18:   HT Protection field encoding

Value	Interpretation
0	Greenfield mode (no protection)
1	Nonmember protection mode
2	20 MHz protection mode
3	non-HT mixed mode

Both the Nongreenfield HT STAs Present field and the Overlapping Basic Service Set (OBSS) Non-HT STAs Present field in the HT Operation Element help determine which protection mode an AP should operate in. When the Nongreenfield HT STAs Present field is set to 1, indicating that a nongreenfield-capable STA is associated to the BSS. The OBSS Non-HT STA Present field reports the presence of unassociated non-HT STAs operating on the primary or secondary channel. When the OBSS Non-HT STA Present field is set to 1, the AP will implement either mode 1, nonmember protection, or mode 3, mixed mode protection.

When set to 1, both the Nongreenfield HT STAs Present field and OBSS Non-HT STA Present field can cause neighboring APs to enable HT protection also.

RTS/CTS and CTS-to-Self

When HT protection is enabled within an HT BSS, an HT STA will precede HT transmissions with either an RTS/CTS control frame exchange or a CTS-to-Self control frame using modulation and coding understandable to the STAs that are being protected against. The Duration ID within these control frames causes STAs to update their network allocation vector (NAV), preventing them from initiating a new transmission until the end of the transmitting HT STA's TXOP.

When protecting the transmission of 40 MHz HT frames against clause 17 (OFDM) radios and clause 19 (ERP) radios, protection mechanism control frames can be sent over the 40 MHz channel using non-HT duplicate transmissions. Non-HT duplicate transmissions allow the two identical 20 MHz non-HT control frames to be transferred simultaneously on both the primary and secondary channels, as pictured in Figure 10.56. Non-HT duplicate transmissions will be sent using clause 17 data rates in the 5 GHz band or clause 19 data rates in the 2.4 GHz band. In Figure 10.56, you can see that non-HT duplicate transmissions are just sending the same data on two adjacent clause 17 or clause 18 20 MHz (52 subcarriers) OFDM channels at the same time. This will cause STAs operating in either the primary or secondary channel to update their NAVs and defer their transmission.

FIGURE 10.56 Non-HT duplicate format

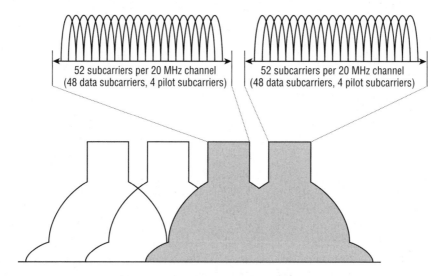

Dual Beacons, Dual CTS, and STBC Beacons

When implementing STBC, the received signal may be improved by up to 8 dB, resulting in greater range (shown in Figure 10.57). An 8 dB increase in signal strength can yield up to 69 percent more range. This increased range will only apply to STBC frames and therefore does not automatically mean an increased BSS size for all STAs.

FIGURE 10.57   STBC increased range

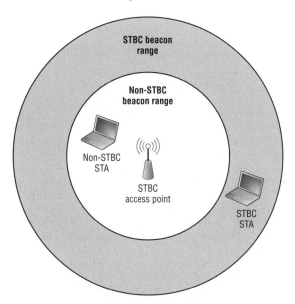

Beacon frames are traditionally sent using the lowest basic data rate; because of backward compatibly requirements, this will not be an STBC MCS. Therefore, the only way to truly increase the BSS size and realize the full potential of STBC is to transmit STBC beacon frames (using the lowest STBC MCS). Because HT 802.11n requires backward compatibility with legacy radios and only HT STBC–capable STAs would be able to hear the STBC beacon frames, access points are also required to transmit a standard non-STBC beacon, referred to as the primary beacon.

When the Dual Beacon field of the HT Operation Element is set to 1, the AP will transmit both a primary beacon and an STBC beacon. The STBC beacon contains the same BSS information as the primary beacon but will have the STBC Beacon field in the HT Operation Element set to 1, indicating it is an STBC beacon.

Although STBC operation using dual beacons increases the range of our BSS for STBC STAs, it also introduces a new hidden node problem. STBC STAs operating at the greater range, indicated by the gray area in Figure 10.57, will not be able to hear the shorter range non-STBC transmission within the BSS; conversely, non-STBC STAs will not be able to understand the STBC transmissions. To combat this dual hidden node problem, the 802.11n amendment introduces a new protection mechanism called *Dual CTS*. Dual CTS sets the NAV in STAs that do not support STBC and STAs that can only associate and communicate use STBC because of their physical distance away from the AP.

An AP implements dual CTS protection by setting the Dual CTS protection field of the HT Operation element to 1; this will cause all non-STBC HT STAs within the BSS to transmit an RTS frame address to the AP at the beginning of every TXOP. In response to this RTS frame, the access point will send two CTS frames. One CTS will be transmitted using an STBC frame, and the other CTS will use a non-STBC frame.

Figure 10.58 shows the Dual CTS procedure where the initiating non-AP STA is STBC capable. Figure 10.59 pictures the Dual CTS procedure where the initiating non-AP STA is not STBC capable.

FIGURE 10.58 Dual CTS, initiating STA is STBC capable

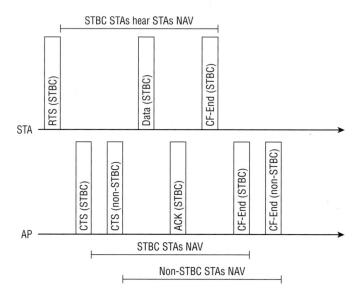

FIGURE 10.59 Dual CTS, initiating STA is not STBC capable

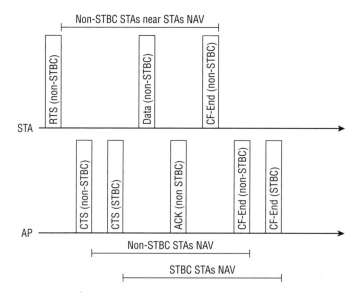

When the non-AP STA is capable of receiving and transmitting STBC frames, as indicated by the TX STBC and RX STBC subfields in the HT Capabilities Element, it will use an STBC frame to transmit the RTS. If the STA is not STBC capable, the RTS will be a non-STBC frame. The first CTS frame transmitted by the access point will match the frame type of the RTS. This means if the RTS is an STBC frame, as shown in Figure 10.58, then the first CTS transmitted by the access point will also be an STBC frame, and the second CTS will be a non-STBC frame. Conversely, if the RTS is a non-STBC frame, as shown in Figure 10.59, the AP will first transmit a non-STBC CTS followed by a STBC CTS.

If a STA finishes sending data before the end of its TXOP, it may truncate the TXOP by sending a CF-End frame, providing the TXOP has enough time left to send the CF-End frame. CF-End frames were defined in the original 802.11 standard as part of the point coordination function (PCF), a contention-free medium access method. The purpose of CF-End frames is to reset a STA's NAV to 0, allowing all STAs to contend for access again. When implementing STBC and Dual CTS, there is no guarantee that all STAs within the BSS will see the CF-End frame transmitted by the non-AP STA. Therefore, the AP will respond by sending dual CF-End frames, one using an STBC frame and one using a non-STBC frame, which guarantees all STAs within the BSS will reset their NAV. Figures 10.58 and 10.59 show this Dual CF-End procedure.

When Dual CTS is enabled within a BSS, throughput will be significantly reduced because of the overhead added to every HT TXOP.

The 802.11n amendment uses the CF-End frame original defined as part of PCF. PCF has never been implemented by wireless vendors. However CF-End frames can now be used to truncate TXOPs and are also used in PCO, which will be described later in the protection mechanisms section. So, do not be surprised when you start to see CF-End frames in your 802.11n packet captures.

L-SIG TXOP

L-SIG TXOP protection is an optional Physical layer protection mechanism, which uses the L-SIG (Legacy Signal) field in the HT mixed PPDU header. Figure 10.60 shows the format of this field. As you have already seen in this chapter, a STA advertises its capability to support L-SIG TXOP protection by setting the L-SIG TXOP Protection Support subfield in the HT Capabilities Info field of the HT Capabilities Element. If all HT STAs within a BSS support L-SIG TXOP protection, the AP will set the L-SIG TXOP Protection Full Support field of the HT Operation Element to 1.

When using the Non-HT legacy PPDU format, the Rate subfield of the L-SIG field identifies the date rate that will be used to transmit the MPDU encapsulated in the PPDU, and the Length subfield identifies the length of the MPDU. From these two subfields, the duration needed to transmit the MPDU can be determined. When using HT mixed PPDU format with L-SIG TXOP protection, the Rate and Length subfields can be set to such values that the calculated duration value is equal to the length of time a non-HT station must not transmit for. Because the L-SIG field is in the non-HT legacy part of the PPDU header, it is readable by all non-HT stations.

FIGURE 10.60 L-SIG field in HT mixed PPDU format

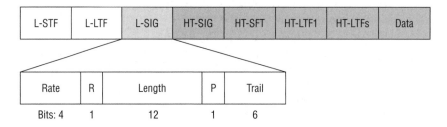

PCO

Another operational mechanism that accounts for the coexistence between 802.11n HT coverage cells and nearby legacy 802.11a/b/g coverage cells is *phased coexistence operation* (PCO). This is an optional mode of operation that divides time and alternates between 20 MHz and 40 MHz transmissions. The HT access point designates time slices for 20 MHz operations in both primary and secondary 20 MHz channels and designates time slices for 40 MHz transmissions.

An STA advertises its capability to support PCO by setting the PCO subfield in the HT Extended Capabilities field of the HT Capabilities Element. A PCO field value of 1 indicates that the STA is PCO capable and a value of 0 indicates that the STA does not support PCO. An AP STA that supports PCO will make PCO active within the BSS when it determines that a PCO BSS would be more efficient than the current BSS or than a 20 MHz–only BSS. When an AP activates a PCO BSS, it will advertise this by setting the PCO Active field of the HT Operation Element to 1 in its beacons.

It is interesting to note that the 802.11n amendment states that the algorithm an AP uses to decide whether it would be more appropriate to enable a PCO BSS than the current BSS or than a 20 MHz only BSS is "beyond the scope of this standard." This leaves the decision on how to implement this down to the individual vendors, if their decision is to implement PCO at all.

When a PCO BSS is active, the AP allocates a time slot for a 20 MHz operational phase and a time slot for a 40 MHz operational phase. The AP switches back and forth between the two phases, as is pictured in Figure 10.61. The access point indicates a change in phases through the use of a new action frame called the Set PCO Phase. Figure 10.62 shows the format for the Set PCO Phase action frame. Within this action frame, the PCO Phase Control Field is set to 0 to indicate the start of a 20 MHz phase and a value of 1 indicates the start of a 40 MHz phase. An AP can also advertise a change of state through the PCO Phase field in the HT Operation Element contained in its beacon frames. This field identifies the current operational phase, with a value of 0 indicating a continuation of or change to a 20 MHz phase and with a value of 1 indicating a continuation of or change to a 40 MHz phase.

FIGURE 10.61   PCO operation

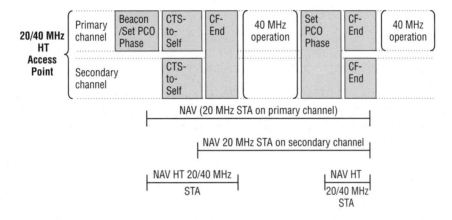

FIGURE 10.62   Set PCO Phase action frame format

Category (16 = HT)	Action (3 = Set PCO Action)	PCO Phase Control
1	1	1

The HT access point uses a non-HT duplicate format CTS-to-Self frame to set the NAV timers of 20 MHz STAs when entering into a 40 MHz phase of operation. It will then send a 40 MHz CF-End frame to reset the NAV in all 40 MHz–capable stations and enter into a period of 40 MHz–only operation. At the end of the 40 MHz period, it will send a Set PCO Phase action frame, indicating the start of a 20 MHz operational phase. This will be followed by a non-HT duplicate format CF-End frame, which will reset the NAV in all 20 MHz STAs, allowing them to contend for access once again. Figure 10.61 shows this procedure.

Both AP and non-AP STAs contain a PCO Transition Time subfield in the HT Extended Capabilities field of the HT Capabilities Element. In an AP, this subfield indicates the transition time between PCO phases of operation. In a non-AP STA, this subfield will be set to the same value as the AP to indicate that it can switch between 20 MHz and 40 MHz phases within the time advertised by the AP. Table 10.19 shows the encoding for this field.

TABLE 10.19   PCO Transition Time subfield

Value	Interpretation
0	Reserved
1	400 µs
2	1.5 ms
3	5 ms

The main advantage of PCO is that no protection mechanisms are needed during the 40 MHz operational phase. PCO might improve throughput in some situations. However, switching back and forth between channels could increase jitter, and therefore PCO mode is not recommended when VoWiFi phones are deployed.

Basic MCS Set

The last field in the HT Operation Element is the Basic MCS Set. This field has a similar format to the RX MCS Bitmask subfield in the supported MCS Set field of the HT Capabilities Element. Unlike the RX MCS Set subfield, which shows the MCS supported by the AP, the Basic MCS Set field shows only MCS values that are supported by all HT STAs within the BSS. Figure 10.63 shows a decode of this field.

FIGURE 10.63   Basic MCS set decode

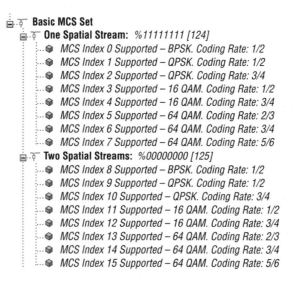

Summary

Well done for getting though this chapter. Having investigated all the fields and subfields of the HT Control field, the HT Capabilities Element, and HT Operation Element, along with their associated methods, operations, and frames, you will now have a better understanding of what the 802.11n amendment defines and how it achieves it. You should also be able to start making sense of those massive HT decodes you have seen in your HT packet captures.

This chapter has covered the HT control frame and how its fields support link adaptation and the Reverse Direction (RD) protocol. The chapter has also described how the Control Wrapper frame is used to encapsulate other control frames in order to add an HT Control field to them. The fields and subfields of the HT Capabilities Element and HT Operation Element were also defined.

We investigated the operations of the following 802.11n features and enhancements:

- TxBF
- ASEL
- STBC
- SM Power Save
- Frame aggregation (both A-MSDU and A-MPDU)
- 20/40 MHz BSS and channel bonding
- Short guard interval
- RIFS
- Forty MHz Intolerant
- Delayed block acknowledgements
- MCSs
- HT protection modes
- Dual CTS
- L-SIG TXOP protection
- PCO

As of this writing, chipset vendors are just starting to release the next generation of chipsets using new silicon, which are capable of supporting all the features of the 802.11n amendment. When vendors will implement these chipsets and which features they choose to implement remains to be seen. It is likely that only the features which are tested by the Wi-Fi Alliance will be implemented initially; see Table 10.6 for a list of these features.

Exam Essentials

Know the three PHY preamble and header formats.   Know the differences between non-HT legacy, HT Greenfield, and HT mixed formats and when and why each would be used.

Define the difference between MIMO and SISO.   Understand that SISO devices use only one radio chain, whereas the MIMO system uses multiple.

Explain HT channels.   Understand the benefit of having additional subcarriers in an HT 20 MHz channel. Be able to explain how channel bonding creates 40 MHz channels and the operation of 20/40 MHz BSS.

Understand the short guard interval.   Explain how the guard interval compensates for intersymbol interferences, and describe the use of both 400- and 800-nanosecond GIs.

Explain modulation and coding schemes.   Explain how MCS are used to define data rates. Identify the packets and fields where you will find the MCS supported by an HT BSS and by an individual STA. Also be able to identify where you will find a list of the MCS supported by all currently associated STAs.

Understand sounding PPDUs.   Know that any 802.11 management, control, or data frame can be carried within a sounding PPDU. Alternatively, when there is no other data to transmit, NDPs can be used to send sounding PPDUs. Understand which HT enhancements use sounding PPDUs and when they are transmitted. Know why and when the NDP announcement subfield is used.

Explain the operation of ASEL.   Understand under what conditions ASEL can be used. Describe how ASEL operation uses the subfields of the HT Control field and ASEL Capabilities field. Be able to describe the operation of both transmit and receive ASEL, understanding when an ASEL Indices Feedback action frame is used and when a CSI action frame is used.

Understand TxBF.   Be able to describe the operation of both implicit and explicit TxBF, and understand how the subfields within the HT Control Field support them. Be able to explain the calibration process and the reason it is needed.

Explain STBC.   Understand how STBC can increase the range of a BSS. Explain how dual beacons and dual CTS are used in a STBC BSS.

Understand SM.   Be able to explain how SM increases throughput. Understand the requirement and operation of SM Power Save.

Explain frame aggregation.   Be able to demonstrate your understanding of frame aggregation. Understand the differences between A-MSDU and A-MPDU and their respective maximum frame sizes.

Understand the subfields of the HT Control field. Know the definition of each subfield within the HT Control field and how they support the Reverse Direction (RD) protocol.

Define the HT Capabilities and HT Operation Information Elements. Understand the interpretation of the fields and subfields found in both the HT Capabilities and HT Operation elements. Know in which management frames these Information Elements are to be found.

Key Terms

Before you take the exam, be certain you are familiar with the following terms:

Antenna Selection (ASEL)

Aggregate MAC Service Data Unit (A-MSDU)

Aggregate MAC Protocol Data Unit (A-MPDU)

Control Wrapper frame

Dual CTS

Forty MHz Intolerant

Frame aggregation

HT Capabilities Element

HT Control field

HT Operation Element

L-SIG TXOP protection

Modulation and coding scheme (MCS)

Multiple-input multiple-output (MIMO)

Phased coexistence operation (PCO)

Protection modes

Reduced Interframe Space (RIFS)

Reverse Direction (RD) protocol

Short guard interval

Single-input single-output (SISO)

SM Power Save

Space Time Block Coding (STBC)

Spatial Multiplexing (SM)

Transmit Beamforming (TxBF)

Review Questions

1. How many subcarriers are there in an HT 40 MHz channel?

   A. 54

   B. 56

   C. 112

   D. 114

2. Which of the PPDU frame formats can be used to protect HT transmissions using L-SIG TXOP?

   A. Non-HT legacy

   B. HT mixed

   C. HT Greenfield

   D. HT protection

3. What is the purpose of the order bit in the MAC header in HT QoS data and management frames?

   A. Indicates the frame contains a HT Control frame.

   B. Indicates the frame contains a HT Capabilities Element.

   C. Indicates the frame contains a HT Operations Element.

   D. Data must be sent using a strictly ordered class of service.

4. Upon receipt of a reverse direction grant (RDG), the receiving station may do what?

   A. Transmit data in the next TXOP to any STA within the BSS

   B. Transmit data back to the source of the RDG within the next TXOP

   C. Transmit data within the current TXOP to any STA within the BSS

   D. Transmit data back to the source of the RDG within the current TXOP

5. 802.11n allows the use of both short and long guard intervals. What are the lengths of the allowable guard intervals?

   A. 100 ns and 200 ns

   B. 200 ns and 400 ns

   C. 300 ns and 600 ns

   D. 400 ns and 800 ns

   E. 500 ns and 1000 ns

6. What type of stations can advertise that they are 40 MHz intolerant?

   A. Only HT 2.4 GHz STAs

   B. Only HT 5 GHz STAs

   C. Both HT 2.4 GHz and 5 GHz STAs

   D. Only non-HT STAs

   E. Both HT and non-HT 20 MHz STAs

7. Each A-MPDU must be acknowledged by _____.

   A. an ACK frame

   B. a non-ACK frame

   C. a BlockAck frame

   D. an A-MPDU ACK action frame

8. Which statement correctly describes transmit beamforming feedback methods?

   A. Both the beamformer and beamformee estimate the channel in implicit feedback.

   B. In implicit feedback, the beamformee estimates the channel, and in explicit feedback the beamformer estimates the channel.

   C. In implicit feedback, the beamformer estimates the channel, and in explicit feedback the beamformee estimates the channel.

   D. In both implicit and explicit feedback, it is only the beamformee that estimates the channel.

9. When looking at an 802.11n packet decode in a protocol analyzer, you notice the NDP Announcement subfield set. Which of the following statements are true?

   A. The NDP Announcement field indicates that the current packet is an NDP.

   B. The next packet you will see in your protocol analyzer will be an NDP.

   C. This packet is requesting the receiver sends an NDP sounding frame.

   D. An NDP will follow the current frame but will not be seen by a protocol analyzer.

10. Over-the-air calibration is used with which of the following HT enhancements?

   A. Implicit transmit beamforming

   B. Explicit transmit beamforming

   C. Antenna selection

   D. STBC

   E. Spatial multiplexing

11. ASEL is a MIMO antenna diversity method that can be used when _____.

   A. a station has more radio chains than antennas

   B. a station has more antennas than radio chains

   C. a station has the same number of radio chains as antennas

   D. a station has more or less radio chains than antennas but not the same.

12. The MFB/ASELC subfield of the HT Control field is interpreted as ASELC when the MAI subfield of the HT Control field is set to which value?

   A. 4

   B. 6

   C. 8

   D. 14

   E. 16

   F. 18

13. Which of the following statements is true with regard to the relationship between the primary and secondary channels?

   A. The secondary channel can be any selectable channel in the same frequency band as the primary channel.

   B. The secondary channel must be one channel directly above the primary.

   C. The secondary channel must be one channel directly below the primary channel.

   D. The secondary channel must be one channel directly above or below the primary channel.

14. In an HT BSS, which has no protection mechanisms enabled, the access point will be in which of the following modes?

   A. Mode 0: Greenfield

   B. Mode 1: Nonmember

   C. Mode 2: 20 MHz protection

   D. Mode 3: HT Mixed

15. Space Time Block Coding improves which of the following? (Choose all that apply.)

   A. The throughput of a BSS

   B. The range of a BSS

   C. The STA capacity of a BSS

   D. The receive signal strength

16. Dual CTS is a protection mechanism required for use with which HT technology?

   A. STBC

   B. TxBF

   C. SM

   D. ASEL

17. Which of the following statements is true regarding PCO?

    A. Dual CTS is used to protect HT transmission during the 40 MHz phase.

    B. HT STAs are not allowed to transmit outside the 40 MHz phase.

    C. No protection mechanisms are needed during the 40 MHz phase.

    D. PCO can only be enabled by an access point when in Greenfield mode 0.

18. The Basic MCS Set field in the HT Operation Element found in Beacon, Reassociation Response, and Probe Response frames advertises which of the following?

    A. All MCS supported by the access point.

    B. MCS supported by all associated STAs.

    C. The MCS that all beacon frames will be transmitted at.

    D. The BSSs required MCS.

19. Which subfield found within a beacon frame lists the HT MCS supported by the access point?

    A. Basic MCS Set

    B. RX MCS Bitmask

    C. TX MCS Set Defined

    D. Support Data Rates

20. What is the purpose of link adaptation?

    A. Establishes STA-to-STA communication

    B. Allows a Beamformer to estimate the channel in order to calculate a steering matrix

    C. Performs over-the-air calibration to reduce the differences between a STA's transmit and receive radio chains

    D. Dynamically assigns an MCS

Answers to Review Questions

1. D. When two 20 MHz HT channels are bonded together, there is no need to reserve the bandwidth at the bottom of the higher channel and at the top end of the lower channel. Therefore, an HT (802.11n) 40 MHz channel uses this spectral space to add two more subcarriers, giving a total of 114 subcarriers instead of 112.

2. B. L-SIG TXOP protection is an optional Physical layer protection mechanism, which uses the L-SIG (Legacy Signal) field in the HT mixed PPDU header.

3. A. The original purpose of this bit was to indicate that data must be sent using a strictly ordered class of service. When set to 1, it tells the receiving station that frames must be processed in order. This is still the correct interpretation of the order bit in non-QoS frames; however, it is rarely used, and you are unlikely to see it set to anything but 0. The introduction of QoS into the 802.11 standard through the 802.11e amendment negated the need for an order bit, and it was always set to 0 in QoS frames. However, with the 802.11n amendment, this unused bit now has a purpose again. When set to 1 in QoS data and management frames, it indicates that they contain a HT Control field.

4. D. When using the RD Protocol, a STA, having obtained a transmit opportunity (TXOP), may grant other STAs (through the use of a RDG) the opportunity to transmit data back within the same TXOP, without requiring the responding STA to contend for the medium before transmission.

5. D. 802.11n uses an 800-nanosecond guard interval; however, a shorter 400-nanosecond guard interval is optional. A shorter guard interval results in a shorter symbol time, which has the effect of increasing data rates by about 10 percent.

6. A. An access point that receives frames with the Forty MHz Intolerant bit set, or reports it, is not allowed to operated a 20/40 MHz BSS. Advertising 40 MHz intolerant is only allowed by HT 2.4 GHz STAs. HT 5 GHz STAs will always set the Forty MHz Intolerant subfield to 0, indicating that 20/40 BSSs are permissible.

7. C. Each A-MPDU must be acknowledged by a BlockAck containing an acknowledgment for each in MPDU within the A-MPDU.

8. C. When using implicit feedback, the beamformer estimates the channel characteristics from the High Throughput Long Training fields (HT_LTF) in PPDUs it receives from the beamformee. When using explicit feedback, the beamformee estimates the channel characteristics from the High Throughput Long Training Fields (HT_LTF) in PPDUs it receives from the beamformer. The beamformee then sends this information to the beamformer to use in calculating its steering matrix.

9. D. The NDP Announcement subfield indicates that an NDP will follow the current frame. Because NDPs are PPDUs that do not contain an MPDU, you will not see them in a protocol analyzer.

10. A. Differences between transmit and receive chains in a STA degrade the performance of implicit beamforming. Through over-the-air calibration, a set of correction matrices can be calculated that reduces the differences between a STA's transmit and receive chains.

11. B. Antenna selection (ASEL) is a MIMO antenna diversity method used when a STA has more antennas than radio chains. An STA uses ASEL to dynamically create a time-variant mapping of antennas to radio chains, picking the combination of antennas that will yield the best signal-to-noise ratio.

12. D. The MAI (MCS request or ASEL indicator) subfield has two interpretations. When set to 14, it is an ASEL indicator, which indicates that we should interpret the MFB/ASELC subfield as an ASEL command (ASELC). Any other value for the MAI subfield is interpreted as an MCS request (MRQ).

13. D. The secondary channel must be one channel directly above or below the primary. The Secondary Channel Offset field in the HT Operation Element indicates whether the primary channel is bonded with the channel above or below.

14. A. In Greenfield mode, only HT radios are in use. All the HT client stations must also have the same operational capabilities. In this mode there is no need for protection.

15. B, D. When implementing Space Time Block Coding (STBC), the received signal may be improved by up to 8 dB resulting in greater range (pictured in Figure 10.57). An 8 dB increase in signal strength can yield up to 69 percent more range.

16. A. Although STBC operation using dual beacons increases the range of our BSS for STBC STAs, it also introduces a new hidden node problem. STBC STAs that are operating at the greater range will not be able to hear the shorter range non-STBC transmission within the BSS. Conversely, non-STBC STAs will not be able to understand the STBC transmissions. To combat this dual hidden node problem, the 802.11n amendment introduces a new protection mechanism called Dual CTS. Dual CTS sets the NAV in STAs that do not support STBC and STAs that can only associate and communicate used STBC because of their physical distance away from the AP.

17. C. The main advantage of PCO is that no protection mechanisms are needed during the 40 MHz operational phase.

18. B. The Basic MCS Set field shows the MCS values that are supported by all STAs within the BSS.

19. B. The 802.11n amendment defines 77 MCSs that are represented by an MCS index from 0–76. The RX MCS Bitmask subfield has one bit for each of the 77 MCSs. A value of 1 indicates support for that particular MCS.

20. D. Link adaptation allows an 802.11n wireless network to use MIMO channel variations and transmit beamforming to dynamically assign an MCS.

Chapter

11

Spectrum Analysis

IN THIS CHAPTER, YOU WILL LEARN ABOUT THE FOLLOWING:

✓ **Spectrum Analyzer Options**

✓ **Review of RF Fundamentals**

  ▪ Cycle

  ▪ Amplitude

  ▪ Frequency

  ▪ Free Space Path Loss

  ▪ Decibel (dB)

  ▪ Received Signal Strength Indicator (RSSI)

  ▪ Noise floor

  ▪ Signal-to-noise ratio (SNR)

  ▪ Receive sensitivity

  ▪ Narrow band vs. spread spectrum

  ▪ Channel widths and spectral masks

✓ **Modulation Schemes**

✓ **How Network Interface Cards (NICs) Work**

  ▪ Wired NICs

  ▪ Wireless NICs

✓ **How Spectrum Analysis Works**

  ▪ Modulation vs. raw energy

  ▪ Frequency domain vs. time domain

✓ **Displaying Spectrum Analysis Data**

- Enter the waterfall plots
- Spectrum density
- Duty cycle
- Noise floor
- Wi-Fi integration

✓ **Locating and Identifying RF Interference Devices**

- Device classification
- Techniques for locating RF devices

✓ **RF Signature Characteristics**

- Shape
- Patterns
- Uniqueness
- Frequency
- Pulse vs. constant
- Duty Cycle
- Frequency hopping

✓ **Example RF Signatures**

- Frequency hopping example
- Analog RF energy
- Jammers
- Wireless video cameras
- Microwave ovens

Before diving into the technical aspect of this chapter, we will define spectrum analysis, since it is a term that is viewed differently by many vendors and support people. Some vendors will say they offer "spectrum analysis" because their management system captures Wi-Fi frame data, and from the frame information they categorize the details about the traffic flow and the channel information that is gathered from this traffic. Thus, according to them, you have analysis by spectrum. Although this information is very important and can be very useful in diagnosing network problems, these types of products are not really providing spectrum analysis but rather frame and channel analysis.

In this chapter, you will focus on "raw" RF spectrum analysis, which means analyzing the RF signals received through the air, regardless of whether they are Wi-Fi frames generated by an 802.11 station or whether they are noise generated by a nearby microwave oven. We will cover the differences between what a Wi-Fi NIC receives and reports, compared with what spectrum analysis devices can see and report. In earlier chapters of this book, you read about the detail, organization, and processing of frames defined by the IEEE's 802.11 specifications. The IEEE additionally defines many specific issues regarding how the RF signals must be processed. One of the abilities of spectrum analysis is to see and confirm these integral pieces of RF communications that are typically unseen parts of the 802.11 protocols.

When talking about the unseen world of RF communications, we often joke about how it would be nice to have RF goggles or Geordi LaForge's visor from the TV show *Star Trek: The Next Generation*. In the fictional TV series, Geordi's visor could see the entire electromagnetic spectrum.

Throughout this book, we show the details surrounding the many different types of 802.11 frames. Wi-Fi NICs do a great job of following these frame-based protocols. Wi-Fi NICs let you see the 802.11 frames and how they are processed. Wi-Fi NICs can process the frames that are transmitted; however, they are unable to analyze the RF that is used to transmit the frames. With a spectrum analyzer, we are able to look at the RF signal itself, getting closer to the capabilities of Geordi's fictional visor.

One of the key tools or components of spectrum analyzers is color. Color is used extensively in all the spectral views that you will be looking at in this book. Although all the figures in the book are presented in black and white, electronic versions of them have been provided on the companion CD. We strongly suggest you look at these files so that you can have a better understanding of how spectrum information is presented.

Spectrum Analyzer Options

Spectrum analyzers range in price from a few hundred dollars to more than $100,000. Along with the vast range in price, there is a vast range in knowledge and skill needed to operate these different units, with operators of the expensive units practically needing advanced degrees in RF and electronics to use and understand them. The advanced units are often designed to listen in on a wide range of frequencies and can be used to analyze radio communications of many types. In this book and on the CWAP exam, you will be concentrating on the different devices that are specifically developed to help you design, maintain, and trouble-shoot an 802.11 wireless LAN.

For consistency's sake, we decided to use the output from one spectrum analyzer to generate all the figures throughout this chapter. You should reference Appendix B, "WLAN Vendor List," for a list of analyzers that are focused on the 802.11-based frequency ranges.

There are many reasons to purchase a spectrum analyzer. Understanding your need for a spectrum analyzer will help you evaluate and select the best unit to address your needs. To help you understand some of the options and features that spectrum analyzers offer, we are including the following list of options and features that are offered by the different spectrum analyzers on the market. This list will also help you understand more about the devices as you progress through this chapter and learn about how to read and interpret the output that these devices produce. Remember that we will be focusing on the options that pertain to spectrum analyzers oriented to the 802.11 market.

Frequency   There are two *frequency* ranges that you need to be concerned with, 2.4 GHz and 5 GHz. In 2009, the 802.11n amendment was ratified. This amendment supports both 2.4 GHz and 5 GHz devices. In addition to the ratification of 802.11n, many, if not the majority, of 802.11 client devices are shipping with support for both 2.4 GHz and 5 GHz transmissions. Even if you are currently only using 2.4 GHz, we recommend that any spectrum analyzer decision support both bands. Also, some spectrum analyzers are capable of monitoring the 5.470 GHz to 5.725 GHz UNII-2E channels, whereas others are not. If this band is important to you, make sure it is supported by the units you are evaluating.

Form Factor   Unfortunately, more and more laptop manufacturers are no longer including *PCMCIA* slots in their machines and instead are transitioning to *Express Card* slots or no slots at all. Some of the spectrum analyzer manufacturers have only PCMCIA units available. You can purchase an adapter to connect a PCMCIA card to an Express Card slot; however, the adapters are typically not convenient to use, especially if you need to walk around with the laptop. Many of the newer spectrum analyzers provide their adapters in a USB form factor. The USB devices are more flexible and easily interchangeable between computers.

Price Here too you will see a wide range of costs and quality. The differences in cost will usually be reflected in the quality of the hardware, along with the robustness and features of the associated software. As we stated earlier in this section, the CWAP exam and book is focused on spectrum analyzers that are geared toward the Wi-Fi market. The least expensive unit is a small USB device starting at around $40, and the most expensive units are specifically designed portable devices that cost more than $9,000, with many others in between.

Hardware Platform Most 802.11-oriented spectrum analyzers are specialty cards or adapters packaged as a USB or PCMCIA device, paired with specialty software that runs on a laptop computer. Some spectrum analyzers are specialty handheld or tablet-sized devices with the sensor either built into the unit or purchased as a module that plugs into the device. The spectrum analyzer hardware may have internal digital signal processors for doing some of the intense RF math calculations onboard; or, to save costs, some vendors use the spectrum analyzer hardware to merely collect the data from the device's antenna and then use the laptop's internal CPU for doing the number crunching and calculations. Others have dedicated chips in their devices to do this work inside the tool.

Resolution Some of the less expensive options do not have the granularity or resolution to see fast-moving frequency-hopping patterns. If you want to see and work with Bluetooth signatures, you need to be aware of this possible limitation. You should check with the vendors before purchasing to confirm that you will be able to visualize your target devices. Like many things in life, you get what you pay for.

Supporting Software Each spectrum analyzer uses software to take the captured signals and put them into human-readable form. Some devices display the data with different views. Nearly all the spectrum analyzers can generate an FFT plot. Plots that may be important to you are waterfall views or swept spectrograms to show historical RF events, duty cycle, channel utilization, device lists, channel interference, and others. What these plots look like and the importance of these plots will be discussed later in this chapter. Some programs are also capable of automatic device classification based upon known RF signatures.

Wi-Fi Integration Wi-Fi cards and spectrum analyzer cards go about seeing the RF world in slightly different ways. The Wi-Fi card can see frames and modulated bits going across the RF medium. It is one thing for a spectrum analyzer to know and recognize a variety of RF interferers' signatures but still another to speculate what the effect of that interferer will be on the wireless LAN. Enter Wi-Fi integration; this is the holy grail of 802.11 spectrum analysis. This may be the secret sauce that puts one vendor in a unique space compared with the competitors. By correlating the raw RF with the data from the Wi-Fi card, you can better understand the effects of various scenarios on your wireless network. As you can imagine, this capability will not be found in the less expensive products.

Look to spectrum analyzer vendors to be adding more integration between both the spectrum analysis cards and Wi-Fi cards. Try to get an appropriate level of Wi-Fi integration that meets your needs. The less you understand about RF fundamentals and 802.11

basics, the more you will need and benefit from the expert analysis software that is built into some of the spectrum analyzers.

> Different vendors label their screens with sometimes inconsistent naming conventions, although they are providing the same fundamental information. Check the vendors' websites to compare what screens and capabilities are offered by each of the vendors you are evaluating. You may be able to download a demo version of each of the products and perform a better comparison before determining which unit to purchase.

Review of RF Fundamentals

Before we move forward and explain the processes that spectrum analyzers use to do their thing, we first will review the basics of both RF and wired NICs to make sure that the proper groundwork and foundation is covered. RF fundamentals need to be reviewed because spectrum analysis relies heavily on RF principles. Wired and wireless NICs also need to be reviewed because it is important to understand the differences between data devices—those NIC devices that can decode bits, combine them into bytes, and then finally into frames; and spectrum analyzer devices that are not even capable of decoding a single bit yet can see a wide swath of the RF spectrum in great detail.

> Please note that there is much more detail available on both of these preliminary subjects in the *CWNA: Certified Wireless Network Administrator Official Study Guide* (Sybex, 2009). This review is merely a quick cursory overview of some of the concepts and vocabulary.

In addition to providing a basic foundation of RF fundamentals, the overview will also give you a shared vocabulary of terms used in the discussion of spectrum analysis. As stated earlier, this is by no means a detailed education in radio frequency issues but a quick review of these terms. Now let us begin our journey toward understanding spectrum analysis.

Cycle

A *cycle* is a wave form that starts at the center; climbs in energy to the highest point, called the *peak*; returns to the center; then drops to the weakest point, called the *trough*; and then finally returns to the center point, as shown in Figure 11.1. The number of cycles that occur during a one-second period of time is measured in *hertz*. Hertz is a term coined for one of the founding fathers of radio transmission, Heinrich Hertz. The distance traveled by one cycle of a wave pattern is called the *wavelength*. Cycle and wavelength are the same distance. Although a cycle is often measured from the center or zero power level, wavelength is often measured from one peak to the next simply because it is easy to identify two sequential peaks.

FIGURE 11.1   RF wave: cycle and wavelength

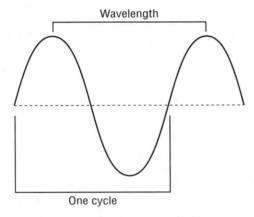

Amplitude

The *amplitude* of a wave is defined as the height, force, or power of the wave (see Figure 11.2). RF power is typically measured in watts; however, the power used by Wi-Fi devices is significantly less, measured in *milliwatts (mW)*, or one-thousandths of a watt. The more energy put into a wave, the larger or taller the wave. This higher wave would have more amplitude; the difference between the lower amplitude and the new higher one is referred to as gain. The opposite of gain is attenuation, also referred to as loss. When the wave gets smaller, or decreases in energy as it travels, we call that attenuation. RF waves attenuate as they pass through different materials. RF even attenuates without passing through any material, simply because of the decrease in energy as the waves travel. This is known as free space loss.

FIGURE 11.2   Amplitude of a wave

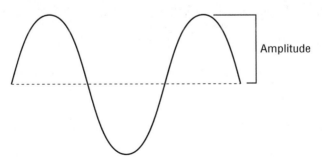

Frequency

Frequency can be defined as the number of cycles that occur within one second. For this discussion, we will be dealing with very large numbers. 2.4 GHz Wi-Fi equipment generates RF waves 2.4 billion times or cycles every second. 5 GHz Wi-Fi equipment generates RF waves 5 billion times or cycles every second. As a point of comparison, AM radio stations transmit down in the much slower range of 500,000 to 2,000,000 cycles per second. Human speech and hearing is exponentially slower still in the range of 400 to 15,000 cycles per second. 802.11 transmissions happen in specific frequencies as defined and approved by various government entities worldwide. The government entities that define and monitor usage of the RF equipment are referred to as regulatory domain authorities.

Free Space Path Loss

Because of the laws of physics, an electromagnetic signal will attenuate as it travels away from the transmitter. *Free space path loss (FSPL)* is the loss of signal energy caused by the natural broadening of the waves, often referred to as beam divergence. The energy of an RF signal spreads over larger and larger areas over time. Think of the waves emanating from a pebble dropped in a pond. At the moment of impact, all the energy of the pebble converts to the wave starting at the point of impact. A second later, the wave now has a much larger circumference. But it still has the same amount of energy that it started with. However, now it must share that energy over a larger area, so the height of the wave decreases or attenuates. Another second later, the circumference of the wave again grows larger, and thus the wave height continues to decrease as the circumference of the wave increases.

In the RF world, we normally work in three dimensions. Like the wave caused by the pebble, RF waves also get weaker as they travel further from their source. The loss of power of the wave is based on the *inverse square law*, originally developed by Isaac Newton.

This law states that the change in power is equal to 1 divided by the square of the change in distance. In other words, as the distance from the source of a signal doubles, the energy is spread out over four times the area, resulting in one-fourth of the original intensity of the signal. There is a logarithmic formula to explain this phenomena, but in short simple terms, as you double the distance from the transmitter, the wave has lost four times its starting energy. If you double the distance, the amount of energy of the wave will be one quarter of its starting energy. In addition to FSPL, any materials the RF signal must pass through only exacerbate the signal loss, which adds even more attenuation.

Here are the logarithmic formulas to calculate free space path loss:

$FSPL = 36.6 + (20\log_{10}(f)) + (20\log_{10}(d))$

FSPL = path loss in dB

f = frequency in MHz

d = distance in miles between antennas

FSPL = 32.4 + $(20\log_{10}(f))$ + $(20\log_{10}(d))$

FSPL = path loss in dB

f = frequency in MHz

d = distance in kilometers between antennas

Decibel (dB)

A *decibel (dB)* is a unit of comparison. You could use dB to compare sound to silence. You could use dB to compare the number of gray hairs today vs. the gray hairs prior to your children being teenagers. dB is merely a unit used to compare numbers, usually for comparing numbers that are drastically different. Comparing 10,000,000 to 3—now that is a big comparison. What kind of chart could you make that would realistically show the difference between 3 and 10,000,000?

Decibels take advantage of the math of logarithms. Normal intelligent people are pretty good at most simple mathematics—adding, subtracting, multiplying, and possibly even doing squares and square roots. But most of us cannot easily do logarithms in our heads. If you want to perform the RF math calculations using the logarithmic formulas, here they are:

dBm = $10 \times \log_{10}(\text{mW})$

mW = $10^{(\text{dBm}/10)}$

With respect to Wi-Fi RF, we normally use a milliwatt to describe the amount of electromagnetic energy used in radio transmissions. You can convert mW to dBm. That is, use the math behind the dB logarithmic formula to change mW to dBm. See Chapter 3 of the *CWNA Official Study Guide* for further details. For this discussion concerning spectrum analysis, we will continue to show our energy received in dBm and leave it to you to convert to milliwatts if you so need. Most, if not all, spectrum analysis can be performed totally using dBm values.

Received Signal Strength Indicator

Received signal strength indicator (RSSI) is a metric that is specified by measuring the amount of energy associated with the bits received via the wireless NIC. Each vendor calculates this value differently. RSSI is sometimes shown in dBm and sometimes converted into a percentage. This is the term most people refer to when they say "signal." RSSI will be discussed in more detail later in this chapter.

Noise Floor

Noise floor is the ambient or background level of radio energy on the specific channel you are analyzing. This can include modulated or encoded bits from other 802.11 stations in the area or nonmodulated energy coming from other devices such as microwave ovens, Bluetooth, portable telephones, and so on.

Signal-to-Noise Ratio

Signal-to-noise Ratio (SNR) can be presented as a dB value or as the difference between the RSSI (signal) and the noise floor (noise) (see Figure 11.3). For example, if the RSSI is -68 dBm and the noise floor is -85 dBm, the SNR would be -68 minus -85 or an SNR of 17dB. SNR is an important value to be familiar with because it is used extensively in RF communications. RF devices often require a minimum SNR to provide a certain level of communications. The SNR requirements often vary between different device types, models, and brands.

FIGURE 11.3 Signal-to-noise ratio

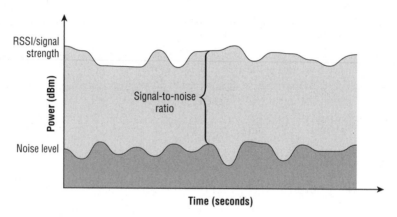

Receive Sensitivity

Receive sensitivity refers to the power level of an RF signal required to be successfully received by the receiver radio. The lower the power level that the receiver can successfully process, the better the receive sensitivity. Vendors develop 802.11 Wi-Fi devices with different abilities to discern a 1 bit or a 0 bit in different RF environments. The receive sensitivity of an 802.11 station is also closely tied to data rates. Different speeds use different modulation techniques and encoding methods, and the higher data rates use encoding methods that are more susceptible to corruption. The lower data rates use modulation-encoding methods that are less susceptible to corruption. Determining what data rate to transmit at often includes monitoring the receive sensitivity, RSSI, SNR, transmission retries, and bit error rates.

Narrow Band vs. Spread Spectrum

Ever since Marconi started working with radio signals, we have used the word *channel* to define the specific frequency or range of frequencies for transmitting and receiving. This has historically meant a small *narrow-band* or range of RF energy grouped tightly around a defined frequency. In developing the protocols to transmit larger amounts of data, 802.11 engineers needed a new broader spectrum to carry more information. They defined new, wider *spread spectrum* groups of frequencies. Figure 11.4 shows a rudimentary comparison of how a narrow-band and spread spectrum signal relate to each other. Sadly, the same word, *channel*, was used to define these larger groups of frequencies. The problem that arises is that these larger groups of defined frequencies (channels) overlap with other channels, as shown in Figure 11.5. Thus, we have issues with co-channel and adjacent-channel interference when unknowledgeable people do not choose channels carefully. Unfortunately, in 2.4 GHz 802.11 we use spread spectrum channels that, if not selected properly, have significant overlap.

FIGURE 11.4   Narrow-band vs. spread spectrum

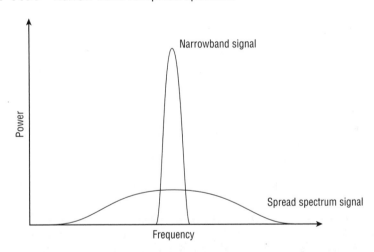

FIGURE 11.5   2.4 GHz channel overlay diagram

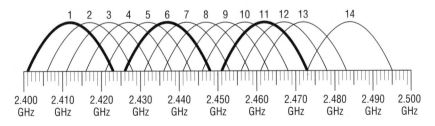

Channel Widths and Spectral Masks

One of the desires with respect to using spread spectrum RF energy was to limit or define a very specific level of energy within this wide band of frequencies. To achieve this, the developers used something called a spectral mask, which is essentially nothing more than a frequency spectrum template.

For 802.11b and its associated data rates of 1, 2, 5.5, and 11, the 22 MHz wide *spectral mask* is used (see Figure 11.6). Note the drastic falling off of energy on both sides. Also notice how wide this mask is and how many frequencies are being used to carry a single "channel" of RF energy.

FIGURE 11.6   22 MHz spectral mask

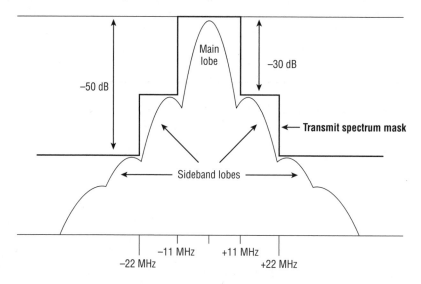

Although it is very common to represent the RF signal of a particular channel with an arch-type line (as shown in Figure 11.5), this is not a true representation of the signal. In addition to the main carrier frequency, or main frequency, sideband carrier frequencies are also generated. The transmit spectrum mask is defined to minimize interference between devices on different frequencies. Even though the sideband carrier frequencies are mere whispers of signals compared to the main carrier frequency, even a whisper is noticeable when the person whispering is close to you. This is true for RF devices too.

Figure 11.7 represents RF signals on channels 1, 6, and 11 (please note that this figure is simplified and not drawn to scale). A signal-level line indicates an arbitrary level of reception by the access point on channel 6. At level 1, meaning the AP on channel 6 receives only the signals above the level 1 line, the signals from channel 1 and channel 11 do not intersect (interfere) with the signals on channel 6. However, at the level 2 line, the signals from channel 1 and channel 11 do intersect (interfere) slightly with the signals on channel 6. At the level 3 line, there is significant interference from the signals from channel 1 and channel 11.

FIGURE 11.7   Sideband carrier frequency interference

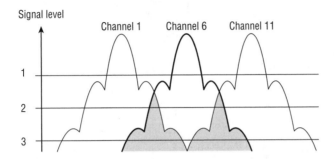

For 802.11g and 802.11a devices that use the OFDM encoding scheme, a 20 MHz spectral mask is used and looks entirely different from the spectral mask for an 802.11b device (see Figure 11.8). OFDM allows for a more dense spectral efficiency, providing higher data throughput than achievable in the BPSK/QPSK encoding schemes of 802.11b.

FIGURE 11.8   20 MHz spectral mask

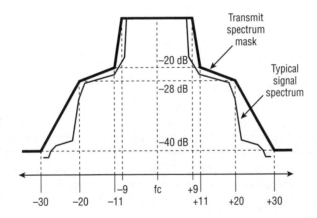

With the advent of 802.11n, we now have an additional spectral mask to deal with. This is the optional OFDM 40MHz channel (see Figure 11.9). Although the 40 MHz wide channel is referred to as channel bonding, it is not two unique 20 MHz channels bonded together but rather an entirely new 40 MHz wide channel that exists across what would have been two 20 MHz channels.

FIGURE 11.9   40 MHz spectral mask

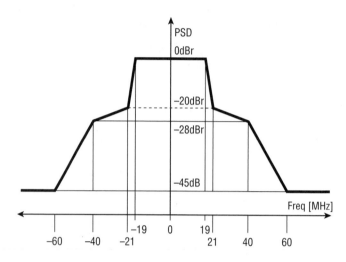

Modulation Schemes

To send data via radio waves, we need to find a way to take the 0s and 1s and encode them into a radio wave in such a way that they can be successfully delivered to the remote device. You could use a very simple encoding scheme. If you want to send a 1, you could send a loud, read strong, wave; and if you want to send a 0, you could send a quiet, or weak wave. Using this very rudimentary method, you could send one bit per cycle. If you were transmitting in the 2.4 GHz frequency range, you would send 2.4 billion bits per second. Though this seems like quite a high rate of data transmission, it is a little misleading. To successfully transmit data, the node that you are sending the data to needs to receive all the data bits in the proper order and without losing any.

When transmitting data, errors can occur. A counter known as *bit error rate (BER)* is used to keep track of transmission errors. There are some very detailed and high-level mathematical ways of showing BER, but to keep it simple, it is essentially counting all the bits sent and comparing that value with the number of bits that showed errors. The result works out to be the number of errors per total bits sent.

So, using our rudimentary *amplitude modulation* scheme, remember a 1 is a loud cycle and a 0 is a soft cycle, transmitted at 2.4 billion bits per second. Using this scenario, let us see how this may work out transmitting frames of data:

   8 bits = 1 byte

   1,500 bytes = 1 frame

Thus:

   1 frame = 12,000 bits

Using the values shown previously, when you send one data frame, you are actually sending 12,000 bits. Even though you send those bits at a very high rate of speed, 2.4 billion bits per second, if you do not have flawless communications, you might have a problem. What if your BER is greater than 1 in 12,000?

If you send one frame and in that frame there is only one single corrupted bit, the receiving device collects all the bits and then runs a CRC error check against the frame. Since one of the bits is bad, the CRC fails. Thus, you must retransmit the data again. When you transmit the data a second time, the BER is still 1:12,000, and you get another error, thus another retransmission. The engineers who developed the modulation schemes used with 802.11 took this issue to bear and designed in very robust, mathematically complex modulation schemes to help take care of the BER issues inherent in RF transmissions. These modulation schemes used in Wi-Fi are called BPSK, QPSK, 16-QAM, and 64-QAM.

Again, you can visit the *CWNA: Certified Wireless Network Administrator Official Study Guide* (Sybex, 2009) for further details. For the sake of this book, you just need to know they exist and use RF waveforms differently.

How Network Interface Cards (NICs) Work

So far in this chapter we have done a quick review of some of the RF fundamentals and terms you need to be familiar with for the discussion of spectrum analysis. Unfortunately, before we can delve into spectrum analysis, we will need to take one more detour and provide some knowledge about how network interface cards (NICs) function. After this section, we promise we will begin discussing spectrum analysis.

Wired NICs

Let us begin by going into the "wayback machine" and traveling to the early 1980s. The team at 3Com took the nascent Ethernet protocol and started selling it to the public. With the introduction of Ethernet cards, the electronics on these cards would allow for transmitting and receiving of frames. These frames were strings of bits. Each bit would have to be transmitted and received.

The protocol used an encoding system called Manchester Encoding (see Figure 11.10). This was a protocol that caused electrical current to change its state in a specific pattern to indicate a 0 or a 1. With Manchester Encoding, a high-to-low transition at the middle of the bit period indicates a 0 bit, and a low-to-high transition at the middle of the bit period indicates a 1 bit. This technique allows for a transmission rate of up to 10 Mbps.

FIGURE 11.10   Manchester signal encoding

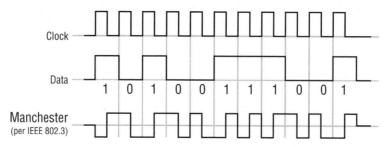

When the various Ethernet vendors were looking to speed up the data transmission speeds, they needed new technical protocol that could transmit and receive more bits of data in shorter periods of time. So, 100 Mbps Ethernet started using new encoding schemes called Non-Return-to-Zero, Invert-on-One and its partner in crime, Multiple Level Transition – 3 Levels (MLT-3). And to answer your question, you do not need to remember these. We are just highlighting that each change in network capability required a change in the encoding methodology.

If you look at the current state of wired networking, you can see that you are using 1 Gbps Ethernet connections, and as you may imagine, gigabit Ethernet has its own encoding process. This one is even more complex and mathematically intricate than previous encoding schemes, which is typical; it is called 8B/10B encoder/decoder and works on entire octets of data rather than single bits. As you move toward 10 Gbps communications protocols, you will see further refinements and advancements in the encoding schemes.

In each of these options, the wired NIC listens across its copper pairs, sensing the changes in electrical current, and interprets these currents as 0s or 1s and combines these bits into strings of data. These strings of bits make up frames, constituted by the Preamble, Header, Data Payload, and finally a Frame Check Sequence (FCS) or CRC, which is used whether or not all of the enclosed bits were received accurately.

The NIC strips off the preamble, checks the destination MAC address to see whether the frame is targeted for this specific NIC or whether the frame is addressed as a multicast or broadcast address. If the MAC address of the frame is not destined for this NIC, then it is discarded. If this frame is addressed to be received by this station or if it is a broadcast or multicast, the header is then stripped off. Finally, the FCS or CRC is calculated to ensure that all the included bits were accurate. At this point, the data payload is sent up the protocol stack to the OS as a designated and approved frame.

Wireless NICs

Enough with the wired side, the CWAP is a wireless certification. It is time to move on to the wireless NICs of today. Unlike their wired counterparts, wireless NICs do not have the advantage of a bounded media like copper or fiber. So instead of using the changes in current or voltage across a copper pair, wireless NICs have to add some additional features.

Instead of the copper connection of an Ethernet NIC, a wireless 802.11 NIC has an antenna. Wireless antennas are designed for specific ranges of frequencies. This allows the antenna to only pass the RF energy for the frequencies that they are designed to operate on. In the case of 802.11b/g, we are referring to radio waves in the 2.4 GHz ISM bands. The antenna is designed specifically to focus on this frequency. Here again, there are some pretty complex mathematics around antenna design, but for the sake of our discussion, these antennas try to block radio waves except 2.4 GHz. Blocking all radio waves from other frequencies is not possible; however, the design of the antennas helps to at least reduce the amount of signal received on other frequencies.

Think for a moment about all the radio waves that you bump into every second of the day. The list is immense, including AM radio, FM radio, satellite radio, police bands, aviation bands, global positioning satellite, HAM operator bands, cell phones, broadcast television, cordless telephones, garage door openers, and many, many more. This list does not even mention any of the devices that radiate RF unintentionally such as lights and motors. To make sense out of all of this RF chaos, the antennas for each of the different types of RF equipment are designed to block the unwanted frequencies or respond to a certain range of frequencies.

So, the first line of defense for the 802.11b/g wireless NIC is its antenna, out there attempting to block all but the 2.4 GHz waves. Unfortunately, even though the antenna focuses on only 2.4 GHz waves, it cannot focus solely on just 802.11b/g signals. Other non-802.11b/g radio signals may be received also. The 2.4 GHz band is an unlicensed band, and many devices are legally able to transmit in this range. Thus, your wireless NIC's antenna will receive RF signals from cordless telephones, Bluetooth transmissions, wireless security cameras, and even microwave oven radiation. All of these devices use the same 2.4 GHz frequency range.

To try to isolate the 802.11b/g signals from the other types of 2.4 GHz signals, the developers of the wireless NICs came up with a second line of defense. This second line of defense is designed to filter out the unwanted RF. To understand this, we refer to our encoding schemes. Since the 10/100/1000 Ethernet encoding schemes are copper dependent, unfortunately they could not be used for wireless communications. Instead, the engineers designed different robust, complex protocols that are capable of discerning 0s from 1s out of RF energy. These encoding schemes are those that we mentioned previously—BPSK, QPSK, 16-QAM, and 64-QAM, like in the ever-increasing and ever more complex world of Ethernet.

As with Ethernet encoding schemes, 802.11 encoding schemes have also become more complex. For Ethernet to move from 10 Mbps to 100 Mbps to 1000 Mbps, the encoding systems increased in complexity. As 802.11 speeds increase, a similar transition occurred with the wireless encoding schemes. Over the years, 802.11 wireless networks have increased the speeds of data transmissions by moving from BPSK used in 1 and 2 Mbps transmissions to QPSK used in 5.5 and 11 Mbps transmissions finally on to the even higher 54 Mbps transmissions supported by OFDM. As the radio signal is processed by this filter, which is based on the encoding systems supported by the wireless NIC, we can now finally see the bits. Just like in the wired NIC, the bits are strung together into a string of 0s and 1s, and in the format of preamble, header, frame body, and FCS. Again, just like the wired NIC, the preamble is discarded, the header is processed to see whether the frame is targeted for the wireless device, and finally the FCS is calculated to ensure that all the included bits were accurate. At this point, the data payload is sent up the protocol stack to the OS as a designated and approved frame.

All of these tasks are just like the ones performed by a wired NIC. However, there are a few differences between the processes performed by the wired and wireless NICs. First, the wireless NIC must use its antenna and encoding filter to keep out all unwanted RF signals and thus unwanted bits as well. There is another unique difference between the way wireless NICs and wired NICs process the incoming data. The wireless NIC will use some of the specific information gleaned from the RF to bit transition process to actually add information to the wireless frame. This additional information is added at the receiving station and is in addition to the bits sent from the source. This added information is called the *Radiotap Header* (see Figure 11.11). It includes date and time stamps, channel stamp, signal stamp, and a noise stamp. The date and time stamps are obvious. The channel stamp is based on the frequency that the NIC was on while it received this bit stream.

FIGURE 11.11   Radiotap Header

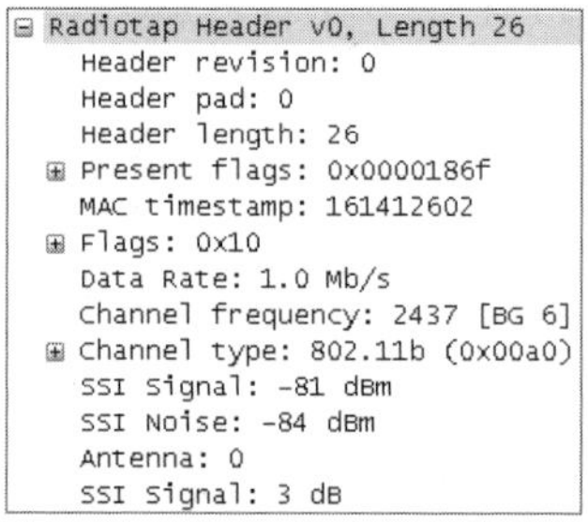

```
⊟ Radiotap Header v0, Length 26
    Header revision: 0
    Header pad: 0
    Header length: 26
  ⊞ Present flags: 0x0000186f
    MAC timestamp: 161412602
  ⊞ Flags: 0x10
    Data Rate: 1.0 Mb/s
    Channel frequency: 2437 [BG 6]
  ⊞ Channel type: 802.11b (0x00a0)
    SSI Signal: –81 dBm
    SSI Noise: –84 dBm
    Antenna: 0
    SSI Signal: 3 dB
```

The next piece of information has its own name and is RSSI. The 802.11-2007 standard defines the RSSI as a relative metric used by 802.11 radios to measure signal strength (amplitude). The 802.11 RSSI measurement parameter can have a value from 0 to 255. The RSSI value is designed to be used by the WLAN hardware manufacturer as a relative measurement of the RF signal strength that is received by an 802.11 radio. RSSI metrics are typically mapped to receive sensitivity thresholds expressed in absolute dBm values, as shown in Table 11.1. For example, an RSSI metric of 255 might represent –30 dBm of received signal amplitude. The RSSI metric of 0 might be mapped to –110 dBm of received signal amplitude. Though RSSI may be calculated differently by various vendors, we still use it and put trust in the number as the true amount of RF energy received by the NIC.

TABLE 11.1   RSSI metrics (vendor example)

RSSI	Receive sensitivity threshold	Signal strength (%)	Signal-to-noise ratio	Signal quality (%)
30	−30 dBm	100%	70 dB	100%
25	−41 dBm	90%	60 dB	100%
20	−52 dBm	80%	43 dB	90%
21	−52 dBm	80%	40 dB	80%
15	−63 dBm	60%	33 dB	50%
10	−75 dBm	40%	25 dB	35%
5	−89 dBm	10%	10 dB	5%
0	−110 dBm	0%	0 dB	0%

We stated that the channel stamp indicated the channel that the NIC was on while it received a bit stream, not the channel that the data was transmitted on. This is an important piece of information for troubleshooting because the transmitter and receiver could be on different channels that are near each other.

It would be very nice if all wireless NIC manufacturers of both stations and access points would adopt a standard for calculating RSSI and presenting RF information from their various devices. But, alas, we do not foresee this happening any time in the near future. The good news is that another measurement, *received channel power indicator (RCPI)*, has in many instances replaced RSSI. RCPI is an 8-bit value ranging from 0 to 220, incrementing by .5 dB. The RCPI values begin at -110 dBm and increment to 0 dBm.

The final bit of information in the Radiotap Header is a variable for noise. To reemphasize, the wireless NIC is not a spectrum analyzer, and though it can transmit and receive data at a prodigious rate, it cannot see raw ambient RF signals. Since the only things getting past the NIC's encoding filter are bits, all of the information reported by the NIC must come from the bits it receives. If you turn on a microwave oven near a wireless NIC, there are no data bits being generated by the microwave, so the NIC will always report a noise variable of zero. Remember that this is because wireless NICs require bits in order to do their magic. You should pause here for a moment to let this fact sink in. In the absence of encoded RF signals coming from other 802.11 devices, the noise variable cannot be used to report the noise floor. We know that you may have seen many screens generated by your various 802.11 devices that display signal (from the RSSI variable) and another value displayed as SNR or signal-to-noise ratio, showing the comparison between the RSSI and the noise floor. The developers of the wireless NICs knew that the RF folks out there "live, breathe, and die" by signal, noise, and signal-to-noise ratio data. These RF engineers demanded a noise variable in order to perform their RF calculations, so various vendor organizations came up with unique ways to guess the noise floor. Since 802.11 wireless NICs can only process bits, they needed to come up with algorithms to calculate a noise variable based on the bits going through the NIC.

By the way, like RSSI, each vendor that manufactures 802.11 equipment calculates noise in a different way. Some vendors flatly refused to make up a number for noise only based on bits. Other vendors have developed very sophisticated algorithms for calculating noise. More recently some 802.11 chip manufactures have figured out how to turn off the encoding filters and use the RF signals coming through the antenna to become rudimentary spectrum analyzers. However, this is in lieu of being an 802.11 NIC capable of processing data. These new chips can be either a lightweight spectrum analyzer or a Wi-Fi card processing data, but never both at the same time. Some of the access point vendors are also using these extra-capable Wi-Fi chips and are adding spectrum analysis as an option for an access point with the appropriate software to take advantage of this extra ability.

With this data resulting from the Radiotap Header information, a wireless NIC can learn about the environment around it by scanning and listening to the different channels available. Many Wi-Fi tools use this technique to learn of the RF environment, such as NetStumbler and inSSIDer. Some vendors also use this same technique of listening in on channels to determine data points to help in their automatic channelizing and power balancing systems. However, none of these devices can see raw ambient RF; they only see what is received in the form of bits or modulated RF encoded by one of our protocols.

How Spectrum Analysis Works

Spectrum analysis is used to determine the spectral composition of audio, electrical, optical, or radio waveforms. We will be discussing spectrum analysis to focus on radio waves in the specific frequencies for Wi-Fi data communications, 2.4 GHz and 5 GHz. In the following sections, we will discuss the fundamentals of spectrum analysis and how it differs from packet analysis.

Modulation vs. Raw Energy

To introduce this section, we want you to remember the first time you used a pixel-based "paint" program, either on a Macintosh or Windows computer. No matter which paint program you used, they both kind of worked alike. It was fun to draw circles and squares and the like. However, if you wanted to edit your drawing, you had to erase and then redraw the section that you were trying to edit. The same was true with drawing and editing text within these programs. It felt perfectly natural to use the keyboard to type words in these paint programs and then to make changes to the font, size, or other features of the text. However, once you saved or committed the text to your drawing, the text, which initially was ASCII characters that you typed, was converted to a picture with the attributes you defined. After the text was converted into a graphic, you could no longer edit the text but had to erase and replace it just like any of the graphics you created.

Remembering that experience, we can delve into one of the key differences between an 802.11 Wi-Fi card and a spectrum analyzer. The Wi-Fi card deals with data, bits, frames, and so on. These are hard-coded into the Wi-Fi card. It can process these bits at astonishingly fast rates of 2.4 billion or 5 billion times a second. Wi-Fi cards are great at decoding the modulated bits encoded into RF energy. Those encoding schemes as we have discussed earlier—BPSK, QPSK, 16-QAM, and 64-QAM—can also be seen by the spectrum analyzer, but the spectrum analyzer does not have the filtering capability to interpret the modulated bits. It is only capable of seeing the raw energy of the RF signal. To the spectrum analyzer, the signal is just graphics with a signature shape. The spectrum analyzer cannot decode any bits at all from the RF energy.

So to recap, a spectrum analyzer can see the graphical shape of encoded RF energy but cannot decode any of the bits. By contrast, a Wi-Fi card can decode the bits at amazingly fast rates but cannot see the graphical shapes of the RF signal.

Frequency Domain vs. Time Domain

Another difference between the two types of cards is the domains they use. We will describe these two domains by using a couple of examples. The first is the *time domain*. The time domain is where the horizontal axis of the graphs you look at is calibrated by time. One example might be in a hospital where you have seen an electrocardiograph (ECG) machine. These machines monitor the electrical impulses that occur in the heart, representing the information over a period of time. Each heartbeat leaves behind a unique signature on the screen. The horizontal axis is time, and the vertical axis is based on the strength of the electrical impulse generated by the heartbeat.

The next domain is the *frequency domain*. In this view, the horizontal axis does not represent time but rather frequency. This is the main view of spectrum analyzers. The horizontal axis is defined by the frequencies of RF energy that you are monitoring, and the vertical axis represents how loud or strong the RF energy is, calibrated to decibels. Figure 11.12 shows the output of a spectrum analyzer displayed in a frequency domain format.

FIGURE 11.12   Sample FFT plot

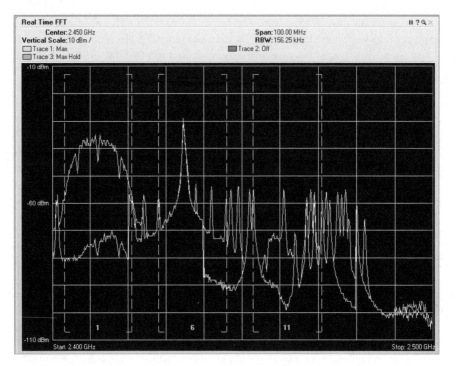

We can use both the time domain and the frequency domain to view the same RF energy. Since the frequencies of RF energy are very high and since we are not able to see or hear them, we will use sound waves to demonstrate this capability. We are using sound waves because most people are familiar with sound and the difference between different frequencies. Additionally, it is likely that sometime in your life you have seen a visual representation of a sound wave either at school, on television, or on the Internet.

We will start with the time domain view of a sound by using something as simple as a tuning fork.

If you plot the time domain view of a tuning fork's sound, it would look much like the image in Figure 11.13. By design, the tuning fork transmits sound waves at a perfect frequency, only slowly dissipating in the height or volume of the wave over time as energy is lost.

Another way to plot the sound generated by this same tuning fork is shown in the frequency domain view (see Figure 11.14). Since the tuning fork has only a solitary frequency, the frequency domain view shows a very simple view: a single spike on that individual frequency.

FIGURE 11.13   Tuning fork in time domain

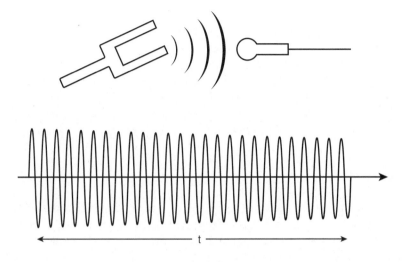

FIGURE 11.14   Tuning fork in frequency domain

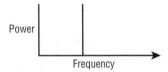

We will explain this a little differently. When you first started to learn algebra, one of the tasks you learned to do was to plot the results of an equation on a graph using a Cartesian coordinate system: the x-axis and y-axis and the little "T"-table. You were probably taught to enter a sequential series of X values and then calculate the corresponding Y values. The X values typically consisted of positive numbers, negative numbers, and 0.

If the equation was something like $y=x^2$ and the X coordinates were whole numbers from -2 to +2, then the T table would like this:

X	Y
-2	4
-1	1
0	0
1	1
2	4

Based on the equation and the T-table, the resulting graph can be plotted, as shown in Figure 11.15, with the graph ending up as a parabola.

FIGURE 11.15   The graph of a parabola

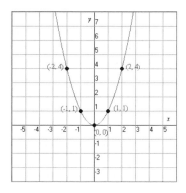

After starting with a simple equation and graph, you then learned that the more complex the equation was, the more complex the graph became. As you moved on in your math career, you learned even more equations and more graphs. You also learned that some graphs such as sine and cosine have repeating patterns. What does all this math have to do with spectrum analysis? To bring all these stories into focus, it is just a quick thought that passed among mathematicians for years—they realized they could make a curve from any equation, but could they get an equation from any curve?

The Fourier Transform in Spectrum Analysis

Joseph Fourier led a very eventful and interesting life—at least more interesting than most mathematicians of his time. An orphan at an early age, he had to live by his wits, and folks around him noticed his quick intelligence. Thus, he was educated at some of the best institutions in France. He was also involved in the politics of the French Revolution, and from that he won an appointment to a prestigious science post.

Noticed by none other than Napoleon Bonaparte, Fourier accompanied the emperor on his conquest of Egypt and was appointed Governor of Egypt for a time. For our part here, we will use his name in spectrum analysis for the process he invented, of taking a known curve and doing a calculation to derive its equation. This has been called a Fourier transform. A faster more efficient algorithm was developed to perform these calculations, which became known as a *fast Fourier transform (FFT)*.

If you take a time domain curve and desire to transform it into a frequency domain curve, you would apply something called a fast Fourier transform (see the sidebar "The Fourier Transform in Spectrum Analysis"). This process takes a complex waveform (see Figure 11.16) and first breaks it into simpler component parts. Then each of these simple parts is graphed against a frequency domain x-axis, as shown in Figure 11.17.

FIGURE 11.16   Complex waveform to component parts

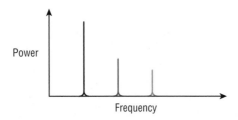

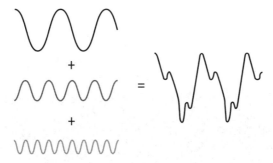

FIGURE 11.17   Converting time domain to frequency domain

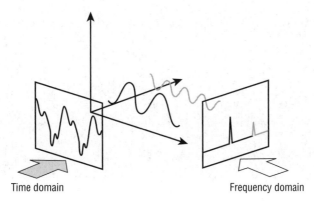

Time domain   Frequency domain

In spectrum analysis, you rely heavily on this FFT process to take the complex wave-forms of RF energy and break them down into their simpler component parts that you can then analyze and plot using a variety of views. This FFT process is fairly CPU intensive. Some vendor products keep their costs down by capturing only the raw RF information and then allowing the laptop's faster CPU to do the FFT process. Other vendor products put custom application-specific integrated circuits (ASICs) on board that can efficiently process the FFTs without relying on the laptop's CPU to perform the calculations.

Displaying Spectrum Analysis Data

Once the received RF energy data has been collected and processed, one of the functions or features of spectrum analyzers is to show the human user this complex data in views to help simplify the understanding. The first view is the real-time FFT plot (see Figure 11.18). In this plot, the FFT realized data is plotted with the horizontal axis as frequency, and the vertical axis is plotted as energy as defined in dBms. Different vendor options may or may not support a real-time FFT plot. This one is fairly CPU intensive and needs a lot of horsepower to plot in near real time (once every second or so). A feature of real-time FFT plots is the ability to plot not only the current FFT data but the average and max hold.

FIGURE 11.18   Real-time FFT plot

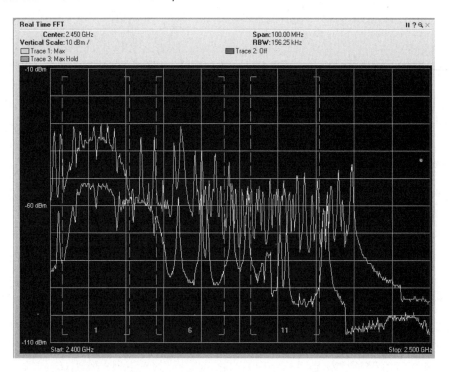

Though the FFT plot shows current RF energy across the watched spectrum, it is displaying "live," and thus you have to pay constant attention to it because it can change quickly. Unfortunately, that can be hard to do, and it is likely that you would miss or forget things that happened in the past.

In the following sections, we will cover the different plots and views that are used to display and analyze spectrum analysis information.

Enter the Waterfall Plots

In a *waterfall plot*, you use the same data from the FFT plot, but you add the dimension of time. In the FFT, the vertical axis was energy, represented in decibels, and the horizontal axis was frequency. With one type of waterfall plot, the swept spectrogram, you use the same frequency on the horizontal axis, but you are using the vertical axis to show historical data, so instead, you code the dB values into colors. You use blue for the weaker signals, then up through green, and finally on to red to show very strong signals.

So, with a waterfall plot (Figure 11.19), the spectrum analyzer takes the RF energy readings post FFT, and instead of plotting the dB values in vertical height, like in the FFT plot, it converts the dB values to color and then plots a single 1-pixel tall line at the bottom of the swept spectrogram plot. Then when the next set of data arrives, this process is repeated, with all the previous data being pushed up the stack by one row of pixels. If the sampling interval is 1 second, in order to look back at what occurred 10 seconds ago, you simply need to look up 10 pixels from the bottom, and you will see the RF energy information received in the past.

In a waterfall view, you can visualize a variety of signature from different RF devices. Some devices leave trails, some look like freckles, some pulse on and off, others are wide, and still others are quite narrow.

FIGURE 11.19   Waterfall plot

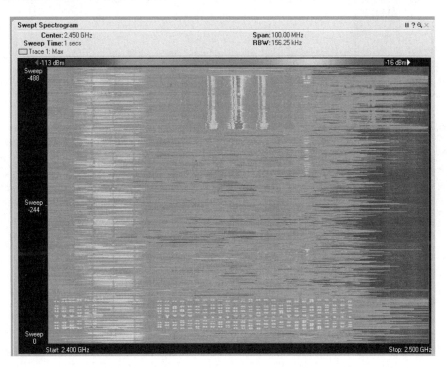

Real World Scenario

Understanding RF Signatures in Spectrum Analysis

A group of five radiology students were on their way to their national exams. They were preparing for one of the largest tests of their life, and so with a little downtime, they were quizzing each other on different X-ray examples.

One of the students would hold up an X-ray, and the others would quickly identify the body part and what symptom was being displayed. So that all five students could study at the same time, a fellow traveler offered to reveal the X-rays and help grade their answers. These guys were fast! The gentleman who was helping them could barely even recognize the bone, when the students would have already done a complete analysis of the patient's problem.

In some ways, you are starting down the same path. You have at your disposal a variety of tools and views of RF energy. Many of these seem very confusing and maybe even downright unintelligible. But you are just starting. Reading and analyzing these various plots is going to take some time and dedicated effort. Please do not get discouraged early on. Keep at it, and soon you too will be seeing the correct things in the views to help you with your wireless LAN troubleshooting.

Waterfall views can also be used to show other data sets. Viewing a duty cycle displayed as a swept spectrogram is a very useful tool to see how badly a device is causing interference.

Sometimes the waterfall type views fall up, meaning the latest information is at the bottom, with historical information moving up on the screen. Other times the most current information is displayed on the top, with the historical information falling down the screen. It does not matter which way the data flows. In either display, the latest information will be inserted in front of the previous data. If the display area is full, the oldest information will be purged from the end of the display.

Spectrum Density

Some vendors' spectrum analysis products also include a spectrum density view. Figure 11.20 shows the spectrum density view from AirMagnet Spectrum XT. In this view, the "popularity" of a specific frequency is highlighted. The horizontal axis represents frequency, and the vertical axis represents energy in decibels, with the brightness of the color being determined by how many times that specific set of information has been captured.

FIGURE 11.20   Spectrum density view

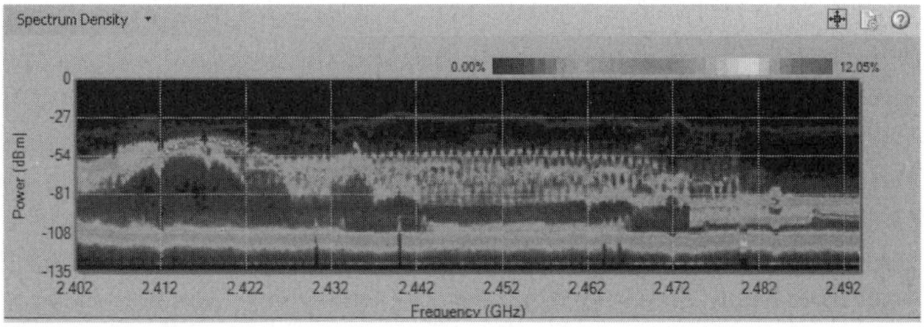

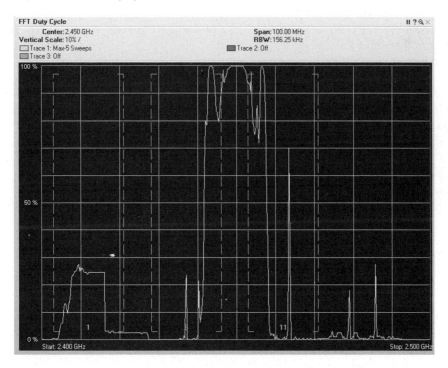

Duty Cycle

The Duty Cycle view of the FFT data gives you the ability to track how harmful the specific RF interference might be (see Figure 11.21). This view displays the percentage of time the ambient RF signal is higher than the noise floor or some other predefined signal threshold. In this view, you can see whether a device is constantly using a frequency. You may also see a very low percentage, meaning that the device was barely pulsing on and did not transmit much of the time.

FIGURE 11.21   Duty cycle view

Paired with the FFT plot, you can compare and contrast between the two. Both the duty cycle and the FFT views display the frequency in the horizontal axis. The FFT view shows vertically how loud the signal is, and the duty cycle view shows how much of a signal there is. Think of the data in these views as water coming through a hose. In the FFT view, the high dB would be a high-pressure burst of water coming through the hose. The duty cycle view is not concerned with pressure but rather the volume or amount of water that comes through the hose. So, you could experience a short high-power burst of energy, which would be displayed on the FFT view. You could also experience an extended period of low-power signal, which would be displayed on the duty cycle view. The worst scenario would be to have a high-power level signal for a high percentage of the time. In general, a high-duty cycle is far worse for RF interference than high dB.

If you are performing a spectrum analysis on a network and you see what appears to be a strong dB device in the FFT view, take a look at the signal from the duty cycle screen. If the duty cycle is very low, even though there may be a strong signal, it is not occurring often, so there is actually not much interference.

Noise Floor

Unlike Wi-Fi devices that need to see encoded and modulated bits in order to register a noise variable, spectrum analyzers can see any type of RF signal. Spectrum analyzers can see RF signals from modulated devices such as Wi-Fi NICs and can see RF signals from nonmodulated devices such as microwave ovens, and a host of other non-Wi-Fi devices. In addition, spectrum analyzers may also have the resolution or scanning sensitivity to even see frequency-hopping devices, either telephones or data devices such as older 802.11 FHSS stations or Bluetooth accessories.

The RF noise floor is defined as all the background RF signal that is received in the frequency range that your device is operating in, from any type of device whether it is generated by an intentional radiator or an unintentional radiator. Earlier in this chapter, we explained how 802.11 NICs are designed to process decoded bits. Therefore, any of the noise floor information that is generated by them is based solely on decodable 802.11 traffic, while any sources of non-802.11 noise are simply ignored. The use of Wi-Fi cards to see non-802.11 transmissions is fraught with errors. Therefore, in order to really see and determine the raw ambient RF noise, you must use a spectrum analyzer.

Because spectrum analyzers are portable and might be located physically close to an access point one minute and then far away the next, their displays have the ability to zoom in to give the user the best possible view of the RF that is being analyzed. This includes the ability to zoom in to a specific channel or to a series of frequencies. You can also use the zoom feature to zoom in on the specific pertinent information you are interested in. The ability to zoom in on specific data is a great option to have. However, like many things with great power, you must use this capability carefully and responsibly. Using the zoom capability, it is possible to recalibrate the display to make a very weak signal appear to be very strong or take a very nasty interfering device and calibrate its signal down so that it looks benign. When reviewing any view generated by a spectrum analyzer, be careful to check the scale and legend of the view. Do not automatically assume that the data you are looking at is being displayed using the default scale.

Wi-Fi Integration

As spectrum analysis tools have matured, more emphasis in their data reporting and analysis has moved toward tighter integration and correlation with Wi-Fi information. We noted earlier how Wi-Fi cards and spectrum analyzers are uniquely different in how they see and interpret RF signals. To provide a much greater overall view of what is happening on a specific channel or frequency range, it is possible to integrate and correlate the data from both of these sources.

Channel utilization is one of the places where integration of both sets of data makes perfect sense. The Wi-Fi card can use 802.11 channel information to capture and analyze the 802.11-encoded data transmitted on a specific channel. The Wi-Fi card can lock on that channel and capture the frames transmitted there. Wi-Fi cards can also scan the other channels to see whether there is data on the adjacent or overlapping channels, which can cause interference. By integrating the raw ambient RF reported by the spectrum analyzer with the channel data from the Wi-Fi NIC, we now have access to a comprehensive view of all that is happening on a given channel or range of channels. Figure 11.22 shows the integration of both spectrum analysis data and Wi-Fi data within the same analysis tool. The first three graphics in the figure are showing spectrum information in the Real Time FFT, Spectrum Density, and Spectrogram graphs. The last graphic, however is displaying individual channel information that is being interpreted from the 802.11 frames being received, since a spectrum analyzer has no knowledge of the channels, only knowledge of the frequencies.

FIGURE 11.22   Wi-Fi Integration with spectrum analyzer

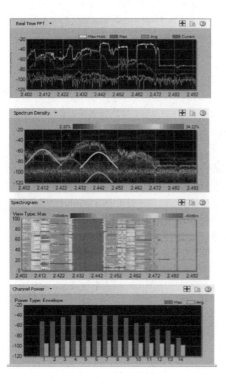

With all wireless analysis products, it behooves the reader to sit down and break open the user guide for your products. There is a wealth of information contained in the spectrum analysis product guides. The user guide will have descriptions of each screen and how the vendor implemented differing spectrum views, which is vital to understanding how to interpret the data. Without this understanding, you will simply be looking at a colorful screen of information without being able to understand what you are looking at. It is also important to realize that not all vendors support all views. Therefore, you need to check your documentation to learn about which views are supported by your product.

This integration can help with performing more detailed analysis. By combining both sets of data, you can see the effects that other Wi-Fi devices have on your network along with the effects that nonmodulated RF signals have on your Wi-Fi network. Having both sets of data can help you identify which of these two different types of RF interference may be causing problems on your network. As you also integrate the errors and reporting from the packet side, you can be even more granular in your analysis by looking at additional data that may allow you to track how the ambient RF affected retry rates on frame transmissions. The ultimate end to this integration will be seen when Wi-Fi cards are fully integrated into spectrum analysis products, as well as when spectrum analyzers are fully integrated into the Wi-Fi-based analyzers and survey tools. How sweet it will be to do a single walk-through of a site and capture both raw ambient RF and passive Wi-Fi data simultaneously. With an integrated site survey, your heat maps will be able to show Wi-Fi coverage along with being able to show any anomalies in the ambient and nonmodulated signals all in one report (Figure 11.23).

FIGURE 11.23   Survey with integrated spectrum analysis

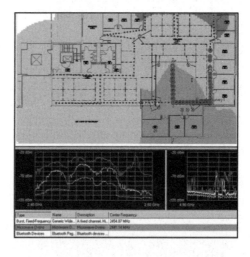

EXERCISE 11.1

Identifying Noise and Wi-Fi Cards

This exercise is designed to help you think about and understand how Wi-Fi cards process RF noise. Imagine yourself in a room that is surrounded by a Faraday cage, essentially an RF shield that prevents any outside RF energy from entering your room. You take out a laptop with a Wi-Fi card and an RF jammer. Except for these two devices, there are no other RF devices in the room. Think about each of the following four scenarios and postulate an answer.

1. With the jammer off, what does the Wi-Fi card register for noise?

2. If you turn the jammer on, now what does the Wi-Fi card register for noise?

3. A friend walks into the room and gives you an access point. The access point is turned on; however, there are no clients connected to it. Now what noise is indicated by the Wi-Fi card?

4. Ten friends with laptops join you in the room. Your friends all connect to the access point, and using FTP, they all begin to wirelessly download a very large (and funny) video file, while the jammer is still turned on. What does your Wi-Fi card report for its noise variable?

Now for the answers:

1. No noise. There are no modulated signals and thus no bits.

2. No noise. There are still no modulated signals and thus no bits to be affected by the jammer.

3. A low amount of noise. Since the access point is only beaconing, there is a small amount of modulated bits riding on RF, the jammer harms those bits, and the Wi-Fi card interprets the broken and harmed modulated bits as noise.

4. A high amount of noise shows up. There are now lots and lots of bits being transmitted across the RF medium in the form of frames. These frames are all hurt by the jammer, with lots of corrupted bits, causing the Wi-Fi card to report a high level of noise.

Note that in these scenarios, the room never changed, the Wi-Fi card never changed, and the jammer never changed. The only change was the number of bits in the air.

One final statement about Wi-Fi cards and their misrepresentation of ambient raw RF. Sometimes if the interfering device is strong enough, when a Wi-Fi device performs a physical clear channel assessment by detecting the RF energy (as opposed to a virtual CCA), it can sense that the frequency is not clear and then refuse to transmit any frames. If this occurs, there would be no frames transmitted in the air, meaning no bits flying across the RF media to be harmed by the interfering device. In this scenario, with your Wi-Fi card monitoring, the RF will show no interference and also no signal since the Wi-Fi devices are not sending any frames at all, but it will display a channel utilization at or near 100 percent.

Locating and Identifying RF Interfering Devices

In addition to identifying different types of devices that are operating near your network, it is often necessary to locate these devices and sometimes disconnect or replace them to prevent interference. In this section, we will discuss a couple of ways to track down interfering devices.

Device Classification

The first step to finding an interfering device is to determine what type of device it is. Many of the professional spectrum analysis tools offer automatic device classification, which can identify and categorize the devices based upon the signal that is received, as shown in Figure 11.24. These tools perform a task known as pattern matching. This process works by mapping the data that your spectrum analyzer is capturing against a database of known RF signatures. In the following section, "Techniques for Locating RF Devices," we will show you some of these signatures. Although computers are wonderful systems of technology and can do many marvelous things, pattern matching is a process that humans still excel at.

FIGURE 11.24   Spectrum analyzer displaying auto device classification

Device	Signal Strength (dBm)	Duty Cycle (%)	Discovery Time	On Time	Channels Affected	Network
⊟ Analog Video [4]						
Device @ 2410.12 MHz	-27.9	64	Sat May 08 13:43:06	00:01:38 (Down)	1..3	
Device @ 2443.61 MHz	-43.8	31	Sat May 08 13:46:10	00:01:07 (Down)	5..9	
Device @ 2450.30 MHz	-26.2	93	Sat May 08 13:45:46	00:01:35 (Down)	7..10	
Device @ 2456.84 MHz	-45.4	32	Sat May 08 13:46:17	00:01:05 (Down)	8..12	
⊟ Bluetooth [5]						
Bluetooth Paging/Inquiry Device(s)	-29.9		Sat May 08 13:52:19	00:02:42 (Down)	N/A	9E:8B:33
⊟ Piconet 1 [1]						
Device 1	-75.2	3	Sat May 08 13:20:20	00:06:04 (Down)	2..8;13..14	BC:F6:C0
⊟ Piconet 2 [1]						
Device 1	-60.9	3	Sat May 08 13:26:39	00:10:25 (Down)	4..8;13..14	BC:F6:C0
⊟ Piconet 3 [1]						
Device 1	-72.5	5	Sat May 08 13:39:44	00:00:05 (Down)	N/A	BC:F6:C0
⊟ Piconet 4 [1]						
Device 1	-63.4	4	Sat May 08 13:39:53	00:33:30	13..14	BC:F6:C0
⊟ Cordless Phones [11]						
DECT-Like Base Station 1	-64.0	7	Sat May 08 13:22:34	00:04:36 (Down)	1..14	10:10:FD:5C:
DECT-Like Base Station 2	-64.5	7	Sat May 08 13:27:35	00:05:16 (Down)	1..14	10:10:FD:5C:
DECT-Like Base Station 3	-28.1	3	Sat May 08 13:35:02	00:01:34 (Down)	153..165	
DECT-Like Base Station 4	-65.9	6	Sat May 08 13:42:15	00:02:21 (Down)	1..14	10:10:FD:5C:
DECT-Like Base Station 5	-63.7	4	Sat May 08 13:45:13	00:02:08 (Down)	1..8;12..14	10:10:FD:5C:
DECT-Like Base Station 6	-67.0	6	Sat May 08 13:52:14	00:03:07 (Down)	1..14	10:10:FD:5C:
DECT-Like Base Station 7	-66.3	8	Sat May 08 13:55:31	00:01:30 (Down)	1..14	10:10:FD:5C:
DECT-Like Base Station 8	-67.4	7	Sat May 08 13:58:48	00:02:32 (Down)	1..2;4..7	10:10:FD:5C:
DECT-Like Base Station 9	-66.8	8	Sat May 08 14:02:26	00:05:11 (Down)	1..14	10:10:FD:5C:
DECT-Like Base Station 10	-65.5	8	Sat May 08 14:12:25	00:01:00	1..14	10:10:FD:5C:
DECT-Like Network 1	-18.6	20	Sat May 08 13:35:44	00:00:50 (Down)	153..165	
⊟ Generic - Continuous [33]						
Device (CW) @ 2410.25 MHz	-46.4	97	Sat May 08 13:24:18	00:01:38 (Down)	1..2	
Device (CW) @ 2415.05 MHz	-44.1	96	Sat May 08 13:26:02	00:00:28 (Down)	1..3	
Device (CW) @ 2465.71 MHz	-83.6	75	Sat May 08 14:06:23	00:00:43 (Down)	10..13	
Device (CW) @ 2465.71 MHz	-83.6	72	Sat May 08 13:57:17	00:08:03 (Down)	10..13	
Device (CW) @ 2465.71 MHz	-84.2	62	Sat May 08 14:08:48	00:03:47 (Down)	10..13	
Device (CW) @ 2465.71 MHz	-84.2	45	Sat May 08 13:51:38	00:00:43 (Down)	10..13	
Device (CW) @ 2471.34 MHz	-34.9	100	Sat May 08 13:30:10	00:00:38 (Down)	11..13	
Device (CW) @ 2475.53 MHz	-34.5	100	Sat May 08 13:28:00	00:00:47 (Down)	12..14	
Device (CW) @ 5776.24 MHz	-58.9	100	Sat May 08 13:28:05	00:00:52 (Down)	157	

Think about the following scenario. You are at the park with your son. He is playing on the big toys along with a group of other children. The birds are chirping, there are traffic noises far away in the background, and people all around you are talking. There are many sounds coming into your brain. Yet with just one word, a very small data point actually, you hear your son yell the word "Dad" with a bit of pain in his voice. Your brain is extremely good at pattern matching, and the voice print of your son's voice is instantly registered, so you quickly turn your head to see what happened.

With respect to the automatic device classification capability that is integrated into many of the spectrum analyzers, these programs use computer algorithms to analyze the received RF data and try to match it to known patterns. One of the downfalls of this process is if there is no pattern for the interfering device in the database of RF signatures. If this were the case, the spectrum analysis software would not be able to classify the signal.

Although the automatic device classification is a great feature, it is important that you learn how to recognize and identify RF signatures yourself. By learning and understanding the signatures that different devices make, you will not have to rely on the computer to do the task for you. This knowledge can also be invaluable if you are using a tool that is not capable of performing automatic device classification. Growing up with a mechanic for a grandfather, I was taught to never buy a car with "idiot lights"—you know, the little indicator lights that go on when there is a problem with your car. I was taught it is always better to have gauges that are capable of showing ranges of values than simple binary on/off indicators. By having gauges and understanding how to read and interpret the gauges, you are more capable of identifying and understanding problems that were occurring with the car, often before they became critical.

This philosophy is also true regarding understanding and troubleshooting using a spectrum analyzer. With the proper training and practice, you will be able to identify and classify the devices on your network whether or not the spectrum analyzer is capable of autoclassifying devices.

Techniques for Locating RF Devices

After you have identified and classified the interfering device, you may already have an idea about where to look for it. If the device is transmitting a modulated signal, you may be able to easily track down the MAC address of the device by looking in the address tables of your wired switches to find the port/jack to which the device is physically connected.

Unfortunately, locating devices is not all that easy. The next technique for locating an RF device requires the use a directional antenna. This assumes your spectrum analyzer has an external antenna connector. If your spectrum analyzer does have an antenna jack, try to use an external antenna that has the tightest beam width possible, along with the least amount of side and back lobes in the antenna pattern. If the antenna's side lobes are too strong, it can make it more difficult to interpret the signal when using it for location tracking.

In addition to the directional antenna, you will need a floor plan of the building that you can write on. During this method of locating a device, we will show how to take RF readings from around the device and try to zoom in on or triangulate the device. To begin the process, from a location in the building, do the following:

1. Hold the directional antenna with it aimed horizontally and away from you.

2. While watching the spectrum analyzer, slowly spin in either direction 360 degrees.

3. During this spin, identify the direction that the antenna is aiming when the signal is at its highest level.

4. On the floor plan, draw a line from your location in the direction of the strongest signal.

5. Now move to a different location at least 15 to 20 meters (50 feet) and somewhere between 45 and 90 degrees to the right or left of the direction of the strongest signal.

6. From this new location, slowly spin 360 degrees, and identify the direction of the strongest signal of the device.

7. On the floor plan, draw a line from your new location in the direction of the strongest signal.

You need to perform this task from at least one additional location.

After looking at the three lines on your floor plan, you may want to try to pick a fourth line from a location that is surrounding or circling the device. After the third and possibly fourth reading, the location where the lines cross should give you a reasonable idea of the location of the device (Figure 11.25). Realize that the beam width of the antenna and the environment can cut down on the accuracy of your readings; however, you should have a fairly reasonable estimate of the device's location.

FIGURE 11.25   Angles and overlapping coverage

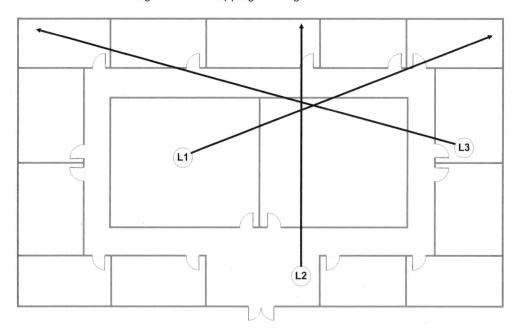

Another method for locating a device does not require a directional antenna. Using this method, you will first divide your floor plan into four quadrants. Go to the center of each quadrant, and take an RF reading. Mark the results either on your floor plan or on a sheet of paper, as shown in the first drawing in Figure 11.26. When you have identified which quadrant has the strongest signal, divide that quadrant into four subquadrants. Now go to the center of each subquadrant and take an RF reading, as shown in the second drawing in Figure 11.26. Again, identify which quadrant has the strongest signal, and divide that quadrant into four smaller subquadrants. Continue subdividing each quadrant as long as there are identifiable RF signal differences in each of the quadrants.

FIGURE 11.26   Quadrant method of finding

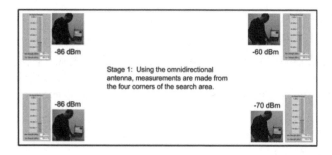

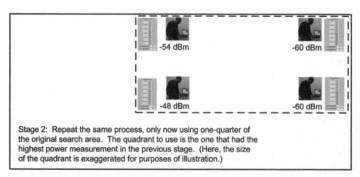

It is important to remember that RF is three-dimensional. You may perform one of these physical locating methods and narrow down your search for a device and not be able to locate the device because it is actually on the floor above or below you. Realize that when you performed the search, you were looking for the location where the signal was the strongest. After you have identified that location, you may need to go to the floor above and the floor below to make sure you are searching for the devices on the correct floor.

RF Signature Characteristics

As you start down your journey of becoming skilled in the art and science of spectrum analysis, you will want to learn the different RF signatures that interfering devices generate. Like the student radiologists in the "Understanding RF Signatures in Spectrum Analysis" example, you will need practice and experience to quickly recognize the characteristics and traits of various devices. In the following sections, you will see some of the traits you will need to look for when trying to identify and manually classify an unknown interfering device.

Shape

One of the first traits to look at is the general shape of the signal that the device is generating. These shapes can vary greatly. Some could be tall and flat on top like the side view of a building. Others could be flat on top but with sloping side, like a geological plateau. Some could be a series of spiky peaks, like what you might see in the ocean during a storm. To fully analyze the shape of the signal, you need to look at it in multiple views, including the FFT plot view, the swept spectrogram view, the spectral density, and other views that your spectrum analyzer may provide. Practice and experience will help you learn to recognize the different shapes that are generated in each of these views along with the types of RF signals that can generate these shapes.

Patterns

Some RF signatures generate specific patterns. When analyzing an RF signal, it is important to see and be able to identify any patterns. Pattern behaviors to look for are things such as if the signature is rock-solid on one frequency, whether it hops around, or whether it merely wavers as it slides between frequencies. Some RF patterns have gaps in them or transition from a random pattern to nonrandom pattern depending upon the state of the device.

Uniqueness

An extremely important concept for analyzing RF signals is to identify what is unique about the specific shape or pattern. When looking at the spectrum pattern or behavior of a device, it is typically necessary to compare it to the patterns and behaviors of known devices. It is important to analyze and identify components of the device that are exactly the same or have similar properties to known devices. To do this, it is important to know and remember the patterns and behaviors of known devices. You need to identify ways that you can use to remember and understand the known devices. Whatever technique or memory aid works for you is fine. Does the pattern or behavior remind you of something else? The Matterhorn Mountain? Teeth of a crosscut saw? An ice pick? Does it have "shoulders"? It does not matter what you use as a memory aid, as long as you remember it. It can be helpful to jot down both text and graphical descriptions as you learn the patterns and behaviors of a new device. Turn the device on and off so that you can learn how it behaves.

Frequency

The patterns of some devices will always show up at a specific frequency or frequency range, while other devices can be set to a specific frequency or channel within a range or selection of valid channels. The pattern of other devices may move or hop between channels or frequencies. Try to identify whether the device operates on a single frequency or channel. If the device is moving between frequencies, try to identify whether it moves in large or small increments across the range.

Pulse vs. Constant

Some devices, such as 802.11 stations, generate traffic that fluctuates on and off, referred to as pulsing traffic. Other devices such as wireless video cameras generate traffic that is steady and constant. Try to understand and interpret the function of the devices and how it handles the data that it is transmitting. If it is a pulsing type of device, see whether there is something memorable or unique with how it turns its transmissions on and off.

Duty Cycle

Another trait that is closely tied to the pulse vs. constant aspect of a device's signal is duty cycle. Be sure to look specifically at each device's duty cycle. It is one sure predictor of RF interference. You might have a interfering device with a very strong, high-power signal, but without a corresponding high-duty cycle it is typically not going to cause much harm to your Wi-Fi network. On the other hand, something with a high-duty cycle but low power could cause much greater harm to your Wi-Fi network.

Frequency Hopping

One of the patterns to look for from RF devices is known as frequency hopping. Frequency-hopping devices operate within a defined range of frequencies. They typically transmit on a single channel or frequency for a short period of time and then switch or hop to another frequency within the operating range and then transmit on that frequency. Frequency-hopping devices usually have a predefined pattern of frequencies that they hop across, although they typically hop so fast that it is virtually impossible to identify the specific pattern.

As an example, Bluetooth devices hop 1600 times per second, across a 79 MHz range of 1 MHz channels. Frequency-hopping devices include but are not limited to Bluetooth peripherals, older 802.11 FHSS networks, baby monitors, and some digital portable telephones. Try to determine whether the pattern changes as the state of the device changes. As an example, some cordless telephones change the way they hop based on if they are "on-hook" or "off-hook."

Another way to classify frequency-hopping devices is by the seemingly randomness of their hopping. Depending upon the actual protocol being implemented, different frequency-hopping devices exhibit different behaviors. Take Bluetooth, for instance. During the discovery process, a Bluetooth device will do a little frequency hopping, but always using the same frequencies. This ends up looking like the teeth of a saw. Looking at this pattern, it is pretty obvious that it is frequency hopping. Initially it may appear to be random. If you look in the waterfall swept spectrogram, you will notice that the little high points look like freckles, but you should choose your own analogy to remember it by. If you continue to do discovery and monitor the swept spectrogram, you will see that these freckles will line up in nice neat columns. That does not sound very random. And it is not. It is pseudorandom. An interesting characteristic of Bluetooth devices is that after discovery is performed and an actual connection is made between the two Bluetooth devices, the little hot spots, or freckles, lose their nice, neat columns and become random across the allowed frequency range. Understanding and interpreting these behaviors is just one more trick to keep up your sleeve when learning to properly classify RF devices.

Example RF Signatures

Our first foray into looking at example RF signatures will be to look at the main devices in wireless LANs: the actual 802.11 devices. Each of the 802.11 Physical layers (PHYs) have unique RF signatures. These are specifically mandated by the protocol. The first is a phase shift keying (PSK) curve (see Figure 11.27). This plot is formed by 802.11b devices or

802.11g devices transmitting at the lower data rates. Note the little notch in the center, designating the center frequency of the channel. You may also note smaller notches on the two sides where the protocol demands a distinct drop in signal. Earlier in this chapter you saw the spectral mask for PSK devices (shown in Figure 11.6). This mask is defined as 22 MHz wide by the protocol.

FIGURE 11.27   PSK curve of access point

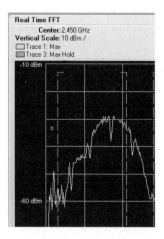

The next modulated signal looks the same for either 802.11g or 802.11a. It is an OFDM signature. The key difference is that the 802.11g plot is in the 2.4 GHz band, and 802.11a plot is in the 5 GHz band. This signature is distinguished by a flat top, as shown in Figure 11.28. Note that the edges tend to fall off in both directions on either side of the flat top. Sometimes, even though you are looking at the RF signature of an 802.11g access point, you will only see the curved signature represented by the PSK plot. The reason why this may occur is that 802.11g access points usually transmit beacon management frames at the lowest supported data rate, which is typically a 1 Mbps or 2 Mbps PSK frame. Thus, you are likely to see the plot of these PSK transmitted management frames.

FIGURE 11.28   OFDM curve—20 MHz

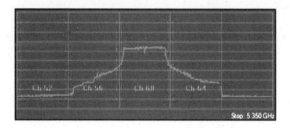

Initially all 802.11a and 802.11g devices used 20 MHz wide channels. With the introduction of 802.11n, you now also have 40 MHz wide channels. They have similar-shaped spectral masks, but you will note the 40 MHz mask is twice as wide (Figure 11.29). The 40 MHz channels are not recommended for 2.4 GHz deployments; however, that does not prevent someone from using them. The 40 MHz channels are commonly implemented 5 GHz deployments for 802.11n Greenfield mode. It is also possible to mix 20 MHz and 40 MHz modes on the same frequencies, but it is not best practice because of an inordinate amount of protection mechanisms that must be put in place. The protection mechanisms will greatly reduce your potential throughput.

FIGURE 11.29   OFDM curve—40 MHz

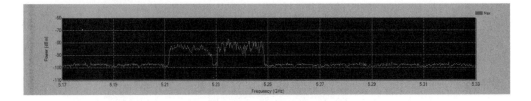

Frequency-Hopping Example

The first frequency-hopping spectrum example is of a Bluetooth device first in discover mode using pseudorandom frequency selection, followed by the personal area network (PAN) mode that happens after connection. Note in the swept spectrogram view during the discovery mode (Figure 11.30) that the little dots line up in nice, clean vertical columns. This is because in discovery mode, when the Bluetooth devices are searching for others to pair with, there is a fixed pseudorandom sequence, thus leaving the vertical lines as the hops are always returning to the same spots. This behavior can also be seen in the FFT plot in Figure 11.31.

Now you will see a Bluetooth device that is functioning in PAN mode. When operating in this mode, you can see in the swept spectrogram view (Figure 11.32), a fully random distribution of hot points. You can still see the peaks in the RF energy, but those are no longer in a fixed pattern. You can also see the random distribution of signal in the FFT plot in Figure 11.33.

FIGURE 11.30   Swept spectrogram of Bluetooth discovery

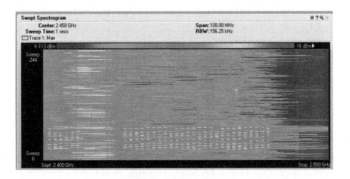

FIGURE 11.31   FFT plot of Bluetooth discovery

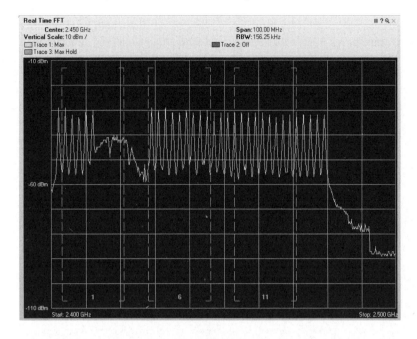

FIGURE 11.32   Swept spectrogram of Bluetooth PAN

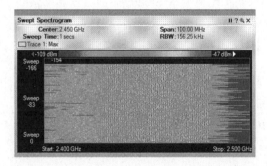

FIGURE 11.33   FFT plot of Bluetooth PAN

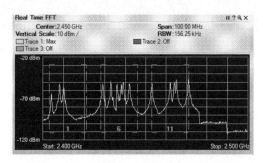

Figures 11.34 and 11.35 show the RF patterns of a couple of frequency-hopping digital portable telephones. Figure 11.34 displays the patterns of a 2.4 GHz telephone, and Figure 11.35 displays the patterns of a 5.8 GHz telephone. These views display the RF patterns of digital telephones you might pick up at a local electronics store. These telephones have very low-duty cycles and by hopping around the spectrum are less likely to interfering with an 802.11 wireless network. Notice that even though these telephones operate in different frequencies, their RF signatures are similar.

Other frequency-hopping technologies that you may run across include some medical telemetry units, very old FHSS 802.11 classic devices, and a variety of proprietary systems.

In evaluating frequency-hopping systems, be sure to not be focused on the FFT and swept spectrogram plots alone. These type signatures may seem to be quite strong, and individual peaks on the hops might actually have a high dB value. However, you must also check the duty cycle. This will help you determine how much actual interference is being transmitted. You might have a device, as shown in this Bluetooth capture, that transmits a high dB signal but uses very little-duty cycle (Figure 11.36) and not have much interfering capacity at all.

FIGURE 11.34   Frequency-hopping portable 2.4 GHz telephone

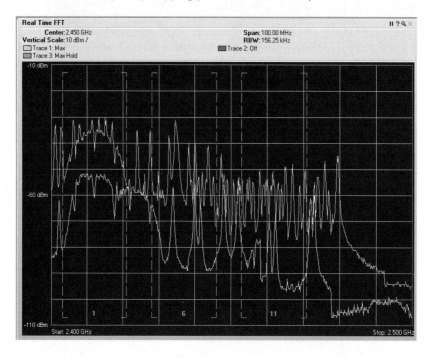

FIGURE 11.35   Frequency-hopping 5 GHz portable telephone

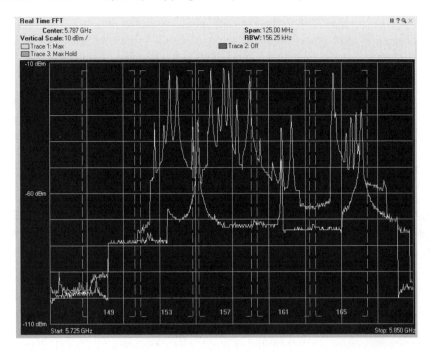

FIGURE 11.36   Duty cycle of Bluetooth discovery

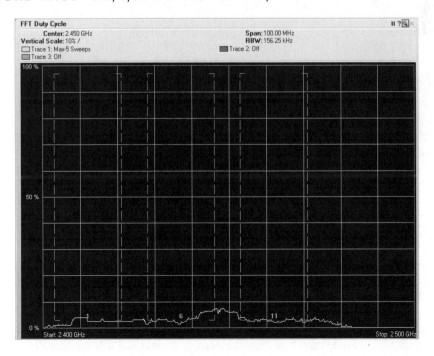

Analog RF Energy

A variety of devices that operate in the 2.4 GHz band use analog radio signals to communicate. Analog radio signals work fine for devices such as a wireless mouse or a cordless telephone carrying voice data. Analog signals have a certain quality to them, transmitting using a very narrow specific frequency, usually with an RF pattern that has much weaker shoulders falling off to both sides.

One of the RF signatures that Figure 11.37 shows is the RF signature of a Logitech 2.4 GHz mouse. This mouse is currently operating around channel 6. As described earlier, it has a very narrow signal that drops off quickly. When viewed in the swept spectrogram (Figure 11.38), the mouse leaves a unique trail, leaving behind a line of hot signal. This signal is generated when the mouse is actually moving and needing to send data to your laptop. This mouse, and many others like it, will also detect interference and move itself to a different frequency when needed.

Another type of analog device is an older model portable cordless telephone. These units operate in the 2.4 GHz and 5.8 GHz frequency ranges. Unlike many of the newer model telephones that automatically switch between frequencies when there is interference, with these older-style telephones, you have to press a "channel" button on the telephone to manually switch to a new channel. When you click the channel button, the frequency does switch but barely. In Figure 11.40, the channel button was pressed five times, but you can clearly see that there are only four different frequencies used. This is because this model of telephone supports only four unique channels, so the fifth pressing of the channel button just returned the telephone to the original channel. Also notice that all four channels are very close together, with all of them operating within the 22 MHz wide area of channel 1.

FIGURE 11.37 Real-time FFT of Logitech analog mouse

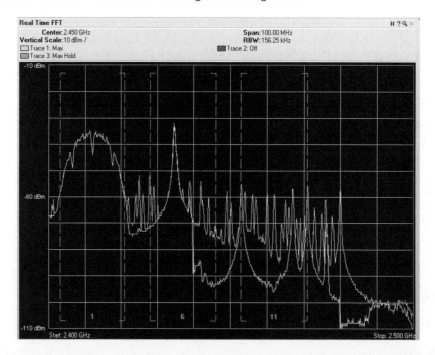

FIGURE 11.38   Swept spectrogram of Logitech analog mouse

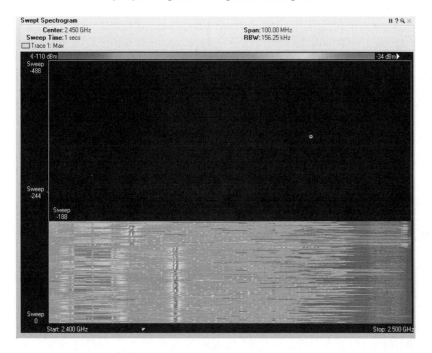

FIGURE 11.39   Real-time FFT of 2.4 GHz analog telephone

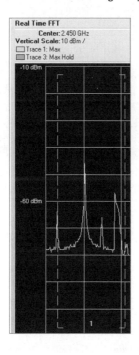

It is important to monitor as much of the frequency spectrum as possible when you are testing equipment or monitoring the RF behavior of a device. In addition to the 2.4 GHz analog telephone, we also monitored a 5 GHz analog telephone. If you look at Figure 11.40, you are actually looking at a swept spectrogram of the 2.4 GHz frequencies. While changing channels on the 5 GHz telephone, we noticed that the 2.4 GHz spectrum was being affected. What do you think is causing this?

The answer to this question is simple and straightforward, although intriguing. A 5 GHz radio uses more electrical energy than 2.4 GHz radio. To prolong battery life in the hand-held telephone, the manufacturer decided to use a 5 GHz signal to transmit from the base station that is plugged directly into a power source and then to use a 2.4 GHz signal to transmit from the handset to the base station. It's not only intriguing but also misleading, especially when the box for the telephone clearly states it is a 5 GHz telephone!

FIGURE 11.40   Swept spectrogram of 5 GHz analog telephone affecting 2.4 GHz spectrum

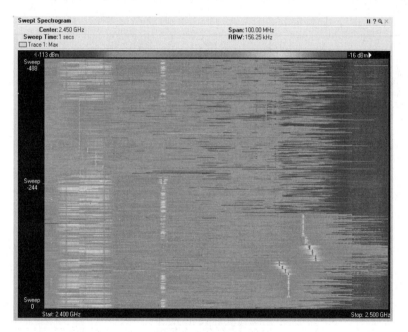

Jammers

An analog narrow-band *jammer* is actually a signal generator that was initially designed to test coaxial RF cable. The one we used to create the figures generates 700 mW of raw analog RF energy. The intended use of it is to first connect it to one end of a cable and to place a watt meter on the other end of the cable. At this point, it can be used to perform different tests. When the signal generator is turned on, the technician can look at the watt meter and identify how much of the generated 700 mW of signal is actually received at the meter. The difference is the loss or attenuation caused by the cables and connector. The technician can also lightly wiggle or shake the cable and watch to see whether the meter on the other end of the cable fluctuates. If the reading on the meter fluctuates, this indicates there is an electrical short or opening internally in the cable or at one of the connectors. However, when the signal generator is connected to an antenna, it becomes a very strong narrow-band jammer. The jammer has a very analog-looking signature (Figure 11.41). What is particularly significant is how much power it is generating, both in decibels (Figure 11.42) and more importantly in the duty cycle (Figure 11.43).

FIGURE 11.41   Swept spectrogram of narrow-band jammer

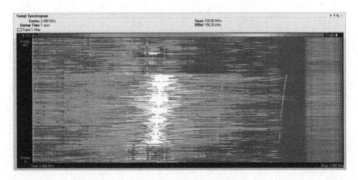

FIGURE 11.42   Real-time FFT of narrow-band jammer

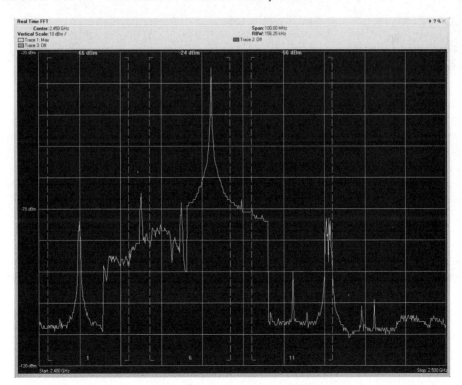

FIGURE 11.43 Duty cycle of narrow-band jammer

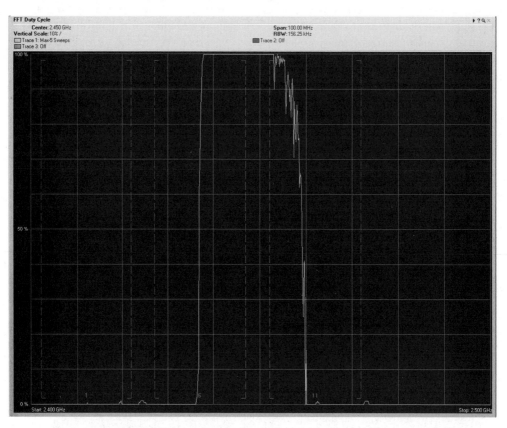

A narrow-band jammer is also useful in wireless LAN penetration testing, because it can be used to disconnect all clients from a specific channel, which in turn will force them to re-associate to other access points, perhaps giving up information useful to the penetration tester.

Another type of jammer, a wide-band jammer, generates interfering signals across an entire frequency range. You can purchase them as a spy camera stopper or as a privacy device, because any of the video cameras mentioned in the section "Video Cameras" would be unable to transmit in the presence of this type of jamming device.

WARNING We will leave it to the reader to research the legality of using jamming devices within the operating environment of your regulatory domain. You should realize that in most countries it is illegal to intentionally cause interference, which is exactly what jammers do.

When operating wide-band jammers, these devices typically transmit across the entire RF band (Figure 11.44). Once the jammer is turned on and viewed using a swept spectrogram, you can clearly see the continuous signal spread across the entire band (Figure 11.45), while the duty cycle view also reaffirms the nearly 100 percent continuous transmission (Figure 11.46).

When a wide-band jammer is powered on, both stations and access points will be unable to transmit any frames—since any time they perform a clear channel assessment, it will fail. This will keep all frames from being transmitted on the media. When you look at the effect of this device with a Wi-Fi card, you will see no noise, as well as no signal.

Another type of jamming device is created by misconfiguring an 802.11 client radio. This is not a task that a typical user can do to their Wi-Fi adapter but rather modifications that hardware and software engineers have performed on certain cards. When following the protocol, an 802.11 chipset will perform a clear channel assessment (CCA) before transmitting any frames. This CCA is performed to make sure that no one else is currently transmitting on this same frequency.

As mentioned, some enterprising folks have hacked into the code on some 802.11 devices and removed or shortened the CCA process, allowing the wireless adapter to continuously transmit without having to first check whether the media is busy. The initial version of this type of device was called the Queensland Attack and was a piece of test software that used any PCMCIA NIC built on a specific chipset. This internally developed test utility was leaked to the public, and with this tool you could put your card into a constant transmit mode. Today you can purchase a device for testing your spectrum analyzer called AirHORN that is capable of generating a variety of test signals, scanning across 2.4 GHz or 5 GHz channels, pulsing, that uses an 802.11 USB device to perform a variety of jamming processes.

FIGURE 11.44   Real-time FFT of 2.4 GHz wide-band jammer

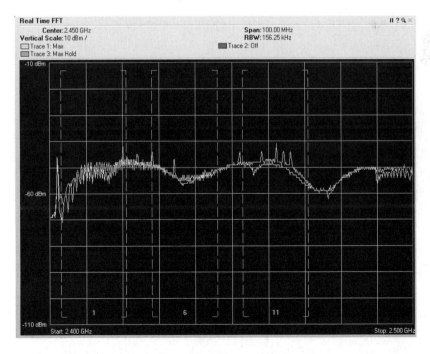

FIGURE 11.45 Swept spectrogram of 2.4 GHz wide-band jammer

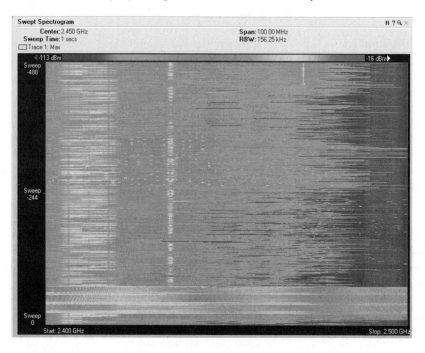

FIGURE 11.46 FFT duty cycle of 2.4 GHz wide-band jammer

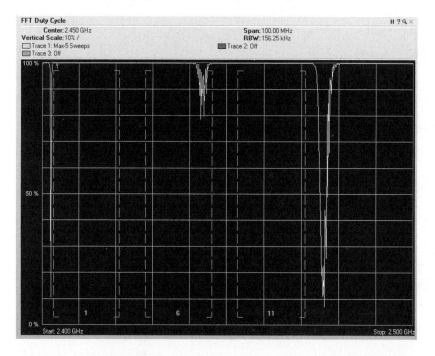

This slight change in the coding allows for a client station, either a PCMCIA or USB form-factor device, to be used in jamming mode. To generate the figures, we used the signal generation product called AirHORN. It can transmit what looks like a standard PSK curve in the FFT plots (Figure 11.47). You will notice near the top of the swept spectrogram (Figure 11.48) that the signal does not look quite right. The shape is the same as a normal 802.11 PSK curve, but it no longer pulses on and off the way a typical Wi-Fi device does. Instead, it is constantly on.

If you look at the duty cycle (Figure 11.49), you will see that this is not like any 802.11 card you have ever seen before. Because of the pulse-like nature of the 802.11 protocol, the spectrum analysis signature of an 802.11 device is unique. These are things that have already been covered in previous chapters, such as DIFS, contention windows, transmitting data, SIFS, and ACKs. These and many other components of 802.11 communications cause many periods of time when there is no transmission on the media.

FIGURE 11.47   Real-time FFT of AirHorn 802.11 jammer

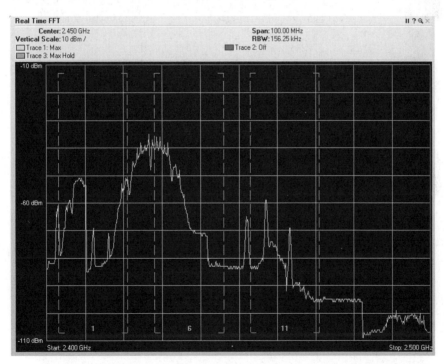

FIGURE 11.48 Swept spectrogram of AirHorn 802.11 jammer

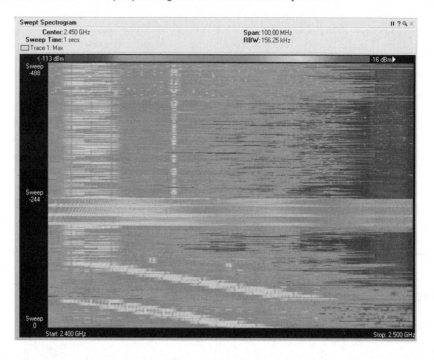

FIGURE 11.49 Duty cycle of AirHorn 802.11 jammer

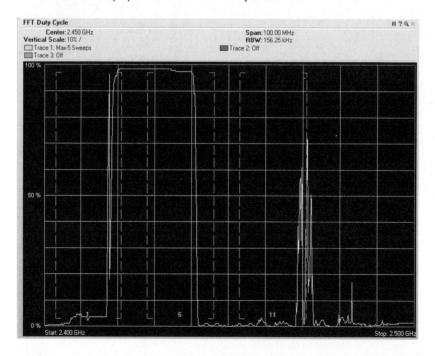

If viewed by a Wi-Fi adapter, since this device is transmitting what appears to be an 802.11 signal, the Wi-Fi card will report this as just a strong access point.

Wireless Video Cameras

These little devices are typically sold as nannycams, as wireless security cameras, or even as remote ways to watch your children while you are gone. There are two key types of video cameras available in the 2.4 GHz spectrum: Wi-Fi based cameras, and non-Wi-Fi based cameras. To begin with, we will be referring to the non-Wi-Fi-based cameras.

These wireless video cameras transmit an analog signal (Figure 11.50), taking up a large chunk of the RF spectrum in the channel 1 area, often as much as one-fourth of the available 2.4 GHZ band, which is about the width of one of the 22 MHz 802.11 channels, as shown in the lower-left corner (Figure 11.51). These wireless video cameras also transmit with near 100 percent duty cycle, as shown on the left side of the plot (Figure 11.52). These analog video cameras do not specifically use any of the 802.11 channels and can cause great havoc to your wireless LAN. Fortunately, many are not very high-powered devices and therefore have a fairly small RF coverage area or footprint. The coverage area where these devices may cause disruption to your wireless LAN is perhaps as small as 10 to 20 meters.

FIGURE 11.50 Real-time FFT of analog video camera

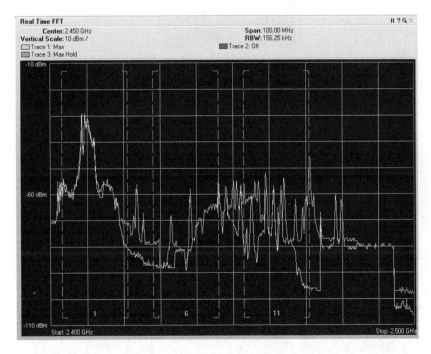

FIGURE 11.51   Swept spectrogram of analog video camera

FIGURE 11.52   Duty cycle of analog video camera

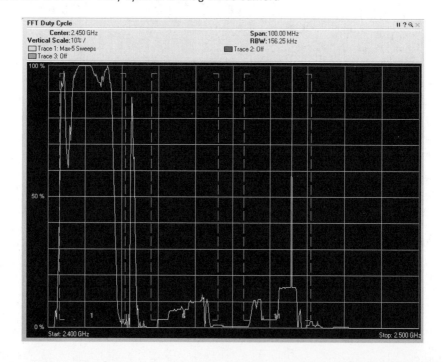

Real World Scenario

Vulnerability of a Layer 1 Denial of Service

When doing wireless penetration testing at client venues, we sometimes enter the premises with one or more of the analog wireless video cameras hidden unobtrusively in a pocket or backpack. To provide power to these cameras, we have created small, portable battery packs. This is a very disruptive activity that we perform to prove to the client that their wireless LAN is always vulnerable to a layer 1 denial-of-service (DoS) attack. It is important to remember that in many parts of the world, the 2.4 GHz and 5 GHz bands that are used for 802.11 networking are also allowed to be used by other non-networking devices. Both of these bands are often unlicensed, allowing anyone to use these bands, providing they stay within the operating standards of the local regulatory domain or agency.

The second type of wireless video cameras is Wi-Fi based. These cameras compete in all the same function arenas as the non-Wi-Fi-based cameras, such as security, remote surveillance, and monitoring. These cameras do not use analog RF signals but instead digitize the video and audio streams and transmit these streams as standard 2.4 GHz or 5 GHz Wi-Fi traffic. Since these cameras transmit their data as standard 802.11 frames, they must contend with any other 802.11 data frames to gain access to the RF medium. These types of digital 802.11 cameras do not have the same interfering capacity of their analog brethren. We have not provided any spectrum analyzer images for these digital cameras, since they are standard 802.11 devices, and therefore their traffic looks just like any other 802.11 device, either generating PSK or OFDM signatures.

If you need wireless security cameras, you will definitely want to be using digital rather than analog. The digital cameras are more likely to have remote control or pan, tilt, and zoom (PTZ) capabilities as well as access to the video and audio streams via IP connectivity.

Microwave Ovens

Simply put, microwave ovens are not supposed to leak. In reality, microwave ovens do leak an extremely minute amount of RF signal. For a microwave oven to be sold in a country, it must pass a certain level of testing that regulates the amount and level of leakage that is allowed. Even though most microwave ovens are designed with multiple locking systems and auto shutoff upon opening the door, after repeated use, or sometimes abuse, microwave ovens may begin to leak more as time goes by. Industrial ovens, such as those used in commercial restaurants, are designed with replaceable door seals, since this is a common place for leaks to occur. However, most home and office microwaves are not reparable, and if they begin to leak, they will need to be replaced instead of being repaired.

Even the smallest microwave ovens are rated at 800 watts of power. In our world of 802.11 devices, client stations normally transmit signals at around 30 mW, and access points can typically transmit at as much as 100 mW. Microwave ovens operate at around

2.45 GHz, which is near channels 8 and 9 in the 2.4 GHz band. Although this frequency is above channel 6 and below channel 11, the width of the microwave signal can cause interference on either of these channels. All of the autoclassification programs have an easy time classifying microwave ovens. Microwave ovens have a very easy-to-read signature. In Figure 11.53, you can see the tip of the RF signature seeming to bend at the top, and it appears to move around quite a bit. Unlike RF systems that use a crystal to lock the frequency, the RF signals of microwave ovens tend to slide around a bit.

FIGURE 11.53 Spectrum plots of a microwave oven

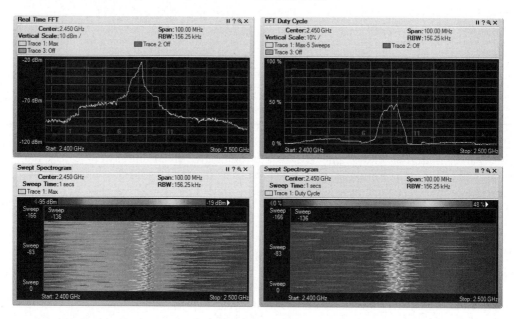

A malfunctioning microwave oven has the potential to cause devastating results to your wireless network. If the RF blocking/absorbing front door were removed from a microwave oven, a single microwave oven could take down all 802.11 activities in the neighboring area. This is not something we suggest you try at home or work, because the nonfunctioning 802.11 networks would be the least of your problems. You should not minimize the importance of how much RF interference can result from a leaking microwave oven or even at times one that is operating and functioning normally. Many times seemingly random client problems on a Wi-Fi network have been traced back to the times when someone was heating up some food in the break room. If you determine that a microwave oven is causing problems on your network, you typically have two ways of addressing the problem—move it or replace it. If you decide that the microwave oven should be replaced, you may need to first have it approved by management. In today's market, the cost of replacing the microwave is far less than the cost of a network technician to troubleshoot further problems caused by the malfunctioning microwave oven. Since a microwave oven is often used by many people in many departments, the problem of replacing it is usually a budget issue, often trying to decide whose budget is going to pay for the replacement.

Summary

In this chapter, you left the world of frames and byte structures that were prevalent in the previous sections and moved into the world of radio frequency.

We began the chapter by discussing some of the different options available to a wireless LAN professional. By understanding these options, you can choose which type of spectrum analyzer will fit your specific situation.

You then took a quick look back at how wired and wireless network interface cards process changes in the electromagnetic spectrum, convert them into encoded bits, and then transport them across a medium. You compared and contrasted the differences between Wi-Fi NICs and spectrum analyzers. The Wi-Fi NIC can decode data at an amazing rate, whereas the spectrum analyzer can see all RF signatures.

Then the chapter covered how spectrum analyzers do their thing. We introduced new views and plots to visualize what happens with both modulated and non-modulated RF and what types of signals might cause interference for our wireless LANs. This chapter also included many graphical examples of a variety of RF signatures so you can start learning and recognizing valid vs. interfering RF devices.

To really get the most out of this chapter, go back and review the different examples. Set up a little lab environment and see for yourself what the different devices in your world look like, what your spectrum analyzer reports, and practice. Reading spectrum analysis plots is a learned skill. Start learning today.

Exam Essentials

Demonstrate appropriate use, features, and configuration of professional spectrum analysis tools.   There are many different types of spectrum analyzers varying in price and capabilities. Understand the different features and capabilities that are available.

Identify common RF device signatures, their operating frequencies, behaviors, and impact on WLAN operations.   An important part of understanding spectrum analysis is to know and understand the RF signatures that different devices generate. By understanding the signatures of common devices and how they impact the wireless LAN, you can better understand how the RF signatures of unknown devices may affect your wireless LAN.

Identify the purpose and illustrate proper interpretation of common types of spectrum measurement, including swept spectrograph, real-time FFT, utilization, duty cycle.   It is important to know the types of plots that spectrum analyzers use to display RF information. Understanding and interpreting an RF signal depends upon being able to read and correlate the information that is generated by the different views. Each view does not present a complete picture or understanding of the RF signal.

Key Terms

amplitude

amplitude modulation

bit error rate (BER)

cycle

decibel (dB)

Express Card

fast Fourier transform (FFT)

free space path loss (FSPL)

frequency

frequency domain

hertz

jammer

milliwatts (mW)

narrow-band

noise floor

PCMCIA

Radiotap Header

received channel power indicator (RCPI)

received signal strength indicator (RSSI)

signal-to-noise ratio (SNR)

spectral mask

spectrum analyzers

spread spectrum

time domain

waterfall plot

wavelength

Review Questions

1. What is the best way to mitigate a leaking office microwave oven causing disruption in your wireless LAN?

    A. Replace the magnetron device.

    B. Use RF-sealing caulk on the door edges.

    C. Replace the entire microwave oven.

    D. Turn the power on the microwave oven to less than 4.

    E. Move the microwave away from the edge of the counter.

2. Looking at the graphic, which of the following devices could have generated this plot?

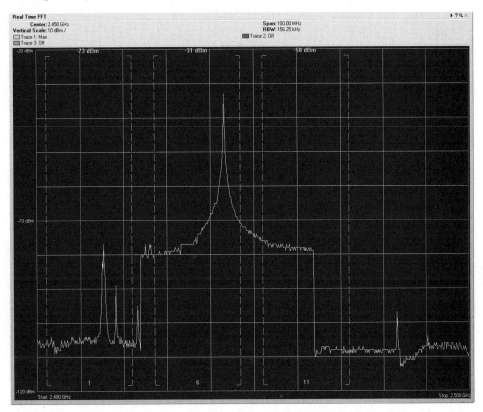

    A. 802.11 OFDM device

    B. 802.11 HR-DSSS device

    C. Wide-band jammer

    D. Narrow-band jammer

    E. Bluetooth headset

3. Looking at the graphic, which of the following devices could have generated this plot?

A. An operating Bluetooth mouse

B. A microwave oven

C. An analog video camera

D. A Bluetooth phone in discovery mode

E. A cordless telephone

4. Which of the following are important items to consider when purchasing a spectrum analyzer? (Choose all that apply.)

A. Frequency range

B. Form factor

C. Resolution

D. Wi-Fi integration

E. GPS integration

5. When performing a spectral analysis, it is important to view the information using different plots, because each plot displays a different aspect of the information. Which of the following are common plots that are used? (Choose all that apply.)

A. Swept spectrogram

B. FFT spectrogram

C. Real-time FFT

D. Frame distribution

E. FFT duty cycle

6. If you were isolated in the middle of a desert and you turn on a microwave oven near your 802.11 wireless NIC, which of the following statements would be true regarding the way your NIC will report noise?

A. Your NIC will report noise if it is set to channel 1.

B. Your NIC will report noise if it is set to channel 6.

C. Your NIC will report noise if it is set to channel 11.

D. Your NIC will report noise regardless of the channel.

E. Your NIC will not report noise.

7. Looking at the graphic, what type of plot is being displayed?

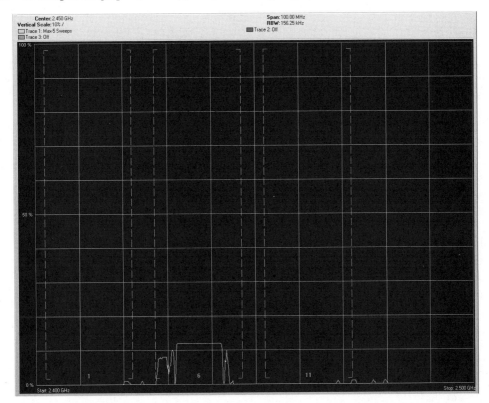

A. Real-time FFT

B. FFT duty cycle

C. Swept spectrogram

D. Spectrum density

E. Waterfall plot

8.   Looking at the graphic, what type of plot is being displayed?

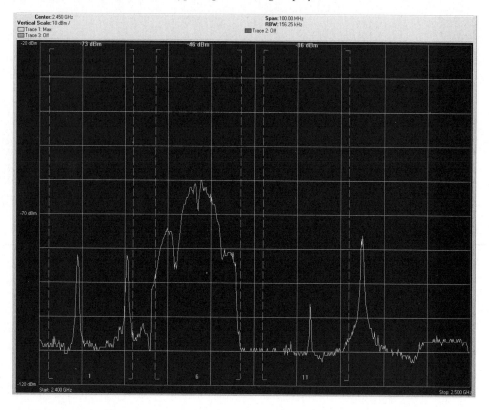

A.   Real-time FFT

B.   FFT duty cycle

C.   Swept spectrogram

D.   Spectrum density

E.   Waterfall plot

9. Looking at the graphic you see a swept spectrogram plot, which is also referred to as what type of plot?

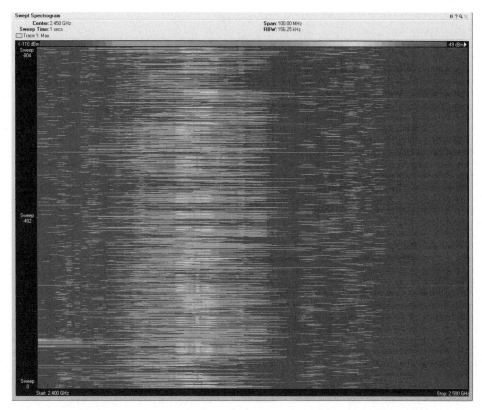

A. Heat map

B. Spectrum density

C. Waterfall

D. Power dispersion

E. Noise dispersion

10. Choose which of the following two conditions has the potential to cause the most RF interference. (Choose all that apply.)

   A. A high-duty cycle

   B. A low-duty cycle

   C. A high-power burst of energy

   D. A low-power burst of energy

   E. Not enough information is provided

11. When analyzing RF signatures, which of the following are key characteristics to analyze? (Choose all that apply.)

   A. Shape

   B. Patterns

   C. Pulse or constant

   D. Uniqueness

   E. Frequency

   F. Duty cycle

12. Which of the following are characteristic of an analog RF device such as a wireless mouse? (Choose all that apply.)

   A. Wide frequency range

   B. Very narrow specific frequency

   C. Continuous transmission

   D. Low transmitting power

   E. Always low-duty cycle

13. Which of the following are characteristics of a non-802.11 wireless video camera? (Choose all that apply.)

   A. Narrow band signal

   B. Uses up to 1/4 of the available frequencies

   C. Low duty cycle

   D. Analog signal

   E. High duty cycle, nearing 100 percent

14. Looking at the graphic, what type of RF signature is being displayed?

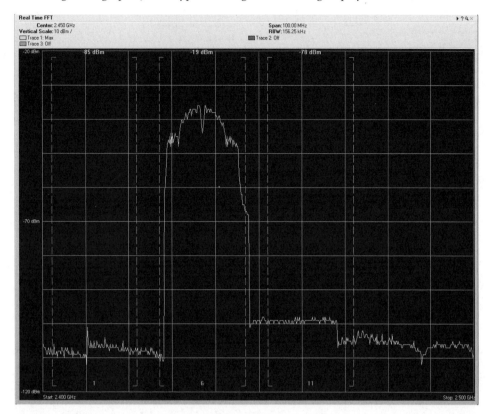

   A. OFDM

   B. ERP-OFDM

   C. FSK

   D. ASK

   E. PSK

15. Looking at the graphic, what type of RF signature is being displayed?

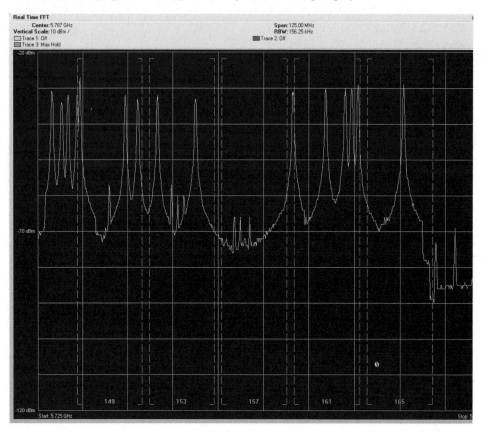

A. Bluetooth device in discovery mode

B. Bluetooth device operating in personal area network mode

C. Frequency-hopping cordless telephone

D. Analog video camera

E. 802.11g OFDM device

16. When analyzing RF information, it is often separated into two different types of domains, known as what? (Choose all that apply.)

A. Power domain

B. Frequency domain

C. Regulatory domain

D. Time domain

E. Signal domain

17. All the nonuseful background RF signal that is received in the frequency range that your device is operating in, from any type of device whether it is generated by an intentional radiator or an unintentional radiator, is known as what?

   A. Interference

   B. Background noise

   C. Spectral noise

   D. White noise

   E. Noise floor

18. What is the name of the additional information that is added to the frame at the receiving station and includes date and time stamps, channel stamp, signal stamp, and noise stamp?

   A. Preamble

   B. Radiohead

   C. Start of frame delimiter

   D. Radiotap Header

   E. Received signal strength indicator

19. What are two systematic methods for dividing and locating or tracking unknown RF devices? (Choose all that apply.)

   A. Triangulation

   B. Follow the leader

   C. Geiger counter

   D. Quadrants

   E. Sectorizing

20. Looking at the graphic showing U-NII 2 channels, what type of RF signature is being displayed?

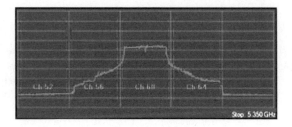

   A. 20 MHz OFDM

   B. 40 MHz OFDM

   C. PSK

   D. ASK

   E. FSK

Answers to Review Questions

1. C. Industrial ovens, like those used in commercial restaurants, are designed with replaceable door seals. However, most home and office microwaves are not reparable, and if they begin to leak, they will need to be replaced instead of being repaired.

2. D. Of the possible answers, a narrow-band jammer is the only device listed that would generate such a strong signal across such a narrow frequency range.

3. D. During the discovery process, a Bluetooth device will do a little frequency hopping, but always using the same frequencies. This ends up looking like the teeth of a saw. After discovery is performed and an actual connection is made between the two Bluetooth devices, the little hot spots, or freckles, lose their nice, neat columns and become random across the allowed frequency range.

4. A, B, C, D. When choosing a spectrum analyzer, it is important to make sure it can monitor the necessary frequency range. Form factor is important to make sure the sensor can connect or plug into your computer. Resolution will provide granularity so that you can see the plots better. Wi-Fi integration will allow you to see both frames and modulated bits on the RF medium at the same time. GPS integration is not typically an available option.

5. A, C, E. The real-time FFT plot displays the FFT realized data plotted with the horizontal axis as frequency and the vertical axis as energy, typically displayed in decibels. The swept spectrogram plot takes the RF energy readings post FFT, and instead of plotting the dB values in vertical height, it converts the dB values to color and then plots a single 1-pixel tall line at the bottom of the plot. When the next set of data arrives, this process is repeated, with all the previous data being pushed up the stack by one row of pixels. The FFT duty cycle plot displays the percentage of the time the ambient RF signal is higher than the noise floor. In this view, you can see whether a device is constantly using a frequency.

6. E. If you turn on a microwave oven near a wireless NIC, there are no data bits being generated by the microwave, so the NIC will always report a noise variable of zero. Remember that this is because 802.11 wireless NICs require bits in order to perform any type of analysis.

7. B. The FFT duty cycle plot displays the percentage of the time the ambient RF signal is higher than the noise floor. Along the side of the plot, the legend is displayed as a percentage from 0 percent to 100 percent. In this view, you can see whether a device is constantly using a frequency. You may also see a very low percentage meaning that the device was barely pulsing on and did not transmit much of the time.

8. A. In a real-time FFT plot, the FFT realized data is plotted with the horizontal axis as frequency and the vertical axis as energy as defined in dBms.

9. C. With a waterfall plot, the spectrum analyzer takes the RF energy readings post FFT, and instead of plotting the dB values in vertical height, like in the FFT plot, it converts the dB values to color and then plots a single 1-pixel tall line at the bottom of the plot. The data flows down the plot, with the latest sampling often at the bottom; however, this can vary by vendor.

10. A, C. The worst scenario would be to have a high-power level signal for a high percentage of the time. In general, a high-duty cycle is worse for RF interference than high dB.

11. A, B, C, D, E, F. All of these are key characteristics for analyzing RF signatures. An additional characteristic to look for is if the signal is generated by a frequency-hopping device.

12. B, D. Analog radio signals work fine for devices such as a wireless mouse or a cordless telephone carrying voice data. Analog signals have a certain quality to them, transmitting using a very narrow specific frequency, usually with an RF pattern that has much weaker shoulders falling off to both sides. A wireless mouse leaves a unique trail, leaving behind a line of hot signal. This signal is generated when the mouse is actually moving and needing to send data to your laptop.

13. B, D, E. Wireless video cameras transmit an analog signal, taking up a large chunk of the RF spectrum, often as much as one-fourth of the available 2.4 GHZ band, which is about the width of one of the 22 MHz 802.11 channels. These wireless video cameras also transmit with near 100 percent duty cycle. These analog video cameras do not specifically use any of the 802.11 channels and can cause great havoc to your wireless LAN. Fortunately, they are not very high-powered devices and therefore have a fairly small RF coverage area or footprint.

14. E. This is a phase shift keying (PSK) curve. This plot is formed by 802.11b devices or 802.11g devices transmitting at the lower data rates. Note the little notch in the center, designating the center frequency of the channel. You may also note smaller notches on the two sides where the protocol demands a distinct drop in signal.

15. C. Looking at the graphic, you will see that the device is operating in the 5 GHz spectrum, which would exclude the Bluetooth devices and the 802.11g OFDM device. Analog cameras typically stick to a range of frequencies and use up a wide range of frequencies, which leaves the choice of the frequency-hopping cordless telephone.

16. B, D. The time domain is where the horizontal axis of the graphs we look at is calibrated by time. The next domain is the frequency domain. In this view, the horizontal axis does not represent time but, rather, frequency. This is the main view of spectrum analyzers.

17. E. The RF noise floor is defined as all the background RF signal that is received in the frequency range that your device is operating in, from any type of device whether it is generated by an intentional radiator or an unintentional radiator.

18. D. The wireless NIC will use some of the specific information gleaned from the RF to bit transition process to actually add information to the wireless frame. This additional information is added at the receiving station, not at the transmitting station, and is in addition to the bits sent from the source. This added information is called the Radiotap Header.

19. A, D. On the floor plan, draw a line from your location in the direction of the strongest signal. Now move to a different location at least 15 to 20 meters (50 feet) and somewhere between 45 and 90 degrees to the right or left of the direction of the strongest signal. From this new location, slowly spin 360 degrees and identify the direction of the strongest signal of the device. On the floor plan, draw a line from your new location in the direction of the strongest signal. You need to perform this task from at least one additional location.

20. A. This is the RF signature for a 20 MHz OFDM RF signature. Note that the edges tend to fall off in both directions on either side of the flat top.

Chapter 12

Protocol Analyzer Operation and Troubleshooting

IN THIS CHAPTER, YOU WILL LEARN ABOUT THE FOLLOWING:

✓ **Understanding Protocol Analyzers**

- ▪ Capture Adapters
- ▪ Analyzer placement

✓ **Protocol Analyzer Features**

- ▪ Channel selection and scanning
- ▪ Protocol decodes
- ▪ Peer map functions
- ▪ Conversation analysis
- ▪ Filtering: capture and display
- ▪ Expert functions
- ▪ Performance analysis
- ▪ Reporting capabilities

✓ **Protocol Analysis Operation**

- ▪ VoWiFi analysis using a protocol analyzer
- ▪ Multiple-channel protocol analysis using multiple adapters and aggregation software
- ▪ Roaming analysis
- ▪ Distributed Protocol analysis and remote packet capture
- ▪ Wired Protocol analysis for WLAN troubleshooting
- ▪ Wired and Wireless Analysis used together

✓ **System Logs**

- ▪ How system logs from wireless network equipment such as wireless controllers, access points and RADIUS servers, can aid the troubleshooting process.

Along with a spectrum analyzer (discussed in Chapter 11), a protocol analyzer is an essential tool for troubleshooting wireless networks. In this chapter, you will learn how wireless protocol analyzers place wireless network adapters into a special mode known as RF monitor mode. Wireless analyzers can be configured either to capture traffic on a fixed channel or to perform a channel scan. After configuring and starting a wireless capture, the many different features of a protocol analyzer will aid the network analyst in troubleshooting by helping them select the traffic of interest quickly and easily and point them in the right direction of a problem.

Expert systems can often be the starting place for analysis, highlighting network events that have been detected in the capture. These events can often lead to packets of one particular conversation being selected or a new more focused capture being started, filtering out any unnecessary traffic. Once the analyst has selected just the packets of interest, the final step in our troubleshooting methodology is to perform some sort of conversation analysis, looking for anything that is different from the expected protocol behavior.

For VoWiFi, a protocol analyzer can be an effective tool to troubleshoot problems. Many problems with VoWiFi networks result from poor roaming. This chapter will discuss the different features wireless analyzers provide to help troubleshoot VoWiFi and roaming issues. In particular, we will examine how the use of multichannel aggregation solves the problem of capturing a client's roam between two access points operating on separate channels.

Distributed analysis allows for a system-wide approach to network analysis, allowing data to be collected across an entire facility, as well as at remote locations. This approach can save both time and money in resolving network problems, as well as allowing for a 24/7 Wireless Intrusion Protection System to operate around the entire organization.

Sometimes to successfully troubleshoot a problem, you need more information than can be obtained from an 802.11 wireless analyzer. In this case, you may need to look at the analysis of the wired network and at system log files.

Understanding Protocol Analyzers

Protocol analyzers provide network visibility into exactly what traffic is traversing a network. Protocol analyzers capture and store network packets, providing you with a protocol decode for each packet captured, which is a readable display showing the individual fields and values for each packet. The power of a protocol analyzer is that it allows you to see exactly which packets different network devices are transmitting and who they are being transmitted to. Protocol analysis is sometimes the only way to troubleshoot a difficult problem.

Many different software products can be classed as protocol analyzers. Table 12.1 lists some of the common 802.11 wireless protocol analyzers.

TABLE 12.1 Common protocol analyzers

Vendor	Product
WildPackets	OmniPeek
Network Instruments	Observer
NetScout	Sniffer
Cace Technologies	AirPcap and Wireshark
TamoSoft	Commview for WiFi
Fluke	AirMagnet WiFi Analyzer
Motorola	AirDefense Mobile

All these products are broadly classed as protocols analyzers because they capture and decode packets, but what they do with this packet information and how they display it depends upon their primary purposes and goals.

Products such as OmniPeek, Observer, Sniffer, and Wireshark started their life as wired Ethernet analyzers and since the publication of the 802.11 standard have adapted their product portfolio to include wireless LAN analysis. These products are your traditional network analysis and troubleshooting tools. Packet analysis, protocol decodes, fault analysis, and network forensics tend to be the strengths of these analyzers. These traditional analyzers also have an advantage of being able to capture traffic from the wired network as well. Why and when you might want to capture traffic from both the wireless and wired network simultaneously will be discussed in more detail later in the chapter.

Unlike the traditional protocol analyzers mentioned earlier, AirMagnet and AirDefense Mobile were created with the sole purpose of monitoring wireless communication and can only capture 802.11 wireless packets. Although at the heart of these products is packet capture and decoding, the default view is often an overview of the wireless environment, showing the overall security and health of your wireless environment. Because of the way these products operate, it might be more accurate to think of them as a portable Wireless Intrusion Detection System (WIDS). Interestingly, both of these vendors have also developed an enterprise-wide Wireless Intrusion Protection System (WIPS). WIPS will be discussed later in this chapter when discussing distributed wireless analysis.

All these products have more or less the same set of features as each other, but factors such as how these features are implemented, their usability, and what information is reported help us classify them. For example, you can get at the packet decodes in WIDS tools; however, it is not always so easy to filter and search them as it might be with your more traditional analyzers. Conversely, although traditional analyzers have many of the same security features such as rogue device detection, they are not always as easy to implement, and reporting is not always as clear as for portable WIDS solutions.

> Although the vendors of these products may see each other as competitors, as wireless consultants, we have both a traditional analyzer and a mobile WIDS in our wireless tool kits and often find that they complement each other well. A mobile WIPS is ideal when trying to gain a quick but informative view of the wireless environment, alerting us to any areas of concern. When troubleshooting a known problem, the more traditional analyzers allow for fast and effective packet analysis. These two tools, along with a good spectrum analyzer, complete our analysis and troubleshooting tool kit and are sufficient for getting to the bottom of most wireless network problems.

Capture Adapters

Ethernet analyzers utilize a computer's *network interface card (NIC)* by placing it into *promiscuous mode*, which instructs the card to pass all packets it receives up to the kernel instead of just the packets that are addressed to it. Promiscuous mode does not prevent normal network operation. For wireless network analysis, promiscuous mode is no longer good enough. This mode would require the wireless card to be associated to an access point and would not capture all wireless frames in the environment. By default, many wireless NIC drivers will not pass up 802.11 management and control frames and therefore would not be visible in the protocol analyzer. 802.11 wireless networks are half-duplex, and wireless NICs cannot listen (receive packets) while transmitting. Because of these issues, wireless analyzers place the NICs into a special mode called *RF monitor mode*; in this mode, the card becomes a passive monitoring device and cannot transmit, and therefore normal wireless network operation is disabled. In RF monitor mode, wireless NICs listen to all 802.11-encoded signals on the channel on which they are currently monitoring.

To be able to place a wireless NIC (adapter) in RF monitor mode, network analyzer vendors have to write a customized driver. Therefore, once you have chosen your network analyzer, you must also get a supported wireless adapter. Most vendors have a list of supported adapters on their websites, listing the wireless adapters for which they have written custom drivers. This list is normally limited by which wireless chip set vendors will release their Hardware Abstraction Layer (HAL) code to the analyzers' vendors, allowing them to write the customized driver.

Having installed your chosen wireless analyzer, you must then install the customized driver for your wireless NIC. Some vendors provide driver installation wizards that step you through the process, as pictured in Figure 12.1. Other vendors require you to carry out the process manually by using the instructions available from their "getting started" guides.

FIGURE 12.1   CommView for WiFi driver installation wizard

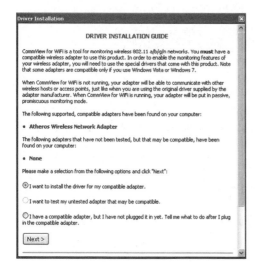

It is important to understand that when you install the customized driver, you are completely replacing the wireless NIC's driver. The new driver should only stop the wireless adapter from working as normal when capturing packets. Once the capture is stopped, the NIC should be reenabled, and normal operation should be restored.

Although installing an analyzer driver should not prevent normal wireless operation while not in RF monitor mode, the analyzer vendor's main focus when writing its driver is wireless capture and not network connectivity. Unlike wireless adapter vendors, analyzer vendors are not as interested in keeping their drivers up-to-date with the latest features, as long as they can still capture traffic. When using your adapter for network connectivity, you will often find that wireless adapters using analysis drivers do not work as well and do not support all the features that would be available in the most up-to-date drivers supplied by the adapter's vendor. It is therefore recommended that you use a separate adapter for wireless capture from the one you use for wireless network connectivity.

Figure 12.2 pictures the Driver tab of the wireless adapter's Properties dialog box in Windows. From here you can roll back a driver if you want to uninstall the analysis driver and revert to the one supplied by adapter's vendor. It is also from this dialog box that you can manually install a customized driver by clicking the Update Driver button. If you are ever unsure which driver you have installed, notice the Driver Provider information, as shown in the example in Figure 12.2.

FIGURE 12.2 Driver tab of the wireless adapter Properties dialog box

Some vendors produce their own dedicated wireless capture adapters, an example being Cace Technologies' AirPcap adapter. The sole purpose of these devices is to be passive monitors. These adapters need no driver other than the one they are supplied with.

Analyzer Location

Identifying the correct location to place a network analyzer is an essential step in performing successful wireless network analysis. Incorrect placement of the wireless analyzer can lead to false conclusions being made. For example, if you are capturing traffic too far away from the source and destination, you might see a lot of corrupted frames; however, the intended recipient may not be experiencing any frame anomalies.

An access point acts as the central point in an 802.11 wireless network, and all traffic must flow through the access point. Therefore, placing the analyzer as close to the AP as possible will allow the wireless analyst to observe the RF environment from the same perspective as the AP. In this scenario, if the analyzer reports a corrupted frame, it is more than likely that the AP also saw the frame as corrupted.

> When capturing packets with a low signal strength transmitted by a client from the edge of a BSS area, it is important to account for a difference in the quality of the receive radios and antennas used by the analyzer to those of the access point. If an access point has a better-quality RF receiver with a lower receiver sensitivity threshold, it could be receiving the packets correctly while the analyzer is reporting corrupted frames. In this scenario, you should look to see whether the access point acknowledges the corrupted frames. If the access point is sending acknowledgments for the frames, you can assume that it received them uncorrupted.

Placing the wireless analyzer as close to the AP as possible often proves to be the best solution. Although there are particular scenarios where this would not be the case, for example, when troubleshooting a problem that affects users in only one particular area, it would probably be best to monitor from the problem area.

Protocol Analyzer Features

Many different brands of wireless network analyzers are available, each with their own set of features. This section aims to outline some of the common features found in wireless analyzers; however, this section is not a minimum requirement list and by no means will all the features mentioned here be in all analyzers. Therefore, it is strongly recommend that you try an analyzer before you buy one. Most vendors provide evaluation and demo versions of their products, which allow you to discover which features they support and whether they can provide you with the required information.

Choosing the right options when configuring a new wireless packet capture is one of the main criteria for successful protocol analysis, because incorrect configuration can prevent the analyzer from capturing the required packets. The common capture options available will be discussed later in this section.

Following a structured troubleshooting methodology can help you perform effective network analysis. The following is an example of such a methodology:

1. Identify a suspect device, protocol, application, or conversation.

Like any sort of investigation, protocol analysis needs to start with some leads, and some of these might lead to dead ends, but sometimes they might lead to the problem. When troubleshooting as a result of a reported problem, you may already have some leads or suspects. For example, if the problem is that users cannot receive their emails, you can start your analysis with a suspect mail server and email protocol. However, sometimes you may not know of any particular problem but are performing proactive analysis to identity any problems before they impact the users. In this scenario, when you do not have any suspects, the analyzer's expert system may be a good place to start your analysis. The expert system will identify applications and conversations where network problems and events have been identified.

2. Having identified a suspicious device, protocol, or conversation, you will then select just the traffic that is of interest. This can be done through the use of display and capture filters.

3. Once the traffic of interest has been selected, conversation analysis can take place. One of the goals of conversation analysis is to identify any unexpected behavior. This does of course mean that you have to know what the expected behavior is and understand how the protocols on your network should operate. Identifying unexpected behavior may involve analyzing protocol decodes.

The features mentioned in the previous methodology will be described in this section of the chapter. By using these features along with an understanding of the protocols described in this book, you can perform effective wireless network analysis.

Capture Options

When initiating a wireless capture, the analyst will be provided with several options. The options available will vary slightly from vendor to vendor, but there are a core set of options available in most products:

- Channel selection and scanning
- Buffer size
- Save to disk
- Packet slicing

These options will be discussed next in the following sections.

Channel Selection and Scanning

It is essential to understand that a wireless NIC can capture packets on only one channel at any given time, making channel selection the most important of the precapture options. Typically two options are available: fixed channel or *channel scanning*. Fixed channel analysis will lock the wireless NIC card onto one channel, enabling it to capture all 802.11-encoded traffic on the selected channel. When channel scanning is selected, the wireless NIC will capture traffic on all selected channels, spending a short amount of time on each channel before moving to the next one.

Fixed Channel

For troubleshooting a particular access point (AP) or station (STA), wireless scanning is not effective. This is because only the packets transmitted at the point in time when the analyzer was capturing on the AP's or STA's operating channel will be captured. The rest of the time the analyzer will be capturing packets on other channels, and therefore many packets from the required conversations will be missing. *Fixed channel analysis* is a much better choice when troubleshooting a particular AP or STA. Figure 12.3 pictures the wireless settings dialog box in Wireshark, showing the configuration for a fixed channel capture set to channel 1.

FIGURE 12.3   Wireshark channel selection

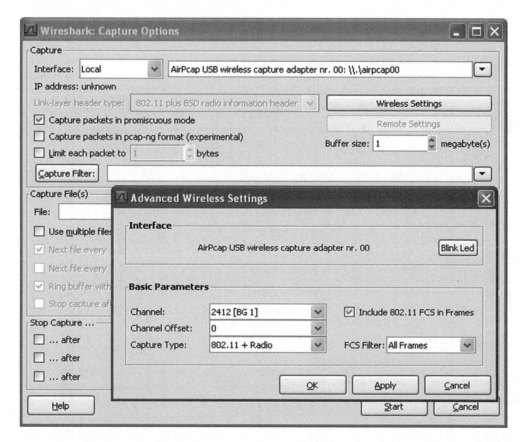

A 40 MHz, 802.11n channel can be selected by selecting the primary channel from the channel drop-down and selecting either a -1 or +1 channel offset to indicate that the secondary channel is either below or above the primary. How 40 MHz 802.11n channels are selected will vary across different vendors' products.

Often an analyst will not know which channel a particular AP or STA is operating on and will therefore initially perform a channel scan in order to identify the correct channel.

Channel Scanning

Wireless scanning provides a good overview of the wireless environment, showing which wireless devices are transmitting on which channels and which security protocols they are using. Figure 12.4 shows the Channel Scanning Options dialog box in OmniPeek. From this dialog box, the channels required to be included in the scan can be selected. In a completely unknown environment, all channels will probably be selected in order to gain an understanding of the wireless environment. However, if you are scanning a known network, with the foreknowledge that all APs are configured on channels 1, 6, or 11, then only these channels need to be selected. This prevents the analyzer from wasting time monitoring channels that contain little or no traffic of interest to you.

FIGURE 12.4 OmniPeek's Channel Scanning Options dialog box

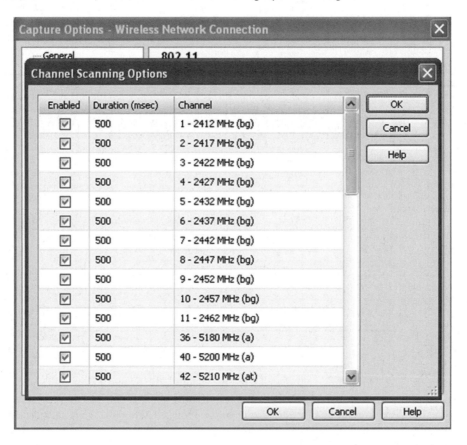

Another parameter that can be set when configuring channel scanning is the amount of time an analyzer will spend capturing on one particular channel before moving to the next. Figure 12.4 shows this duration set to the default value of 500 msec in OmniPeek.

Figure 12.5 shows the packet's view when channel scanning is enabled; notice how the analyzer jumps channels, capturing only a few packets per channel.

Country Code

Within a given frequency band, every country has its own regulations that govern which channels are allowed to be used. These regulatory authorities govern RF communication in terms of power, bandwidth and use; in the United States, for example, this is done by the Federal Communications Commission (FCC), and in the United Kingdom, it is regulated by OfCom. In the 2.4 GHz band, there are 11 channels available for use in the United States, but 13 are available in most countries across Europe.

FIGURE 12.5   Channel scan, packet view

acket	Source	Destination	Flags	Channel	Signal dBm	Data Rate	Size	Protocol
184	06:8B:5D:A3:84:CA	Ethernet Broadcast	*	1	-90	1.0	158	802.11 Beacon
185	ThomsonTel:0A:91:D9	Ethernet Broadcast	*P	1	-93	1.0	123	802.11 Beacon
186	00:8B:5D:A3:84:CA	Ethernet Broadcast	*P	1	-89	1.0	217	802.11 Beacon
187	0A:8B:5D:A3:84:CA	Ethernet Broadcast	*	1	-89	1.0	153	802.11 Beacon
188	06:8B:5D:A3:84:CA	Ethernet Broadcast	*	1	-89	1.0	158	802.11 Beacon
189	0A:8B:5D:A3:84:CA	Ethernet Broadcast	*	2	-89	1.0	153	802.11 Beacon
190	06:8B:5D:A3:84:CA	Ethernet Broadcast	*C	2	-89	1.0	158	802.11 Beacon
191	00:8B:5D:A3:84:CA	Ethernet Broadcast	*P	2	-89	1.0	217	802.11 Beacon
192	00:8B:5D:A3:84:CA	Ethernet Broadcast	*P	2	-89	1.0	217	802.11 Beacon
193	0A:8B:5D:A3:84:CA	Ethernet Broadcast	*	2	-89	1.0	153	802.11 Beacon
194	06:8B:5D:A3:84:CA	Ethernet Broadcast	*	2	-89	1.0	158	802.11 Beacon
195	00:8B:5D:A3:84:CA	Ethernet Broadcast	*P	3	-91	1.0	217	802.11 Beacon
196	06:8B:5D:A3:84:CA	Ethernet Broadcast	*C	3	-90	1.0	158	802.11 Beacon
197	06:8B:5D:A3:84:CA	Ethernet Broadcast	*	3	-91	1.0	158	802.11 Beacon
198	00:8B:5D:A3:84:CA	Ethernet Broadcast	*PC	3	-90	1.0	217	802.11 Beacon
199	Netgear:EB:E5:12	Ethernet Broadcast	*P	4	-89	1.0	138	802.11 Beacon
200	Ethernet Broadcast	Netgear:EB:E5:12	#	4	-89	1.0	14	802.11 CTS
201	Netgear:EB:E5:12	Ethernet Broadcast	*PC	4	-88	1.0	138	802.11 Beacon
202	Netgear:EB:E5:12	Ethernet Broadcast	*PC	4	-89	1.0	138	802.11 Beacon
203	ThomsonTel:80:13:87	Ethernet Broadcast	*P	5	-83	1.0	97	802.11 Beacon
204	Netgear:EB:E5:12	Ethernet Broadcast	*PC	5	-86	1.0	138	802.11 Beacon
205	ThomsonTel:80:13:87	Ethernet Broadcast	*P	5	-83	1.0	97	802.11 Beacon
206	ThomsonTel:80:13:87	Ethernet Broadcast	*P	5	-83	1.0	97	802.11 Beacon
207	Netgear:EB:E5:12	Ethernet Broadcast	*P	5	-86	1.0	138	802.11 Beacon
208	ThomsonTel:80:13:87	Ethernet Broadcast	*P	5	-83	1.0	97	802.11 Beacon
209	AskeyCompu:D9:14:13	Ethernet Broadcast	*P	5	-87	1.0	297	802.11 Beacon
210	ThomsonTel:80:13:87	Ethernet Broadcast	*P	5	-83	1.0	97	802.11 Beacon

After installing a customized analysis driver, you might find that you have the wrong number of channels available within your wireless analyzer. This is likely to be because the driver is configured with an incorrect country code. Often the country code or region can be changed in the advanced driver properties for the wireless adapter, as pictured in Figure 12.6.

FIGURE 12.6 Setting the country code/region

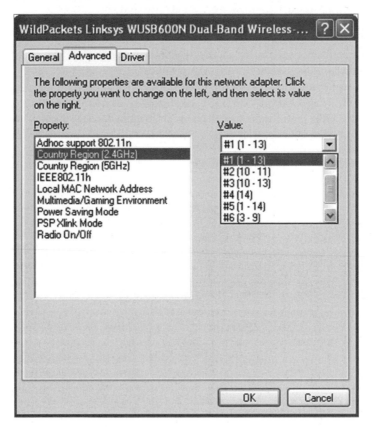

2.4 GHz Channel Overlap

Because the channels in the 2.4 GHz ISM band overlap, it is quite common to capture packets on channels other than the one on which they were originally transmitted. The channel a frame was captured on is displayed in the packet information at the top of every packet decode, as shown in Figure 12.7.

When performing a full channel scan in a multichannel architecture (MCA) environment that uses only channels 1, 6, and 11, do not be surprised when you capture packets on all 2.4 GHz channels.

FIGURE 12.7 Capture channel information

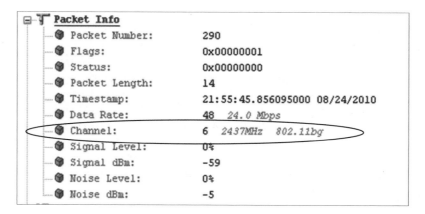

```
⊟ ▼ Packet Info
   ─◉ Packet Number:      290
   ─◉ Flags:              0x00000001
   ─◉ Status:             0x00000000
   ─◉ Packet Length:      14
   ─◉ Timestamp:          21:55:45.856095000 08/24/2010
   ─◉ Data Rate:          48   24.0 Mbps
   ─◉ Channel:            6   2437MHz   802.11bg
   ─◉ Signal Level:       0%
   ─◉ Signal dBm:         -59
   ─◉ Noise Level:        0%
   ─◉ Noise dBm:          -5
```

To determine the channel a frame was transmitted on, you need to start examining the packet decode. A 2.4 GHz AP advertises the channel the BSS is operating on in the Direct Sequence Parameter Set information element contained in the beacon and probe response frames, as shown in Figure 12.8. So, for beacon and probe response frames, the transmitted channel is right there in the packet. However, a bit more work is required if you are going to determine which channel other frame types were transmitted on, because the transmitted channel information is not recorded within the frame. The following three-step procedure can be used to determine the transmit channel of a 2.4 GHz packet:

1. Determine the BSSID from the packet in question. You can find this in the MAC header.

2. Find a beacon frame with a matching BBSID. This could be done using a filter or search.

3. Look up the BSS channel in the Direct Sequence Parameter Set information element.

FIGURE 12.8 Direct Sequence Parameter Set information element

```
⊟ ▼ Direct Sequence Parameter Set
   ─◉ Element ID:      3   Direct Sequence Parameter Set [65]
   ─◉ Length:          1 [66]
   ─◉ Channel:         6 [67]
```

This method works for all frames transmitted as part of a BSS. However, it is not possible to determine the channel of a probe request frame, because these frames are used for BSS discovery and are transmitted on all channels by stations performing active scanning. The BSSID in a probe response frame is set to the broadcast ID of all 1s.

Buffer Size

When configuring a wireless capture, as well as selecting your channel settings, another configuration option is the capture *buffer size*. The capture buffer is an allocation of memory (RAM) that will be reserved for your packet capture. This memory is used by your analyzer to store captured frames. Selecting the right buffer size will largely depend upon the amount of memory available in the computer running the analyzer software. The default behavior of network analyzers is to fill the capture buffer and stop capturing or to implement a ring buffer with a "first in, first out" policy. For short-term packet captures such as wireless environment channel scans, the analyzer's default buffer size is normally sufficient. On busy networks, if you find the capture buffer is being filled too quickly, one option is to increase the buffer size; just make sure that there is enough computer memory free to accommodate the extra buffer size, without compromising performance.

Save to Disk

If you need to capture packets over a sustained period of time, just selecting a large capture buffer will probably not provide enough storage, so the other option is to save the packets to disk. Captured packets are still placed into the capture buffer initially. Once the buffer is full or reaches a specified level, the packets are written to disk along with a date and time stamp applied to the end of the filename. These steps are repeated for the length of the capture.

Over a long period, these save-to-disk captures can produce many files. Some analyzers provide a forensic search facility for searching through a set of capture files (or trace files) and selecting just the packets that match the search criteria, displaying them in a new window. Save-to-disk captures are especially useful when trying to troubleshoot an intermittent problem. As an analyst, it can be amazing how, at the time when you are capturing packets, the problems just disappear, and everything works as it should. It is for situations like this when you want to leave a save-to-disk capture running and go for coffee. Just make sure there is someone around to record the time when the problem recurs.

Packet Slicing

Save-to-disk captures allow you to perform long-term packet captures; however, they can have the drawback of eating up your hard disk space. This is where *packet slicing* can help. Packet slicing allows you to just capture the first so many bytes of each packet, disregarding the rest of the frame. Often the only information we are interested in is the header information, and we do not have any interest in the data elements of the packets. This is especially the case on wireless networks when encryption is used and the data is unreadable. By using packet slicing, you can store a significantly larger number of packets to disk.

When encryption is used on a wireless network, the data element can sometimes still be of some use to the analyst, providing they know the encryption key. If a preshared key is used for encryption, some analyzers allow the key to be entered when configuring captures. The analyzer will then decrypt the packets in real time as they enter the capture buffer. When analyzing unencrypted packets, layer 2–7 header information is available. If you want to use packet slicing to remove the data element of a packet but still leave the MAC, IP, and TCP/UDP and application protocol headers in place, slicing packets at 128 bytes normally works quite well.

 Real World Scenario

No Data for You!

A wireless analyst, who was hired to troubleshoot a slow response time for a bespoke application running on wireless handheld terminals, realized after analyzing the wireless network that this might be an application problem and wanted to troubleshoot the TCP responses. However, the network he was monitoring was encrypted with a WPA pre-shared key. Although the consultant had signed an NDA, the organization was reluctant to provide the key to the consultant because it was company policy to not allow company data on any machine that would be leaving the premises. The consultant was able to demonstrate that, through packet slicing, the analyzer could be configured to strip off the data elements to all packets, leaving only the IP and TCP header information he required. Satisfied that no company data would be stored, the IT manager entered the key in the analyzer's configuration, enabling the analyst to solve the problem.

Protocol Decodes

At the very heart of protocol analysis are *protocol decodes*. Network analyzers can decode hundreds of network protocols, and these protocol decodes are used to decode the captured packets. Analyzing the detail within these packet decodes is often the last step in protocol analysis. Protocol analysis will often begin with looking for interesting or suspect protocols, devices, or events; these are often flagged by the expert features within analysis products. Next you can focus your analysis on just a particular device, protocol, or conversation, and finally, we can examine the packets and their decodes.

Protocol analyzer packet decode screens are traditionally split up into three areas: decode window, hex view, and ASCII view, as shown in Figure 12.9. Each of these three areas displays the captured packet. The decode window splits the packet down into its individual fields and displays a meaningful decode for each field. The hex view shows the raw hexadecimal value for each byte in the packet, and the ACSII view displays the ACSII character for each byte. The ASCII view is typically shown to the right of the hex view. If a protocol sends its data in clear text, the data will be readable in the ACSII view. Some analyzers also include an option to show EBCDIC encoding too.

FIGURE 12.9 Wireshark packet decode screen

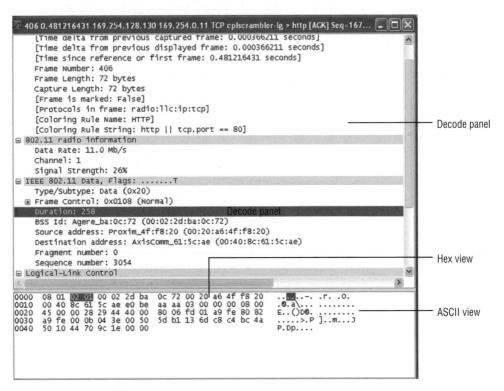

Figure 12.10 shows an example of an 802.11 protocol decode. The protocol decode window is arranged with the lower layers of the OSI seven layer model at the top; as you travel down the window, the layers go up. At the very top of the decode window is the packet information section, which displays information decoded about the packet by the analyzer such as packet number, length, and time stamp, as well as information passed up from the PHY layer such as signal strength, modulation type, and data rate.

Following the packet information section, the packet decode begins. All 802.11 packets begin with a layer 2 (data link) MAC header. What follows depends upon whether the packet is encrypted. When no encryption is used, the next header will be the second Data-Link sublayer, the Logical Link Control (LLC). In Figure 12.10, this is followed by an IP header, followed by a TCP header, and finally followed by an application layer HTTP header. When encryption is used, the encryption header and encrypted data directly follow the MAC header, as shown in Figure 12.11.

FIGURE 12.10   Example decode of an unencrypted wireless frame

```
⊟ ⊤ Packet Info
    ─ ● Packet Number:        23
    ─ ● Flags:                0x00000000
    ─ ● Status:               0x00000000
    ─ ● Packet Length:        346
    ─ ● Timestamp:            15:18:45.144702000 06/06/2001
    ─ ● Data Rate:            22  11.0 Mbps
    ─ ● Channel:              11  2462MHz  802.11bg
    ─ ● Signal Level:         90%
    ─ ● Noise Level:          0%
⊟ ⊤ 802.11 MAC Header
    ─ ● Version:              0 [0 Mask 0x03]
    ─ ● Type:                 %10  Data [0 Mask 0x0C]
    ─ ● Subtype:              %0000  Data [0 Mask 0xF0]
  ⊟ ⊤ Frame Control Flags:    %00000001 [1]
      ─ ●                        0... .... Non-strict order
      ─ ●                        .0.. .... Non-Protected Frame
      ─ ●                        ..0. .... No More Data
      ─ ●                        ...0 .... Power Management – active mode
      ─ ●                        .... 0... This is not a Re-Transmission
      ─ ●                        .... .0.. Last or Unfragmented Frame
      ─ ●                        .... ..0. Not an Exit from the Distribution System
      ─ ●                        .... ...1 To the Distribution System
    ─ ● Duration:             314  Microseconds [2-3]
    ─ ▦ BSSID:                00:A0:F8:8B:20:1F  SymbolTech:8B:20:1F [4-9]
    ─ ▦ Source:               00:A0:F8:9B:B9:AA  SymbolTech:9B:B9:AA [10-15]
    ─ ▦ Destination:          00:A0:C5:E2:6D:A8  ZyxelCommu:E2:6D:A8 [16-21]
    ─ ● Seq Number:           1672 [22-23 Mask 0xFFF0]
    ─ ● Frag Number:          0 [22 Mask 0x0F]
⊟ ⊤ 802.2 Logical Link Control (LLC) Header
    ─ ● Dest. SAP:            0xAA  SNAP [24]
    ─ ● Source SAP:           0xAA  SNAP [25]
    ─ ● Command:              0x03  Unnumbered Information [26]
    ─ ● Vendor ID:            0x000000 [27-29]
    ─ ● Protocol Type:        0x0800  IP [30-31]
⊞ ⊤ [32-51]    IP:           S=192.168.0.11 D=192.216.124.4
⊞ ⊤ [52-71]    TCP:          S=rmiactivation D=http SEQ=859976888 ACK=190996474 W=17520
⊞ ⊤ [72-340]   HTTP:         C=GET URI=/
⊟ ⊤ FCS - Frame Check Sequence
    ─ ● FCS:                  0x3877C861  Calculated
```

FIGURE 12.11 Example decode of an encrypted wireless frame

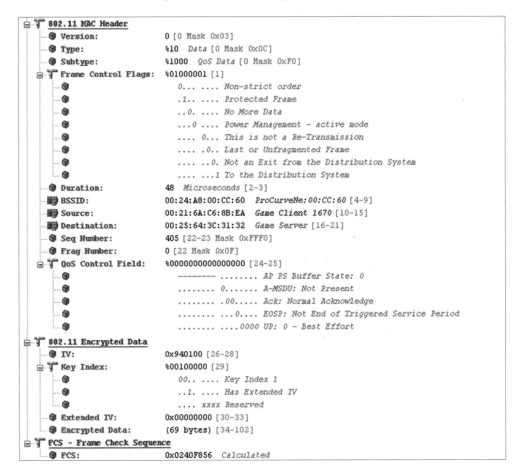

When a preshared key is used to encrypt traffic, such as WEP, WPA-PSK, or WPA2-PSK, some analyzers allow this key to be entered into the analyzer's configuration, as shown in Figure 12.12. Once a preshared key is configured, the protocol analyzer can then decrypt packets, displaying the protocol decodes as if no encryption had been used.

FIGURE 12.12   Encryption key configuration

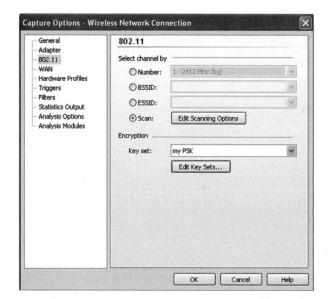

When reading protocol decodes, you see three pieces of information displayed: the field name, value, and decode, as identified in Figure 12.13. The field name is often a self-explanatory name, such as source address, SSID, or beacon interval, and this is followed by the field value. The field value can be displayed in either binary, hexadecimal, or decimal—whichever is the most appropriate for that field. Most vendors follow the convention shown in Figure 12.14: when just a number is displayed, it is a decimal value; when the value is preceded with a 0x, it is a hexadecimal value; and when preceded with a %, it is a binary value. The last piece of information is the field decode, which is an interpretation of the field value. Figure 12.12 shows a deauthentication reason code value of 2; the decode helpfully interprets the reason code 2, which is "Previous authentication no longer valid."

FIGURE 12.13   Field decode information

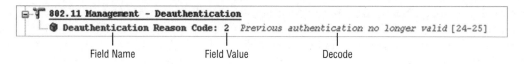

Field Name   Field Value   Decode

FIGURE 12.14   Decode value interpretations

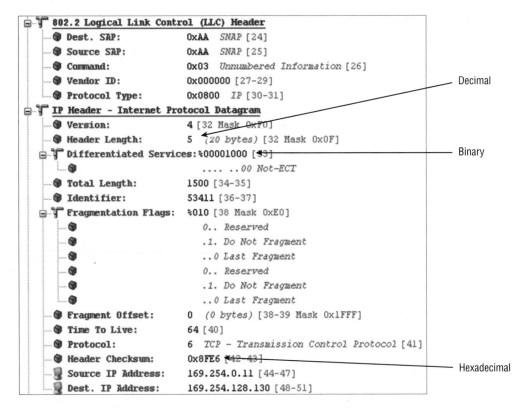

Peer Map Functions

A *peer map* is a visual representation of which STAs are communicating with each other. Lines between peers indicate communication. The peer map feature in OmniPeek, pictured in Figure 12.15, indicates the volume of traffic between the communicating peers through the thickness of the line joining them. A thicker line indicates more traffic has been communicated. You will also notice from Figure 12.15 that a dot is associated with each node; the size of the dot indicates the volume of traffic that each node has transmitted.

When troubleshooting network traffic, one of the first big questions that often needs to be answered is, "Where did the packets come from, and where are there going?" Both physical and logical peer maps can help you answer this question. The peer map shown in Figure 12.15 is a physical peer map.

FIGURE 12.15   OmniPeek peer map

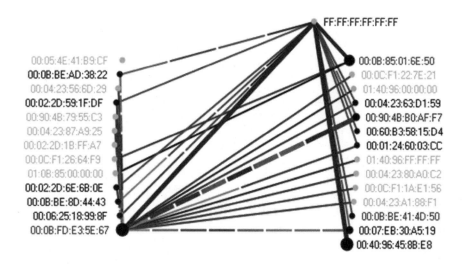

Physical peer maps identify which physical devices (identified by their MAC address) are communicating. Physical peer maps draw lines between the source and destination MAC address within the MAC header. On a physical peer map, traffic addressed to or from a device on an external subnet will be shown as traveling to and from the default gateway/router.

To help explain this, take a look at the simple network diagram shown in Figure 12.16. In this diagram, the wireless analyzer has captured a packet traveling between the wireless client and access point. The captured packet and its address fields are also pictured. Because the ultimate destination of this packet is a server on another network, as indicated by the destination IP address in the IP header, it is sent to the client's default gateway. The default gateway is the client's known route to other networks. So, when we look at the MAC header of this packet, the source address is 00:00:00:00:00:00, which is the client's MAC address, and the destination address is 22:22:22:22:22:22, which is the router's (client's default gateway) interface on the network that contains the wireless network. On a physical peer map, this packet would cause a line to be drawn between these two MAC nodes.

Logical (layer 3) peer maps are also available. On an IP logical peer map, lines are drawn between the source and destination address in the IP header. So, the packet captured in Figure 12.16 would cause a line to be drawn between 192.168.0.10 (the wireless client) and 192.168.2.20 (the server).

Peer map displays can be configured to make a much more readable display. Figure 12.17 shows a peer map created from a filtered packet capture showing only frames to and from a wireless VoIP handset. A floor plan background has been added, and the nodes have been named and placed on to the background. You can now clearly see that the VoIP handset has communicated with each of the access points in this room.

FIGURE 12.16   Example network diagram

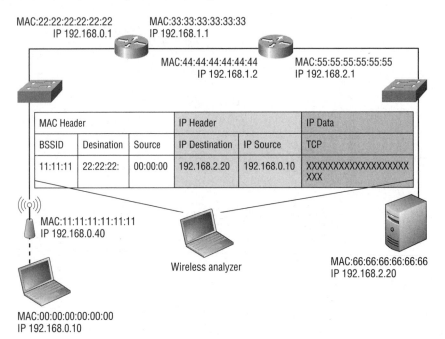

MAC Header			IP Header		IP Data
BSSID	Desination	Source	IP Destination	IP Source	TCP
11:11:11	22:22:22:	00:00:00	192.168.2.20	192.168.0.10	XXXXXXXXXXXXXXXXXXXXX

MAC:22:22:22:22:22:22
IP 192.168.0.1

MAC:33:33:33:33:33:33
IP 192.168.1.1

MAC:44:44:44:44:44:44
IP 192.168.1.2

MAC:55:55:55:55:55:55
IP 192.168.2.1

MAC:11:11:11:11:11:11
IP 192.168.0.40

Wireless analyzer

MAC:66:66:66:66:66:66
IP 192.168.2.20

MAC:00:00:00:00:00:00
IP 192.168.0.10

Peer maps have many different features and configurations, which allows you to quickly identify and select the traffic you are interested in. For example, right-click a node to select and display all traffic addressed to or from the device, or alternatively click a line to bring up details of a particular conversation.

FIGURE 12.17   Example peer map display

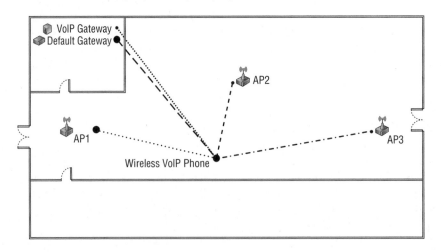

VoIP Gateway
Default Gateway
AP2
AP1
Wireless VoIP Phone
AP3

Conversation Analysis

Often the final step of protocol analysis is analyzing an individual conversation. Most protocol analyzers have a conversation view, listing the individual conversations and their statistics such as the number of packet sent/received, the number of bytes sent/received, the duration, and the throughput. Figure 12.18 shows Wireshark's conversation window. The conversation window can provide a good starting place when selecting the conversation or flow that you would like to analyze in more detail. Analyzers that include an expert system will also list any events or alarms, which have been detected by the expert system. Expert systems help identify which conversations need analyzing in more detail and will be discussed in more detail in the expert system section of this chapter.

FIGURE 12.18   Wireshark conversation window

Address A	Address B	Packets	Bytes	Packets A->B	Bytes A->B	Packets A<-B	Bytes A<-B	Rel Start	Duration	bps A->B	bps A<-B
Intel_18:2f:2a	Cisco_9d:3e:f2	7	1051	2	363	5	688	15.253030777	0.0392	74143.29	140525.01
Invensys_54:f8:20	AxisComm_61:5c:ae	7	1964	6	432	1	1532	19.556760788	30.5579	113.10	N/A
Intel_81:bb:d3	Cisco_9d:3e:f2	27	3643	21	2698	6	945	4.762403488	46.9003	460.21	161.19
Intel_81:bb:d3	Broadcast	42	5437	42	5437	0	0	2.542194366	50.1275	867.71	N/A
Intel_61:b5:2a	Cisco_9d:3e:f2	123	137066	20	5366	103	131700	1.139770508	46.4518	924.14	22681.57
Intel_64:42:8d	Cisco_9d:3e:f2	298	203435	123	33919	175	169516	1.256290436	43.8544	6187.57	30923.44
Intel_4d:c9:9f	Cisco_9d:3e:f2	727	296120	330	108568	397	187552	14.631919861	38.0080	22851.61	39476.32
Proxim_4f:f8:20	AxisComm_61:5c:ae	10562	10917093	3480	250560	7082	10666533	0.000000000	52.7593	37992.92	1617387.92

Selecting just the traffic that you want to analyze is a key troubleshooting step. This may be one particular conversation, or it may be a set of conversations, such as all the conversations that one particular problematic station has had. Two main methods of packet selection are available:

- Display filters
- Select related

These methods hide any unwanted traffic from your analyzer's display. Which of these are available to you will depend upon your preferred analyzer's capabilities. Post capture filters will be described in more detail in the next section on filters. The select-related method allows the analyst to click or right-click a node, protocol, packet, or conversation in any screen within the analyzer and select the packets related to that object. For example, you can right-click a node in the peer map and select all packets transmitted to and from that node. Or in the protocol view, right-click the HTTP protocol, and select all the web traffic.

Having selected the conversation(s) of interest, you can then start to examine conversation flow and packet decodes. When performing this type of analysis, you are looking for any unexpected behavior or error messages. If you are going to be able to detect unexpected behavior, you need to know what the expected behavior is. It is at this point that knowing your protocols, and all you have learned in this book, becomes important.

If a user was experiencing network connectivity problems, you would want to understand the procedure a station would go through under normal conditions to connect to the network. For example, this might be as follows:

1. Network discovery

    1.1 Probe request

    1.2 Probe response

2. Open system authentication

    2.1 Authentication message 1: open system request

    2.1 Authentication message 2: authentication success

3. Association

    3.1 Association request

    3.2 Association response

4. EAP authentication

    4.1 EAPoL START

    4.2 EAP request: identity request

    4.3 EAP response: identity response

    4.4 EAP request: client challenge

    4.5 EAP response: challenge response

    4.6 EAP request: server challenge

    4.7 EAP response: challenge response

    4.8 EAP success

5. RSN four-way handshake

    5.1 EAPoL KEY

    5.2 EAPoL KEY

    5.3 EAPoL KEY

    5.4 EAPoL KEY

6. DCHP

    6.1 Discover

    6.2 Offer

    6.3 Request

    6.4 Acknowledge

If you know what the expected behavior is, you can then compare this to your captured packets and identify at what point it fails. Does the association fail? Are you not getting a response to the EAPol START message? There are many different places within in this procedure that a failure could occur. On an encrypted network, the DHCP packets in step 6 would be encrypted, making the DHCP messages unreadable. However, if the procedure up to the end of the four-way handshake had been successful but the client was not obtaining an IP address, you could correctly point the finger at the DCHP procedure, because you know this is the next expected behavior. If you wanted to analyze the DCHP procedure, this could be done with an Ethernet analyzer on the wired network.

EXERCISE 12.1

EAP Conversation Analyses

In this exercise, you will use a protocol analyzer to analyze a client's authentication and association using EAP/802.1x. The following directions should assist you with the installation and use of WildPackets' OmniPeek protocol analyzer demo software. If you have already installed OmniPeek, you can skip step 1.

1. A demo copy of OmniPeek Enterprise is included on the CD that comes with this book. Locate the file `OmniPeek65ademo.exe`. Double-click the installation file, and follow the installation prompts. You will need to be connected to the Internet to activate the license.

2. This exercise will use frame captures that are on the CD that comes with this book. If you want to use OmniPeek for live captures, you will need to install the proper drivers for your Wi-Fi radio card. Verify that you have a supported Wi-Fi card. You can find information about the supported drivers at `www.wildpackets.com/support/downloads/drivers`. Review the system requirements and supported operating systems. Install the proper driver for your Wi-Fi card.

3. From Windows, choose Start ➢ Programs ➢ WildPackets OmniPeek, and then click the OmniPeek icon. The OmniPeek application should appear.

4. Click the Open Capture File icon, and browse the book's CD.

5. Open the packet capture file called `EAPauth1.apc`.

6. In the left column, click Capture ➢ Packets. Drag the Protocol column so that it can be viewed within the window.

7. Scroll down to packet 134; you will notice it is a probe request message. Examine the packet decode to see the requested SSID.

8. Packet 135 shows the probe response from the access point. Examine the packet decode, and find the matching SSID.

9. Right-click the probe response (packet 135), and select Insert Into Name Table.

10. In the resulting dialog box, enter the name **AP**, and choose a blue color from the color drop-down.

Continues

11. Click OK, and a second dialog box will appear. In this box, enter **Client** as the name, and pick a red color from the color drop-down; then click OK. You should now notice that the source and destination MAC addresses have changed to the AP and Client labels you have just given them. If you do not see these labels in the source and destination columns, then from the menu select View ➤ Display Format and make sure Show Address Names is selected.

    In packets 147–154, you see the client open authentication and associate to the access point. In packet 155, the client initiates the EAP protocol exchange.

12. Follow the EAP exchange through. Was it successful?

13. Open EAPauth2.apc.

14. Find the EAP exchange in this file. Was it successful?

Filtering: Capture and Display

In a busy 802.11 wireless environment, an unfiltered packet capture will generate a large number of packets for analysis. The sheer quantity of data can make it very difficult to find the information you require. When dealing with large amounts of the data like this, filters become an essential analysis tool, allowing you to quickly locate the data you require. Filters can be configured to hide traffic that is of no interest to the analyst or to select only the interesting traffic. The three main methods for creating filters are as follows:

- Regular expression
- Proprietary scripting language
- Proprietary filter creation GUI

Which of these are available to you and what criteria can be used to create the filters will depend on your choice of analyzer. At a very basic level, you should be able to create filters on address, protocol, and port.

Filter Conditions and Operators

Address filters allow the selection of traffic based upon physical (MAC) or logical (Network layer) addresses. As well as individual addresses, address filters allow the use of wildcard entries that enable the selection of IP subnets. MAC address wildcard entries allow the analyst to filter on a particular vendor's organizationally unique identifier (OUI). OUIs are the first three bytes of every MAC address and are uniquely assigned to vendors by the IEEE Registration Authority. For example, 00:1E:5D:*:*:* is assigned to Cisco-Linksys. If you only ever deploy one or two different vendors' equipment, by filtering out their OUIs, you can quickly see whether there are any noncompliant devices in your RF environment.

Having entered an address into a filter, the default behavior is to filter all traffic traveling to or from that address or subnet. However, address filters can be configured to filter only that traffic being sent to the configure address or from the configured address. Alternatively, you can just filter traffic traveling between two different addresses or subnets. Figure 12.19 shows the different address filter options.

FIGURE 12.19 Address filter options

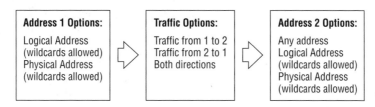

Protocol and TCP/UDP port filters allow the analysis to focus their filters on a particular type of traffic. Protocol and port filters can be used in conjunction with address filters or separately. For example, you might want to look simply at all email traffic, or you might want to look at all email traffic from a particular server.

The address, protocol, and port are not the only criteria that can be used to create a filter condition. More advanced filters can be created through the use of other criteria. Some of the other common options available are shown here:

Value/Offset   This is probably the most powerful filter criteria, allowing any byte or bit of a packet to be filtered on. The byte(s) to be filtered is referenced with an offset from the beginning of the packet. If less than one byte is of interest, a bit mask can be used to select the individual bits required. This is a great way of filtering on a particular flag within a packet. One word of warning: with offset filters, unless you are filtering on something generic within the MAC header, always use a protocol filter as well. For example, if you were filtering on the 35th byte offset in a beacon frame looking for the privacy flag being set, it is important you at look at the 35-byte offset only in beacons and not in all frames.

Pattern   This matches a particular data pattern in ASCII or hex anywhere within the packet or between two configured offsets.

Length   This filters packets that have a size between a minimum and maximum length.

Wireless   Filters can be created based on 802.11 wireless conditions, such as channel, signal strength, data rate, and BSSID.

When combining multiple filter conditions, such as address and protocol within one filter, you can AND the conditions together, which will result in only the traffic that matches both the conditions being filtered. You can also OR the conditions together, which filters any traffic matching either of the conditions. A NOT operator can also be applied to a filter condition, resulting in any traffic that does not match the condition being filtered. Through the use of multiple conditions and operators, you can create complex and powerful filters.

Applying Filters

When applying filters, a choice can be made to either collect packets matching the selected filters or to reject packets matching the selected filters. Filters can be applied at capture time, or they can be applied after the capture as display filters.

Capture Filters

Capture filters are applied to the packet stream before the packets enter the capture buffer. Anything filtered out at capture time is not stored and therefore cannot be recovered later. Capture filters can make your packet captures more readable by removing unneeded traffic.

Wireless captures can become crowded by beacon and probe request/response messages. This is because access points send beacon frames typically every 100ms, and clients will often transmit probe request messages searching for new and better access points, even when associated. If beacon and probe request messages are not of interest, then filtering them out at capture time will provide for a cleaner capture window, allowing the needed information to be found more easily. When performing a long-term capture and saving the packets to disk, an unfiltered capture can needlessly eat away at your hard drive space. By only saving the packets of interest through capture time filtering, you reduce the risk of filling your hard drive.

Display Filters

Display filters or post-capture filters provide a way of hiding from view unwanted packets. An advantage of display filters is that the packets are only hidden and can be retrieved if required. When you are not sure what information you will require and system resources are not a problem, capturing everything and using display filters to home in on what you need can often be the best approach. This way, if you filter out some data that you later discover you need, you can just remove the filter.

Expert Functions

Expert analysis is the automatic detection of network events, errors, and problems by an analyzer. Expert analysis is a term used by the more traditional protocol analysis vendors, whereas the WIDS vendors tend to refer to their expert analysis as a set of alarms. There are two types of expert analysis, threshold-based and heuristic-based. An explanation of these two types follows.

Threshold-Based

Threshold-based expert analysis collects network statistics and compares them to configured threshold values. When the statistics exceed the configured threshold, an expert event is triggered, and a notification is sent. An example of a threshold-based expert event would be "Too many retransmissions," where the threshold value is configured to trigger this event when retransmissions reach an unacceptable level. A good default value for this event may be three retransmissions within a 10-second period. Although like all threshold-based expert events, the value should be tweaked to match the network and wireless environment being monitored. Figure 12.20 pictures the expert setting in OmniPeek.

FIGURE 12.20 OmniPeek event finder settings

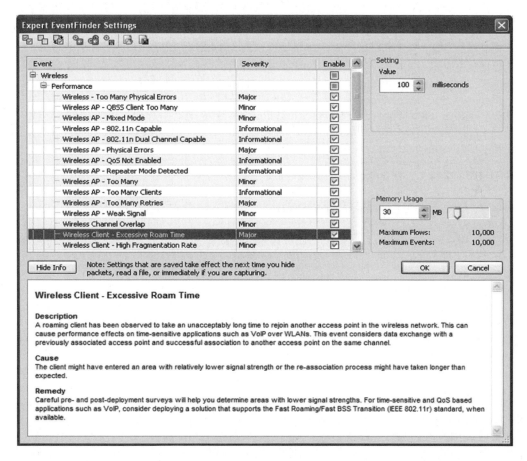

If an expert event is triggering regularly and after investigation you believe it not to be an issue for your network, then you should change the threshold value to a more appropriate level for your network. There may even be some expert events and alarms that you want to disable because they are not appropriate for your environment. Having configured your expert settings, it is good practice to export a backup copy of the settings so that they can be easily reloaded if needed. When using a portable analyzer to monitor many different networks, the default expert settings will probably work well, because they have been designed by the vendors to work for typical network deployments. If you find yourself analyzing a group of networks on a regular basis, you could have expert event settings files for each network, which get reloaded for each network.

Heuristic-Based

Heuristic-based expert analysis looks for patterns in the traffic flow and compares them to a set of rules. Traffic that does not conform to these rules is reported. A good example of a heuristic-based expert event would be "Inefficient client," which looks for clients sending data using only small packet sizes. Some expert events are a combination of both threshold-based and heuristic-based analysis.

Expert systems save network analysts time by automating some of the basic analysis tasks. The events report by the expert system provides a good starting place for further analysis and can point the analyst in the right direction of a problem.

Because of the large number of expert events or alarms that vendors implement, it is not always easy to know what every alarm is and how it is triggered. To help combat this, analysis tools contain a database of events/alarms with a description of the event and a possible mitigation technique. Figure 12.21 shows the alarm description window in AirDefense.

FIGURE 12.21   AirDefense alarms details

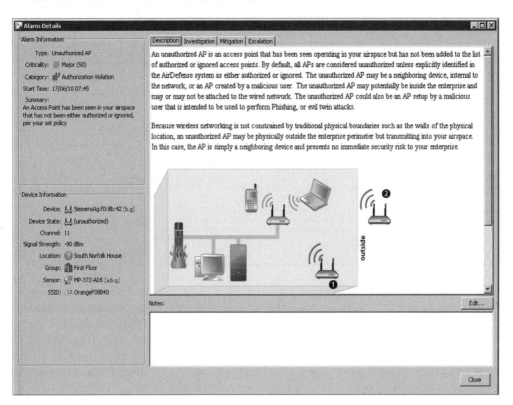

Wireless Policies

Many wireless analysis vendors allow the configuration of a wireless policy to be entered into the analyzer. Configuring a wireless policy is similar to the configuration of a wireless service on a wireless LAN controller. Wireless policies allow the analyst to specify the wireless network, which is analyzed in terms of the following:

- SSID
- Channel set
- Security mechanism (authentication and encryption)
- Vendor

Any traffic captured that does not conform to the configured policy will be reported. This can help identify misconfigured or rogue devices.

Performance Analysis

The main metrics used for measuring network performance are availability and throughput. Maintaining a wireless network that provides all users with the required throughput and a high level of availability is a difficult task. Many different factors affect wireless network performance, some of which are listed here:

- High volumes of associated clients to a single access point
- Clients communicating at low data rates because of physical distance from the access point
- Mixed modulation types and protection mechanisms
- Co-channel and adjacent channel 802.11 interfering devices
- Non-802.11 RF interference
- Inefficient roaming
- Physical environment: multipath, obstructions, and absorption
- Channel hops because of Dynamic Frequency Selection (DFS)

Poor network performance manifests itself in wireless network analyzers as follows:

- High level of retransmissions
- High level of corrupted packets
- Weak signal
- Excessive RTS/CTS packets
- Excessive data rate changes
- Too many clients associated to the same AP
- High wireless utilization
- Slow roaming times

Many of these performance-related issues will be detected by an analyzer's expert system or a performance-related alarm in WIDS. Examples of the performance-related events and alarms that wireless analyzers can detect are shown in Figures 12.21 and 12.22.

FIGURE 12.22 AirDefense Mobile performance alarms

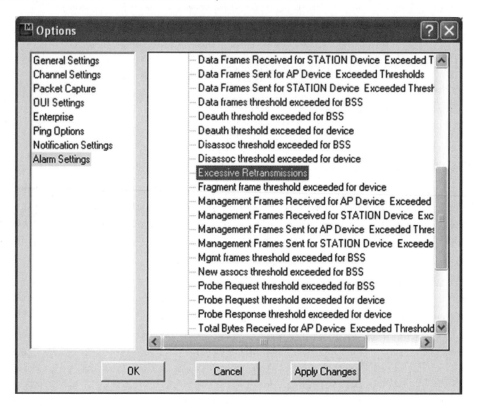

Reporting Capabilities

Most analyzers have some built-in reporting capabilities. This can be anything from creating an HTML report showing the same statistics, events, and graphs visible in the GUI to providing a full regulatory compliance report. Analyzers often provide different levels of reports, ranging from an executive summary report, which just provides the overall health, performance, and security of your wireless network, to a full detailed report, which includes statistics on the protocols, devices, and conversations observed on the network, plus all expert events and alarms that have been detected.

A WIPS is often the most comprehensive reporting tool, allowing the creation of custom reports through a report building wizard, as pictured in Figure 12.23. WIPS also have many report templates for different types of security and performance-related reports, these including ones that will be required for regulatory compliance, such as the PCI report pictured in Figure 12.24.

FIGURE 12.23   AirDefense Report Builder

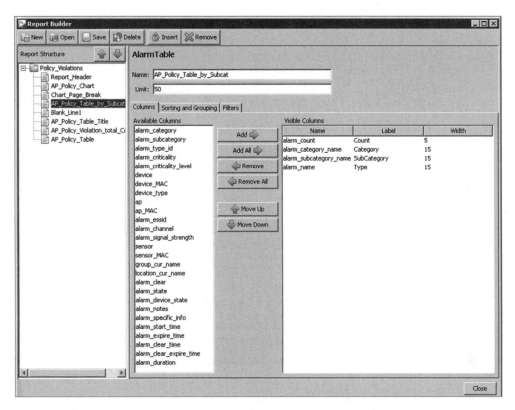

PCI DSS

The Payment Card Industry Data Security Standard (PCI DSS) is a security standard defined by the Card Industry Security Standards Council. The aim of the standard is to help organizations that process card payments to prevent fraud. Organizations that process or store card details must be compliant with the standard.

The PCI DSS standard includes minimum security requirements for wireless networks and also requires that a test to detect the present of rogue wireless access points be carried out at least quarterly. For more information on the wireless requirements outlined by PCI DSS, a Security Standards Council document titled "Information Supplement: PCI DSS Wireless Guidelines" has been included on this book's CD.

FIGURE 12.24 AirDefense PCI report

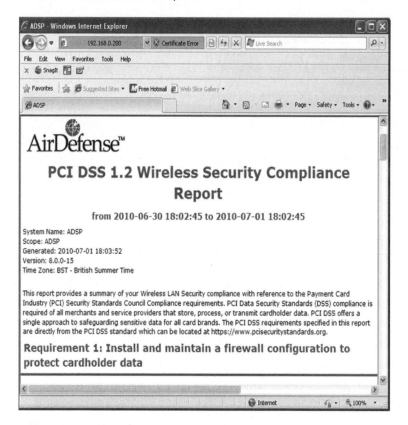

Many analyzers allow 24/7 monitoring captures to be performed. These captures work in one of two ways:

- By using a ring buffer, where the oldest packets are removed from the buffer in order to make way for the new ones coming in
- By only recoding the statistics about each packet, without storing the packets themselves

Although both of these methods throw away packets, the statistics about all packets are still recoded from whenever the capture was started.

The automated reporting capabilities of a network analyzer can be used along with a 24/7 monitoring capture to save an HTML-formatted report to an internal web server every five minutes. This will create an internal website showing the current status of the wireless network, which can be accessed by the whole networking team. Distributed analysis platforms often provide this functionally also through a dashboard view accessible from remote consoles or via a web GUI.

Protocol Analysis Operation

Understanding the common features of a protocol analyzer and the use of a basic trouble-shooting methodology are great for troubleshooting many problems; however, there are some situations where you will find yourself requiring more advance analysis procedures and operations. One such situation is when analyzing a real-time application such as Voice over IP (VoIP), which requires Quality of Service (QoS) end-to-end across the entire network, not just the wireless segment. Often Voice over Wi-Fi (VoWiFi) problems are caused by problems with a voice handset roaming. Troubleshooting roaming problems is not easy when using a signal wireless capture adapter because the adapter can capture packets on only one channel at any given time. The solutions to these analysis problems will be discussed next in this section.

Any analyst will know that the worst type of problem to troubleshoot is an intermittent one. You can guarantee that when you are on-site performing a packet capture, everything will be operating perfectly. Distributed analysis can help solve this problem by giving the analyst the power to start a capture at a remote site at the time a problem occurs. Having the ability to monitor and troubleshoot your entire wireless environment from one central location can save valuable time and resources. The different distributed analysis architectures and their uses will be discussed in this section.

VoWiFi Analysis

As with all application-based protocol analysis, the level of VoWiFi analysis that can be performed if encryption is used on the wireless network will be limited. If you are not able to decrypt the packets, some analysis of VoIP calls and signaling will be able to be performed from the wired network.

Although we cannot analyze VoIP calls and their signaling on an encrypted network, we can still analyze two of the most import requirements for voice on a wireless network: QoS and fast efficient roaming. Roaming problems are one of the most common causes of dropped calls or glitches on a VoWiFi system. Analysis of roaming will be discussed in the "Roaming Analysis" section later in this chapter.

WMM Analysis

As you have already learned in previous chapters, QoS on a wireless network is achieved through the use of wireless multimedia (WMM). WMM-capable access points will advertise their WMM capabilities in beacon frame, as shown in Figure 12.25.

FIGURE 12.25 WMM Information Element

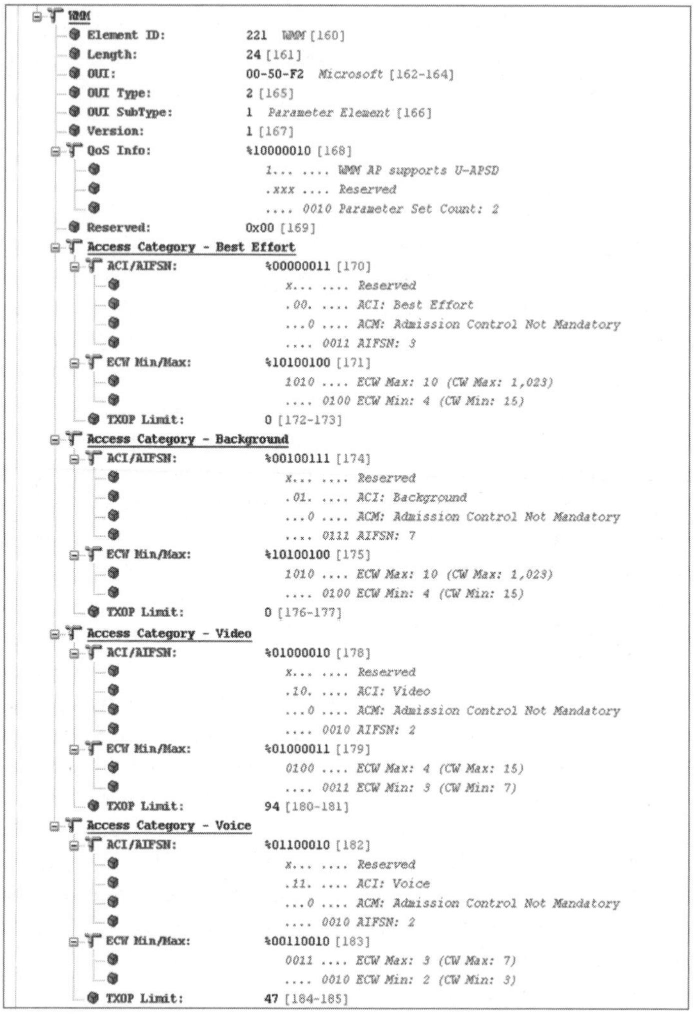

```
☐ ☋ WMM
   │  ● Element ID:        221  WMM [160]
   │  ● Length:            24 [161]
   │  ● OUI:               00-50-F2  Microsoft [162-164]
   │  ● OUI Type:          2 [165]
   │  ● OUI SubType:       1  Parameter Element [166]
   │  ● Version:           1 [167]
   ☐ ☋ QoS Info:          %10000010 [168]
   │  ● ─────────────      1... .... WMM AP supports U-APSD
   │  ● ─────────────      .xxx .... Reserved
   │  ● ─────────────      .... 0010 Parameter Set Count: 2
   │  ● Reserved:          0x00 [169]
   ☐ ☋ Access Category - Best Effort
   │  ☐ ☋ ACI/AIFSN:       %00000011 [170]
   │  │  ● ──────────      x... .... Reserved
   │  │  ● ──────────      .00. .... ACI: Best Effort
   │  │  ● ──────────      ...0 .... ACM: Admission Control Not Mandatory
   │  │  ● ──────────      .... 0011 AIFSN: 3
   │  ☐ ☋ ECW Min/Max:     %10100100 [171]
   │  │  ● ──────────      1010 .... ECW Max: 10 (CW Max: 1,023)
   │  │  ● ──────────      .... 0100 ECW Min: 4 (CW Min: 15)
   │  ● TXOP Limit:        0 [172-173]
   ☐ ☋ Access Category - Background
   │  ☐ ☋ ACI/AIFSN:       %00100111 [174]
   │  │  ● ──────────      x... .... Reserved
   │  │  ● ──────────      .01. .... ACI: Background
   │  │  ● ──────────      ...0 .... ACM: Admission Control Not Mandatory
   │  │  ● ──────────      .... 0111 AIFSN: 7
   │  ☐ ☋ ECW Min/Max:     %10100100 [175]
   │  │  ● ──────────      1010 .... ECW Max: 10 (CW Max: 1,023)
   │  │  ● ──────────      .... 0100 ECW Min: 4 (CW Min: 15)
   │  ● TXOP Limit:        0 [176-177]
   ☐ ☋ Access Category - Video
   │  ☐ ☋ ACI/AIFSN:       %01000010 [178]
   │  │  ● ──────────      x... .... Reserved
   │  │  ● ──────────      .10. .... ACI: Video
   │  │  ● ──────────      ...0 .... ACM: Admission Control Not Mandatory
   │  │  ● ──────────      .... 0010 AIFSN: 2
   │  ☐ ☋ ECW Min/Max:     %01000011 [179]
   │  │  ● ──────────      0100 .... ECW Max: 4 (CW Max: 15)
   │  │  ● ──────────      .... 0011 ECW Min: 3 (CW Min: 7)
   │  ● TXOP Limit:        94 [180-181]
   ☐ ☋ Access Category - Voice
   │  ☐ ☋ ACI/AIFSN:       %01100010 [182]
   │  │  ● ──────────      x... .... Reserved
   │  │  ● ──────────      .11. .... ACI: Voice
   │  │  ● ──────────      ...0 .... ACM: Admission Control Not Mandatory
   │  │  ● ──────────      .... 0010 AIFSN: 2
   │  ☐ ☋ ECW Min/Max:     %00110010 [183]
   │  │  ● ──────────      0011 .... ECW Max: 3 (CW Max: 7)
   │  │  ● ──────────      .... 0010 ECW Min: 2 (CW Min: 3)
   │  ● TXOP Limit:        47 [184-185]
```

WMM needs to be configured on both the access point and the wireless VoIP handset. If correctly configured, wireless VoIP packets should be transmitted using QoS data frames. QoS data frames contain a QoS Control field in the 802.11 MAC header, as shown in Figure 12.26. By looking at the QoS Control field, you can confirm that the packet is being transmitted using the correct access category (AC). Voice traffic should be marked with a very high priority and therefore put in to the Voice access category, as pictured in the QoS Control field decode in Figure 12.27.

FIGURE 12.26   The 802.11 MAC header

Frame Control	Duration/ ID	Address 1	Address 2	Address 3	Sequence Control	Address 4	QoS Control	HT Control	Frame Body	FCS
2	2	6	6	6	2	6	2	4	0–7955	4

FIGURE 12.27   QoS Control field decode

```
⊟ ⊤ QoS Control Field:     %0000000000100111 [24-25]
   ●                       ------- ........ AP PS Buffer State: 0
   ●                       ........ 0....... A-MSDU: Not Present
   ●                       ........ .01..... Ack: No Acknowledgement
   ●                       ........ ...0.... EOSP: Not End of Triggered Service Period
   ●                       ........ ....0111 UP: 7 - Voice
```

Figure 12.27 shows the TID (Traffic Identifier) subfield of the QoS Control field set to 7, indicating a UP (User priority) of 7; this UP is mapped to the Voice AC, as shown in the decode text. By creating a filter on the TID subfield of QoS Control field, you can identify all devices currently sending data using the voice AC. By doing this, you can check two things:

- That it is only our VoIP handsets using this high-priority AC
- To confirm how many VoIP calls are currently active in the BSS

Looking at the number of devices actively sending out voice AC traffic is a good way to identify the number of voice calls on an encrypted network. Tagging frames alone does not guarantee good voice quality because interference or bad wireless design can also affect call quality. What tagging does do is give your voice packets the best chance of getting to the access point fast enough to not cause an audible problem.

For our VoIP system to work successfully, you must ensure QoS end-to-end across the whole network. Network analysis confirming the operation of QoS over the wireless network is only half the job; you must also ensure the traffic prioritization is working across the whole network. This may involve analysis of the VoIP frames on the wired Ethernet network, confirming the Differentiated Services Code Point (DSCP) priority in the IP header and confirming that the 802.1Q VLAN tags are carrying the right priority across trunk connections.

If at any point across the network traffic priorities are not upheld, VoIP traffic could get held up behind large data packets, impacting the call quality. This can become a problem when all wireless traffic is being sent from an access point to a wireless LAN controller/ switch in a propriety encrypted tunnel. Encrypting wireless traffic across the wired network in this way is a method commonly used by wireless LAN vendors to contain the wireless traffic until the wireless LAN controller has processed the packet through its own firewall and made a decision about its destination VLAN. This effectively makes the wireless LAN controller the network entry point for the wireless LAN packets. To help understand why this can be a problem when trying to ensure end-to-end QoS, let's consider the network pictured in Figure 12.28.

FIGURE 12.28 Example path from access point to controller

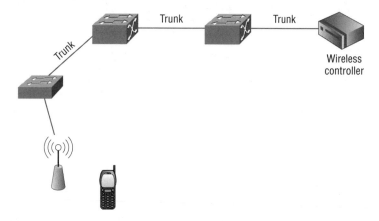

In the example network pictured in Figure 12.28, when the access point receives a VoIP packet from the wireless handset transmitted using the voice AC, it forwards this packet on to the wired network, and the UP priority should be honored in the Differentiated Services field in the IP header. When this packet traverses a trunk again, the priority should be honored in the VLAN tag. This will ensure the wireless VoIP packet has priority on the three trunk connections between the access point and controller, over other network traffic. However, when propriety layer 2 tunneling is used between the access point and the wireless controller, the entire wireless frame is encrypted and sent to the controller in a proprietary layer 2 frame. When this frame is received by a wired switch, it cannot read the priority identified in the IP header because it is encrypted and therefore treats the frame equally to all other network traffic. It is not until the frame is decrypted and forwarded by the wireless controller that the prioritization will be honored again across the network. Unfortunately, in the diagram shown in Figure 12.28, by that point, the packet has already traveled across three VLAN trunk connections and has been significantly delayed. It should be noted that this is only a problem when using layer 2 priority tunneling. When layer 3 tunneling is used, the priority from the inner frame can be transferred to the outer layer 3 frame. Most wireless vendors support the ability to use layer 3 tunneling. However a few wireless vendors default behavior is still for an access point to try and connect using layer 2 tunneling first.

Call Analysis

On unencrypted networks or on networks where you can enter a preshared key to decrypt the packets, you are able to analyze the call and signaling information of your VoIP conversations. Some network analyzers include special VoIP analysis features:

- Call list
- Call quality metrics (MOS and R-Factor)

- Signaling diagrams
- Call replay
- VoIP expert events

Figure 12.29 shows an example call list , which lists each call and its associated signaling. Quality metrics are also shown for each call.

FIGURE 12.29   Observer call list

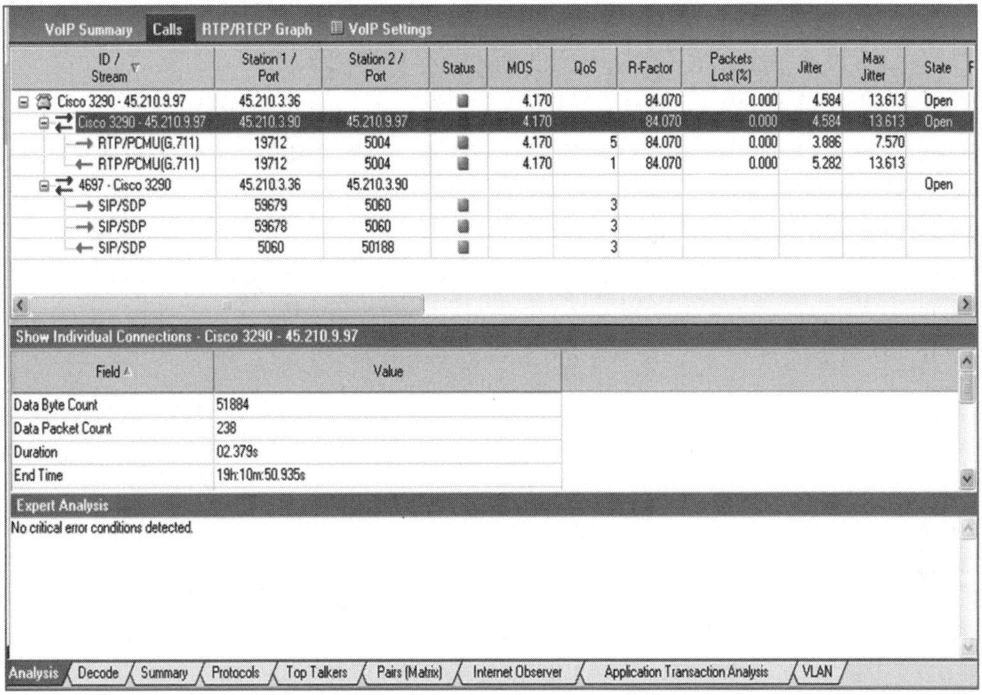

The *mean opinion score (MOS)* is a value from 1 to 5 that indicates the perceived quality of a call. MOS scores were originally derived by playing a test message to a group of listeners who rated the quality of the message using the rating scheme shown in Table 12.2. The average rating is taken to be the MOS score for that particular communications medium.

Because protocol analyzers do not have lots of tiny people inside listening to each call, they are not able to calculate a true MOS score, and therefore the MOS score displayed by your protocol analyzer is what is called passive MOS. Passive MOS is calculated from another quality metric that you will see displayed in your protocol analyzer, called R-Factor. *R-Factor* is calculated from measurable information such as jitter (the variation in packet delay over time), packet loss, and latency. R-Factor is a value from 0 to 100. Table 12.3 shows the mapping between R-Factor and MOS.

TABLE 12.2   Mean opinion score

MOS	Quality	Impairment
5	Excellent	Imperceptible
4	Good	Perceptible but not annoying
3	Fair	Slightly annoying
2	Poor	Annoying
1	Bad	Very annoying

TABLE 12.3   R-Factor and MOS mapping

R-Factor	MOS	Quality
90	4.3	Excellent
80	4.0	Good
70	3.6	Fair
60	3.1	Poor
50	2.6	Bad

When the MOS and R-Factor values indicate poor call quality, the reason for this is often flagged by the analyzer's VoIP expert events. Figure 12.30 shows an example of an analyzer's display, showing VoIP expert events.

Many network analyzers can display a list of calls as shown in Figure 12.30; it is from here that many of an analyzer's advanced VoIP features can be accessed, such as call playback, as pictured in Figure 12.31. The audio data is extracted from the VoIP packets and reconstructed into an audio file, which can be played to the analyst. The analyzer will honor the packet time stamps when reconstructing the audio, so the analyst can hear the effects of delay, packet loss, and jitter. This could end up sounding worse than it would to the actual end VoIP user because VoIP handsets have built-in jitter buffers that help mask the effects of delay and jitter from the user. Therefore, analyzer vendors allow a jitter buffer to be configured in the VoIP playback tools, which can be set to the same value as configured in the VoIP handsets. The analysts can then hear the calls as they would be perceived by the end users.

FIGURE 12.30 OmniPeek VoIP expert

Call ... ▲	Name	Call Status	End Cause	Codec	Media Type	Start	Duration	MOS-Low
○ 1	Cisco 3290-->4697	Closed	over timeout	G.711 µ-law	Voice	07/10/2010 23:31:36	45.493431000	3.56
2	Cisco 3290-->3359	Closed	Temporarily Not Available	(no media flows)		07/10/2010 23:32:39	0.164445000	
○ 3	Cisco 3290-->4672	Closed	BYE	G.711 µ-law	Voice	07/10/2010 23:32:58	00:02:10.186113000	2.96
○ 4	Cisco 3290-->3358	Closed	truncated	G.711 µ-law	Voice	07/10/2010 23:34:04	00:01:22.035135000	2.31

◁ Details ⟋ Event Summary ⟍ Event Log   ▷

Layer	Event	Count ▼
🔵 VoIP	RTP Late Packet Arrival	16
ℹ️ Client/Server	One-Way Traffic	12
⚠️ VoIP	Low MOS-CQ	7
⚠️ VoIP	RTP Excessive Packet Loss Detected	6
⚠️ VoIP	RTP Excessive Jitter Detected	6
⚠️ VoIP	RTP Excessive Packet Loss Reported	4
⚠️ VoIP	SIP Client Error	2
🔵 VoIP	RTP Packet Out of Sequence	1
🔵 VoIP	RTP Not Marked for QoS	1

FIGURE 12.31 Wireshark call playback

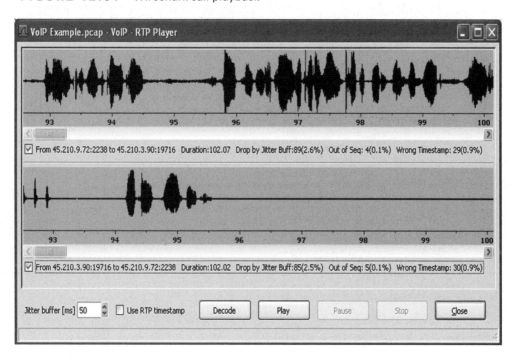

When a VoIP call is made, three main data flows occur. The first data flow is the signaling protocol that manages the VoIP session including establishing and tearing down the call. There are many different types of signaling protocol, including many propriety ones. Some commonly used signaling protocols are Session Initiation Protocol (SIP), H.323, and Cisco's Skinny.

Voice information is encoded using a codec such as G.711 into Real Time Protocol (RTP) packets. A telephone call requires data to flow in both directions. Once a call is established, two RTP streams are created, one carrying voice packets *from* the caller and one carrying voice packets *to* the caller. Many analyzers provide advance features for analysis of both the signaling and RTP conversations, as pictured in Figures 12.32 and 12.33.

Because each direction of a call is carried in a unique RTP session, each RTP session will have its own quality metrics. When voice quality problems occur, you might find one direction has a good MOS score and the other direction is poor. You may have experienced this on your VoIP phone or your cell phone when you can hear the other person perfectly but they cannot hear you.

FIGURE 12.32 Wireshark signal analysis

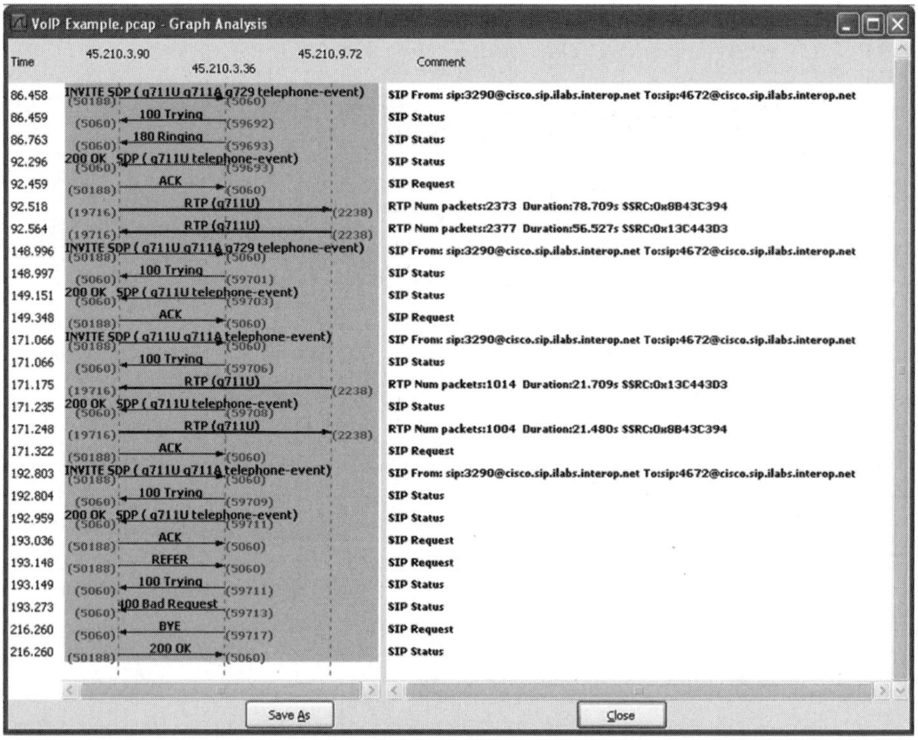

If encryption is used and you cannot decrypt the wireless traffic but still want to get at the call and signaling information, you need to capture this information on the wired network by capturing the traffic traveling to and from the access point or wireless LAN controller. However, when looking at call quality metrics (such as MOS & R-factor), it must be remembered that, for packets flowing toward the wireless network, effects of access point queuing buffers, wireless contention, and transmission will not have been taken into account.

FIGURE 12.33   Wireshark RTP analysis

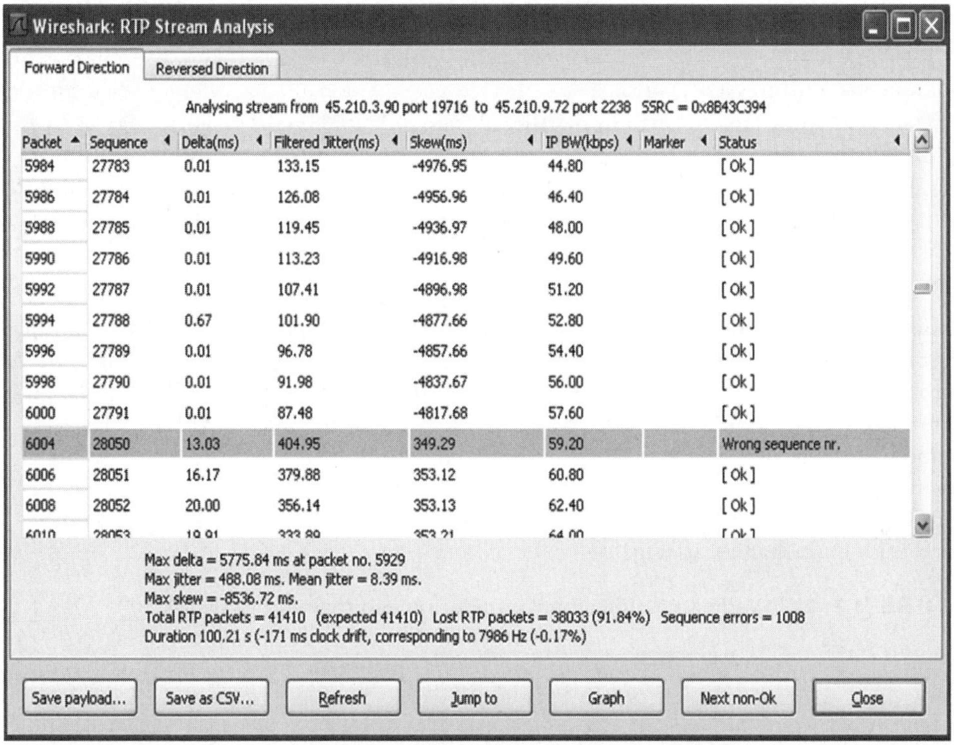

By comparing the wired traffic to the encrypted frames transmitted within the wireless cell, you can probably work out which encrypted frames belong to which call. By looking at the differences between the delay of these encrypted frames and packets captured on the wired side, you can work out whether any excessive delay is being introduced by the wireless network.

Multiple-Channel Protocol Analysis

One method of capturing traffic on different channels is to configure your wireless analyzer to perform channel scanning. The limitation of channel scanning is that the wireless capture adapter is capable of capturing packets on only one channel at a time and therefore only captures a snapshot of what is happening on each channel. Any sort of conversation analysis or detailed troubleshooting is impossible, because too many of the required packets will be missing. When performing conversation analysis, it is better to configure the wireless analyzer for a fixed channel. Problems with this approach occur when troubleshooting an MCA environment with roaming clients. Roaming analysis requires the use of multiple capture adapters. This can be achieved by using one of the following approaches:

Multiple Network Analyzers   In an MCA environment, where the channel sets 1, 6, and 11 have been deployed, this approach would involve three separate analyzers on three separate laptops, with each analyzer configured for a different channel. This would produce three separate packet trace files.

Simultaneous Captures and Multiple Adapter Support   Some analyzers support the ability to start simultaneous captures from different network adapters. The advantage of this approach is that you need only one protocol analyzer; however, you are still left with three separate capture files—one for each channel. One solution to this problem is a tool shipped with OmniPeek by WildPackets called Peekcat. `Peekcat.exe` is a command-line tool that concatenates trace files together into one file and can optionally merge packets by their time stamp.

Multichannel Aggregation   *Multichannel aggregation* takes capture streams from multiple adapters and aggregates them together into one capture. Each adapter can be configured for a different channel. Figure 12.34 pictures the AirPcap solution from Cace Technologies, where three USB capture adapters are connected to the analyzer via a UBS hub. This method has one big advantage over the other two methods, which is that all packets are captured straight into one capture file, making for easy analysis of clients' activities as they roam from access point to access point. Figure 12.35 pictures the configuration of OmniPeek's multichannel aggregator.

FIGURE 12.34   AirPcap multichannel monitoring and roaming analysis

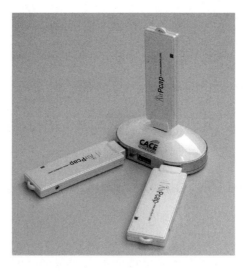

FIGURE 12.35   OmniPeek's multichannel aggregator configuration

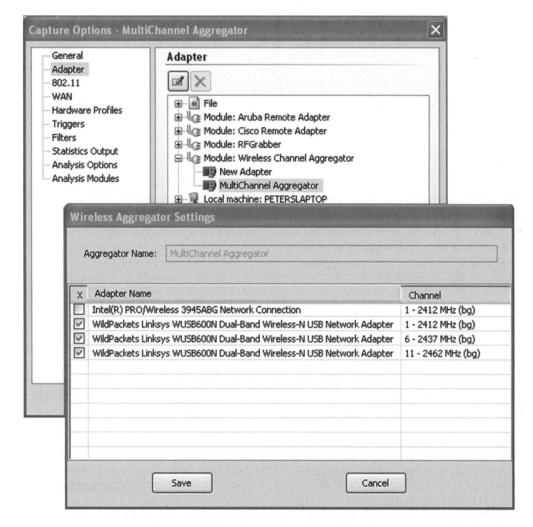

 A white paper entailed "The Triple Blendy: Multi-Channel Capture for Mobile Clients" by Devin Akin is included on the CD of this book. This paper details the equipment you will require and provides step-by-step instructions on the configuration of a multichannel aggregated capture.

Roaming Analysis

Roaming is the method by which client stations move between RF coverage cells in a seamless manner. Client stations switch communications through different access points. Seamless communications for stations moving between the coverage zones within an extended service set (ESS) is vital for uninterrupted mobility. One of the most common issues that you'll need to troubleshoot is problems with roaming. Roaming problems are usually caused by poor network design. Because of the proprietary nature of roaming, problems can also occur when radio cards from multiple vendors are deployed. Changes in the WLAN environment can also cause roaming hiccups.

Client stations, and not the access point, make the decision on whether to roam between access points. Some vendors may involve the access point or WLAN controller in the roaming decision, but ultimately, the client station initiates the roaming process with a reassociation request frame. The method by which client stations decide how to roam is entirely proprietary. All vendor client stations use roaming algorithms often based on multiple variables. The variable of most importance will always be received signal strength. As the received signal from the original AP grows weaker and a station hears a stronger signal from another known access point, the station will initiate the roaming process. However, other variables such as SNR, error rates, and retransmissions may also have a part to play in the roaming decision.

Because roaming is proprietary, a specific vendor client station may roam sooner than a second vendor client station as they move through various coverage cells. Some vendors like to encourage roaming, whereas others use algorithms that roam at lower received signal thresholds. In an environment where a WLAN administrator must support multiple vendor radios, different roaming behaviors will most assuredly be seen. For the time being, a WLAN administrator will always face unique challenges because of the proprietary nature of roaming.

The best way to ensure that seamless roaming will commence is through proper design and a thorough site survey. When designing an 802.11 WLAN, it is recommended that at least two APs should provide the desired minimum signal level in all roaming locations. The only way to determine whether proper design is in place is by conducting a coverage analysis site survey.

Roaming problems will occur if there is not enough overlap in cell coverage. Too little overlap will effectively create a roaming dead zone, and connectivity may even temporarily be lost. On the flip side, too much cell overlap will also cause roaming problems. For example, if two cells have 60 percent overlap, a station may stay associated with its original AP and not connect to a second access point even though the station is directly underneath the second access point. This can also create a situation in which the client device is constantly switching back and forth between the two or more APs. This often presents itself when a client device is directly under an AP and there are constant dropped frames.

Another design issue of great importance is latency. The 802.11-2007 standard defines the use of an 802.1X/EAP security solution in the enterprise. The average time involved during the authentication process can be 700 milliseconds or longer. Every time a client station roams to a new access point and 802.1X/EAP security solution has been deployed, reauthentication is usually required. The time delay that results from the authentication process can cause serious interruptions with time-sensitive applications. Protocols such as VoIP requires end-to-end delays of less than 150 milliseconds to maintain good quality. When roaming a station, performing a full 802.1x/EAP authentication can take as long as 500 milliseconds to reauthenticate. Many vendors have implemented fast secure roaming (FSR) solutions to keep the reauthentication time to less than 100 milliseconds. Currently, the implemented FSR solutions are proprietary, although the 802.11i amendment defines optional FSR.

Two new IEEE 802.11 amendments published in 2008 will ideally standardize fast secure roaming in the enterprise. 802.11k amendment has defined the use of radio resource measurement (RRM) and neighbor reports to enhance roaming performance. The 802.11r amendment also defines faster handoffs when roaming occurs between cells in a wireless LAN using the strong security defined in a robust security network (RSN).

Chapter 7 of the *CWSP: Certified Wireless Security Processional Official Study Guide* by authors David Coleman, David Westcott, Bryan Harkins and Shawn Jackman (Sybex, 2010) provides a full description of the proprietary FSR algorithms currently used and those defined by the 802.11k and 802.11r. Also, a white paper has been included on the CD of this book entitled "Robust Security Network (RSN) Fast BSS Transition (FT)" by Devin Akin. This is highly recommended reading. You will also find a brief description of FSR in Chapter 9 of this book.

The best way to troubleshoot a roaming problem is to use an analyzer that supports multichannel aggregation and to configure one adapter for each of the channels used by the wireless network. If possible, follow a client around as it roams from access point to access point capturing its packets each time it roams. Filtering the capture to show just the packets to and from that particular client should allow you to quickly identify any roaming problems, including the time taken for each roam. Some analyzers have special displays that show roaming statistics. Figure 12.36 shows OmniPeek's Roaming plug-in.

FIGURE 12.36   OmniPeek's roaming plug-in

Name	MAC	IP	Time	Latency (sec)	Source AP	Destination AP	Source Channel	Destinatio
Wireless VoIP Phone	00:03:2A:01:F2:B5		15:10:16.344 16/09/2008	0.571	Cisco:ED:F8:02	Cisco:E7:FE:A0	6	1
Wireless VoIP Phone	00:03:2A:01:F2:B5		15:10:39.202 16/09/2008	0.359	Cisco:ED:F8:02	Cisco:EE:54:10	1	1
Wireless VoIP Phone	00:03:2A:01:F2:B5		15:10:54.391 16/09/2008	0.417	Cisco:EE:54:10	Cisco:E7:FE:A0	1	1

marquest phone roam2.pkt - by AP ✕

Name	MAC	Roam Count	Avg Roam Time (sec)
Cisco:E7:FE:A0	00:13:60:E7:FE:A0	2	0.494
Cisco:EE:54:10	00:11:92:EE:54:10	1	0.359

marquest phone roam2.pkt - by Node ✕

Name	MAC	IP	Roam Count	Avg Roam Time (sec)	Current AP	Current Channel
Wireless VoIP Phone	00:03:2A:01:F2:B5		3	0.449	Cisco:E7:FE:A0	1

Real World Scenario

Ping-Pong Roaming

A wireless network was deployed in a very large sports center with the sole purpose of providing the staff with telephony services via VoWiFi handsets. After installing the access points, the center IT manager confirmed coverage by using laptop-based site survey software. Since rolling out the VoWiFi system, many complaints about long silences and dropped calls in certain areas of the center have been reported.

The sports center engaged the services of a wireless analyst to identify the problem. The analyst performed a channel aggregated capture, with three capture adapters configured for channels 1, 6, and 11 (matching the channel set used for the installed access points). Having configured a capture time filter to look at all traffic to and from a particular VoWiFi handset, the analyst followed the IT manager on a tour of the building while on a test call. The IT manager reported every occurrence of a problem with the call. In problem areas, the analyst observed the client roaming repeatedly between two access points.

The VoWiFi handsets were configured with a -75 dBm roaming threshold. Although the IT manager had confirmed wireless coverage, he had not confirmed that he had greater than -75 dBm coverage everywhere. In some areas between two of the installed access points, the client could not hear either access point at a signal strength greater than -75 dBm. The VoWiFi handset would realize that its current access point was below its roaming threshold and roam; having roamed, it would again realize that its current receive signal strength was below its roaming threshold and roam again. The handset would continue to ping-pong between the two access points until it moved close enough to one access point to receive a signal strength greater than -75 dBm.

The analyst correctly identified that the wireless network coverage was not designed for the chosen VoWiFi handsets; it had been designed following all the guidelines for a data network. Generally, as was the case in this network, VoWiFi networks require more access points than a data network. The problem was fixed by adding more access points in the areas where the signal strength was low, ensuring that in all places there was at least one access point that was greater than the roaming threshold.

Distributed Protocol Analysis

This chapter has so far focused on portable wireless analysis that utilizes wireless protocol analysis software installed on a laptop or tablet. The main limitation with using a portable analyzer is that an analyst must go on-site in order to capture data, and sending an engineer to remote sites can be an expensive exercise. It is not just remote sites that can be problematic for portable analysis; analyzing a network at a large site can involve a lot of walking, and just the process of collecting captures at different locations around the facility can take a full day, if not more.

By using portable analyzers, an analyst can only ever look at the wireless traffic at their current location; there is no way of seeing the wireless traffic across the whole network.

Distributed analysis addresses the limitations of portable analyses through the deployment of wireless sensors (or probes). Wireless sensors are remote capture devices that monitor the wireless environment and report their statistics/packets to an analyzer or server.

A variety of architectures exist for distributed analysis. The three most common architectures shown here will be described next:

- Wireless analyzer with remote capture probes
- Wireless analyzer with remote engines
- Centralized server with wireless sensors (WIPS)

Wireless Analyzer with Remote Capture Probes

Some analyzer vendors sell remote *wireless probes*. These devices look a lot like access points and are installed at remote locations. Instead of going on-site when a problem occurs, the analyst can simply launch their protocol analyzer, and instead of selecting a local adapter, they can select the remote probe as their capture adapter. The probe can be configured to perform a channel scan or configured to capture on a fixed channel. All the packets captured are sent across the network to the network analyzer.

The main disadvantage with this approach is that all the packets are sent back over the network, using up valuable network bandwidth. This can be a particular problem when connecting to a probe at a remote site over a low-bandwidth WAN link. To help alleviate some of this extra traffic from the network, many remote probes support hardware filtering, allowing capture-time filters to be applied, and therefore the probe only sends the traffic of interest back across the network.

Instead of using an analyzer vendor's own probe, some wireless infrastructure vendors' access points can be converted into remote capture adapters. Figure 12.37 pictures the Capture Options dialog box from OmniPeek; notice that as well as the option to capture from an RFGrabber (WildPackets' own wireless probe), the option to use Aruba and Cisco access points as remote adapters is also available. To use a Cisco access point as a remote probe, you must first place the access point into sniffer mode. Figure 12.38 pictures the configuration for this on a Cisco Wireless LAN controller.

Many network analysis vendors now support wireless software agents, which are software-based remote probes that utilize the computer's wireless adapter. Any computer can be turned into a remote probe by connecting to a supported USB wireless adapter and installing the software agent. This can be a cost-effective way of adding wireless analysis to small remote sites.

FIGURE 12.37   OmniPeek capture options dialog

FIGURE 12:38   Cisco WLC access point configuration in sniffer mode

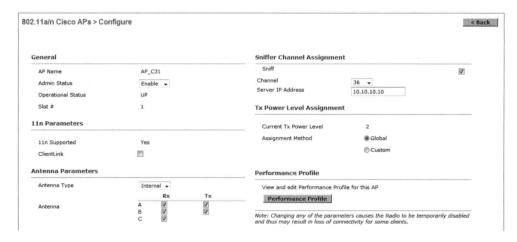

Wireless Analyzer with Remote Engines

As described earlier, the problem with remote capture probes is that they send all the traffic back over the network, using up valuable bandwidth on WAN links. *Remote engine*s are software services that run on dedicated hardware or existing servers. Packet capture, filtering, decoding, and analysis are all performed on the engine. All packets are stored on the engine or attached storage. The analyst can connect to an engine, configure captures, and perform analysis from a console application. The console application has the same look and feel as a local portable analyzer, but only small screen updates are sent back across the network and not the packets.

For wireless capture, a supported wireless adapter can be connected to the engine. Multiple USB wireless adapters can be connected to a USB hub, which in turn can be connected to a remote engine. This engine can then be configured to use the multichannel aggregator and create a remote probe capable of capturing all wireless traffic within your remote environment. Alternately, some vendors provide dedicated intelligent wireless sensor hardware with a remote engine built-in.

Centralized Server with Wireless Sensors

The third deployment model is the one favored by Wireless Intrusion Protection Systems vendors. This model utilizes *wireless sensor*s that monitor the wireless environment 24/7 and send their statistics to a centralized server. A consolidated view of wireless security and performance can be accessed from a console application. Figure 12.39 pictures the default dashboard view from Motorola AirDefense Enterprise.

FIGURE 12:39   Motorola AirDefense Enterprise dashboard

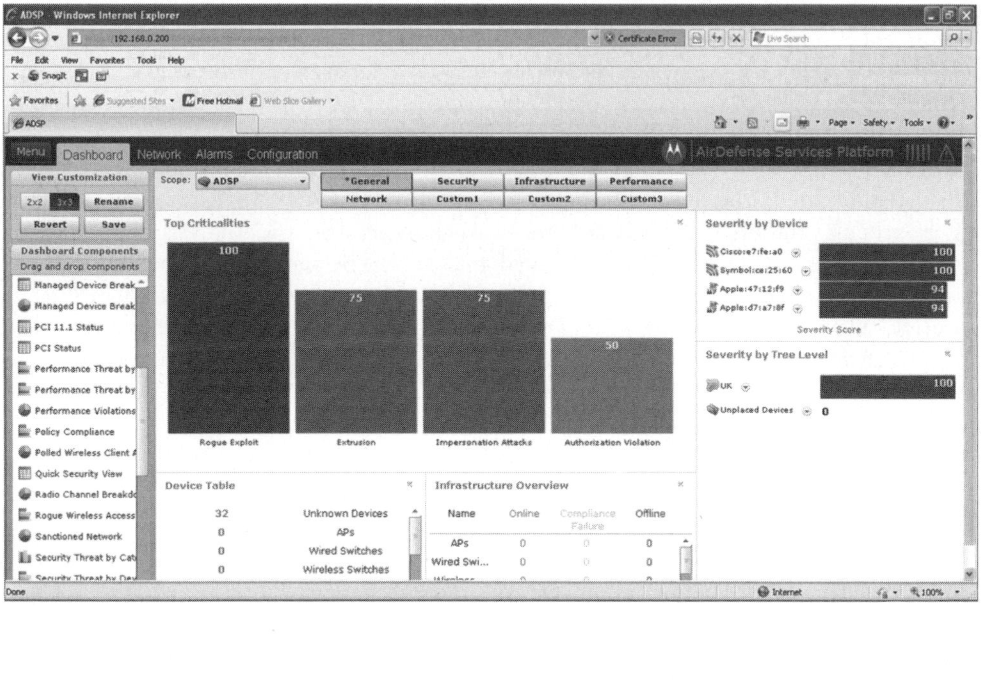

The primary purpose of a WIPS is to protect the network against potential security threats. For detailed information about how a WIPS protects against security threats, see Chapter 10 in the *CWSP: Certified Wireless Security Processional Official Study Guide* by David Coleman et al. (Sybex, 2010). As well as threat detection and prevention, WIPS also includes features to report the overall performance of a wireless network with detailed analysis and forensics software modules.

Wireless sensors can be a dedicated hardware device or a converted radio within a supported access point. A wireless sensor overlay network can be deployed to provide 24/7 monitoring of your wireless environment; as a rule of thumb, we say one sensor for every four access points. This 1:4 rule works well for analyzing and troubleshooting your existing wireless network, but when deploying a WIPS for security protection as well, more sensors may be required for areas where you do not currently have wireless coverage but are still at risk from rogue devices.

Converting one of the radios in a dual radio access point to be a dedicated wireless sensor removes the need to install both types of device, that is, wireless sensors and access points. Dual radio access points can support both 2.4 GHz clients and 5 GHz clients; however, when converting one radio to be a dedicated wireless sensor, the access point will only be able to support clients in one frequency band (either 2.4 GHz or 5 GHz). Because of this limitation, vendors such as Motorola supply tri-radio access points where one radio is used as a dedicated 24/7 wireless sensor and the other two radios provide wireless access, one at 2.4 GHz and the other at 5 GHz.

WIPS monitor the wireless environment and trigger alarms, which can in turn raise a notification against a whole host of different security and performance-related events. As well the detection of security events, a WIPS system can take action to mitigate the threat. For example, a sensor could turn from passive monitor to active transmitter and start transmitting deauthentication frames to nullify the risk from rogue devices; alternatively, if a rogue access point is detected as being connected to the wired network, the WIPS server could communicate with the switch via Simple Network Management Protocol (SNMP) and disable the port to which the access point is connected.

For the majority of the time, WIPS sensors perform channel scans, providing an overview of the wireless environment. However, advanced forensics and analysis features of WIPS software can fix the channel on a particular sensor, allowing it to capture all traffic from a particular station. Figures 12.40 and 12.41 show the Forensic Analysis and Live View modules from AirDefense where detailed analysis can be performed on a particular station. Many wireless sensors can be configured to perform full packet capture, which is very useful when troubleshooting a problem at a remote location. The captured packets either can be analyzed in the WIPS's own analysis module or can be saved to a file and opened in your preferred network analyzer.

FIGURE 12.40   AirDefense forensic analysis

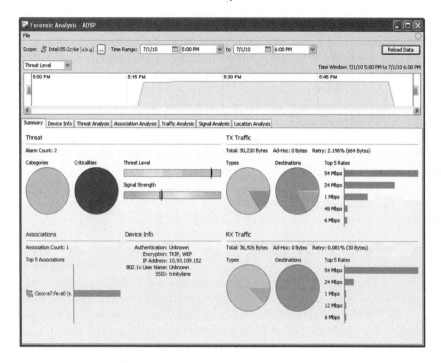

FIGURE 12.41   AirDefense live view

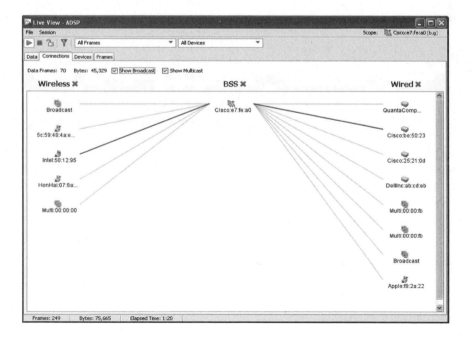

Wired Analysis

Wireless analysis alone will often not provide you with enough information, and analysis of the wired network is also required. This is especially the case when encryption is used on the wireless network. If you want to troubleshoot layer 3–7 protocols on an encrypted wireless network, you would either have to be able to decrypt the wireless traffic or capture the data in the wired network.

To capture data frames traveling to or from the wireless network, you must first identify where on the wired network the required traffic will be visible and second decide on how you are going to get access to the traffic. The obvious answer to the first question is the point where an access point connects to the wired LAN. Although placing an analyzer behind the access point will work for autonomous access points, it will be no good for access points that send all their packets back to a wireless controller/switch over an encrypted tunnel. In these cases, the best place would be the wireless controllers' network uplink connection.

Having identified the best location for capturing your unencrypted data packets, you must now consider how you are going to get the packets into your network analyzer buffer. Where and how do you connect your network analyzer? If you wanted to place your analyzer behind an access point to monitor all traffic flowing to and from the access point, one easy option would be to place a network hub between the access point and its network connection. You would then connect your analyzer to the hub. Because a network hub forwards all packets out on all ports, you will see all traffic traveling to and from the access point. The main disadvantage with this method is that you have to break the access point's network connection in order to place and remove the hub. When placing a hub in-line with a PoE powered access point, if there is not already a PoE injector between the hub and access point you will need to insert one.

WARNING   It is getting increasingly hard to buy a true network hub. That is to say, not all hubs are hubs. Many modern devices that are sold as network hubs are really just small unmanaged switches and therefore do not forward all traffic out of all ports and are no good for network analysis. So if you have any old network hubs lying around, do not throw them away, because they are useful for network analysis, and you might find it hard to find another one.

Many 802.11n access points have gigabit Ethernet ports. When connected to a 10/100 Mbps network hub, 802.11n access points will autonegotiate down to a 100 Mbps half-duplex connection. For a highly utilized wireless network, this may cause a bottleneck and could result in dropped packets.

An alternative traffic access approach would be to span or mirror the switch port connected to the access point or controller. Having connected the network analyzer to a spare port on the network switch, *port spanning* (sometimes called *port mirroring*) can be configured to send a copy of all traffic traveling on the access point's port on the switch to the analyzer's switch port. Port spanning is often a good way to access the wireless controller's traffic because disconnecting the wireless controller in order to place a network hub could potentially disrupt the entire wireless network. Because network hubs are only 10/100 Mbps half-duplex devices, it is very likely that they would not be able to cope with the volume of traffic traveling to and from the wireless controller on a large network.

The wireless controller might have more than one connection to the wired network. Some switch vendors allow multiple ports to be spanned onto the analyzer's port, providing that the total volume of traffic does not exceed the bandwidth of the analyzer's port. If the switch does not allow multiple ports to connect to one span port or the controller is physically connected to different switches, the alternative is to configure multiple span sessions and aggregate their captures together. In just the same way as with the multichannel aggregator, multiple Ethernet adapters can be configured to capture their packets into the same capture buffer.

One disadvantage of port spanning is the extra load added to the switch's back plane. When spanning busy network connections, the extra traffic caused by port spanning could also cause the switch to drop packets. Typically, switch vendors allow only one or two span sessions per switch. An alternative approach is to use a network tap. Passive network taps sit in line and send a copy of the data to a separate port for the network analyzer. Network taps may at first sound a bit like going back to the idea of a hub; however, a tap is a dedicated device designed to provide monitoring tools access and has the following advantages:

- The traffic on 1 Gig and 10 Gig links can be accessed through a network tap.

- Because the device is a completely passive device, should the device fail, the link will continue to work.

- Network taps are designed to be permanently installed in locations where you would want to monitor regularly.

Wireless encryption does not render the wireless analysis useless, because all wireless specific information is still transmitted "in the clear." All 802.11 management and control frames are transmitted unencrypted, and the 802.11 MAC header of every frame is also transmitted unencrypted. Therefore, wireless specific issues can still be effectively troubleshooted on encrypted networks.

802.11w: Protected Management Frames

The 802.11w amendment published by the IEEE in 2009 increases the security of management frames. This builds on the security mechanisms defined by the 802.11i amendment and applies them to certain management frames such as deauthentication and disassociation frames. This helps to thwart certain denial of service (DoS) attacks. From an analysis point of view, it will mean that more of your wireless traffic is now encrypted.

Wired and Wireless Analysis

There are times when you might want to monitor both the wired and wireless networks simultaneously. This could be achieved through the use of a separate wired and wireless analyzer or alternatively by using an analyzer that supports both wired and wireless capture. One example when you might want to capture both wireless and wired traffic is when analyzing 802.1x/EAP authentication problems. If a client cannot authenticate, you need to determine where the problem lies. This could be a problem with any of the following:

- Incorrectly configured client
- Incorrectly configured access point
- Incorrectly configured RADIUS server

To correctly identify where the authentication procedure is failing, you must analyze both the access point's conversation with the client and the access point's conversation with the RADIUS server. Figure 12.42 pictures both a wired and wireless capture of an 802.1x/EAP authentication exchange in OmniPeek.

FIGURE 12.42   Wired and wireless analysis

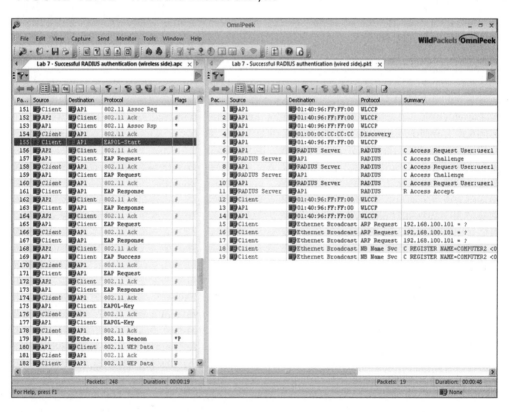

System Logs

Before we finish the discussion of protocol analysis, we'll cover how the information contained within system logs can help support protocol analysis in the troubleshooting process. Most network systems and devices produce log files or messages. The information within these log files and messages can help the analyst get to the root cause of a problem. Many Windows applications write error messages to the log files found in Event Viewer. Figure 12.43 shows the System log in Event Viewer with some TCP/IP network events written to the log file by the network adapter driver.

FIGURE 12.43   Windows Event Viewer, System log

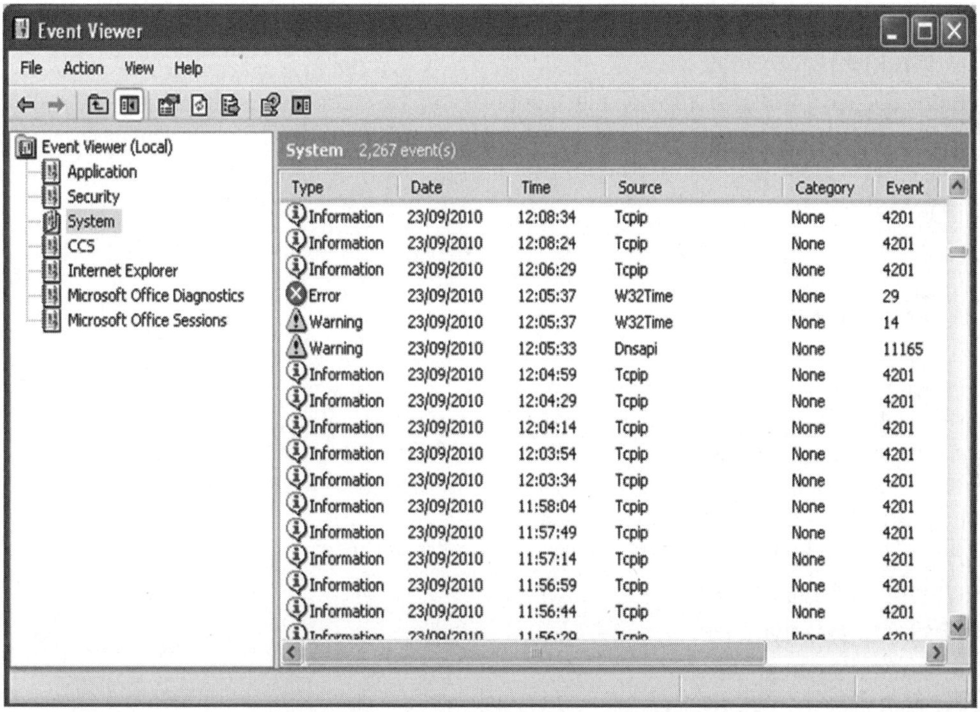

Many applications and network devices generate their own log files and often can generate syslog messages. syslog allows network devices and applications to send their system messages to a syslog server that handles the reporting and analysis, providing the network manager with a centralized location for all logs.

If you take the example of analyzing an 802.1x/EAP authentication exchange from the previous section, you can see how protocol analysis and logs can be used together to troubleshoot a network problem. A client's authentication is failing, and when analyzing the conversation between the access point and the RADIUS server, you can see the access point send the initial access request to the RADIUS server. However, no response is received, not even a error message. Having confirmed that the message is going to the correct IP address and after confirming that the RADIUS service is running on the server, the RADIUS logs would be the next obvious place to look. When looking at the log file, you notice that the RADIUS server is reporting a silent disconnect, indicating that it has received an "access request" message from an invalid network access server (NAS), in this case the access point. This would suggest that the access point is not known to the RADIUS server. After looking at the server configuration, you can see that an entry for the access points exists. However, the access point's IP address has been entered incorrectly. In the previous example, by using both protocol analysis and the information in the log file, you were able to identify that it was the RADIUS server not responding and then quickly identified the area where the configuration error was.

The consolidation of syslog messages on a syslog server can help speed up the troubleshooting process. Along with syslog messages from wireless controllers, access points, and RADIUS servers, expert events and alarms from a protocol analyzers can be sent as syslog messages to a syslog server. Therefore, the information from different systems can be correlated together to form a more complete and system-wide view of network issues.

Summary

This chapter has looked at how a protocol analyzer works, discussing how a customized driver needs to be installed in order to place an 802.11 wireless adapter into RF monitor mode, allowing it to become a passive monitoring adapter. The common options available when configuring a wireless capture were discussed, including the difference between fixed channel analysis and performing a channel scan.

The following analyzer features and their uses were outlined:

- Protocol decodes
- Peer map functions
- Conversation analysis
- Filtering: capture and display
- Expert functions
- Performance analysis
- Reporting capabilities

The chapter also investigated how both the QoS and calls of VoWiFi systems can be analyzed. The problem of analyzing a roaming client using just one capture adapter was identified, and the solution of using multiple adapters and a multichannel aggregator was defined. The way distributed analysis addresses many of the shortfalls of portable analysis was discussed, along with a description of the different approaches and architecture available to achieve a distributed analysis environment.

The chapter concluded with a look at how both wired analysis and system logs can aid a wireless network analyst in troubleshooting network problems.

Exam Essentials

Understand the installation and configuration of a protocol analyzer.   Know how to install a customized analysis driver and understand that the customized driver places the wireless capture adapter into a special mode called RF monitor mode. Understand the different capture options available and that channel scanning can be used to gain a good understanding of your wireless environment. For detailed analysis, a fixed channel should be configured.

Define generic features common to 802.11 protocol analyzers.   Describe the functions of the following common analyzer features: protocol decodes, peer map functions, filtering, and expert systems.

Understand expert analysis and troubleshooting methodologies.   Understand how expert events can provide the network analyst with a starting point for further detailed analysis. Demonstrate how filtering can be used to select the packets that are of interest and how conversation analysis is applied to troubleshoot the problem.

Define VoWiFi and roaming analysis procedures.   Understand the VoIP-specific features of a protocol analyzer and when you would use them. Know that troubleshooting QoS is an end-to-end task and will involve wired analysis too. Explain how multichannel aggregation enables effective roaming analysis.

Explain distributed wireless analysis.   Explain the benefits of distributed analysis over portable analysis. Understand the difference between a wireless probe and remote engine.

Understand the use of system logs in troubleshooting.   System logs can provide additional and supporting information to the troubleshooting procedure. Understand how a syslog server can consolidate log information from many different networking tools and devices into one centralized location.

Key Terms

buffer size

capture filters

channel scanning

display filters

distributed analysis

expert analysis

fixed channel analysis

heuristic-based expert analysis

Mean Opinion Score (MOS)

multichannel aggregation

network interface card (NIC)

packet slicing

peer map

port spanning

protocol decodes

remote engine

RF monitor mode

R-Factor

threshold-based expert analysis

wireless probe

wireless sensor

Review Questions

1. Network analyzers place the wireless adapter into which mode?

    A. RF monitor

    B. RF capture

    C. RF sniff

    D. RF scan

2. Channel scanning is the best option when doing which of the following? (Choose all that apply.)

    A. Performing conversation analysis

    B. Summarizing the wireless environment

    C. Detailed troubleshooting

    D. Reporting the overall security and performance of a wireless network

3. Having the wrong country code configured could cause which of the following problems?

    A. The protocols decodes to be in the wrong language

    B. The wrong number of channels available

    C. The protocol analyzer software to crash

    D. Your access points to switch channels

4. Which of the following are true regarding packet slicing? (Choose all that apply.)

    A. Reduces the size of capture files

    B. Can be configured to capture only the header information, disregarding the data

    C. Is required when performing distributed analysis over a WAN connection

    D. Removes unwanted packets from the capture buffer

5. How is a protocol decode window most commonly laid out?

    A. The OSI layers go from high to low as they travel down the decode window with packet information at the top.

    B. The OSI layers go from high to low as they travel down the decode window with packet information at the bottom.

    C. The OSI layers go from low to high as they travel down the decode window with packet information at the top.

    D. The OSI layers go from low to high as they travel down the decode window with packet information at the bottom.

6. Which of the following security solutions settings could be configured into the analyzer to enable encrypted packets to be decrypted? Choose all that apply.

   A. PEAP

   B. WEP

   C. PSK

   D. EAP-FAST

7. In a peer map, lines between nodes show what?

   A. The access points to which a roaming client has associated

   B. The wired infrastructure

   C. The VLAN that each wireless clients is in

   D. Communication between stations

8. Which of the following are common protocol analyzer features? Choose all that apply.

   A. Peer map

   B. Filtering

   C. RADIUS authentication service

   D. Expert analysis

9. Which of the following best describes expert analysis?

   A. The automatic detection of network events, errors, and problems by an analyzer

   B. The removal of unwanted traffic from the capture buffer

   C. The visual representation of which STAs are communicating with each other

   D. The collection of network statistics based upon the captured packets

10. What does heuristic-based expert analysis do?

   A. Collects network statistics and compares them to configured threshold values

   B. Looks for patterns in the traffic flow and compares them to a set of rules

   C. Automatically performs active attacks against rogue devices

   D. Uses SMNP to monitor wireless infrastructure

11. Which two elements of a VoWiFi network can be analyzed on an encrypted network?

   A. Per-call MOS-quality metrics

   B. Signaling

   C. QoS tagging

   D. Roaming

12. Where in the packet can you see its access category?

    A. QoS Control Field

    B. WMM Information Element

    C. IP Header

    D. Frame Body

13. An MOS score of 4 indicates what level of quality?

    A. Excellent

    B. Good

    C. Fair

    D. Poor

    E. Bad

14. Which of the following is true regarding voice calls?

    A. Both directions of the call are carried in the same RTP session and therefore will have the same MOS scores.

    B. Both directions of the call are carried in the same RTP session but can have different MOS scores.

    C. Each direction of a call is carried in a separate RTP session and therefore may have different MOS scores.

    D. Each direction of a call is carried in a separate RTP session but will always have the same MOS score because they belong to the same conversation.

15. Multichannel aggregation performs which of the following tasks?

    A. Allows separate captures to be created from different capture adapters within the same analyzer

    B. Takes capture streams from multiple adapters and aggregates them together into one capture

    C. Enables a signal capture adapter to capture up to three separate channels simultaneously

    D. Simultaneously connects to several remote probes configured for different channels

16. Which of the following are common roaming problems? Choose all that apply.

    A. Too little cell coverage overlap

    B. Too much cell coverage overlap

    C. Free space path loss

    D. CSMA/CA

    E. Hidden node

17. What are the advantages of distributed analysis over portable analysis? Choose all that apply.

  A. Remote off-site analysis

  B. Real-time decodes

  C. Expert analysis

  D. Enterprise-wide statistics

18. To confirm that the wireless QoS priorities are being preserved on the wired network, you decide to capture the traffic traveling to and from the network uplink on your wireless controller. You do not want to disrupt the operation of the wireless controller by breaking its network connection. What method should you use to obtain a copy of the wireless controller's traffic?

  A. Place a network tap in line with the wireless controller.

  B. Use a wireless analysis to capture the packets from the air.

  C. Place a network hub in line with the wireless controller.

  D. Configure port spanning on the switch connected to the wireless controller.

19. As the expert in wireless analysis within your company, you are sent a unfiltered trace file from a colleague who captured the file at a site were users where unable to authenticate to the wireless network. The trace files consist of more than 5,000 packets, and 70 percent of trace file is made up of beacon, probe request, and probe response frames. What is one the first things you would do?

  A. Configure a display filter to hide any unwanted traffic.

  B. Ask your colleague to take another capture, with filters configured to remove beacon, probe request frames, and probe response frames.

  C. Reconfigure the access points with a greater beacon interval.

  D. Start looking through each packet decode in turn, looking for anything unusual.

20. Address filters can select traffic based on which of the following? (Choose all that apply.)

  A. IP address

  B. MAC address

  C. Subnets

  D. Switch port

Answers to Review Questions

1.   A.   Wireless analyzers place the NICs into a special mode called RF monitor mode; in this mode, the card becomes a passive monitoring device and cannot transmit, and therefore normal wireless network operation is disabled.

2.   B, D.   Wireless scanning provides a good overview of the wireless environment, showing which wireless devices are transmitting on which channels and which security protocols they are using. WIPS sensors perform channel scanning to provide a consolidated view of wireless security and performance.

3.   B.   After installing a customized analysis driver, you might find that you have the wrong number of channels available within your wireless analyzer. This is likely to be because the driver is configured with an incorrect country code.

4.   A, B.   Packet slicing allows you to just capture the first so many bytes of each packet, disregarding the rest of the frame. Often the only information you are interested in is the header information, and you do not have any interest in the data elements of the packets. Because packet slicing reduces the size of capture files, you can store a significantly larger number of packets to disk.

5.   C.   The protocol decode window is arranged with the lower layers of the OSI seven-layer model at the top. As you travel down the window, the layers go up. At the very top of the decode window is the packet information section.

6.   B, C.   When a preshared key is used to encrypt traffic, such as WEP, WPA-PSK, or WPA2-PSK, some analyzers allow this key to be entered into the analyzer's configuration to decrypt packets, displaying the protocol decodes as if no encryption had been used.

7.   D.   A peer map is a visual representation of which STAs are communicating with each other. Lines between peers indicate communication.

8.   A, B, D.   The following are all common protocol analyzer features: protocol decodes, peer map functions, filtering, and expert functions.

9.   A.   Expert analysis is the automatic detection of network events, errors, and problems by an analyzer.

10.   B.   Heuristic-based expert analysis looks for patterns in the traffic flow and compares them to a set of rules. Traffic that does not conform to these rules is reported.

11.   C, D.   Although you cannot analyze VoIP calls and their signaling on an encrypted network, you can still analyze two import requirements for voice on a wireless network: QoS tags and fast efficient roaming.

12.   A.   By looking at the QoS Control field, you can confirm that the packet is being transmitted using the correct access category (AC).

13. B.   The mean opinion score (MOS) is a value from 1 to 5, which indicates the perceived quality of a call. 5 = Excellent, 4 = Good, 3 = Fair, 2 = Poor, and 1 = Bad.

14. C.   Because each direction of a call is carried in a unique RTP session, each RTP session will have its own quality metrics. When voice quality problems occur, you might find one direction has a good MOS score and the other direction is poor.

15. B.   Multichannel aggregation takes capture streams from multiple adapters and aggregates them together into one capture. Each adapter can be configured for a different channel.

16. A, B.   Roaming problems will occur if there is not enough overlap in cell coverage. Too little overlap will effectively create a roaming dead zone, and connectivity may even temporarily be lost. If two RF cells have too much overlap, a station may stay associated with its original AP and not connect to a second access point even though the station is directly underneath the second access point.

17. A, D.   Distributed analysis enables wireless probes to be installed at remote locations, and instead of going on-site when a problem occurs, the analyst can simply launch their protocol analyzer. Instead of selecting a local adapter, they can select the remote probe as their capture adapter. Wireless sensors that monitor the wireless environment 24/7 and send their statistics to a centralized server can be deployed across the entire enterprise, providing a consolidated view of wireless security and performance statistics.

18. D.   Having connected the network analyzer to a spare port on the network switch, port spanning (sometimes called *port mirroring*) can be configured to send a copy of all traffic traveling on the wireless controller's port to the analyzer's port. Port spanning is often a good way to access the wireless controller's traffic because disconnecting the wireless controller in order to place a network hub or tap could potentially disrupt the entire wireless network.

19. A.   Because clients are reporting an authentication problem, hiding all nonauthentication traffic using a post capture filter would provide a way for the analyst to see clearly just the packets of interest.

20. A, B, C.   Address filters allow the selection of traffic based upon physical (MAC) or logical (Network layer) addresses. As well as individual addresses, address filters allow the use of wildcard entries, which enable the selection of IP subnets.

Appendix

About the Companion CD

IN THIS APPENDIX:

✓ What You'll Find on the CD

✓ System Requirements

✓ Using the CD

✓ Troubleshooting

What You'll Find on the CD

The following sections are arranged by category and summarize the software and other goodies you'll find on the CD. If you need help with installing the items provided on the CD, refer to the installation instructions in the "Using the CD" section of this appendix.

Some programs on the CD might fall into one of these categories:

Shareware programs are fully functional, free, trial versions of copyrighted programs. If you like particular programs, register with their authors for a nominal fee and receive licenses, enhanced versions, and technical support.

Freeware programs are free, copyrighted games, applications, and utilities. You can copy them to as many computers as you like—for free—but they offer no technical support.

GNU software is governed by its own license, which is included inside the folder of the GNU software. There are no restrictions on distribution of GNU software. See the GNU license at the root of the CD for more details.

Trial, *demo*, or *evaluation* versions of software are usually limited either by time or by functionality (such as not letting you save a project after you create it).

Sybex Test Engine

The CD contains the Sybex test engine, which includes all the assessment test and chapter review questions in electronic format, as well as two bonus exams located only on the CD.

Electronic Flashcards

These handy electronic flashcards are just what they sound like. One side contains a question, and the other side shows the answer.

System Requirements

Make sure your computer meets the minimum system requirements shown in the following list. If your computer doesn't match up to most of these requirements, you may have problems using the software and files on the companion CD. For the latest and greatest information, please refer to the ReadMe file located at the root of the CD-ROM.

- A PC running Microsoft Windows 98, Windows 2000, Windows NT4 (with SP4 or later), Windows Me, Windows XP, Windows Vista, or Windows 7

- An Internet connection

- A CD-ROM drive

Using the CD

To install the items from the CD to your hard drive, follow these steps:

1. Insert the CD into your computer's CD-ROM drive. The license agreement appears.

> The interface won't launch if you have autorun disabled. In that case, click Start ➢ Run (for Windows Vista or Windows 7, Start ➢ All Programs ➢ Accessories ➢ Run). In the dialog box that appears, type **D:\Start.exe**. (Replace *D* with the proper letter if your CD drive uses a different letter. If you don't know the letter, see how your CD drive is listed under My Computer.) Click OK.

2. Read the license agreement, and then click the Accept button if you want to use the CD.

The CD interface appears. The interface allows you to access the content with just one or two clicks.

Troubleshooting

Wiley has attempted to provide programs that work on most computers with the minimum system requirements. Alas, your computer may differ, and some programs may not work properly for some reason.

The two likeliest problems are that you don't have enough memory (RAM) for the programs you want to use or you have other programs running that are affecting installation or running of a program. If you get an error message such as "Not enough memory" or "Setup cannot continue," try one or more of the following suggestions and then try using the software again:

Turn off any antivirus software running on your computer. Installation programs sometimes mimic virus activity and may make your computer incorrectly believe that it's being infected by a virus.

Close all running programs. The more programs you have running, the less memory is available to other programs. Installation programs typically update files and programs, so if you keep other programs running, installation may not work properly.

Have your local computer store add more RAM to your computer. This is, admittedly, a drastic and somewhat expensive step. However, adding more memory can really help the speed of your computer and allow more programs to run at the same time.

Customer Care

If you have trouble with the book's companion CD-ROM, please call the Wiley Product Technical Support phone number at (800) 762-2974. Outside the United States, call +1(317) 572-3994. You can also contact Wiley Product Technical Support at http://sybex.custhelp.com. John Wiley & Sons will provide technical support only for installation and other general quality-control items. For technical support on the applications themselves, consult the program's vendor or author.

To place additional orders or to request information about other Wiley products, please call (877) 762-2974.

Glossary

Numbers

4-Way Handshake   Under the 802.11i amendment, two stations (STAs) must establish a procedure to authenticate and associate with each other as well as create dynamic encryption keys through a process known as the 4-Way Handshake.

802.11-2007 standard   On March 8, 2007, the most current iteration of the standard was approved: IEEE Std. 802.11-2007. This new standard is an update of the IEEE Std. 802.11-1999 revision. The following documents have been rolled into this latest revision, providing users with a single document that has all the amendments published to date. This new standard includes the following:

IEEE Std. 802.11-1999 (R2003)
IEEE Std. 802.11a-1999
IEEE Std. 802.11b-1999
IEEE Std. 802.11d-2001
IEEE Std. 802.11g-2003
IEEE Std. 802.11h-2003
IEEE Std. 802.11i-2004
IEEE Std. 802.11j-2004
IEEE Std. 802.11e-2005

802.11g protected mode   See *protection mechanism*.

802.11e   An approved 802.11 amendment that defines QoS enhancements.

802.11n   The 802.11n-2009 amendment defines high throughput (HT) clause 20 radios that use multiple-input multiple-output (MIMO) technology in unison with Orthogonal Frequency Division Multiplexing (OFDM) technology.

802.1p   A protocol that defines eight levels of priority for 802.3 wired networks.

802.1X   The 802.1X standard is a port-based access control standard. 802.1X provides an authorization framework that allows or disallows traffic to pass through a port and thereby access network resources. An 802.1X framework may be implemented in either a wireless or wired environment. The three main components of an 802.1X framework are the supplicant, the authenticator, and the authentication server.

A

access point   The CWNP definition is a half-duplex wireless device with switch-like intelligence. In reality, an access point is simply a hub with a radio card and an antenna. Access point radios must contend for the half-duplex medium in the same fashion as the client station radio cards.

acknowledgment (ACK)   The ACK frame is one of the six control frames and one of the key components of the 802.11 CSMA/CA media access control method. Because 802.11 is a wireless medium that cannot guarantee successful data transmission, the only way for a station to know that a frame it transmitted was properly received is for the receiving station to notify the transmitting station. This notification is performed using an ACK. The ACK frame is a very simple frame consisting of 14 octets of information.

Active mode   Active mode is the default power management mode for most 802.11 stations. When a station is set for Active mode, the wireless station is always ready to transmit or receive data. Active mode is sometimes referred to as Continuous Aware mode, and it provides no battery conservation. In the MAC header of an 802.11 frame, the Power Management field is 1 bit in length and is used to indicate the power-management mode of the station. A value of 0 indicates that the station is in Active mode. Stations running in Active mode will achieve higher throughput than stations running in Power Save mode, but the battery life will typically be much shorter.

add traffic stream (ADDTS) frames   This is used to carry TSPEC and optionally TCLAS elements to set up and maintain traffic streams.

adjacent channel   This is the next or previous numbered channel.

adaptive rate selection   This is also known as *dynamic rate shifting*, *dynamic rate selection*, or *automatic rate selection*. It is a process that client stations use to shift to lower-bandwidth capabilities as they move away from an access point and to higher-bandwidth capabilities as they move toward an access point. The objective is upshifting and downshifting for rate optimization and improved performance.

Advanced Encryption Standard (AES)   The AES algorithm, originally named the Rijndael algorithm, is a block cipher that offers much stronger protection than the RC4 streaming cipher. AES is used to encrypt 802.11 wireless data by using an encryption method known as *counter mode* with Cipher Block Chaining Message Authentication Code (CCMP). The AES algorithm encrypts data in fixed data blocks with choices in encryption key strength of 128, 192, or 256 bits.

Aggregate MAC Protocol Data Unit (A-MPDU)   This is a frame aggregation technique that combines multiple frames into a single frame transmission. All the 802.11 frames (MPDUs) do not need to have the same destination address. Also, the data payload of each MPDU is encrypted separately by using the multiple dynamic encryption keys that are unique between the access point and each individual client.

Aggregate MAC Service Data Unit (A-MSDU)   A frame aggregation technique that combines multiple MSDU payloads into a single frame transmission. The aggregated MSDUs will have a single destination when wrapped together in a single frame. Multiple MSDUs are encrypted by using the same dynamic encryption key.

all-band interference   All-band interference is RF interference that occurs across the entire frequency range that is being used. The term *all-band interference* is typically associated with frequency-hopping spread spectrum (FHSS) communications that disrupt HR-DSSS and/or ERP-OFDM channel communications.

amplitude   This is the height, force, or power of a wave; it is often referred to as *signal strength*.

amplitude modulation   See *amplitude shift keying (ASK)*.

amplitude shift keying (ASK)   ASK varies the amplitude, or height, of a signal to represent the binary data. ASK is a current state technique, where one level of amplitude can represent a 0 bit and another level of amplitude can represent a 1 bit.

announcement traffic indication message (ATIM)   This is a unicast frame that is used in an IBSS network when Power Save mode is enabled. If a station has buffered data for another station, it will send an ATIM frame to the other station, informing it that it must stay awake until the next ATIM window so that it can receive the buffered data. Any station that either has buffered data for another station or has received an ATIM will stay awake so that the buffered data can be exchanged.

antenna selection (ASEL)   This is a method to increase signal diversity by dynamically selecting which antennas to use when an STA has more antennas than radio chains.

arbitration interframe space (AIFS)   The AIFS is used for WLANs that support 802.11e QoS.

ARC4   This is a stream cipher that was designed by Ron Rivest of RSA Security in 1987. RSA never released the algorithm, so unofficial versions of it are often referred to as *Arcfour* or *ARC4*, which stands for "Alleged RC4."

Arcfour   See *ARC4*.

associated   After a station has authenticated with the access point, the next step is for it to associate with the access point. When a client station associates, it becomes a member of a basic service set (BSS). Association means that the client station can send data through the access point and on to the distribution system medium.

association request   This is the first frame sent in the association phase from the requesting station to the AP (or a station in an IBSS).

association response   After reception of the Association Request frame, if the AP is granting access to the cell, the association response frame is sent.

association identifier (AID)   Any time a station associates to an access point, the station receives an association identifier (AID). The access point uses this AID to keep track of the stations that are associated and the members of the BSS.

authentication   Authentication is the verification of user identity and credentials. Users must identify themselves and present credentials, such as usernames and passwords or digital certificates. More secure authentication systems exist that require multifactor authentication where at least two sets of different credentials must be presented.

authentication algorithm number   This field in the authentication frame describes which authentication system is used (0 for Open System and 1 for Shared Key).

authentication frame   This validates the device type, verifying that the requesting station has proper 802.11 capabilities to join the cell.

authentication server (AS)   When an 802.1X/EAP solution is deployed, an authentication server validates the credentials of the supplicant that is requesting access and notifies the authenticator that the supplicant has been authorized. The authentication server will maintain a user database or may proxy with an external user database to authenticate user credentials.

Authentication Transaction Sequence Number   A 2-byte field that indicates the current state of progress through the multistep authentication transaction.

authenticator   When an 802.1X/EAP solution is deployed, a device that blocks or allows traffic to pass through its port entity is known as the *authenticator*. Authentication traffic is normally allowed to pass through the authenticator while all other traffic is blocked until the identity of the supplicant has been verified.

authenticator nonce (ANonce)   This random numerical value is generated one time only and is used by the authenticator during a 4-Way Handshake frame exchange.

automatic rate selection   A process that client stations use to shift to lower-bandwidth capabilities as they move away from an access point and to higher-bandwidth capabilities as they move toward an access point. The objective of ARS is upshifting and downshifting for rate optimization and improved performance.

B

basic rates   This is the set of data rates that a client station must be capable of communicating with in order to associate with an access point successfully. Basic rates are required rates with a basic service set (BSS).

basic service set (BSS)   The 802.11 standard defines three topologies known as *service sets*. One topology, known as the basic service set (BSS), involves communications between a single access point and client stations that are associated with the access point.

basic service set identifier (BSSID)   The BSSID address is a 48-bit (6-octet) MAC address used as a unique identifier of a basic service set. In either a BSS or ESS topology, the BSSID address is simply the MAC address of a single access point. In an IBSS topology, the BSSID address is a virtual address.

basic service set (BSS) load element   This provides information on the cell load, from the AP point of view. It is typically sent by the AP (although the 802.11 standard does not restrict it to APs only) and used by the receiving stations to decide how to roam.

beacon interval   This field in the beacon management frame represents the number of time units (TUs) between target beacon transmission times (TBTTs).

beacon management frame   This is one of the most important 802.11 frame types, commonly referred to as the *beacon*. Beacons are essentially the heartbeat of the wireless network. They are sent only by the access point of a basic service set. Client stations transmit beacons only when participating in an IBSS, also known as *ad hoc mode*.

best effort   This is the third highest priority access category used with 802.11 QoS.

bit   A bit is a basic unit of information storage and communication.

bit error rate (BER)   This is a counter used to keep track of transmission errors. There are some very detailed and high-level mathematical ways of showing BER, but to keep it simple, it is essentially counting all the bits sent and comparing that value with the number of bits that showed errors. The result works out to be the number of errors per total bits sent.

Bitmap Control   This is one of the TIM information element fields. The Bitmap Control field is 1 byte that has two purposes. The first bit of the byte is used only in a DTIM beacon, and its purpose is to indicate whether broadcast/multicast frames are buffered at the AP.

Bitmap Offset   The remaining seven bits of the bitmap control, which may have any value between 0 and 127, are used as a space saver.

block acknowledgment (BA)   Introduced in the 802.11e amendment, the block acknowledgment mechanism improves channel efficiency by aggregating several acknowledgments into one single acknowledgment.

block acknowledgment request (BlockAckReq) frame   The originator requests acknowledgment of all the outstanding QoS data frames by sending a BlockAckReq frame.

broadcast address   This group address indicates all stations that belong to the network.

buffer   This is temporary memory on the AP used for storing data that could not be delivered because of Power Save mode.

buffer size   This is also referred to as the *capture buffer size*. It is an allocation of memory (RAM) that will be reserved for the packet capture.

byte   This is a unit of digital information comprised of 8 bits.

C

Capability Information field   This is a 2-octet field contained in many management frames that contains a number of subfields that are used to indicate requested or advertised optional capabilities.

calculation fields   These are all the fields of the MAC header and frame body that the frame check sequence is calculated over.

capture filters   These are filters applied to the packet stream before the packets enter the capture buffer. Anything filtered out at capture time is not stored and therefore cannot be recovered later.

carrier frequency   This is the nominal frequency of a carrier wave.

carrier sense   This check is performed by an STA to see whether the medium is busy.

Carrier Sense Multiple Access with Collision Avoidance (CSMA/CA)   This is the media access control method used by 802.11 networks. Four mechanisms are used together to ensure that only one station is transmitting at any given time on the half-duplex RF medium. The four mechanisms are physical carrier-sense, virtual carrier-sense, interframe spaces, and the random back-off algorithm.

CBC   See *cipher-block chaining.*

CBC-MAC   See *cipher-block chaining message authentication code.*

CCM   See *counter mode with Cipher Block Chaining Message Authentication Code (CCMP).*

CF-End frame   This is a 20-octet frame that is used to indicate the end of a contention-free period.

CF-End+CF-Ack frame   This is a 20-octet frame that is used to indicate the end of a contention-free period and acknowledge receipt of a frame.

channel scanning   This is analysis that captures traffic on all selected channels, spending a short amount of time on each channel before moving to the next one.

channel switch announcement   This is used by the AP to inform the cell that all stations had to move to another channel because radar was detected on the current frequency.

chips   This is a series of bits that represent a single bit of data. To prevent confusion, the data is referred to as a *bit*, and the series of bits are referred to as *chips* instead of bits.

chipping   This process of converting a single data bit into a sequence of bits known as *chips* is often called *spreading* or *chipping.*

cipher-block chaining   This is a mode of operation for a block cipher in which a sequence of bits is encrypted as a single unit or block with a cipher key applied to the entire block.

cipher-block chaining message authentication code   This is a layer 2 authentication and integrity method.

clear channel assessment (CCA)   This is a layer 1 process that determines whether the RF medium is busy. 802.11 radios cannot transmit if the RF medium is busy.

clear to send (CTS)   See *request to send/clear to send (RTS/CTS).*

complementary code keying (CCK)   This is a spreading/coding technique used by 802.11b cards to provide higher data rates (HR-DSSS).

contention free (CF)   This is an optional 802.11 operating mode when PCF medium access method is implemented and operating. Although defined by the standard, CF and PCF medium access method have not been implemented.

contention-free period (CFP)   This occurs when the access point is functioning in PCF mode. During the contention-free period, the access point polls only clients in PCF mode about their intention to send data. This is a method of prioritizing clients.

contention-free burst   The data frame transmissions within a TXOP are called a contention-free burst (CFB).

contention window   After a station has waited while performing both virtual and physical carrier senses, the station may contend for the medium during a window of time known as the contention window.

control frames   Control frames help with the delivery of the data frames. Control frames must be able to be heard by all stations; therefore, they must be transmitted at one of the basic rates. Control frames are also used to clear the channel, acquire the channel, and provide unicast frame acknowledgments. They contain only layer 2 header information.

controlled port   This is a virtual port used during 802.1X/EAP authentication. The authenticator maintains two virtual ports: an uncontrolled port and a controlled port. The uncontrolled port allows EAP authentication traffic to pass through, while the controlled port blocks all other traffic until the supplicant has been authenticated.

Control Wrapper frame   The Control Wrapper frame is a new control frame introduced by the 802.11n amendment. Its purpose is to carry other control frames along with an HT Control field.

convolutional coding   This is a form of error correction. Convolutional coding is not part of OFDM but rather part of 802.11a and 802.11g. It is a forward error correction (FEC) that allows the receiving system to detect and repair corrupted bits. There are many levels of convolutional coding.

counter mode with Cipher Block Chaining Message Authentication Code (CCMP)   This is the default encryption method defined under the 802.11i amendment. This method uses the Advanced Encryption Standard (AES) cipher. CCMP/AES uses a 128-bit encryption key size and encrypts in 128-bit fixed-length blocks. An 8-byte message integrity check (MIC) is used that is considered much stronger than the one used in TKIP. CCMP/AES is the default encryption method defined by WPA2.

CTR   See *counter mode with Cipher Block Chaining Message Authentication Code (CCMP)*.

CTS-to-self   A protection mechanism for mixed-mode environments. One of the benefits of using CTS-to-self over RTS/CTS as a protection mechanism is that the throughput will be higher, because there are fewer frames being sent.

cycle   This wave form starts at the center; climbs in energy to the highest point, called the *peak*; returns to the center; then drops to the weakest point, called the *trough*; and finally returns to the center point.

cyclic redundancy check (CRC)   This is an error-detecting code.

D

Data-Link layer   This is the second layer of the OSI model. The Data-Link layer is subdivided into two sublayers: the upper LLC sublayer and the lower MAC sublayer.

data encoding   This is the process of spreading data across a channel.

data frames   802.11 data frames carry the layer 3–7 MSDU payload. The MSDU is usually encrypted for data privacy purposes.

deauthentication frame   This is a notification frame used to terminate an authentication. Because authentication is a prerequisite for association, disassociation will also occur. Deauthentication cannot be refused by either party.

decibel (dB)   Decibel is derived from the term bel. It is a measurement of the ratio between two powers: decibels = $10 \times \log_{10}(P_1/P_2)$.

delivery traffic indication message (DTIM)   This is a special type of TIM that is used to ensure that all stations are awake when multicast or broadcast traffic is sent.

delete traffic stream (DELTS) frame   This is a traffic stream deletion frame sent from the station or the AP.

delta time   This is the time difference between transmitted frames.

destination address (DA)   The MAC address that is the final destination of the frame.

de-spreads   This means converting a chip sequence back into a single data bit.

differential binary phase shift keying (DBPSK)   This is a modulation technique used to transmit 802.11 DSSS data at 1 Mbps.

differential quadrature phase shift keying (DQPSK)   This is a modulation technique used to transmit 802.11 DSSS data at 2 Mbps.

differentiated service code point (DSCP)   This is used to indicate QoS in the IP header. This uses the 8 eight priority levels as main markers and adds 3 three other bits to determine subpriorities called drop precedences.

direct sequence parameter set element   An element used by both DSSS and OFDM systems on both 2.4 GHz and 5 GHz spectrums that indicates the current channel.

direct sequence spread spectrum (DSSS)   This is a spread spectrum technology originally specified in the 802.11 standard. Provides 1 Mbps and 2 Mbps RF communications using the 2.4 GHz ISM band. DSSS 802.11 radio cards are often known as clause 15 devices.

direct sequence spread spectrum-OFDM (DSSS-OFDM)   This is an optional PHY defined by the 802.11g ratified amendment.

disassociation frame   This is an 802.11 notification frame used to terminate an association. Disassociation is considered a polite way of terminating the association. Disassociation cannot be refused by either party.

display filters   Also known as postcapture filters, these filters are applied to the stored packets, hiding the unwanted packets from view, while retaining them for future use.

distributed analysis   This is analysis using wireless sensors or remote capture devices to monitor the wireless environment and report their statistics/packets to an analyzer or server.

distributed coordination function (DCF)   CSMA/CA is provided by DCF, which is the mandatory access method of the 802.11 standard.

distributed coordination function (DCF) interframe space   This is a period of time used with DCF clear channel assessment. During a contention period, if the medium is continuously idle for a DCF Interframe Space (DIFS) duration, only then should it transmit a frame.

delivery traffic indication map (DTIM) count   One of the TIM information element fields, this count indicates the number of incremental beacon frames until the next DTIM beacon.

delivery traffic indication map (DTIM) period   This is the number of beacon frames between DTIM beacons.

distribution system (DS)   The DS is a system used to interconnect a set of basic service sets (BSSs) and integrated local area networks (LANs) to create an extended service set (ESS). The DS consists of a medium used for transporting traffic as well as services used for transporting traffic.

distribution system medium (DSM)   The DSM is a logical physical medium used to connect access points. Normally, the DSM is an 802.3 Ethernet backbone; however, the medium can also be wireless or some other type of medium.

distribution system service (DSS)   This is a system service built inside an autonomous access point or WLAN controller usually in the form of software. The distribution system service is used to transport 802.11 traffic.

doze   When Power Save is enabled, this is the energy conservation move.

driver   This is software that tells the operating system or a program how to communicate with a hardware device.

Dual CTS   Dual CTS sets the Network Allocation Vector (NAV) in STAs that do not support STBC and STAs that can only associate and communicate used STBC because of their physical distance away from the AP.

Duration/ID field   This is a field in an 802.11 frame header that is typically used to set the NAV timer in other stations. This is used with virtual carrier sense.

dwell time   This is a defined amount of time that the FHSS system transmits on a specific frequency before it switches to the next frequency in the hop set. The local regulatory body typically limits the amount of dwell time.

dynamic frequency selection (DFS)   This is used for spectrum management of 5 GHz channels for 802.11a radio cards. The European Radio communications Committee (ERC) originally mandated that radio cards operating in the 5 GHz band implement a mechanism to avoid interference with radar systems as well as provide equable use of the channels. The DFS service is used to meet the ERC regulatory requirements. This requirement has since become a requirement of other regulatory bodies, such as the FCC in the United States.

dynamic rate shifting   See *automatic rate selection.*

dynamic rate switching (DRS)   See *automatic rate selection.*

E

end-of-service period (ESOP)   This is a 1-bit subfield of the QoS Control field that is used by the hybrid coordinator (HC) to indicate the end of the current service period (SP).

Enhanced Distributed Channel Access (EDCA)   As defined by the 802.11e amendment, Enhanced Distributed Channel Access (EDCA) is an extension to DCF. The EDCA medium access method provides for the prioritization of traffic via the use of 802.1d priority tags.

energy detection   This is a power-level measurement that varies between devices. If modulated bits are detected at this level, the CCA will go busy for 15 microseconds.

Exclusive-OR (XOR)   Part of an exclusive disjunction, this type of logical disjunction on two operands results in a value of true if exactly one of the operands has a value of true.

expert analysis   This is the automatic detection of network events, errors, and problems by an analyzer.

ExpressCard   This hardware standard is replacing PCMCIA cards.

extended interframe space (EIFS)   If a previously received frame contains an error, then the transmitting station must wait an EIFS duration instead of DIFS before transmitting.

Extended Rate Physical (ERP)   This is a Physical layer specification (PHY) defined for clause 19 radios. This PHY operates in the 2.4 GHz ISM band and uses ERP-OFDM to support data rates of 6 Mbps to 54 Mbps. ERP/DSSS/CCK technology is used to maintain backward compatibility with HR-DSSS (clause 18) radios and DSSS (clause 15) radios.

Extended Rate Physical DSSS/CCK   802.11g clause 19 radios must maintain backward compatibility with 802.11 (DSSS only) and 802.11b (HR-DSSS) radios. A Physical layer (PHY) technology called Extended Rate Physical DSSS (ERP-DSSS/CCK) is used for backward compatibility and for supporting the data rates of 1, 2, 5.5, and 11 Mbps. This PHY layer operates in the 2.4 GHz ISM band.

Extended Rate Physical OFDM (ERP-OFDM)   This is a Physical layer (PHY) technology used by 802.11g clause 19 radios to achieve greater bandwidth. This uses OFDM as defined in the 802.11a amendment. Therefore, data rates of 6, 9, 12, 18, 24, 36, 48, and 54 Mbps are possible using OFDM technology. This PHY layer operates in the 2.4 GHz ISM band.

Extended Rate Physical PBCC (ERP-PBCC)   This is an optional PHY defined by the 802.11g ratified amendment for clause 19 radios.

extended service set (ESS)   The 802.11 standard defines three topologies known as *service sets*. One topology, known as the extended service set (ESS), involves communications between multiple access points that share a network infrastructure. An ESS is one or more basic service sets that share a distribution system medium.

extended service set identifier (ESSID)   This is the logical network name of an extended service set, also known as a *service set identifier* (SSID).

extended supported rates element   This is used in conjunction with the supported rates element to identify the supported rates.

Extensible Authentication Protocol (EAP)   The Extensible Authentication Protocol (EAP) is used to provide user authentication for an 802.1X port-based access control solution. EAP is a flexible layer 2 authentication protocol that resides under Point-to-Point Protocol (PPP).

Extensible Authentication Protocol (EAP) – PEAPv0 (EAP-MSCHAPv2)   Microsoft's EAP-PEAPv0 (EAP-MSCHAPv2) is the most common form of PEAP. The protocol used for user authentication inside the tunnel is EAP-MSCHAPv2. The credentials used for this version of PEAP are usernames and passwords. Client-side certificates are not used and are not supported.

Extensible Authentication Protocol (EAP) PEAPv0 (EAP-TLS)   A type of PEAP from Microsoft, EAP-PEAPv0 (EAP-TLS) uses the EAP-TLS protocol for the inner tunnel authentication method. EAP-TLS requires the use of a client-side certificate. The client-side certificate is validated inside the TLS tunnel. No username is used for validation because the client-side certificate serves as the user credentials.

Extensible Authentication Protocol (EAP) PEAPv1 (EAP-GTC)   This is Cisco's implementation of PEAP authentication. EAP-PEAPv1 (EAP-GTC) uses EAP-Generic Token Card (EAP-GTC) for the inner-tunnel authentication.

Extensible Authentication Protocol (EAP) Transport Layer Security (EAP-TLS)   Defined in RFC 5216, this is a widely used security protocol, largely considered one of the most secure EAP methods used in WLANs today. It requires the use of client-side certificates in addition to a server certificate.

FT 4-way handshake   This occurs during the first association. The PTK and GTK encryption keys are created during the FT 4-Way Handshake, and the 802.1X controlled port is unblocked.

FT action frame   This is sent over the air between the STA and the current AP. The action frame is used as a transport mechanism for data that is destined for the target AP.

FT initial mobility domain association   The FT action frames are sent over the air between the STA and the current AP. The Action frame is used as a transport mechanism for data that is destined for the target AP.

fast basic service set transition (FT)   This is a set of fast secure roaming mechanisms defined by the 802.11r-2008 amendment.

Fast basic service set transition information element (FTIE)   This includes information needed to perform the FT authentication sequence during a fast BSS transition.

fast Fourier transform (FFT)   This is a more efficient algorithm for calculating a Fourier transform.

fast Fourier transform (FFT)-Duty Cycle   This view displays the percentage of the time the ambient RF signal is higher than the noise floor.

Forty MHz intolerant   When the Forty MHz Intolerant subfield is set to 1, it prohibits the use of 40MHz channels. An access point that receives frames with the Forty MHz Intolerant bit set, or reports it, is not allowed to operate a 20/40 MHz BSS.

Fourier transform (FT)   This is a process of taking a known curve and performing a calculation to derive its equation.

fixed channel analysis   This is analysis that locks the wireless NIC on to one channel, enabling it to capture all 802.11-encoded traffic on the selected channel.

forward error correction (FEC)   This is a technology that allows a receiving system to detect and repair corrupted bits.

fragment burst   This is a burst of fragments in which the transmitting station takes control of the medium and does not release it until all fragments are transmitted.

Fragment Number subfield   This is a field that is part of a fragmented frame that contains a 4-bit number assigned to each fragment of an MSDU.

fragmentation threshold   This is the threshold value at which an MSDU will be fragmented.

frame   This is a unit of data at the Data-Link layer.

frame aggregation   Frame aggregation allows multiple smaller MSDUs or MPDUs to be grouped together into a single frame, reducing the amount of overhead that would have been necessary for each individual frame.

frame body   This is part of the MPDU that is considered the unit of data of the frame.

frame check sequence (FCS)   This is the extra characters added to a frame and used for error detection and correction.

frame control field   This is a 16-bit field that includes information about the frame being sent and specific protocol operations.

frame subtypes   Each of the frame types is divided into multiple subtypes, with each subtype providing a different function and having a different frame structure.

frame types   802.11 defines three different frame types: control frames, data frames, and management frames.

free space path loss (FSPL)   This is the loss of signal energy caused by the natural broadening of the waves, often referred to as *beam divergence*.

frequency   This is a term describing a behavior of waves. How fast the waves travel—or more specifically, how many waves are generated over a one-second period of time—is known as *frequency*.

frequency domain   This is the representation of a graph where the horizontal axis is calibrated by frequency.

frequency hopping spread spectrum (FHSS)   This is a spread spectrum technology that was first patented during World War II. FHSS was used in the original 802.11 standard and provided 1 Mbps and 2 Mbps RF communications using the 2.4 GHz ISM band. FHSS works by using a small frequency carrier space to transmit data and then hopping to another small frequency carrier space and transmitting data and then to another frequency, and so on.

From DS field   This 1-bit field is part of the Frame Control field, indicating whether the frame is originating from the distribution system (DS).

G

gain   Also known as *amplification*, gain is the increase of amplitude or signal strength. The two types of gain are active gain and passive gain.

group address   This is a multiple destination address, which could be used by one or more stations on a network.

group key handshake   This is used only to issue a new group temporal key (GTK) that has already formed previous security associations. Effectively, the Group Key Handshake is identical to the last two frames of the 4-Way Handshake. The purpose of the Group Key Handshake is to deliver a new GTK to all client stations that already have an original GTK generated by an earlier 4-Way Handshake.

group master key (GMK)   This is part of the 4-Way Handshake that is randomly created on the access point/authenticator and is used to create the group temporal key (GTK).

group temporal key (GTK)   This is used to encrypt all broadcast and multicast transmissions between the access point and multiple client stations.

guard interval   The guard interval (GI) is the time that a transmitter waits between sending symbols. Short GI is 400 nanoseconds vs. the traditional GI of 800 nanoseconds.

H

hertz (Hz)   This is a standard measurement of frequency, which was named after the German physicist Heinrich Rudolf Hertz. An event that occurs once in 1 second is equal to 1 Hz. An event that occurs 325 times in 1 second is measured as 325 Hz.

heuristic-based expert analysis   This is analysis that looks for patterns in the traffic flow and compares them to a set of rules. Traffic that does not conform to these rules is reported.

high throughput (HT)   High throughput (HT) provides PHY and MAC enhancements to support wireless throughput of 100 Mbps and greater. HT is defined by the 802.11n amendment for clause 20 radios.

high throughput (HT) protection modes   There are four protection modes used by 802.11n to ensure backward compatibility with older 802.11 a/b/g radios.

high-rate DSSS (HR-DSSS)   The 802.11b 5.5 and 11 Mbps speeds are known as high-rate DSSS (HR-DSSS).

honeypot   This is a trap set for potential hackers to detect and possibly counteract unauthorized access of a computer network.

hop time   In a frequency-hopping spread spectrum network, this is the amount of time it takes for the transmitter to change from one frequency to another.

hopping sequence   This is a predefined hopping pattern or set used in frequency hopping spread spectrum. The hopping sequence comprises a series of small carrier frequencies, or *hops*. Instead of transmitting on one set channel or finite frequency space, an FHSS radio card transmits on a sequence of subchannels called *hops*. Each time the hop sequence is completed, it is repeated.

hops   These consist of a series of small carrier frequencies used by frequency hopping spread spectrum radios.

HT capabilities element   This contains a number of fields that are used to advertise optional HT capabilities of an HT STA. It is present in beacon, association request, association response, reassociation request, reassociation response, probe request, and probe response frames.

HT Control field   The HT Control field carries important PHY and MAC information regarding link adaptation, antenna selection, and calibration among other information.

HT-Greenfield   This is one of the new PPDU formats defined by the 802.11n amendment.

HT-mixed   This is one of the new PPDU formats defined by the 802.11n amendment

Hybrid Coordination Function (HCF)   The 802.11e amendment defines enhanced medium access methods to support QoS requirements. Hybrid Coordination Function (HCF) is an additional coordination function that is applied in an 802.11e QoS wireless network. HCF has two access mechanisms to provide QoS: Enhanced Distributed Channel Access (EDCA) and Hybrid Coordination Function Controlled Channel Access (HCCA).

Hybrid Coordination Function Controlled Channel Access (HCCA)   As defined by the 802.11e amendment, Hybrid Coordination Function Controlled Channel Access (HCCA) is similar to PCF. HCCA gives the access point the ability to provide for prioritization of stations via a polling mechanism. Certain client stations are given a chance to transmit before others.

HT operation element   The HT Operation Element is found in beacon, (re)association response, and probe response frames transmitted by an AP. The operation of HT STAs in the BSS is controlled by the HT Operation element.

I

idle   This is one of the three awake states that a station can operate in, when Power Save mode is enabled.

independent basic service set (IBSS)   The 802.11 standard defines three topologies known as service sets. One topology, known as an independent basic service set (IBSS), involves direct communications between 802.11 client stations without the use of an access point. An 802.11 IBSS network is also known as a peer-to-peer network or an ad hoc network.

individual address   This is an address assigned to a unique station on the network (also known as a *unicast address*).

industrial, scientific, and medical (ISM)   The ISM bands are defined by the ITU-T in S5.138 and S5.150 of the radio regulations. Although the FCC ISM bands are the same as defined by the ITU-T, the usage of these bands in other countries may be different because of local regulations. The 900 MHz band is known as the industrial band, the 2.4 GHz band is known as the scientific band, and the 5.8 GHz band is known as the medical band. It should be noted that all three of these bands are license-free bands, and there are no restrictions on what types of equipment can be used in any of the three ISM bands.

The ISM bands are as follows:

902–928 MHz (26 MHz wide)

2.4000–2.4835 GHz (83.5 MHz wide)

5.725–5.875 GHz (150 MHz wide)

information elements   These variable-length fields are optional in the body of a management frame.

information fields   These are fixed-length mandatory fields in the body of a management frame.

initialization vector (IV)   The IV is utilized by the RC4 streaming cipher that WEP encryption uses. The IV is a block of 24 bits that is combined with a static key. It is sent in clear text and is different on every frame. The effective key strength of combining the IV with the 40-bit static key is 64-bit encryption. TKIP uses an extended IV.

inner identity   EAP methods that use tunneled authentication have two supplicant identities. These two supplicant identities are often called the *outer identity* and *inner identity*. The outer identity is effectively a bogus username, and the inner identity is the true identity of the supplicant.

interframe space (IFS)   This is a period of time that exists between transmissions of wireless frames.

integrity check value (ICV)   This is a data integrity checksum that is computed on data before encryption. The ICV is used to prevent data from being modified.

International Organization for Standardization (ISO)   The ISO is a global, nongovernmental organization that identifies business, government, and societal needs and develops standards in partnership with the sectors that will put them to use. The ISO is responsible for the creation of the Open Systems Interconnection (OSI) model, which has been a standard reference for data communications between computers since the late 1970s. The OSI model is the cornerstone to data communications, and understanding it is one of the most important and fundamental tasks a person in the networking industry can undertake. The layers of the OSI model are as follows:

Layer 1—Physical

Layer 2—Data-Link

Layer 3—Network

Layer 4—Transport

Layer 5—Session

Layer 6—Presentation

Layer 7—Application

J

jammer   This is a device that generates nonmodulated signals into the air with the intent of disrupting legitimate modulated signals.

jitter   This is a variation of latency.

L

L-SIG TXOP protection   This is an optional Physical layer protection mechanism, which uses the L-SIG (Legacy Signal) field in the HT-mixed PPDU Header.

latency   Latency is the time it takes to deliver a packet from the source device to the destination device.

Lightweight Directory Access Protocol (LDAP)   This is an application protocol for querying and modifying directory services running over TCP/IP. LDAP-compliant databases are often used with RADIUS solutions during proxy authentication.

listen interval   This is a field in association and reassociation requests used to indicate to the AP how often a station in Power Save mode wakes to listen to beacon management frames.

Logical Link Control (LLC)   This is the upper portion of the Data-Link layer in the IEEE 802.2 Logical Link Control (LLC) sublayer, which is identical for all 802-based networks, although not used by all IEEE 802 networks.

Long PPDU   This is a PPDU consisting of a 144-bit PLCP Preamble, which consists of a 128-bit Sync field and a 16-bit Start of Frame Delimiter (SFD).

M

MAC header   This is part of the MPDU that contains frame control information, duration information, addressing, and sequence control information.

MAC Protocol Data Unit (MPDU)   This is an 802.11 frame. The components include a MAC header, an MSDU (data payload), and a trailer.

MAC Service Data Unit (MSDU)   The MSDU contains data from the LLC and layers 3–7. A simple definition of the MSDU is the data payload that contains the IP packet plus some LLC data.

management frame protection (MFP)   These are techniques used to deliver management frames in a secure manner with the hope of preventing many layer 2 denial-of-service attacks.

management frame protection capable (MFPC)   This is a bit that an STA uses to advertise that it is capable of using protected management frames but does not require them.

management frame protection required (MFPR)   This is a bit that an STA uses to advertise that it requires the use of protected management frames.

management frames   A majority of the frame types in an 802.11 network are this type. Management frames are used by wireless stations to join and leave the network. Another name for an 802.11 management frame is a Management MAC Protocol Data Unit (MMPDU). Management frames do not carry any upper-layer information. There is no MSDU encapsulated in the MMPDU frame body, which carries only layer 2 information fields and information elements.

Management MAC Protocol Data Unit (MMPDU)   This is another name for an 802.11 management frame.

maximum transmission unit (MTU)   This is the largest-size packet or frame that can be transmitted across the network. The size varies depending on the protocol.

mean opinion score (MOS)   This is a type of VoIP analysis that uses a value from 1 to 5, which indicates the perceived quality of a call.

Media Access Control (MAC)   This is the bottom portion of the Data-Link layer, which is identical for all 802.11-based networks.

Message Integrity Check Code (MIC)   TKIP uses a data integrity check known as the Message Integrity Code (MIC) to mitigate known bit-flipping attacks against WEP. The MIC is sometimes referred to by the nickname *Michael*. This is also sometimes referred to as a *message integrity check*.

Microsoft Point-to-Point Encryption (MPPE)   MPPE is a 128-bit encryption method that uses the RC4 algorithm. MPPE is used with Point-to-Point Tunneling Protocol (PPTP) VPN technology.

milliwatt (mW)   This is a unit of power equal to 1/1000 of a watt.

mixed mode   This is the default operational mode of most 802.11g access points. Support for both DSSS/HR-DSSS and ERP is enabled; therefore, both 802.11b and 802.11g clients can communicate with the access point. See *protection mechanism*.

mobility domain   This is a set of basic service sets (BSSs), within the same extended service set (ESS), that support fast BSS transitions between themselves.

mobility domain controller (MDC)   Some WLAN vendors refer to their WLAN controllers as MDCs.

mobility domain information element (MDIE)   This is used to indicate the existence of a mobility domain as well as the method of fast BSS transition.

mobility domain identifier (MDID) field   This is a unique identifier of the group of APs that constitute a mobility domain.

mobility domain information element (MDIE)   This is used to indicate the existence of a mobility domain as well as the method of fast BSS transition.

modulation   Modulation is manipulating a signal so that the receiving station has a way of distinguishing 0s and 1s.

modulation and coding schemes (MCS)   As mandated by the 802.11n-2009 amendment, data rates for clause 20 HT radios are defined by multiple variables known as *modulation coding schemes (MCSs)*. Non-HT radios that used OFDM technology (802.11a/g) defined data rates of 6 Mbps to 54 Mbps based on the modulation that was used. HT radios, however, define data rates based on numerous factors, including modulation, the number of spatial streams, channel size, and guard interval.

More Data field   This is a 1-bit field used with Power Save mode to indicate whether the access point has more buffered data for the station.

More Data flag   See *More Data field*.

More Fragments field   This is a 1-bit field used with fragmentation to indicate whether there are more fragmented frames waiting to be transmitted.

multicast-group address   This is an address used by an upper-layer entity to define a logical group of stations.

multichannel aggregation   This is analysis that takes capture streams from multiple adapters and aggregates them into one capture. Typically each adapter is configured for a different channel.

multipath   This is a propagation phenomenon that results in two or more paths of a signal arriving at a receiving antenna at the same time or within nanoseconds of each other.

multiple-input multiple-output (MIMO)   This is any RF communications system that uses multiple antennas at both the transmitter and receiver to improve communication performance. MIMO communications are used by 802.11n radios.

N

narrow-band   A small narrow-band or range of RF energy grouped tightly around a defined frequency.

near/far   This is when a low-powered client station that is a great distance from the access point could become an unheard client if other high-powered stations are very close to the access point. The transmissions of the high-powered stations can raise the noise floor to a higher level at which the lower-powered station cannot be heard. This scenario is referred to as the *near/far problem*.

Network Allocation Vector (NAV)   This timer mechanism maintains a prediction of future traffic on the medium based on the Duration value information seen in a previous frame transmission. When an 802.11 radio is not transmitting, it is listening. When the listening radio hears a frame transmission from another station, it looks at the header of the frame and determines whether the Duration/ID field contains a Duration value or an ID value. If the field contains a Duration value, the listening station will set its NAV timer to this value. The listening station will then use the NAV as a countdown timer, knowing that the RF medium should be busy until the countdown reaches 0.

network interface card (NIC)   This is a computer hardware adapter that interfaces the computer to a network.

noise floor   This is a measurable level of background noise. This is often compared to received signal amplitudes. See *signal-to-noise ratio (SNR)*.

nonce   This is a random or pseudorandom value issued in an authentication protocol to ensure that previous communications cannot be reused in replay attacks.

nonadjacent channel   This is any channel after an adjacent channel.

non-HT PPDU   This is a PPDU defined by the 802.11n amendment, often referred to as a *legacy format* because it was originally defined by clause 17 of the 802.11-2007 standard for OFDM transmissions.

nonoverlapping channels   When defined by DSSS, these are channels that have at least 30 MHz of spacing between the center frequencies. When defined by HR-DSSS, these are channels that have at least 25 MHz of spacing between the center frequencies.

null data frame   Client stations sometimes use null data frames to enable or disable Power Save mode, which is indicated by a bit in the frame control field. The use of the null data frame allows a station to communicate with another device without requiring it to transmit data.

O

octet   This is a series of 8 bits used to form a single byte.

Open System authentication   Open System authentication is the simpler of the two 802.11 authentication methods. It provides authentication without performing any type of client verification. It is essentially an exchange of hellos between the client and the access point.

Order field   This is a single bit set to 1 in any non-QoS data frame when a higher layer has requested that the data be sent using a strictly ordered class of service, which tells the receiving station that frames must be processed in order. The field is set to 0 in all other frames.

organizationally unique identifier (OUI)   This is a 24-bit number that is purchased from and registered with the Institute of Electrical and Electronics Engineers (IEEE). It is intended to be an identifier uniquely given to a vendor, manufacturer, or other organization that reserves a block of each possible type of derivative identifier (such as MAC addresses) for the exclusive use of the assignee.

Orthogonal Frequency Division Multiplexing (OFDM)   Orthogonal Frequency Division Multiplexing is one of the most popular communications technologies used in both wired and wireless communications. As part of 802.11 technologies, OFDM is specified in the 802.11a and 802.11g amendments and can transmit at speeds of up to 54 Mbps. OFDM technology is also used by 802.11n HT radios. OFDM transmits across separate, closely and precisely spaced frequencies, often referred to as *subcarriers*.

over-the-air fast BSS transition   The client station communicates directly with the target AP using standard 802.11 authentication with the FT authentication algorithm. The PMK-R1 key is the seeding material for the over-the-air fast BSS transition process that creates the final pairwise transient key (PTK).

over-the-DS fast BSS transition   Client station sends an FT Action request frame to the original AP. The FT Action request frame is forwarded over the distribution system (DS), which is the wired infrastructure. The target AP responds to the client station over the DS with an FT Action response frame.

outer identity   See *inner identity*.

P

packet   This is a unit of data at the network layer.

packet analysis   This means decoding frames to determine content, frame type, origin, and destination.

packet slicing   This feature allows you to capture a selected amount or piece of a packet, not the entire packet. This is often used with packet streams that are encrypted, since the encrypted data is often unusable and therefore extraneous.

packet spoofing   This means creating and transmitting fake traffic with the intent of masquerading as a different device, disrupting service, or compromising a device or network.

pairwise master key (PMK)   This is a cryptographic key that is used to derive lower-level keys.

pairwise transient key (PTK)   Used to encrypt all unicast transmissions between a client station and an access point, each PTK is unique between each individual client station and the access point. Every client station possesses a unique PTK for unicast transmissions between the client STA and the AP. PTKs are used between a single supplicant and a single authenticator.

partial virtual bitmap   This is one of the TIM information element fields. It is a series of flags (bits set to either a 1 or a 0) indicating whether each associated station has unicast frames buffered at the AP.

PC Card   The PC Card standard specifies three types of PC Cards. The three card types are the same length and width and use the same 68-pin connector. The thickness of the cards are as follows: Type I = 3.3 mm, Type II = 5.0 mm, and Type III = 10.5 mm.

PCMCIA   See *Personal Computer Memory Card International Association.*

peer map   This is a visual representation of which STAs are communicating with each other. Lines between peers indicate communication.

Personal Computer Memory Card International Association (PCMCIA)   PCMCIA is an international standards body and trade association. The PCMCIA has more than 100 member companies and was founded in 1989 to establish standards for peripheral cards and to promote interchangeability with mobile computers. A PCMCIA adapter is also known as a PC Card. A radio card can be used in any laptop or handheld device that has a PC Card slot. Most PC Cards have integrated antennas. Some cards have only external antenna connectors, while others have external antennas and external connectors.

phased coexistence operation (PCO)   This is an optional 802.11n mode of operation that divides time and alternates between 20 MHz and 40 MHz transmissions.

physical carrier sense   This is performed constantly by all stations that are not transmitting or receiving data. It determines whether a frame transmission is inbound for a station to receive or whether the medium is busy before transmitting. This is known as the *clear channel assessment* (CCA).

Physical layer   This is the first layer of the OSI model. The Physical layer is divided into two sublayers. The upper portion of the Physical layer is known as the Physical Layer Convergence Procedure (PLCP) sublayer, and the lower portion is known as the Physical Medium Dependent (PMD) sublayer.

Physical Layer Convergence Procedure (PLCP)   This is the upper portion of the Physical layer. PLCP prepares the frame for transmission by taking the frame from the MAC sublayer and creating the PLCP Protocol Data Unit (PPDU).

Physical Medium Dependent (PMD)   This is the lower portion of the Physical layer. The PMD sublayer modulates and transmits the data as bits.

pilot carriers   These are OFDM subcarriers used as references for phase and amplitude by the demodulator, allowing the receiver to compensate for distortion of the OFDM signal.

plain text   This is unencrypted information or data.

PLCP header   Part of the PLCP Protocol Data Unit (PPDU), this header is 48 bits long and contains the Signal (8 bits), Service (8 bits), Length (16 bits), and CRC (16 bits).

PLCP Preamble This is a string of 0 and 1 bits that are used to synchronize incoming transmissions.

PLCP Protocol Data Unit (PPDU) When the PLCP receives the PSDU, it prepares the PSDU to be transmitted and creates the PLCP Protocol Data Unit (PPDU). The PLCP adds a preamble and PHY header to the PSDU.

PLCP Service Data Unit (PSDU) This is equivalent to the MPDU. The MAC layer refers to the frame as the MPDU, whereas the Physical layer refers to this same frame as the PSDU.

Point Coordination Function (PCF) This is an optional 802.11 medium access method that uses a form of polling. Although defined by the standard, the medium access method has not been implemented.

point coordinator (PC) The polling device in an 802.11 PCF network.

port spanning This is also known as *port mirroring*. A network switch is configured to send a copy of all traffic traveling on the access point's port on the switch to another port that has an analyzer connected to it.

power management field This is a single-bit field in the 802.11 MAC header that is used by a client station to notify the AP that the station is going into Power Save mode.

power management flag See *power management field*.

Power Save mode This is an optional mode for 802.11 stations. A wireless station can shut down some of the transceiver components for a period of time to conserve power. The station indicates that it is using Power Save mode by changing the value of the Power Management field to 1.

Power save multi-poll (PSMP) This power management method builds on scheduled automatic power save delivery (*S-APSD*). S-APSD comes from the 802.11e amendment. It is the power management method primarily defined for networks that use hybrid coordination function (HCF) controlled channel access (*HCCA*).

Power save poll (PS-Poll) frame When Power Save mode is enabled, if an access point has buffered data for a station when the station wakes up, the station will send a 20-octect frame to the access point, notifying the access point that the station is awake. When the access point receives the PS-Poll frame, it will send the buffered unicast frame to the station.

Pre-robust security network associations (pre-RSNAs) The 802.11-2007 standard defines WEP as a legacy encryption method.

probe request This is an 802.11 management frame that is transmitted during active scanning. A client station that is looking for an SSID sends a probe request. Access points that hear the probe request will send a probe response, notifying the client of the access points' presence. If a client station receives probe responses from multiple access points, signal strength and quality characteristics are typically used by the client station to determine which access point has the best signal and thus to which access point it should connect.

probe response   An 802.11 management frame that is transmitted during active scanning. After a client station sends a probe request, access points that hear the probe request will send a probe response, notifying the client of the access points' presence. The information that is contained inside the body of a probe response frame is the same information that can be found in a beacon frame, with the exception of the traffic indication map (TIM).

processing gain   This is the task of adding additional, redundant information to data. In this day and age of data compression, it seems strange that we would use a technology that adds data to our transmission, but by doing so, the communication is more resistant to data corruption. The system converts 1 bit of data into a series of bits that are referred to as *chips*.

protocol decodes   Network analyzers can decode hundreds of network protocols, and these protocol decodes are used to decode the captured packets.

Protected frame field   This is a single-bit field used to indicate whether the MSDU payload is encrypted. Originally the field was called the WEP bit.

protection mechanism   For the legacy 802.11 DSSS stations, 802.11b HR-DSSS stations and 802.11g ERP stations to coexist, the ERP stations enable a protection mechanism, also known as protected mode. RTS/CTS or CTS-to-Self is used by the ERP stations to avoid interfering with the DSSS and HR-DSSS stations.

Protocol version field   A consistent 2-bit field indicates which protocol version of 802.11 is being used by the frame.

pseudo-random function (PRF)   This hashes various inputs to derive a pseudorandom value and expands a key and a seed to a pseudorandom output, usually of a variable length.

Q

quadrature amplitude modulation (QAM)   This modulation technique is a hybrid of phase and amplitude modulation. It is used for transmission of OFDM 24 Mbps, 36 Mbps, 48 Mbps, and 54 Mbps data by 802.11a and 802.11g radios.

quality of service (QoS)   This is an attempt to prioritize and provide certain levels of predictable throughput along a shared access medium.

quality of service data frame   This is any Data Type frame where the most significant bit (MSB) of the Subtype field (bit b7) is set to 1. This bit is defined as the quality of service (QoS) subfield, specifying that the frame is a QoS data frame.

QoS control field   This 16-bit field identifies the traffic category (TC) or traffic stream (TS) to which the frame belongs and various other QoS-related information about the frame.

quality-of-service basic service set (QBSS)   This 802.11 basic service set provides quality of service (QoS). An infrastructure QBSS contains an 802.11e-compliant access point.

Queensland Attack   This DoS attack exploits the CCA functionality in a WLAN, making devices believe the medium is busy and not allowing the devices to transmit since they are forced to back off.

R

R-Factor   This metric is calculated from measureable information such as jitter, packet loss, and latency. R-Factor is a value in a range from 0 to 100.

Radiotap   RF information that is grabbed from the RF to Bit transition process by the wireless NIC and then added to the wireless frame. The Radiotap Header includes date and time stamps, a channel stamp, signal stamp, and a noise stamp.

random backoff   During the CSMA/CA process, after waiting for a DIFS period of inactivity, a random backoff value is chosen, and the STA proceeds to count down for this period of time.

RC4   The RC4 algorithm is a streaming cipher used in technologies that are often used to protect Internet traffic, such as Secure Sockets Layer (SSL). The RC4 algorithm is used to protect 802.11 wireless data and is incorporated into two encryption methods known as WEP and TKIP.

reason code   This field is used to indicate the reason that an unsolicited notification management frame of type Disassociation, Deauthentication, DELTS, DELBA, or DLS Teardown was generated.

reassociation   When a client station decides to roam to a new access point, it will send a reassociation request frame to the new access point. It is called a *reassociation*, not because it is reassociating to the access point but because it is reassociating to the SSID of the wireless network.

reassociation request   This frame is sent by a station to an access point (never from an AP to a station or from a station to a station in an IBSS) and is used when the station is already associated to the ESS and wants to associate to another access point connecting to the same ESS.

reassociation response   After reception of the reassociation request frame, if the AP is granting access to the cell, the reassociation response frame is sent.

receive   This is one of the two core functions of the wireless network. The other is transmit.

receive DTIMS   This station setting can enable or prevent the station from receiving DTIM beacons.

receive sensitivity   The amount of signal a wireless station must receive in order to distinguish between data and noise.

received amplitude   The received signal strength is most often referred to as *received amplitude*. RF signal strength measurements taken during a site survey is an example of received amplitude.

received channel power indicator (RCPI)   This 802.11 signal measurement consists of an 8-bit value ranging from 0 to 220, incrementing by .5 dB. The RCPI values begin at −110 dBm and increment to 0 dBm.

received signal strength   This is a measurement of the amount of signal received.

received signal strength indicator (RSSI)   This optional 802.11 parameter has a value from 0 to 255. It is designed to be used by the hardware manufacturer as a relative measurement of the RF power that is received. The RSSI is one of the indicators that is used by a wireless device to determine whether another device is transmitting, also known as a *clear channel assessment (CCA)*.

receiver   The receiver is the final component in the wireless medium. The receiver takes the carrier signal that is received from the antenna and translates the modulated signals into 1s and 0s. It then takes this data and passes it to the computer to be processed.

receiver address (RA)   This is the MAC address of the 802.11 radio that receives the incoming transmission from the transmitting station.

regulatory domain authority   Local regulatory domain authorities of individual countries or regions define the spectrum policies and transmit power rules.

Remote Authentication Dial-In User Service (RADIUS)   A networking protocol that provides centralized authentication, authorization, and accounting (AAA) management.

remote engine   Remote engines are software services that run on dedicated hardware or existing servers. Packet capture, filtering, decoding, and analysis are all performed on the engine. All packets are stored on the engine or attached storage. The analyst can connect to an engine, configure captures, and perform analysis from a console application. The console application has the same look and feel as a local portable analyzer; however, only small screen updates are sent back across the network and not the packets.

Retry field   This is a single-bit field of the Frame Control field indicating whether the frame is being retransmitted (1) or whether it is an original transmission of the frame (0).

Request to send   See *request to send/clear to send (RTS/CTS)*.

request to send/clear to send (RTS/CTS)   This mechanism performs a NAV distribution and helps prevent collisions from occurring. This NAV distribution reserves the medium prior to the transmission of the data frame. RTS/CTS can be used to discover hidden node problems. RTS/CTS is one of the two protection mechanisms used in mixed-mode environments.

Reverse Direction (RD) protocol   This improves the efficiency of data transfer between STAs. Legacy devices must contend for access to the medium before initiating a data transfer. When using the RD protocol, an STA, having obtained a Transmit Opportunity (TXOP), may grant other stations the opportunity to transmit data back within the same TXOP, without requiring the responding STA to contend for the medium before transmission.

RF monitor mode   This is a special operating mode in which a wireless card becomes a passive monitoring device and cannot transmit. In this mode, wireless NICs listen to all 802.11 encoded signals on the channel on which they are currently monitoring, and normal wireless network operation is disabled.

reduced interframe space (RIFS)   This is a new interframe space that is used in 802.11n and is even shorter in time than an SIFS. A RIFS interval can be used in place of an SIFS interval, resulting in less overhead during a frame burst.

Rijndael algorithm   This is a cipher developed by two Belgian cryptographers, Joan Daemen and Vincent Rijmen.

robust security network (RSN)   A robust security network (RSN) is a network that only allows for the creation of robust security network associations (RSNAs). An RSN utilizes CCMP/AES encryption as well as 802.1X/EAP authentication.

robust security network associations (RSNAs)   As defined by the 802.11i security amendment, two stations (STAs) must establish a procedure to authenticate and associate with each other as well as create dynamic encryption keys through a process known as the 4-Way Handshake. This association between two stations is referred to as a robust security network association (RSNA).

robust security network information element (RSNIE)   Often referred to simply as the RSN information element, an information element is an optional field of variable length that can be found in 802.11 management frames. The RSN information element can identify the encryption capabilities of each station. The RSN information element will also indicate what whether 802.1X/EAP authentication or preshared key (PSK) authentication is being used.

S

scheduled automatic power save delivery (S-APSD)   This is an enhanced power management method introduced by the IEEE 802.11e amendment.

security associations (SA)   This is the establishment of shared security information between two network devices to support secure communication.

Sequence number field   A 12-bit number assigned sequentially by the sending station to each MSDU and MMPDU. The value range is 0 to 4095.

service set identifier (SSID)   The SSID is a logical name used to identify an 802.11 wireless network. The SSID wireless network name is the logical name of the WLAN. The SSID can consist of as many as 32 characters and is case sensitive.

service set identifier (SSID) element   This is present in all beacons, probe requests, probe responses, association requests, and reassociation requests. The element ID is 0. The length section defines the length of the SSID string, in octets. The SSID string is a text string, with each character being coded over one octet. It contains as many octets as it has characters, with a maximum of 32 characters.

service periods   Contiguous periods of time scheduled at regular intervals, during which one or more downlink unicast frames can be sent to the station and/or one or several unicast uplink frames can be polled from the station. This is used to provide expected QoS levels.

Shared Key authentication   The more complex of the two 802.11 authentication methods. Shared Key authentication uses WEP to authenticate client stations and requires that a static WEP key be configured on both the station and the access point. In addition to WEP being mandatory, authentication will not work if the static WEP keys do not match. The authentication process is similar to Open System authentication but includes a challenge and response between the AP and client station.

short guard interval   See *guard interval*.

short interframe space (SIFS)   This is a short gap or period of time that is used during the transmission of data.

Short PPDU   This is a PPDU consisting of a 72-bit PLCP Preamble, which consists of a 56-bit Sync field and a 16-bit Start of Frame Delimiter (SFD).

Signal field   This is a field in the PLCP Header that indicates which modulation method will be used to transmit the PSDU portion of the PPDU.

signal strength   This is the magnitude of the electric field at a reference point that is a significant distance from the transmitting antenna.

signal-to-noise ratio (SNR)   The SNR is the difference in decibels between a received signal and the background noise. The SNR is an important value because if the background noise is too close to the received signal, data can get corrupted and retransmissions will increase.

simple data frame   This is an 802.11 data frame whose subtype is *data*. Simple data frames carry MSDU payloads.

single-input single-output (SISO)   This is a system that makes use of a single radio chain.

slot time   This is a period of time that differs between the different spread spectrum technologies. It is a large enough time to allow for receive-to-transmit radio turnaround, MAC processing, and clear channel assessment (CCA).

SM power save   See *spatial multiplexing power save (SMPS)*.

source address (SA)   This is the MAC address of the original sending station.

spatial multiplexing (SM)   MIMO radios transmit multiple radio signals at the same time. Each independent signal is known as a *spatial stream*, and each unique stream can contain different data. SM increases overall throughput.

spatial multiplexing power save (SMPS)   High throughput stations are able to transmit multiple data streams at once by using spatial multiplexing in order to increase throughput or extend range, but that causes a drain in battery life. SMPS involves disabling spatial multiplexing temporarily so that batter life can be extended.

Space-Time Block Coding (STBC)   This is a method to improve the reliability of data transfer by transmitting different copies of the data stream from different antennas. This adds a level of redundancy to data communication. By increasing the signal quality, the range is also increased.

spectral mask   This is a frequency spectrum template.

spectrum analysis   Locating sources of interference in the 2.4 GHz ISM and 5 GHz UNII bands is considered mandatory when performing an 802.11 wireless site survey. Using a spectrum analyzer to determine the state of the RF environment within a certain frequency range is known as *spectrum analysis*.

spectrum analyzer   Spectrum analyzers are frequency domain measurement devices that can measure the amplitude and frequency space of electromagnetic signals. A spectrum analyzer is a tool that should always be used to locate sources of interference during an 802.11 wireless site survey. Spectrum analyzers are also used for security purposes to locate layer 1 DoS attacks. Most spectrum analyzers are stand-alone devices, but distributed solutions exist that can be used as layer 1 intrusion detection systems.

spread spectrum   Spread spectrum transmission uses more bandwidth than is necessary to carry its data. Spread spectrum technology takes the data that is to be transmitted and spreads it across the frequencies that it is using.

spreading   This is the process of converting a single data bit into a sequence. It is also known as *chipping*.

Start of Frame Delimiter (SFD)   This is a 16-bit portion of the PPDU that indicates that the information found in the PLCP Header is being transmitted next.

station (STA)   The main component of an 802.11 wireless network is the radio card, which is referred to by the 802.11 standard as a station (STA). The radio card can reside inside an access point or be used as a client station.

station service (SS)   This is one of two major categories of 802.11 services used by all 802.11 client stations including access points.

station-to-station link (STSL)   This is a direct link established between two stations.

status code   This is a field in the ADDTS response action frame. This accepts or rejects the stream and specifies why. The reasons can range from a lack of bandwidth to wrong parameters.

subcarriers   OFDM transmits across separate, closely and precisely spaced frequencies referred to as *subcarriers*.

Subtype   See *frame subtypes*.

Subtype field   This 4-bit field indicates the subtype of the frame.

supplicant   When an 802.1X/EAP solution is deployed, a host with software that is requesting authentication and access to network resources is known as the *supplicant*.

supported rates   This is the set of data rates that the access point will use when communicating with an associated station.

Supplicant nonce (SNonce)   This is a random numerical value that is generated one time only and is used by the supplicant during a 4-Way Handshake frame exchange.

swept spectrogram   A spectrum analysis plot is a waterfall plot that converts the dB values to color and then plots a single, 1-pixel tall line at the bottom of the swept spectrogram plot. Then when the next set of data arrives, this process is repeated, with all the previous data being pushed up the stack by one row of pixels. If the sampling interval is one second, in order to look back at what occurred 10 seconds ago, you simply need to look up 10 pixels from the bottom, and you will see the RF energy information that was received in the past.

Sync field   This is part of the PPDU that alerts the receiver that a potentially receivable signal is present.

T

Temporal Key (TK)   The temporal encryption key used to encrypt/decrypt the MSDU payload of 802.11 data frames between the supplicant and the authenticator.

Temporal Key Integrity Protocol (TKIP)   TKIP is an enhancement of WEP encryption that addresses many of the known weaknesses of WEP. TKIP starts with a 128-bit temporal key that is combined with a 48-bit initialization vector (IV) and source and destination MAC addresses in a complicated process known as per-packet key mixing. TKIP also uses sequencing and uses a stronger data integrity check known as the message integrity check (MIC). TKIP is the mandatory encryption method under WPA and is optional under WPA2.

Temporal Key Integrity Protocol (TKIP) countermeasures　Countermeasures are used to protect against active attacks against the TKIP MIC.

Temporal Key Integrity Protocol (TKIP) mixed transmit address and key (TTAK)　After the 128-bit temporal key is created, the two-phase key mixing process begins. A 48-bit TKIP sequence counter (TSC) is generated and broken into 6 octets labeled TSC0 (least significant octet) through TSC5 (most significant octet). Phase 1 key mixing combines the appropriate temporal key (pairwise or group) with the TSC2 through TSC5 octets of the TKIP sequence counter as well as the *transmit address (TA)*. The TA is the MAC address of the transmitting 802.11 radio. The output of the Phase 1 key mixing is the creation of the TKIP-mixed transmit address and key (TTAK).

threshold-based expert analysis　This expert analysis system collects network statistics and compares them to configured threshold values. When the statistics exceed the configured threshold, an expert event is triggered, and a notification is sent.

time domain　This is the representation of a graph where the horizontal axis is calibrated by time.

time stamp　This is an 8-byte field in the beacon and probe response frames, containing a value representing the time on the access point, which is the number of microseconds the AP has been active. The stations in the cell use the time stamp value to adjust their own clock.

To DS field　This 1-bit field is part of the Frame Control field, indicating whether the frame is being sent to the distribution system (DS).

traffic identifier (TID)　This is used by QoS to specify differentiated services on a per-MSDU basis.

traffic indication map (TIM)　The traffic indication map (TIM) is used when stations have enabled Power Save mode. The TIM is a list of all stations that have undelivered data buffered on the access point waiting to be delivered. Every beacon will include the AID of the station until the data is delivered.

transition security network (TSN)　An 802.11 wireless network that allows for the creation of prerobust security network associations (pre-RSNAs) as well as RSNAs is known as a *transition security network*. A TSN supports 802.11i-defined security as well as legacy security, such as WEP, within the same BSS.

transmit　This is one of the two core functions of the wireless network. The other is receive.

transmit address (TA)　This is the MAC address of the transmitting 802.11 radio.

transmit beamforming (TxBF)　This means multiple antennas are connected to a signal processor. The processor feeds the individual antennas with signals of different relative phases, creating a directed beam of RF signal aimed at the client device. The 802.11n draft amendment proposes this as an optional PHY capability. The technology uses phased-array antenna technology and is often referred to as *smart antenna* technology.

transmit opportunity (TXOP)   This is a limited-duration controlled access phase, providing contention-free transfer of QoS data.

transmit opportunity (TXOP) holder   During TXOP operations, the TXOP holder has unfettered access to the channel for data frame transmissions.

transmit opportunity (TX) limit   This is the duration of the TXOP interval.

transmit power control (TPC)   This is part of the 802.11h amendment. TPC is used to regulate the power levels used by 802.11a radio cards. The ERC and the FCC mandate that radio cards operating in the 5 GHz band use TPC to abide by a maximum regulatory transmit power and are able to alleviate transmission power to avoid interference. The TPC service is used to meet the ERC and FCC regulatory requirements.

transmit spectrum mask   A mask that defines the frequencies and power levels that a transmission signal and its sidebands must operate within.

transmitter address (TA)   The MAC address of an 802.11 radio that is transmitting the frame onto the half-duplex 802.11 medium.

Transport Layer Security (TLS)   This is a cryptographic protocol normally used to provide secure communications. Just like SSL, the TSL protocol uses end-to-end encryption at the Transport layer of the OSI model.

traffic specification (TSPEC)   This is a field of the ADDTS request frame that contains the set of parameters that define in detail the characteristics and QoS expectations of a traffic flow, such as packet size, quantity, expected rate, and so on.

type   See *frame types*.

Type field   This is a 2-bit field indicating the type of the frame.

U

uncontrolled port   This is a virtual port used during 802.1X/EAP authentication. The authenticator maintains two virtual ports: an uncontrolled port and a controlled port. The uncontrolled port allows EAP authentication traffic to pass through, while the controlled port blocks all other traffic until the supplicant has been authenticated.

unicast   This is a transmission that is directed to a unique or individual station.

unicast address   This is a destination address on a frame assigned to a unique station.

Unlicensed National Information Infrastructure (UNII)   The IEEE 802.11a amendment designated OFDM data transmissions within the frequency space of the 5 GHz UNII bands.

The 802.11a amendment defined three groupings, or bands, of UNII frequencies, known as UNII-1 (lower), UNII-2 (middle), and UNII-3 (upper). All three of these bands are 100 MHz wide, and each has four channels. The IEEE 802.11h amendment introduced the capability for 802.11 radios to transmit in a new frequency band called UNII-2 Extended with 11 more channels. The 802.11h amendment effectively is an extension of the 802.11a amendment.

The UNII bands are as follows:

UNII- 1 (lower) is 5.15–5.25 GHz.

UNII-2 (middle) is 5.25–5.35 GHz.

UNII-2 Extended is 5.47-5.725 GHz.

UNII-3 (upper) is 5.725–5.825 GHz.

unscheduled automatic power save delivery (U-APSD)   This is an enhanced power-management method introduced by the IEEE 802.11e amendment. The Wi-Fi Alliance's WMM Power Save (WMM-PS) certification is based on U-APSD.

V

video   This is the second highest access category used with 802.11e QoS.

virtual carrier sense   This is a CSMA/CA mechanism used by listening 802.11 stations. When the listening radio hears a frame transmission from another station, it looks at the header of the frame and determines whether the Duration/ID field contains a Duration value or an ID value. If the field contains a Duration value, the listening station will set its NAV timer to this value. The listening station will then use the NAV as a countdown timer, knowing that the RF medium should be busy until the countdown reaches 0.

voice   This is the highest access category used with 802.11e QoS.

Voice over IP (VoIP)   This stands for Voice over Internet Protocol and is the transmission of voice conversations over a data network using TCP/IP protocols.

Voice over Wi-Fi (VoWiFi)   Any software or hardware that uses Voice over IP communications over an 802.11 wireless network is known as VoWiFi. Because of latency concerns, VoWiFi requires QoS mechanisms to function properly in an 802.11 BSS.

W

waterfall plot   See *swept spectrogram*.

wavelength   This is the distance between similar points on two back-to-back waves. When measuring a wave, the wavelength is typically measured from the peak of a wave to the peak of the next wave.

Wi-Fi Alliance   The Wi-Fi Alliance is a global, nonprofit industry trade association with more than 300 member companies. The Wi-Fi Alliance is devoted to promoting the growth of wireless LANs (WLANs). One of the Wi-Fi Alliance's primary tasks is to ensure the interoperability of WLAN products by providing certification testing. During the early days of the 802.11 standard, the Wi-Fi Alliance further defined the 802.11 standard and provided a set of guidelines to ensure compatibility among vendors. Products that pass the Wi-Fi certification process receive a "Wi-Fi CERTIFIED" certificate.

Wi-Fi Protected Access (WPA)   Prior to the ratification of the 802.11i amendment, the Wi-Fi Alliance introduced Wi-Fi Protected Access (WPA) certification as a snapshot of the not-yet-released 802.11i amendment, supporting only the TKIP/RC4 dynamic encryption key management. 802.1X/EAP authentication was required in the enterprise, and passphrase authentication was required in a SOHO environment.

Wi-Fi Protected Access 2 (WPA2)   WPA2 is based on the security mechanisms that were originally defined in the IEEE 802.11i amendment defining a robust security network (RSN). Two versions of WPA2 exist: WPA2-Personal defines security for a small-office home-office (SOHO) environment, and WPA2-Enterprise defines stronger security for enterprise corporate networks. Each certified product is required to support WPA2-Personal or WPA2-Enterprise.

Wi-Fi Protected Setup (WPS)   Wi-Fi Protected Setup defines simplified and automatic WPA and WPA2 security configurations for home and small-business users.

wildcard BSSID   This is an address of all 1s (hex FF:FF:FF:FF:FF:FF), making the address a broadcast address.

Wired Equivalent Privacy (WEP)   WEP is a layer 2 encryption method that uses the RC4 streaming cipher. The original 802.11 standard defined 64-bit and 128-bit WEP. WEP encryption has been cracked and is not considered a strong encryption method.

wireless distribution system (WDS)   Although the distribution system (DS) typically uses a wired Ethernet backbone, it is possible to use a wireless connection instead. A wireless distribution system (WDS) can connect access points together, using what is referred to as a *wireless backhaul*. WLAN bridges, repeaters, and mesh access points all use WDS connectivity.

wireless intrusion detection system (WIDS)   A WIDS is a client/server solution that is used to monitor constantly for 802.11 wireless attacks such as rogue APs, MAC spoofing, layer 2 DoS, and so on. A WIDS usually consists of three components: a server, sensors, and monitoring software. Wireless intrusion detection uses policies and alarms to classify attacks properly and to alert administrators to potential attacks.

wireless intrusion prevention system (WIPS)   A WIPS is a wireless intrusion detection system (WIDS) that is capable of mitigating attacks from rogue access points. WIPS use spoofed deauthentication frames, SMNP, and proprietary methods effectively to render a rogue access device useless and to protect the network backbone.

wireless local area network (WLAN)   The 802.11 standard is defined as a wireless local area network technology. Local area networks provide networking for a building or campus environment. The 802.11 wireless medium is a perfect fit for local area networking simply because of the range and speeds that are defined by the 802.11 standard and its amendments. The majority of 802.11 wireless network deployments are indeed local area networks (LANs) that provide access at businesses and homes.

wireless probes   These are remote sensors that typically look like access points and are installed in remote locations. Analysts can use these sensors to remotely capture packets and send them across the network to the network analyzer.

wireless sensor   This monitors the wireless environment 24/7 and sends its statistics to a centralized server. A consolidated view of wireless security and performance can be accessed from a console application.

Index

Note to the Reader: Throughout this index **boldfaced** page numbers indicate primary discussions of a topic. *Italicized* page numbers indicate illustrations.

B

C

U

X

The Best CWAP Book/CD Package on the Market!

Get ready for your Certified Wireless Analysis Professional (CWAP) certification with the most comprehensive and challenging sample tests anywhere!

The Sybex test engine features the following:

- All the review questions, as covered in each chapter of the book

- Challenging questions representative of those you'll find on the real exam

- Two full-length bonus exams available only on the CD

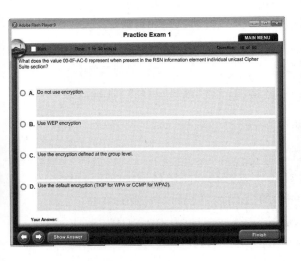

- An assessment test to narrow your focus to certain objective groups.

Use the electronic flashcards to jog your memory and prep last-minute for the exam!

- Reinforce your understanding of key concepts with these hardcore flashcard-style questions.

- Now you can study for the CWAP exam anytime, anywhere.

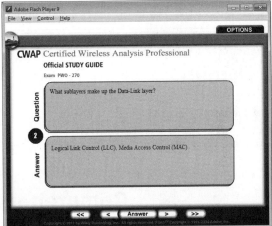

Expert

Design

Secure

Troubleshoot

Earn all 3 Professional Level Certifications to earn CWNE

Comprehend

Network engineers and adminstrators, begin with CWNA to gain the foundational RF knowledge required to implement and manage enterprise Wi-Fi. CWNA is required for CWSP, CWAP, CWDP, and CWNE.

Begin

Newbies, non-techies, project managers, and technical sales professionals, start your wireless career with CWTS.